D1714693

NATIONALISM

Nationalism

A WORLD HISTORY

ERIC STORM

PRINCETON UNIVERSITY PRESS

PRINCETON & OXFORD

Published by Princeton University Press
41 William Street, Princeton, New Jersey 08540
99 Banbury Road, Oxford OX2 6JX

press.princeton.edu

All Rights Reserved

Library of Congress Cataloging-in-Publication Data

Names: Storm, Eric, 1966– author.
Title: Nationalism : a world history / Eric Storm.
Description: Princeton, New Jersey : Princeton University Press, [2024] |
    Includes bibliographical references and index.
Identifiers: LCCN 2024015293 (print) | LCCN 2024015294 (ebook) | ISBN
    9780691233093 (hardback) | ISBN 9780691234052 (ebook)
Subjects: LCSH: Nationalism—History—Cross-cultural studies. |
    Globalization—Cross-cultural studies. | Citizenship—Cross-cultural
    studies. | Identity politics—Cross-cultural studies. | BISAC: POLITICAL
    SCIENCE / Political Ideologies / Nationalism & Patriotism | PHILOSOPHY /
    Political
Classification: LCC JC311 .S76 2024 (print) | LCC JC311 (ebook) | DDC
    320.5409—dc23/eng/20240415
LC record available at https://lccn.loc.gov/2024015293
LC ebook record available at https://lccn.loc.gov/2024015294

British Library Cataloging-in-Publication Data is available

Editorial: Ben Tate, Josh Drake
Production editorial: Elizabeth Byrd
Jacket: Heather Hansen
Production: Danielle Amatucci
Publicity: Kate Hensley (US), Carmen Jimenez (UK)

This book has been composed in Arno

Printed in the United States of America

10 9 8 7 6 5 4 3 2 1

CONTENTS

LIST OF ILLUSTRATIONS

I concluded that it would be more fruitful to study the past with a comparative approach, first focusing on Spain, France, and Germany—writing books on the rediscovery of El Greco and the construction of regional identities—and then on Europe as a whole. But I quickly realized that Europe was not isolated from the rest of the world. Thus, unlike most other practitioners of world history, I arrived to the field with primarily European expertise. A changing educational environment at Leiden University provided a strong incentive for my increasingly global orientation. Since the 2010s I have been teaching in various international programs, with students from around the world. As a consequence, I decided to broaden my teaching by giving seminars on the rise and evolution of nationalism around the world.

A collective research project at the Institute for Advanced Studies in Sofia on the conceptual history of European meso-regions—such as Scandinavia and the Balkans—showed me that I really enjoy writing broad, ambitious overviews. My task was to write a chapter on the role of these meso-regions in art history. The organizers, Diana Mishkova and Balázs Trencsényi, pushed all collaborators to examine developments over more than two centuries and not to limit our focus to Western and Central Europe. Xosé Manoel Núñez Seixas and I decided to repeat our experience in Sofia by editing a volume on regionalism in modern Europe, for which I wrote a chapter on the impact of tourism on regional identities throughout the Continent and during the entire long twentieth century. I really relished reading about areas and topics about which I had very little previous knowledge, while detecting many surprising shared trends and patterns.

Another major stimulus to write *Nationalism: A World History* was a lecture course on the history of states and nations from 1500 to the present, which we teach every two years with various colleagues from the general history section of Leiden University. The only global overview available was Azar Gat's *Nations: The Long History and Deep History of Political Ethnicity and Nationalism.* I felt a great unease about using this study, even though it undoubtedly has a lot of merits. As a political scientist, Gat has little sense of the profound historical changes that took place during the thousands of years that he explores in his book. In addition, as an expert on warfare, he focuses primarily on expressions of nationalism in exceptional, violent circumstances. In the end, my frustration with this situation inspired me to write an alternative account that focuses on the period since the age of revolutions and on nationalism in normal circumstances, and with more attention to the fundamental transformations that happened during the last few centuries in the fields of both politics and culture. Fresh input was provided by a workshop I organized with Stefan Berger on the various theoretical approaches to investigating the history of nationalism and in which we could count on the collaboration of a great group

WHEN I BEGAN my studies at the University of Groningen in the Netherlands, I had little direct knowledge of the world. I was born in a provincial town close to the German border. My parents had thrilling stories to tell, about their childhoods under German occupation during the Second World War, for instance. My mother had grown up on a barge and my father had been an officer in the merchant marine, sailing to Africa, India, and Australia during the height of the decolonization era. My father's only brother had emigrated to New Zealand, and my other uncles had either a barge or a coaster and roamed parts of Western Europe. During my own youth, however, we barely traveled. Because of my mother's poor health, we stayed in the vicinity for our yearly vacations, not even crossing one national border, which is quite difficult in a tiny country like the Netherlands. So when I enrolled at university, I was determined to catch up. Profiting from the European Erasmus program, I went on exchange to Spain, where I studied for nine months at the University of Salamanca. Before embarking on a PhD, I spent a year in Berlin working at the trade fair and as a tourist guide, and as a doctoral student I lived in Madrid for another year. While immersing myself in these new environments, I became interested in national differences.

I encountered the topic of nationalism when studying the 1905 commemoration of *Don Quixote* for my dissertation on Spanish political debates during the Belle Époque. The tercentenary of the publication of the novel was celebrated on grand scale throughout Spain. The goal was to bring the nation together after the humiliating defeat in the Spanish-American War while instilling pride in the country's great literary heritage. I was amazed at the amount of effort and money spent to commemorate a book about a fictional hero fighting windmills. At the same time, the newspapers were full of stories about the dissolution of the Soviet Union, the war in Yugoslavia, and the genocide in Rwanda. Nationalism, therefore, became one of the main topics of my research, and indirectly it has continued to be over the last twenty years.

But why write a world history of nationalism? From early on, as an outsider to Spanish history, I wondered why phenomena that also occurred in other parts of Europe were explained by examining only domestic developments.

of authors from various parts of the world. The end result of all these experiences now lies in front of you.

This book would not have seen the light of day without the enthusiastic support from Princeton University Press, where Ben Tate and Josh Drake faithfully guided me through the editing process, and Alfabet Uitgevers, which at an early stage was willing to publish a Dutch translation and where Catharina Schilder gave me very useful feedback. I have also profited from the generous support of many colleagues and friends. I feel very privileged to be part of the Institute for History of Leiden University, where over the years Wim van der Doel, Jeroen Duindam, Henk te Velde, and Bernhard Rieger have encouraged me in my academic endeavors. The Institute also awarded me a sabbatical in 2019 to 2020, part of which I spent at the Friedrich Meinecke Institute of the Free University in Berlin. Its great library collections and the inspiring conversations with, among others, Sebastian Conrad (my host at the global history section), Nader Sohrabi, Fidel Tavárez, and Ben Van Zee, provided a very stimulating environment in which to conduct my research. I received extremely useful tips from a large number of Leiden colleagues, including Joost Augusteijn, Eric Jorink, Henk Kern, Leo Lucassen, Damian Pargas, Walter Nkwi Gam, Dennie Oude Nijhuis, Judith Pollmann, Andrew Shield, Soledad Validiva Rivera, and Carolien Stolte. Colleagues at other universities, such as Mark Bassin, Paul Betts, Wessel Krul, Joep Leerssen, Matthijs Lok, Siniša Malešević, Fernando Molina, Ben de Pater, José María Portillo, and Andreas Stucki, also provided me with great feedback. Others were so kind to read early drafts of one or several chapters. I certainly have to mention Patrick Dassen, Dario Fazzi, Anne Heyer, Maartje Janse, Geoffrey Jensen, Kenan van de Mieroop, Raúl Moreno Almendral, Javier Moreno Luzón, Herman Paul, Alejandro Quiroga, Anne-Isabelle Richard, Diederik Smit, Maarten Van Ginderachter, Peer Vries, and Claire Weeda. Very inspiring also were the many lectures and debates organized in collaboration with André Gerrits of the Leiden University Nationalism Network and the online events we organized with Marco Antonsich (Loughborough University), Szabolcs Pogonyi (Central European University), and Gezim Krasniqi (Edinburgh University). Finally, I would like to thank my students at Leiden University. During the various seminars I have taught on the topic of nationalism, they provided me with great questions, fresh insights, and fascinating papers that have inspired several passages in *Nationalism: A World History*.

Introduction

NATIONALISM AS A GLOBAL PHENOMENON

NATIONALISM IS CLEARLY on the rise. Populist politicians with a nationalist program have recently won elections in many parts of the world. Viktor Orbán did so in Hungary in 2010, Narendra Modi in India in 2014, Rodrigo Duterte in the Philippines in 2016, Donald Trump in the United States in 2016, and Jair Bolsonaro in Brazil in 2018. They all argue that their nation's identity and interests should be protected against globalization, immigration, and assertive minorities. Meanwhile, the United Kingdom voted to leave the European Union in order to "gain back control." It also seems that xenophobic incidents occur more frequently. Notwithstanding the emphasis these right-wing populists put on national independence and the protection of their unique traditions and culture, it is quite curious that this nationalist wave seems to have occurred simultaneously around the world.

Moreover, the forms in which nationalism expresses itself are also strikingly similar throughout the globe. During the football World Cups, a "feel-good nationalism" can be found almost everywhere, even quite prominently in relatively new countries such as those in sub-Saharan Africa. As in many other parts of the world, people in Cameroon—a five-time winner of the Africa Cup of Nations—gather with family and friends to watch the matches of the national team. Radio shows, television programs, and internet forums discuss the performance of the squad for weeks, producing a national conversation in which supporters from all walks of life participate. Football—known as soccer in the United States—strongly contributes to the reproduction of the imagined community of the nation. However, the nation is not just imagined, it is also performed. At international matches, fans come to the stadium wearing the national jersey and waving the national flag. Some attend the game with painted faces, wigs in the national colors, or spectacular hats, while others even dress up in fantastical costumes inspired by various national stereotypes (figure I.1). Some play typical music on characteristic instruments or special songs composed for the occasion.[1]

FIGURE 1.1 Senegalese fans on stands at the FIFA World Cup, Moscow, June 2018. These supporters, also known as the Twelfth Lion, are dressed in the national colors and have painted their bodies with letters forming the word "Senegal." At the national team's important matches they are accompanied by musicians and perform traditional dances.

Nationalism tends to be associated with chauvinist demagogues, xenophobic movements, wars of conquest, ethnic-cleansing campaigns, or even genocide. However, at World Cups, it can also bring people together. Moreover, nationalism can even be used to pacify a tense or warlike situation. In Ivory Coast, the national football team actually contributed to the consolidation of a fragile peace agreement between the government and northern insurgents. In 2007, team captain Didier Drogba insisted that the next qualifying match for the World Cup would be played in Bouaké, which had been the center of the rebel forces. The 5-0 win over Madagascar, with the final goal by Drogba himself, provoked an outburst of collective joy that helped in bringing the two parts of the country together.[2]

Even in sub-Saharan countries with highly artificial borders and very diverse populations, nationalism has taken hold of the imagination and has a strong impact on everyday life. Cameroon, for instance, has around 280 ethnic groups and hundreds of languages. Nonetheless, its inhabitants express their national feelings en masse during sporting events, cheering their national representatives.[3] But what is the nation that they identify with? Membership is clearly not determined by ethnicity or culture. In fact, the nation consists of the community of citizens, the *demos*, and is defined primarily by the state.

There are also many nations that can be characterized in a very different way: as an *ethnos*, a large group of people sharing the same ethnic background, language, and culture. However, many nations defined in such terms, such as the Kurds or Catalans, do not have their own state and consequently could be described as nations without a state, or state-seeking nations. There are many such culturally unified nations, but they are all excluded from World Cups because the International Association Football Federation (FIFA)— just like the International Olympic Committee and the United Nations— only admits independent states. These state-seeking nations moreover cannot alone determine their fate. This became clear in the autumn of 2017, when both the Kurds and the Catalans organized independence referendums based on the right to self-determination, which received broad support from the voters. However, since these plebiscites were not authorized by the governments of Iraq and Spain, respectively, the international community did not recognize Kurdistan and Catalonia as independent nation-states. They therefore remain barred from international organizations and sports contests.[4]

Yet, the cases of Kurdistan and Catalonia are less straightforward than they seem. In fact, political entities tried to become independent in 2017, not national communities. In the Kurdish case, it was the autonomous Kurdistan Region within Iraq that organized the plebiscite, while in Spain, the government of the autonomous region of Catalonia took the initiative. Moreover, both regions are not ethnically or linguistically homogenous, and many speakers of Kurdish and Catalan live in adjacent territories. Thus, large Kurdish minorities can be found in Syria, Turkey, and Iran, while lots of Catalan speakers live in neighboring regions of Spain, the principality of Andorra, Southern France, and on the Italian island of Sardinia. So nationalism is not so much the spontaneous expression of feelings of belonging by members of a particular community; it is mostly channeled through territorial authorities and institutions such as nation-states, education systems, armies, political parties, national football teams, and regional governments.

So we may conclude that the conventional understanding of the nation as a large group of people united by common descent, a shared language, culture, or religion that has—or strives for—its own state does not reflect reality. Actually, there is a profound mismatch between the number of states and the number of potential nations. Currently, the United Nations has 193 member states, and according to a recent estimate there are 7,151 living languages in the world. Moreover, only a fraction of the existing states is ethnically or culturally homogenous.[5]

But whereas ethnically or culturally homogenous states are an exception, the nation-state model has been adopted throughout the world. The nation-state was invented in the United States and France during the age of revolutions, and it was fundamentally different from existing forms of statehood such as tribal federations, city-states, autocratic empires, and absolute monarchies. A nation-state has a clearly bounded territory and is based on the sovereignty of the nation, which expresses itself in a (written) constitution, equality before the law, and an institutionalized form of political participation. As a result, the nation is formed by the community of citizens—the *demos*—which therefore is not necessarily ethnically or culturally homogenous. Remarkably, the nation-state has been an extraordinary success. By now, almost all countries have adopted the nation-state model, leaving only a handful of exceptions such as the absolute monarchies of Saudi Arabia and Brunei, or religiously defined states such as Vatican City and the Islamic Emirate of Afghanistan.[6]

Thus, nationalism—defined as striving for or loyalty to a nationally defined state—is a complex phenomenon. Nations can be characterized in terms of *demos* or *ethnos*, they can be based on state-oriented or state-seeking nationalism, they can focus on what binds people together or on excluding outsiders, and they can be both peaceful and violent. And as every historian knows, things profoundly change over time, and so do nations and nationalism. In order to get a good understanding of the history of nationalism across the globe, we need to explore both the enormous success of the nation-state and the variegated impact of nationalism on people around the world.

A Fresh Approach

Since the revival of openly expressed nationalism in the 1980s and 1990s, the number of studies on this topic has grown enormously, profoundly improving our understanding of the evolution of nationalism in the different parts of the world.[7] Nonetheless, a fresh approach is needed. In general, existing studies have five serious flaws: (1) they mostly take *ethnos*-type nations as a starting point; (2) they focus excessively on nationalist activists; (3) they mostly interpret nationalism as being transferred from the West to "the rest"; (4) they see the replacement of empires by nation-states as largely inevitable; and (5) they tend to suffer from various forms of methodological nationalism.

First, scholars still primarily use an ethnic or cultural definition of the nation. This is particularly true of authors studying expressions of national consciousness before the late eighteenth century, as they generally emphasize the continuity between older ethnic identities and modern nations.[8] Surprisingly, many scholars focusing on modern forms of nationalism equally assume that nations have a cultural core. This is even the case with some of the classical modernist studies that continue to be points of departure for most investigations. Both Benedict Anderson and Ernest Gellner assign a crucial role to language and culture, the former by emphasizing the role of print capitalism in standardizing vernacular languages and thus creating cohesive national cultures, and the latter by arguing that mass education in a national language was required in industrial societies.[9] However, the invention of the nation-state during the age of revolutions was the consequence of a conflict about political legitimacy in which ethnic, cultural, and language differences did not play a substantial role. So in order to understand the rise of the nation-state model, we primarily need to take into account the nation as a *demos*, a community of citizens.

Second, the traditional focus on nationalist movements and their leaders has been challenged by the historical sociologist Andreas Wimmer, who in *Waves of War* (2013) uses big data and sophisticated statistical analysis to refute the almost exclusive focus on domestic actors. His study demonstrates that even if a population enthusiastically embraced the ideals propagated by nationalist activists, the most important factor in determining whether a nationalist movement succeeded in creating a sovereign nation-state was the existence of an international "window of opportunity." Independence mostly can be explained by widespread geopolitical instability or substantial international power shifts. Internal factors such as the strength of a nationalist movement— or socioeconomic modernization—had a modest impact, at best. Examples of such windows of opportunity are the Atlantic Revolutions, the Second World War, and the fall of the Berlin Wall, each of which enabled the creation of a wave of new independent nation-states.[10]

Third, the spread of nationalism has generally been interpreted as a process of dissemination from the West to the rest, largely linked to the advance of the modernization process. It first affected Western Europe and the Americas, after which nationalist movements arose in Central and Eastern Europe. By the end of the First World War, the nation-state had become the norm in the West, inspiring anti-imperial activists in the colonies to start claiming independence.[11] Wimmer, however, repudiates the view that nationalism is the consequence of a linear modernization process. The modernity of the economy, an expanding infrastructure, or high literacy rates—like the strength of the nationalist movement—were not very relevant for explaining the dissemination of the nation-state model during the nineteenth and twentieth century.[12] Recent studies, moreover, have shown that at the end of the eighteenth century the world was much more connected than we previously thought. Activists and statesmen from around the world felt inspired by the new nation-state model and immediately tried to adopt various of its aspects. This means that nationalist ideas were widely present in the non-Western world long before the rise of the anticolonial independence movements.[13]

Fourth, the view that empires were outdated and inexorably would be replaced by modern nation-states has been refuted as well. Recently, various scholars have made clear that nation-states and empires were not completely opposed forms of statehood. Actually, until the 1960s, most Western European nation-states were also colonial empires. At the same time, many traditional empires adopted various elements of the nation-state. Hybrid forms such as imperial nation-states and nationalizing empires were very common during much of the nineteenth and twentieth centuries. This means that in many cases, the emergence of the nation-state was not a sudden conversion, but rather the result of a gradual transformation.[14] As a consequence, reformist politicians in traditional states in Eastern Europe, Asia, and Africa probably had a more important role in appropriating and disseminating the nation-state model than Western propagandists or anticolonial movements. Moreover, even at the height of the decolonization process, many newly independent countries tried to create broad federations. So it was only toward the end of the 1960s, when most of these federations had ended in failure, that the nation-state achieved a hegemonic position, turning the international system based on sovereign nation-states into the natural order of things.

Finally, various forms of methodological nationalism have distorted the understanding of the history of nationalism. The overwhelming majority of investigations are case studies that primarily examine developments within one national context, while focusing mostly on individual actors and events.[15] This is a logical approach for historians. Traditionally, historians argue that in order to understand a society, one has to study its roots. However, this generally encourages scholars to explain developments almost exclusively from a national perspective by focusing primarily on domestic actors and ignoring foreign influences and transnational patterns, resulting in exceptional paths for each nation. Thus, existing studies largely emphasize national differences, while often implying that every nation—as a dedicated nationalist would also argue—is unique.[16] More ambitious historical overviews tend to focus on one continent, while also portraying developments in the area under study as exceptional.[17] Truly global interpretations of the history of nationalism, on the other hand, are almost nonexistent or outdated.[18]

Nationalism: A World History, therefore, breaks new ground by analyzing the rise and evolution of nationalism as a global process. It also aims to escape the stranglehold of methodological nationalism by avoiding the excessive focus on individual cases, singular events, and national differences. Instead of examining the nationalists themselves and their roles in exceptional situations such as wars and political conflicts, the goal of this book is to understand the structural impact of nationalism on the wider population. This should be done accurately, and since the causal relationship between the propagation of nationalist ideas—primarily based on the *ethnos*—and the advance of the nation-state model—mostly based on the *demos*—is very weak, both topics will be studied in parallel. The aim is to show both how people became receptive to the nationalist message and how they related to the nation-state.

This will be done with an indirect method. A real bottom-up approach—giving a voice to hundreds or thousands of individuals from the past—would be an enormous challenge but would hardly provide a meaningful picture of the manifold ways in which nationalism influenced the world. Therefore, I will focus on the practical effects of the rise and evolution of nationalism, by exploring the advance of the nation-state model and the nationalization of the cultural realm as two interrelated but separate processes. This book will analyze these processes by focusing on four themes: (1) the creation of new nation-states, (2) the meaning and reach of citizenship, (3) the impact of nationalism on the cultural realm, and (4) the nationalization of the physical environment.

By systematically studying these four themes, it will become clear that the rise of new nation-states was determined mostly by major shifts in the international context, that the relationship between nation-states and their citizens evolved largely according to global patterns, and that worldwide intellectual trends affected both the nationalization of the cultural sphere and the nationalization of the physical environment. Actually, the main watershed moments were global and often affected all four realms in a similar way.

Structure of the Book

The book adopts a chronological format in order to show that nationalism changed profoundly over time and that its evolution was far from linear. It opens with a chapter that provides a brief overview of the evolution of national identities from the Middle Ages until the age of revolutions. This is followed by seven chronological chapters that examine a period of about thirty to forty years and which are divided by major international turning points: the beginning of the American War for Independence in 1775, the Congress of Vienna of 1815, the Revolutions of 1848, the start of modern imperialism as a result of the Berlin Conference of 1885, the beginning of the First World War in 1914, the end of the Second World War in 1945, and finally 1979, the year that saw the international breakthroughs of neoliberalism with the election of Margaret Thatcher and of identity politics with the Iranian Revolution.

Within the chapters, the approach will be thematic. Developments are largely examined by clusters of countries—for instance, by continent, by empire, or by focusing on a number of neighboring states—or by subthemes, such as the impact of nationalism on specific scientific disciplines or cultural domains. The emphasis will be on structural mechanisms, shared patterns, and general trends. *Nationalism: A World History* will not systematically chart the transnational contacts and networks that enabled the quick spread of nationalist ideas. Although international contacts will be mentioned occasionally in the text, it is clear that the awareness of nationalist developments elsewhere was widespread; most activists had extensive transnational networks, and more often than not, inspiration came from outside sources.

As for the geographical reach of the book, the first chapters will concentrate on Europe, as it was there that the nation-state ideal arose. But even at this stage, the Americas already played an important role, and short references to similar developments in Asia and Africa will appear now and then. From the early nineteenth century on, the story will become more global. The aim of the book is not to be all-encompassing; not all countries or cultural domains can be discussed in detail, and for the most part a few relevant examples from various parts of the world are used to illustrate a more general trend.

In the first section of each chapter, I will discuss the rise and spread of the nation-state model. The nation-state was invented during the American and French Revolutions. The ideal of the sovereignty of the nation, which implied legal equality and political participation, was particularly attractive for members of the middle classes around the world, but their leverage was quite limited. Reformist rulers of traditional states would have more impact. They quickly became aware that nation-states mostly had the upper hand in international conflicts, and as a consequence, they aimed to strengthen their states by adopting some of its most useful elements. A major international power shift, exemplified by a humiliating defeat, often provided the incentive for traditional states like the tsarist and Ottoman Empires, Madagascar, Persia, Siam, and Japan to drastically change course. Using the concept of isomorphism, I will elucidate the mechanisms that subsequently gave rise to a growing number of remarkably uniform (nation-) states.[19] In order to strengthen the state, reformist politicians introduced conscription, a centralized bureaucracy, individual property rights, legal equality, and secular education. Many of these innovations were introduced in the European colonies as well, while the process of decolonization—which equally was connected to large-scale geopolitical crises—came to imply the wholesale adoption of the nation-state model. From 1789, most new states, first in Europe and the Americas and then in the rest of the world, adopted a constitution, a form of representative government, and several of the other institutions that had become inextricably linked with the nation-state model. During the twentieth century, this isomorphic process of nation-state formation was reinforced by international organizations such as the United Nations and the International Monetary Fund, which, directly or indirectly, require member states to adopt similar institutions and procedures.

The second section, on citizenship, shows how inhabitants were connected to the nation-state. Initially, the criterion of "civilization" was used to
exclude women, Indigenous populations, and people of color from (full)
civic and political rights. During the nineteenth century, national citizenship
often was attractive to middle-class males only: they were given the right to
vote. At the same time, it was mostly experienced as a burden by the lower
classes, especially in the countryside, where the introduction of the nation-
state was accompanied by direct rule, conscription, and rising taxes. Racial
ideas gained currency toward the end of nineteenth century and served to
exclude ethnic minorities and specific immigrant groups. Some ethnic communities were made the target of eugenic measures, ethnic-cleansing campaigns, or programs of forced assimilation. Over time, however, nation-states
provided more services to their citizens, and many adopted the model of the
welfare state. In addition, the emancipation of women, Indigenous populations, and the LGBTQ+ community gave (more) civic rights to wider sections
of the population, more fully integrating them into the nation. Recently, the
guarding of national borders has been strengthened, especially against the
entry of poor immigrants.

But how and when did ideas and practices related to the nation become
relevant for large sections of the population? This is the topic of the third section of each chapter. Although vague conceptions of nationhood existed before
the eighteenth century, ethnic and cultural differences did not play a significant
role in the invention of the nation-state during the Atlantic Revolutions. The
conceptual framework needed to delineate a secular domain of human cultural
activity came into being only during the Enlightenment, when umbrella terms
such as culture, civilization, art, society, and progress received their modern
meanings. The nationalization of the creative activities of humanity began in
earnest during the Romantic era, when the nation was increasingly defined as
a linguistic and cultural community. As a consequence, a single (Christian)
civilization was largely replaced by a growing number of distinct national cultures, each with a standardized national language. In the humanities and social
sciences, the nation increasingly became the basic unit of analysis, and by constructing national histories, defining national canons, and even gathering
national statistics, the nation was reified in scholarly discourse. Artists, musicians, and writers did the same by representing and characterizing the nation
in many of their works. The impact of racial ideas on the cultural sphere was
most profound from the 1890s until the 1940s. Although after 1945 avant-garde
modernism propagated a kind of placeless cosmopolitanism, mass media continued to naturalize the division of the world into discrete nations, each with
their own characteristics. The affirmation of culturally defined national identities has made a strong comeback since the late 1970s, as testified by the rise of

identity politics and populism. Recently, collective identities have been strengthened by the echo chambers of social media.

The fourth section deals with the nationalization of the physical environment, which began during the Romantic era when the first national museums and monuments appeared in European and American capitals. Throughout the nineteenth century, new monumental state buildings, statues of national heroes, nationalist street names, and the preservation of cultural heritage helped to nationalize public spaces throughout large parts of the world. Toward the end of the century, extraordinary landscapes, characteristic buildings, and many aspects of the domestic sphere were nationalized as well, including the decorative and culinary arts, the design of gardens, and pets. World's fairs, tourism, and later, UNESCO's World Heritage List were instrumental in disseminating standardized representations of national identity such as vernacular buildings, artisanal products, traditional costumes, typical dishes, folklore, and characteristic souvenirs, which could be defined as a process of cultural isomorphism. Moreover, the branding of products as originating from a specific nation—such as Camembert, tequila, sushi, Volkswagen, and Ikea furniture—became an established marketing strategy during the twentieth century. In all these ways, the common association that exists between national identities, the physical environment, and various aspects of everyday life were normalized and became second nature to people around the globe.

A last word on more practical issues. In a book that targets a global audience, non-English terms are avoided as much as possible, so most of them are translated. Exceptions are only made for widely used terms, such as "samurai." I have tried to respect the East Asian tradition of mentioning first the family name and then the first name. For pragmatic reasons, I have adopted the transcription of names from other writing systems by adopting the form used by some of the main English-language authors on which my argument in that particular instance is based.

1

Early Conceptions of Nationhood

SCHOLARS GENERALLY concur that the nation-state was invented toward the end of the eighteenth century, but they strongly disagree about whether nations or early forms of nationalism already existed before then. According to the dominant modernist view, they did not; nations and nationalism are a consequence of the rise of modernity. In *Imagined Communities*, Benedict Anderson argues that the nation as a limited and sovereign community only became possible as the consequence of a long process of secularization that undermined the divinely sanctioned power of monarchs and the existing religious conceptions of time and history, and with the replacement of sacred script languages by national print languages—two developments that began only in the early modern period.[1] In *Nations and Nationalism*, Ernest Gellner focuses on a later period: the transition from agricultural to industrial society. According to him, modern industrial societies require mass education in a standard language and thereby turn a generally very heterogenous population into a culturally homogenic nation. This means that ethnic minorities have the option to either assimilate into the dominant nation or begin their own nationalist movement.[2] Eric Hobsbawm largely agrees with Gellner, arguing that nations are constructed from above by states and nationalist movements. For both Gellner and Hobsbawm, nations are the product of nationalism and not the other way around.[3]

Although the modernist interpretation is accepted by most scholars who deal with modern forms of nationalism, it is heavily contested by experts who focus on earlier periods of history. This has led to two almost separate fields of study whose practitioners barely communicate with each other, and when they do, discussions easily get heated, which happened for instance at the 1995 Warwick debates between Ernest Gellner and his former student Anthony D. Smith, or more recently, at the occasion of the publication of ambitious studies by Caspar Hirschi and Azar Gat that attack the modernist consensus.[4] However, those who oppose the modernist view do not agree on an alternative explanation for the rise of nationalism.[5] Some argue that human beings have a primordial inclination to identify with people who are related to them; thus, members of an ethnic group or nation naturally bond together. Others assert that national societies have always existed, while a third group of authors claim that most modern nations are based on earlier ethnic communities and have largely adopted their myths, symbols, and narratives.[6]

Historians generally are quite pragmatic and do not try to develop a comprehensive theory to explain the rise of nationalism. However, those who deal with earlier forms of nationhood provide a wide variety of often conflicting interpretations. Some assert that nations, or at least a form of national consciousness, could be found in the European Reformation.[7] Others search for their origins in the Middle Ages or Renaissance,[8] while another group of scholars detects their presence in biblical times[9] or in ancient Greece, Egypt, or China.[10] Even when dealing with a particular case, opinions diverge. Some have argued that a certain awareness of the English nation can already be found in the early eighth century. Other experts situate the nation's origins in the Norman invasion of 1066, in the growing opposition against the Norman "oppressors" in the following centuries, in the loss of the French possessions during the Hundred Years' War and the growing role of the English language, or in the destruction of the traditional feudal elite during the sixteenth century that led to unprecedented social mobility and a community of more or less equal citizens.[11] Thus, before the nation-states provided legal rules to define who exactly belonged to the nation, these writers used a variety of cultural, social, and political criteria ranging from collective awareness to language use, social homogenization, civic equality, collective resistance, and territorial unification.

Although the focus of *Nationalism: A World History* is on the nation-state, it is useful to assess the role of conceptions of nationhood before the age of revolutions. The new model of the nation-state was quickly adopted around the world, but it arose primarily as a consequence of (Western) European developments. This chapter, therefore, provides a brief overview of the various conceptions of nationhood in Europe from the Middle Ages until the late eighteenth century and it examines several political and intellectual trends that preceded the invention of the nation-state, including the consolidation of powerful territorial states.

This does not mean that Western Europe was unique. In an ambitious comparative study, Victor Lieberman has shown that there were many striking parallels between the state-building processes in East Asia and Western Europe. He argues that from about the ninth century until the early nineteenth, state formation in large parts of the Eurasian continent, responding to almost synchronic economic, climatic, and military developments, evolved along similar lines. He detects four cycles of political consolidation, the third and main one beginning in the early seventeenth century. New forms of warfare—with cannons and firearms—led to the consolidation of larger, more centralized states. This happened not just in Europe but also in Burma (modern-day Myanmar), Siam (Thailand), Vietnam, China, and Japan, leading to demographic growth, an expanding tax base, economic integration, and, crucially, growing cultural uniformity. In fact, the Chinese Empire had already achieved considerable cultural unity under the Song dynasty (960–1276) thanks to the civil service examinations, which spread a uniform set of ideas based on Confucianism. These were absorbed not just by a significant number of state officials but also by a much wider group of literati. Moreover, the Chinese language based on characters enabled written communication between educated elites regardless of the vernacular languages they spoke. During the seventeenth and eighteenth centuries Burma, Siam, and Vietnam also became more culturally uniform. The monarchies succeeded in limiting the autonomy of religious institutions, literacy rates rose, and the elite culture of the dominant ethnic group was increasingly adopted by both the lower classes and the populations of peripheral areas. The state clearly favored this process.[12] Lieberman defines this growing synergy of economic, political, and cultural integration as "politicized ethnicity," meaning that a dominant ethnic group increasingly identified with the state. However, according to Lieberman, this was still fundamentally different from modern nationalism because these early modern Asian states continued to be strongly hierarchical, took legal and linguistic pluralism for granted, and promoted a universal religious worldview, which also sanctioned the right of the monarch to rule.[13]

Other authors have shown that the introduction of gunpowder, too, led to the consolidation of large centralized states in other parts of Asia and in Africa. The Muslim empires of the Ottomans, the Safavids, and the Moghuls initiated this process in the sixteenth century. State-building in their realms led to economic prosperity, demographic growth, and more cultural unity. Largely based on the same principles, the kingdoms of Dahomey and Oyo in West Africa also began to expand during the early seventeenth century.[14] The question now is, what conceptions of nationhood existed in premodern Europe, and how were processes of state-building and growing cultural homogenization related to the invention of the nation-state during the age of revolutions?

Ethnic Identities and State-Building in Late Medieval and Early Modern Europe

During the Middle Ages, the Bible and classical antiquity were the main sources for the identification of territories and their inhabitants. The division of the world into Asia, Africa, and Europe—which had its origins in classical

Greece—was linked to Noah's sons Shem, Ham, and Japheth, and another biblical story, about the Tower of Babel, explained the existence of different languages. In the context of the Crusades, clerics from various parts of Europe began to argue that their community had a special bond with God, that they were the "chosen people" or the "New Israelites." On the other hand, many cities, peoples, and dynasties claimed to have been founded by mythical heroes from classical antiquity such as Alexander the Great, and many Roman names for territories (such as Britannia, Germania, Gallia) and tribes (Franks, Scythians, and Goths) were still widely used.[15]

Concepts from classical Rome that categorized people or defined feelings of belonging remained in circulation, such as *populus* (people), which generally referred to fellow Romans (excluding slaves and aliens), whereas people from outside were defined as *gens* (related to "descent") or *natio* (connected to land of birth). *Patria* (fatherland) could refer to *patria naturae*, the place where one had grown up, which was connected to family and nostalgia, and to *patria civitatis*, the political community, defined by freedom, the common good, and laws sanctioned by the gods, to which one owed allegiance and loyalty.[16]

Differences between ethnic groups were addressed frequently in the later Middle Ages. There were lists of ethnic groups with their specific virtues and vices, ethnic slanging matches occurred frequently at universities, and populations were regularly characterized in literary and historical narratives. The attributes assigned to ethnic groups were derived from ancient myths and etymology; names were seen as a tool to decipher hidden meanings of God's creation. Hippocratic-Galenic medical theories on man's humoral complexion, which had been rediscovered in the eleventh century through Arabic sources, and Aristotle's *Politics* provided the main sources of inspiration for relating the influence of the climate on human temperament to the specific characteristics of entire communities. More mundane factors were also taken into account, such as diets (wine and olive oil, for instance, versus beer and dairy products), martial attitudes, and supposed degrees of civility. As a result, many lasting stereotypes, such as Spanish pomp and German strength, came into circulation.[17]

The way individuals defined themselves in a territorial sense depended on the actual context. During the Crusades, inhabitants of the Kingdom of France tended to identify themselves as belonging to the *natio Francorum*," while closer at home they probably referred to themselves as the inhabitants of a duchy or county, such as Gascons or Burgundians, or of a specific town or village. Sometimes a people's collective identity was linked not to a territory but to an ethnic group such as the Celts, or to a territorial entity that did not exist anymore, such as the Roman province of Italia. In any case, in feudal societies borders were diffuse and shifted frequently; personal loyalties to local

barons or to the king prevailed over specific territorial attachments. That countries were not yet an obvious frame of reference becomes clear by looking at
international encounters. In many European cities, merchants and students
were classified in "nations," more or less according to language group, which
did not lead to neat divisions. The University of Paris distinguished between
Gallic, Norman, Picard, and Anglican nations: Germans, Poles, and Scandina-
vians belonged to the Anglican nation, whereas Greeks, Italians, and Spaniards
were classified as Gallicans. The University of Orléans meanwhile had ten nations, eight of which referred to different provinces of France; the German
nation, on the other hand, consisted of students from the Holy Roman Empire,
England, Denmark, Poland, Dalmatia, and Italy.[18] At church councils, division
into "nations" had become common as well. At the Council of Constance, the
German nation included representatives from Hungary, Croatia, Bohemia,
Poland, Denmark, and Sweden.[19]

Religious differences between Christians, Jews, Muslims, and heathens
were much more important than those between "nations," and the identarian
boundaries between them were much sharper. Christianity was seen as a fundamentally coherent unity. Both the papacy and the Holy Roman Empire
cherished the Roman heritage and had universal pretensions. This entailed a
bipolar relationship with the non-Christian world, which was seen as essentially
inferior.[20] The view was not very different in the Muslim empires—which
drew a sharp distinction between the "territory of Islam" and the "territory of
war"—or in China.[21]

Due to the feudal system, political and military authority was highly fragmented in Europe. Social and legal differences were very pronounced, and
members of the different social groups—nobles, clerics, burghers, and
peasants—behaved and dressed in distinct ways, which were often codified in
sumptuary laws. Often, peasants and serfs were not even regarded as fully
human; they were depicted as degraded, dark-skinned creatures who were
ignorant of the true faith and therefore barely distinguishable from animals.[22]
"Nations," as a consequence, were not stable, fixed entities; instead, they were
categorized according to circumstance. Moreover, the often quite vague "ethnic" boundaries rarely overlapped with state borders, which in this period
were equally fluid. Social and religious cleavages were much more pronounced,
and these often coincided with differences in rights, language, and behavior.

The rise of centralized states in Europe from the late medieval period onward
slowly undermined the supremacy of the pope and the emperor and seriously
weakened the territorial power of the landed nobility, leading to a new, multi-
polar state system. The process of state centralization started around the
twelfth century, when improved infrastructures and the growing use of written
communication increased the center's hold over local affairs. Military

innovations, however, were critical. By the fourteenth century, mounted knights, which had formed the core of a feudal army, were being defeated by well-organized infantry forces, which happened for instance at the Battle of Crécy in 1346 during the Hundred Years' War. The introduction of the cannon (a Chinese invention) at about the same time fatally undermined the independent military power of the aristocracy; city walls and castles could easily be breached with the rapidly improved artillery. Cannons, mercenary armies, and new types of fortresses hugely inflated the costs of warfare and induced states to become more centralized and to increase their tax revenues. This process continued in the early modern period. The size of new standing armies kept growing and soldiers needed more training, while long sieges of strategic cities replaced short, decisive battles. As a consequence, small states and those that did not successfully follow the new centralizing tendencies became vulnerable, and only enterprising mercantile states like Venice, Portugal, England, and the Dutch Republic could compete with strong monarchic states such as Spain, France, Sweden, and Austria.[23]

In Europe, the state-building process was further reinforced by both the Reformation and the age of exploration. The sixteenth-century Reformation disrupted the fundamental unity of Western Christianity, and the wars of religion finished off the universal aspirations of the Holy Roman Empire. Principalities that went over to Protestantism dismantled the independent power of the Catholic Church by confiscating monastic properties and creating new state churches, as in England and the Lutheran parts of Europe. Although Catholic monarchs did respect the earthly possessions of the Church, they also succeeded in increasing their control over the clergy. At about the same time, the exploration of the sea routes to Asia and the "discovery" and conquest of the Americas strengthened the European states on the borders of the Atlantic, which now became the most dynamic part of the Old World. Long-distance trade (which was largely organized through chartered companies) and colonial settlement required protection by the navy and, in many instances, the presence of armed forces as well, so state support was crucial.[24]

As a consequence, states had to increase their fiscal resources, which also implied more control over their territory, both at the borders and in the interior. Many states began to adopt mercantilist policies, supporting domestic industries and shipping while reducing internal tariffs, all with the goal of increasing the country's wealth. Internal communications were improved by the construction of new roads. Maps increasingly showed state borders, and fortifications were built to protect the territory of the state. To this end, toward the end of the seventeenth century, Louis XIV, the French "Sun King" who became the embodiment of royal absolutism, ordered Vauban to construct hundreds of new fortresses to defend the borders of the kingdom.[25]

The inhabitants of these states were not passive bystanders in this process. They actively requested protection from the monarch when needed, providing further opportunities for the state to enhance its territorial reach. But central control was not always welcomed. Indeed, because the state was associated with taxes and warfare. it was often seen as a burden by large parts of the population.[26] Some critics, especially among Protestants in France, the Low Countries, and England, began to theorize about the right to resist a despotic monarch who did not respect traditional liberties—which were, in fact, corporate privileges. Inspired by uprisings against monarchs in the French religious wars, the Dutch Revolt, the English Civil War, and the Glorious Revolution, they developed ideas about a social contract between the ruler and his subjects. This way, religious legitimizations of royal power, especially the divine right theory and other forms of sacred kingship, were slowly being replaced by a more secular interpretation. As a result, the idea of a patrimonial monarchy, in which the state was seen as the private patrimony of the ruling dynasty, was slowly being abandoned as the interests of the king were separated from those of the state.[27]

The growing strength of the state also had an impact on the way territorial identities were formulated. According to Caspar Hirschi, the Renaissance brought new interpretations, particularly by reworking the ideas of classical authors such as Cicero and Tacitus. In the Italian city-states, authors like Leonardo Bruni and Niccolò Machiavelli tried to revive the civic republican tradition from classical antiquity, based primarily on the ideas of Cicero. According to this statesman of the late Roman Republic, the duty of a virtuous citizen was to defend the patria on the battlefield, to vindicate the public good in the political arena, and to praise the fatherland in speech and writing.[28] Humanists in Italian city-states and elsewhere in Western Europe followed Cicero's model of the learned orator by lauding their patria. However, most of these historians, legal experts, and political theorists did so in the service of princes.[29] Interestingly, writers from Italian city-states also promoted "Italy" by depicting other Europeans as mere "barbarians." German and French humanists countered by defending the honor of their "nations" vis-à-vis their Italian colleagues; paradoxically, most German humanists did so in Latin, and by updating classical ideals. The diffuse nature of the concept also became evident in Spanish America, where many authors praised their patria in numerous publications. "Patria" could refer to their home city, their province or viceroyalty, or even to America as a whole, as many scholars defended the New World against disparaging views from Europe.[30] Nonetheless, the more critical aspects of civic republicanism—promoting an active attitude of the citizens in the service of the public realm, while defending civic liberties—did not disappear and were taken up in the following centuries by political thinkers across the Western world.[31]

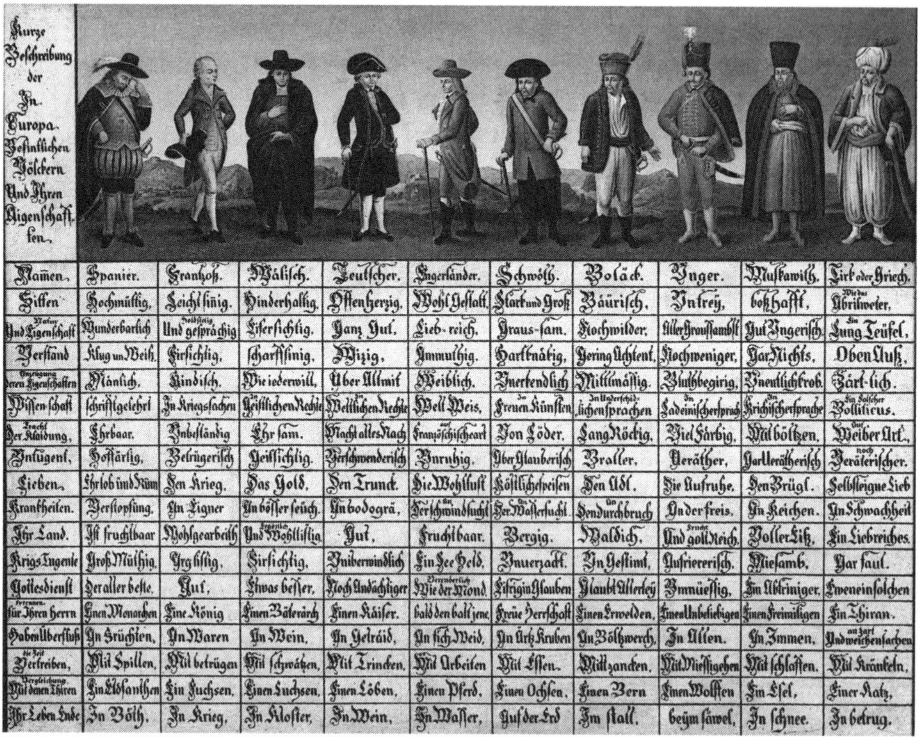

Namen.	Spanier.	Frantzoß.	Wälisch.	Teutscher.	Engerländer.	Schwödt.	Polack.	Unger.	Muskawith.	Tirk oder Griech.
Sitten	Hochmütig,	Leicht sinig.	Hinderhaltig.	Offenhertzig.	Wohl Gestalt	Starck und Groß	Bäurisch,	Untreu,	boßhafft,	Wie das Aprilweter,
Natur Und Eigenschaft	Wunderbarlich	Und holdseelig gesprächig	Eifersichtig.	Ganz Gut,	Lieb-reich.	Graus-sam.	Noch wilder,	Allergraussambst	Gut Ungerisch.	Ein Lung Teüfel,
Verstand	Klug und Weiß.	Fürsichtig,	scharffsinig,	Witzig,	Anmuthig.	Hartnäckig,	Gering Achtent,	Noch weniger,	Gar Nichts,	Oben Auß,
Anzeigung deren Eigenschaften	Männlich,	Kindisch.	Wie iederwill,	Über Allmit	Weiblich.	Unerkendlich	Mittlmässig.	Bluthbegirig,	Unentlich grob.	Zärt-lich.
Wissen-schaft	schriftgelehrt	In Kriegssachen	In Geistlichen Rechte	In Weltlichen Rechte	Welt Weis,	In Freuen Künsten	In Underschid-lichen sprachen	In Lateinischer sprach	In Krichischer sprache	Ein falscher Bolliticus.
Tracht Der Klaidung,	Ehrbaar.	Unbeständig	Ehr sam.	Macht alles Nach	auf Französische art	Von Löder.	Lang Röckig,	Viel Färbig,	Mit böltzen,	auf Weiber Art,
Untugent,	Hoffärtig,	Betrügerisch	Geilsichtig.	Verschwenderisch	Unruhig.	Über Glauberisch	Praller,	Verräther,	Gar Verrätherisch	noch Verräterischer.
Lieben.	Ehrlob und Rüm	Den Krieg,	Das Gold,	Den Trunck.	Die Wohllust	Köstliche speisen	Den Adl,	Die Aufruhr,	Den Prügl.	Selbsteigne Lieb
Kranckheiten.	Verstopfung,	An Eigner	An bösser seüch.	An Podogrä,	An Der schwindsucht	An Der Wassersucht.	An Dendurchbruch	An der freis.	An Keichen.	An Schwachheit
Ihr Land.	Ist fruchtbaar	Wohlgearbeith	Und Fruchtbar Wohllistig.	Gut,	Fruchtbaar.	Bergig.	Waldich,	Und Frucht gold Reich.	Voller Eiß,	Ein Liebreiches.
Krigs Tugende	Groß Müthig,	Arg listig,	Fürsichtig.	Unüberwindlich	Ein See Held,	Unverzagt.	Ungestimt,	Aufrierrerisch.	Miesamb,	Gar faul.
Gottesdienst	Der aller beste,	Gut,	Etwas besser,	Noch Andächtiger	Veränderlich Wie der Mond	Eifrig im Glauben	Glaubt Allerley	Unmüessig,	Ein Abtriniger,	Zweneinsolchen
Erkennen für Ihren herrn	Einen Monarchen	Eine König	Einen Päterärch	Einen Käiser.	bald den bald jene,	Freüe Herrschaft	Einen Erwölden,	Einen Unbeliebigen	Einen Freiwilligen	Ein Thiran.
Haben Überfluß	An Früchten,	An Waren	An Wein,	An Getraid,	An fisch Weid,	An Ertz Gruben	An Bölzwerch,	In Allen.	An Immen,	An zart und weichen sachen
Die Zeit Vertreiben,	Mit Spillen,	Mit betrügen	Mit schwätzen,	Mit Trincken,	Mit Arbeiten	Mit Essen.	Mitt zancken,	Mit Miessiggehen	Mit schlaffen.	Mit Kränkeln,
Vergleichung Mit denen Thiren	Ein Elöfanthen	Ein Fuchsen,	Einen Luchsen,	Einen Löben,	Einen Pferd.	Einen Ochsen,	Einen Bern	Einen Wolffen	Ein Esel,	Einer Katz,
Ihr Leben Ende	In Böth.	In Krieg,	In Kloster,	In Wein,	Im Wasser,	Auf der Erd	Im stall.	beym säwel,	In schnee.	In betrug.

FIGURE 1.1 *Styrian Table of Peoples*, around 1725, oil on canvas, 104 × 126 cm. This *Völkertafel* contains a stereotypical comparison of ten European peoples, briefly characterizing their appearances, personalities, clothing, diseases, war virtues, and pastimes, among other things.

The writings of Tacitus, which were rediscovered during the Renaissance, rapidly gained popularity as well. The Roman author, who grew up during the reign of Emperor Nero, was very critical of the decadence he saw around him, and he praised the rustic virtues of various Germanic tribes. Tacitus thus became a source for various myths of origins. Germanic tribes were now presented as the ancestors of the Germans; the Batavians and the Anglo-Saxons became the forefathers of the Dutch Republic and the English, respectively. Peoples were also routinely compared to each other, for instance in the so-called table of peoples (figure 1.1), which were still largely based on Hippocrates's theories on climate and temperament. Historians, meanwhile, paid less attention to the role of dynasties as the embodiment of a territory, in favor of the inhabitants. During the sixteenth and seventeenth centuries they also began to integrate the new religious differences between Catholics and various strands of Protestants into their narratives. After the recognition of the territorially bounded, sovereign state by the Peace of Westphalia of 1648, which put an end to the European wars of religion, scholars focused more on the relationship between the population and the state.[32]

As a kind of intellectual continuation of the ethnic slanging matches and the tables of peoples, several authors documented the great historical achievements of the patria. In various countries, scholars provided overviews of the great literary authors of the past. Initially, most of these works were written in Latin. Others honored their fatherlands' main virtues in a more didactic manner. Cardinal Richelieu, the powerful chief minister of Louis XIII, for instance, commissioned a portrait gallery of twenty-five French monarchs, ministers, and generals, each embodying a specific virtue, for his new Parisian palace. In 1777 Ove Malling published an extensive *Lives of Eminent Danes, Norwegians, and Holsteinians*, in which he illustrated each important virtue with several short biographies of great individuals from the three parts of the composite Danish kingdom.[33]

In most parts of Europe, the identification of the inhabitants with the state was on the rise. However, the terminology used to refer to peoples and the inhabitants of a state still lacked coherence. Raúl Moreno Almendral argues that in early modern Europe, four different conceptualizations of nationhood can be found; to these, a fifth could be added. Two of the five are primarily cultural and three are more political. First, the term "nation" was applied to a loosely defined group of people sharing the same geographical background or speaking similar languages; from the later Middle Ages this frequently occurred with communities of students, merchants, and clergymen in an international setting. Second, there existed a more consistent classification of the civilized world into "ethnotypes"—that is, more closely defined "peoples," each with its own characteristics. These probably had their origin in the tables of peoples, but now they were based primarily on the virtues Tacitus ascribed to the various Germanic tribes. A third, more political conceptualization was derived from the Roman idea of patria as a political community of citizens. This ideal of civic republicanism was revived during the Renaissance and applied primarily to city-states and small republics. Fourth, "ethnotypes" were often connected to a specific kingdom or realm. As a consequence, a kingdom's "national character" was supposedly also reflected in its specific institutions and the ensemble of its corporate rights. An updated version of this Aristotelian theory was expressed in Montesquieu's *Spirit of the Laws* (1748), in which he argued that political systems were heavily influenced by geographic and climatic conditions.[34] Finally, one may add to this list as a fifth conceptualization the "aristocratic nation," which was particularly used to characterize the Polish-Lithuanian Commonwealth, in which a large group of nobles elected the monarch. This term was also applied to the Kingdoms of Hungary and

Bohemia, where the nobility, which actively distinguished itself from the rest of the population, had a similar predominant position. Even in Western Europe, "nation" often applied only to the elite groups who were represented in the Estates General, Parliament, or the Imperial Diet.[35]

Despite the fact that the meaning of nationhood remained rather vague and the actual meaning could vary considerably, people often appealed to patriotic sentiments. Monarchs, for instance, demanded support from the population, especially when they were in dire straits. During the Hundred Years' War, French kings requested the payment of taxes "for the defense of the patria," and Charles V in his campaign to get elected emperor of the Holy Roman Empire in 1519 presented himself as more German than his competitors.[36] Patriotic feelings could also be invoked to justify an uprising against the legitimate sovereign. At the beginning of the seventeenth century, the Dutch revolt against the king of Spain—which had already been going on for decades and was also a civil and religious war—was successfully framed as a war to defend the traditional liberties of the provinces against a foreign tyrant. Stories from the revolt were popular among the population of the Dutch Republic, while elsewhere, heroes who had fought a foreign enemy, such as Wilhelm Tell and Joan of Arc, lived on in popular memory too.[37]

In the end, it is obvious that the division of humanity into peoples with different, ill-defined characteristics was widely acknowledged. Moreover, many people felt loyal to their king or state and if needed, were willing to defend their own community; in times of war or natural disasters, outsiders were easily blamed. Nevertheless, it is also clear that conceptions of nationhood were very different from their modern equivalents. First of all, the boundaries of these communities and the terms to refer to them were quite fluid. More fundamental was the lack of internal unity; legal pluralism was the norm in early modern societies. One could be a citizen of a city, but not of a state, and this entails that in most cases, local communities decided who was native and who a foreigner.[38] Nobles, clerics, burghers of towns, guild members, free farmers, and serfs had different rights, obligations, and privileges, and these differences were even more pronounced in the case of Indigenous populations and slaves in overseas territories. In most states, geographical variations were considerable, too. Taxes and legal and administrative procedures, as well as measures and coins, differed from province to province and from city to city, and military, political, and religious districts often did not coincide. Colonies, territories of chartered companies in the Americas and Asia, areas inhabited by Indigenous populations, and border zones often had a special status. Although over time many monarchs succeeded in centralizing their realms—for instance, by sending intendants to outlying provinces—most of this complex administrative patchwork continued to exist. Moreover, the supposedly more efficient central administration did not comply with modern bureaucratic standards. Most offices, especially at the local level, did not come with a fixed salary but instead depended on levies and fees for services rendered. In desperate need of additional funding, many monarchs resorted to tax farming and the sale of offices. Thus, large parts of the state's administration were effectively in the hands of private individuals.[39]

England might seem somewhat of an exception. Feudal power relations and landholdings had largely disappeared by the end of the Middle Ages, and common law applied to all residents. The Glorious Revolution of 1688 introduced new civil liberties while curtailing the power of the king in favor of Parliament. Nevertheless, at the local level, the country still consisted of an irregular patchwork of overlapping jurisdictions, and there was no political equality. Voting rights were limited, and the criteria for jury membership were even more restrictive. Moreover, Catholics, dissenters, and Jews were excluded from office.[40]

The legally enshrined social differences were generally reinforced by linguistic pluralism. Almost everywhere, the clergy used a dead but sacred language for liturgic purposes: Latin for Catholicism, Church Slavonic or Byzantine Greek for Orthodox Christianity, Hebrew for Judaism, Classical Arabic for Islam, Sanskrit for Hinduism, and Pali or Classical Tibetan for Buddhism. Often, these languages were also used in the scientific realm, in courts, and in the state administration. In Europe, Latin was the main language of international diplomacy until it was largely displaced by French during the seventeenth century. In many cases, monarchs and aristocrats spoke a prestigious literary language. Thus, thanks to the glamorous court of Versailles, French became the dominant language of the polite classes in Western Europe, while Persian had a comparable role in large parts of the Islamic world and Chinese was predominant in East Asia. In some specific domains, other languages had a dominant position. Dating from the late medieval period, Lower German had an important role in commerce in Northern Europe, whereas in the southern parts of the continent Italian had a similar function. Italian terms were also widely used in the fields of architecture and music, while in England, law courts continued to use French until the beginning of the eighteenth century.[41] The large majority of the population used a multitude of dialects that often belonged to different language families, such as French, Basque, Flemish, and Breton patois in France and Romanian, Hungarian, and German dialects in Transylvania.

This situation—in which language use was largely determined by social group or professional domain, while not overlapping with territorial borders— continued to exist in Eastern Europe until the late eighteenth or early nineteenth century. In Muslim and Orthodox areas, the printing press was ignored or prohibited, and primary education was not a priority. Here, literacy rates remained below 10 percent. As a consequence, elite languages continued to have a dominant position. In 1724 the new Russian Academy of Sciences adopted Latin as its main working language, while Old Church Slavonic remained the main administrative language of the tsarist empire until the second half of the eighteenth century. In Catholic areas, the dominant position of Latin in the religious domain and the administration was reinforced during the Counter-Reformation. This began to change after the dissolution of the Jesuit Order in 1773; it was only then that Polish became the sole official language in Poland. In the Habsburg Empire Latin remained the main language of the administration until 1784, and in the Hungarian half of the empire the use of Latin was finally abolished only in 1867.[42]

In Western Europe, on the other hand, vernacular languages became more important. Between the fourteenth and sixteenth centuries, states in Western Europe replaced Latin with English, Italian, Spanish, Portuguese, French, Dutch, Danish, or German as their official language. This process was reinforced by the invention of the printing press, which lowered the price of books and pamphlets. Although print capitalism certainly favored the standardization of vernacular languages—as famously argued by Benedict Anderson—this was not an automatic process, and in many cases it took centuries. Moreover, most printed books were still in Latin.[43] A crucial role was played by the Reformation, which boosted the diffusion of religious texts. Unlike Catholic and Orthodox Christians, Protestants prioritized written over ritual or symbolic communication, encouraging individual access to the Holy Scriptures. They preferred vernacular languages over Latin, even for liturgic and administrative purposes, thus dissolving the strict separation between the religious sphere and everyday life. New Bible translations such as those by Martin Luther and the King James Version contributed to a process of linguistic standardization. Protestants also put more emphasis on primary education—and Catholics in adjacent areas followed suit—but except in the urban areas of Northwestern Europe, progress was generally slow.[44]

In the cultural domain, social differences were more important than territorial ones. The outlook of elite groups, consisting of the well-educated parts of the clergy, nobility, and urban middle classes, was very cosmopolitan. Classical antiquity and Christianity continued to be the primary frames of reference, whereas Latin remained the main vehicle of communication for the sciences and philosophy. Humanists and men of letters from the different parts of Europe read each other's work, corresponded frequently, and were quite mobile, forming a closely interlinked network, the so-called Republic of Letters.[45] After the decline of the Italian Renaissance, the French court began to set the tone in architecture, art, music, dance, fashion, and manners. Everywhere, princes and aristocrats built the same classicist palaces, and even wealthy bourgeois acquired furniture, paintings, and tapestries that followed the latest trends from Paris and Versailles.

Nonetheless, courts could also have a unifying impact on countries, as local elites adopted social and cultural norms from the capital. In France, the government created royal academies, first for the French language in 1635 and later for sciences and fine arts. The monarchy also promoted the use and standardization of the French language and the founding of provincial academies, and Louis XIV urged the high nobility to reside part of the year at his new palace in Versailles, thus transmitting not just a more homogenous form of French but also new standards in fine arts, high fashion, and civilized behavior. In Japan, several decades earlier, the shogun had obliged the high nobility to reside part of the time in Edo (present-day Tokyo). This likewise helped in spreading the Edo dialect and the refined manners and customs of the shogun's court to the lower nobility and well-to-do civilians in the provinces. In England after the Glorious Revolution, Parliament functioned as a similar cultural focal point. The aristocracy met in London during the season and their sons received a homogeneous education, for instance at the public school of Eton and the universities of Oxford or Cambridge. After the union with Scotland, the Scottish nobility was quickly integrated, creating a rather unified British elite.[46]

In contrast, the popular culture of the European lower classes, expressed mainly in dialect, consisted of a baffling patchwork of regional forms and local traditions. Ordinary people primarily identified with their family, with others of the same social standing, and with their village or town. Religious identifications were vital, and many people felt attached to their parish or to particular saints, local shrines, or chapels. Special meanings attached to objects and locations such as holy trees, magic wells, and places that memorialized specific events such as natural disasters or battles. Only in exceptional cases historical sites had a wider popular appeal, such as the chapel of Wilhelm Tell, the hero who initiated the Swiss uprising against their Habsburg overlords, and the monumental tomb in Delft for William of Orange, the leader of the Dutch Revolt. Popular culture certainly was not immune to influences from learned groups, and the literacy of urban artisans was on the rise. However, during the early modern era, social differences increased because the upper classes began to turn their backs on local popular festivities and traditions. By replacing the model of the knight with that of the courtier, the nobility distanced itself from the lower classes, and by drawing the nobility to Versailles, Louis XIV only increased this divide. During the sixteenth and seventeenth centuries the clergy also became better educated because of the Reformation and the Counter-Reformation. They put more emphasis on decorum and they increasingly frowned on the excesses and superstitions associated with many popular traditions.[47]

Interestingly, between the regionally diverse popular culture and the cosmopolitan learned culture, a market for cultural products in a standardized vernacular arose in countries with a significant well-educated urban population. In the main cities, the role of the Church, the monarchy, and the aristocracy as the main patrons of artists and writers was supplemented or taken over by commercial actors. In Western Europe, a rich literature in vernacular languages had already been produced in the late Middle Ages. The invention of the printing press spurred the publication of books, journals, and broadsheets; novels, poetry, history books, and plays were also produced for a growing middle-class audience. In the sixteenth and seventeenth centuries clearly distinguishable national theater traditions arose in England, with Shakespeare as the most important author, and in Spain, with Lope de Vega, whereas in France, theater was embodied by Molière. Other countries followed their example, but commercial theater in German was institutionalized only toward the end of the eighteenth century. Slowly, learned publications also appeared in vernacular languages. Descartes, for instance, published his *Discourse on the Method* (1634) in French instead of Latin, and Newton opted for English for his book on optics (1704).[48]

A similar process could be detected in many parts of East Asia. In Japan, a vibrant commercial culture emerged in major cities with theater performances, literature, and various other art forms for a broad, socially mixed audience. Its secular perspectives and hedonism even began to influence the cultural life of the lower nobility, while at the same time undermining the hierarchical and rigidly segmented social structures. In Russia, on the other hand, where the gap between the French-speaking elites and the ordinary population was particularly wide, it was not until the early nineteenth century that authors such as Karamzin and Pushkin created a Russian literary language by combining Church Slavonic, Western European terminology, and everyday speech.[49]

More unified commercial cultural practices also arose in other domains. During the sixteenth and seventeenth centuries a considerable market for smaller works of art with realistic depictions of everyday life developed in the Low Countries. At about the same time, cookbooks, grocery shops, and standardized fish and dairy products enabled middle-class housewives in the Dutch Republic and England to create a "middling cuisine," each with its own characteristics and typical dishes. In this way they steered a middle course between the scant meals of the poor, who ate what they could get, and the elaborate culinary wonders created by famous cooks from the French court, which could also be encountered in the dining rooms of the "civilized classes."[50] Still, these new "national" cultural practices remained limited to a small middle-class audience in the most affluent parts of the Continent, and they did not yet have political implications.

Eighteenth-Century Enlightenment

Many of the centralizing and nationalizing tendencies that could be detected in most parts of Europe in the early modern period continued during the eighteenth century. There was one major difference: the process of secularization, which had been initiated during the Renaissance, gained momentum because of the Scientific Revolution and the Enlightenment, profoundly transforming both the world of politics and the cultural realm. This did not mean that large parts of the population became irreligious, but rather that in fits and starts, more and more parts of the universe, nature, and society were explained and understood in rational and worldly terms.

Anderson already has drawn attention to some of the cultural implications of the secularization process. First, he points to the replacement of sacred with vernacular languages, which began in the fourteenth century. Sacred script languages were considered "emanations from reality" and therefore an "inseparable part" of the divine truth, and this was not the case with the new standardized vernacular languages. Secularization, according to Anderson, also led to a different conception of time. Depicting biblical figures wearing contemporary garments was no issue within the premodern Christian cosmology. This messianic time, in which different periods were connected in a mystical way, was slowly replaced by "homogeneous, empty time," which was divided in exact rational units by the clock and the calendar.[51]

Other authors have argued that this new conception of time also led to the transition from a cyclical to a linear view of history, which implied that the past was increasingly understood as a fundamentally different world. Thus, toward the end of the seventeenth century, French academics already were debating whether modern scholarship and literature had surpassed those of the ancients. In this so-called Quarrel of the Ancients and the Moderns some still defended classical antiquity, while the idea of progress was championed by the "moderns."[52] But this progress could be detected only by measuring the improvements in the field of human achievements, for which a new conceptual framework had to be created.

In classical antiquity, it was not difficult to distinguish a well-educated citizen from a plebeian or a barbarian. However, more abstract concepts such as culture, civilization, and art did not exist. Art was not fundamentally different from artisanal products, and both were embedded in a religious worldview. The Roman *ars* referred to skilled practitioners. Nevertheless, the Romans distinguished between the "vulgar" or "mechanical arts," which involved payment and physical labor, and the "liberal arts," which were associated with learning that was considered more appropriate for members of the upper classes. During the Middle Ages, the liberal arts—consisting of the trivium of grammar, rhetoric, and logic and the quadrivium of arithmetic, geometry, astronomy, and music—continued to dominate the curriculum of higher education, and in the sixteenth century, history and moral philosophy were added. At the same time, brilliant representatives of the "vulgar arts" such as Raphael and Michelangelo gained great reputations. Nonetheless, they still were hired for specific assignments, and as with other artisans, their contracts usually stipulated the size of the work, the subject matter, and the materials.[53]

As a result of the spectacular rise of the natural sciences during the seventeenth and eighteenth centuries, the traditional classification of the liberal arts was slowly replaced by a new division in terms of the natural sciences, humanities, and fine arts. According to Larry Shiner, new phenomena such as art academies, exhibition salons, architectural associations, secular concerts, and copyright profoundly altered the status of professional artists, who now increasingly worked for an anonymous market. As a consequence, imaginative and original artists were distinguished from mere entertainers and artisans, who now became associated with routine and imitation, while women were increasingly relegated to amateur status or to minor arts such as embroidery. Nevertheless, many were still hesitant to use the term "creation" for a work of art, because only God had the power to create. The new artistic performances also required a new "aesthetic" behavior from the public—calm attentiveness, and reading, listening, or contemplating in silence, which set the refined classes apart from the rest of the population.[54]

With the rising awareness that the contemporary era surpassed earlier societies in producing both more and better knowledge and more skillful and beautiful artefacts, new overarching concepts were needed. During the second half of the eighteenth century, enlightened thinkers broadened the already existing terms of culture and civilization, which now came to refer to an autonomous domain of human creativity. In Roman times, "culture" was an agricultural term that referred to the cultivating of the land. Over time, the concept was broadened and could also refer to individuals in the sense of educating or caring for oneself. "Civilization" was derived from *civis* and thus connected to cities and citizenship; in later centuries it became associated with civilized life and manners. During the Enlightenment, both terms were increasingly used to refer to a larger collective and encompassed all domains of human activity. Nevertheless, most eighteenth-century authors primarily spoke about human civilization while largely ignoring cultural differences. Enlightened thinkers such as the Marquis of Condorcet and Thomas Paine put a strong emphasis on abstract values such as reason, liberty, and morality, and as a consequence, they focused on the progress societies could make from a state of barbarity via different stages of civilization toward absolute perfection.[55]

The emancipation of the cultural domain can also be detected in exhibition practices. Cabinets of curiosities in the early modern period provided an inventory of God's creation by showing both artefacts (created by human beings) and *naturalia* (items from natural history). Objects were classified by themes and species, so, for instance, a painting depicting an animal was juxtaposed with a stuffed figure of the animal. Geography and chronology were irrelevant in this all-encompassing taxonomy. Thus, the arts were part of a broader, religious cosmology.[56] From the sixteenth century, in some princely collections, artefacts were separated from the rest, although paintings were still exhibited together with scientific instruments and other "artisanal" products. This changed only during the eighteenth century, with the rise of specialized art exhibitions in France and England.[57]

Remarkably, this new classification also meant that time and space became meaningful categories. The sixteenth-century writer Giorgio Vasari, who provided biographies of the most important Italian architects, painters, and sculptors, had ordered his book according to the main cities of the Italian Peninsula. During the eighteenth century, art was classified into national schools, with French, German, Dutch and Spanish schools. In 1761, the Society for the Encouragement of Arts, Commerce, and Manufactures in Great Britain organized an ambitious first exhibition of British art, which clearly had mercantilist aims, as it primarily sought to encourage domestic production. Shortly afterward, with similar economic motives, enlightened princes such as Joseph II of Austria and his brother Grand Duke Leopold of Tuscany began to display parts of their collections according to "nationality." By viewing the growth, maturity, and decline of the arts in their own realm, current-day artists could find inspiration and contribute to a new heyday. These new conceptions of space and time also influenced the arts themselves. The British American painter Benjamin West made a number of innovative history paintings, including the famous *Death of General Wolfe* (1770; figure 1.2), in which the protagonist—who succumbed during the capture of Quebec in the Seven Years' War—and his fellow officers were depicted not in classical attire, but in contemporary dress.[58]

Similar tendencies could be found in other domains. In France, several books praising the country's great men and sometimes even women were published during the eighteenth century. They contained biographies of monarchs, generals, and statesmen, but also scientists, artists, and writers, usually in a loose chronological order. Elsewhere, authors sometimes preferred an alphabetical ordering, which was in line with the famous *Encyclopedia* edited by Diderot and d'Alembert. This was the case with the *Hungarian Athenas*, published by Péter Bod in 1766, which contained biographical notes on more than five hundred Hungarian writers. The *Historical Dictionary of the Most Illustrious Professors of Fine Arts in Spain*, published in 1800 by Juan Augustín

FIGURE 1.2 Benjamin West, *The Death of General Wolfe*, 1770, oil on canvas, 153 × 214 cm. A famous painting of the death of a British general at the Battle of Quebec in 1759. Contrary to existing conventions, West depicted the figures in contemporary clothes.

Ceán Bermúdez, was even more extensive. These publications also included entries on foreigners who had worked in Hungary and Spain, and thus they were more inventories of great authors, artists, and works of art that had been created in the states' territories than canons of culturally defined nations.[59]

This new spatial and chronological mapping of cultural highlights was in line with new developments in scientific thought. God's creation was increasingly studied by empirical means, and supernatural or mythical aspects received less attention or were completely ignored. Immanuel Kant in his *Critique of Pure Reason* (1781) even dispelled metaphysics from the realm of science. Nevertheless, even during the Enlightenment, most scholars understood the natural world as the work of divine creation. Geographers continued to understand the natural and human world as evidence of God's design until well into the nineteenth century. Even so, God's creation could be disentangled by close scrutiny. As a consequence, explorers and scholars had to find a logical explanation for geographical differences, both in nature and in human societies. The Count de Buffon even rejected Montesquieu's geographical determinism, arguing that human beings had largely liberated themselves from the tyranny of nature, thus separating human culture and society further from the natural world.[60]

The impact of the wider secularization process can also be detected in historical studies. Before the eighteenth century, historians generally viewed the particular past they analyzed—usually the history of a city, an order of the Church, a dynasty, or a state—as part of a universal Christian story that led from the Creation via the birth of Christ to the Day of Judgement. Their task was to disclose the signs of God's providence, while the past was primarily seen as a treasure trove of examples of both vices and virtues for the present. Although secular tendencies can be detected in humanist histories since the Renaissance era, rational analysis of the past in worldly terms became dominant only during the Enlightenment. This also meant that the focus on examples of virtues and the traces of God's will was succeeded by a new emphasis on chronology and human progress. Thus, in his *Essay on Universal History, the Manners, and the Spirit of Nations* (1756), Voltaire wrote a history in which India, China, and the Ottoman Empire received some attention, but Europe—and particularly France—represented the apex of civilization.[61]

The secularization process also affected the political realm. Anderson has argued that the religious legitimacy of dynastic rule in Western Europe began its decline in the seventeenth century.[62] Other scholars have made clear that increased international competition induced state authorities to improve and rationalize the administration of their territories, while Enlightenment thinkers paved the way for a radical restructuring of politics and society. Major international wars among the great powers occurred in quick succession. The Nine Years' War (1688–1697) had barely ended when the War of the Spanish Succession (1701–1714) broke out. The War of the Austrian Succession (1740–1748) largely overlapped with the War of Jenkins' Ear and was swiftly followed by the Seven Years' War (1756–1763), which in turn coincided with the French and Indian War. The American Revolutionary War (1775–1783) also involved many European powers. The nature of warfare also changed. Under Louis XIV, the French state had taken on the supply, finances, and organization of the navy and the army. Other armies followed suit, and as a consequence, they did not have to live off the land, which had been common practice previously. This considerably raised the costs of the armed forces, and generals therefore preferred to conduct sieges of strategic cities rather than risking their well-trained mercenaries in hazardous adventures or decisive battles.[63]

Most of these wars were financed by loans, and these had to be repaid in peacetime. Consequently, governments tried to raise their tax revenues by boosting the economy. This was done by increasing the productivity of agriculture and industry and improving domestic transports. As a result, physiocrats in France, cameralists in the German states, and enlightened reformers elsewhere in Europe tried to free indentured labor, combat the power of the guilds, remove restrictions on the sale of land, and improve access to markets. Many of these reforms were also introduced in the Spanish and Portuguese colonies in the Americas, while similar developments can be detected in various East Asian polities. Many states began to measure up their territories in order to produce reliable cadastres and standardize taxation. Colonial expansion abroad or on the frontiers was combined with the colonization and reclaiming of land at home; King Charles III of Spain, for instance, attracted thousands of Catholics from Central Europe to largely deserted and insecure parts of Andalusia.[64]

These reformers were inspired by Enlightenment ideas. In the late seventeenth century, Isaac Newton had discovered that the motion of celestial bodies and objects on Earth could be explained by one and the same principle: the law of universal gravitation. As a result, many Enlightenment thinkers began to argue that God's creation was an ordered whole that could be understood by rational inquiry. Like the universe, society was supposedly ruled by equally simple laws. If they could understand social processes, human beings could then apply their knowledge to improve and rationalize society. But the eighteenth-century philosophes did not agree on how this could be done. Some proposed limited improvements without fundamentally changing the existing social order. This aligned with the views of the Baron de Montesquieu, who advocated a separation of powers, and Voltaire, who between 1750 and 1753 acted as an adviser to Frederick the Great of Prussia. Others such as Denis Diderot and Baron d'Holbach were more radical and hoped to abolish the society of orders, including serfdom and slavery, while creating a new rational, secular, and egalitarian society. Since this second, more radical current could easily mobilize social discontent. it rapidly gained influence toward the end of the eighteenth century.[65]

This enlightened focus on ratio and progress did not remain just the view of a small group of writers and reformist politicians; it also had profound social implications. Between 1720 and the 1780s, the overall literacy rate in France increased from about 34 to over 50 percent.[66] Jürgen Habermas has argued that this was not a mere quantitative change, since it led to the rise of a fundamentally different "public sphere." In salons and coffeehouses throughout Europe and the Americas, all kinds of issues were debated among a growing number of well-educated people. Thus a new egalitarian and meritocratic sphere came into being, where the strength of a person's argument no longer depended on their social standing or religious authority, but on the argument's coherence and persuasiveness. At first, these public debates were concerned primarily with cultural, scientific, and philosophical topics, but politics was increasingly a subject of interest.[67]

This can easily be detected in England. Printing presses had been allowed outside of London since 1695, and the first daily newspaper appeared in the

British capital in 1702. Two years later, the first weekly newsletter was published in Boston, in the American colony of Massachusetts. Current events were widely discussed in coffeehouses and taverns, while peddlers spread the news to the countryside. During the second half of the eighteenth century, King George III was often caricatured in the popular press, but because he was timid and mentally unstable he was not seen as a dangerous tyrant, at least not in Great Britain. As Robert Darnton has shown, discussion in the public sphere in France was not limited to uplifting, rational debates; semi-pornographic tracts, vitriolic pamphlets, and scurrilous attacks on the privileged orders and the monarchy were soon published as well.[68] In the long run, the extension of the public sphere would seriously undermine the authority of the absolute monarchy, while also debilitating the power of tradition throughout the Western world.

Both oppositional groups and supporters of the monarchy responded to these developments by increasingly portraying themselves as serving a new, secular "common good." After the death of the Sun King in 1715, privileged groups in France tried to reestablish their former preeminence. Some of them did so by resorting to the language of civic republicanism, arguing in favor of an active patriotism. In the new public sphere, authors invoked the "patria," the "nation," and "society." The monarchy also began to use the language of patriotism, while the king presented himself as the father of the people. This became particularly evident during the Seven Years' War, when the state attempted to rally the population behind the war effort while fiercely denouncing not just the British king, but the English people as a whole. In 1771, when Lord Chancellor René Nicolas de Maupeou attempted to centralize the French judicial system by a kind of royal coup, those who defended the traditional liberties of France called themselves the "patriotic party," assuming that they, more than the king and his ministers, represented the fatherland. Similar tendencies could be found among oppositional groups elsewhere in Europe.[69]

Some enlightened monarchs such as Catherine the Great, Frederick the Great, Gustaf III of Sweden, and Charles Emmanuel III of Sardinia responded to the new demands of the population by rationalizing their governments and awarding more rights to their subjects. They initiated projects to codify and standardize the laws of their realm, or even completely redrew the institutional structures of the state. They also increasingly justified their reign in secular terms; thus, although power remained firmly in his hands, Frederick legitimized his rule as king of Prussia by presenting himself as the first "servant of the state." In 1755 the newly founded state of Corsica adopted a ten-page written constitution, clearly anticipating the invention of the nation-state a few decades later.[70]

Conclusion

Nation-states and national citizenship did not exist before the end of the eighteenth century. Since the late Middle Ages most Europeans had been aware that the Continent was inhabited by a number of vaguely defined peoples. However, there were various different conceptions of nationhood. These could refer to cultural or political communities, and none of them were very precisely circumscribed. Moreover, religious and social differences were much more important than territorial or ethnic distinctions. Social boundaries were hardened by legal pluralism. Each group had its own rights and obligations, and this social and legal diversity was reinforced by linguistic and cultural differences between privileged groups and the popular classes.

Nonetheless, in Western Europe important changes took place during the early modern era. Because of the growing costs of warfare, states felt compelled to centralize, increase their tax returns, and improve the administration. The rise of standardized vernacular languages, fueled by the introduction of the printing press, created a new public sphere between the provincial domain where dialects continued to dominate and the cosmopolitan realm of the upper strata where Latin or French was the lingua franca. A more "national" culture, based on a commercial market of middle-class customers, arose primarily in highly urbanized and well-developed areas in Western Europe. But a conceptual framework to define the field of human achievements was missing until the eighteenth century. A process of secularization broke the spell of an all-encompassing religious worldview, and new terms such as "culture" and "civilization" were coined to describe and celebrate human progress. However, nations, polities, and cultures were not yet intimately linked together.

2

The Birth of the Nation-State, 1775–1815

THE NATION-STATE was born out of a worldwide imperial crisis. Wars had become more disruptive during the early modern era because of the global military revolution. In many parts of the world, the almost continuous warfare put a heavy strain on the already overburdened finances of the rulers and exhausted their sources of manpower. Without profound modifications of the state structure, these problems proved difficult to solve. Wartime devastation, rising taxes, and growing state debts led to economic hardship and social unrest and undermined the legitimacy of the ruling dynasties. Many regimes failed the test. Early in the eighteenth century, the Persian Safavid Empire was the first to collapse. Toward the end of the century, the Moghul Empire in India ran into serious trouble, and the centralized monarchies of Burma, Siam, and Vietnam fell apart. There were major uprisings led by Yelmenyan Pugachev in tsarist Russia and by Túpac Amaru II in the Spanish viceroyalty of Peru. The historian Linda Colley has argued that in this dire situation rulers needed to mobilize the support of the population, and this could be done by devising new ways to legitimize the state. Another precondition for the rise of the nation-state was the acceptance of new enlightened ideas about political legitimation, and although the Enlightenment had repercussions outside the Western world, its revolutionary impact was felt primarily in Europe and the Americas.[1] There, "patriots" began to contest the traditional legitimacy of the existing monarchical regimes. In the end, it would be the Seven Years' War—fought on a global scale, between 1756 and 1763—that ignited an imperial crisis in both Great Britain and France, which resulted in the birth of the nation-state.

The United States can be seen as the first nation-state, but it was a curious one. Differences in language and culture did not play a role during the American War of Independence. What began as an old-fashioned tax revolt turned into a civil war, before ending in the unforeseen independence of thirteen of the nineteen British colonies in North America. Moreover, the inhabitants tended to identify with their state rather than with the union, so if there was a nation, it was rather fragile and its demarcations were not very clear. The French Revolution, which turned France into a powerful centralized nation-state, would have much greater impact, creating the model of the nation-state that was adopted rapidly throughout Europe and Latin America and that had long-term repercussions around the globe.

The Birth of the Nation-State in the United States and France

The age of revolutions began in a peripheral part of the eighteenth-century world: the thirteen British colonies on the east coast of North America. The French and Indian War (1754–1763)—which coincided with the Seven Years' War—had ended in a British victory and the annexation of all French territories east of the Mississippi, but the British state debt had increased enormously. During the war, the settlers in the thirteen colonies had paid emergency taxes, but with the removal of the French threat, there was little incentive to continue to pay large sums for British military protection. The British government, however, aimed to share the burden with the American colonies by introducing legislation for new taxes, such as the Stamp Act of 1765. The colonies were governed directly by the Crown and had no representatives in Parliament. The royal administration consisted of barely more than a governor in each colony, and local affairs were firmly in the hands of colonial assemblies. The introduction of new taxes accordingly went against tradition, and as a consequence, the slogan "No taxation without representation" resonated among the settlers in the thirteen colonies. In the British colonies in the Caribbean, settlers feared slave rebellions above all, so they preferred to continue to rely on British troops. The situation in North America escalated when the British authorities took harsh repressive measures after the Boston Tea Party of 1773.[2]

When open hostilities in the thirteen mainland colonies began, the rebels complained that a despotic king had infringed their "rights of Englishmen." However, they did not follow the customary script by requesting the restoration of their traditional liberties, as petitioners had done during earlier rebellions such as the Dutch Revolt and the Glorious Revolution.[3] The delegates of the colonies who met in Philadelphia in 1775 to raise an army and coordinate resistance against the British instead adopted the enlightened ideals, such as contract theories and natural rights, which had become popular among urban elites throughout the Western world. By appealing to "the people," the leaders of the rebellion tried to mobilize support for the war effort among broad strata of the population, and as a result, they also extended the suffrage—which in the rather egalitarian settler societies was already quite broad—to between 60 and 90 percent of all white males. However, this was not merely a war between the American colonies and Great Britain, it also was a civil war between "patriots" and a very considerable group of "loyalists"; many settlers preferred to stay loyal to the Crown and rejected the idea that power should be in the hands of "the people." On the July 4, 1776, the Second Continental Congress pushed ahead by issuing a declaration of independence that stated that "all men are created equal" and are endowed with certain "unalienable rights." Subsequently all thirteen states drew up a constitution. A government needed the "consent of the governed," and therefore "the people" had the right to throw off an unjust government and institute a new one. Thus, they solemnly proclaimed that "these united Colonies are . . . Free and Independent States."[4]

In order to create some sort of political unity, the Second Continental Congress drafted the Articles of Confederation, but after the war against Great Britain and the loyalists was won in 1783—largely thanks to the military interventions of France, Spain, and the Dutch Republic—the central government of the new republic proved to be too weak to pay off the war debts and play a serious role in the international arena. Moreover, the inhabitants' primary loyalties were to their states. In order to avoid the collapse of the union, Congress drafted a federal constitution, which was adopted in 1788. Nonetheless, the historian David Hendrickson defines the Constitution as a kind of international "peace pact," arguing that full sovereignty rested with the states.[5]

The nation-state that was created as a consequence of the revolution in France is a less ambiguous case. Like Great Britain, the French state had accumulated huge debts due to almost continuous warfare during the eighteenth century. Fiscal reforms were urgent to avoid bankruptcy. In addition, the international position of France was threatened by the rise of Prussia and the tsarist empire and the growing dominance of Great Britain at sea. After several attempts to introduce new taxes had failed, King Louis XVI decided to convene the Estates General during the spring of 1789, a measure the Bourbons had avoided since 1614. The Third Estate represented 96 percent of the population, and as a concession, it was given double the number of representatives in its assembly. However, according to tradition, voting was done separately, by order, so it was unlikely that the privileged First and Second Estates—the clergy and the nobility—would give up their tax exemptions. This dismayed the reform-minded representatives of the Third Estate, who also wanted to address other pressing issues related to the old order. To unlock the stalemate that developed almost immediately, the Third Estate invited the members of the other estates to join them and allow voting to proceed by head. This was not an attractive option for most members of the First and Second Estates, and a week later, the Third Estate renamed itself the National Assembly, unleashing revolution. The first measure the assembly took was to declare all taxes unlaw-ful, although they provisionally adopted them until they were replaced by a new fiscal system. The implication was clear: sovereignty was no longer in-vested in Louis XVI, king by the grace of God, but in the nation as represented by the members of the assembly.[6]

Three days later, the king shut down the building where the National As-sembly met. The representatives responded by swearing not to disband until they had adopted a constitution. When the nation is sovereign, they argued, the state should treat its members equally and enable them to control the govern-ment through an elected parliament. To establish equal rights for all citizens, the next step was to abolish the manifold remnants of feudalism. On the night of August 4, radical deputies stepped forward to renounce the special privileges of the social bodies they represented: the nobility, the clergy, the provinces, and the cities. Now everyone was equal, but it was not clear what that entailed. Therefore, three weeks later, the assembly produced the Declaration of the Rights of Man and of the Citizen, which listed the natural and universal laws, such as freedom of speech and religion, that applied to all citizens of France.[7]

Shortly afterward, corporations were abolished as well; they were seen as symbols of a society based on privilege and as obstacles to individual freedom. In response to the collapse in tax receipts, the National Assembly confiscated all properties of the Church and placed them "at the disposal of the nation." That winter, all monastic orders were dissolved. Priests and bishops, having lost their source of income, were made elected officials of the state, and they had to swear an oath of loyalty to the nation. The guilds were abolished in June 1791. The end of feudalism and privileged corporations resulted in the removal of all formal social and territorial barriers: all members of the nation now had the same rights and were treated equally by the state. The revolution-ary transformation of the country into a nation-state was completed by the adoption of the constitution in September 1791. France was now a constitu-tional monarchy in which sovereignty resided in the nation, while its citizens controlled the executive through an elected legislative assembly. But the revo-lution did not stop there. When the king tried to flee, he was imprisoned, and in September 1792 a republic was proclaimed. This quickly led to a radicaliza-tion of the regime under Maximilien Robespierre, but his Reign of Terror ended in the summer of 1794. Under the Directorate, the Consulate, and Na-poleon Bonaparte's empire, the regime became more authoritarian, but until the very end in 1815 it would continue to be based on a constitution and a parliamentary system with regular elections.[8]

The long-lasting success of the nation-state model as it was created during the first years of the French Revolution depended not only on the rapidly growing popularity of the notion of the sovereignty of the nation—which im-plied legal equality of all citizens, political participation through free elections, and a written constitution—but also on the military innovations related to the idea of the nation in arms. Although plans for a national army had been voiced before, they would take effect only after the revolutionary wars began.

In April 1792 France declared war on the Austrian monarchy, and a few months later, Prussia and an army of French émigrés joined the Austrian forces and invaded France. The French armies were in disarray. Many aristocratic officers had gone into exile, and those who remained were distrusted. There was no money to hire new mercenaries, most volunteers lacked training, and provisioning was difficult in a country in turmoil. Setbacks on the battlefield were compensated with new recruitment efforts. In February 1783 three hundred thousand men were drafted, and seven months later, the new republic announced the famous *levée en masse*, ordering that until "our enemies have been chased off the territories of the Republic, all Frenchmen are on permanent requisition for military service."[9] This national call to arms aimed to mobilize the entire population for the war effort. The decree stipulated that "the young men shall go to battle; the married men shall forge arms and transport provisions; the women shall make tents and clothes, and shall serve in the hospitals; the children shall turn old linen into lint; the old men shall . . . stimulate the courage of the warriors and preach the unity of the Republic and hatred of kings."[10]

By the end of the year, the republic had more than one million soldiers. But it was not so much the skills of a new, meritocratic officer class or the nationalist fervor of the fresh recruits that was responsible for the string of victories of the revolutionary and Napoleonic armies—as the myth of the nation-in-arms suggests—but rather a number of tactical innovations that addressed the desperate situation of unexperienced soldiers and lack of supplies. In contrast to the royal armies that still followed the tradition of the cabinet wars, the French revolutionary forces operated in autonomous divisions that had to live off the land. Instead of using a defensive line and focusing on rapidly succeeding volleys by well-trained mercenaries, the revolutionary armies resorted to targeted attacks by massive columns of soldiers using bayonets as their most effective weapons, assisted by free-firing skirmishers and a flexible artillery. This meant that the strength of armies was determined primarily by the number of potential recruits, and that wars became much more aggressive and bloody, as well as more socially disruptive, as supplies were requisitioned from the local population.[11]

The Rise of the Nation-State Model
in Europe and Latin America

The Revolutionary and Napoleonic Wars provided a window of opportunity to disseminate the nation-state model. Dozens of new nation-states were created, and their success largely depended on the geopolitical context. The revolutionary innovations, however, were not imposed from the outside. There were many people who sympathized with the ideals of the French Revolution, and news about developments in France spread quickly through publications, commercial contacts, émigrés, and travelers. This rapidly affected Europe, the Americas, Asia, and Africa. Jacobin clubs were founded even in Constantinople, Aleppo, and Seringapatam, the capital of Mysore in South India, while news about successful slave rebellions in the French colonies quickly reached not only other parts of the Americas but also the Pacific and the coasts of West Africa, forming a source of inspiration for local Maroon communities.[12]

The Dutch Republic actually anticipated the French. In the mid-1780s revolutionary "patriots" took over various Dutch cities, threatening the military authority of the stadtholder, the prince of Orange. In 1787, the Prussian king Frederick William II intervened by sending troops to restore order. Soon after, the radical innovations of the French Revolution inspired people elsewhere to take matters into their own hands. In August 1789 the so-called Happy Revolution forced out the prince-bishop of Liège, turning the independent princedom into a republic. Shortly afterward, the Southern Netherlands rose up, proclaiming their independence from the Austrian Habsburgs and establishing the United States of Belgium. In the end, it took the Austrian troops more than a year to reconquer the rebellious provinces. In Poland, "patriots" collaborated with the enlightened King Stanisław II Augustus to adopt a liberal constitution in May 1791. This served as an excuse for the great powers to intervene. Invited by a group of conservative Polish aristocrats, Catherine the Great of Russia invaded the Polish-Lithuanian Commonwealth. The subsequent Second Partition of Poland, which began in January 1793, diverted the attention of Russia and Prussia, preventing a massive military intervention that might have ended the revolutionary experiment in France. Five years later, another French-inspired rebellion, that of the United Irishmen, which capitalized on the widespread social unrest in the conservative Irish countryside, was brutally suppressed by the British army.[13]

Although the French revolutionaries did nothing to effectively help their Polish brethren, with the arrival of the republic, they radicalized their foreign propaganda. At the end of 1792 the National Convention declared that "it will grant fraternity and assistance to all peoples who wish to recover their liberty, and . . . grant assistance to these peoples and . . . defend those citizens who have been— or may be—persecuted for their attachment to the cause of liberty." French revolutionary armies would help the "liberated" areas by establishing "free and popular" governments and abolishing aristocratic privileges and other remnants of feudalism.[14] However, many of the newly elected assemblies in the liberated territories "demanded" to be incorporated into the French Republic. Between 1791 and 1795, this was the case with Avignon, the Duchy of Savoy, the County of Nice, the Republic of Mainz on the left bank of the Rhine, and the Southern Netherlands. One curious exception was the Basque province of Guipúzcoa, whose representatives expressed the wish to regain the independence they had lost to the Spanish monarchy five hundred years before, while maintaining their traditional privileges and their Catholic religion. But the French military commanders, who had already occupied part of the province in the summer of 1794, rejected the proposal of the Guipuzcoans, which demonstrated that "liberated" territories were not entirely free to determine their own fate. In the end, the French revolutionaries revived Louis XIV's dream of making the Rhine the natural border of the country. This meant that the southern part of the Dutch Republic had to be annexed, but after also "liberating" the Netherlands in 1795, the new Batavian Republic remained nominally independent.[15]

Even after Napoleon took command in France—first, informally, as the most powerful general, then in 1799 as first consul, and finally as emperor— the abolishment of the remnants of feudalism and the introduction of a constitution, elections, and a parliament remained part of the package bestowed on all newly conquered territories (map 2.1). This happened in the Ligurian Republic, the Cisalpine Republic, the Helvetian Republic, and the Republic of Danzig. The same recipe was also applied to vassal states, such as the Kingdom of Italy, the Kingdom of Naples, the Kingdom of Westphalia, and the Kingdom of Spain. In 1798 Napoleon even set up a short-lived enlightened regime in Egypt. This also meant that French revolutionary and Napoleonic administrative reforms were adopted in most parts of Western and Central Europe.[16]

Even Napoleon's absolutist enemies Prussia and Austria felt obliged to adopt many elements of the new nation-state model. Both Frederick the Great and Joseph II had already introduced reforms during the late eighteenth century, but their successors were reluctant to introduce more enlightened measures after the French Revolution had made clear that elected assemblies could take control. Nevertheless, the crushing military defeats in 1805 and 1806 compelled them to change course. In Austria, Emperor Francis tried to increase popular support by improving education, adopting a civil law code that applied equally to all inhabitants, and undertaking some limited administrative reforms. The most important new institution was a citizens' militia, which mobilized all men between eighteen and forty-five.[17] Prussia's more thorough reforms were led by Heinrich Friedrich Karl vom und zum Stein and Karl August von Hardenberg. They abolished serfdom, introduced greater civil equality and some basic freedoms, eliminated the monopolies of the guilds, and extended the powers of the provincial assemblies; they even had plans to create a national parliament. By rationalizing the state, they hoped to mobilize civil society and inspire a sense of national unity among the Prussian population, but in the end, power remained in the hands of the monarch.[18]

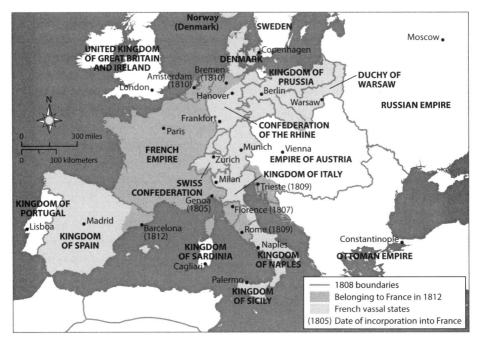

MAP 2.1 Napoleonic Europe around 1808, with the territories annexed by
France and its vassal states.

The nation-state model was also adopted outside of Europe. In 1795 conservative Boer settlers in Graaff-Reinet and Swellendam rebelled against the
Dutch colonial authorities in Cape Town, wearing the tricolor cockade and
adopting the slogan "Liberty, equality, and fraternity." They hoped to create an
independent government according to "the French system," but their hopes
were dashed by a British military intervention. The British also blocked an
attempt by Loyalist Black Americans to create an independent nation-state
in Sierra Leone. Many African American soldiers from the British army had
been brought to Nova Scotia after the American War of Independence, while
others had traveled to London. British abolitionists then created companies
to resettle them and their families in Sierra Leone, founding Freetown in 1792,
and promised land, liberty, and political representation. However, the African
Americans were quickly disappointed when they received only small plots and
learned they would have to pay considerable rents and would be governed by
white directors. In September 1800, the inhabitants of Freetown rebelled, drew
up their own law code, and instituted a bicameral parliament. A few weeks
later, a British ship arrived with five hundred Maroon warriors—free Blacks
from Jamaica who hoped to resettle in Sierra Leone. The Maroons sided with

the British authorities and quickly quelled the rebellion, nipping in the bud the first attempt to create a self-governing Black colony or independent nation-state on the west coast of Africa.[19]

Obviously, the revolutionary shockwaves were quickly felt in most French colonies, including Mauritius, the French outposts in India, and Saint-Domingue. Various colonial assemblies were set up, and they mostly tried to steer a course independent of Paris. Spanish and Portuguese colonies also felt the impact, although it was decades before the full effects materialized. In fact, outside North America and Europe, new nation-states were established only in Latin America. However, independence was not caused by the strong revolutionary convictions of local enlightened elites, but was primarily a consequence of further imperial crises. Moreover, the struggle for independence was—just like in the United States—actually a civil war.[20] This was also the case in Saint-Domingue, the first Caribbean colony to become independent, as Haiti.

The impact of the revolution on the French plantation colony of Saint-Domingue was immense. There were already many grievances concerning the restrictions on trade, the subordinate position of free people of color, and the inhumane treatment of the enslaved. In 1790 a colonial assembly was elected by white males. The local "patriots," representing mostly the poor whites, adopted a constitution, declared autonomy, and opened the harbor to foreign ships, a measure that was opposed by the local elite and the metropolitan authorities. The large property owners and the free people of color (who remained excluded from political decision-making) opposed the "patriots." The conflict rapidly escalated into a full-scale civil war in which all groups mobilized slaves, who made up the majority of the population. Like other slave communities in the Americas, they were not resigned to their fate, and they took the opportunity to rise up and claim freedom. Toussaint L'Ouverture, a freed slave, emerged as their successful leader. Spain, which integrated L'Ouverture's army into their own, and Great Britain also intervened in order to weaken France's international position. In February 1794, the National Convention in Paris decided to abolish slavery in all French territories, in a desperate attempt to regain control. L'Ouverture now changed his allegiance from Spain to the French Republic and became commander of the western province; within a few years, he effectively controlled the entire colony. In 1802, Napoleon sent a large expedition force to the island to reintroduce slavery, and L'Ouverture was arrested, deported, and jailed in France. Finally, the French army was defeated by the troops of Jean-Jacques Dessalines, another former slave, and the colony declared its independence in 1804. The next year, Haiti adopted a constitution, becoming the first nation-state in Latin America.[21]

The imperial crisis in Spanish America resembled the one in Saint-Domingue, but it was even more complex. There was widespread discontent about trade restrictions and the enlightened reforms of King Charles III, whose main aim was to improve the financial situation of the state. One of the most controversial measures of his centralization policy was the exclusion of American-born residents—so-called Creoles—from the highest functions in the administration. Haiti's emancipation of its mixed-race population and the island's successful slave revolt made Spanish American Creole elites wary of revolutionary experiments. In the end, the establishment of new nation-states was triggered by the Napoleonic invasion of Portugal and Spain, which began in 1807. The Portuguese royal family almost immediately fled to Brazil, making Rio de Janeiro the de facto capital of Portugal while implicitly ending the colonial status of the various, largely disconnected Brazilian provinces.[22]

Meanwhile, Napoleon used a dynastic conflict between King Charles IV of Spain and Crown Prince Ferdinand to gain control over Spain. In the spring of 1808 he summoned the Spanish royal family to the French city of Bayonne, where he pressured both father and son to abdicate. He then put his own brother Joseph on the Spanish throne and convened a parliament of Spanish notables to adopt the Statute of Bayonne, a constitution he had written largely by himself. The new king immediately was confronted with a mass uprising. After a few months, a Supreme Central Junta was established to coordinate the war efforts of the many local juntas that had sprung up in areas the Bonapartes did not have under control. To strengthen its legitimacy, the Supreme Central Junta summoned a Cortes, which according to the new enlightened ideals was elected by all male homeowners from both the Spanish metropole and the overseas territories. The new Cortes, which convened in the city of Cádiz under the protection of the British navy, immediately began to write a liberal constitution and to abolish the remnants of feudalism and forced labor. Thus, after the implosion of royal authority there were three different and more or less legitimate regimes: the Bourbon king, who was effectively a prisoner in France; King Joseph Bonaparte, who tried to govern from Madrid; and the newly elected Cortes in Cádiz.[23] This caused a lot of confusion in Spanish America, which had been mostly cut off from Spain by a British blockade for several years.

In most parts of Spanish America, opposition to the Supreme Central Junta and the viceroys came from city councils led by Creole elites. It was only in the viceroyalty of New Spain, where Spaniards controlled Mexico City, that opposition was concentrated in the provinces. There, warfare began in 1810 when Miguel Hidalgo, a conservative priest, gathered a large army composed mostly of poor farmers to combat the continued dominance of the Spanish-born, while at the same time defending the rights of both Ferdinand and the Catholic Church. Elsewhere, city councils created their own, more enlightened juntas, and in 1810 various regional councils were convened and argued that in the absence of the king, sovereignty reverted to the people. In 1811 the first constitutions and republics were proclaimed in cities including Caracas, Cartagena de Indias, Santa Fe de Bogotá, Buenos Aires, and Santiago, which in many instances led to open warfare with other cities and the surrounding countryside. Most liberal "patriots" still wavered in their aims between an autonomous kingdom within a larger Spanish monarchy, a Spanish constitutional regime, and outright independence, but the refusal of the Cortes in Cádiz to grant the American colonies equal representation, some form of autonomy, and free trade seriously affected their loyalty to the new regime.[24]

There was further political uncertainty at the end of Napoleonic period with the return of Ferdinand VII, who immediately abrogated the constitution in order to restore an absolute monarchy. A large expeditionary army succeeded in subduing many parts of Spanish America, but the violent repression of the "rebels" by the royalist armies alienated many Spanish Americans from Madrid. A liberal interregnum between 1820 and 1823 added to the confusion, reversing sympathies and alliances, and the new Cortes refused to give in to the key American demands. Although Ferdinand hoped to get military support from the conservative European powers united in the Holy Alliance, this did not materialize, partly because Great Britain and the United States opposed outside intervention. Without international support, and in dire financial straits, Spain was too weak to defeat the "liberation armies," which were led by Simón Bolívar in Venezuela and New Granada and by José de San Martín in Río de la Plata and Peru. By 1826, all parts of the Spanish American mainland had become independent and adopted constitutions and parliamentary elections. Another liberal revolution in Portugal, in 1820, provided the opportunity for Brazilian elites to declare independence and put onto the throne Prince Pedro, who had been left behind as regent when the royal family returned to Portugal. Like the United States, the new American nation-states were weak—the legal framework of the nation-state was not buttressed by well-developed national institutions—and there were fierce debates over the nature of the new political system. Should it be a centralized state with a strong executive, should supreme power reside in the parliament, or would a decentralized federal republic be the best option?[25]

Citizenship

Thus, the nation-state was a product of the Atlantic Revolutions, but what actually constituted the nation, which now had become sovereign? First of all, the geographical boundaries of the new nations were not fixed. With the Treaty of Paris in 1783 the United States received a huge swath of land between the Appalachian Mountains and the Mississippi River, which included the so-called Indian Country. In 1802 the United States bought Louisiana from

France, and in 1819 it acquired Florida from Spain. The new French nation-state annexed a number of territories to achieve a natural border along the Rhine, and under Napoleon, parts of Italy, the Illyrian Provinces, the Kingdom of Holland, northwest Germany, and Catalonia were added as well, increasing the number of potential army recruits.[26] In Spanish America, the demarcations between the various new nation-states would take several decades to crystallize. Many provincial cities were not willing to subordinate themselves to new capitals such as Bogotá or Buenos Aires and instead tried to create separate republics; Bolívar and San Martín attempted to form larger states such as the United Provinces of South America, Gran Colombia, and the Confederation of the Andes, which all ended in failure. Finally, the captaincy generals of Venezuela, Chile, and Central America seceded from the viceroyalties to which they belonged, and peripheral provinces such as Uruguay, Paraguay, Bolivia, and Ecuador also gained independence (map 2.2). Even Haiti, with the sea as a natural boundary on three sides, did not have stable borders during the first decades of its existence. Two years after achieving independence, the country was split into two parts, north and south, after Dessalines was killed during a coup d'état. In 1820, the new strongman in the south, Jean-Pierre Boyer, succeeded in unifying Haiti. Two years later he annexed Santo Domingo, bringing the entire island of Hispaniola under his authority, but this would last for only about two decades.[27]

As a consequence, language and culture were largely irrelevant when defining a nation. They did not play a significant role in the creation of the United States, nor in the independence of the Latin American states, since both metropole and colonies used the same standard language, and cultural differences between the dominant elites on both sides of the Atlantic were minimal. Moreover, the inhabitants of newly added territories often did not speak the dominant language of the expanding nation-state. Even if we ignore dialects and languages that were seen as "uncivilized," the United States had to integrate a considerable number of French and Spanish speakers, Haiti had to deal with Spanish speakers, and revolutionary France had incorporated territories where most inhabitants spoke German, Dutch, or Italian. In Spanish America, too, cultural and linguistic differences were not a factor when drawing the new borders.

Whereas cultural and linguistic boundaries did not matter, political borders did. The geographic extension of national communities was determined by existing borders. Surprisingly, transatlantic empires were often defined as one nation. We have seen that the early North American "rebels" defended their "rights as Englishmen." In Spain and Portugal, Enlightenment reformers had already represented the American colonies and the European metropolis as a "single national body," and when these early modern monarchical empires became nation-states, their "national" assemblies represented the inhabitants of all territories, including the American possessions and colonies elsewhere, such

MAP 2.2 The Americas around 1830. The map was very different from today, with other borders (for instance, between the United States and Mexico) and large states that have disappeared since then, such as Gran Colombia and the United Provinces of Central America.

as the Philippines and Macao. The constitutions of Spain and Portugal—adopted in 1812 and 1822, respectively—defined the nations as consisting of "the sum of all Spaniards," and Portuguese "of both hemispheres." Likewise, the French constitutions of 1793 and 1795 included the overseas territories as part of the nation.[28]

Smaller territories that adopted a constitution or proclaimed independence also defined themselves as nations. This was the case with the Republic of Mainz in 1792—which designated itself a Rhenish-German nation—as well as Lombardy in 1796 and Naples in 1799. In the Batavian Republic, some politicians opposed a unitary state, arguing that the ancient Dutch provinces constituted nine different nations.[29] Even those who opposed the revolutionary principle of national sovereignty used the term to refer to smaller political units. In Prussia, Stein pleaded for "the participation of the people" in creating a "general national representation," and in 1810 Hardenberg used the term "nationalism" in a positive sense; both of them were not referring to the German but rather the Prussian nation. In Austria, the staunchly Catholic, antirevolutionary inhabitants of the County of Tyrol referred to themselves as the "Tyrolean nation."[30] Thus, the term "nation" was applied primarily to the inhabitants of political units, be they empires, traditional kingdoms, provinces, or new nation-states.

What mattered most when defining who belonged to the *demos* of the nation—and accordingly, who was allowed to participate in politics—was the supposed level of "civilization." This was particularly evident in France. The French National Assembly no longer represented the various estates and corporations of the kingdom, but rather a nation of citizens. In order to know the true aspirations of the people—or the "general will," as Jean-Jacques Rousseau had famously called it in *The Social Contract* (1762)—voting was done in assemblies, first locally and then at a departmental level, and not in secret. It was deemed crucial that every individual could freely determine their vote. This meant that voters should be autonomous and capable of rational reasoning. As a consequence, the Constituent Assembly excluded minors, first up to the age of twenty-five and later up to twenty-one. The intellectually disabled, criminals, and vagabonds were also disqualified. Domestic servants were excluded because they were thought to depend on their masters, and members of monastic orders were not seen as independent either. Like minors, the intellectually disabled, and domestic servants, women were given only passive citizenship. According to Pierre Rosanvallon, they were not seen as completely autonomous individuals; this was based on their supposedly inferior intellectual capacity (an argument rejected by prominent revolutionaries such as Olympe de Gouges and the Marquis de Condorcet) and on their place in the family—if they were married, their husbands reputedly represented them. On the other hand, male foreigners who had a clear link to France through marriage or work and who had resided at least five years in the country could acquire full citizenship by swearing an oath of loyalty. After some debate, French Jews were also awarded citizenship. However, many Ashkenazi Jews in Alsace were far from enthusiastic about giving up their separate jurisdiction and religious laws in return for becoming a member of the French nation.[31] Many of these provisions, such as the inclusion of religious minorities and the exclusion of women and servants, were also introduced in most other constitutions during the revolutionary and Napoleonic era.[32]

The exclusion of people who were not "civilized" white males was more obvious in the United States. Citizenship was awarded by the individual states, but slaves were excluded everywhere, as had been the rule in the colonial assemblies. In a compromise with the Southern states, three-fifths of the total population of slaves were counted when determining the number of seats allocated to states in the House of Representatives, which depended on the states' populations. Voting rights were denied to women and in most cases also to free people of color. Native Americans who paid taxes were considered citizens, and often they were included in the electoral rolls, but most Native Americans belonged to "foreign nations" and did not possess U.S. citizenship. The first Naturalization Act, which was adopted in 1790, was even more explicit, awarding U.S. nationality only to "free white people" of "good character." In most British and French colonial assemblies the Indigenous population was excluded, as were slaves and, in most instances, free people of color.[33]

The Spanish and Portuguese constitutions of 1812 and 1822, both of them short-lived, also excluded slaves. However, Spain had a problem: the population of the American territories was greater than that of metropolitan Spain. This implied that the American representatives would constitute a majority in Spain's new parliament. To avoid this, the constitution stipulated that free Blacks and mixed-race persons with an African ancestor did not possess suffrage rights. Most Spanish American constitutions awarded citizenship to free Blacks and mixed-race persons, and the same was true for Brazil. But there were property qualifications to vote, and in some cases, literacy was a requirement as well. In this way, large sections of the population—including almost all Blacks and mixed-race persons—were excluded. In Peru and Bolivia, the special statute for Indians was reintroduced under a new guise. They had to pay a special fee (which had been an important source of revenue for the colonial administration) but were exempt from the national sales tax and conscription, which in fact turned them into second-rate citizens.[34]

The French constitutions of 1793 and 1795 were quite generous. They awarded citizenship to free people of color, and in 1794 the French Republic even abolished slavery. When the situation in Saint-Domingue was under control again, Napoleon changed course. In the constitution of 1799 he separated the colonies from the motherland by proclaiming that "the regime of the French colonies will be determined by special laws." In 1802, he reinstituted slavery in the Caribbean territories. As Josep Fradera has forcefully argued, the legal separation between the European metropole (a nation-state with a constitution) and the overseas colonies, which had "special," more restrictive laws, would become the dominant model in the nineteenth and large parts of the twentieth century. As a consequence, the invention of the nation-state replaced the legislative pluralism of the ancien régime with legal equality and written constitutions in the metropolitan areas. At the same time, it hardened the

boundaries between insiders (mostly white male property owners) and outsiders (women, people of color, Native Americans, and foreigners) and between metropole and colonies.[35]

National Awareness

Older conceptions of nationhood endured during the age of revolution. In a
thorough analysis of autobiographical writings in four Western European countries, Raúl Moreno Almendral shows that people continued to use cultural
"ethnotypes" that referred to the specific characteristics of ethnic communities,
such as Germans or Italians. Ethnic, cultural, or religious groups that did not
have their own territory were generally defined as peoples, but because they
lacked their own states, they could not become sovereign nations. French politicians, for instance, spoke of the need to unify all the "peoples" of France, while
French Jews and German-speaking Alsatians were not recognized as a nation,
but referred to as "peoples." Political "ethnotypes" were more important, as
some revolutionaries argued that their country already possessed an "ancient
constitution." As a consequence, they preferred to use the medieval names of
their modern national assemblies, such as the Cortes in Spain. The Batavian and
Helvetian Republics explicitly adopted the names of the tribes that according to
Tacitus had inhabited their territories in Roman times, and in the Americas,
revolutionaries integrated indigenous symbols into their national emblems and
flags.[36] Nevertheless, all new regimes adopted the nation-state model. An appeal
to the country's ancient traditions could be used to reject revolutionary ideals,
which was what happened in Guipúzcoa and with Hidalgo in Mexico. In both
cases, the defense of the traditional rights of the Church was a crucial element.

The most important older conception of nationhood during the Atlantic
Revolutions was, without a doubt, the idea of patria, which was closely linked
to the ideal of civic republicanism and which had already been on the rise
during the eighteenth century. Most revolutionaries defined themselves as
"patriots" determined to defend freedom and the common good.[37] This was
logical in France, where the revolutionaries took over the state and where loyalty to the state became synonymous with loyalty to the new revolutionary
principles, such as the sovereignty of the nation. After the war broke out, the
state expanded its borders not just to liberate other territories from feudal
oppression, but also to add citizens who could be recruited to defend the "patria." Elsewhere, adopting the label of patriot was, in fact, quite paradoxical. In
the Americas, many "patriots" fought against "tyranny," but they did so by
rejecting the states to which they had belonged. Apparently, the loyalty to the
smaller patria of the city, the colony, or the imperial province was more important than loyalty to the dynastic state. Moreover, they were willing to fold their

local patria into new territorial units such as the United States of America or Gran Colombia. The same was also true in many of the smaller nation-states in Europe, such as the duchy of Savoy and the Republic of Mainz, where revolutionaries agreed to abolish their own patria and become part of France. One could argue that the revolutionaries were worried not so much about loyalty and the common good, but about who held the reins of power—the nation or the monarch—and the state or the patria actually was replaceable. However, the dominant conception of the nation as a sovereign community of citizens was totally new. As a consequence, we can also conclude that the age of revolutions constituted a fundamental break and that there was no significant form of cultural continuity, as anti-modernist scholars generally posit.

But who actually identified with the new nation that now had become sovereign? It is obvious that in Europe, those who lost their privileges, such as the nobility and large parts of the clergy, opposed the revolutionary conception of the nation, and so did many conservatives, royalists, and Catholics. On the other hand, there was widespread support, especially among urban, enlightened elites, for many of the radical reforms such as the introduction of equality before the law, the recognition of the sovereignty of the nation, and the adoption of a constitution. The abolition of feudal dues and manorial rights was generally hailed by the inhabitants of the countryside. However, the measures against the Catholic Church were much more controversial, and they rapidly alienated wide strata of the population in France, while Catholics elsewhere became very suspicious of the "godless" revolutionaries. The radicalization of the revolution after the proclamation of the republic in 1792, the execution of the king, and the subsequent Reign of Terror further weakened support. Thus, after a first moment of exaltation, interest in revolutionary politics waned. The turnout at elections quickly dropped to only 10 percent in September 1792. In a similar vein, the enthusiasm to defend the nation by volunteering for the army rapidly dwindled. The 1793 levy of three hundred thousand soldiers caused a grand-scale rebellion in the department of the Vendée. Conscription was widely dodged—often through self-mutilation—and many deserted at the first opportunity. The hardships of the war, the economic downturn, and the radicalization of the National Convention also led to an uprising of more moderate revolutionaries—the so-called Girondins—in major cities like Marseille, Lyons, and Bordeaux, which was fiercely repressed by the army in the late summer of 1793.[38]

Elsewhere, small groups of enlightened "patriots" supported revolutionary reforms and often even welcomed the French troops that brought "liberation." Republics with a new form of representative government were created throughout Europe and the Americas, whenever circumstances allowed. In general, the inhabitants of the countryside were more reluctant to accept the new revolutionary regime, and in many instances opposed it outright. Michael

Broers argues that in many parts of Europe and Spanish America the revolution degenerated into a civil war between well-educated urban elites and more conservative rural folk. Although peasants welcomed the repeal of seigneurial dues, many resented the attacks on the monarchy and organized religion. In Catholic countries, peasants supposedly profited from the abrogation of tithes and the sale of Church lands, but in practice, most of them were unable to buy new land, and higher rents and new taxes had a detrimental effect on their economic position. The Church, too, was unable to continue many of its charitable works. The replacement of traditional channels of self-government with elected assemblies, which were generally dominated by urban middle classes, was not appreciated either. On top of that, the new state increased taxes, interfered more directly in their affairs, and conscripted young males. Moreover, the new form of warfare meant that armies had to live off the land, so requisitions and billeting imposed a heavy toll on the countryside. From about 1793, widespread rural uprisings occurred not only in the Vendée but also in Brittany, the Southern Netherlands, Switzerland, Tyrol, and various parts of Italy. After 1808, they also took place in Spain and its American colonies.[39]

Many of these rural rebels were made into national heroes later in the nineteenth century. They supposedly fought against "foreign invaders" and "oppressors" while making a significant contribution to a war of "independence" or "liberation," but in fact, they hardly qualify as nationalists. Most of them refused to fight outside of their villages or region. This was the case in both the Vendée and Brittany, but also in many parts of Spain and Spanish America. In the Peninsular War, guerrilla fighters from Guadalajara were unwilling to liberate the nearby city of Valencia; in Galicia, a large peasant army largely disappeared after the French troops had been expelled from the region. These peasants apparently did not concern themselves about their fellow nationals. In southwest Germany, farmers were willing to defend their village against the French but refused to take up defensive positions along the Rhine, just a few kilometers away.[40] Francisco Espoz y Mina, a successful guerrilla leader in Northern Spain, allegedly showed his disgust for the Constitution of Cádiz—which invested the Spanish nation with sovereign powers—by having a copy "executed" by a firing squad. In Spanish America, patriotic armies that introduced conscription had to introduce heavy penalties for dodging and desertion, and in many areas peasant communities easily switched sides or continued to support the time-honored rights of the Crown and the Catholic Church.[41]

Revolutionary officials and Napoleonic officers, on the other hand, refused to see uncivilized peasants as rightful members of the nation; many even compared these "backward bandits" to barbarians or beasts. Broers argues that many officers distinguished between the core parts of the empire, such as Northern France, Holland, the Rhineland, and Northern Italy, where "civilized men" behaved decently and accepted the new laws, and the backward areas—which included large parts of rural France—where "wild communities" had to be tamed by a "civilizing mission" and, if needed, brutal repression. This context explains the campaign under the Committee of Public Safety to replace regional languages and dialects with a rationalized and purified French. Using patois was seen as a sign of backwardness and a reactionary mentality. Some historians argue that a policy of "linguistic terror" was conducted in Alsace and Roussillon, where German and Catalan were widely spoken. Linguistic uniformity was promoted not to secure the cultural attachment to the French nation, but as a rational measure to remove obstacles to communication, to civilize the population, and to combat counterrevolutionary tendencies.[42] In the end, though, even many revolutionaries lost heart and traded the much-desired republic for an empire. This happened in France in December 1804, but empires were also proclaimed—often, relatively briefly—in Haiti in 1804, in Mexico in 1821, and in Brazil in 1822.

The Nationalization of Everyday Life, Culture, and the Physical Environment

Although the identification of the population with the nation was limited, the introduction of an enlightened nation-state model had momentous implications, and this was most particularly true for France, where the revolutionaries had the time, power, and means to apply many of their ideas. There, a process of universalist nationalization set in, affecting everyday life. Before 1789, one's social position was largely defined by an individual's standing and legal status. Thus, the clergy, the nobility, burghers of a city, members of a guild, free farmers, and the rest of the population were subject to different rules. Formal regulations, often reinforced by social conventions, determined the way people dressed and behaved, while generally restricting their social interactions and the choice of marriage partners to those of similar standing. Enshrined by the law, social position was everything. Moreover, in many instances, these rights and regulations were different in various parts of the kingdom. Even disregarding further complexities in the overseas possessions, France was a patchwork of overlapping jurisdictions. With the introduction of a constitution based on legal equality, all inhabitants of France suddenly were subject to the same rules, and there was one tax regime for all. This meant that all Frenchmen became equal and that one's nationality—or one's membership of the *demos*—now was more important than social identities.

It was not just legal rules that were codified on a national scale. Many institutions that had been provincial or royal now became national, such as the National Assembly, the national treasury, the national archive, and national tribunals, while new institutions were added, such as the National Garde and national museums. This did not mean they became culturally French, but that they belonged to the French nation. Moreover, the French Revolution was characterized by a large-scale attempt to reconstruct state and society largely from scratch, by applying rational and uniform rules in almost every domain. Thus, local measures and weights were replaced by a uniform metric system. The removal of internal tolls and trade barriers created a national market. A uniform civil registry replaced the baptism registers of the Church. The irregular mosaic of provinces, cantons, and cities was replaced by a rational grid of uniform departments of almost equal size, with new names that referred not to the past but to geography (usually rivers or mountains) and with their capitals at the center. Most of the uniform rules were also introduced in those parts of Europe that came under French influence. At about the same time, the United States adopted an even more rigorous geometrical grid, not only to define state borders but also to determine the layout of settlements and landholdings.[43]

Moreover, after the proclamation of the republic, the memory of the royalist past was erased. Signs of "feudalism" were removed from the physical landscape. Streets, cities, and villages that referred to royals, nobles, or the Church received new names using terms taken from the revolutionary nation-state, such as "revolution," "constitution," and "liberty." A similar revolutionary iconoclasm could be found outside of France as well, although the transformation of the built environment was for the most part less radical. In 1793 a new, secular calendar (figure 2.1) was adopted in France—beginning with the proclamation of the republic instead of the birth of Christ—in which names were based on nature. The months referred to the typical weather of each season, while the days no longer referred to saints but to animals, trees, fruits, and agricultural tools. The calendar was also rationalized; each week had ten days and each month thirty days, and the six extra days became national holidays.[44]

The nationalization of the population of France progressed not just because the national framework became much more prominent in daily life—there were also conscious attempts to connect the inhabitants to the new nation-state. However, almost all of the symbols used to mobilize the population (e.g., the tree of liberty, the patriotic altar, and the liberty cap) celebrated the revolution rather than a culturally distinct French nation. The same was true with memorabilia, such as stones of the Bastille and commercial products like engravings and commemorative objects, and new customs, such as addressing each other as "citizen," preferring the egalitarian *tu* (you) to the more deferential *vous* (thou), and avoiding powdered wigs and extravagant dress. The many festivals with elaborate rituals that were organized throughout the country also were focused on the revolutionary ideals. Radicals even converted Notre-Dame into a Temple of Reason, and Robespierre organized a deistic Festival of the Supreme Being.[45] Only the red, white, and blue cockade, the tricolor flag, and

FIGURE 2.1 Philibert-Louis Debucourt, *French Revolutionary Calendar*, 1793. Completely rational calendar with weeks of ten days, months of thirty days, and six national holidays. The names for days and months were invented from scratch and mostly refer to nature.

Marianne referred to France in an abstract way, but in other countries they were easily replaced by a Belgian, Italian, or Mexican equivalent. Moreover, the "Marseillaise," like most of the other symbols of the republic, was widely adopted by revolutionaries outside of France.

The primary aim was not to encourage national feelings, but to create a new, enlightened human being. This revolutionary ideal was hammered home through speeches, pamphlets, images, festivals, and primary education, for which thorough reforms were planned. And this ideal was clearly gendered: men should be rational and upright citizen-soldiers, and women would primarily take a nurturing role, by giving birth, bringing up the citizens of the future, and supporting their husbands. Although women had participated actively in the early stages of the revolution, they were increasingly excluded from political participation, and in 1799 they (along with foreigners and servants) were debarred from wearing the revolutionary cockade. The French Revolution thus hardened the boundaries between a male public and a female domestic sphere.[46]

The revolution and the invention of the nation-state also had a great impact on the cultural realm. Many writers, artists, and architects became enthusiastic messengers of the new gospel. Some art forms, such as opera, were not very suitable for revolutionary propaganda because they were too intimately connected with the world of the court and the aristocracy. Theater, on the other hand, was well suited for conveying the revolutionary message, and a wide variety of propagandistic plays were staged, attracting a broad audience. Songs such as "Ça ira" and the "Marseillaise" were even more suitable, since they were a very democratic art form and could be performed everywhere and at almost all occasions.[47]

More lasting effects were achieved through the establishment of new revolutionary institutions, of which the Louvre Museum was the most important. These new cultural establishments have been interpreted as a crucial step in the invention of "heritage" and "art," and they actually nationalized both.[48] Neither process started from scratch, but the French Revolution accelerated developments and, in the end, became a watershed moment. In 1750, parts of the royal art collections were opened to the public at the Palais du Luxembourg in Paris. The goal was both to give wider public access to a selection of masterpieces and to revitalize the training of young artists. But the revolution would turn the Louvre Palace into a grandiose art museum. With the secularization of the properties of the Church in November 1789, the French state came into possession of a large number of precious objects. Soon after, the properties of émigrés were confiscated, and after the proclamation of the republic the royal possessions were also nationalized. In 1790 the new Monument Commission was tasked with making an inventory of valuable objects of art, industry, and science that needed to be saved and protected, turning conservation into a public responsibility. This resulted in the foundation of four national museums—the Louvre, the Museum of French Monuments, the Conservatory of Arts and Métiers, and a Museum of Natural History—while at about the same time, the royal book and manuscript collection became the National Library.[49]

But what should the state do with all the valuable treasures that now belonged to the nation? Most artistic objects were sold, some were demolished, and others were saved. During the Terror, in an attempt to create a radically new society, aristocratic coats of arms were removed from buildings, and religious statues and the royal tombs in Saint-Denis were destroyed. Many royal tapestries were melted down to recover the precious metals of the gold and silver threads. There were widespread debates on how rigorous the purification campaign had to be. In August 1793 the revolutionary painter Jacques-Louis David criticized the new Central Art Museum of the Republic in the Louvre, arguing that the many luxurious decorative objects reminded visitors more of "aristocratic cabinets" than of an "imposing school."[50]

Another problem was the politically undesirable messages expressed in many artworks, such as those that glorified the monarchy or propagated religious "fanaticism" or "superstition." Even more modest genre paintings were seen as problematic because they lacked an uplifting message. However, when these canvasses and sculptures were removed from churches, royal palaces, and aristocratic mansions and integrated into museums, they acquired a new secular meaning. The focus was now on the form, on the aesthetic quality of the artworks rather than the content, and thus these objects of worship or royal glorification were converted into cultural heritage. An official report of May 1794 argued that the "marks of superstition, flattery, and debauchery" could best be obliterated by arranging the works of art in a rational order as "a continuous and uninterrupted sequence revealing the progress of the arts and the degrees of perfection attained by various nations that have cultivated them."[51] Nevertheless, in a detailed analysis of the Louvre, Andrew McClellan has shown that under Napoleon, when the museum took a more definitive form, the wish to achieve a symmetrical and visually pleasing display was more important than a chronological arrangement according to national schools.[52]

In the more modest Museum of French Monuments, Alexandre Lenoir succeeded in imposing a strict chronological order. His museum was a continuation of the National Depot, which had been created to store the most impressive sculptures, tombs, and architectural fragments that had been removed from confiscated properties. When Robespierre's policy of destroying remnants of the feudal past was condemned as "vandalism" after the Terror ended, Lenoir used the new political context to turn the depot into a museum. By building period rooms, he created an historical overview of French sculpture with a clear progression from the "Dark Ages" to the era of liberty and enlightenment that had been inaugurated by the Revolution.[53] In this way, not only did the confiscated artistic objects belong to the nation, but the chronological arrangement of the rooms also created a clear picture of the nation's artistic progress, while implicitly suggesting a cultural essence.

An important goal of all four museums was to make the nation's treasures accessible to the people. Another objective was to make them available for study, and this was particularly the case with the Louvre. Revolutionaries criticized the traditional education at the Royal Academy, where each aspiring artist was assigned to the studio of an established master, which encouraged the "slavish" copying of his work. In the new Louvre, the great masterpieces of the past had become accessible and students now had the freedom to choose the master they wanted as a guide. Most of the time, the museum was open exclusively for artists.[54]

The Louvre was not conceived as a narrowly defined national museum. Actually, many French works of art went to Versailles, and in 1797 the empty palace was converted into the Special Museum of the French School. The best French artworks would stay in the Louvre, where they were shown together with the masterpieces of the Italian and Northern schools. Moreover, the Louvre was continuously enriched by fresh arrivals. When the Southern Netherlands was annexed in 1794, the new territory was supposed to contribute "monuments of interest to the arts and sciences" to the national collections, just as other departments had done. This plan was repeated in the following decades with all of France's conquests, even if the new territories remained nominally independent. These confiscations of art were presented as an act of "liberation" from despotism, as the treasures returned to the reputed land of liberty and equality. The best art of the past would find a "final home" in Paris, which would succeed Rome as the "capital of the arts," and the Louvre would become a universal source of inspiration for artists from all over the world.[55]

Instead of showcasing the evolution of French fine art, the Louvre exhibited the artistic highlights of (Western) civilization, and pieces from the early modern period were arranged according to national schools. However, this past was tainted by feudalism and superstition. Accordingly, the revolutionaries had a strong preference for classical antiquity, from which they could draw more uplifting aesthetic and moral lessons. In early 1797, when the troops of Napoleon conquered Rome, among the hundred works of art confiscated from the pope were eighty-three classical statues, of which the *Apollo Belvedere* was seen as the most important trophy. It received its own room of honor in the new classical sculpture gallery of the Louvre. Whereas classical antiquity still set the tone in sculpture, in painting the summit had been reached during the Italian Renaissance. Raphael was seen as the greatest painter of all time, and his best works comprised the focal point of the Grand Gallery.[56]

This tendency to hold classical antiquity and its revival during the Renaissance in great esteem was also seen in other fields. Many revolutionary plays had classical themes, political rhetoric followed classical examples, and neoclassicism—mostly in an austere, monumental version—would become the dominant style of revolutionary artists, architects, and designers in France and elsewhere. Neoclassicism had already come into vogue a few decades earlier, particularly as a consequence of the rediscovery of the spectacular archaeological remains of Pompeii and Herculaneum.[57] During the Terror, Gabriel Bouquier, a French painter-revolutionary, explained his preference for neoclassicism by arguing that "effeminate works," "false taste," and "monarchical routine" had to be overcome by a "virile and energetic style," "dignified colors . . . a bold brush, a volcanic genius."[58]

The painter whose work and activities best embodied the new ideals was Jacques-Louis David, whose vigorous neoclassical style had already won him

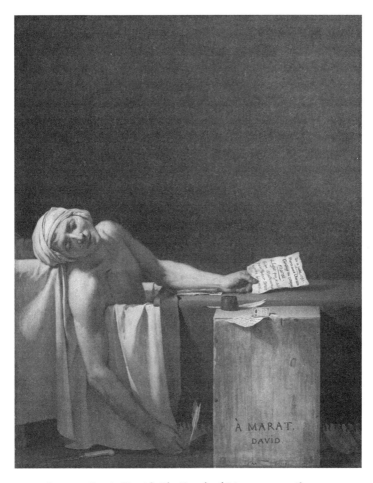

FIGURE 2.2 Jacques-Louis David, *The Death of Marat*, 1793, oil on canvas, 162 × 128 cm. Iconic image of a French revolutionary leader, stabbed to death by Charlotte Corday in his own bath, by David, the most prominent neoclassical painter of the time.

a name before the Revolution. In his early paintings he depicted examples of patriotic virtue in ancient Greece and the Roman Republic. After 1789 he produced a number of magnificent paintings that documented contemporary events, such as *The Oath on the Tennis Court* (1790–1794) and *The Coronation of Napoleon* (1806). He also painted life-sized, iconic images of revolutionary heroes, such as *The Death of Marat* (1793; figure 2.2) and *Napoleon at the Saint-Bernard Pass* (1801). His revolutionary career took off with the organization of the procession that carried the mortal remains of Voltaire to the newly installed Pantheon, and it culminated during the Terror. As a member of the National Convention, David voted for the execution of the king; he also

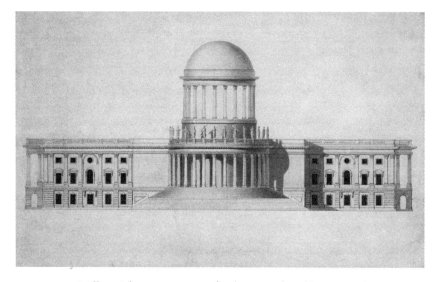

FIGURE 2.3 William Thornton, *Design for the Capitol Building in Washington D.C., West Elevation*, 1793, drawing, 38 × 61 cm. Thornton's neoclassical design combined perfectly with L'Enfant's grandiose plan for the layout of the city of Washington, D.C.

directed many of the revolutionary festivals, such as the one dedicated to the Supreme Being.[59]

In architecture, the connection with classical antiquity, supposedly the cradle of human civilization, was even more obvious. The meeting room of the new National Assembly was modeled on an ancient amphitheater, the festival terrain on the Parisian Champ de Mars was inspired by a Roman circus, the Temple to Great Men by the Pantheon in Rome, and most new public buildings by classical temples. Under Napoleon, the central Rue de Rivoli and the Arc de Triomphe were also designed in a monumental neoclassical style. During the Terror, architects developed ambitious plans to redesign the city of Paris and aimed to strictly supervise the construction of civic buildings in the rest of the country, which according to François Loyer would have resulted in a "truly architectural dictatorship." However, the unstable political and financial situation meant that most projects did not get off the ground. This was not the case for furniture and fashion, where the neoclassical empire style would become very popular. And the revolutionary preference for classical antiquity was not limited to France. In the United States, the French American architect Pierre Charles L'Enfant designed a grandiose plan for the development of the new federal district in Washington, which included a president's house and the Capitol Building (figure 2.3), both of which were built beginning in 1791 in an imposing neoclassical style. In the parts of Europe dominated by France, grandiose buildings and urban plans in a monumental neoclassical style were developed in, for example, Milan and Karlsruhe.[60] Thus, although the artistic past was now arranged along national lines, the artistic preferences of the revolutionary elites were very cosmopolitan, while Paris and other cities aimed to become classicist centers of Western civilization. Revolutionaries in the Americas and the rest of Europe followed the French lead, and as a consequence, national differences were largely disregarded and no conscious attempt was made to create a distinct national culture.

Conclusion

The nation-state that arose during the age of revolution was very different from what we are accustomed to today. Nation-states could be tiny, such as the cities of Mainz and Cartagena de Indias, or they could span various continents, like Spain and its colonial empire. Their boundaries were not stable; their territories were often expanded without taking into regard cultural and linguistic differences. After the nation became sovereign, foreigners often obtained citizenship easily, but people who were thought to be lacking in civilization—that is, not in the possession of a fully independent, rational mind—such as women, children, the intellectually disabled, slaves, people of African descent, and most Native Americans—were excluded from political participation and sometimes even from passive citizenship. Nevertheless, the introduction of the nation-state and the abolition of all remnants of feudalism had huge implications for the way political power was legitimized, replacing the king's absolute power with the sovereignty of the nation. After the legal equality of all citizens was proclaimed, social identities became largely irrelevant and nationality now determined one's legal status. However, the newly created nations were not defined in cultural terms. During their most radical phase, the French revolutionaries tried to create a new rational society by breaking with the past. This affected all spheres of life, but left no room for national peculiarities. Cultural life continued to be highly cosmopolitan, and the frame of reference remained classical antiquity. With the new national cultural institutions the first steps were taken to define a national heritage and canon, but artistic taste—in rhetoric, literature, painting, fashion, and architecture—was dominated by neoclassicism, a universal artistic trend.

3

Romantic Nationalism, 1815–1848

THE IMPOSITION OF the nation-state in large parts of Europe through the force of French arms was met with resistance. Anti-French feelings became particularly pronounced in German lands after Napoleon inflicted another crushing defeat on Austria and Russia at Austerlitz in December 1805. The French emperor decided to rearrange the German principalities—most of which had become French client states—by creating the Confederation of the Rhine. A few months later, Napoleon humiliated the Prussian army in the battles of Jena and Auerstädt. Most of Prussia was occupied, and King Frederick William III had to sign a punitive peace treaty. In this context, the poet Ernst Moritz Arndt declared that every virtuous German could not but hate the French, the philosopher Johann Gottlieb Fichte proclaimed the superiority of the German language and culture, and Friedrich Jahn began gymnastic clubs to physically prepare young German men for throwing off the French yoke.[1]

This kind of hostility toward a "foreign" enemy was not a German peculiarity; it could be found almost everywhere during the manifold conflicts that broke out during the age of revolution. In the United States, violence against "enemies of American liberty" was widespread. At the proclamation of independence of Haiti in 1804—after about half of the population had succumbed in more than a decade of violence—Jean-Jacques Dessalines pledged "to kill every Frenchman who soils the land of freedom with his sacrilegious presence." In a manifesto issued shortly after the Napoleonic invasion of Spain in 1808, the Supreme Central Junta called the French monstrous and incited the population to "kill these ferocious animals." When uprisings began in Spanish America, rebels in New Spain and in Venezuela targeted persons born in Spain for death and confiscation of their possessions.[2]

Azar Gat argues that since the earliest beginnings of humankind, communities of kindred people bonded together to resist an outside invasion or to fight a foreign oppressor.[3] Aggressive proclamations and sentiments of hatred toward the enemy are not unusual in a warlike situation. Nevertheless, in the case of the Americas, cultural differences did not play a role. Although political leaders and intellectuals attempted to frame their struggle as a war between an innocent and harmless "people" and an aggressive foreign oppressor, most conflicts during the Atlantic Revolutions were also civil wars, and this certainly was the case in German lands, Spain, and the Americas. Thus, the wars that accompanied the creation of the first nation-states in fact were not waged over unsurmountable cultural differences between "us" and "them," but over different conceptions of political legitimacy.

The Rise of Romantic Nationalism

Yet, intellectuals began to formulate an alternative to the Enlightenment interpretation of the nation as a sovereign community of equal citizens, as defended in both the American and French Revolutions. As a response to the excesses of the Jacobin Terror, this occurred even in France, by authors such as François-René de Chateaubriand and Germaine de Staël.[4] But this reaction was best articulated in German lands. In *Addresses to the German Nation* (1807–1808), a lecture series at the Royal Academy of Sciences in a Berlin occupied by French troops, Fichte defined the nation as a linguistic community that throughout history had developed its own distinct culture. Language, according to him, was not just a transparent vehicle of communication—it reflected both the history and the cultural peculiarities of the "nation" or "people," terms he used interchangeably. As a consequence, Germans should remain faithful to their own language and culture, because this was the only way they could make a significant contribution to the progress of humanity. This exactly was the problem with France; although its inhabitants descended primarily from the Franks—a Germanic people—they had adopted a "foreign" language derived from Latin. According to Fichte, the nation also gave meaning to individual existence. People could make a creative contribution to the development of their nation's culture and by enduring over time, the nation conferred a transcendent meaning to individual acts. Fichte argued that because the German states had lost their political independence, the cultivation of this unique German culture—and ultimately, the fatherland—was now more urgent than ever.[5]

This cultural interpretation of the national community did not come out of the blue. An important source of inspiration for Fichte was the ideas of Johann Gottfried Herder. In his *Treatise on the Origin of Language* (1772) Herder had argued that every language was adapted to the living conditions of a people and reflected its mentality and characteristics. He did not assert that any language was superior to others; in God's eyes, they were all equal. In order to understand the character of a people, one had to study its interaction with the physical environment over time. His emphasis on cultural differences and "primitive" folk traditions as the best expression of a people's way of thinking clashed frontally with the abstract universalism and cosmopolitan elitism of the Enlightenment. Nevertheless, Herder's ideas fell on fertile soil because at about the same time, a new generation of authors—known as Sturm und Drang (storm and stress)—including Johann Wolfgang Goethe and Friedrich Schiller began to oppose the dominance of French classicist theater at the princely courts. Their own plays, written in German, often dealt with heroes of the past who rose up against oppression, such as Goethe's *Egmont* (1788) and Schiller's *Wilhelm Tell* (1804).[6]

This reaction against neoclassicism, aristocratic decadence, and French cultural hegemony could also be found elsewhere in Europe. The Celtic epic poems of Ossian, the Norse Edda sagas, and the German *Nibelungenlied* were "rediscovered." They conferred on peripheral languages an ancient poetic tradition that rivalled Homer and classical antiquity. These stories about mythical heroes could presumably still be found in primitive peasant communities, which as a consequence began to embody the authentic source of a people's cultural traditions. The writings of Jean-Jacques Rousseau, such as *Discourse on the Origin and Basis of Inequality among Men* (1754) and the epistolary novel *Julie, or the New Heloise* (1761), also praised the authenticity of primitive societies and idealized the simple life in the countryside. These books were rapidly translated and read all over Europe.[7]

However, what languages were a suitable basis for a true national culture and potentially independent statehood? The connection between language, culture, and nation was quite straightforward in most parts of Western Europe and the Americas, where vernacular languages had long been "civilized" by being extensively used for administrative, literary, and scholarly purposes. Most scholars argued that Indigenous languages in the Americas and dialects and less widely spoken languages in Europe were ill-suited for modern civilized life; they lacked the sophisticated terminology for philosophical, medical, or scientific discourse, and would probably vanish. Herder assumed that even the Hungarian language was doomed. This was particularly worrying for young intellectuals in East-Central Europe, where sacred script languages like Latin, Byzantine Greek, and Old Church Slavonic still had a dominant position, whereas well-educated elites mostly used German or French.[8]

The new focus on language and culture had opposite effects in different parts of the Continent. In Western Europe, Romantic nationalism was mostly state-centered. In German and Italian states, it legitimized the call for national unification, whereas in Eastern Europe it led to emancipatory movements. This was evident, for instance, in the role of cultural associations such as learned societies, reading rooms, and male choirs, which during the early nineteenth century became important vehicles for nationalist mobilization. In German lands, their activities focused mostly on celebrating a shared German fatherland. In

East-Central Europe they propagated the use and study of the vernacular language, whereas in France, they professed a more state-centered patriotism.[9]

The efforts to standardize vernacular languages and turn them into a sound base for a flowering national culture had impressive results. Polish and Czech, both of which had been chancery languages in the past, were quickly revived. In 1807 Samuel Linde initiated the publication of a monumental six-volume Polish dictionary, and between 1792 and 1821 Josef Dobrovský wrote a history of the Czech language and literature, a grammar, and a German-Czech dictionary.[10] Elsewhere, language activists similarly produced dictionaries, grammars, and textbooks, effectively transforming dialects into languages and replacing foreign loanwords with neologisms. Jernej Kopitar, an employee of the Court Library in Vienna, composed a Slovene grammar and inspired others to publish a dictionary, a translation of the Bible, a literary history, and collections of folk songs and proverbs. He also supported Vuk Stefanović Karadžić, who published a Serbian grammar and dictionary, and translated the New Testament into Serbian. This implied that a new language-based nationalism slowly replaced the older patriotism based on principalities or Crown lands; thus Bohemian patriotism was replaced by a German and Czech nationalism that both referred to wider communities.[11]

Other scholars standardized languages such as Hungarian, Romanian, and Finnish. Dictionaries for Bulgarian, Albanian, Lithuanian, and other less common languages would follow toward the end of the century. In the context of missionary work, many languages were codified in non-Western parts of the world as well. In order for a language to be taken seriously as a "civilized language," multivolume encyclopedias and lexicons with technical terms were also needed. But standardizing a language was not always a straightforward affair. Were Slovak and Moravian separate languages, or mere dialects of Czech? A similar situation existed in Russia: many accepted that there were differences between Great Russia, Little Russia (Ukraine), and White Russia (Belarus), but the assertion that Ukrainian and Belarussian were independent languages was heavily contested. In other places there was a conflict over the correct version of the national language. In Greece, some intellectuals preferred to take Classical Greek as a starting point, while others advocated for the language the people actually spoke in daily life, the "demotic." In the 1830s, Katharévousa, a compromise between demotic and Classical Greek, was adopted by the state. In Norway, which had been part of the composite Danish Kingdom until 1812, there are two official versions of the Norwegian language: Bokmål, which is very close to Danish, and Landsmål, or Nynorsk. Landsmål (language of the land) was developed by Ivar Aasen based on dialects of the interior, which according to him were closer to the original language of the Norwegians.[12]

Even in large Western European countries such as France, the United Kingdom, and Spain, less common languages—most of them spoken primarily by peasants—became an object of antiquarian interest. Between 1807 and 1827, Jean-François Le Gonidec published a Celtic-Breton grammar and dictionary and translated the Bible into Breton. Many thought that languages such as Gaelic, Welsh, Frisian, Breton, Occitan, Basque, and Catalan were doomed to disappear; others saw them as the linguistic sediment of separate peoples with their own unique cultures, and during the nineteenth century, they began to revive these languages.[13] Even ignoring the many linguistically mixed areas in Europe, this suggests that the boundaries of linguistically defined nations were far from clear and that those boundaries depended on which languages were considered "civilized."

Although Romantic nationalism rapidly gained ground in Europe and beyond, the Enlightenment ideal of national sovereignty and older conceptions of nationhood had not disappeared. The situation became more complex as nationalist ideals became entangled with the new political ideologies that sprang up during the period between 1815 and 1848. One could argue that the rise of modern politics had been an unintended consequence of the invention of the nation-state. During the ancien régime, politics had been either very specific (e.g., protests against the impairment of a local privilege) or very general, exemplified by the famous blueprints for an ideal society produced by Locke, Montesquieu, and Rousseau. After royal absolutism, aristocratic privileges, and the remains of feudalism had been abolished during the French Revolution, the domain of politics was entirely open. What powers should be given to the parliament? Who should get the vote? Who should pay what taxes? And what would be the division of tasks between the central state, local authorities, and civil society?[14]

At first, many radicals thought there would be one rational solution to all new political questions. Robespierre, for instance, argued that his policies embodied the "general will." But during the early decades of the nineteenth century, it became clear that various answers were possible. Many nationalist activists, including the French historian Jules Michelet and the Italian revolutionary Giuseppe Mazzini, still espoused the left-wing Jacobin ideal of an independent democratic nation-state, in the form of a republic based on popular sovereignty. Moderate liberals preferred a juste-milieu solution, rejecting both the unrestrained popular sovereignty of the republicans and a strong executive dominated by the monarch. Instead, they embraced the nation-state in the form of a constitutional monarchy, which recognized the equality before the law of all citizens while limiting suffrage rights to property owners.[15]

Many conservatives, rather than defending the privileges of the ancien régime, learned to speak on behalf of the nation as well. Some did so by building on older conceptions of nationhood, such as existing political "ethnotypes." Edmund Burke, in his famous *Reflections on the Revolution of France* (1790), rejected the abstract principles on which the revolutionaries aimed to build a new government and praised the British political system, which according to him was derived from the "inheritance from our forefathers." In German lands, many conservatives understood that the new revolutionary ideals could not be totally rejected. Conservative Prussian aristocrats were willing to accept limited citizen rights and provincial assemblies while replacing the egalitarian fraternal model of the republicans with a more hierarchical paternalist one. Others proposed that the existing German states should collaborate and adopt a federal constitution.[16]

Conservative intellectuals also sought to reconcile the nation with Christianity. In *The Genius of Christianity* (1802) the French aristocrat François René Chateaubriand reconnected the French nation with its Catholic faith, presenting patriotic feelings—meaning, primarily, attachment to the native soil—as a gift from God. Patriotism was chiefly associated with love of the fatherland and increasingly lost its radical political implications. Sergei Uvarov, the minister of education under Nicholas I, instructed Russian schools to inculcate the "joint spirit of Orthodoxy, Autocracy, and Nationality." A quite curious proposal was made by Vincenzo Gioberti, who suggested in his best-selling book *On the Moral and Civil Primacy of the Italians* (1843) that the Italian principalities unite in a federation with the pope as its head, thus reconciling nationalism with the Catholic Church and royal power with limited forms of political participation.[17] In the end, the mixture of Enlightenment and Romantic ideals and conservative and more liberal views would have profound implications.

Nation-State Formation in Europe

Anti-French sentiments received a strong boost during the Napoleonic era, and many military and political leaders now summoned their populations to rally behind their flags. In 1808 Spanish patriots incited the population to rise up against the oppressor, reminding them of earlier heroic exploits. Tsar Alexander I called on the Russian people, the "descendants of valiant Slavs," to take up arms against the Napoleonic invasion. After much hesitation, Frederick William III decided to side with the tsar, and in March 1813 he appealed to the Prussian population to support the war effort. Others summoned all Germans to rise up against the French in order to liberate the "fatherland." In the end, the number of volunteers in these so-called German Wars of Liberation was relatively small—the free corps contributed about thirty thousand men—but many people made donations to save the fatherland, and almost six hundred women's associations were created to sustain the cause.[18]

Although nationalist ideas were clearly on the rise during the Romantic era, they had a very limited effect on the existing international order. After the defeat of Napoleon, most state authorities lost interest in mobilizing the population in the name of the fatherland. Moreover, they were very suspicious of the idea of popular sovereignty and scarcely interested in cultural differences. This became evident at the Congress of Vienna, where the victorious powers of Russia, Austria, Prussia, and Great Britain gathered in 1814. They rearranged borders without taking into account the "nationalities" or wishes of the populations. Strong buffer states along the borders of France such as the United Kingdom of the Netherlands and a reinforced Kingdom of Sardinia would provide protection against future French aggression. Great Britain retained the Dutch possessions of Ceylon and the Cape Colony, which they had taken over during the war, and the continental powers also wanted to be given new territories. The language, culture, and wealth of the areas concerned were ignored; the only criterion that mattered was the territory's number of "souls," meaning the number of potential military recruits, which was a crucial factor in the new type of warfare introduced by the French revolutionaries. Thus, Prussia was enlarged with various German principalities, Austria annexed the Illyrian Provinces, Venice, and Lombardy, and the Duchy of Warsaw and the Grand Duchy of Finland were awarded—in a personal union—to the Russian tsar. As a compensation for losing Finland, the Swedish king received Norway at the cost of the Danish king, who together with some German principalities had fought on the side of Napoleon until the very end.[19]

In addition to the Final Act of the Congress of Vienna, Tsar Alexander I, King Frederick William III, and Emperor Francis signed the treaty of the Holy Alliance, in which they promised, as "members of one and the same Christian nation," to uphold the "precepts of Justice, Christian Charity and Peace," which in fact meant that a league of traditional monarchs would collaborate in order to avoid further revolutionary experiments. This became clear in 1819, when the Austrian chancellor Clemens von Metternich—worried by the activities of nationalist students—convinced the states of the German Confederation to introduce censorship, to prohibit Jahn's gymnastic clubs, and to closely monitor student fraternities. The next year, Metternich convened a meeting of the great powers in Troppau to discuss the military uprising in Naples that had forced King Ferdinand I to adopt a liberal constitution. Russia and Prussia endorsed the intervention by the Austrian army, which quickly restored the autocratic power of the king. Two years later, at the Congress of Verona, the French were authorized to invade Spain, where a coup had brought to power the liberals, who had immediately restored the Constitution of 1812. Tsar Alexander offered to "mediate" in the conflict between Spain and its American colonies, but Great Britain rejected the proposal.[20] Thus the continental powers effectively blocked the spread of the nation-state model in Europe, though they could not fully control the hearts and minds of their subjects.

After 1815, monarchs in Eastern and Southern Europe largely returned to the old order, but this was not a realistic option in the areas where the impact of the revolution had been most profound. There it was inconceivable to reinstate the feudal dues and obligations that had been abolished, to undo the sale of church lands, and to return to the irregular patchwork of jurisdictions, taxes, and privileges of the ancien régime. The fact that it was virtually impossible to break with the nation-state model was most clearly visible in France, where the Bourbons were restored to the throne. Although Louis XVIII reintroduced the white Bourbon flag and proclaimed that all acts adopted since 1791 were null and void, he granted his "subjects" a constitutional charter that recognized legal equality and civil liberties and he installed a parliament with limited powers, elected by a very restricted suffrage.[21]

The constitutional monarchies that remained after 1815 were the United Kingdom of Great Britain and Ireland, the United Kingdom of the Netherlands, the United Kingdoms of Sweden and Norway, and Congress Poland; constitutional charters had been adopted in France and in some smaller German and Italian states. Elsewhere, the ideal of a written constitution had not disappeared. As we have seen, liberal uprisings led to brief constitutional monarchies in Naples and Spain in 1820, and in Portugal two years later. Even in autocratic Russia, Tsar Alexander toyed with the idea of granting a constitutional charter, and one of the main demands of the failed Decembrist revolt of 1825 was a constitution.[22]

During the next two decades no fundamental liberal breakthrough was reached, although some progress was made. Several German principalities adopted a constitution, and the Revolution of 1830 caused a change of dynasty in France, where Louis Philippe presented himself as a "citizen king." The following year, the new state of Belgium adopted a liberal constitution, and several countries extended the suffrage. Reforms were also introduced in the United Kingdom, bringing the country more in line with the new nation-state model, with equal rights for all citizens. Influenced by the recognition of the rights of French-speaking Catholic Quebecois in British North America, the Roman Catholic Relief Acts of 1791 and 1829 removed almost all obstacles for Catholics in Great Britain and Ireland to exert their citizenship rights, while the repeal of the Test Act in 1828 opened public office to Dissenters and Catholics. Moreover, in 1832 the Reform Act revised the boundaries of more than one hundred counties and boroughs in the United Kingdom, with the aim of making parliamentary representation fairer to those areas where the population had grown considerably.[23]

In most countries in the western half of the European continent, nationalism was expressed primarily as a longing for a constitutional nation-state;

apart from reactionary groups who advocated a return to the ancien régime, all political currents adopted its ideals. Particularly the rapidly growing liberal mainstream, in both its moderate and more radical forms, embraced the nation-state model, making nationalism largely invisible as a distinct political ideology. Things were different in many parts of East-Central Europe. Nationalist movements in German lands, on the Italian Peninsula, and in Polish areas not only aimed to change the political system but also aspired to change the borders of the state by uniting various shattered territories into a new nation-state.[24] In the Austrian and Russian Empires, meanwhile, small numbers of activists tried to turn the members of their own ethnic communities into self-conscious nations.

In Italy, nationalist opposition to French rule had been organized in secret societies, of which the Carbonari were the most famous. After Napoleon's failed Russian campaign, the British collaborated with the Carbonari to spark a national uprising, but this did not have much effect. These nationalist secret societies, which also included many Freemason lodges—continued their activities after 1815. The Carbonari, for instance, provoked uprisings in various Italian principalities, but the 1820 revolution in Naples and the 1830 insurrections in the Papal States, Modena, and Parma were quickly repressed by Austrian military intervention.[25] Other well-known secret societies were the German League of Virtue, which was created in 1808, and the Greek Society of Friends, which was founded in Odessa in 1814, both of which tried to spark nationalist uprisings. A second group of secret societies was created in the wake of the failed Revolution of 1830. Mazzini used his exile in Marseille to create his own society, Young Italy, which was intended to continue the propaganda efforts of the Carbonari and organize further insurrections. Under his charismatic leadership, Young Italy rapidly gained adherents, and the formula was copied elsewhere, generating Young Germany, Young Poland, and Young Ireland. Three years later, Mazzini created Young Europe with fellow exiles from Germany and Poland, presaging the peaceful coexistence of clearly delineated nation-states in the future.[26]

Ottoman Empire and Beyond

The nation-state model advanced (albeit quite slowly) not only because it was attractive to middle-class activists, but also because it was enticing for ambitious political leaders outside of the Western world. Military innovations had already propelled forward a process of state centralization in the early modern era, but now this was combined with conscious attempts to strengthen the state by adopting various aspects of the nation-state. Although the early European and American nation-states were quite diverse, they all seemed to connect their inhabitants more closely to the state, while enabling economic growth. The Ottoman Empire and various other states in the Eastern Hemisphere now sought to emulate the success of the Western nation-states by adopting the elements they found useful.

The introduction of new weapons, especially muskets, transformed traditional warfare practices in many parts of the world and fueled a process of political centralization. Successful warriors could rapidly strengthen and expand their realm, but to consolidate their power they had to extract more resources from the population. Rulers therefore tried to increase the productivity of the land, while state officials directly dealt with the population, bypassing traditional chiefs and intermediate military castes. This process was visible in the South Indian state of Mysore, where Haidar Ali usurped power in 1760. His innovative standing army, which combined a traditional mobile cavalry with a highly disciplined infantry, was modeled on European examples, and for it, he recruited French aid. He also built a modern navy, and he sidestepped the traditional landowning warrior class by imposing a direct tax on the peasants. His son, Tipu Sultan, who succeeded him in 1782, introduced further reforms. He increased tax revenues by helping the peasants improve their output, and he founded a state company to encourage international trade. Adopting the terminology of the age of revolutions, Tipu defined himself as a "citizen prince." When it appeared that the rapidly expanding state of Mysore was seeking French military support, the British intervened and finally defeated Tipu's army in 1799.[27]

Elsewhere in the Indian and Pacific Oceans, the introduction of European muskets also disrupted traditional balances of power while encouraging state centralization, but the outcome—that is, either the consolidation of a centralized state or European intervention—depended largely on the geopolitical context. The musket wars among Maori tribes in New Zealand initially reinforced the power of a relatively small number of warrior chiefs. In 1835, British interference induced them to create the United Tribes of New Zealand, with a national flag and a declaration of independence. The 1840 Treaty of Waitangi, however, brought the islands under the protection of the British monarchy. In the Pacific archipelago of Tonga, the outcome was different. There, the decentralized political system, with many local chiefs, was transformed by the introduction of European weapons. Several chiefs competed for European aid, while strengthening their power bases at home by increasing agricultural output and centralizing their polities. In the end, Taufa'ahau, one of the most powerful chiefs, created a unified monarchical state, and when he was baptized in 1831 he adopted the name George I.[28] Because of its peripheral position, the Kingdom of Tonga remained independent, but in the age of high imperialism it sought British protection by signing a treaty of friendship.

Similar processes could be encountered in other island states, such as Hawaii, where in 1840 King Kamehameha III adopted a constitution and a bicameral parliament. By that time most of his subjects had converted to Christianity, and about 70 percent of Hawaiians were literate. By presenting Hawaii as a civilized Christian nation-state, Kamehameha hoped to stave off foreign intervention. However, the fate of many modernizing island states was determined largely by the interests of the great powers, and in 1898 Hawaii was annexed by the United States.[29]

Another fascinating example can be found in Madagascar. In 1817 Radama I, the ruler of the expanding highland kingdom of Imerina, signed a treaty with the British in which he was recognized as the king of Madagascar. He used British support to modernize his country and extend his rule. He introduced conscription, adopted the Latin alphabet, created a centralized bureaucracy, and employed foreign experts to build an arms factory and improve craft manufacturing, while missionaries provided modern education. Radama even adopted European dress, table manners, and hairstyles (figure 3.1). Nonetheless, the economy continued to be based on conquest, slavery, and forced labor.[30]

The nation-state model also had a profound impact on the Ottoman Empire. This process has been studied primarily in various national research traditions, thus largely overlooking how developments in the different parts of the empire were closely interrelated. Although Enlightenment ideals also penetrated Muslim society,[31] they primarily influenced the more cosmopolitan Christian communities, which could count on moral (and sometimes military) support from the major European powers. Thus, nationalism undermined the Ottoman Empire by having contrary effects on Muslim and Christian communities. Whereas the authorities mostly pursued a reform course in order to strengthen and centralize the Ottoman Empire or some of its provinces, nationalist activists in the predominantly Christian Balkans aimed to carve out their own national state by means of peasant rebellions and foreign support. While Frederick Anscombe claims that religious motives were more important than nationalist ones in the Ottoman lands, I would argue that the rise of nationalism deepened religious cleavages.[32]

Like other states of the time, the Ottoman Empire felt the impact of new types of warfare. Rulers drew inspiration from the nation-state model to centralize the state, strengthen the army, raise taxes, and abolish existing privileges. These goals were thoroughly connected. The main privileged social group in the Ottoman Empire was the Janissaries, which during the seventeenth and eighteenth centuries had evolved from a formidable slave infantry army into a "part-time militia of shop owners" whose primary aim was to defend its own legal privileges and tax exemptions.[33] After crushing defeats in 1791 and 1792 at the hands of Austria and Russia, it was clear that something

FIGURE 3.1 Robert Jacob Hamerton, *Portrait of King Radama I of Madagascar*,
date unknown, lithograph. In the 1820s, this African monarch modernized his
kingdom and adopted European costumes and hairstyles.

had to be done. Thus, Sultan Selim III introduced a modern-style army, trained
by French officers sent by the Directory regime and dressed in European uniforms. He also rationalized the state administration and took measures to increase tax receipts. However, he was openly criticized by Muslim clerics and
did not dare to abolish the old army. In 1807 he abdicated after a successful
revolt of the Janissaries.[34]

More successful was Mehmed Ali, who in 1805, as an officer of a group of
Albanian mercenaries in the service of the sultan, became governor of Egypt,
a relatively autonomous and wealthy Ottoman province. After consolidating
his position by massacring the local Mamluk elite—the Egyptian equivalent
of the Janissaries—he embarked on an ambitious course of reform. Profiting
from the high grain prices during the Napoleonic era, he improved the

irrigation system, extended private ownership, and encouraged the cultivation of cash crops. In his efforts to strengthen the economy, he introduced new trades and set up arms and textile factories. On the request of the sultan, his army quelled a Wahhabi rebellion in the Hijaz, conquering the holy cities of Mecca and Medina. Soon after, he also annexed Sudan. In desperate need of fresh recruits, in 1821 he decided to conscript Egyptian peasants into the army to protect his empire within an empire. Mehmed Ali was inspired by Selim's attempt at military reform, but he also was a great admirer of Napoleon. He employed French military advisers and set up modern academies to train officers, engineers, and doctors. The army quickly became a disciplined fighting machine, and within a decade, it had more than one hundred thousand soldiers. However, it was not yet a truly national army. First, it recruited only Muslims. Second, native Arab-speaking recruits could not rise above the rank of lieutenant, leaving officer posts to Ottoman Turks like Mehmed Ali. And third, the governor did not make his subjects citizens; he refused to grant them legal equality and the right to participate in politics.[35]

In the Balkans, the nation-state model entered the Ottoman Empire by other means. During the second half of the eighteenth century, Orthodox intellectuals and merchants became interested in new Enlightenment ideas, overcoming the traditional hostility toward the West. Many of them were inspired by the French Revolution, Rhigas Velestinlis prepared a revolutionary proclamation for a Hellenic republic with a bill of rights, an anthem, and a constitution. The uprising never materialized, though, and in 1797 the Austrian authorities handed Velestinlis over to the Ottomans. His draft constitution recognized the sovereignty of the nation and favored religious tolerance, and it was intended that the republic would encompass all areas with a significant Orthodox population: the entire Balkan Peninsula, the Aegean Islands, and the western parts of Asia Minor.[36]

Another option to advance the national cause was to use a traditional peasant rebellion, which is what happened in Serbia in 1804. Led by Karageorge Petrović, the rebels set up a rudimentary government, while volunteers arrived from other Ottoman territories and the Austrian Empire. The Russian tsar also promised support. Eight years later, benefiting from the turmoil in Europe connected to Napoleon's invasion of Russia, the Ottoman army reconquered the Serbian territories. A new uprising in 1815, this time led by Miloš Obrenović, again received protection from Russia. The more diplomatic Obrenović succeeded in carving out an autonomous polity in Serbia, not unlike that of Mehmed Ali's Egypt. Citizens' rights, however, were not on his mind.[37]

More openly nationalist was the uprising in 1821 that was instigated from the outside by Alexander Ipsilantis, the leader of the Society of Friends, the Odessa-based secret society. He focused on Wallachia and Moldavia, two

Romanian principalities that were tributary states of the Ottoman Empire, ruled by princes with a Greek merchant background. But the lack of active Russian support and the difficult combination of disgruntled peasants (most of whom spoke Romanian dialects) and Greek nationalist aspirations rapidly led to defeat. The uprising also affected the Peloponnese, where it managed to survive. Atrocities were committed on all sides, and although internal disputes within the Greek camp escalated into civil war, the main dividing lines in the conflict were religious. Greek rebels killed tens of thousands of Muslims and about five thousand Jews; in retaliation, Orthodox Christians were being ha-rassed and killed in many parts of the Ottoman Empire. Meanwhile, a Greek national assembly set up the institutions of a fledgling Greek state and drew up a constitution that reserved citizenship for Orthodox Christians.[38]

In Western Europe there was much sympathy for the Greek cause, and many philhellenes, including the famous British poet Lord Byron, joined the fight, while others donated money or provided loans. But the rebels—who were often portrayed as direct descendants of the ancient Greeks—did not succeed in fending off the Ottomans. In 1824 the sultan secured the assistance of Mehmed Ali, whose new army was much more effective than his own. In the end, Great Britain, France, and Russia intervened on behalf of the rebels. Their joint fleet quickly won the Battle of Navarino against the Ottoman-Egyptian navy. This was followed by a French "humanitarian" intervention in Greece and a Russian invasion of the Ottoman Empire from the north. In 1830, the three allies concluded the London Protocol, making Greece an independent state. Under Russian pressure, Moldavia, Wallachia, and Serbia became self-governing provinces under a hereditary prince, and all three adopted a constitution.[39]

Embarrassed by the weak performance of the Janissaries in the Greek uprising, Sultan Mahmud II decided to follow the example of his Egyptian governor and create a new Western-style army, this time assisted by Prussian instructors. He also centralized the administration, established advisory coun-cils, and opened a medical school for the army, a military academy, and a trans-lation bureau. This was a significant step, as he now openly showed his willing-ness to learn from the "infidels"; he even stipulated Western clothes for his officials. Unlike his predecessor, he ruthlessly got rid of the old army in 1826. Without the Janissaries, the traditional balance of power in the Ottoman Em-pire tipped toward the central state.[40] Nevertheless, Mahmud first had to ward off an internal threat to his reign. The sultan had not rewarded Mehmed Ali for his contribution in the war against the Greek insurgents, and in 1831, the Egyptian governor decided to snatch it for himself by conquering Syria. His forces defeated various Ottoman armies and even advanced into central Ana-tolia. The Ottoman Empire was on the brink of collapse and was finally rescued by the promise of Russian military assistance. Pressured by France and Great Britain, Mehmed Ali accepted the governorship of the Syrian provinces for himself and his son, ensuring the survival of his dynasty. However, Mehmed Ali did not feel secure in his position, and in 1838 he tried to obtain independence for Egypt. This was blocked by the Western powers, who feared that this would lead to the final dissolution of the Ottoman Empire. When the conflict between Constantinople and Cairo escalated into open warfare, the British decided to interfere on behalf of the sultan. Although the Egyptian armies had the upper hand, Mehmed Ali finally accepted the offer to become hereditary governor of Egypt, while giving up his holdings in Syria and abandoning the idea of independence. Although it is clear that Mehmed Ali's victories could have led to an all-out war over the spoils of the Ottoman Empire, there is no doubt that the Western powers saw him as a formidable rival, and in contrast to their attitude toward Greece, they did not favor the creation of an independent Egyptian state. Apparently, different standards were applied to Christians and Muslims.[41]

In response to the humiliating defeats against Mehmed Ali, the Ottoman Empire began to reinforce the bond with its population by allowing them more rights and hesitantly also adopting other aspects of the nation-state model. In 1839 the new sultan, Abdülmecit, initiated an era of reform, known as the Tanzimat, which would last until 1876. First, a new edict—drafted mainly by Great Vizir Mustafa Resid Pasha, who had been ambassador in Paris and London—promised to guarantee the life, honor, and property of Ottoman subjects. This was particularly relevant for civil servants, who until then had been at the mercy of the sultan. Paid tax collectors replaced the existing system of tax farming, although in some areas this proved to be more expensive, and there, the measure was reversed. In order to better assess the available resources, a census was held and cadastral surveys were introduced. New law codes were drawn up, largely following French models, which in principle resulted in equality before the law. Mahmud II had already mandated the fez as the headdress for all male subjects, regardless of their religion or social status. However, Muslims continued to have the right to present their case for a religious court applying the shari'a.[42]

Citizenship

One of the crucial issues debated during the Restoration era in Europe was citizenship rights, which tended to become more restricted where they had already been granted. Many statesmen agreed that one of the main causes of the radicalization of the French Revolution had been the political influence of the "plebs," who had exerted pressure in the streets, through clubs, and at electoral assemblies. Time-consuming, indirect elections in market squares and assembly halls tended to block the lower classes from access to seats in the National Assembly, but not well enough. In France, moderate liberals like François Guizot devised a new system of political representation, which would quickly be adopted in many parts of Europe and Latin America. Instead of mobilizing the population by granting all male citizens the vote, they now restricted suffrage to those with "sufficient" intellectual capacities. At first, this meant that only successful members of society who paid a certain amount of taxes—and thus had a direct stake in the affairs of the state—were given the vote. Under Louis Philippe the census threshold was slightly lowered, and those with a higher education were also granted the vote. Moreover, direct elections were preferred in order to establish a close link between members of the parliament and their constituencies. In the 1830s the suffrage in France was restricted to about two hundred thousand men, but Prime Minister Guizot argued that it was open to all—people just had to "enrich themselves."[43]

Restrictions were also imposed on foreigners. During the Revolutionary Wars, many governments had introduced state control over foreign travelers, requiring them to have a passport. In most cases, passports were issued by the central state, replacing the letters of recommendation that formerly had been drafted by clergy, guilds, or high-ranking individuals. These restrictions were not lifted after the end of the Napoleonic Wars. Control at the local level also remained important. Since poor relief was the responsibility of local authorities, beggars and vagabonds were expelled whenever possible. For most people, then, rights of residence mattered more than citizenship. This also meant that freedom of movement did not exist in most European countries. Travelers often had to pay high fees to cross international borders, and formal barriers affected the poor more than the well-to-do, so legal equality was more apparent than real.[44]

The exclusion of women from active citizenship rights was tightened as well. This had already begun during the most radical phase of the French Revolution. In 1793 revolutionary clubs for women were outlawed, and women were barred from voicing their opinions in other public venues. Napoleon's Civil Code made married women subordinate to their husbands, to whom they owed obedience. In most constitutional texts, active citizenship was tied directly to military service, which was a male preserve. Professionalization—in art academies, museums, and universities, for instance—increasingly excluded women from the public realm as well, largely relegating them to the domestic sphere.[45]

A similar tendency was apparent in the treatment of religious minorities. Many states continued to have an official religion, and Dissenters and Jews were, at best, second-class citizens. Napoleon considered the Alsatian Jews a "nation within a nation" and tried to force their assimilation. In 1808, he put restrictions on their allegedly abusive practices in moneylending and commerce, obliged all

young men to serve in the army, and tried to mandate intermarriage with
non-Jewish citizens. These measures were not renewed after the end of his regime. After 1815, only France and the Netherlands continued to grant Jews full
citizenship rights. In the Austrian Empire, the civil code that guaranteed equality
before the law did not apply to Jews. In many German states their legal rights
were rescinded, and some states even decided to expel them. This situation
changed temporarily during the Revolutions of 1848.[46]

In Great Britain, where the emancipation of Dissenters and Catholics had
made considerable headway in the late 1820s, the same was not true for Jews.
In the 1830s several legal barriers were removed, and in 1847 the first Jewish
candidate was elected in the House of Commons, but because he was required
to swear an oath "on the true faith of a Christian," Jews were effectively barred
from taking their seats. This situation was remedied only in 1866 when the
formula of the oath became more neutral ("so help me God"). Surprisingly, in
view of the discriminatory regulations against Jews that continued to exist in
most European countries, the great powers required new states, beginning
with Greece, to adopt freedom of religion.[47]

In the Americas, formal and informal methods were used to exclude not just
women and the lower classes from the electoral lists, but also people of color
and Native Americans. Introducing literacy qualifications was an efficient
measure to disqualify most of these groups. Another method of exclusion was
invented in the United States: relocations. In 1819 the American Colonization
Society was founded with the explicit aim of removing emancipated African
Americans from the United States by helping them emigrate to the new Black
homeland of Liberia. Thousands of free Blacks were shipped to West Africa, and
in 1847 these settlers helped make Liberia the first African nation-state by issuing
a declaration of independence and adopting a constitution.[48]

Less voluntary were the relocations of Native Americans living in the
Southeast of the United States. Officially, Native American "tribes" were seen
as "sovereign nations" with which international treaties could be concluded,
but at same time, they were considered "wards," and consequently, the treaties
between these unequal partners could be annulled. Particularly striking was
the case of the Cherokees, who adopted individual landownership, invented
an alphabet, and published newspapers. Many converted to Protestantism,
and in 1827 they even adopted a written constitution. But their attempts to
become a fully "civilized" nation were to no avail. In 1830, instead of recognizing them as an independent nation-state or giving them individual citizenship,
President Andrew Jackson signed the Indian Removal Act, which led to the
forced relocation of the Cherokees and four other Native American "nations"
to Indian Territory in present-day Oklahoma. Thousands of people lost their
lives in this forced migration known as the Trail of Tears.[49]

The main argument for denying citizenship rights to certain populations was that they were not "civilized" enough. This was not just the view of intellectuals and politicians from the West; statesmen on the European periphery also claimed that the populations of their countries were not yet ready for legal equality and political participation. Although Tsar Alexander had given liberal constitutions to the Grand Duchy of Finland and the Kingdom of Poland, he thought that the Russians did not yet have the capacity to be governed by constitutional means. Reshid Pasha, the driving force in the early phase of the Tanzimat reforms, argued that the Ottoman population was too "ignorant" to be governed by a parliament and constitution. In Egypt, Mehmed Ali similarly reasoned that he could not copy Western laws because they were designed for "enlightened and civilized people" and were not suitable for his own subjects, whom he compared to "wild beasts." More than thirty years later, his grandson Ismael mentioned the beneficial effects of a parliamentary regime in "civilized countries" at the inauguration of the Chamber of Delegates (which had only consultatory powers), implying that the Egyptians had not yet reached this stage. Even in Liberia, the Black settlers excluded the Indigenous population from the suffrage because they were not yet "civilized."[50]

National Awareness

So who was drawn to the idea of the nation-state or even became a nationalist activist in the period between 1815 and 1848? The main victims of the age of revolutions—monarchs, nobles, and clergy—were not very keen to promote or even accept the nation-state model, which had led to the abolition of their ancient privileges. Although some of them adopted the nationalist rhetoric and tried to give it a more conservative bent, most remained wary of its revolutionary and egalitarian implications. The reactionary position was probably best symbolized by the coronation ceremony of Charles X in Reims Cathedral in 1825. In the presence of members of the royal family, the court, the highest officers of the army, and representatives of the clergy and the nobility, the new French king took the oath with his hand on the Bible and a relic of the True Cross. He was crowned by the archbishop of Reims, reconfirming the alliance between altar and throne. At the end of the magnificent ceremony, the doors were opened to the people waiting outside, incense filled the air, five hundred doves were released, and salutes were fired on the city's ramparts. A few days later, the king made a ceremonial entry into the city of Paris and again, all the splendor of the ancien régime was used to impress his subjects. But since the French Revolution had broken the sacred aura of the monarchy, many will have seen the royal spectacle as a mere masquerade.[51]

Very different was the composition of the National Assembly that gathered in Frankfurt in 1848 to write a constitution for the new unified German nation-state. Well-educated urban professionals dominated the assembly. About 95 percent of the 830 representatives had attended secondary education, and almost three-quarters had a university diploma. The number of nobles and clergy was relatively low, and there were only a few artisans and farmers. At the opening ceremony, these upper-middle-class parliamentarians were escorted by the city's militia, which also was the preserve of the male urban elite.[52] These were the people who strove for legal equality, a constitution, and an elected parliament that represented the interests of the nation. Obviously, the well-educated middle classes were much more numerous and influential in Western Europe than on the southern and eastern fringes of the Continent or in Latin America, where cities were few and literacy rates still extremely low.

In general, the lower classes and especially the peasants were much less receptive to the nationalist message, nor were they impassioned by constitutions and elections. In 1820 a revolution in Piedmont failed in a matter of weeks because the majority of the population was not interested in adopting a liberal constitution or "liberating" their fellow Italians. In many instances, nationalist activists tried to mobilize the masses, mostly by appealing to economic or religious grievances. In the Belgian Revolution of 1830, middle-class intellectuals used widespread social and religious discontent among the Catholic population to force a secession from the United Kingdom of the Netherlands, which was dominated by Protestants from the north. In both Greece and Serbia, most people revolted against the abuse of power by tax collectors and local Ottoman officials, while the main societal cleavages were religious. Many military leaders even preferred recognition by the sultan or a position of warlord over the construction of a modern nation-state.[53] The lack of enthusiasm was even more obvious during the Polish Uprising of 1846, which was organized by intellectuals and nobles from the Free City of Cracow with the aim of resurrecting the Polish state. Polish-speaking serfs in the surrounding Galician countryside—who referred to the nationalist rebels as "the Poles"—sided with the Austrian emperor against their aristocratic landlords. As a result, hundreds of Polish noblemen were slaughtered by the peasants.[54]

The Rise of National Cultures

During the Romantic era, most thinkers continued to accept the Enlightenment view that progress was possible, but they clearly rejected the mechanical worldview of the enlightened authors, which emphasized rationalism, universalism, and linear progress. Instead, time and space were profoundly historicized, and individual inspiration, imagination, and creativity replaced the emphasis on classical composure. Romantic authors—many of whom came from German lands, where the universities became intellectual breeding grounds—focused on international differences, arguing that communities had adapted themselves over time to the particular geographic and climatic conditions of their natural environments. However, humans also adjusted their natural surroundings to their own needs, refined the solutions found by their ancestors, and passed the cultural forms they developed to their descendants. Thus, over the centuries, each people or nation—defined, following Herder, as language communities—had developed its own personality and culture.[55]

Herder's ideas about the development of the singular character of each people as a consequence of its interaction with the surrounding nature interlinked with earlier notions and stereotypes, facilitating their acceptance. But the older cultural and political "ethnotypes" were quite static—and mostly rather superficial—because they were based on humoral theories, differences in climate and food habits, judgments from classical authors, or exaggerated patriotic panegyrics. According to the new Romantic view, each nation's collective personality—or popular "spirit" or "soul"—had to be studied in terms of its historical development in order to understand its origins, its golden age, and its periods of decline. Knowledge of the national past was crucial in order to better cope with both the present and the future. Innovations, moreover, should be adapted to the particular national circumstances before they could be absorbed.[56]

These Romantic ideas about the nation were strongly influenced by radical new ideas on nature. Authors such as Jean-Baptiste Lamarck, Charles Lyell, and Alexander von Humboldt distanced themselves from a literal biblical interpretation of nature as God's creation and the more mechanical interpretation that had become popular as a consequence of the Scientific Revolution. Their views would profoundly influence Charles Darwin, who in the 1830s began his scientific explorations. In 1801 Lamarck had introduced the principle of evolution in the field of biology, thus historicizing the animal world, and a few decades later, Lyell did the same for geology, demonstrating that the earth must be much older than what could be deduced from the Bible. But most influential were the best-selling travel writings of Humboldt, a Prussian aristocrat who published most of his works in French. According to him, the geology, climatic influences, nature, and populations of specific areas had to be studied together as an intimately connected web of life. Beginning in the Revolutionary era, he undertook extensive travels through Europe, Spanish America, and the Russian Empire to closely examine these interactions on a global scale. He understood the world in secular terms, as an interwoven organic web of animated forces that could not be unraveled just through exact measurements, but which also needed the recourse of the imagination. His writings profoundly historicized the natural world while embedding human societies in their natural surroundings. This also had effects in the real world. For military reasons, governments had already shown a keen interest in mapping their realms by triangulation. Now, they also began to chart the geological, botanic, and ethnographic particularities of their territories, which together determined the possibilities for human life.[57]

Influenced by this new organic worldview, many authors argued that a nation's character could best be observed in its purest form, reversing established hierarchies, by studying the distant past and peripheral rural communities where people still had intimate contact with the surrounding nature. Simple peasants were more important sources of knowledge about the people's true customs and wisdom than autocratic rulers, stylish aristocrats, and the urban middle classes, most of whom had lost contact with the nation's origins, were unfamiliar with its natural surroundings, and were under the spell of cosmopolitan fashions. But in order to uncover the true personality of the nation, perspicacious scholars were needed. They should not limit themselves to book learning, but also go out to the more remote areas of the countryside to dig up the remains of the nation's most authentic traditions.[58]

Herder had been one of the main instigators of this trend, having published a collection of folk songs from various parts of Europe in 1778, which in a second edition was titled *The Voices of Peoples in Songs*. In the early decades of the nineteenth century, there was an avalanche of similar publications that attempted to reveal the "spirit" of each particular nation. In 1812, the brothers Jacob and Wilhelm Grimm published a first, extremely influential collection of German folktales that they had uncovered by perusing old books and interviewing elderly people throughout the German lands. Tapping these sources, they hoped to get a glimpse of the original customs, values, and norms of the German people. Similarly, Friedrich von Savigny, a professor of law who had lectured the Grimm brothers at the University of Marburg, argued that new laws should reflect the moral sentiments of the people, thus distancing himself from the Enlightenment ideal of rational, universal law codes. As a consequence, he developed a profound interest in the customary laws of the primitive Germanic tribes and the ways later German statesmen had assimilated Christian precepts and Roman law.[59]

Language, too, conveyed the nation's culture and had a significant history. In the 1780s, William Jones, the founder of the Asiatic Society in Calcutta, popularized the idea that Sanskrit was related to Greek and Latin, and probably to Persian, Gothic, and Celtic languages as well. This insight was quickly taken up by many European scholars, and in *The Speech and Wisdom of the Indians* (1808), Friedrich Schlegel further historicized the new discipline of comparative linguistics by arguing that Sanskrit was the original source from which the other languages (which were soon defined as Indo-European) derived. He supposed that new branches that broke away from the trunk had been the result of people migrating to other areas. Since the Germanic tribes had been one of the last groups to leave the Central Asian mountains, they and their language, according to the German scholar, were more closely related to the original than the other European languages. This exaltation of the German language as the bearer of a unique German culture, which was equally prominent in Fichte, also led to the editing of a historical dictionary that would include all words that had been used in the German language. The project was begun in 1838 by the Grimm brothers and would take more than a century to finish; it finally consisted of thirty-three massive volumes. This example was followed elsewhere, resulting in, for instance, the *Oxford English Dictionary*, on which composition began in 1857.[60]

German authors were not the only ones who studied their nation's "spirit" by browsing old publications and searching the countryside for the remnants of a supposedly authentic folk culture. All over Europe and in the Americas, scholars felt inspired by the same ideas and avidly read Herder, Grimm, Savigny, and Humboldt. In particular, the study of history thrived. Antiquarian and historical societies were created and new historical journals were published, while academies of sciences gave more attention to historical research. Historical documents had to be preserved, too. In 1819, on the initiative of Baron von Stein, a historical society began to publish important documents from the German medieval past as the *Monumenta Germaniae Historica*. This example was quickly followed all over the Continent.[61]

By studying the past through a national lens, historians shifted their attention from classical antiquity, whose influence was increasingly seen as foreign and detrimental (except in Greece and Italy), to the primitive origins of the nation and the Middle Ages. Golden ages, national heroes, and great victories were particularly highlighted, but so were tragic defeats. Imperial invasions were rejected as foreign occupations, and rebellions were often reinterpreted as national resistance movements. A national view not only became the norm, it also informed the method. The chronological narrative largely ignored external influences and transnational trends, explaining the evolution of the nation as being caused primarily by internal factors. Local history and developments related to social classes or religions were studied within a national framework. By taking the nation as a container in which developments were studied, historians nationalized the past, and each nation seemed to have a unique character and to follow its own special path. Since most scholars investigated the history of their own country or people, implicitly identifying with their main protagonists and often even interjecting chauvinistic remarks, the nationalist character of most studies was very pronounced.[62]

Most historians in Western Europe focused on the state, as did the profoundly historicizing philosopher Georg Wilhelm Friedrich Hegel. He made a sharp distinction between historical and "unhistorical nations," meaning "uncivilized" peoples who did not progress and as a consequence were relegated to the discipline of ethnography.[63] Historians, for their part, focused on the political and military history of "civilized countries," dealing primarily with kings, battles, diplomats, and parliaments. According to the famous historian Leopold von Ranke, a state had to reflect the character of its people, which suggested that the people needed to be free to develop their own political institutions. It was the task of the historian to uncover this national essence by studying the past. Other historians tried to explain the histories of their countries in terms of the specific genius of the people. In France, Jules Michelet wrote a triumphant national narrative focused on the French Revolution, when the people finally liberated themselves from the shackles of feudalism and absolutism. In Great Britain, Thomas Babington Macauley created the Whig master narrative of England's progressive march toward political and religious liberty, which similarly culminated in the Glorious Revolution. In East-Central Europe, where most language communities did not yet have a state of their own, historians tended to focus more on the "people" as the main subject of their story.[64]

In the Americas, a vital issue was the question of origins. Conservative historians like Francisco Adolfo de Varnhagen in Brazil tended to underscore the link with the European motherland, which had Christianized and "civilized" the New World. Liberal historians such as Carlos María de Bustamante in Mexico, on the contrary, deplored the colonial occupation and generally preferred to study the pre-Hispanic past or the glorious struggle for independence, which in theory assigned a more honorable role to the Indigenous population. Historians in the United States such as George Bancroft presented the arrival of the first settlers to the "virgin lands" of the New World as a "new beginning."[65] This new interest in the past also led to the establishment and rapid growth of adjacent academic disciplines such as archaeology, ethnology or folklore studies, literary history, philology, and art history. All these branches of science now began to chart the development of the nation's character and its main cultural expressions.[66]

Nationalism also had a great impact on the arts. For the Romantics, poetry was the highest art form because it enabled both the spontaneous expression of individual emotions and the intuition of higher truths about external reality. They rejected the rigid metric patterns of classicist genres and preferred ballads, free verse, and fragments. Many of them collected folk stories and songs, and in Finland, Elias Lönnrot turned them into a magnificent national epic, the *Kalevala* (1835). William Wordsworth used folk stories as source of inspiration for his own *Lyrical Ballads* (1798), which in simple language evoked everyday life in the countryside, portraying both the local color of the surrounding landscape and the folk wisdom of the rural population. Others, including Felicia Hemans, adopted the older tradition of patriotic hymns, but in her case, this mainly meant celebrating peoples who fought foreign oppressors, such as the Spaniards who rose up against Napoleon, or the Greeks who (supposedly) longed for their own state. She also wrote more sentimental poems about her own homeland, such as "Welsh Songs" and "The Stately Homes of England." Meanwhile, Adam Mickiewicz glorified another uprising—against the tsar—in his *Pan Tadeusz* (1834), which quickly became the national epic of Poland.[67]

Composers participated in this Romantic quest for national authenticity. Franz Schubert used folklore as a source of inspiration for his own song cycles, and Frédéric Chopin adopted themes from folk dances such as mazurkas and polonaises in his compositions. Music was also explicitly used to arouse national feelings. Arndt's hymn "What Is the German Fatherland?" (1813) received a more catchy melody and became hugely popular in German lands. Composers like Mikhail Glinka and Giuseppe Verdi included patriotic stories from the past in their operas, such as, respectively, *A Life for the Tsar* (1836) and *Nabucco* (1842), with the famous "Va, pensiero" chorus, which became the unofficial anthem of Italian nationalists.[68]

The historical novel rapidly gained popularity, thanks in large part to the gripping stories of Walter Scott. Many of his novels deal with the struggle against tyranny, such as *Waverley* (1814), about the last Jacobite revolt, and *Ivanhoe* (1819), about a twelfth-century nobleman of Saxon descent who lived in an England dominated by the Normans. Scott revived a significant moment of the national past by telling the dramatic story of a fictional character and depicting the historical setting convincingly, with detailed descriptions of costumes, customs, buildings, and interiors. Many authors had a strong preference for the Middle Ages, exemplified by Victor Hugo's *The Hunchback of the Notre-Dame* (1842), while Honoré de Balzac extensively documented the nation's more recent past. Love stories like Alessandro Manzoni's *The Betrothed* (1827) mostly provided a central intrigue and emotive content that was directly linked to struggle against foreign oppression. Sometimes the story was set around a historic battle, as in Hendrik Conscience's *The Lion of Flanders* (1838), which thematized the Battle of the Gulden Spurs of 1302, when the Flemish cities beat back an army of French knights. Conscience's novel was hugely popular and provided an impetus for the rise of the Flemish movement.[69]

History painting became the dominant genre in art exhibitions. Artists shifted their attention away from religious topics and classical antiquity to portray crucial events in the nation's history, filled with antiquarian details.

FIGURE 3.2 Eugène Delacroix, *Liberty Leading the People*, 1830, oil on canvas, 260 × 325 cm. The female figure of Liberty, with the French tricolor in her hands, leads the people of Paris during the Revolution of 1830. Although Delacroix was a prominent Romantic painter, he depicted the Enlightenment concept of the sovereignty of the nation: power belonged to the community of citizens.

The huge images typically were highly theatrical, focused on the central hero, and had a didactic message. Eugène Delacroix also depicted contemporary events, as in the *Massacre at Chios* (1824), which attested to his support for the Greek war of independence, and *Liberty Leading the People* (1830; figure 3.2), which showed a bare-breasted woman with a liberty cap, a musket, and the tricolor urging on Parisians at the barricades during the Revolution of 1830. Other painters sensitively depicted the nation's natural environment. The transcendental landscapes of the German painter Caspar David Friedrich contained Gothic ruins, native trees such as oaks and firs, and a few melancholic observers. John Constable captured the spirit of the English countryside, for instance in *The Hay Wain* (1821; figure 3.3), depicting a farm wagon crossing the River Stour. In the United States, painters tended to focus more on

FIGURE 3.3 John Constable, *The Hay Wain*, 1821, oil on canvas, 130 × 185 cm. This is one of the paintings in which the artist tried to capture the essence of rural England.

primeval landscapes, impressive mountains, and magnificent waterfalls, as in Thomas Cole's *The Oxbow* (1836), a panorama view of the Connecticut River Valley after a thunderstorm.[70]

As a consequence of the writings and activities of scholars, authors, and artists in Europe and the Americas, the transnational Republic of Letters of the eighteenth century, with its emphasis on a shared European or Western civilization, was fragmented into a growing number of national cultures, each with its own folklore, history, and artistic highlights. Each linguistically defined culture supposedly had evolved organically by adapting itself to its specific natural environment. Even the American nation-states that were not primarily defined by their languages developed cultures of their own.

The Nationalization of the Physical Environment

The new Romantic interpretation of the nation also had direct consequences in everyday life. Many members of the upper classes, especially in East-Central Europe, began using a standardized vernacular instead of an international lingua franca. There were also spectacular changes in the physical realm, although during the first half of the nineteenth century they were largely limited to the major capitals. In Paris, for example, the royal library, archive, and art gallery had been nationalized during the French Revolution. Since their treasures now belonged to the nation, they had to be protected and made accessible. Other European and American countries quickly followed suit by creating a national library and a national archive. A national theater, where the country's best plays could be staged in a dignified way, was also needed. Most of the new national theaters were magnificent buildings in eye-catching locations. A somewhat curious example was the Hungarian National Theatre in Pest, which still staged plays in the German language when it opened its doors in 1810.[71]

National museums were often housed in even more prominent buildings, since they displayed the country's artistic heritage and should attract foreign visitors. Royal museums were opened in Sweden in 1792, in Spain in 1819, and in Bavaria in 1826. New states also quickly created their own national museums; Greece did so in 1829 and Belgium in 1842. Aspiring nations in the Austrian and Ottoman Empires also founded national museums, beginning with Hungary in 1802. Bohemia followed in 1818, Slovenia in 1821, and Serbia in 1844; understandably, they were mostly the work of private associations. In 1835, Mehmet Ali established the Egyptian Museum in Cairo, meant primarily for foreign travelers. These museums also used the nation as a starting point for their layout and focus. Thus, Karl Friedrich Schinkel's 1830 Alte Museum in Berlin, the first building expressly designed as an art museum, showed objects and sculptures from classical antiquity in the basement and first floor. On this foundation of Western civilization, the second floor was dedicated to a chronological overview of the Italian and Dutch-German schools, the first ending with the rather insipid academic art of the seventeenth century and the second culminating in the highly original paintings of Rubens and Rembrandt, providing a source for inspiration for contemporary German artists.[72]

The recent past was also shown in a livelier manner in dioramas, panoramas, and wax cabinets, the most famous of which was Madame Tussaud's. During the French Revolution she made a large number of wax heads of the most famous revolutionaries, sometimes directly after they had been guillotined. In 1802 she brought them over to England, where she toured the country before opening her own museum in London in 1835. Historical museums tended to be more dignified, while providing a nationally framed chronological overview. In 1837, King Louis-Philippe hoped to boost his popularity by opening the Palace of Versailles as a national historical museum. Its centerpiece was the Gallery of Battles, which exhibited thirty-three huge paintings of the country's main victories from the fifth to the nineteenth century. All victories, whether they were fought by Frankish tribes, by mercenaries defending the dynastic interests of the king, by revolutionary armies, or by the multinational troops of Napoleon's empire, were claimed for the French nation, forging a continuous national narrative.[73]

Historical museums could house small objects and architectural fragments, but what to do with larger monuments and ancient buildings that had been damaged or were in a state of decay? Instead of worthless piles of rubble or useful quarries, they were now seen as tangible signs of the nation's creativity in the past. In German lands, Goethe and Schinkel advocated the conservation of ancient monuments, and plans were made to finish the impressive Gothic cathedral in Cologne. In 1842, Frederick William IV of Prussia decided to financially support its completion, presenting it as a patriotic task. Five years earlier, the French minister of the interior François Guizot had created the Commission of Historical Monuments, led by the writer Prosper Mérimée and with the collaboration of Victor Hugo and the architect Eugène Viollet-le-Duc. Mérimée quickly drew up an inventory of old monuments in urgent need of repair. One of the first projects undertaken by Viollet-le-Duc was the restoration of the Notre-Dame in Paris, which was made more typical than it had ever been before by adding all kinds of Gothic elements such as spires and gargoyles. The example of the French commission was followed elsewhere in Europe, although in some countries private initiatives predominated, as in Great Britain, where the Anglican Church, individual aristocrats, and the Royal Institute of British Architects took the lead in preserving the country's heritage.[74]

Another way to acquaint the population with the nation's history and its main heroes was through the establishment of a national pantheon. In 1791 the French revolutionaries turned the new Church of Sainte Geneviève into a mausoleum of famous Frenchmen. Soon after, the House of Commons recommenced the tradition of honoring great Britons with a commemorative sculpture in Westminster Abbey. But the most spectacular example was the newly built Walhalla (figure 3.4), a Greek temple on a hill overlooking the Danube near Regensburg, which King Ludwig of Bavaria inaugurated in 1842 to commemorate the great men of Germany. Around 160 monarchs, politicians, artists, and scientists were honored with a bust or plaque. The king's conception of Germany apparently was quite broad, since his collection included tributes to the Flemish painter Peter Paul Rubens, the writer Erasmus of Rotterdam, and the Dutch stadtholder-king William III.[75]

Public monuments followed. Most of the early monuments in Europe were dedicated to the wars against Napoleon—which received pompous nationalist names such as the "Wars of Liberation" (Germany), the "War of Independence" (Spain), the "Patriotic War" (Russia)—whereas in the Americas they logically referred to the "Wars of Independence." The commemoration of these wars began early on. In 1814, the Spanish parliament decided to commemorate the

FIGURE 3.4 Leopold von Klenze, *Walhalla*, 1842, Regensburg, color photo-
chrome, circa 1900. King Ludwig of Bavaria ordered the construction of a Greek
temple on a hill overlooking the Danube. He decreed that it should serve as a
national pantheon for Germany.

start of the popular uprising against the French army in May 1808. The court
painter Francisco Goya, who had also worked for King Joseph Bonaparte, proposed to immortalize the most heroic scenes of "our glorious insurrection
against Europe's tyrant." To earn his way back into King Ferdinand's good graces,
he produced two impressive paintings showing how the ordinary people of Madrid had attacked Napoleon's troops and how, on the following day, many of
them had been executed (figure 3.5). But the new king was not very fond of this
interpretation of the war—especially because of its democratic implications—
and so the paintings ended up in the warehouse of the Prado Museum and the
commemoration was not resumed in the following years.[76]

   In Germany, Arndt immediately proposed commemorating the Battle of
the Nations in Leipzig, but this proved more difficult than originally thought.
Most monuments that commemorated the Wars of Liberation were erected
by the princely states. In 1821 the Prussian king proffered Schinkel's neo-Gothic

FIGURE 3.5 Francisco Goya, *The Third of May 1808*, 1814, oil on canvas,
268 × 347 cm. The court painter, who had collaborated with King Joseph
Bonaparte, made this painting for the returning Bourbon King Ferdinand VII.
His dramatic representation of the ordinary heroes of the Spanish "War of
Independence," because of its democratic implications, was not to the liking of
the new monarch.

National Monument for the Liberation Wars on the Kreuzberg—depicting
the main battles and generals—to his "people." The Bavarian king Ludwig followed in 1863 with the Hall of Liberation in Kelheim, designed by Leo von
Klenze. The Monument to the Fallen for Spain in Madrid was inaugurated by
the successor of King Ferdinand in 1840, and the column at Trafalgar Square
with which Great Britain honored Admiral Nelson was finished three years
later.[77] In the United States, most monuments were dedicated to George
Washington, whereas in Latin America, statues of Bolívar and San Martín
abounded.[78]

Many of the new national institutions and public monuments were built in
a neoclassical style, which gave them a dignified and timeless air. Schinkel's
Alte Museum in Berlin, Klenze's Glyptothek in Munich and the Walhalla in

Regensburg, and Nelson's Column were all done in an austere neoclassical style, whereas a neo-Egyptian obelisk was used for the Monument to the Fallen in Madrid and the Washington Monument in Washington, D.C. However, it was hard to express a nation's specific character in the neoclassical idiom. Other revival styles were developed as well, and neo-Gothicism became particularly popular. Original Gothic buildings had been produced by anonymous people working in guilds, and they were untainted by classical influences. Thus, they best represented the nation's popular soul, and so they were claimed by British, French, and German architects as being characteristic of their own nations. The Kreuzberg monument in Berlin and the impressive monument to Sir Walter Scott, inaugurated in 1844 in Edinburgh, were done in an exuberant Gothic style. The Gothic cathedral in Cologne was finished, and Notre-Dame in Paris was one of the first buildings to be restored. When London's Houses of Parliament burned down in 1834, Augustus Pugin's neo-Gothic design was selected to recreate the magnificent Palace of Westminster. Ironically, in 1850, it was a German art historian who discovered that the Gothic style had been invented in France.[79]

Coda: 1848

The new Romantic conception of the nation, which understood the nation as a historically grown language community with a shared culture, had advanced considerably by 1848. It now heavily influenced the perception of the countryside and the view of the past, leading to the appreciation of vernacular languages and folklore, the proliferation of nationalist literary and artistic works, a new focus on the national past, the creation of museums to exhibit the highlights of the nation's heritage, the restoration of ancient monuments, new commemorative practices, and the construction of new buildings with clear nationalist connotations. These changes mainly affected the realm of high culture, while contributing to the naturalization of the existence of linguistically defined nations among well-educated people in the Western world.

The political ideal of a state that primarily served the nation, in which the citizens were equal before the law and could actively control the government, also lived on and played a major mobilizing role during the Revolutions of 1848. However, now it would be combined with the new Romantic conception linking nations to language and culture. Mazzini, probably the best-known nationalist of his time, thought that culturally defined nations had been created by God, that everyone naturally belonged to one of them, and that if all nations had their own democratic state, there would be no more need for foreign aggression.[80] However, the Revolutions of 1848 would make clear that prospective nation-states were quite prone to wage war. Moreover, the actual coming into existence of new nation-states depended mostly on the geopolitical situation, which finally proved to be not very favorable.

The revolution originated in Paris in February 1848 and rapidly spread to several parts of the Old Continent, due to comprehensive socioeconomic and political grievances. Power collapsed not only in Paris, but also in Vienna, Berlin, and many other European capitals. Revolutionaries demanded elections, a broad franchise, a constitution, and the abolishment of the remnants of feudalism where these still existed. In countries where only the nature of the regime was at stake, such as in the Netherlands and Denmark, the revolutions were resolved quite smoothly after the kings accepted liberal constitutions. The kings of Prussia and Sardinia—also known as Piedmont—quickly gave in to revolutionary demands, too, implicitly recognizing the sovereignty of the politically defined Prussian and Sardinian nation. In France, it took more time for things to settle down: a failed social revolution—the June Days—was followed by the election of Louis Bonaparte, the nephew of Napoleon, as president of the Second Republic.[81]

In many cases, it was not just the regime that was contested, but the nature and boundaries of the state itself. Here, the revolutionary demands for a liberal constitution were accompanied by nationalist demands for independence or the unification of all territories belonging to a culturally defined nation. In the United Kingdom, a revolt of Young Irelanders was quelled rapidly. In Italy, Sicily rose up in January, revolts in Lombardy and Venetia followed in March, and almost a year later, Mazzini—assisted by Giuseppe Garibaldi—established a short-lived republic in Rome. Since there was no coordination between these revolts, the Austrian and Neapolitan forces quickly reinstated order in their territories, whereas a French army corps restored the Papal States in Rome, quashing any remaining dream of Italian unification.[82]

In March 1848, when most German states had given in to the demands of the local revolutionaries, a group of liberals called for elections in the German Confederation. Citizens from all German states thus elected a national assembly in Frankfurt, which then produced a constitution for a unified German state. The main question was whether the new state should be led by Prussia and exclude Austria or be headed by the Austrian emperor. In the end, the "smaller German solution" was chosen, but by then, a number of nationalist conflicts had broken out in border areas, as German interests openly clashed with Danish, Polish, and Czech nationalist demands.

In March the new constitutional regime in Denmark decided to fully integrate into the state the Duchy of Schleswig, which together with the neighboring Duchy of Holstein formed a personal union with the Danish kingdom. The inhabitants of Schleswig and Holstein, most of whom saw themselves as German, revolted. They also participated in the elections for the German national assembly. The conflict quickly escalated, and Prussian troops invaded Schleswig, a move that was approved by the Frankfurt Parliament. International pressure from Russia and Great Britain then forced Prussia to withdraw, but it was clear that according to most members of Parliament, the new nation-state should include these duchies because the majority of the population spoke German.[83]

Posen, a province of Prussia annexed during the First and Second Partitions of Poland and thus officially outside of the German Confederation, also elected members to the Frankfurt Parliament, who were provisionally admitted. Most Polish-speaking inhabitants of Posen were not very keen on becoming part of a new German nation-state. Nationalist activists, who initially could count on the sympathy of many German revolutionaries, hoped to restore the Polish state by fighting Russia. But the war did not come; instead, Poles were given autonomy within a small part of Posen, but the rest would be incorporated into Prussia and thus become part of the new German state. As a result, tensions between Polish and German nationalists mounted, and quickly escalated into violence.[84]

In Bohemia and Moravia, which were part of both the Austrian Empire and the German Confederation, most Czech speakers boycotted the elections for the Frankfurt Parliament. This was met with incomprehension from many German liberals. Why would bilingual intellectuals, such as the famous historian František Palacký, not want to become a citizen of a highly civilized and powerful German nation-state? Palacký, like many other Czech activists, wavered between supporting an autonomous Kingdom of Bohemia within the Austrian Empire, a collaboration of all Slav peoples in the empire, and a more narrowly defined Czech nationalism. But he was clear that the protection of the Austrian Empire was crucial for the less numerous "peoples" of Central Europe: if the empire had not existed, it would have to be invented. Therefore, independence was not his goal. Mounting tensions between Czech and German activists in Bohemia were defused by the restoration of imperial control by Habsburg troops.[85]

In Hungary, a similar process could be observed as the revolution turned the ancient kingdom into an autonomous state within the Austrian Empire. Although Hungarian had been a co-official language (with Latin) since 1844, the revolutionaries—led by Lajos Kossuth—declared that Hungarian would be the only language of the new constitutional assembly, and they abolished the special status of Transylvania and Croatia. This met with hostility from many of those who had a different mother tongue and now felt treated like second-class citizens. Croats, Serbs, Slovaks, and Romanians convened their own national assemblies. The revolution spilled over into adjacent territories, which officially still were part of the Ottoman Empire. Serb activists in Hungary maintained contacts with sympathizers in Serbia. and some pleaded for uniting all South

Slavs in a Yugoslav kingdom. Romanian activists in Transylvania had close rela-tionships with revolutionaries in Wallachia and Moldavia, and there, some ar-ticulated the ideal of unification of all Romanian territories.[86]

Thus, nations were defined either along historical borders, as in the German Confederation and the Kingdom of Hungary, or along linguistic lines, which easily led to tensions, violent incidents, and even wars because of the existence of so many linguistically mixed areas. In general, the revolutionaries tried to include as much territory as possible, but nobody advocated the liberation of foreign territories or the necessity of natural frontiers, which had been com-mon during the Atlantic Revolutions. Within the Austrian Empire—except in Hungary, where revolutionaries were fighting an all-out war in 1849 with the Austrian army—autonomy or a federal state was the goal, not independence. The same was true in many parts of the British Empire, including Cape Colony and Mauritius, where activists demanded representative assemblies, but independence was not an issue.[87]

In the end, Russian troops helped the Ottoman and Habsburg Empires defeat the revolutionaries in Wallachia and Hungary. The tsar and the emperor also put pressure on Frederick William IV—who had succeeded in revoking political reforms in Prussia and restoring order in Posen—to refuse the impe-rial title offered to him by the national assembly in Frankfurt. He declined the honor, stating that he did not want to accept a crown from the "gutter" or let himself be "chained" like a dog to the Revolution of 1848.[88] So it was not the unification of Germany that he rejected, but the liberal character of the new state, where power would be in the hands of ordinary citizens.

Conclusion

Although a new Romantic conception of the nation as an organically grown language community made important inroads in the Western world during the first of half of the nineteenth century, it would begin to have political ef-fects only during the Revolutions of 1848, when various nationalist movements for the first time violently clashed over disputed territories. In fact, most na-tionalist activists were still inspired by the Enlightenment ideal of the sover-eignty of a nation of equal citizens. Nevertheless, power was mostly in the hands of conservative or reactionary monarchs, and the appeal of nationalism barely reached beyond the well-educated urban middle classes. When new nation-states arose, it was usually because they were tolerated or even encour-aged for strategic reasons by the great powers. This was the case with Greece and Belgium, whereas Poland and Ireland, because of their geopolitical situa-tions, had no chance to become independent. It also seems that a double stan-dard applied, because Egypt, a quickly rising Muslim power, was not allowed to become independent, and supposedly "uncivilized" groups like people of color and Native Americans were largely excluded from citizenship in the Americas. Many countries on the European periphery, which reached into the Indian and Pacific Oceans, began to adopt certain aspects of the nation-state model, particularly those that enabled them to survive in the international arena, such as a conscripted army, a centralized administration, direct taxation, and modern education. Some rulers even (hesitantly) adopted constitutions, legal equality, and limited political participation.

In the meantime, nationalism had a profound influence on the cultural realm, where history, language, and folklore became favorite objects of study, and were analyzed primarily within a national, historicist framework. Artists, writers, and musicians also began to integrate national themes into their paintings, ballads, novels, and songs, which reached a broad audience. As a result, the relatively unified Western civilization of the eighteenth century was divided up into new linguistically defined national cultures, each with their own highlights. The built environment also began to be nationalized with the construction of national monuments, national museums, and national theaters, which mostly affected major urban centers. Lastly, a beginning was made in the preservation of a newly invented national heritage.

4

Nation-Building, 1848–1885

THE FAILURE OF the Revolutions of 1848 in Europe set in important changes. Many revolutionaries slowly became aware that their nationalist ideals were hard to realize and that a Europe of democratic nation-states would not automatically bring everlasting peace. In the following decades, strong, old-fashioned statesmen such as Cavour and Bismarck profited from a more favorable geopolitical situation by annexing new territories to the states they served—Piedmont and Prussia—and ended up with an Italian and a German nation-state. These were not achieved by mass mobilization, elections, or revolutions, but through war, skillful negotiations and conquest. This turn to realpolitik was accompanied by an equally clear shift toward realism in the cultural sphere. The Romantic search for the nation's soul and its authentic roots was replaced by a more professional, realist and positivist attitude. Hard facts, scientific research, and truthful representations would provide a more exact picture of the nation's nature and characteristics. This, however, did not impair the position of the nation as the self-evident framework for politics and culture.

At about the same time, the Industrial Revolution began to have more concrete effects on daily life. Standards of living in Western Europe and North America improved due to rising incomes and the availability of more affordable industrial products. Trains, steamships, and the telegraph facilitated transport and communication over longer distances. More people got educated, and the quality of publications such as newspapers and books increased while they became accessible to wider groups in society. This had a double effect. First, the extension of the public sphere made possible a more sustained political mobilization of the masses. In many European and American countries the suffrage was slowly extended, and by traveling, reading, and voting, more people became acquainted with a world consisting of nation-states. But the forces of the ancien régime had not been defeated definitively. Moreover, the violent workers' uprising during June Days in Paris had revealed the new specter of socialism, which could potentially replace the nation-state with the international solidarity of the working classes and a dictatorship of the proletariat. As a consequence, people had to be made aware of their nationalities, mostly so they could be loyal to the existing nation-state, but in some cases, also so they could strive for independent nationhood.

The economic success of the newly industrializing countries was also expressed in their expanding political power, which made itself felt outside the Western world as well. Societies were modernized, either by imperial powers imposing administrative and economic reforms in their colonies, or by independent states adopting many aspects of the nation-state model in order to keep the European powers at bay.

Rise of Nation-States

The Revolutions of 1848 clearly revealed the popularity of the nation-state model. For most activists, political reform implied a constitution, the broadening of the suffrage, and parliamentary control. In 1848, Denmark, the Netherlands, Piedmont, Switzerland, and some smaller German states adopted liberal constitutions, while in 1850 Prussia got a constitution that was more restrictive than the one the king had granted under pressure of the revolution. As a consequence, most countries in Western Europe now were nation-states with a parliament, elections, and the recognition of equality before the law. In the Austrian Empire, the revolutionary abolishment of feudal remnants such as serfdom and the tithe was not undone. Elsewhere, activists had tried to create new nation-states, either by reestablishing ancient kingdoms, as in Poland, Hungary, and Bohemia, or by founding new unified nation-states, which was attempted in Germany and Italy. A similar longing for national unification had been expressed by the South Slavs and Romanians.

In the German Confederation, the German Customs Union, which had been a Prussian initiative, signified an important step toward greater union. It encouraged not just the economic integration of parts of the confederation, but also the cooperation between states, companies, and individuals.[1] In order to redraw boundaries in Central Europe a favorable geopolitical constellation was needed, and this would come about in the 1850s and 1860s. In the United Kingdom, both the general public and political elites assumed that "civilized" nations would want to rule themselves, and most Britons were willing to support them unless it negatively affected the interests of the British Empire. Moreover, in the late 1850s, developments in Asia such as the Indian Rebellion and the Second Opium War required the attention of the government. In France, too, the nation-state was widely taken for granted as the model of the future. Napoleon III—burdened by the memory of his uncle—was willing to engage in foreign adventures and was confident that France could take up the role of protector of new nation-states.[2] Austria and Russia, for their part, had been opposed to revolutionary change and threats to the international order since

the early 1790s. However, the Revolutions of 1848 had exposed the internal
weakness of the Austrian Empire, and Russia would suffer a tough defeat in
the Crimean War (1853–1856). These developments upset the international
order that had been created in 1815.

Adroit statesmen who could take advantage of this window of opportunity
were needed as well. In Piedmont, Camilo Benso, Count of Cavour, was appointed prime minister in 1852, and he quickly became the indisputable leader
of the kingdom. As a French-speaking aristocrat, his main aim was to faithfully
serve the state, but he grasped that the mobilizing and legitimizing potential
of nationalism could be used to enlarge Piedmont. There was no clear master
plan for the unification of Italy; it was the outcome of skillful maneuvering by
Cavour and a high dose of luck. King Victor Emmanuel had already induced
the state to participate in the Crimean War on the Anglo-French-Ottoman side
to create goodwill for Piedmont's expansionist plans. In 1859, with French
backing, Cavour provoked a war with Austria in order to conquer Lombardy.
After two months, Napoleon III abandoned his ally and signed an armistice
with Austria. Yet Piedmont received Lombardy. During the war, the governments in smaller Italian states such as Tuscany, Parma, and Modena were
toppled. Newly elected parliaments asked for the integration of their states
into Piedmont, which was agreed after overwhelming victories in local plebiscites. Shortly afterward, Giuseppe Garibaldi's irregular Redshirt volunteers
invaded Sicily and quickly overthrew the unpopular Bourbon monarchy in
Naples. In a preemptive move, Piedmont's troops occupied the Papal States
to avoid a revolutionary takeover by Garibaldi. The latter acceded in holding
a plebiscite in Naples on its unification with the rest of Italy under King Victor
Emmanuel, creating a unified Italian nation-state, to which only Venetia and
Rome would be added in 1866 and 1870, respectively.[3]

German unification happened along similar lines. The Prussian chancellor
Otto von Bismarck—another aristocrat—used German nationalist sentiment
to justify Prussia's expansionist drive. The process started in 1862, when King
William I clashed with the Prussian Diet over increasing the military budget.
Instead of giving in to the parliamentary majority, he appointed Bismarck as
the new chancellor, and Bismarck immediately appeased Russia by offering
Prussian troops to help quell a Polish uprising. The next year, Christian IX
ascended to the Danish throne, integrating Schleswig into his reign. This provided the perfect reason for Bismarck to seek Austria's help to defeat Denmark.
Within two years, Austria and Prussia were quarreling over how the newly
conquered Duchies of Schleswig and Holstein should be administered, which
led to another war—this time, between Austria and Prussia. Bismarck succeeded in securing the active support of various Northern German states.
After a decisive victory, Prussia dissolved the German Confederation, annexed
several Northern German principalities, and forced the rest of them into a new

MAP 4.1 The German Empire in 1871. The new unified nation-state had adopted the "lesser German solution" and was much smaller than the German Confederation, which had been dissolved in 1866. However, it included Prussia's Polish territories in the East and Alsace-Lorraine—annexed from France—in the West.

North German Confederation dominated by Prussia. In 1870, Bismarck provoked a war with Napoleon III (map 4.1). This time, he received the support of the Southern German states, who, after another quick win, accepted the offer to become part of a new German empire that would retain a federal structure. In the new constitution—which would become a model for conservative rulers around the world—the appointment of the government remained the privilege of the emperor, and the government could not be held accountable by parliament. However, since the Imperial Diet had to approve new laws and the budget, it could not be completely ignored.[4]

The successful unifications of Italy and Germany had consequences elsewhere. Understandably, many Poles, Serbs, and Romanians—who were also dispersed in various states—were inspired by these examples, which also reinforced the already existing idea that only larger nation-states had a viable future. Mazzini doubted the possibility of an independent Irish nation-state, for instance, and others saw no future for Belgium or Portugal. Eric Hobsbawm has defined this as the "threshold principle."[5] Accordingly, some intellectuals and politicians argued that peoples belonging to the same language family should collaborate or even unite in a (federal) state, which led to various pan-movements. The best known of these was the pan-Slavic movement, which was created by Czech and Slovak intellectuals but also had enthusiasts among the South Slavs. In 1848, Palacký had convened the Slavic Congress in Prague. At about the same time, a pan-Turanian movement—consisting of Finnish and Hungarian intellectuals looking for ancestors and brethren in Central Asia—as well as a pan-Celtic movement came into being.[6]

Pan-movements could also be found in independent nation-states. In Spain and Portugal, writers began to promote a closer economic and political cooperation between the two Iberian states. Some even proposed the introduction of an Iberian customs union, while others aimed to create a federal republic, the United States of Iberia.[7] In Denmark, Sweden, and to a lesser extent, Norway, intellectuals advocated a pan-Scandinavian union—with proposals ranging from a political alliance to a federation or a united kingdom—partly so that the countries would be less vulnerable to foreign intervention. In 1873, this led to the creation of the Scandinavian Monetary Union.[8] Similar arguments could be heard in the remaining British colonies in North America. The unstable international situation—with the civil war in the United States, the urgency to improve transborder communications by train, and the need to find a solution for the French-speaking Catholics of Quebec—led to the creation in 1867 of the Dominion of Canada.[9]

Toward the end of the nineteenth century, after ever-smaller nation-states were created, especially in the Balkans, where the Ottoman Empire was forced to retreat, the threshold was lowered. In 1867 the Austrian Empire reacted to its crushing defeat in the war against Prussia by giving in to the Hungarian demand for autonomy, creating the Dual Monarchy of Austria-Hungary. As a counterreaction, nationalist activists in other parts of the empire, especially in Bohemia and Croatia, began to request autonomy. The fierce Ottoman repression of a peasant rebellion in Bosnia-Herzegovina and a nationalist revolt in Bulgaria sparked another Russian intervention in 1877, with the tacit approval of the other great powers. The subsequent Treaty of Berlin confirmed the independence of Serbia, Montenegro, and Romania, and Bulgaria became autonomous.[10] The independent existence of these small nation-states provided a fresh stimulus for activists in Ireland, Finland, and Flanders to stand up for their collective rights.

Strengthening the Austrian, Russian, and Ottoman Empires

Military defeats were the main trigger for political reforms in the Austrian, Russian, and Ottoman Empires, and from the 1840s, this would also be the case in the East Asian empires. The Western European nation-state model was the main source of inspiration for the increasingly global process of isomorphism—a concept used in sociological institutionalism to show how state institutions throughout the world increasingly adopted similar forms after the Second World War.[11] Military humiliations provided a strong incentive in these traditional realms for the adoption of conscription. In order to pay for a modernized army, new taxes were introduced, and a more centralized state bureaucracy was needed for their implementation. Social reforms such as the abolishment of traditional privileges and exemptions and the introduction of new law codes, modern education, and private property would stimulate the economy while providing more rights and opportunities to the population. A constitution and political participation were adopted only hesitantly, since they would undermine the power of the monarch and the governing elites.

In general, the innovations concerned certain policies or institutions, not the entire nation-state package. The Austrian Empire was be the exception; there, reform had been relatively gradual and not much out of step with what was happening elsewhere in Western Europe. Since the beginning of the nineteenth century, for instance, it had had a civil code, and Franz Joseph I began a moderate reform course after reestablishing order in 1849. The bureaucracy became more standardized, education was improved, new municipal councils allowed political participation at the local level, freedom of profession put an end to the privileges of the guilds, and Protestants had the same rights as Catholics—although Jews would have to wait until 1867. After defeat at the hands of Piedmont and France, the emperor also created a bicameral parliament. The lost war against Prussia led to the Compromise of 1867, in which both Hungary and Austria received constitutions. In this way, the empire was in fact split into two multiethnic nation-states, each of which consisted of a patchwork of crown lands and was held together by the monarchy and the army.[12]

The Russian Empire had been more hesitant with reforms. The enormous army—consisting of peasants who were drafted for life—had performed reasonably well during the Napoleonic Wars. The empire thus continued to be one of the major European powers and also acted as a kind of international policeman suppressing revolutions and nationalist movements whenever this was in line with Russia's geopolitical interests and possibilities. Alexander I and Nicholas I were wary of introducing reforms; the only major change was the codification of Russian customary law in 1835. However, the Crimean War exposed the structural weakness of the empire. Confronted with the military forces of France and Great Britain, it became evident that Russia lacked modern rifles, well-educated officers, and railways. A drastic change of course was needed; this had already been a major topic of debate between so-called Westernizers and Slavophiles, the former being in favor of a thorough modernization along Western lines and the latter proposing a renewed emphasis on native values.[13]

In the 1860s and 1870s the Russian government introduced a modern judicial system, elected municipal councils, new military colleges, and conscription. The construction of an extensive railway network, funded primarily through foreign investments, enabled the economic integration of the country. But the most important reforms were done half-heartedly. The abolishment of serfdom in 1861 made the peasant communities collectively responsible for the redemption sum, binding most of the former serfs to their villages for an extended period of time and hampering the development of a market-oriented agricultural sector. Political participation was permitted only at the municipal and regional levels, and the new provincial assemblies had almost no power. Tsar Alexander II confided to Bismarck (the Prussian ambassador at the time) that the Russian elites did not have a sufficient level of education for representative government—but improving the education of both the general population and the upper classes was not his priority either.[14]

The weak performance of the Ottoman army during the Crimean War and the intensive contacts with its British and French allies led to a new round of reforms in the Ottoman Empire, too. By curtailing slavery and introducing legal reforms at the start of the Tanzimat era, the sultan was in some respects ahead of the tsar. In 1856 legal equality was enhanced with the final abrogation of the head tax for Christian and Jewish subjects and the introduction of obligatory military service for all men. However, this was met with resistance from tribal communities in the peripheries and many non-Muslim groups. In the end, a new military tax that exempted Christians and Jews from military service replaced the head tax. The empire continued to be an Islamic state, in which the sultan occupied the position of caliph—the leader of the faithful— and wars were often defined in terms of jihad. Reformist elites who adopted European dress were often ridiculed by traditionalist Muslims.[15]

In terms of political participation, developments in the Ottoman Empire did not lag behind Russia either. In 1864 regional assemblies were introduced, followed by the establishment of the Council of State. The outcry in Europe over the so-called Bulgarian massacres of 1876, in which local Muslims retaliated against a nationalist uprising, quickly led to the deposition of Sultan Abdülaziz. In order to avoid foreign intervention, the new sultan gave in to demands for a constitution from the Young Ottomans, a small group of Muslim intellectuals who advocated combining liberal reforms with upholding the Islamic tradition of justice. Grand Vizier Midhat Pasha—who had already proven to be an able modernizer in the Danube Province and Bagdad—was inspired by the new constitution of the German Empire and hoped to create a similar system in which an elected parliament would be combined with an efficient central government and a more autonomous position for provincial authorities. However, after a few months, Midhat Pasha was sacked by

Abdülhamid II, and in the context of the war with Russia, which would result in
the loss of a large part of the Balkans, the sultan also suspended the constitution.
Like Tsar Alexander III, who came to power in 1881, he preferred autocracy
over constitutional experiments. But there was one major difference: whereas
Russia used foreign investments to modernize its infrastructure and economy,
in 1881 the sultan's state went bankrupt and was forced to accept the long-term
tutelage of European banks in the form of the Ottoman Public Debt Administration, which seriously hampered its economic progress.[16]

In Egypt a similar pattern can be detected. The largely autonomous Ottoman province was moving toward the nation-state model, but instead of encouraging this development—as they did with the nationalist movements
among the Christian inhabitants of the Balkans—the European powers set up
extra hurdles. In 1838, when the Ottoman sultan was in dire straits because of
Mehmed Ali's advance in Syria, the British signed a free trade agreement with
the Ottoman Empire. This gave the British (and other European powers) almost free access to the Ottoman markets, while undermining a vital source of
income for Mehmed Ali's Egyptian administration by prohibiting state monopolies. Reforms in Egypt continued, albeit at a slower pace. In 1855, in line
with Ottoman policies, Said, the son of Mehmed Ali, abolished the head tax
for Christians and began to conscript them into the army, thus introducing
equal obligations for Christians and Muslims. His successor, Ismael, created a
consultative assembly. Egypt also embarked on an ambitious scheme of infrastructural works, including the Suez Canal. This was largely financed by foreign
loans, and instead of boosting the economy, it rapidly led to an unsustainable
situation. In 1876 Ismael was forced to install the Public Debt Commission,
which handed over control of Egypt's finances to the French and British. Protests
against foreign influence, together with plans to introduce a constitution and
an elected parliament, triggered a British military intervention in 1882 that
turned Egypt into an informal colony of the United Kingdom.[17]

East Asian Empires

Western influence also began to undermine the existing political models in
East Asia. The Qing Empire in China, which had expanded considerably during the seventeenth and eighteenth centuries, was the mightiest power. The
emperor was seen as the "Son of Heaven" who presided over "all under
Heaven." Rulers in Korea, Vietnam, Siam, and Burma recognized the supremacy of the Chinese emperor by sending regular tribute missions; during the
Tokugawa shogunate Japan stopped paying tribute, but it too was part of the
broad Chinese sphere of influence. Confucian ideals and Chinese political
institutions had been adopted in many parts of East Asia, and until the late

nineteenth or early twentieth century, Chinese was the main administrative language in Korea, Japan, and Vietnam and the lingua franca for scholars and well-educated people throughout East Asia. Communication was mostly in written form, through letters or in person, sitting together with paper and brush. Because Chinese characters can be pronounced in many different ways (depending on dialect or language) even within China, oral communication was almost impossible unless both speakers were from the same area or fluent in Mandarin, the dialect used at the court in Beijing.[18]

European countries or merchants who wanted to trade with China had no option but to comply with the Chinese tribute system, which permitted access only through the harbor of Canton (now Guangzhou). European powers increasingly rejected this. In 1793, a British diplomatic mission failed to improve the trading options because its leader refused to kowtow(perform the traditional bow kneeling and touching his forehead to the ground) before the Chinese emperor. At the time, the power balance between the agricultural Qing Empire and the dynamic mercantile empire of Great Britain was quickly changing: in England the Industrial Revolution had just started, whereas the Chinese economy began a prolonged downturn. The British East India Company was eager to acquire Chinese tea and other luxury products, but until it discovered the potential of opium from Bengal, it did not have many attractive wares for exchange. Although the Chinese authorities quickly prohibited the use of opium, demand grew rapidly. The situation escalated when the imperial court enforced a strict antidrug policy and seized foreign stocks. The British government decided to intervene by sending the navy to defend the interests of its merchants and the principle of free trade. The British maritime forces—which included steamships with heavy guns—were far superior to the Chinese junks and could easily bombard several cities. The Treaty of Nanjing, which ended the First Opium War in 1842, stipulated the opening of five ports to foreign trade, a considerable indemnity, and the transfer of Hong Kong to the British.[19]

In 1856, after two minor incidents—the execution of a French missionary and the seizure of a British smuggling ship—France and Great Britain sent a joint expeditionary force to China, at exactly the time when the Qing government was occupied with the suppression of a major uprising, the Taiping Rebellion. After various allied victories, a first peace agreement was negotiated. But the British refused to adapt to the hierarchical tributary system, and in 1860 a British-French army conquered Beijing and sacked the emperor's summer palace, ending the Second Opium War. The Xianfeng Emperor, who had already awarded the right to collect international trade duties to the new Imperial Maritime Customs Service administered by foreigners, now also had to concede religious freedom, the right for foreigners to travel in China, the opening of ten more port cities where foreigners received extraterritorial rights, the legalization of the opium trade, and the establishment of foreign embassies in Beijing. In fact, China was obliged to submit to the Western standards of international relations—between (notionally) independent and equal states—by signing another "unequal treaty."[20]

The humiliating defeat put the Qing Empire in the same position as the Ottoman Empire and the Russian tsar after the Crimean War. Basically, there were three options for dealing with the new situation: nativism, authoritarian reform, or Westernization. The nativist option meant rejecting all foreign influences. This was usually religiously motivated, and in times of crisis it often resonated with xenophobic sentiments among the general population. The second, more realistic option was a course of moderate reform focusing particularly on areas that seemed most urgent, such as modernizing the armed forces, while reinforcing the powers of the central state. This could be done in a rather technocratic way, or by dressing innovations in a traditional guise and reinforcing religious and monarchical feelings among the population. Authoritarian reform was the favored option of most Eurasian empires. The third option, favored mostly by a small group of progressive intellectuals and officials, was to thoroughly Westernize not just the army and the administration but also society. Many argued that a strong state was possible only when supported by a modern civic society. According to them, mass education, citizen rights, and political participation should be a vital part of any reform package.

The Chinese Empire opted for a feeble authoritarian reform. The central government was seriously weakened by the Taiping Rebelling and the Second Opium War, and the situation would remain difficult for several years, with floods, droughts, famines, and mass migration. After the death of the Xianfeng Emperor in 1861, most of his successors were infants, and power was effectively in the hands of bureaucratic elites and Cixi, the empress dowager. They began the self-strengthening movement, which emphasized a stern Confucian morality that included obedience, self-discipline, and ritual propriety, while adopting Western technology, especially for the armed forces. The only institutional reform was the creation in 1861 of the General Affairs Bureau, which functioned as a ministry of foreign affairs. In the following years, modern language and translation schools, naval academies, arsenals, and a defense industry would follow. However, the court did not deem it necessary to follow the "barbarians" in other areas by adopting more profound social or political reforms.[21]

These moderate reforms could not prevent further setbacks and the rapid dismantling of China's sphere of influence. Siam and Burma stopped sending tribute missions to Beijing, while Great Britain began to penetrate Burma. In the 1870s Japan annexed the Ryukyu Islands, sent a punitive expedition to Taiwan, and forced Korea to open itself to international trade. During the Sino-French War of 1884 to 1885 China succeeded in repelling a French invasion, but the new fleet was almost completely destroyed, and Indochina was colonized by France.[22]

The Kingdom of Siam also opted for authoritarian reform, and in the end it was more successful than the Qing Empire in warding off the Western threat, although this probably was helped by the imperial rivalry between Great Britain and France. Burma modernized at a faster pace during the 1850s and 1860s, but because of its strategic value at the eastern border of India, it was annexed by the British in 1886.[23] In Siam, a new dynasty ascended the throne in the late eighteenth century. The capital, Bangkok, rapidly became a thriving, cosmopolitan port city, and King Mongkut was very interested in Western innovations. In 1855, in order to avoid the fate of China, the Siamese government established a state monopoly on the sale of opium, and it negotiated a trade deal with Great Britain. King Chulalongkorn, Mongkut's young successor, traveled to several European colonies in Southeast Asia to learn from their experiences with modern reforms. After reaching majority in 1873, he immediately began to centralize the administration. To forestall a clash with the nobility, most of the reforms—including the abolition of forced labor and the introduction of direct rule, a uniform law code, and conscription—were made gradually, over almost four decades. He refused to permit a constitution or a parliament. According to him, the Siamese kings strictly followed Buddhist ethical principles, so there was no need for political control through Western institutions like a parliament.[24]

Japan similarly drew lessons by observing how the Qing Empire was overcome by the Western powers. Under the Tokugawa shoguns, who had ruled—theoretically, in the name of the emperor—since the early seventeenth century, the country had prospered, even though it had been almost entirely shut off from the outside world. Through information from a small Dutch settlement in the harbor of Nagasaki and contacts with Asian traders, Japanese elites were relatively well aware of what was going on elsewhere in the world. The Chinese defeat in the First Opium War came as a shock, and in 1854, Commodore Perry forced Japan to enter into diplomatic negotiations with the United States. On this occasion only minor concessions were made, such as the opening of two ports for the provisioning of foreign ships. Four years later, while China was losing again, in the Second Opium War, the United States persuaded Japan to sign another treaty, opening six ports to foreign merchants. Opium trade was forbidden, though, and freedom of religion applied only to foreigners.[25]

There was much debate among the country's ruling elites about which course to follow. A few favored a thorough modernization along Western lines; a more substantial group advocated the self-strengthening strategy adopted in China, combining domestic values—derived primarily from Confucianism, Shintoism, and the samurai warrior code—with Western technology and science. Radicals adopting the nativist option wanted to repel all foreigners. The powerful lords of Satsuma and Choshu sided with radical samurai who adopted the slogan "Revere the emperor and expel the barbarians." In 1863 and 1864 they openly challenged the foreign powers, but after their domains were bombarded by Western fleets, they understood that a return to international isolation was no longer an option. Instead, they focused on fighting the shogunate, which in the next year was abolished after a short civil war. All power then reverted to the young Meiji Emperor.[26]

Japanese officials began to study Western knowledge, make trips abroad, and employ foreign experts. Many became convinced that a thorough modernization course was needed, but this was camouflaged by an appeal to tradition. In 1868 the court announced the Restoration of Imperial Rule of Old, while the emperor promised, in good Confucian spirit, that the "just laws of Nature" would be followed. The leadership of the country was now dominated by able samurai administrators from Satsuma and Choshu, who rapidly created an efficient centralized state by dismantling feudal society. This was done with tact. Thus, the great lords were first turned into governors of their fiefs. Soon after, they had to give up their political power, but in return they each received a pension and a new aristocratic title, while their domains were integrated into newly drawn prefectures. The introduction of conscription made the traditional role of the samurai—the lower nobility—superfluous. They received modest financial compensation and had to start new lives. At the same time, a land tax was introduced, and agricultural holdings were turned into private property. Peasants, artisans, and merchants were now free to move and to choose their own professions, creating a more dynamic, capitalist society.[27]

Economic modernization was crucial, and a start was made with the construction of railways and industrial development. However, the government was restrained about taking foreign loans that could pull it into a financial morass, which in the case of the Ottoman Empire and Egypt had resulted in foreign tutelage.[28] Japan became a clear example of what Stefan Berger and Alexei Miller have called a "nationalizing empire," as an active nation-building policy was conducted in the core areas. A centralized mass-education system was installed in 1872, followed six years later by prefectural assemblies. These were elected, but had only an advisory function, like their equivalents in Russia and the Ottoman Empire. In 1884 a modern cabinet system, led by a prime minister, was introduced, and the first political parties began to demand national elections. In 1889 the emperor proclaimed a constitution, which also entailed the creation of a bicameral parliament (figure 4.1). Inspiration was found in Bismarck's conservative constitution for the German Empire. Sovereignty still rested with the emperor, who also was the supreme commander of the armed forces and could veto new laws. The inhabitants, moreover, were

FIGURE 4.1 Eisaku Wada, *Ceremony for the Proclamation of the Constitution at the Imperial Palace in Tokyo February 1889*, 1936. This painting was made for the Meiji Memorial Picture Gallery, which was built in the 1920s. Eighty large paintings documented the most important scenes of the emperor's life. Here we see the official ceremony in which the emperor handed the constitution over to the prime minister. The emperor, his family (including female members), the government, and all other guests wore modern Western uniforms, costumes, or dresses.

defined as "subjects," while suffrage was very restricted. A few years later, a new civil code, inspired mostly by French examples, implicitly confirmed Japan's new status as a "civilized" nation-state.[29]

Administrative and economic modernization also was an important objective in the European empires in South and Southeast Asia. However, there

were some important differences between the reformist policies of the nominally independent states that were trying to "catch up" and what happened in
the colonies, where power remained firmly in the hands of the imperial authorities, territorial unification often was undermined by a divide-and-rule
strategy, and the metropolitan economic interests generally reigned supreme.
Thus, Indian tariffs reflected the British metropolitan interests, and opium
became the main source of income of the East India Company. In 1830 in Java,
the Dutch introduced a "cultivation system" in which farmers were required
to cultivate cash crops for the colonial authorities on one-fifth of their lands,
which generated huge profits.[30]

The most important colony was British India. As a result of the Seven Years'
War the commercial East India Company had become a major territorial
power by conquering not just French trading posts but also the province of
Bengal, whose ruler had allied with France. Subsequently, it occupied large
parts of the Indian subcontinent, converting most of the remaining principalities into vassal states. Many of the mechanisms we have seen in Europe and the
Eurasian empires could be detected here as well. The company needed a large
standing army to protect its territories, and in order to pay the rising costs, it
had to augment the tax revenue, for which a growing professional bureaucracy
was needed. Western education in English was introduced to enable the recruitment of Indians in the lower ranks of the administration. In order to standardize legal procedures, the indigenous laws of both Hindus and Muslims
were codified. The collection of taxes was systematized by reforming land ten-
ancy, with legally enshrined property titles. Land now became a commodity
that was measured and could be sold, while informal customary rights were
disregarded. Tribal territories and nomadic practices were increasingly seen as
an anomaly, and even forests and wastelands began to be exploited commercially. After the Great Rebellion of 1857, the British state took over the Indian
possessions of the East India Company and implemented some minor reforms
such as appointing a number of Indians to the Imperial Legislative Council and
more systematically surveying landed property to better assess the amount of
taxes that could be paid. In 1871 a full-scale census was conducted.[31]

Citizenship

The Revolutions of 1848 made clear that the demand for citizen rights, constitutions, and political participation was widespread. In the following decades,
many European and American governments decided to gradually extend the
suffrage and soften repressive laws. In the early 1870s the French Third Republic, the German Empire, and the United States all adopted universal male suffrage, setting a new standard. Still, there were various ways to mitigate the

influence of voters or to manage electoral results. Revolutionary politicians and parties could be banned. More subtle methods included employing single-member districts to raise the bar for parliamentary representation, which was the case in Great Britain and many European and American countries. Prussia and Austria adopted a three-class franchise system, in which the wealthiest taxpayers and the middle classes each received the same number of seats as the large majority of poor voters. In most countries the conservative countryside was overrepresented, diminishing the role of the "unruly" urban electorate. Another option was to redraw electoral boundaries, to "neutralize" the electoral impact of a working-class neighborhood, for instance—a practice known as "gerrymandering" in the United States, but utilized elsewhere as well.

Other frequently used practices were more dubious. Under Napoleon III, "official candidates" received the full support of the administration, while districts that voted for an opposition politician were punished, by halting investments in schools and infrastructure, for example. In many parts of Southern Europe and the Americas, politics functioned primarily through patronage networks in which concrete favors were more important than ideological differences in determining electoral outcomes. Italian governments could control most electoral seats in the largely illiterate South by enabling pro-government candidates to use the spoils of the state to serve their "clients." In Spain, in order to avoid the political instability and violent military coups that had characterized politics in the 1850s and 1860s, the Liberal and Conservative Parties agreed to alternate holding power by using their respective countrywide patronage systems. Election results were determined beforehand at the Ministry of the Interior, and local bosses ensured the desired outcome.[32] As a consequence of both these legal and extralegal practices, moderate parties—mostly conservatives and liberals—had no difficulty in dominating parliamentary politics.

Women continued to be excluded from the suffrage. As a reaction to the supposedly radical influence of female activists during the Revolutions of 1848, many German states introduced laws that explicitly forbade women to found political organizations, take part in their meetings, or publish newspapers. It was the responsibility of men to defend the fatherland, participate in politics, and contribute to the economic well-being of the nation; women were supposed to raise children, create an orderly home, and care for the elderly and sick. The citizenship ideal was strongly gendered: men should be rational, productive, strong, and composed, while women were seen as self-effacing, tender, and affectionate. These ideals reflected the middle-class male breadwinner model, which also began to be adopted by many aristocrats and the blue-collar elite. But in some aspects, the strict division between these separate spheres slowly faded. Women increasingly devoted themselves to public matters by being active in charity work and associations that were focused mostly on humanitarian issues such as poor relief, temperance, or missionary activities, but also more politically sensitive topics such as abolitionism and pacificism. The education of girls received more attention from the authorities; as future mothers, they would be responsible for the biological and cultural reproduction of the nation. In some countries, women were admitted to positions that until then had been the exclusive domain of men. In Great Britain during the late 1860s, the first woman was inscribed in the medical register, female students were admitted to the University of Cambridge, and in some local areas women were permitted to vote for district councils and school boards.[33]

During the second half of the nineteenth century, restrictions on travel, which particularly targeted the poor, were lifted in most parts of Europe. The German Customs Union had already liberalized trade in German lands, but the growing demand for labor from the industry and the simultaneous expansion of railway transport and postal systems made it less convenient to strictly supervise the movement of persons. Governments slowly adopted the free trade ideology, and as a result, passport and visa requirements were lifted. In 1867 the North German Confederation abolished the documentary controls on movement, both for citizens and foreigners, and the introduction of freedom of movement was accompanied by measures to encourage freedom of profession and settlement.[34] The opposition against restrictions on movement also had effects elsewhere. The unequal treaties imposed on many East Asian states—which traditionally had restricted foreign travel—usually included a clause allowing unhampered access for foreigners and freedom of residence, at least in some treaty ports. And as we have seen, the Japanese government, which took the most drastic path of reform among the traditional empires, rapidly adopted freedom of labor and movement for its own population.

Unfree labor was increasingly seen as a relic of the past. Serfdom was abolished in the Austrian Empire in 1848 and in Russia in 1861. Great Britain abolished slavery in its colonies in 1833 and France did the same in 1848, while the victory of the North in the Civil War also meant an end to slavery in the United States. In 1888 Brazil followed suit, and slavery was also phased out in Siam. But in addition to individuals and labor, the soil also had to be freed. In Catholic countries such as Italy, Spain, and Mexico, the vast possessions of the Church were disentailed, and so were common lands and communal landholdings of Indigenous communities. Land was also turned into private property in the Ottoman Empire, Japan, and most European colonies. Elsewhere, virgin lands were rapidly occupied and turned into privately owned farmland. This was accelerated by the construction of new railway lines. In 1862 the United States adopted the Homestead Act, which opened up the West for settlers. The same happened in Canada, and similar developments could be seen in Siberia and Patagonia.[35]

This liberalization of the national labor and land markets implied that peasants, artisans, and the poor lost many of their traditional rights and collective safety nets, such as grazing rights on common lands, protection by guild rules, and local poor relief. Most authorities argued that the new economic opportunities, together with hard work and thrift, could turn the majority of the population into prospering workers or even modest land and business owners. National welfare systems to assist the poor and needy would not be created until the end of the nineteenth century.[36] More devastating were the effects on traditional Indigenous populations. In the United States the settlers' quest for land had made Native Americans into an obstacle. In 1871 they lost their status as "nations" with whom treaties could be concluded. Reservations were created where they were meant to settle as farmers with individual plots and learn to lead a "civilized" life; citizenship, however, was awarded only in 1924. In most parts of Latin America, community lands were privatized on the assumption that individual farmers would be more productive. In Argentina, the Conquest of the Desert "cleared" Patagonia of Indigenous inhabitants, opening it up for white immigrants. At about the same time, Meiji Japan forced the traditional Ainu communities on Hokkaido to adopt an agrarian lifestyle. Similar processes can be detected in most colonies, both those dominated by white settlers, such as South Africa and Australia, as in India or the Dutch Indies, where the presence of Europeans was more limited. In British India, forests were cleared or exploited ruthlessly, while traditional Indigenous practices such as hunting, collecting wood for fuel, and grazing livestock became clandestine activities.[37] A capitalist mentality, diligence, and individual self-reliance apparently were seen as indispensable elements of good citizenship.

Fixed ideas about a "civilized" lifestyle also tended to exclude those who did not fit the image of the national community. In the United States, the polygamy practiced by the Mormons in Utah was prohibited in 1862 as being barbarous. After the end of the Civil War, the federal government tried to settle emancipated slaves as independent farmers, while encouraging them to marry and adopt the male breadwinner model. But Reconstruction was not a success. The Freedmen's Bureau, which assisted former slaves, was closed in 1872, new Black Codes were adopted by many Southern states, and African Americans were effectively excluded from voting. The "separate but equal" doctrine rapidly led to racial segregation that made Blacks second-rate citizens. Similar ideas and practices existed in Latin America. In the 1850s the Chorographic Commission in New Granada—current-day Colombia—recommended better education and technical training for the white inhabitants of the central highlands, forced labor for the "lazy" people of African descent in the tropical lowlands, and the submission of the Indians in the "unhealthy" borderlands.[38]

The trend to exclude "uncivilized" people also led to a hard separation between metropole and colonies. We have already seen that Napoleon had adopted a clause in the constitution of 1799 stipulating that the text applied only to metropolitan France. Having a different legal regime for colonies became increasingly common during the nineteenth century. When Spain adopted a liberal constitution in 1837, it literally copied Napoleon's clause that "overseas colonies shall be governed by special laws." In taking over India from the East India Company in 1858, Great Britain implicitly also adopted special laws for the largest of its colonies. Shortly after the Morant Bay Rebellion on Jamaica in 1865, the British authorities concluded that the attempt to turn the island's freedmen into "civilized" peasants had failed. As a consequence, the elected assemblies on the British Caribbean islands were abolished, even though they had been dominated by the white planters, and a special regime was introduced in the West Indies. Only the white settler communities in Canada, Australia, New Zealand, and the Cape Colony continued to have their own assemblies and a form of self-government.[39]

In France, the turning point was related to Algeria. After the invasion of 1830, it took a long time to "pacify" this former province of the Ottoman Empire. In 1848 the fertile coastal area was annexed and turned into three more French departments, awarding full citizenship to the growing number of settlers. Napoleon III made the Indigenous population French subjects. In theory, they could acquire citizenship and suffrage rights by rejecting Islamic and customary laws, but this was not a feasible option for the overwhelming majority of the Arab and Berber population. A few years later, the government of the Third Republic decided that property would be subject to the French Civil Code, thus dividing communal landholdings into individual plots, which could more easily be acquired by European settlers. The division between citizens and subjects finally led to the drafting of the Indigenous Code of 1881, which contained harsh "special rules" that were also applied to the Indigenous populations of Indochina and France's new African colonies.[40]

National Awareness

In Europe and the Americas, the nation-state was becoming a fact of life. Moreover, the national awareness of the population was clearly on the rise. In many ways, this was an almost automatic consequence of a general modernization process. The improvement of the infrastructure—the building of new roads, canals, telegraph lines, and above all, railways—connected the different parts of the country. As a result, economies became more integrated, creating truly national markets. People became more mobile and thus knowledge of the diversity and riches of the fatherland increased. The state bureaucracy also grew rapidly in size. More people received elementary education and became fluent in the national standard language.[41]

This also enabled the expansion of the public sphere. Printing became cheaper and the circulation of newspapers and magazines increased enormously. The provincial middle classes and many workers now became part of a national readership, and this happened not just in Europe and the Americas, but also in various parts of Asia and Africa. Many individuals now simultaneously read articles about the same national events, creating common topics of conversation among people who had never met before and who might even come from different parts of the country.[42] Michael Billig has shown how the national frame was reinforced through the press, for instance by distinguishing between foreign and domestic news; by emphasizing the national aspects of a wider phenomenon, such as an economic crisis; by portraying the world as consisting of different nations, each with its own identity and territory; and in times of international conflicts, by drawing a distinction between "us" and "them." But the nation was also flagged in a more subtle and banal way, by addressing the members of the nation as "we" or by speaking generally about "society," "the government," or "taxes," while readers knew that what was meant was the society, government, and taxation of their own country. When discussing foreign affairs, the actions of a president or government were described in national terms: "France" adopts a new policy, or "the Mexicans" take action. Even the weather forecast took national borders for granted.[43]

The invention of lithography and the rotary press made it easier to publish images. Thus, from the 1840s, the illustrated press—in both cheap, sensationalist publications and in high-end magazines—conveyed to a rapidly growing public a world consisting of visually different countries. In most maps each country was represented by a different color, and characteristic landscapes, well-known landmarks, typical costumes, and traditions helped people to distinguish nations from each other, while also getting to know the characteristics of their own. This development was reinforced in the 1880s when new techniques enabled the mass reproduction of photographs. Journalists, then, contributed to the naturalization of the nation.[44]

It was not only the nation-state that was taken for granted; nationalism also was increasingly becoming self-evident. Even though nationalists had been defeated in 1848 in most parts of Europe, the subsequent reforms undertaken by the victors made it clear that a (partial) return to the ancien régime was no longer an option. Most monarchs, aristocrats, and members of the clergy began to accept nationalism and the nation-state—or, as Cavour, Bismarck, and Japan's samurai leadership did, they used it to enlarge and strengthen the state while maintaining a central position for the monarchy, the nobility, and in many instances, established religion as well. Nonetheless, it was the well-educated urban middle classes who continued to be the mainstay of nationalism. This had become evident in 1848, but it was also visible in their active support for the unification of Italy and Germany, and middle-class intellectuals had a leading role in nationalist movements all over Europe.[45]

The bulk of the population was opposed, indifferent, or at best lukewarm vis-à-vis nationalist demands. In times of crisis, peasants, artisans, and laborers could be stirred against unpopular rulers, local officials or tax collectors, but many of the reforms related to the creation of the nation-state, such as higher taxes, conscription, and the abolishment of the guilds and common lands, were met with outright hostility. The extension of the suffrage made the issue of the national awareness of the masses and their loyalty to the fatherland all the more urgent. As a consequence, nationalist intellectuals and politicians began to target them, which could be done in two different ways, depending on whether nationalists were state-seeking or already had an established nation-state.

In the parts of Europe where nationalists did not yet have their own independent state, nationalism could become the main mobilizing force in the political arena. This was the case in Ireland and Finland, where the people resented the political supremacy of Great Britain and Russia, respectively, and in many parts of East-Central Europe. There, political mobilization occurred mostly along linguistic lines, by Czech politicians in Bohemia, for example, addressing Czech audiences in the Czech language, primarily defending Czech national interests—and prompting German politicians to rally the German-speaking Bohemians in a similar way. Nationalists tried to reach out to the lower classes to show that the whole nation stood behind them. This could be done through nationalist associations, publications, festivals, and political or social campaigns. Schools particularly became a battleground, because they determined the language and the "nationality" of the future generations. Sometimes material incentives were used, like free school books. More negative campaigns such as boycotting shops, products, or people, which gave an active role to women, were also used to mobilize the rank and file.[46]

In general, nationalism was not a divisive issue in established nation-states such as France, Sweden, Denmark, the Netherlands, Spain, and Portugal, where borders were not contested (except in a few disputed areas such as Schleswig-Holstein and Alsace-Lorraine) and therefore nationalism was much less visible. Nonetheless, the extension of the suffrage made the loyalty of the new voters a vital issue Here the powers of the state could be used for the national cause. The best example of a conscious nation-building strategy can be found in the French Third Republic. In the late 1870s, when the republicans finally defeated the various monarchist parties in the general elections, they immediately tried to enhance the population's connection to the republic.

First, they emphasized that all adult males, in their role as voters, jurors, and soldiers, had been given the responsibility for the well-being of the nation. In 1889 military conscription was reformed, reducing the term of service to three years and eliminating most of the exemptions that had favored the well-to-do, thus creating a truly national army where all classes of society mingled. Second, by increasing the presence of the state, they showed that the authorities did not just extract resources from the population, but actually cared about their interests. Thus, in 1881 to 1882 free compulsory education was introduced. In fact, the educational system was nationalized by eliminating the significant input of religious orders and centralizing its organization.[47]

Education was an important issue. In France, around 1850, over 40 percent of the population was illiterate. Twenty years later, still only about half of the population had French as their mother tongue. Some of the other languages and dialects spoken in the country, such as Occitan, Catalan, and Italian, were closely related to French, but this was not the case with Alsatian, Flemish, Breton, and Basque. An educational offensive would disseminate knowledge of the French language to all corners of the hexagon. At the same time, primary education was no longer limited to reading, writing, and arithmetic; history, geography, and gymnastics would instill patriotic feelings. A widely used textbook, *The Tour of France by Two Children* (1877), told the story of André and Julien traveling the country, discovering the beauty and riches of its constituent parts. Pupils were introduced to the glories of the past through Ernest Lavisse's *History of France* (1884), and gymnastics prepared the boys for their future role in the army. In the end, this nation-building process, which Eugen Weber has characterized as a top-down assimilation process or even colonial conquest, succeeded in turning peasants and artisans into Frenchmen.[48]

Although not all established nation-states had the means and drive of the Third Republic, most European states implemented similar nation-building policies. American states were much less active in this area—illiteracy in Latin America around 1900 was well above 50 percent, though Argentina emulated France by introducing free compulsory and secular primary education in 1884.[49] Some governments chose a different strategy, targeting the enemy within. Bismarck, for instance, developed a policy that Hans-Ulrich Wehler has defined as "negative integration," taking repressive measures against domestic "enemies" such as Catholics and socialists. The idea was that this would rally the majority of the population behind the government. Although Bismarck remained in power until 1890, in the end, this policy was not very successful—both the Catholic Center Party and the Socialist Party increased their followings considerably. Nevertheless, they also accepted the German Empire as their primary frame of reference.[50]

The Nationalization of Culture

The nationalization of the cultural realm gained ground, but in a more subtle way than in the preceding era. The failure of the Revolutions of 1848 left many European intellectuals and scholars disillusioned about the Romantic dreams. Subjective and metaphysical speculations about "national souls" and "popular spirits" would make room for numbers and empirical research. The rather arbitrary collecting of stories and artefacts was replaced by a scientific approach, and the focus shifted from the distant past and remote rural areas to contemporary society. Although many Romantic ideas and interpretations were now rejected as subjective, the nation-state and the nation as a language community continued to be the main frame of reference for social thought. This manifested itself unambiguously in the humanities, the new social sciences, and even in the field of statistics.

Governments increasingly needed detailed information for taxing landed property, charting economic activities, conscripting young men, and creating electoral districts. Many states already conducted censuses, usually at ten-year intervals. A federal census was introduced in the United States in 1790 to decide on the number of congressmen for the House of Representatives. Napoleon created a Bureau of Statistics in France in 1800. Nevertheless, national statistics offices became a permanent feature of most states in Europe and the Americas only halfway through the nineteenth century. International Statistical Congresses, the first of which was held in Brussels in 1853, enabled the standardization of categories, questions, and calculation methods, creating internationally comparable data.[51]

The introduction of statistics offices also meant that the main geographical unit of analysis was the nation-state, which was often just referred to as "society." This was not an issue in Western Europe and the Americas, but in East-Central Europe many national and state borders were contested. In order to objectively measure the demographic sizes of nationalities, the Prussian statistician Richard Böckh suggested that census questionnaires include an item on language. His proposal was accepted in 1872, and after then, most censuses took the language of daily use as an indicator of national belonging. This implied that respondents should declare just one language, rendering bi- and multilingual persons invisible, while dialects and "jargons" such as Yiddish were ignored. This meant that especially in the Habsburg Empire, language communities, most of which were, in fact, recent inventions, were reified by the statistical bureaus. Censuses even became a battleground as nationalist activists did their best to boost the presence of their "nation."[52] Similar processes can be detected in the colonies, where censuses were conducted as well. A complete census was taken in both British India and Ceylon in 1871, for

example. Since populations had to fit into neatly delineated categories, boundaries between castes, religions, and ethnic communities—defined as either
"nationality" or "race"—became much harder.[53]

This methodological nationalism could also be found in other disciplines.
They mostly took the nation or nation-state as the basic unit of analysis,
ignored transnational influences, and equated society with a supposedly homogenous national community.[54] National academies of sciences and myriad
learned societies took the nation-state as their main unit of analysis and began
to take stock of its geological, geographical, botanical, and archaeological
riches. Universities created new chairs to study the history of the nation, its
economy, and the national language. The seminar system as it had developed
in German lands, with a strong emphasis on research, was adopted by universities around the world, leading to a professionalization of scientific investigations and increasingly presenting the nation as an objective reality.

This professionalization can be observed in the discipline of history, where
German influence was profound. Many universities created a chair for
the study of history, which in most cases meant national history. Many of these
professors were involved in the creation of historical journals, which set
benchmarks for professional research. Archives with professional staffs were
established, and they often published source collections. The professionalization and institutionalization of historical research also meant that amateurs
were increasingly excluded, and that borders with other disciplines such as
philology, archaeology, and philosophy were reinforced. A new positivist emphasis on facts, primary sources, and truthfulness led to a rejection of the
hero-worshipping and exalted national histories of the preceding age. Nonetheless, the focus on the nation was not abandoned, but made even stronger.
In fact, the historical discipline took the national frame for granted; almost all
historians, archives, journals, and publications focused on national history. In
order to understand the present, one had to study the historical roots of current society, thus creating unique trajectories for each individual nation. The
national focus was quite obvious in new states like Germany, Italy, Romania,
and Serbia, but also evident in old states such as Great Britain and Russia, and
in aspiring nations such as Ukraine, Ireland, and Catalonia. A similar but
somewhat slower process of professionalization, institutionalization, and nationalization of history writing can also be detected in the Americas.[55]

A modern form of national history writing also arose in the Ottoman Empire and East Asia. First, a vocabulary had to be developed, coining new terms
for European concepts such as nation, civilization, culture, progress, and freedom. Of course, these terms were also new in Europe, where they took on their
modern meanings only in the late eighteenth or early nineteenth century.
Narodnost, the Russian word for nationality, gained currency only in the 1820s.

The Turkish *vatan* and the Arab *watan*—meaning fatherland or homeland—began to be heard more often in the middle of the nineteenth century. At the start of the Tanzimat period, terms like "civilization," "rights of men," "freedom," and "people" were introduced into Ottoman Turkish and Arabic, and the same happened in Persia. A few decades later, Japanese, Chinese, and Korean intellectuals began to adopt this vocabulary by creating new equivalents or redefining existing concepts.[56] In this way, another process of global isomorphism made headway in the cultural sphere, introducing not only a homogenic conceptual framework but also similar institutions such as modern educational establishments, museums, and exhibitions, and similar practices such as doing scientific research, producing modern art, preserving heritage, and defining national canons.

History writing, which mostly had taken the form of chronicles describing the major feats of the dynasty, had to be adapted as well. In the Ottoman Empire, modern historical studies were produced in a close dialogue with Western scholarship. This was particularly true in Egypt, which had attracted extensive scholarly attention since the Napoleonic invasion. The Antiquities Service and the Egyptian Museum, both founded in 1858, were led by European archeologists, while Egyptians were admitted only in minor positions. Nevertheless, in 1868, Rifaa al-Tahtawi published a first volume of the history of Egypt. Under Mehmed Ali he had been sent to Paris for studies, and on his return he became director of the new School of Languages and translated a French history of ancient Egypt. He personally knew the leading Western scholars active in Egypt, and his own book traced the history of Egypt from its earliest beginnings until the Islamic conquest. Like his European counterparts, he also injected doses of chauvinism into the narrative, asserting that under the pharaohs, Egypt had been "the mother of all nations of the world" and that classical Greece was "the daughter of Egypt," and presenting the Romans as foreign conquerors. His approach differed from those of foreign Egyptologists only in minor details—by beginning with a Quranic quotation, for example. In the text he also interspersed a few moral lessons derived from the Quran and Arabic authors. The following decades saw more modern historians, including Ahmad Kamal, a curator at the Egyptian Museum who was the most prolific and published in both French and Arabic.[57]

In Japan, the state tried to continue the traditional form of history writing by creating a new office in 1868 that would compile *A Chronicle History of Great Japan*, written in Chinese. The office would help legitimate the Meiji Restoration's ending of almost seven centuries of shogun rule. Its staff members confirmed that the first emperor had descended from the Sun Goddess and that the Japanese imperial dynasty had ruled the country for over two millennia. Over time, however, the main historians of the office began to combine the

Chinese "evidential research" tradition of closely scrutinizing ancient texts with contemporary Western source criticism. After the staff switched to the new Tokyo Imperial University in 1888, they founded the Japanese Historical Association and a scientific journal. Some of them began to publish more critical interpretations of Japan's official past, casting doubt on the divine origins of the first emperor, for instance, and portraying Shintoism as a historically grown form of nature worship—views that caused them serious trouble.[58]

Intellectuals also began to publish modern historical and geographical works. A crucial author was Fukuzawa Yukichi. He had learned Dutch, but soon realized that English was a more important language. He participated in the first Japanese diplomatic missions to the United States and Europe. On his return, he published the first, best-selling volume of *Conditions in the West* (1866–1870), didactically explaining the functioning of Western taxation, schools, hospitals, museums, and so on. Three years later, he began his *All the Countries of the World*, aimed at children and women, in which he discussed all countries by continent, and in which he presented Europe—not China—as the pinnacle of civilization. Moreover, he very much valued national independence and encouraged his fellow countrymen to follow the examples of Egypt, Brazil, and Chile in trying to catch up with Europe. In his *Outline of a Theory of Civilization* (1875), he criticized traditional, morally charged history writing. He looked for inspiration instead from François Guizot and Henry Thomas Buckle, who had written histories of European and English civilization, respectively. Fukuzawa adopted their linear view of progress, distinguishing between barbarian lands, semicivilized countries such as the Ottoman Empire, China, and Japan, and the civilized West. China and Japan, he asserted, had failed to progress because they disregarded practical learning and stuck with age-old customs—such as Confucianism—and a feudal mentality. Fukuzawa argued that the only way for the Japanese to protect their "nationality" and "sovereignty" was to embrace Western civilization.[59]

In China and Korea, it took more time for a modern historicist interpretation to make inroads. In the 1880s, the influential Chinese thinker and politician Kang Youwei reinterpreted Confucius as progressive reformer. Around the turn of the century, other intellectuals and historians, influenced by Western and Japanese authors, gave up the Sinocentric worldview and critically scrutinized historical myths, such as the Yellow Emperor being the ancestor of the Han Chinese, and Tan'gun—the "grandson of heaven"—founding the first Korean kingdom. Probably the most influential historicist author was Liang Qichao, who together with his mentor Kang had to flee China after their involvement in the Hundred Days of Reform. In his productive exile in Japan, Liang deepened his knowledge of Western scholarship and was impressed by Fukuzawa's publications. In 1902, he founded a biweekly, *New Citizen Journal*, which would quickly reach a broad audience. In the following years he published biographical sketches of European nationalists such as Mazzini, Garibaldi, Cavour, and Kossuth, positively assessing their struggles for national liberation. He also toyed with the idea of writing a general history of China, but in the end he finished only two introductory chapters. He rejected the traditional chronicles, which recounted the cyclical succession of dynasties without providing a rational analysis of cause and effect. Instead, he aimed to examine how the geographical circumstances had had an impact on the evolution of Chinese civilization and how humans could change the course of history. Like Fukuzawa, he exhorted his fellow countrymen to see themselves as equal participants in a world of nations and abandon inherited traditions that held them back. If China was to make progress and ward off further foreign interventions, its population should learn to become active and responsible citizens of a modern nation-state.[60]

In Europe, the intertwined processes of professionalization, institutionalization, and nationalization could also be seen in the field of art history. Beginning in Germany, many universities created a chair for the new discipline. Art history was very Eurocentric; indeed, in most historical overviews the non-European world was largely absent. Sometimes—as in Franz Kugler's voluminous *Handbook of Art History*, published in the 1840s—the art of pre-Columbian America, ancient Egypt, the Middle East, India, and China was squeezed in between European prehistory and the birth of Western art in classical Greece and Rome, and a short intermezzo in the European Middle Ages was dedicated to Islamic art. This made it clear that a progressive evolution of the arts had occurred only in Southern and Western Europe. From the Renaissance onward, the history of art was discussed mostly by country, and Scandinavia, Eastern Europe, and the Balkans were barely mentioned. National schools—Italian, French, German, Dutch-Flemish, British, and Spanish—had already been defined in the eighteenth century. Art historical studies were now structured as chronological narratives that connected the artistic expressions in a particular country in a meaningful account. This implied that a specific national style, a golden age, and a national canon were defined, and in most instances, foreign artists were excluded from the story. Scholars also began to write national art histories for non-Western countries. In the 1870s Shyamacharan Srimani praised the ancient arts of India in a historical overview, arguing that although British authors tended to see these artistic expressions as merely decorative, they really belonged to realm of the fine arts.[61]

This methodological nationalism could have curious implications. Thomas DaCosta Kaufmann has shown that at various seventeenth-century Central European courts there had been many Dutch sculptors and architects working in the exuberant baroque Counter-Reformation style that was fashionable at the time. During the nineteenth century they were largely excluded from overviews of Dutch art because their work did not follow the sober, Calvinist, Dutch artistic style found primarily in genre paintings for middle-class customers. Moreover, as foreigners, they were also ignored in studies on seventeenth-century German, Czech, and Polish art. Another fascinating case can be found in Spain, where Spanish followers of Raphael were rejected as mere imitators whose Italianate idealism was foreign to the country's realist disposition, whereas El Greco—who had been born on Crete and educated in Venice—was held up as the founder of the Spanish school. As a highly original painter whose apostles seemed to come straight from the mountains of Toledo, he was a better exemplar for a clearly distinguishable national artistic evolution. Nevertheless, most art historians agreed that the Spanish golden age culminated in the work of Diego de Velázquez, who was born and raised in Seville.[62]

A turn away from Romantic idealism in favor of a more down-to-earth, direct observation of the surrounding environment can also be detected among artists, writers, and musicians. Their works were less explicitly nationalist, but the reality they represented was mostly a national reality. In the case of painting, this was made possible by the invention of the paint tube in 1841 and the construction of railway lines. Painters now began making trips to the countryside to work en plein air. Beautiful hamlets in easily accessible areas close to major capitals, such as Barbizon, quickly became flourishing artists' colonies, and soon after, fishing villages such as Saint Ives and Skagen also attracted many artists. Realist artists produced less dramatic landscape paintings, while trying to immerse the viewer in the scene. Painters like Gustave Courbet and Jean-François Millet plainly depicted the life of the rural poor or ordinary events in small towns, which is attested in the former's enormous painting *A Burial at Ornans* (1849–1850; figure 4.2).[63]

Although the impressionists have been interpreted as having started the first cosmopolitan avant-garde movement, in fact, they documented scenes from everyday life in their immediate surroundings. Moreover, by capturing the atmosphere and light of a specific moment of the day, they even claimed to convey a more truthful snapshot of reality than their precursors. They mostly focused on city life in Paris, but also made trips to depict other parts of France, such as the city of Rouen and the Normandy coast. Hundreds of juste-milieu painters from Europe and the Americas incorporated the innovations of the impressionists while portraying the urban and rural life of their own countries, as exemplified by Ilya Repin's magnificent *Barge Haulers on the Volga* (1870–1873; figure 4.3). Through art exhibitions, the public got an idea of what their country looked like. Some significant parts—such as capital cities and impressive river landscapes of the Rhine, the Seine, the Volga, and the Hudson—were represented more than others.[64] Artists in the Ottoman

FIGURE 4.2 Gustave Courbet, *A Burial at Ornans*, 1849, oil on canvas, 315 × 660 cm. The painter aimed to depict the reality of French provincial life on a monumental scale, including its more negative aspects, such as poverty and sorrow.

Empire and India, such as Osman Hamdi Bey and Raja Ravi Varma, also adopted Western-style realism to depict their own fatherland, while the first Japanese painters, such as Kuroda Seiki, went to Paris to become acquainted with plein-air painting and the impressionist brushstroke.[65]

Meticulous attention to the realities of daily life in the countryside and the cities, without ignoring the grimmer parts of national societies, was also characteristic of the realist and naturalist writers of the time. Novels like Charlotte Brontë's *Jane Eyre* (1847) and Gustave Flaubert's *Madame Bovary* (1856) provided candid portraits of the provincial middle classes in the writers' countries, while authors such as Charles Dickens and Fyodor Dostoyevsky explored the fates of dropouts and social climbers in the large cities of their fatherlands. Leo Tolstoy and Mark Twain presented enthralling pictures of the interaction between urban and rural milieus. Harriet Beecher Stowe's *Uncle Tom's Cabin* (1852) and Émile Zola's *Germinal* (1885) revealed the heinous treatment of enslaved African Americans and the plight of French coal miners, respectively. Historical novels that realistically portrayed specific national episodes through the eyes of ordinary people were published by, among others, Benito Pérez Galdós in Spain and Bankimchandra Chattopadhyay in India.[66]

Nationalism had a greater impact on classical music during this period. Verdi had become a national hero, and his "Va, pensiero" was intoned by nationalists everywhere in Europe, while "Rule Britannia"—written in 1740—became popular in the United Kingdom. Many operas were dedicated

FIGURE 4.3 Ilya Repin, *Barge Haulers on the Volga*, 1870–1873, oil on canvas, 132 × 281 cm. This painting combines a truthful depiction of rural poverty with a magnificent view of the Volga, Russia's most important river.

to famous historical figures, like Modest Mussorgsky's *Boris Godunov* (1874). Folk melodies, typical instruments, and religious chants gave compositions a national flavor. Franz Liszt claimed the music of the Romani in his *Hungarian Rhapsodies* (1846–1853), Edvard Grieg composed *25 Norwegian Folk Songs and Dances* (1869), and Richard Wagner became an international celebrity by thematizing Germanic mythology in his stupendous *Ring of the Nibelung* (1876). Others used their compositions to describe the beauties of their homelands. Bedřich Smetana's *The Moldau* (1879), for instance, evoked two small streams coming together, flowing through the different parts of Bohemia, and slowly evolving into a majestic river.[67]

Artists, writers, and musicians also produced works about other countries. Gioachino Rossini wrote an opera about the Swiss hero Wilhelm Tell (1829), Johannes Brahms composed *Hungarian Dances* (1869, 1880), and the Egyptian khedive commissioned Verdi to write *Aida*. Many painters made trips abroad, while scores of foreign artists living in Paris depicted the city and its environments. In general, though, they singled out the most salient aspects of a country's history, folklore, and landscape, and in some cases they succeeded in inventing a new national myth. *Carmen*, the tragic love story about a Sevillian girl of Romani background, was written by the French novelist Prosper Mérimée in 1845, then adapted for theater, and in 1875 the French composer Georges Bizet turned it into an opera. The overwhelming international success of the opera transformed the fictional character into a Spanish archetype.[68]

The Nationalization of the Physical Environment

Until 1848, nationalist propaganda had mostly taken the form of lectures, historical novels, and history paintings. These were consumed primarily by a middle-class audience in salons, museums, learned societies, and reading rooms throughout Europe and the Americas. National institutions, monuments, and statues were built mostly in the capitals and a few other big cities. During the second half of the century, scholars and artists tried to be more objective and less openly nationalistic—which implicitly meant that they took for granted a world divided into discrete nations. Nevertheless, thanks to the (illustrated) press, their reach had increased substantially. At the same time, nation-building activities became more vigorous and increasingly took to the streets. Now, almost all cities and towns obtained impressive state buildings such as hospitals, schools, town halls, and post offices. Statues dedicated to famous members of the nation were erected in almost every major square, and streets, avenues, and parks were named after national heroes or major national events. Although in many cases individual citizens or private associations took the initiative, support from state authorities was crucial, especially for more ambitious projects. This meant that it was much more difficult for nationalist movements without a state to put their stamp on public spaces, although nationalist activists in Bohemia, Poland, and Flanders, for example, could enlist the support of municipal authorities in some of their regional strongholds.

Many states began to beautify their capitals. This was done by building new imposing national institutions and monuments and by dignifying urban spaces. Georges-Eugène Haussmann, Napoleon III's prefect of Paris, ordered the demolition of overcrowded inner-city quarters to make room for new spacious boulevards, many of which ended in grandiose buildings such as the Arc de Triomphe and the new Opéra Garnier. At the same time, the areas around ancient monuments such as Notre-Dame were cleared of surrounding houses. This example of ruthless urban reform was quickly followed in other European capitals. Brussels, for instance, built several new avenues, one of them leading to Joseph Poelaert's new Palace of Justice (1866–1883), the largest building of the nineteenth century. Budapest constructed new boulevards and a splendid neo-Gothic parliament (1885–1904) along the Danube, and in Rome, a new avenue connected the Colosseum with the Altar of the Fatherland, the imposing monument to King Victor Emmanuel II, which was begun in 1885 (figure 4.4). In the Americas, many capitals, including Buenos Aires, adopted the Parisian model. Haussmann's influence was felt even in Egypt. Expropriation was more complicated in Northern Europe and the Anglo-Saxon world, where new majestic

FIGURE 4.4 Giuseppe Sacconi, *Victor Emmanuel II Monument*, 1885–1911, Piazza Venezia, Rome. This grandiose neoclassical monument, also known as the Altar of the Fatherland, was dedicated to the first king of a unified Italy. The photo was almost certainly taken at the festive inauguration of the monument in June 1911.

national spaces were created mostly at the edges of existing cities, such as Berlin's Victory Column (1873) at the King's Square and Amsterdam's Rijksmuseum (1885) and Royal Concert Hall (1888) at Museum Square.[69]

The new avenues, squares, and parks not only became more impressive, they were also thoroughly nationalized. This was done by naming them after national heroes or important historical events and decorating them with statues. A clear democratizing tendency could be detected in these dedications: in addition to members of the royal family, generals, statesmen, battles, and colonial possessions, now renowned writers, artists, and scientists were honored, too. Nationalist street names also appeared outside the capital cities, and statues of national heroes, mostly of local provenance, were erected in small towns and villages. New states and new regimes that were in need of legitimation and recognition were particularly active. The Third Republic, for instance, decreed that each of the more than thirty thousand municipalities should have a post office and a town hall.[70]

The preservation of heritage also attracted more attention. In 1877 the Society for the Protection of Ancients Monuments was created in Great Britain. Soon, similar associations were founded in other countries, such as Germany, the Netherlands, Italy, France, and Egypt. These organizations published their own journals and reports documenting the conditions of monuments. They often put pressure on local and national authorities to take action whenever an old building was under threat. Initially, preservationists focused on well-known monuments such as palaces, castles, and cathedrals, but they increasingly paid attention to lesser-known gems in small towns and the countryside, broadening the nation's heritage.[71] In the United States—where old European-style buildings were scarce—the preservation of nature began to be taken seriously. As in Europe, characterizing something as worth being preserved meant nationalizing it as the collective heritage of the people. Yellowstone, created in 1872, was the first "national park" (figure 4.5). To preserve the notion of America as a pristine land open to European settlers, "savage" Native Americans, who were seen as a nuisance, were increasingly removed from the area. In the 1870s and 1880s this model was adopted in Canada, Australia, and New Zealand.[72]

More ephemeral events also gained importance. Commemorations had mostly been royal, religious, or local affairs, but during the second half of the nineteenth century the trickle of festivities with a clear nationalist substance developed into a wave. Many centenaries were dedicated to national literary heroes, such as Schiller and Burns in 1859, Shakespeare in 1864, Dante in 1865, Rousseau and Voltaire in 1878, and Camões and Pushkin in 1880. Others were devoted to famous battles, politicians, or warriors, but also to composers, painters, inventors, and scientists. The commemorations often were very elaborate, with festivities throughout the country lasting several days. Although the most solemn occasions were generally by invitation only, organizing committees increasingly tried to involve the general population, including workers, women, and children. The programs therefore included pageants, public concerts, and the publication of special editions of the main works of the commemorated hero, sometimes adapted for children. All these activities were extensively covered by the press and thus reached almost the entire nation. State funerals of national heroes could have a similar unifying function, which was the case with the burial of Victor Hugo in 1885, when millions of people lined the route to pay him a last tribute (figure 4.6).[73]

Many new states began commemorating their declaration of independence or proclamation of the constitution on an annual basis. In the United States, the Fourth of July was celebrated regularly, but it became an official holiday only in 1870. In the first decades after its independence, Brazil had five different commemoration days, each with its own ideological implications. In Europe, when Greece began to celebrate its independence in 1838, it chose a religious

FIGURE 4.5 *Great Falls at Yellowstone*, 1872. Yellowstone in the United States was the first national park in the world. It nationalized an exceptional scenery, while confirming the myth of the West as consisting of virgin lands, open to white settlers.

FIGURE 4.6 *The Funeral Procession of Victor Hugo Arrives at the Pantheon,* June 1, 1885, Paris. Millions of people lined the streets to pay a last tribute to the author of *The Hunchback of Notre-Dame* before he received a state burial at the Pantheon.

feast day, Annunciation, the same day that the uprising against the Ottoman Empire had begun. In Denmark the proclamation of the constitution was commemorated from 1849, although until 1890 this was an ordinary working day. In Spain and Germany, attempts to make the start of the uprising against Napoleon or the Battle of the Nations at Leipzig a national holiday did not get off the ground for lack of state support. Sedan Day—marking victory over France in 1870—began to be celebrated in various parts of Germany, but Bismarck refused to make it a national holiday on the grounds that this would damage the traditional legitimacy of the dynasty by enthroning the nation.[74]

The Third Republic played a crucial role in the standardization of national holidays, flags, and anthems. Flags had already existed for centuries, mostly as royal flags or ensigns, and were used by the army and at sea. Specific religious hymns or military marches had been played at official occasions, but national anthems began to be institutionalized only during the nineteenth century. In fact, the French Revolution had already invented the symbolic repertoire of the nation. In the 1790s Bastille Day became a national holiday, the tricolor the national flag, the "Marseillaise" the anthem, and Marianne the personification of the French Republic. Subsequent regimes discontinued this tradition, and in 1830 only the tricolor flag was reintroduced. Around 1880, the Third Republic also reinstated Marianne, the "Marseillaise," and Bastille Day. Although these symbols were heavily contested by the Church, the royalists, and the conservatives, the republicans succeeded in getting the population to accept them, probably at the cost of rendering them banal. The flag was raised on all state buildings, the anthem was played at official occasions, and every town hall had a bust of Marianne, who also appeared on emblems, coins, and monuments. On Bastille Day, the civic, military, and religious authorities participated in the official ceremonies such as the military parade and a banquet; other festivities such as concerts, balls, and fireworks were aimed at the entire population and were organized even in small towns and villages.[75]

This example was quickly followed in other countries such as the Netherlands, Belgium, Hungary, Switzerland, and Sweden. In the Netherlands, liberal politicians were increasingly worried about the growing political role of the population. A national holiday could unify the people, but it also provided "civilized" entertainment for the lower classes. Since King William III was rather capricious and unpopular, liberal politicians decided to celebrate instead the birthday of Crown Princess Wilhelmina, who was still a young girl. It started as a local initiative in 1885, but it was quickly adopted by the rest of the country. The British elites apparently did not feel the need to create a national holiday, but the golden and diamond jubilees of Queen Victoria in 1887 and 1897 were celebrated with much pomp and thus fulfilled a similar nation-building function. National holidays were also celebrated before a country was actually independent, as the cases of Norway and Ireland demonstrate. Interestingly, many of the popular festivities of Saint Patrick's Day, such as the famous street parade, were developed first by Irish immigrant communities in the United States and Australia.[76]

World's fairs probably had the greatest impact on the diffusion and standardization of national identities during this period. In 1851, the Great Exhibition of the Works of Industry of All Nations, held in London's Crystal Palace, had been a great success, with over six million visitors. This first world's fair was framed as a peaceful international contest. Each of the twenty-five participating countries displayed its contributions to human progress in the forms of raw materials, machines, industrial products, and works of art. Although most world's fairs were held in Europe and the United States, the phenomenon rapidly spread to other parts of the world. Moreover, there was an even greater number of ambitious regional and national exhibitions, which often stretched over dozens of hectares. The press covered these splendorous events in special illustrated editions and extensive reports.[77]

World's fairs developed various ways that national identities could be represented. First, the number of sections increased rapidly, often depending on the preferences of the organizing country. At the second world's fair, held in New York in 1853, entertainment had a prominent place, and in 1855 France added agriculture. But it was difficult to distinguish countries from each other through machinery, industrial products, or fine arts, so for the Paris Universal Exposition of 1867 it was decided that each country would build a national pavilion to display its own characteristic heritage. This plan was successful, and it was adopted at all successive world's fairs. A country's particular national heritage could be exhibited by adopting certain templates that had proven their worth on earlier occasions, such as a national pavilion built in a typical architectural form, a display of wax figures dressed in traditional costume, or dioramas with historical scenes, adding yet another process of isomorphism. New formats were also introduced, such as magnificent open-air exhibits with "authentic" inhabitants. Both the Austrian and Russian Empires built typical rural villages at the Universal Exposition of 1867. Picturesque representations of the East—such as a street of Cairo and a Moroccan quarter—could be visited at the Paris world's fair of 1878. In 1884, the South Kensington International Health Exhibition displayed twenty-five full-scale reproductions of ancient buildings forming Old London. These old cities and ethnographic villages attracted large crowds and were repeated at later expositions.[78]

A magnificent world's fair could boost the host country's national pride, and it was a perfect occasion for countries to define themselves. The Third Republic organized an enormous universal exposition in 1889 to celebrate the centenary of the French Revolution. The purpose-built Eiffel Tower, with 1,789 steps, functioned as an observation platform and became a permanent landmark of the city, connecting the French Republic with modernity and progress. Often, participating countries had to conform to the expectations of both the organizers and the visitors. For the universal exposition of 1867, Brazil was asked to prepare an "original" presentation of its "Indians, farmers, and gauchos"; a huge stage design of a pristine tropical forest was one of the most popular attractions in its pavilion. At the Universal Exposition of 1889, Mexico tried to combine antiquity with modernity by constructing an Aztec palace of steel.[79]

From the very start, world's fairs involved almost all parts of the world. At the Great Exhibition in 1851, the Ottoman Empire, Egypt, Tunisia, Persia, and China participated with their own sections. This meant that they adopted the nation-state model in which each nation had a particular character embodied by its past, the ordinary people of its countryside, and its cultural heritage. At the 1867 Universal Exposition in Paris, Egypt erected three typical buildings: a pharaonic temple, a lavishly decorated medieval reception room, and a caravansary that included artisans, a few camels, and donkeys. Western colonies also participated in this process of national identity construction. In India, for instance, colonial officers and Indigenous elites collected the best specimens of artisanal work from the subcontinent to display as typical "Indian" crafts. Indeed, all countries presented their "typical" face by presenting the most exceptional, spectacular, and extraordinary aspects of their heritage to attract attention at these mega events; Joep Leerssen calls this the "typicality effect."[80]

The role of world's fairs as part of a global learning process was particularly clear in the case of Japan, which was very eager to get acquainted with the outside world after the Meiji Restoration. Thus, the government sent a large delegation to the 1873 World's Fair in Vienna to study all the exhibits, which resulted in an exhaustive report of ninety-six volumes. The country appealed to the expectations of the visitors by representing itself with a pagoda, a Japanese garden, and a Shinto shrine. However, it also had to adapt to the exposition's official classification schemes, which distinguished between a large number of product categories. The Japanese were not familiar with the Western conceptualization of art, and they had difficulty categorizing some of their precious ancient objects; thus, a beautiful golden teakettle was displayed in the metal industry section. In order to be taken seriously as a "civilized nation," they had to distinguish between fine arts, applied arts, objects of worship, and ordinary industrial products.[81] In fact, they had to create a national culture from elements that previously had belonged to transnational religious or civilizational domains on the one hand or local vernacular and folkloric traditions on the other, and pour them into Western molds that were rapidly defining global standards. Even in Europe, this process had been initiated less than a century earlier.

In the end, it is clear that the nationalization of the physical environment had advanced enormously since 1848; it affected more countries, spread from the capitals to the provinces, and encompassed more domains. State authorities and national activists nationalized streets and landscapes by dotting them with statues, giving them nationalist names, and creating national parks. The global diffusion of the nation-state model, best exemplified at the world's fairs, also standardized what was required for admission to the international community of "civilized nations." Every country—and even empires and colonies—needed to have a flag, an anthem, a national holiday, a well-documented glorious past, a national heritage, national heroes, characteristic buildings, and folklore. Preferably, they also had a few national icons who were known throughout the civilized world.

Conclusion

Nationalism made much progress between 1848 and the 1880s. Most of the Americas and Western Europe now consisted of nation-states. Piedmont's and Prussia's wars of conquest created unified nation-states in Italy and Germany, and many aspects of the nation-state model were adopted by the autocratic empires in East-Central Europe, by traditional monarchies in East Asia, and in European colonies. Although the colonies had no choice but to apply the formulas imposed by imperial authorities, many independent countries, too, felt compelled to follow the Western lead in order to survive. They had three basic options: a nativist rejection of all foreign influences, an authoritarian course of reform, or a thorough process of Westernization. Most opted for authoritarian reform; only Austria and Japan adopted the entire package, including legal equality, a constitution, and political participation. At the same time, citizenship remained very restrictive. Women and supposedly "uncivilized" people such as the inhabitants of the colonies, Indigenous populations, and people of color were by formal or informal means excluded from political participation. Nonetheless, the population's national awareness was clearly on the rise, even in the non-Western world, where growing numbers had access to the printed press and modern education.

The nationalization of the cultural realm also made a great deal of progress during this period, especially because the nationalist content of most scientific and artistic work was less evident. Yet, by prioritizing the national framework in their "objective" depictions of reality, scientists, writers, and artists succeeded in naturalizing the nation in the minds of educated people throughout the world. Impressive monuments and statues, nationalist street names, and heritage preservation nationalized the built environment in small cities and even villages too, and newly invented national parks protected specific exceptional landscapes. National identities were increasingly standardized, and every country needed to adopt a flag, an anthem, and a national holiday. World's fairs proved crucial in disseminating global templates for presenting an extraordinary and recognizable national heritage to an international audience, paradoxically making national identities increasingly uniform and homogenous.

5

Nationalist Radicalization, 1885–1914

THE OPTIMISTIC, forward-looking atmosphere in most parts of Europe, the Americas, and Japan—the result of a prolonged period of technological innovation, economic prosperity, and political liberalization—came to an end toward the end of the nineteenth century. This was caused by a complex mixture of a socioeconomic crisis, a profound intellectual revolution, and growing international tensions. The introduction of steamships and trains had brought many advantages, but it also created a global market for industrial and agricultural products, putting pressure on prices. During a prolonged economic depression from about 1873 to 1896, it even led to deflation. Lower transport costs made it possible for farmers in Russia, the United States, and Argentina to directly compete with their colleagues elsewhere in the world, who often had smaller plots and employed less efficient techniques. Dramatically falling prices caused a profound agrarian crisis. This not only led to a rural exodus to cities, new industrial areas, and immigrant countries, but also brought an end to the era of free trade. Many European politicians felt inclined to support the farmers in the rural heartlands, which often formed a crucial part of their electorate. The German Empire and Italy had already introduced the first protective measures in the late 1870s, and the United States and France adopted high tariffs in the early 1890s. Most other countries fell in line as well.[1]

The same shift from free trade to protectionism was visible in the way imperial powers treated the rest of the world. At the Berlin Conference of 1885, convened by Bismarck to deal with colonial issues, participants established the exact dimensions of the new Congo Free State (a private venture of the Belgian king) and decided that its territory would be open for international trade. They also decided that new colonial claims had to be made effective on the ground in order to be recognized. Instead of calming matters, this led to a scramble for new colonies, in which imperial powers tried to prevent the expansion of their rivals by quickly occupying new territories. Moreover, rather than opening up the newly conquered areas, they claimed them for exclusive exploitation by the occupying power's own traders and companies. Thus, free trade and a spirit of cooperation—at least in the Western world—were increasingly replaced by international competition and rivalry.[2]

A similar shift from optimism to pessimism can be detected in domestic affairs. During the second half of the nineteenth century, many observers thought that the integration of the working classes was going quite smoothly. Growing prosperity and rising levels of education would slowly improve the situation of the workers. Through hard work, thrift, and prudence they would be able to establish a family, acquire some property, and provide a decent education for their children. However, toward the end of the nineteenth century, many liberals and conservatives became aware that this was not an automatic process. Karl Marx's critique of capitalist society as inevitably leading to capital accumulation among the few and impoverishment of the many began to strike a chord. In fact, instead of producing a free market of equal players, the negotiation power of the workers was dwarfed by that of the ever-growing industrial conglomerates. Moreover, instead of voting for established parties, workers increasingly created their own movements, many of which aimed to break with the existing liberal constitutional order while advocating the international solidarity of the workers. Large-scale strikes in 1889 in the London harbor and in coal mines in the Ruhr area, for example, brought entire economic sectors to a halt and seemed to be a first step toward a social revolution. In 1890, in what would become an annual tradition, the socialists celebrated International Workers' Day on a massive scale in the heart of many Western cities. That year, the German Socialist Party won almost 20 percent of the vote in the Reichstag elections. At about the same time, anarchist terrorists adopted a different strategy, murdering numerous monarchs, politicians, generals, and other "enemies of the people." Most conservatives and liberals became aware that urgent reforms were needed to better integrate the working classes into the nation in order to avoid a revolutionary takeover.[3]

A further blow was the intellectual assault on the very foundations of Western philosophy and science. Heavily influenced by Friedrich Nietzsche, young intellectuals radicalized Immanuel Kant's enlightened theory of knowledge, which implicated that we cannot truly know whether reality really conforms to our perceptions. Kant had assumed that God guaranteed that we do not live in a world of illusions. But when Nietzsche declared that "God is dead," he distanced himself not only from the religious underpinnings of Kant's rationalism, but also from the moral value system of Christianity. Another supposition that underlay the optimistic, rational worldview that had been dominant during the second half of the nineteenth century was that education would lead to better behavior and thus indirectly improve society. But who guaranteed that more knowledge and rationality would really motivate people to behave better? And what is good, anyway? Indeed, Nietzsche rejected the idea of absolute moral standards. His turn away from rationalism and his disdain for the masses and the idea of human equality was embraced by many intellectuals and artists of a younger generation. This led to a rapidly growing fascination with irrational aspects of human existence—which engendered, for example, symbolist art and Sigmund Freud's psychoanalysis—as well as a pronounced elitism and a widespread longing for a more spiritual and authentic way of life. Although these developments did not immediately lead to a clear political alternative, Nietzsche's views clearly undermined the rational and egalitarian ideals of the constitutional nation-state.[4]

Another crucial cultural development was the growing influence of biological thinking. Differences in "civilization" had been explained primarily by pointing to "backward" traditions and "superstition," which could be remedied in the long term by modern education and encouraging rational behavior. Nevertheless, inspired by the impact of Darwin's theory of evolution and the rise of racial theories, differences between societies were increasingly cast in biological terms, in terms of innate intellectual and physical capacities. The same was true for the way the underclass was viewed; education would not be able to overcome congenital deficiencies. According to social Darwinists like Francis Galton and Ernst Haeckel, the principle of the survival of the fittest could also be observed among individuals and societies. The degeneration of the underclass had to be countered by eugenic measures, and in the international arena, only the strong would survive. This was the natural way of things, and as a result, there was no need to feel pity for the weak.[5] It also implied that national identities were not just the product of rather arbitrary historical developments; they were increasingly seen as having a biological basis—some peoples were superior to others as a consequence of a process of natural selection.

Nation-State Formation

Although the decades before the First World War are often seen as a period of rising nationalism, it was not an uncontested heyday of the nation-state. The scramble for Africa engendered a tense international political constellation in which many nation-states tried to acquire colonies and create an empire. Imperial status was seen as indispensable for a "civilized" power. So it was not only existing colonial powers such as the United Kingdom, France, the Netherlands, Spain, and Portugal that expanded their realms; new nation-states such as the United States, Belgium, Italy, Germany, and Japan also conquered overseas territories.

Irredentist movements became more active as well, aiming to include fellow nationals living outside the national borders by enlarging the country's territory. The fact that these fellow nationals lived mostly in ethnically mixed areas was not seen as a major issue. In Italy, irredentism received growing support, and in Germany the new Pan-German League rapidly became popular. Many of the Young Turks, who had gained power in the Ottoman Empire in 1908, were in favor of uniting all Turkish-speaking peoples in one state, and in 1910 the notion of Greater Greece was embraced by the government of Eleftherios Venizelos.[6] Further east, the radical nationalist Zhang Binglin argued that a future Chinese republic should include Vietnam and Korea, because they used the Chinese written language and had comparable customs. By the same token, he also admitted that Tibetans, Muslims, and Mongols had very little in common with the Chinese and could be given the option to have their own states.[7]

In this heated climate, it is no surprise that dynastic unions came under pressure. A first union that was dissolved without regret was the one between Luxembourg and the Netherlands. Because the succession of women was not permitted, Queen Wilhelmina, who ascended the Dutch throne in 1890, could not become grand duchess of Luxembourg. In Norway, growing tensions were related to the democratization process. In 1814 Norway had formed a dynastic union with Sweden, but it had kept its own constitution and parliament. The level of cultural, economic, and political integration was limited and the relations between the two halves were not hostile, but this began to change in 1885, when the Swedish parliament succeeded in getting a say over the union's Ministry of Foreign Affairs, which until then had been answerable only to the king. The growing power of the Swedish legislature was seen as an affront in Norway, where the Norwegian assembly did not get the same rights. As a consequence, opposition to the union increased. Norwegian nationalism was further exacerbated by the introduction of protectionist policies for the entire union, which primarily favored Swedish commercial interests. In 1905 the Norwegian parliament voted for the dissolution of the union. In a plebiscite, the overwhelming majority of the population voted in favor of independence. The outcome was accepted by Sweden and effectively created an independent Norwegian nation-state.[8]

Many European empires also came under strain. The first to collapse was Spain, which after the loss of the Latin American mainland had become a secondary power, although it still had valuable colonial possessions, including Cuba, which was particularly profitable. Constitutional rule, which was adopted in Spain in 1837, did not apply to the overseas colonies. As a consequence, colonial elites began to demand political autonomy and the recognition of civil and political rights. British colonial assemblies and, after 1867, Canadian political autonomy served as important models to reform-minded Cubans. But Spanish authorities refused to make meaningful concessions. This led to a large-scale rebellion on Cuba that started in 1868 and would last ten years. Inspired by writers like José Martí and José Rizal, new nationalist uprisings broke out in Cuba in 1895 and in the Philippines in 1896. In Cuba, repression of the uprising was severe. Finally, the United States interfered in order to "liberate" the Cuban people. After a short war in which the United States inflicted a humiliating defeat on Spain, Puerto Rico was annexed and the Philippines became a colony. Cuba became independent but was in fact an informal protectorate of the United States, and the same happened a few years later with the newly independent state of Panama.[9]

Meanwhile, the defeat in the Spanish-American War produced a backlash in Spain, where Catalonia and the Basque Country, the most advanced and prosperous parts of the country, increasingly turned their backs on Madrid. Democratization also played a role. The political system, which was based on extensive patronage networks, began to be fiercely criticized, while the manipulation of the elections became increasingly difficult in urban areas. The reactionary Basque Nationalist Party, which had been created in 1895, started to made electoral inroads after it moderated its tone. The Catalan language and culture had already received broad scholarly attention from the late Romantic era onward, and toward the end of the century a rapidly growing Catalanist movement began to claim autonomy, with the Austro-Hungarian Compromise of 1867 as their main source of inspiration. But it was only after the loss of the last colonies of a once-glorious empire that the Catalan economic elites relinquished their bond with the governing parties and the new Regionalist League scored its first electoral victories. The party rapidly became a dominant force in the four Catalan provinces. Hoping to stem the discontent with the strongly centralized political system, and inspired by Irish Home Rule plans, the Spanish government granted Catalonia a limited form of regional autonomy in 1914.[10]

Similar tendencies and tensions could be found in the British Empire, but with one major difference: the United Kingdom was at the zenith of its power, and as a consequence, the government could impose its will more easily. The growing political awareness of the population and the extension of voting rights led to fresh demands for self-government. This was most easily awarded to the white settler colonies, which, following the example of Canada, were given dominion status. In the 1850s and 1860s most of these colonies had already secured an elected assembly and "responsible government." In 1901 the six Australian colonies created a federation and adopted a constitution; the same happened with the merger of various colonies into the Union of South Africa in 1910. New Zealand became a dominion in 1907.[11]

The situation in Ireland was more complicated. In 1801, the personal union under the king of England had been transformed into a United Kingdom of

Great Britain and Ireland, which meant that the Parliament of Ireland was abolished in return for a number of seats in Westminster Parliament. The relationship between Ireland and Great Britain had been very troubled, with several rebellions. The extension of the vote enabled the mobilization of the electorate behind a nationalist program. The Home Rule movement started in the 1870s, but it only gained real traction in later decades. Led by Charles Stewart Parnell, the Irish Parliamentary Party consistently won the majority of the Irish districts. Parnell convinced the government to draw up a Home Rule Bill, which was adopted on the third attempt in 1914, only to be immediately suspended because of the outbreak of the First World War. Inspired by Parnell, in 1886 Scottish activists created a Scottish Home Rule Association, which began to lobby for devolution. However, the Government of Scotland Bill of 1913 was suspended for the same reason its Irish equivalent was.[12]

Although nationalist movements also existed in other parts of the British Empire, they had even less of a chance of getting substantial concessions. Colonel Ahmad Urabi protested foreign control over Egypt's state finances, using the slogan "Egypt for the Egyptians" and demanding a constitution in the "name of the people." However, the 1882 Urabi rebellion triggered a full-scale British military intervention that made the Ottoman province effectively a British protectorate. Three years later, the Indian National Congress was formed to defend the interests of the inhabitants of British India, including equal access to government jobs and limited forms of political participation. It was only in 1909, when members of a new generation of well-educated Indians had become more vocal, that some concessions were made. The Indian Councils Act awarded more seats in the central and provincial councils to Indian representatives, although the majority of seats were still allocated by the colonial authorities. That independence was not an option when it affected the interests of London was made clear during the Anglo-Boer War of 1899 to 1902, which led to the integration of the white settler republics of Transvaal and Orange Free State into the British colonial empire. Nevertheless, as supposedly "civilized" white statelets, they retained the right to self-government, and in 1910 they became part of the new Union of South Africa.[13]

Austria-Hungary was less equipped to deal with similar centrifugal forces, and therefore it relied primarily on soft power. Although the Dual Monarchy was a multiethnic empire, it had adopted all the crucial elements of a nation-state. It had a constitution with legal equality, the bureaucracy and the legal system functioned well, and it had an army of conscripts. In 1907 the Austrian half of the empire even adopted universal male suffrage. Although the dominant group of German speakers constituted only about a third of the population and consequently was not in the position to pursue a policy of assimilation, politics became polarized around the language issue. Secondary education continued to be taught in German, but minority languages had equal status in primary education. In 1868 Austria had created a public school system and required all children to attend school for eight years. This quickly led to attempts by various nationalist movements to control school boards, increasing political polarization between communities. By institutionalizing the language policy, a pragmatic issue was turned into a question of national rights. Nevertheless, practical compromises at the level of the crown lands (could still be reached in the early decades of the twentieth century (on the language issue in Moravia, Bukovina, and Galicia, for instance). Moreover, the state authorities consciously tried to encourage the traditional feelings of loyalty to the emperor, which culminated in an impressive celebration of the golden jubilee of Franz Joseph in 1898.[14]

After the Compromise of 1867, the Hungarian government began an active assimilationist policy. Around 1850, somewhat less than half of the population of the Kingdom of Hungary had Magyar as their mother tongue. This linguistic situation was not much different from France's; the main differences were that Magyar had become the sole official language only in 1867, and none of the minority tongues were part of the same language family, making it hard for others to learn the national language. Moreover, when compared to the nation-building activities of the Third Republic, there were a few significant disadvantages. First, the army remained imperial and its language of command was German, while minority languages—including Romanian, Slovak, and Serbian—functioned as regimental languages. As a consequence, the armed forces did not function as a Hungarian nationalization machine. Second, suffrage in Hungary was very restricted, so politics remained the domain of the largely Magyar-speaking nobility. There was no urgency to convert peasants into Hungarians, and accordingly, the budget for nation-building activities was limited. A third factor was that primary schools were largely in the hands of the various churches, which in general were divided along ethnic and linguistic lines. Their priority was religious education, not nationalist indoctrination, although over time they were obliged to adopt Magyar as the main language of instruction. In 1902, classes on Hungarian history, geography, and citizenship were added to the curriculum. Only in 1907 was education was free and compulsory. Finally, linguistic assimilation from below was not an important factor either, since Hungary could not offer many jobs in an expanding bureaucracy, nor did it have colonies, which could have served as attractive destinations for ambitious youngsters. Nonetheless, the share of Magyars in the census increased from 41.5 percent in 1850 to 54.4 in 1910. But except for Jews, who mostly adopted the Hungarian language, members of other ethnic minorities saw Magyarization policies as a form of coercion, which encouraged them to create their own nationalist associations, or to emigrate to neighboring countries or the United States.[15]

Nationalizing Empires

To some extent, Austria-Hungary could be defined as a "nationalizing empire." It was an empire that implemented many aspects of the nation-state, and Hungary pursued an active nation-building strategy.[16] The Russian Empire also was a nationalizing empire, although as a major, conservative power, it had been less inclined to adopt the more liberal aspects of the nation-state model. Regional assemblies had been introduced in 1865, but since then no further measures had been taken. The humiliating defeat in the war against Japan in 1905 was accompanied by widespread social unrest, which in the end forced Tsar Nicholas II to make new concessions. Russia finally received a constitution and a national parliament, the Duma, but as in Germany and Japan, the government was answerable to the monarch alone. Censorship was eased, and various civil rights were recognized. However, when the moderate land reform that would have enabled the peasant to leave the village community did not get the support of the majority of the representatives, the Duma was dissolved. Shortly afterward, the suffrage became more restrictive. The emancipation of the Jews, another government proposal, was vetoed by the tsar. Indeed, some high officials scapegoated Jews and disseminated antisemitic conspiracy theories. The authorities were at best passive during two waves of pogroms, first after the assassination of Alexander II and again between 1903 and 1906.[17]

Many scholars have argued that instead of a policy of liberalization, the empire pursued a Russification strategy that promoted the unity between the tsar and the population, of which about 65 percent spoke Russian or a closely related dialect/language. Nevertheless, recent studies have questioned the existence of a conscious, consistent, and protracted nation-building strategy. They hold that the assimilation of Poles, Jews, most Muslims in the Central Asian provinces, and nomadic peoples in Siberia was never the goal of the Russian government. Moreover, education was not a top priority; the literacy rate increased from less than 10 percent in 1880 to about 25 percent thirty years later. What did exist were worries about nationalist activities in the western provinces and an active policy to resettle farmers in the southern and eastern borderlands. In new industrial centers and along the Siberian frontier, Russian did become the lingua franca among the newcomers. In the west, large-scale uprisings in Congress Poland in 1830 and 1863 caused major headaches for the Russian government. In 1864 the Polish territories were integrated into the empire, and Russian became the language of administration and education. Likewise, the authorities were concerned about the loyalty of the other territories that had been part of the Polish-Lithuanian Commonwealth; there, the Polish Uprising of 1830 had found widespread resonance. In the 1830s, the Uniates—members of the Orthodox Church who in 1438 had accepted the authority of the pope in Rome—were forced to unify with the Russian Orthodox Church. Moreover, Ukrainian and Belarusian were treated as Russian dialects, so education and publications in these "would-be languages" was strongly discouraged. After the Second Polish Uprising in 1863, the emphasis on the use of Russian clearly increased. In 1899 Nicholas II even attempted to fully integrate the Grand Duchy of Finland into the empire, which until then had been connected to the tsar by personal union. Russian became the language of the administration, and Finns were conscripted into the imperial army. This Russification policy backfired, strongly encouraging the rise of Finnish nationalism, and the same happened with other minority groups in the more developed western provinces of the empire.[18]

In the Ottoman Empire, reforms stalled after the suspension of the constitution in 1878. Like the Russian tsars, Sultan Abdülhamid II pursued an authoritarian course, in which economic development was combined with a renewed emphasis on religion—foregrounding his role as caliph—and traditional loyalty to the dynasty. However, because of financial difficulties and the absence of a serious self-strengthening policy, not much progress was made in the modernization of the administration, the army, and the educational system. Literacy rates lagged behind even those of Russia. In 1908, a military coup by the Young Turks restored the constitution. The new regime aimed to strengthen the Ottoman state but had difficulty remaining in power. It made conscription obligatory for both Muslims and non-Muslims, centralized the bureaucracy, put greater emphasis on Ottoman Turkish as the language of administration and education, and added citizenship classes to the curriculum.[19]

As elsewhere, democratization led to renewed nationalist polarization, but there were also major religious fault lines. After the independence of Romania, Serbia, and Montenegro in 1878, the Christian minority had become considerably smaller. At the same time, about 1.5 million Muslims emigrated from the newly independent Christian states to the remaining parts of the empire. In earlier decades, as many as two million Muslims had fled territories along the Black Sea and the Caucasus after they were conquered by the Russian Empire, which added to the feelings of beleaguerment and persecution. Resentment among the Muslim majority was fanned by the fact that many modern sectors of the economy, such as commerce, industry, and banking, were dominated by non-Muslims such as Jews, Armenians, and Greeks.[20]

Many of the Christian minorities, on the other hand, expected outside support. Most new Balkan countries had come into existence thanks to foreign diplomatic or military intervention. With the Treaty of Berlin, the Western powers had obliged the sultan to promise reforms in the Eastern Anatolian provinces, where Christian Armenians formed a substantial minority. Around 1890, Armenian nationalists became a factor in the neighboring provinces of the

Russian Empire, and they subsequently began a terrorist campaign in the Ottoman Empire (which later spread to Russia) to draw attention to the oppression of the Armenian population. In response, the government created Kurdish militias to maintain order in the Ottoman borderlands. In 1894, a tax revolt in Sasun led to a massacre of its Armenian population, and violence soon spilled over to other parts of the Ottoman Empire. Although further pogroms against Armenians in Russia in 1905 and the Ottoman Empire in 1909 would move Western public opinion, no serious attempts were undertaken to come to their rescue. Because the Armenians did not have a territory where they formed a majority, and because they were living in faraway borderlands between the Russian, Persian, and Ottoman Empires, geopolitics did not work in their favor. Nonetheless, other Christian minorities (on Crete and in the Balkans, for instance) pursued a similar strategy of engaging in violent protests to capture the attention of the Western powers. The growing polarization, combined with centralizing efforts by the Young Turks and open warfare during the Balkan Wars of 1912 to 1913, also led to nationalist mobilization among Muslim minorities such as Arabs and Albanians, eventually leading to the creation of a new Albanian nation-state in 1912 (map 5.1).[21]

The economic and political turbulence in Russia in 1905 also triggered a revolution in the neighboring Persian Empire. Similar to what happened to other patrimonial states, military defeats during the early decades of the nineteenth century had forced the Qajar dynasty to strengthen and modernize the state, but most reforms were very modest or were abandoned after several years. At the beginning of the twentieth century, central power was weak and the empire was still governed largely indirectly, through local notables and tribal leaders. The turmoil in Russia affected the Persian economy, and the subsequent sociopolitical unrest forced Muzaffar al-Din Shah to announce elections for a constituent assembly. The new constitution was modeled on the liberal Belgian example and recognized all kinds of civil rights. Nevertheless, Shi'i Islam was declared the official religion of the state, and religious courts remained responsible for implementing shari'a. In 1911 the new government introduced universal male suffrage. However, without a modern bureaucracy and heavily curtailed by foreign intervention—customs had been under European control since 1900, and seven years later the United Kingdom and the Russian Empire divided Persia into zones of influence—the Persian authorities had no means to reinforce their presence in the countryside, leaving ample space to provincial warlords and tribal leaders.[22]

Another weak nationalizing empire was China. The reticent policy of the Qing regime, wavering between reactionary nativism, authoritarian reform, and full-scale Westernization, became untenable after the humiliating defeat in the war with Japan over the domination of Korea in 1895. This triggered

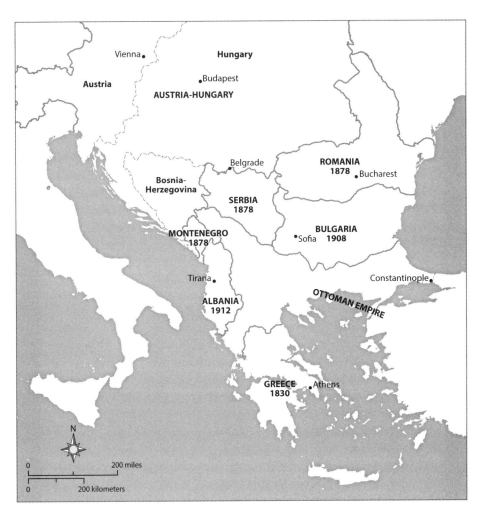

MAP 5.1 The Balkans in 1912. The former Ottoman province of Bosnia-Herzegovina had been annexed by Austria-Hungary in 1908. Greece, Serbia, Montenegro, Romania, Bulgaria, and Albania had seceded from the Ottoman Empire, often with open support from major European powers. The date of independence for each country is indicated on the map.

another round of foreign encroachments whereby Western powers extended their concessions and spheres of influence. Kang Youwei now prompted the young Guangxu Emperor to modernize the administration, the army, the educational system, and the examinations system, but Empress Dowager Cixi ended the Hundred Days of Reform by putting her nephew, the emperor, under house arrest. The strength of conservative forces also became clear during the Boxer Rebellion of 1899 to 1901. Popular unrest had been focused by the Boxers United in Righteousness, a semireligious mass movement that used martial arts and magic spirits to drive out the foreigners. The traditionalist violence against foreigners and Chinese Christians—who were made scapegoats, much like the Armenians and Jews in the Ottoman and Russian Empires—triggered a military intervention by eight major powers, including Japan. They quickly defeated the Boxers and the Qing army, occupied Beijing, and sacked the new Summer Palace.[23]

The Chinese government understood that more radical reforms were needed, and many were introduced in the following decade. It had to draft modern law codes, abolish collective and physical punishments, and prepare a constitution—modeled on Japan's—before it could abolish the unpopular extraterritorial rights of foreigners. The civil service examinations were abrogated, and after local and provincial assemblies were introduced, China elected a national parliament in 1910. Loans, nationalizations, and tax reforms would provide the resources for modern schools and new provincial armies. However, there was mounting discontent with the Manchu Qings, who were now seen as a "foreign" dynasty. A local uprising in the summer of 1911 rapidly escalated into a widespread revolt, which finally toppled the empire. Sun Yat-sen, the leader of the Guomindang, the recently established Chinese nationalist party, proclaimed a democratic republic. But the actual strongman of the new regime was Yuan Shikai, who led the strongest modern army corps. He became a kind of military dictator, and in 1915 he even tried to revive the empire. With his death in the following year, the authority of the central government was fatally undermined, effectively conferring power on the regional military governors, who established themselves as warlords.[24]

Democratization also led to polarization along national lines, but this happened mostly in peripheral parts of the empire that had not been fully integrated into the state. Although the linguistic diversity within China proper was very considerable, the use of a common script based on characters enabled communication between literate elites. Moreover, the exam system had encouraged the cultural assimilation of wide strata of the population by teaching a shared canon of classical texts. By the end of the nineteenth century there were about five million classically trained literati. Under the Qing, the empire had been extended into Manchuria, Mongolia, Xinjiang, and Tibet, which continued to be governed indirectly through their own feudal elites. The authorities in these areas tried to prevent assimilation of the population by discouraging intermarriage, immigration, and learning the Chinese language. Nevertheless, during the nineteenth century the number of Han Chinese migrants into Manchuria and Xinjiang had grown massively. The 1911 Revolution was accompanied by strong anti-Manchu feelings, and although the official rhetoric now spoke of a five-nation republic consisting of Han, Manchus, Mongols, Tibetans, and Muslims, the new regime was effectively dominated by the Han Chinese majority. Moreover, the principle of civic equality threatened the privileges of feudal elites in the periphery. As a consequence, when the empire disappeared, the traditional Buddhist leadership of Tibet and Mongolia, encouraged by Great Britain and Russia, respectively, decided to relinquish their bonds with China and proclaim independence, but without adopting the nation-state model, which by that time had become quite exceptional.[25]

Japan was by far the most successful of the Eurasian empires in adopting the nation-state model. In 1889 the government granted a constitution and a national parliament. Although the Diet could not force the government to resign, it flexed its muscles by frequently rejecting the budgets of individual ministers. In the late nineteenth century, Japan also introduced conscription, equality before the law, and a civil code. Ethnic diversity was not really an issue; nevertheless, the Japanese government pursued an active nation-building policy. In 1872 it had already introduced centralized primary education along the same lines as France. Over time, influenced by modern pedagogical ideas, there was more emphasis put on ethics, combining Western ideas on character building and traditional Confucian ideas. Finally, as in Austria and the Ottoman Empire, the authorities encouraged loyalty to the emperor—who, as a descendent of the Sun Goddess, provided the religiously colored legitimization for the new regime. Japan also gained international respect by inflicting crushing defeats on China in 1895 and the Russian Empire in 1905.[26]

Foreign recognition was a very sensitive issue. Japanese politicians were aware of the fates of China, Egypt, and the Ottoman Empire, not to mention the many parts of the world that had been colonized by European powers. In 1894 Japan renegotiated the trade agreement with Great Britain and succeeded in abolishing the extraterritorial rights of British citizens and restoring full Japanese sovereignty. It could now determine its own tariffs. Other Western powers quickly followed, abrogating the hated unequal treaties. The question of extraterritoriality was crucial, and it can uncover some of the mechanisms of the dissemination of the nation-state model. In most parts of Asia, and in early modern Europe, legal pluralism had been the rule, while monarchs generally claimed sovereignty over subjects rather than over territories. This changed with the invention of the nation-state. The French Revolution did away with legal pluralism and turned the borders of the state into hard legal boundaries. Thus, when the trade treaties between Western powers and Asian states gave Europeans the right to have their own consular courts to deal with the legal issues of their citizens residing in the Asian monarchies, this was in accordance with traditional practices. But Ottomans, Chinese, and Japanese did not have the same rights in European or American countries; the idea of allowing foreigners or minorities to settle their own legal issues clashed with the territorial jurisdiction that had become the norm in the Western nation-states. Moreover, Europeans and Americans argued that they could not submit themselves to the "barbarous" legal practices, such as torture and corporal punishment, that were still the rule in many Asian countries. Japanese discussions from the 1870s onward make clear that many intellectuals were aware that the "unequal treaties" could be abolished only by adopting "civilized" legal and penal practices. Abolishing corporal punishments, adopting a constitution, introducing modern civil and criminal codes, and installing an independent judiciary were crucial preconditions for being treated as an equal, "civilized" partner in the international arena. The alternative would be to abolish the treaties unilaterally, but this would be unacceptable to the Western powers and would lead to conflicts.[27]

So revision of the treaties—and implicitly, recognition of Japan's full national sovereignty—was viable only after Japan had become a constitutional state that adopted the rule of law according to Western standards. Japan was not obliged by force to conform to these norms, but it had no option but to comply if it wanted to be taken seriously as an equal partner, which shows how isomorphism functioned. The institutions of the nation-states showed a clear tendency to become similar, and in many cases almost identical, and the same was true for legal codes, bureaucratic procedures, rules for citizenship, forms of education, and so on. Sometimes these changes were imposed by an external power, which usually happened in colonies and protectorates. In independent states, this occurred through attraction or mimesis; Japan is the perfect example of this.

Nationalization Processes in Southeast Asia and Africa

In the colonies, various aspects of modern statehood were introduced by the imperial authorities, a process that was already well underway in Asia, where European powers were expanding their colonial possessions. The Netherlands, for instance, brought the East Indies under more effective control, also conquering Aceh and Bali, while the British expanded their control over Burma, the Straits Settlements, and the Federated Malay States. Increased taxation, improved infrastructures, a more commercially oriented agriculture, legal codifications, and the introduction of modern education profoundly affected local societies. Following the example of British India, Westminster also introduced legislative councils in Singapore and Burma, but the majority of the Indigenous members were appointed and the colonial authorities preserved veto rights. Unlike in the dominions, power remained firmly in British hands.[28]

Modern political institutions were not introduced by France, which incorporated its recent colonial acquisitions in Southeast Asia in the Indochinese

Union in 1887. Although the union was not a centralized colony, the development of export sectors such as rice and rubber was strongly encouraged in all
parts of it, and railroads were constructed and Western education extended.
A romanized script was introduced to replace the use of Chinese characters
and pull Indochina away from the Chinese sphere of influence. Like elsewhere,
these reforms were financed largely by raising taxes.[29]

U.S. policies in the Philippines might seem more enlightened—the goal
was to civilize and educate the inhabitants in self-government—but they took
off only after the archipelago had been brutally pacified. The new administration quickly installed a public school system using the English language, improved the infrastructure, and imposed public health measures. In 1907 the
first elections for a Philippine assembly were held, with the franchise restricted
to literate, tax-paying males. Although the elections were won by the Nationalist Party, which was in favor of immediate independence, the governor-general
retained extensive veto powers and blocked many initiatives of the new representative institutions.[30]

A similar process of modern state-building began in Africa, but it was far
from straightforward. The Conference of Berlin resulted in a quick scramble for
African territories. In subsequent treaties, the European powers decided on the
exact—mostly straight—borders between their respective colonies. The sub-
jection of the population took more time, with uprisings occurring frequently
until the first decade of the twentieth century. Because of the general contempt
with which Europeans viewed the "savage" inhabitants, "rebellions" were
usually repressed with extraordinary violence. The goal of the occupation of
African lands was economic profit; hence, many territories, and in some cases,
entire colonies, were given to commercial companies. The German East Africa
Company, the South Cameroon Company, and the British South Africa Company received mining concessions and large swaths of land for plantations, and
often also the right to use forced labor and collect taxes, thus opening up many
parts of the continent to commercial agriculture and mining, while uprooting
the traditional livelihoods of large segments of the Indigenous population. It
was only in exceptional cases—such as French West Africa, where the military
was in charge—that more attention was given to public health care, modern
education, and infrastructure. Efforts to build a modern bureaucratic apparatus
were minimal, though this slightly changed after states began to take over the
administration from companies and Indigenous rulers.[31]

Modern state-building also occurred outside the new colonial empires, first
in small independent settler states such as Liberia, Transvaal, and Orange Free
State. But this process can also be detected in many indigenous states; Madagascar and Ethiopia are the best illustrations of this. We have already seen how
Radama I of Madagascar had modernized his kingdom during the first decades

of the nineteenth century. In the 1860s the Westernization process was taken up again. Queen Ranavalona II and her husband, Prime Minister Rainilaia-rivony, converted to Christianity, undermining the traditional religious legiti-mization of the monarchy. In later years, a cabinet system was introduced, laws were codified, taxation was rationalized, African slaves were emancipated, and primary education became mandatory. However, the modernization of the economy was very limited, and the government became increasingly indebted to European creditors. After two French military interventions to protect European interests, Madagascar became a French colony in 1897.[32]

Ethiopia was a feudal state, in which various kings recognized the suzer-ainty of the emperor. Central power had been weak until Tewodros II as-cended to the imperial throne in 1855 and modernized the army. However, the technical assistance he hoped to get from Europe's fellow Christian powers did not materialize. One of his successors, Emperor Yohannes IV, succeeded in warding off an Egyptian invasion, frustrating Khedive Ismael's attempts to create a great African empire. After Yohannes's death, Menilek II, who had expanded his own kingdom substantially, proclaimed himself emperor in 1889. Meanwhile, Italy tried to expand its colonial acquisitions in Eritrea and Somaliland by turning Ethiopia into a protectorate. But Menilek secured his domestic power base and quickly increased his modern weapon arsenal, ac-quiring firearms from commercial dealers, but also from Italy and France. In 1896, when the Italian army advanced into Ethiopian territory, it suffered a humiliating defeat in Adwa against the emperor's much larger and well-equipped forces. Similar to what happened in Siam, the emperor consolidated his country's independence and even extended his territories by steering a middle course between French and British colonial interests. Menilek also embarked on a moderate authoritarian course of reform, modernizing the country's infrastructure. In 1908, Ethiopia became a member of the Universal Postal Union, and in 1917 the new capital, Addis Ababa, was connected by railway to the port of Djibouti. Menilek also adopted the cabinet system, a royal council, and a centralized administration of justice. He streamlined taxa-tion by measuring land holdings and introducing individual property rights, and he oversaw the first steps to introduce modern education. After 1917, Me-nilek's modernization course would be continued by Ras Tafari, first as regent for Empress Zawditu, and after 1930 as Emperor Haile Selassie.[33]

Citizenship

From about 1885, modern states began to interfere more actively in the economy. Not only did they become more directly involved in the economic exploitation of the colonies, they also raised tariffs to protect domestic markets, enacted antitrust laws, and adopted laws protecting workers. As a result of the Long Depression, there was widespread awareness in Europe, the Americas, and East Asia that poverty, unemployment, and the unhealthy living conditions of millions of people threatened the social fabric. Moreover, liberalizing travel and residence restrictions had implicitly made poor relief a national responsibility, while the extension of the suffrage had increased the electoral clout of the lower classes. As a consequence, governments began to protect workers against accidents, ruthless exploitation, and the temporary imbalances of the economic system. The German Empire pioneered the establishment of a social security system, both to safeguard the productivity of the labor force and as a response to a rapidly growing socialist movement. In 1883 and 1884 Bismarck had introduced insurances against sickness and accidents, and a pension system was adopted in 1891. In Great Britain, social housing schemes were developed at about the same time, and from 1906 to 1914 Liberal governments introduced a package of social reforms that included old-age pensions, free school meals, and compulsory health insurance. Other European countries adopted similar measures, binding working-class citizens closer to the state.[34] Governments in the Americas and Japan were much less actively involved, though they did take measures in the areas of labor regulations, public health, and urban planning. Voluntary associations and company insurance schemes were more common, partly because trade unions were often counteracted or prohibited by the authorities. In the Americas they tended to be weak because of the predominant position of agriculture, the large influx of fresh immigrants, and the high mobility of workers.[35]

Following the example of religious minorities and workers, women also began to fight for equal rights such as the vote, which was secured in New Zealand and Australia in the early 1890s. Finland and Norway followed suit in 1906 and 1913. Elsewhere, the spectacular protests by British suffragettes drew much attention. Feminists (the term was coined in France around the turn of the century) also demanded better employment and schooling opportunities, childcare, and access to birth control, challenging traditional views on gender roles. Many countries adopted protective laws that prohibited women from working at night or in dangerous industries, and some conservatives even proposed introducing family wages that would allow married women to be excluded from the job market. Although feminists did not approve of all of these measures, women increasingly were integrated into the nation and their situation became a topic for political debate.[36]

At the same time, measures to exclude "dangerous" members from the national community became harsher. Influenced by the new theories on evolution, scholars began to scrutinize hereditary factors to explain deviant behavior among the underclass. In the 1870s and 1880s most researchers still hoped that improving the "degenerate" living conditions of the urban poor could reduce crime, alcoholism, mental illness, and sexual depravity. Others, such as Cesare Lombroso, thought that skull measurements could help detect atavistic savages to exclude them from participating in the civic life of the nation. But with the more competitive international arena and the more pessimistic cultural climate of the turn of the century, many academics became increasingly worried. In Great Britain, in the context of the Boer Wars, there were serious concerns about the declining fitness of potential recruits. Some hoped that physical exercise might increase the well-being of the nation, but there was also growing support for Frances Galton's call for drastic "eugenic" measures. He argued that the urban poor procreated more rapidly than the "civilized" classes, upsetting the natural selection process described by Darwin. In France, many scholars and politicians argued that society should be shielded from incurable criminals and psychologically disturbed persons.[37]

These new ideas had practical consequences. In Germany, for example, there was a growing preoccupation with the emigration of millions of Germans to the New World. German nationalists called them "diaspora Germans," regretting their loss and implying that the bonds with the fatherland should be maintained. In 1913 their wishes were fulfilled when a legal reform decreed that German citizenship no longer expired after ten years and also that it was conferred on offspring. The purity of the German "race" was another concern. In 1905 mixed marriages in the colonies were banned, and immigration and naturalization laws were used to exclude and even expel Poles and Jews.[38] Racial exclusion was an important issue not only in the colonies, but also in the Americas. Since the 1870s and 1880s, Jim Crow laws had enforced racial segregation of public facilities in the U.S. South. In 1913, President Woodrow Wilson established segregation of the federal administration. The immigration of unwanted groups was also discouraged. In 1882 the United States barred Chinese laborers from citizenship and prohibited their immigration. Whereas Canada, Australia, and most Latin American states welcomed European migrants, they too discriminated against Asians, often even prohibiting their entry into the country.[39]

National Awareness

Toward the end of the nineteenth century, nationalism clearly swung to the right and tended to become more radical and pervasive. This was possible because the left largely abandoned the open, cosmopolitan nationalism that had been espoused by earlier generations. Now that legal equality and broad suffrage rights had become a reality, working-class parties began to strive for social justice, and they did so by becoming internationalist, proclaiming the solidarity of all workers. Nevertheless, they still were organized along national lines, and at the outbreak of the First World War they rallied behind the national flag. At about the same time, cosmopolitan free-trade liberals were outflanked by the more interventionist social liberals—also known as new liberals, progressives, or regenerationists—who were more focused on national issues, while traditional conservatives lost ground to a new populist right, for which Maurice Barrès now claimed the term "nationalist." New movements such as French Action, the Italian Nationalist Association, the Union of Russian People, and the Pan-German and Christian Social Parties in Germany and Austria used a mix of nationalist, antisemitic, and imperialistic rhetoric to mobilize the masses.[40]

Although there can be no doubt that nationalism affected many more people, its reach was still limited. Outside Western Europe and the Americas, the enthusiasm for a constitutional nation-state was not very widespread. Those in power in the traditional Eurasian empires understood that changes were needed to strengthen the state, but most opted for authoritarian reforms and opposed popular participation. When the revolutionary wave that began in 1905 jeopardized their survival, this had more to do with the burdens they placed on the population (e.g., higher taxes, conscription, economic dislocations) and their lack of success than with a deeply felt longing for a constitution and an elected parliament. Only small groups of intellectuals and officials, such as the Young Turks, the Russian Constitutional Democrats, and the Guomindang, welcomed a thorough democratization along Western lines. Nationalist activists in India and Indochina such as Phan Boi Chau pursued similar ideas, although their main concern was to transform or overthrow colonial rule. In Japan a constitution was adopted mostly so that the unequal treaties with foreign powers could be revised. Even in established nation-states, support for the constitutional system was limited; political patronage flourished in many countries as voters and politicians put their personal interests before those of the nation.

The idea that each nation has its own culture and heritage that needed protection was still foreign to most people, even those in powerful positions. In 1908 the Coptic patriarch of Egypt wanted to melt down old church vessels and gospel covers to salvage the silver, but he was stopped by Marcus Simaika, a notable with a clear historical interest who brought together the money to buy the precious objects and exhibit them in a small museum. A few years later, on the occasion of the visit of the U.S. president Theodore Roosevelt, another notable suggested giving the most valuable manuscript of the collection to their guest of honor. In Colombia, the Conservative president Carlos Holguín bought a recently discovered pre-Columbian treasure to show in the Colombian section at the American Historical Exposition in Madrid and Chicago's World's Columbian Exposition. Afterward, instead of preserving these important archaeological finds, he offered many of the best pieces to the Spanish queen regent, and the rest was sold in the United States.[41] Similar attitudes could be found among European peasants. When in 1908 two Russian folklorists wanted to record traditional peasant songs in the region of Belozersk, they were met with suspicion: these strangers with their devilish phonograph could be secret police or even Japanese spies, and their own "backward tunes" were of no interest whatsoever. At about the same time, well-to-do German farmers in Mecklenburg preferred to construct new modern urban houses rather than the picturesque rural dwellings proposed to them by an architect, arguing that these buildings reflected their supposedly ancestral traditions.[42]

On top of that, many people in Europe and the Americas did not know to which nation they belonged. In this regard, a fascinating case is Macedonia, which was constituted by three ethnically mixed Ottoman provinces where Slav-speaking Orthodox Christians formed a small majority. People identified themselves primarily by their religion or occupation, not by ethnicity or nationality. The area was claimed by Bulgaria, because the dialects spoken by most inhabitants were closely linked to Bulgarian. Serbia defined the population as Southern or Old Serbs, while Greece referred to them as Slav-speaking Greeks, thus staking their own claim. Since education was organized largely through religious communities, the Orthodox children who went to school were taught in Greek. A bloody conflict arose in 1870 when next to the Greek Orthodox Church an autonomous Bulgarian exarchate was created; both tried to convince parishes to come over to their side, which also meant control over Church properties, schools, and language of education. In 1893 the clandestine Internal Macedonian Revolutionary Organization was created, and it used violence to force the Ottoman authorities to grant the region autonomy. Some of its members wanted unification with Bulgaria, while others pleaded for a "Macedonia for the Macedonians" that ultimately would become an autonomous part of a wider Balkan federation. An uprising in 1903 was meant to spark foreign intervention, but the limited interference of the great powers brought no enduring solution. As a result, Macedonia became the main prize for all its neighboring countries during the Balkan Wars of 1912 and 1913.[43]

The national classification of populations was not very obvious in other parts of East-Central Europe either, especially where religious and ethnic boundaries did not overlap, as in the cases of Ukrainian Catholics, Albanian Orthodox Christians, and Serbian and Bulgarian Muslims. Moreover, many people felt strong affinities with various imagined communities. One could be Breton and French, Welsh and British, Sardinian and Italian, or Bavarian and German.[44] Even in the 1920s Polish and Soviet officials still found it hard to determine the nationality of the inhabitants of the borderlands, where Polish and Ukrainian dialects were hardly distinguishable and people identified as "peasants," "Catholics," or "people from here." In many parts, farmers who spoke different languages lodged their children with each other to enable them to become bilingual, and children were sent to the "wrong" school to enhance their chances for the future. Intermarriage was common, and many people were bilingual or trilingual. Switching "sides" in return for material rewards such as free schooling, or because of changing political contexts, happened very often. Nevertheless, similar forms of "national indifference" could also be found in Western Europe, where peasants often opposed the schooling of their children and Catholic priests used dialects or minority languages to communicate with their flocks. In 1908, activists proposed that Moresnet, a tiny neutral territory located between Belgium, Germany, and the Netherlands, should adopt the artificial international language Esperanto, an idea that was well received but in the end, failed to materialize.[45]

Nationalization of Culture

During the decades around the turn of the century, many academics tried to ground nations more firmly in the past. Instead of defining nations on the basis of language, which could be changed relatively easily by learning another tongue, many now became interested in more enduring biological factors and the long-term impact of the natural environment. Although this period certainly was characterized by an intensification of nationalist sentiments, the national framework surprisingly was less taken for granted. Some scholars argued that racial categories were more important than national boundaries for understanding human differences. Radical ideas about the unsurmountable differences between races, such as those voiced by Robert Knox and Arthur de Gobineau in the 1850s, became more fashionable toward the end of the century. Probably inspired by the new imperialistic mood after the scramble for Africa, a fresh wave of publications reached a much wider audience; these included Georges Vacher de Lapouge's *The Aryan: His Social Role* (1899), Houston Chamberlain's *The Foundations of the Nineteenth Century* (1899), and the fiercely antisemitic *Jewish France* (1886) by Edouard Drumont.[46] Although racial theories would have a huge impact on many (right-wing) nationalists, in most instances, racial categories did not overlap with existing nation-states or with ethnically or culturally defined nations.

These theories were also adopted outside of Europe and the Americas. In India, for instance, the ideas about a shared Indo-European language that had originated in an Aryan homeland in Central Asia were popularized by the Oxford philologist Max Mueller, who argued that the "southern Aryans" had conquered India. The Brahmins and other upper-caste Indians accordingly were the descendants of these fair-complexed speakers of Sanskrit, while the lower castes and the Dalits descended from the Indigenous population. From about the 1870s, these ideas were taken up by Hindu authors. In 1875 in Bombay, Dayananda Saraswati founded the Society of Aryans, which aimed to disseminate the idea of the Aryans as the original inhabitants of the world, to whom the word of God was revealed in the form of the Vedas, the sacred texts of the Hindus. He also associated the upper castes with the Aryans, although he rejected the idea of the hereditarian character of the caste system. Other activists argued that the British and the Hindus were in fact two branches of the same "Aryan race"; in *The Arctic Home in the Vedas* (1903) the Indian nationalist Bal Ganghadar Tilak went further, claiming that the "southern Aryans," unlike the European branch, had preserved their original, superior civilization. At about the same time, the British colonial official Herbert Hope Risley conducted an ambitious ethnographic survey, largely based on the physical measurements of members of the population, which aimed to prove that the higher castes and the peasants from Northern India were of Aryan stock, whereas the lower castes and most inhabitants of the South belonged to the less civilized Dravidian "race."[47]

In the recently institutionalized academic discipline of geography, scholars also frequently referred to larger areas, especially in the debate on "geopolitics," a term introduced by Rudolf Kjellén. A crucial question was whether maritime or continental empires would dominate the world. Alfred Thayer Mahan defended the importance of sea power, whereas Halford Mackinder thought that land empires would have the upper hand. Both of them divided the world in enormous geopolitical regions. In 1904 Mackinder discerned three regions: the pivot area (the large Eurasian mass that at the time was dominated by the Russian Empire), a marginal crescent around it, and an outer insular crescent. Other scholars devised a more fine-grained division, distinguishing, for instance, Central Europe, the Baltic area, and Eastern, Southern, and Western Europe, while implicitly arguing that it was logical for each of these geographical areas to be dominated by one power. These authors apparently saw a kind of Darwinian struggle for survival among the major powers as a self-evident fact. Friedrich Ratzel, for instance, interpreted states as living organisms that were determined by the interaction between a population and its natural environment and that expanded or decreased, depending on their vitality. Therefore, he argued, it was natural for strong states to conquer "living space" and dominate others.[48]

Interestingly, geographers also began to contest the internal homogeneity of existing nation-states. Paul Vidal de la Blache argued in *Geographical Tableau of France* (1903) that his fatherland consisted of a variety of different regions, each with its own geographic, climatic, and natural peculiarities. The inhabitants were strongly impacted by these circumstances, but the influence was reciprocal. By cultivating the land and using its resources, they created particular ways of life and at the same time, transformed the land. As a result, each region had its own peculiar culture. This did not necessarily lead to conflicts: most regions complemented each other, forming a harmonious national whole—at least in the case of France. Elsewhere, similar ideas were put into practice. Patrick Geddes also propagated a regional geographical approach, applying it to various parts of Scotland, India, and Palestine. In 1919, Charles Bungay Fawcett presented a map of England in which the existing counties, with their rather arbitrary boundaries, were replaced by larger provinces based on more objective natural and cultural criteria. This way, it was easier to take into account the peculiar circumstances of each area.[49]

In the field of biology, nature was also studied in its regional embeddedness. New disciplines such as ecology, plant geography, and plant sociology studied the rootedness of "plant communities" in specific geological, geographical, and climatic conditions. Remarkably, many scholars focused on the regional variety within existing countries, thus taking national borders for granted. The influential garden architect Willy Lange divided Germany into three different zones: mountainous, intermediate, and plain landscape. His American colleague, Frank A. Waugh, similarly distinguished four landscape types for the United States.[50]

A strong focus on substate regions can also be detected in folklore studies, which made a comeback toward the end of the nineteenth century. The number of associations and journals grew rapidly, while the first chair for folklore was created in 1886 at the University of Oslo. Folklorists documented the folk tales, traditions, songs, and customs that could shed light on the interaction between a local population and their natural environment over the ages. In many regions these popular traditions had largely disappeared, but among peasants and fishermen in more peripheral "relic areas," such as Dalarna in Sweden, the Zuiderzee area in the Netherlands, and Karelia in Finland, they were still very much alive. To determine the spatial distribution of these traditions, the next step was to create ethnographic atlases, which, again, took national boundaries as their starting point. At about the same time, the interest in the "authentic" folkloric traditions of Indigenous communities was rapidly growing, both in the Americas, where until then they had been generally disregarded as relics of a bygone era, and in Japan, where Yanagita Kunio began to study the folkloric traditions of the Japanese countryside.[51]

Art historians and cultural critics also began to utilize a variety of geographical levels in their studies. Julius Langbehn, whose *Rembrandt as Educator* (1890) became a bestseller in Germany, used the Germanic-speaking areas as a meaningful demarcation while presenting Rembrandt and Shakespeare as important sources of inspiration for a rebirth of German culture—they had been the most individual and therefore the most "German" creative geniuses. At the same time, he distinguished various Germanic tribes, each with its own character traits, while arguing that Lower Germany—where he himself was born—would lead the country's spiritual rebirth. Interestingly, he did not describe his views as an objective analysis of the past, but as a call for the future. All cultural expressions had to be rooted in the best ancestral traditions, and "unhealthy" foreign influences that did not fit the nation's personality should be excluded. About twenty years later, the German art historian Wilhelm Worringer contrasted the Gothic, transcendental inclinations of Nordic artists—among whom he included the Germans—with the more realist and "emphatic" art of Mediterranean peoples. In turn, the Mediterranean or Latin heritage was defended by influential authors such as Charles Maurras, José Ortega y Gasset, and Eugenio d'Ors, whose ideas were taken up by artists such as Aristide Maillol and Giorgio de Chirico. Further east, artists and intellectuals such as Alphonse Mucha, Nikolai Roerich, Wassily Kandinsky, Abanindranath Tagore, and Okakura Kakuzō became fascinated by primitive Scythian, Slav, Eurasian, and Asian artistic traditions.[52] At about the same time in Latin America, José Enrique Rodó defended Latin "spirituality" against Anglo-Saxon materialism, while Swami Vivekananda, a reformist Hindu monk, and the poet Rabindranath Tagore defended Asian spirituality against the materialism of the West.[53]

A fascinating case of this search for origins, which fundamentally questioned accepted boundaries, can be found in the iconoclastic work of the Austrian art historian Josef Strzygowski. In his publications he replaced the traditional south-north orientation of art history, in which Greece, Rome, and Italy were presented as the cradle of Western civilization, with a new east-west axis connecting Northern Europe with the Middle East and Central Asia. In *Orient or Rome* (1901) he asserted that European medieval art had its roots in the Hellenic, Coptic, and Byzantine worlds. In subsequent years, he studied early artistic expressions from Anatolia, Armenia, Persia, and Central Asia in order to show that their decorative patterns and construction techniques had a decisive impact on the Germanic and Nordic worlds. During the First World War he radicalized his views, arguing that the traditional focus on monumental architecture and figurative art had excluded the decorative art and wooden architecture of the Nordic peoples, which they shared with their "tribal brothers" in Iran and India. He thus combined an exceptionally broad geographical reach with a profound German nationalism; toward the end of his life, he would become a dedicated Nazi.[54]

Nevertheless, the majority of art historians, like most of their colleagues in the humanities and social sciences, continued to take the framework of the nation for granted. Admittedly, many historians examined the impacts of ancient tribes, such as the rivalries between Anglo-Saxons and Celts in what was now the United Kingdom or between Franks and Gauls in France. Others focused on the role of geography, the prime example being Frederick Jackson Turner's explanation of the development of American self-reliance and democratic spirit from the frontier mentality of the settlers. More emphasis was also put on the contributions of individual countries to the "glorious" history of Western expansion and the civilizing mission in the colonies, but most scholars continued to narrate the political and cultural evolution of their own nations. The nation-state also constituted the main framework for new disciplines such as sociology, economics, and political science, where scholars such as Alfred Marshall, Émile Durkheim, and Max Weber, focused primarily on differences within "society," which clearly meant "national society."[55]

The nation-state also was the starting point for the academic discipline of international law, which had been institutionalized during the second half of the nineteenth century. Whereas earlier experts had focused on the concrete actions of princes and diplomats, a new generation of professional scholars, including Gustave Rolin-Jaequemyns, Johann Kaspar Bluntschli, and John Westlake, argued that international law was founded not in the legislation of sovereigns but in the society of states, by which they meant the "family of advanced nations." In the "civilized world," peoples governed themselves, while respecting the rights of individuals. International law, as a result, depended on the civilized behavior of the Western states among themselves. Whereas the Ottoman Empire and Meiji Japan were seen as dubious aspirant members of this international community of "civilized" states, "barbaric" countries such as Persia, China, and Siam were excluded. Although treaties could be concluded with them, because they were "fanatical" and lacked "restraint" they could not be trusted to put Western individuals on trial. Western citizens deserved to be judged by civilized powers. "Savage tribes" fell entirely outside of the realm of international law, although many scholars argued that as "minors" they should be treated with "gentleness" and "persuasion." However, this humanitarian discourse had its limits, especially after the rise of social Darwinian ideas and modern imperialism. The agreements on the rules of war adopted at the peace conferences of The Hague in 1899 and 1907 applied only to the "civilized" signatory powers, and as a consequence, they were not valid in colonial wars. Thus, in 1900, when the German emperor dispatched his troops to quell the Boxer Rebellion in China, he urged them to fight in the spirit of the "Huns," as the Chinese were not an integral "subject" of international law. This also implicates that treaties between colonial powers and Indigenous kingdoms or tribes were not recognized in international law cases because the latter did not possess sovereign powers. Remarkably, this is still relevant for border disputes in Africa.[56]

Both the intensification of the nationalist sentiment and the interest in a broad variety of territorial identities could be seen in the cultural realm as well. Artist colonies became more significant, in both the number of colonies and the

FIGURE 5.1 Carl Bantzer, *Communion at a Hessian Village Church*, 1892, oil on canvas, 160 × 249 cm. The artist painted an idyllic picture of a rural German community. In fact, however, social relations in Willingshausen were very tense, and his models were drunk day laborers instead of respectable independent farmers.

number of artists. Enterprising hotel owners often played a crucial role by providing lodgings, credit, models, and traditional costumes and other attributes.[57] Many painters began to more faithfully document the specific characters of individual regions and villages by focusing on vernacular buildings, characteristic landscapes, and folkloric traditions, mostly transmitting the image of a rural idyll of hard work, harmony, and fulfillment, which contrasted sharply with the episodes of class war in industrial areas. In fact, though, social relations between landlords, independent farmers, and the large population of day laborers were frequently very tense in these supposedly arcadian communities. This was the case in Willingshausen, which was the favorite location for Carl Bantzer's paintings. The residents of the area elected a virulently antisemitic populist as their representative in the Reichstag, and in order to produce an "authentic" image of the region's proud and self-conscious farmers in his *Communion at a Hessian Village Church* (1892; figure 5.1), Bantzer had to resort to recruiting destitute and drunk laborers to sit as his models.[58]

Many Western artists explicitly wanted to document the nation's traditions and its characteristic landscapes. The openly nationalist artists Ferdinand Hodler and Joaquín Sorolla both painted series of huge canvasses that represented the people, landscapes, and traditions of the various regions of their fatherlands, adopting painting styles that presumably conformed to national traditions and reflected the "archaic" brutality of the Swiss mountains and the luminosity of the Mediterranean coast, respectively. Akseli Gallén-Kallela and Alphonse Mucha focused on the mythological histories of Finland and the Slav peoples, respectively.[59] Curiously, both Mucha and Sorolla received financial support from wealthy American patrons, Charles Crane and Archer Huntington, who appreciated picturesque images of traditional rural communities. Most of the residents of the European artist colonies were foreigners as well—there was usually a large contingent of British and American painters. They played a pioneering role in selecting the motifs that were recognized and appreciated by the public in the Parisian salons and other art exhibitions. The folkloric image of the Netherlands—with fishing villages, windmills, tulip fields, and wooden shoes—was created mainly by American and German painters such as George Hitchcock, Gari Melchers, and Max Liebermann. A good example is Melchers's *In Holland* (1890; figure 5.2), depicting two traditionally dressed girls descending a sand dune, with a windmill and the red roofs of a village in the background.[60]

European artists also went to the colonies, where artistic societies and art academies were established and where they tried to capture the essence of the local "popular spirit." Their art has often been denigrated as orientalist or imperialist, but implicitly they contributed to the definition of national identities in the non-Western world. This trend, moreover, was also taken up by Asian artists who focused on picturesque topics and began to develop proper national styles. In 1898 Okakura Kakuzō and likeminded artists such as Yokoyama Taikan established the Japan Art Institute, where indigenous artistic traditions were the principal source of inspiration. Motivated partly by Okakura's visits to India, Abanindranath Tagore made the Government College of Art in Kolkata the base for a new Bengal school that focused on the artistic heritage of India and East Asia. Inspired by Mughal miniatures, Tagore painted *The Passing of Shah Jahan* (1902; figure 5.3), which depicted the emperor lying on his deathbed, with his daughter at his feet, looking out over the Taj Mahal, the famous mausoleum he had built for his favorite wife.[61]

Avant-garde artists generally had a very cosmopolitan outlook, but many also worked for longer periods in rural or seaside artist colonies. Paul Gauguin stayed in Pont-Aven, the fauves worked in Collioure, and Murnau became a springboard for the careers of expressionists such as Wassily Kandinsky and Gabriele Münter. In their drive to break with the academic and realist traditions of Western art, they were also fascinated by non-Western art. Gauguin moved to Tahiti, Vincent van Gogh was fascinated by Japanese prints, Pablo Picasso used African masks as a source of inspiration, and Franz Marc and

FIGURE 5.2 Gari Melchers, *In Holland*, 1890, oil on canvas, 277 × 198 cm. Foreign artists, like this American painter, had a crucial role in creating a stereotypical image of the Netherlands, with fishing villages, windmills, red-tiled houses, and folkloric costumes.

Kandinsky included not only children's drawings, peasant art, and medieval works in their famous almanac of the Blaue Reiter (Blue Rider), but also non-Western "primitive" art. At about the same time, Igor Stravinsky used "primitive" pagan traditions in his *Rites of Spring* to break with some of the stifling conventions of classical music. This longing for cultural innovation could also have nationalist implications. Marc and Kandinsky, for instance, argued that

FIGURE 5.3 Abanindranath Tagore, *The Passing of Shah Jahan*, 1902, oil on board, 35 × 25 cm. The painter drew inspiration from India's past by adopting formal aspects from traditional Mughal miniatures and by depicting a historical scene: the final moments of Emperor Jahan, who had built the famous Taj Mahal—which can be seen in the background—for his favorite wife.

they were looking for a new collective style that could express the widely felt sense of loss in an increasingly chaotic world. Based on the insights of Worringer, authors such as Paul Fechter interpreted this transcendental longing for meaning as a typical German character trait, which could be detected in both the Nordic Gothic cathedrals of the Middle Ages and the new expressionist paintings.[62]

Composers also showed a renewed interest in folk music, and some of them combined traditional music with national themes. Jean Sibelius composed the

Karelia Suite (1893), inspired by folk music from what was considered to be the most authentic part of Finland. His *Kullervo* (1892) and *Lemminkaïnen Suite* (1895) were based on the *Kalevala*, the Finnish national epic that had been the topic of many paintings of Gallén-Kallela. Sibelius's *Finlandia* (1900) evoked the struggle for national liberation of the Finnish people suffering under the increasingly repressive Russian yoke. In Spain, young composers such as Isaac Albéniz, Manuel de Falla, and Enrique Granados incorporated Andalusian folk music into their pieces and dedicated compositions to great figures of the Spanish cultural heritage such as Francisco Goya and Miguel de Cervantes. Many musicians, such as Béla Bartók, went out into the countryside to collect traditional songs. The English Folk-Song Society was particularly active in this respect. Lucy Broadwood and Cecil Sharp collected thousands of songs from various parts of the United Kingdom, and Sharp also revived the traditional Morris dances. Their work inspired many composers to write pieces capturing the "soul" of specific regions, such as Gustav Holst's *The Cotswolds* (1900) and *Somerset Rhapsody* (1907).[63] Similar trends can be detected outside of Europe. Chinnaswami Mudaliar studied the Carnatic music of southern India, and Vishnu Narayan Bhatkhande did extensive fieldwork and published thousands of orally transmitted "Hindu" compositions in a six-volume work. In the Dutch Indies, local elites became interested in the traditional gamelan music from Java. Larger geographical traditions were also incorporated into national canons. Thus, Japanese scholars investigated Asian musical traditions, while in Latin America—particularly in Brazil—the African musical heritage was incorporated into contemporary compositions.[64]

Regional identities were also explored by a large number of writers, most of whom were from provincial backgrounds themselves. Frédéric Mistral, who is best known for his long poem *Mirèio* (1859) in the Provençal dialect, was awarded the Nobel Prize in 1905. Toward the end of the nineteenth century, a growing number of European and American poets and novelists tried to grasp the specific character of a region and its vernacular traditions in their literary creations.[65] Probably the most famous nationalist author of the time was Maurice Barrès. In 1889 he was elected to the National Assembly as a follower of the populist General Boulanger. His program consisted of "nationalism, protectionism, and socialism,"—to which he later added antisemitism, as one of the leaders of the anti-Dreyfus camp. In influential novels like *The Uprooted* (1897) and in essays, he argued that love for the fatherland spread out from the family to the region and then to the nation. The fatherland, moreover, did not just belong to the current inhabitants; it also formed a heritage that was passed on to the following generations. Therefore, artists and writers should be truthful to the ancestral traditions and listen to the "voice of the blood and the instinct of the soil."[66]

Nationalization of the Physical Environment

After conquering the streets of the main cities, nationalism began to transform the countryside and the domestic sphere. Earlier trends such as the beautification of capitals and the erection of statues to national heroes intensified during the decades before the First World War, and national holidays and commemorations were celebrated in grand style. The standardization and naturalization of national identities continued to progress, for example through the illustrated press and world's fairs. And as nationalist culture underwent profound changes, the nationalization of the physical environment took on new forms as well.

Higher levels of education and the widening of the public sphere contributed to a growing self-awareness in the provinces. During the nineteenth century the number of local learned societies had grown considerably, but their reach had been rather limited. Toward the end of the nineteenth century, new regional associations began to target broader groups in society by making excursions to the surrounding countryside and cherishing their unique regional heritages, which consisted of not just archeological remains or historical objects that required considerable background knowledge, but also colorful traditional costumes and popular handicrafts. New local museums were created, and preservation efforts began to target guild houses and vernacular buildings in the countryside. Sometimes entire communities became part of the national patrimony—in 1900 the municipal authorities of Bavaria's Rothenburg ob der Tauber decided to actively protect the entire medieval town.[67]

In the colonies, the restoration of major monuments such as Angkor Wat and Borobudur commenced in the early years of the new century. Indigenous elites such as Kromodjojo Adinegoro, the regent of Mojokerto, were active in field of heritage preservation, founding a museum for the archaeological remains of the late medieval Majapahit Empire in Java, which was opened in 1911. Interest in the local vernacular heritage was also on the rise. On the initiative of the French-British artist Baron Rudolph d'Erlanger, who also was an expert on traditional Arab Andalusian music, all existing buildings in the Tunisian village of Sidi Bou Said received official protection, preserving their terraces, whitewashed façades, traditional balconies, and cast-iron balusters. Thus, the village quickly became more typical than it had ever been before, as everything that did not conform to the idealized notion of a traditional Arab building was proscribed (figure 5.4).[68]

At about the same time, the preservation of characteristic landscapes became a priority too, resulting in the foundation of the Society for the Protection of French Landscapes in 1901 and, soon after, the German Association for the Protection of the Homeland. Touring clubs, tourism activists, hunters, and alpinists also took a keen interest in the matter, and in 1909 the International

FIGURE 5.4 *Village of Sidi Bou Said*, Tunisia, circa 1935. On the initiative of Baron d'Erlanger this traditional village obtained monumental status and quickly became more typical than it had ever been. Here we see Café El Alia, in the center of the village. All wooden elements are painted blue, which beautifully contrasts with the whitewashed walls.

Conference for the Protection of Landscapes convened in Paris. By then, France had already adopted a law to protect typical landscapes, such as the spectacular stretches of rocky coast in Brittany. Modern addition like posters, billboards, and unsightly buildings had to be removed. In the colonies, the preservation of characteristic landscapes and their animals was often related to hunting. In Indochina, the first hunting regulations to protect wildlife were already in place in 1890, forbidding the Indigenous population from using firearms. The decline of the number of characteristic animals such as elephants and rhinoceros led to the creation of hunting reserves in 1914, for which permits were strictly regulated. The same process can be seen in Africa. The Convention for the Preservation of Wild Animals, Birds and Fish in Africa was signed in London in 1900. Several colonial powers introduced game reserves, which in many cases deprived the Indigenous populations of their sources of income, removed them from their land, and turned traditional hunting practices into poaching. Many of these reserves became national parks. The famous Kruger National Park, which was founded in 1926, also had its origins in a game reserve.[69]

The growing interest in the natural and vernacular patrimony of the provinces was visible at the national level, too. In many countries new ethnographic museums were created, and the open-air museum was invented in Stockholm in 1891. People could visit typical vernacular buildings from various parts of the country, inhabited by "authentic" farmers and their animals or by craftsmen in traditional costumes demonstrating their skills. This picturesque spectacle was an instant success and was rapidly copied elsewhere.[70] Similar exhibits that showed the fatherland as a unity in diversity could also be seen at various expositions. Ethnographic villages with dozens of buildings and up to hundreds of inhabitants were a major attraction at the Swiss National Exposition in Geneva (figure 5.5), the Millennial Exhibition in Budapest, and the International Exhibition of Art in Rome. Smaller and more geographically circumscribed ethnographic villages could be visited at regional expositions in Lemberg/Lviv, Dresden, Leipzig, and Nancy. At world's fairs in the United States, one could see Native American villages, old plantation exhibits (with African Americans reenacting slavery in the antebellum South), and Wild West shows.[71]

Many of these exhibits were intended to present an appealing national image abroad. Thus, a large German village could be visited at the World's Columbian Exposition in Chicago in 1893, and the Swiss village shown at Geneva in 1896 was rebuilt at the Paris Universal Exposition of 1900. It contained characteristic buildings from each individual canton, a real lake, a cascade, and an artificial mountain. Existing borders were not always recognized, and when taking stock of the national vernacular heritage, ethnicity often trumped citizenship. At the Jubilee Exhibition in Bucharest, for example, the nation was defined in an expansive way: the Romanian ethnographic village contained "Romanian" vernacular constructions from Transylvania, Banat, Bukovina, and Macedonia; buildings from Bessarabia were missing only because of the obstruction of the Russian authorities. At the rural village at the Czechoslavic Ethnographic Exhibition, held in Prague in 1895, the vernacular heritage of German-speaking Bohemians was excluded on ethnic grounds.[72]

FIGURE 5.5 *Village Suisse*, Swiss National Exhibition, 1896, Geneva. The ethnographic village contained replicas of buildings from all Swiss cantons, a fake mountain, a lake, and a real cascade, and was inhabited by over three hundred traditionally dressed villagers performing all kinds of agricultural and artisanal jobs. The exhibit was such a success that it was reconstructed for the Paris world's fair of 1900.

Surprisingly, many of these ethnographic villages—like most of the colonial villages that could be seen at these international exhibitions—were commercial undertakings staffed by professional showmen. Brown and Sons, a soap company that marketed its products as quintessentially Irish, constructed a "typical" village called Ballymaclinton, with replicas of well-known monuments, Irish cottages, and traditionally dressed girls, at almost every major international exhibition between 1908 and 1924. Other exhibits went on tour; the best-known was Buffalo Bill's Wild West show, which reenacted a romanticized version of the struggle between cowboys and Native Americans throughout the Western world. Many colonial exhibits also were taken on tour as a kind of traveling "human zoo."[73] Generally, these villages and shows focused on some of the most salient folkloric features to portray a striking and recognizable picture of a country or one of its regions or tribes. Even though many of the people on show—especially the inhabitants of colonies and Native

Americans—were seen as uncivilized "savages," their picturesque heritages presumably represented their countries' true characters.

The nationalization of the countryside received a decisive boost from the rapid growth of tourism. The construction of secondary railway lines, the mass production of bicycles, and the introduction of automobiles and buses made it easier to visit more remote parts of the countryside. Rising standards of living enabled more people to go on vacation or make a day trip, while youth groups such as the Boy Scouts organized hiking and camping trips. Favorite destinations were parts of the countryside that had unique natural features, characteristic buildings, or "authentic" folkloric traditions.[74]

Local authorities, ambitious entrepreneurs, railway companies, and automobile clubs did their best to foster the growing demand for regional attractions. Most of the tourism infrastructure had already been in place since the 1840s and 1850s, with travel agencies such as Thomas Cook and the modern travel guides of Murray, Baedeker, and Joanne, and many cities already had a fair number of hotels and restaurants. Around the turn of the century, camping grounds and youth hostels provided new budget options. Train companies advertised new destinations to encourage travel, while Michelin began publishing travel guides and maps, highlighting tourist routes, and using stars to indicate whether an attraction merited a detour. The tourist information office was pioneered in the French city of Grenoble in 1889, and local authorities and associations quickly began to produce posters, leaflets, and local guides to advertise the specific beauties of their city or region. This example was soon followed elsewhere, even outside Europe. The Welcome Society was established in Japan as early as 1893, and in the following decades, tourist offices were created in colonies such as Jamaica, the Dutch Indies, and Indochina.[75]

Those with a stake in the tourist business did not just facilitate access to attractions; in many ways, they created them. In fact, they selected what ought to be seen, by creating itineraries, signposts, parking areas, and footpaths with panoramic viewpoints. Entire regions were redefined by the invention of catchy names such as Côte d'Azur, Costa Brava, and Little Switzerland. Many traditional festivities were transferred to the summer season, and entirely new ones were invented, such as the Festival of Blue Nets in the Breton coastal town of Concarneau. Old neighborhoods such as Seville's miserable Barrio de Santa Cruz were restored by making them much more traditional, using cobblestones, decorative tiles, and cast-iron street lamps. Often, new buildings in a characteristic style were added; in Seville, this made the neighborhood more archetypically Andalusian than it had ever been. The same formula was used in the restoration of the other medieval neighborhoods, such as the city center of Bruges.[76]

This process of "touristification" had an even greater impact on the non-Western world. Foreign visitors to Bali, some of whom resided for longer periods on the island, created the image of a peaceful tropical paradise and encouraged the local population to package their music, dance, costumes, and skillfully crafted objects into folkloric traditions, art, and crafts by separating them from their original religious context.[77] This creation of separate domains for religion, fine arts, artisanal works, and folklore could also be seen elsewhere. World religions such as Christianity, Islam, Hinduism, and Buddhism reformulated their doctrines, becoming more standardized. The rise of a more secular worldview paradoxically increased the impact of these world religions on social life, to the detriment of local customs and beliefs.[78] At about the same time, a separate cultural domain—now largely emancipated from a religious cosmology—came into existence, in which picturesque vernacular traditions were redefined as folklore or part of the national heritage. Tourism thus had a secularizing impact, and it was driven mainly by capitalist motives.

Nationalism not only penetrated the more peripheral rural areas, it also entered the domestic sphere. Influenced by the arts and crafts movement, architects began to use natural materials, local artisanal techniques and constructive traditions to design buildings that fitted well into the surrounding landscape, while taking into account local climatic conditions and the personal needs of the owner. Cottages, villas, and country houses in a neo-vernacular style—which was clearly distinguished from the historicist styles that had dominated the nineteenth century—became very popular in suburban neighborhoods and garden cities, and as second homes, hotels, and restaurants in tourist zones. Architects pretended that their new creations followed national or regional traditions, while mostly taking extraordinary colorful or picturesque vernacular constructions as their main sources of inspiration. As a consequence, they invented a broad range of labels, sometimes referring to a region (neo-Norman), a town (the Polish Zakopane style), a landscape (Frank Lloyd Wright's prairie style), an ethnic group (Pueblo), or a particular building (mission revival). Other architects found inspiration in broader geographical trends, inspired either by prehistoric times, such as Celtic, Germanic, or Turanian constructive and decorative trends, or by vernacular traditions connected to a religion, such as the neo-Byzantine style in the Balkans or the revival of the pagoda style in the Buddhist parts of Asia. In the Americas there was a strong transnational interest in the pre-Columbian and colonial heritage, which led to various revival styles.[79]

In general, the most salient aspects of prehistoric, indigenous, religious, colonial, and vernacular legacies were seamlessly connected to the nation. In Germany, both the picturesque vernacular and the sturdier Germanic influences were seen as modern German architectural trends. In France, the large geographical and climatic differences led to the definition of various regional traditions such as neo-Basque and neo-Provençal, while Celtic elements were

NATIONALIST RADICALIZATION 169

incorporated in neo-Breton buildings, celebrating the country's unity in diversity. In the United States, in relatively new states such as California and New Mexico, local Indigenous and colonial legacies were a source of inspiration, demonstrating that the architectural heritage of the Southwest was older and more picturesque than the colonial buildings of New England. Some city councils even actively encouraged the adoption of such a neo-vernacular style for all new buildings in the city; this happened in Hamburg, where a neo-Hanseatic brick tradition was reinvented, in Seville, where "regionalism" became the favored building style, and in Santa Fe.[80]

The nationalization of the domestic sphere was not just limited to the outer shell of the house. Most architects also designed the interior decoration and the furniture for homes, and many built on the revival of the arts and crafts that had begun in the 1860s in Great Britain, where activists such as William Morris renovated the traditional handicrafts by encouraging a close collaboration between artists and artisans in guildlike associations. The arts and crafts movement quickly spread to other parts of the world, and while initially, many activists shared the cosmopolitan and reformist socialist views of Morris, strong nationalist tendencies soon became visible. Crafts, for instance, had a prominent role in ethnographic villages and open-air museums, where they represented the authentic traditions of the fatherland. At many artists' colonies, craftsmen were employed to make products designed by painters or sculptors, and many of them increasingly took national artisanal traditions as a starting point for new work. In the Hungarian artist colony Gödöllő, all kinds of decorative arts were produced that were inspired by the local "peasant culture," while the Iris workshop, led by Count Louis Sparre in the Finnish town of Porvoo, produced everyday objects in an explicitly national style. At the Russian artist colony of Abramtsevo a ceramics factory produced Old Russian majolica, while the Russian painter Sergey Malyutin invented the matryoshka doll, which would become a national icon thanks in part to its success at the Paris Universal Exposition of 1900. In the United States, María Martínez—advised by archeologists to make her designs more typical—revived the traditional ceramics of the Pueblo Indians in New Mexico.[81]

It was not only houses and their interior decoration that were nationalized—so were cooking practices. Obviously, food habits differed enormously around the globe, but in general they were connected to social classes, religious traditions, or zones of cultivation, and not to nations. Haute cuisine, which had originated at the court of Versailles, dominated the tables of the rich and the menus of refined restaurants and luxurious hotels throughout the world, while the poor ate whatever they could afford. Toward the end of the nineteenth century, cookbooks, women's magazines, and cheap restaurants increasingly offered simpler dishes. Recipes were standardized and dishes received names, which usually referred to a specific village, town, or region, thus becoming part of a national culinary legacy. Cookbooks for male chefs continued to follow the gastronomic standards that were set in Paris, but most publications targeting middle-class housewives focused on a specific country and propagated a newly invented national cuisine. This process can be detected throughout Europe and the United States, but also in countries such as Mexico and Japan.[82]

The nationalization trend can be detected in other domestic practices, too. Gardens were laid out with care, increasingly using indigenous plants and flowers that were both pleasing to the eye and adapted to the local climatic and geological conditions. Gardening now was profiled as typically English, while certain cleaning habits (e.g., having "snow-white" linens and curtains) began to be framed as characteristic of "proper" German housewives.[83] Even pets were nationalized. Toward the end of the nineteenth century, dog breeding spread from Great Britain to other parts of the world, and national kennel clubs began to define the characteristics of each type of dog, giving them names that mostly referred to nations or regions, such as German shepherd and Yorkshire terrier. Animals of foreign origin—such as Persian and Siamese cats—were also increasingly converted into purebreds, thus fixating territorial identities in the animal realm and further naturalizing national classifications in everyday life.[84]

Finally, the human body was nationalized as well. Gymnastic associations had become popular throughout the Western world, and they generally had a clear nationalist undertone. In 1862 Miroslav Tyrš founded the Czech nationalist Sokol (Falcon) movement, which was quickly copied in Moravia, Slovenia, Poland, Ukraine, and Serbia. At around the same time, European immigrants founded gymnastic associations in the United States and Canada. Physical exercise became an integral part of educational programs at British public schools, Japanese schools, and U.S. colleges. After the military defeat against Prussia, French authors promoted physical education in order to strengthen the nation. Traditional games—which were often rude, chaotic, and violent, and played according to local rules—were regulated, leading to the invention of soccer and rugby at English public schools, and American football at Harvard and Princeton. Other sports such as track and field, swimming, boxing, skating, and rowing were also standardized toward the end of the nineteenth century. The idea was that sports would not only increase the fitness of male students but also shape their characters by promoting discipline, courage, self-reliance, respect for rules, and fair play. Sports should prepare boys to become good soldiers, productive workers, and perfect gentlemen. Physical exercise was much less important for women; generally, it was deemed useful only to help women become vigorous mothers of the nation's future generations.[85]

Whereas gymnastics was focused on group cohesion through cooperative exercises and mass performances, sports was based on competitive contests.

Sports was quickly disseminated throughout the world, and myriad regional and national competitions were organized. Thus the English Football Association set up a national soccer championship in 1871, and the American National League for baseball began in 1876. This meant that sports also reinforced the national framework. Teams from various clubs met each other to compete for a national title. This way, the local loyalty of a rapidly growing fan base was strengthened, as was their awareness of the nation, which in almost all cases coincided with the boundaries of the nation-state. Nevertheless, there were exceptions. England, Scotland, Wales, and Ireland each had their own national competitions and teams. This also was the case with Bohemia in Austria-Hungary. Another type of exception was the exclusion of people based on ethnic or racial criteria. As a response to the growing antisemitism, separate Jewish sports clubs were founded in different parts of Europe; some defined their aim as developing a "muscular Jewry." In French Algeria the Indigenous population was excluded, and in the United States African Americans were barred in various ways: while the National League applied an informal color ban, other professional baseball leagues explicitly prohibited the participation of Black players.[86]

Certain sports or sporting events became closely associated with a particular nation. A good example is the Scottish Highland Games, which originated in local traditions mostly connected with an annual fair. During the nineteenth century the games were standardized and turned into festive events with traditional sporting contests, bagpipes, kilts, and folkloric dances. It was a clear source of inspiration for the Gaelic Athletic Association, which was founded in Ireland in 1884. Although it also encouraged Irish music and dance, the focus was on Irish sports such as hurling and Gaelic football. The association was openly nationalist, and it forbade its members to play and watch "foreign" games, which referred primarily to popular English sports such as soccer and rugby. In the United States, baseball was presented as a quintessential American game, reflecting the core values of the American way of life such as individualism, equality, team spirit, and competitiveness. Baseball games became an indispensable part of Independence Day celebrations. Other sporting events were invented with a clear nationalist purpose in mind. In 1903, the Parisian sports newspaper L'Auto organized a three-week bicycle race through France to boost its sales during the summer month of July. The Tour de France also showed the beauty of the various parts of the country as it connected towns and villages—including in the contested region of Alsace-Lorraine—on its yearly changing route. In 1922, the Swedish Vasaloppet, a ninety-kilometer cross-country ski race, was organized in honor of King Gustav Vasa, who had led the country's war of liberation against Denmark. The race quickly became a mass event that was intended to harden Swedish bodies and to commemorate a historical event by practicing a national sport in the country's heartland of Dalarna.[87]

With the growing popularity of sports, international matches began to be played and international federations were established for individual sports in order to impose uniform rules and organize regular encounters between national teams. FIFA, the International Federation of Association Football, was founded in 1904. The greatest international sports event, the Olympic Games, was reinvented in 1896 in Athens. The first games were relatively minor affairs, organized as sideshows during major international exhibitions, but they initiated a tradition of regular international meetings in which individuals and teams representing their own countries could peacefully compete for the highest honor.[88]

Conclusion

Toward the end of the nineteenth century, nationalist tensions were on the rise. Many dynastic unions came under stress. Norway gained independence, and nationalism was growing in Eastern Europe, Ireland, Finland, and Catalonia. Traditional empires such as Russia, the Ottoman Empire, China, and Persia felt compelled to adopt various aspects of the nation-state model but had difficulty remaining politically stable. Many nation-states, meanwhile, began to participate in the imperial race, acquiring colonies in Africa or the Pacific and thus becoming nationalizing empires, too. At the same time, the exclusion of racial outsiders—such as Chinese immigrants in the Americas—was reinforced.

Nationalism also reached further into everyday life. The nationalization of the countryside and the domestic sphere was realized mostly through the promotion of all kinds of striking vernacular traditions (e.g., recipes, artisanal products, building traditions) as essential parts of a regionally diversified national heritage. Although many people were still indifferent to or unaware of the nation to which they "belonged," most European nation-states tried to bind the inhabitants closer to the state by introducing social reforms such as health insurance and old-age pensions. Meanwhile, nationalism became more pronounced in several scientific disciplines, but surprisingly, other territorial identities, including substate regions and larger areas defined by geographical features, culture, or race, received scholarly attention as well. This was also visible in the fine arts, music, and literature. Many of these tendencies undermined the self-evident nature of the existing international order and therefore helped prepare the ground for the cataclysmic global wars of the following decades.

6

The Clash between Extremes, 1914–1945

THE FIRST WORLD WAR WAS an important turning point. Most traditional land-based empires collapsed and were replaced by nation-states. The prolonged carnage also subverted the global leadership of the "civilized" European powers and the hegemonic position of the liberal nation-state. Initially, the war was greeted with enthusiasm; most Europeans expected a short decisive conflict, like the wars of Italian and German unification. Although some socialists and pacifists opposed the war, and many ordinary people were worried about the consequences, most people rallied around the flag. Many politicians saw the war as inevitable; it would show who would prevail in the international struggle for survival. Many intellectuals greeted the war as an opportunity for social and cultural renewal, as a kind of purification that would bring down the prevalence of materialistic concerns and replace stifling cultural conventions with more authentic, spiritual values.[1]

From the start, the Central powers distanced themselves from the rules of international law regulating the relations between "civilized" European nation-states. In 1908 Austria-Hungary had used the occasion of the Young Turks' seizure of power to annex Bosnia-Herzegovina. This measure violated the treaty of 1878 and was opposed by most inhabitants of the region, particularly the Muslim population and a growing group of South Slav nationalists. After the assassination of Crown Prince Franz Ferdinand by a Bosnian Serb activist in Sarajevo in June 1914, the Dual Monarchy issued an ultimatum to Serbia, whose army officers had provided logistical support. The ultimatum contained a large number of demands that would be unacceptable to any independent state, but Serbia seemed to accede to all of them except the requirement that officials from Austria-Hungary be allowed to participate in the prosecution of suspects in Serbia. This was rejected by Belgrade as being contrary to the Serbian constitution. On July 28, Austria-Hungary declared war on Serbia.[2]

The German Empire, too, consciously broke with the accepted views of the international order. Since 1848, most wars on the European continent had been fought on the basis of nationalist claims, which implied that conquering parts of the "civilized world" not inhabited by fellow nationals was illegitimate. But the war aims formulated in September 1914 by Chancellor Theobald von Bethmann Hollweg made it clear that Germany did not want to merely adjust borders according to the nationality principle. The German plans to annex the iron-ore mines in northeast France and the ports of Dunkirk and Antwerp were justified by their economic and strategic value, and a newly established Polish state and the Baltic provinces would not be sovereign nation-states but instead would be made subordinate to German economic and political interests. Even neutral states like the Netherlands, Switzerland, and the Scandinavian countries would be drawn closely into the German orbit, thus implementing on the European continent imperialist ideas that had been routinely applied in Asia and Africa.[3] In February 1917, in a desperate attempt to win the war, Germany resumed unrestricted submarine warfare in the waters around the United Kingdom. This inevitably led to casualties among the citizens of neutral countries, triggering the United States' entry into the war.[4]

The Entente powers claimed they were defending the international order by rejecting Germany's occupation of Belgium and aiming to return Alsace-Lorraine to France. This was most poignantly formulated in President Wilson's Fourteen Points speech. All occupied territories had to be evacuated, and Belgium and even Poland would be restored as independent states. However, the principle of national self-determination that Wilson formulated shortly afterward did not apply to the non-Western world, and this led to widespread disappointment in Asia and parts of Africa.[5] The disillusionment increased even further when in the end, many of the promises made during the war to both the inhabitants of the European colonies and many (potential) allies were not kept.

It was not just the European colonial powers that lost prestige; the same was true for the nation-state model. A basic tenet was that the state should serve the nation, but during the war it often seemed that the opposite was true. The ease with which new recruits were sent to the front lines to live a miserable life in the trenches, get wounded, or die in droves in another futile assault seriously affected the deference generally shown to military and civil authorities. Moreover, the full mobilization of the economy for the war effort required huge sacrifices, and the longer the conflict lasted, the more war-weariness grew. From 1916 onward, protests, strikes, mutinies, and revolts occurred ever-more frequently in most of the participating countries. The dislocations brought on by the demobilization of millions of soldiers after the war, the new conflicts that broke out over the control of various disputed territories in many parts of East-Central Europe and Anatolia, and the scenes of outright civil war in Russia added to a general postwar economic slump, further eroding support for the existing order. Moreover, the Soviet Union offered a fresh communist alternative to the liberal nation-state. At the peace conference in Paris and in the offices of the new League of Nations, the principle of national self-determination made the nation-state the model for the future, but many people began to lose their trust in constitutional governments. Thus, instead of a new era of peaceful cooperation—which seemed to begin during the second half of the 1920s—the following decades were mostly a time of turmoil and growing tensions, which resulted in a new catastrophic global war that ended only in 1945.[6]

Although this period was known for its extreme forms of nationalism, the nation-state was not taken for granted. Imperial tendencies were stronger than ever, and in the social sciences and humanities both larger and smaller regions still attracted broad attention. Society was interpreted from many different angles, from geographical determinism and racial theories to cultural relativism. This diversity can also be detected in the cultural realm and the physical domain. Many artists, musicians, and architects had recourse to vernacular sources of inspiration or were openly nationalist or xenophobic. Others espoused a placeless modernism that radically broke with the (national) past.

New Nation-States: The Impact of the First World War

In Europe, many new states were created as a consequence of the collapse of the Russian, Austro-Hungarian, and Ottoman Empires, but the fall of these continental empires was not inevitable. Initially, the war provoked feelings of loyalty to the existing states. Many people expected a rapid victory, and as a consequence there were frequent patriotic demonstrations, in which the participants expressed their loyalty to the tsar, emperor, or sultan. That unity vanished as the state failed to win a quick victory, to effectively mobilize the economy, and to provide help to those in need. Poor relief and aid to refugees was organized mostly along religious and ethnic lines. Economic hardship and general insecurity heightened tensions between ethnic communities, some of which were suspected of sympathizing with the enemy. This was the case with Italians and various Slavic groups (e.g., Serbs, Czechs, and Ruthenians), in Austria-Hungary, and with ethnic Germans and Turkic peoples in the Russian Empire. In the early days of the war, authorities had used denunciations and rumors to imprison, deport, and execute thousands of suspects from such minority groups. Confiscations, plundering, and rape occurred frequently. The war was also seen by some as an opportunity to "resolve the Gypsy question," either by internment or deportation. In Russia, Jews were targeted, and many were "evacuated" from the zones closest to the front. In the Ottoman Empire, too, removals of suspect minority groups occurred frequently; many Greek merchants and Arab nationalists suffered persecution, but the main victims were Armenians.[7]

The Christian Armenians lived in ethnically mixed areas on both sides of the border between the Russian and the Ottoman Empires. In the preceding decades, separatist violence and anti-Armenian pogroms had already poisoned interethnic and interreligious relations in the area. Ottoman authorities suspected that many Armenians would sympathize with the Russian Empire. Moreover, the memory of Christian uprisings receiving aid from foreign powers and the presence of large numbers of Muslims expelled from territories lost to Russia and the new Balkan states—a new wave had arrived as a consequence of the Balkan Wars of 1912 to 1913—did not favor a benevolent attitude toward the remaining religious minorities. In the winter of 1914 to 1915, Russian troops inflicted a heavy defeat on the Ottoman army in the Caucasus. Enver Pasha, the Ottoman commander in chief, put the blame on the Armenians. Soon after, the army decided to disarm non-Muslim soldiers and turn them into labor battalions. The next step was the evacuation of the Armenian population from the zones close to the front. The Armenians were deported to improvised camps in the Syrian desert, but this was not an ordinary evacuation. Many men were deliberately killed before departure, and many more deportees perished on the way. Within a few months, central and eastern Anatolia were "cleared" of Armenians and, to some extent. of Assyrians, another Christian minority. This operation, often characterized as a genocide, cost the lives of at least six hundred thousand people.[8]

Tensions between ethnic groups were also exacerbated by the occupation authorities' courting of some minorities and by the warring parties' opportunistic promises to nationalist movements in enemy territory. This started during the early months of the war when the use of Russian was discouraged in favor of local languages in German-occupied parts of the tsarist empire. In occupied Belgium, the German military authorities made Dutch a state language. They even separated Wallonia and Flanders administratively and made Dutch the official language of the University of Ghent, which had been a longstanding demand of Flemish nationalists.[9]

The warring parties also tried to get neutral powers on their side by promising territorial expansion, especially in areas where "fellow nationals" were living. Thus, Bulgaria entered the war on the side of the Central powers in 1915, while the Entente powers enticed Italy into their camp in 1915, Romania in 1916, and Greece in 1917.[10] Further promises were made to a variety of nationalist movements. At the start of the war, Russia, Austria, and Germany vowed to create a Polish nation-state, which had to be situated largely on territories belonging to the enemy. Germany actively encouraged Finnish and Ukrainian nationalists, and in the spring of 1916, Berlin supported an Irish uprising, attempting to supply weapons to Roger Casement. In January 1917, the German state secretary of foreign affairs, Arthur Zimmermann, aimed to forge a military alliance with Mexico by promising German support for the recovery of Texas, New Mexico, and Arizona, but Zimmermann's secret telegram was intercepted and published by the British secret service, causing an uproar in the United States.[11]

The Ottoman Empire applied the same tactics. The sultan-caliph proclaimed jihad against the empire's enemies, both to galvanize support from the large majority of his own subjects and to instigate Muslim uprisings in India, Central Asia, Egypt, and French North Africa. The Ottoman government also made efforts to inspire rebellions among Turkish peoples in the Russian Empire and Persia. Meanwhile, German authorities tried to convince captured colonial soldiers from North Africa and India to enlist in the Ottoman army. The German military also created "national" battalions with Finnish, Georgian, and Ukrainian prisoners of war.[12]

The British government, for its part, tried to undermine the Central powers. In 1914 it made Egypt a formal protectorate, breaking its remaining ties with the Ottoman Empire. Two years later, it supported Hussein bin Ali, the sharif of Mecca, in rising up against the sultan as a self-proclaimed king of the Arabs. This was followed in November 1917 by Foreign Secretary Alfred Balfour's promise of a national home for the Jewish people in Palestine. The French and British governments also welcomed national committees set up by Polish, Czechoslovak, and Yugoslav exiles, consisting of Serbs, Croats and Slovenes. In April 1918, Italian activists convened the Congress of Oppressed Nationalities of the Austro-Hungarian Empire to advocate for the breakup of the Dual Monarchy. The Entente powers also created Polish, Czech, and Czechoslovak legions, recruited among exiles, prisoners of war, and migrants.[13]

This did not mean that the continental empires were toppled by strong nationalist movements. Nationalist uprisings against imperial authorities were rare and did not constitute a real threat. In 1916, both the Easter Rising in Ireland and an uprising in Turkestan—a response to the Russian decision to draft Central Asian Muslims into labor battalions—were quickly and harshly repressed. In the end, the continental empires were not overthrown by nationalist unrest in the periphery—instead, they imploded at the center, creating a void that was filled largely by nationalist movements. The first to collapse was the Russian Empire. Support for the tsarist regime was eroded by military defeats and by its failure to solve the problems at the home front, such as rampant inflation and the lack of food and fuel. In Saint Petersburg, a demonstration of female textile workers in February 1917 escalated into protests that finally led to the abdication of the tsar. The new provisional regime made Russia into a democratic republic, with individual rights for all citizens, and the autonomy of Finland and Poland was restored. Although land reform and the supply of basic necessities were the most pressing issues, political mobilization developed largely along ethnic and religious lines, as communication was easier when appealing to shared sentiments in one's own language. Moreover, social cleavages often coincided with ethnic and religious divides, with Ukrainian peasants opposed to Polish and Russian landowners, for instance. The new Ukrainian Central Council requested both regional self-government and a solution to the land question, and Estonian, Moldavian, and Kazakh nationalists also demanded political autonomy. A national assembly of Muslims was created, as well as a score of other nationalist parties representing smaller minorities.[14]

During the summer of 1917, while the provisional government postponed major reforms until after the war, the Bolsheviks promised peace, land, and national self-determination, and their coup d'état was welcomed by a war-weary population. The chaotic situation created by the war and the October Revolution provided a window of opportunity for nationalist movements. In territories occupied or "protected" by the German Empire, activists created the new nation-states of Poland, Lithuania, Latvia, Estonia, Ukraine, Belarus, and Finland, while Moldavia, Georgia, Armenia, and Azerbaijan seceded from Russia. Some of these states had an ephemeral existence: after the Bolshevists prevailed in the Russian civil war, Ukraine, Belarus, and the Transcaucasian states were incorporated into the new Soviet Union.[15]

The next to fall was Austria-Hungary. With German support, the Austro-Hungarian army had performed better than its Russian counterpart, but the domestic situation was far from rosy. Scarcity was the order of the day, and rations were reduced during the final years of the war. There were many destitute refugees and displaced persons, and ethnic tensions increased in most parts of the empire. A wave of strikes and protests in January 1918 exposed the breadth of the discontent. After the French government revealed that separate peace overtures had been made by the new emperor, the Germans obliged their ally to prove its loyalty in a new offensive on the Italian front in June, which predictably ended in disaster. In October, Emperor Karl made an attempt to reconcile the rising nationalist movements by proposing a federalization of Austria, but it was too late. When the defeat of their German ally was imminent, Austro-Hungarian troops deserted in droves. As local and provincial authorities were focused on practical issues such as maintaining order and addressing the dire food situation, new national committees provided the clearest alternative for the future. Thus, the empire was replaced by the new nation-states of Poland, Czechoslovakia, and Yugoslavia and small Hungarian and Austrian rump states.[16]

The Ottoman state, the weakest of the continental empires, did not collapse because of the war, but as a consequence of the peace. After initial setbacks on the Russian front, it defended its territories surprisingly well. The situation of the Ottoman Empire became untenable only with the defeat of the German Empire. In October 1918 an armistice was signed with the Entente powers, which in fact amounted to a capitulation. Sultan Mehmet VI succeeded his brother, and the Young Turk wartime leaders left the country. But the new government was not treated with leniency by the victors, who had to reconcile many conflicting promises made during the war. The concessions made to the Russian tsar—such as control over the Bosporus—could be ignored, but Italy and Greece claimed substantial parts of the Anatolian coast, France and Great Britain had divided the Arab provinces, and Armenians and Kurds claimed extensive territories for an independent nation-state, possibly under the tutelage of one of the Entente powers (map 6.1). Only the interior of Asia Minor would remain for a small Turkish rump state. Anticipating final decisions, in May 1919 the Greek army occupied the areas around Izmir/Smyrna, a predominantly Greek city on the Anatolian coast. This triggered a Turkish resistance movement, led by Mustafa Kemal (better known by his later name, Atatürk), who as military inspector of the Ottoman army in Eastern Anatolia became its indisputable leader. With the help of the Soviet Union, Kemal succeeded in undoing the plan for an Armenian nation-state and also making an autonomous Kurdistan a chimera. In 1922 he defeated the Greek troops. The Treaty of Lausanne, signed in July 2023, was much more advantageous for the new Turkish republic.[17]

Meanwhile, the Arab provinces of the Ottoman Empire were divided largely according to the secret Sykes-Picot Agreement, which was made by the United Kingdom and France in 1916 and which contradicted Britain's earlier promise of an Arab kingdom to Sharif Hussein; he received only a modest kingdom in the Hijaz, which in 1925 would be lost to Ibn Saud. France received Syria, from which Lebanon was separated to create a state dominated by Maronite Christians, while Great Britain obtained Iraq, Transjordan, and a newly defined state of Palestine, to honor the promises made by Balfour to the Zionists. Thus, in the drawing of borders, the Entente powers clearly favored Christians and Jews over Muslims. All states were governed as mandates assigned by the new League of Nations. The populations of these territories supposedly lacked the civilized attitude needed for self-government.[18]

All major decisions concerning the fate of the Ottoman Empire and the drawing of borders in East-Central Europe were made at the Paris Peace Conference, which began in January 1919. The expectations were high, especially among the many nationalist movements to whom various promises and concessions had been made. In the final months of 1918 the new nation-states of Poland, Czechoslovakia, and the Kingdom of Serbs, Croats, and Slovenes (later renamed Yugoslavia) were created. The Bolsheviks had already embraced the principle of national self-determination, which also targeted the colonial world. Wilson's support for national self-determination, which

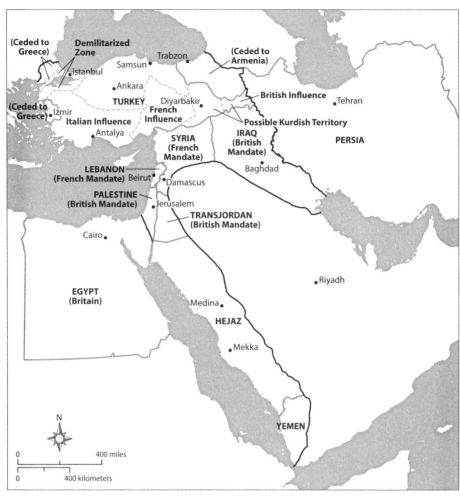

MAP 6.1 The Treaty of Sèvres of 1920 formalized the partition of the Ottoman Empire by the Allies. The sultan had to cede extensive territories to Greece and a new Armenian state, while large parts of Eastern Anatolia were defined as possible Kurdish territories. Italy, France, and Great Britain received large zones of influence in Anatolia, where only a small Turkish rump state would remain independent. Further south, instead of creating a unified Arab nation-state, Iraq, Transjordan, and Palestine became British mandates whereas Syria and Lebanon were allotted to France.

principally referred to the consent of the governed, had more immediate impact, because it was combined with the prospect of peaceful international cooperation within the framework of the new League of Nations. In the short term, instead of creating a stable new international order, the Wilsonian moment had a strong destabilizing effect.[19]

Although the principle of national self-determination sounded logical, the question now was, What nations would be allowed to determine their own fate? In the chaos after the fall of the Russian and Austrian-Hungarian Empires, there were many new states created that did not endure. Some of them, such as Ukraine and Armenia, were quite substantial and could count on the support of well-developed nationalist movements; others, such as the Western Ukrainian Republic, the Hutsul Republic, German Bohemia, and German Southern Moravia, disappeared almost without a trace. Other alternatives did not materialize. For instance, Austrians appealed to the principle of self-determination to request unification with Germany. Irish and Catalan nationalists used the Wilsonian moment to advance their claims. Regional movements in Brittany, Corsica, Spanish Galicia, and Wales now claimed to represent a nation, as did Romansh-language activists in Switzerland. In Southern Germany, some pleaded for a Great Swabian nation-state that encompassed Swabia, Baden-Württemberg, the German-speaking parts of Switzerland, and Alsace. They argued that since the inhabitants of these areas descended from the same Swabian tribes and spoke closely related dialects, they should be recognized as a nation and therefore deserved their own state.[20]

Even in the case of recognized nations that were seen as deserving their own state, it was far from clear where the exact boundaries should be and what should be done with the millions of people who ended up in the "wrong" state. The new borders were drawn at the Paris Peace Conference, but in most instances they merely reflected the military reality on the ground. The armies of Romania, Czechoslovakia, and Yugoslavia, backed by the Entente, had occupied large swaths of the newly independent nation-state of Hungary, which bitterly fought to resist these losses. Further south, a new Croatian Committee, with strong support in the countryside, violently opposed the merger of the South Slav Habsburg lands with Serbia, but it was quickly defeated. The Czech army incorporated Slovakia and the territories of the West Ukrainian Republic while it clashed with Poland over the mixed Teschen District. The new Polish state was implicated in violent uprisings in the Polish-speaking parts of Germany, and wars were fought with Lithuania, Ukraine, and the Soviet Union. When a peace treaty was signed in 1921 with the Soviet Union, Poland annexed extensive territories inhabited largely by Lithuanians, Jews, Ukrainians, and Belarusians.[21]

The promises made during the war and Wilson's proclamations about national self-determination also raised expectations among nationalists outside

Europe. Their hopes were on President Wilson and the Paris Peace Conference, but they ended in disappointment. Emir Feisal, the son of Sharif Hussein, had the strongest case, and he was allowed to address the Supreme Council of the Peace Conference. But his pleas for self-determination for the Arabs, implying the creation of an Arab constitutional monarchy in Greater Syria—which included Lebanon and Transjordan and could be extended to other Arab lands—clashed with the British and French plans to divide the Middle East. In order to buy time, the Big Five decided to send a commission to the Middle East, but its report was shelved. Back in Damascus, Feisal mobilized society to support the demand for sovereignty. In March 1920, the Syrian General Congress declared independence, with Feisal as king. A few months later, Feisal was deposed by a French army. Meanwhile, Great Britain united the three Ottoman provinces of Basra, Baghdad, and Mosul, while promising the inhabitants a "national government." The British authorities forbade a delegation of local notables to visit the Paris Peace Conference to plead for the creation of an Iraqi nation-state. When the League of Nations made Iraq a British mandate in April 1920, protests quickly escalated into a full-blown uprising, which was brutally put down by the British army. In the end, the British decided to create a kingdom led by Feisal, a proposal that was approved in a plebiscite by the Iraqi population.[22]

Social unrest also occurred in various British colonies. They had made huge sacrifices for the war, contributing vital supplies and large numbers of soldiers and laborers. Moreover, shortages and rising costs of living had put a heavy burden on the population. Taking advantage of the new international constellation after the war, Egyptian politicians argued that their country was entitled to self-determination. However, Said Zaghlul, vice president of the legislative assembly and the leader of the new Wafd (Delegation) Party, was denied permission to present the Egyptian case in Paris. After widespread protests, strikes, and disturbances, the British authorities gave in and a delegation made it to France, only to hear that the Americans had just recognized the British protectorate.[23]

Elsewhere, too, nationalism became a mass movement. In December 1916, the Indian National Congress and the Muslim League demanded Home Rule for India. Secretary of State Edwin Montagu responded by promising the "gradual development of self-governing institutions." As a consequence, in 1919, Great Britain introduced the Government of India Act, in which it extended the suffrage for elections to the legislative assembly, while provincial governments and assemblies received autonomy in matters of health care, education, and agriculture. Nonetheless, the British viceroy retained extensive veto powers, and the Rowlatt Act extended wartime restrictions on civil rights in order to combat security threats. These concessions were seen as too limited, and together with objections against repressive measures such as the Amritsar massacre, they led to an all-India protest movement, guided by Mahatma Gandhi, the new charismatic leader of the Indian National Congress. His tactics of nonviolent resistance succeeded in involving broad sections of the population.[24]

Imperial Japan faced similar reactions, especially in Korea, which had been a Japanese colony since 1910. At the end of 1918 a group of nationalists sent a petition to Wilson, arguing that Korea, as a civilized nation with a distinct language and culture, had the right to self-determination. Soon after, Korean students in Tokyo read out a declaration of independence, and others proclaimed independence in Seoul. This was met with repression, triggering countrywide demonstrations. The prominent Korean nationalist Syngman Rhee established a provisional government in Shanghai and Korean migrant organizations held the First Korean Congress in Philadelphia, appealing to both to the U.S. government and the general public. Although their pleas for an independent nation-state were ignored in Paris, the Japanese authorities felt compelled to grant them a limited measure of self-government, which failed to appease most Korean nationalists. The decision to award Japan the former German concession of Shantung also sparked a widespread protest movement in China, which had joined the war against the German Empire in August 1917. Its main demand was the restoration of China's full territorial sovereignty, including the annulment of the unequal treaties and the recovery of Shantung.[25]

The Interwar Period and the Second World War

More nation-states were created during the interwar period, mostly as offshoots of the British Empire. First, the United Kingdom was confronted with nationalist demands for self-determination in Ireland. The Easter Rising of 1916 had ended in failure, but the fierce crackdown on the rebels and their sympathizers backfired. In the elections of December 1918 Home Rule was on the agenda, and Sinn Féin (We Ourselves), a new nationalist party that embraced the Wilsonian message of self-determination, won a landslide victory. In January, the Sinn Féin delegates created a separate parliament, proclaimed independence, and sent a delegation to the Paris Peace Conference. Violence commenced almost immediately; the British government was not willing to accept these illegal acts, nor were the Protestant Ulster unionists. As a response, David Lloyd George's coalition government adopted the Government of Ireland Act, which awarded Home Rule to both Southern and Northern Ireland. Reciprocal attacks did not subside, and it was only in December 1921 that the Anglo-Irish Treaty led to the creation of the Irish Free State as a self-governing dominion.[26]

Elsewhere in the empire, British authorities similarly attempted to placate nationalist forces by granting self-government. In 1922 Egypt became independent, although Great Britain would continue to control the Suez Canal, supervise the country's diplomatic relations, and safeguard the extraterritorial rights of foreigners. Soon after, Iraq adopted a constitution. After ratifying the Treaty of Preferential Alliance, which allowed Great Britain to retain two air bases and the right of transit for troops, Iraq became independent in 1932. The Statute of Westminster of 1931, meanwhile, turned the five dominions—which actually were already member states of the League of Nations—into fully sovereign nation-states, and six years later, the new Republic of Ireland adopted a constitution and rescinded all formal bonds with the British Empire. Great Britain also introduced limited forms of self-government in some of its Asian colonies. Ceylon was given a unicameral legislature in the form of a state council, which was elected with universal male and female suffrage. In 1935 the British government adopted the Government of Burma Act, which included an elected assembly and a cabinet led by an Indigenous prime minister. In the same year, Great Britain conceded responsible self-government on a provincial level to India, although governors retained ample powers to safeguard British interests. The reforms at the federal level, however, did not become effective, because of opposition from India's princely states.[27]

France was less inclined to grant self-government. In the Spanish protectorate of Morocco, an uprising led by Abd el-Krim al-Khattabi, a tribal leader from the Rif Mountains, spilled over to the French zone. In 1921, he inflicted a devastating defeat on an advancing Spanish army and created an independent Republic of the Rif, appealing to the principle of self-determination. In April 1925 he invaded the French protectorate, proclaiming holy war to drive out the infidels. France and Spain sent massive reinforcements and used aerial bombings, artillery, and chemical weapons to subdue the "rebellion." Meanwhile, Druze forces, conservative Islamists, and urban nationalists in Syria decided to use the opportunity to mount a coordinated uprising o obtain independence. After quelling the "revolts" in both Morocco and Syria, French authorities understood that concessions were needed. In 1926 Lebanon was granted a constitution and self-government. A similar solution was agreed for Syria in 1930. Because the French colonial lobby was very strong, further reforms were blocked.[28]

Outside of Europe, political sovereignty continued to be identified with an independent nation-state with a written constitution, an elected parliament, and a cabinet. This was true not only for nationalist movements and protectorates, but also for independent states. After the Guomindang succeeded in defeating most of the regional warlords, China received a new constitution in 1930; with it, the government of Chiang Kai-shek recovered control of some foreign concessions and reduced the extraterritorial rights of foreigners. The next year, Emperor Haile Selassie adopted a constitution for Ethiopia, and after a bloodless coup in 1932, the Kingdom of Siam also became a constitutional state with an elected parliament. Still, in all three countries, democratic rights remained curtailed; large parts of the population were still deemed politically immature.[29]

Nevertheless, during the interwar era, the liberal nation-state model came increasingly under fire. The crisis of classical liberalism that began in the late nineteenth century and the First World War had undermined its prestige. Was a parliamentary system really the best and most efficient way to serve the nation's interests? Alternative political models were developed in the Soviet Union, in many dictatorial states, and in Fascist Italy and Nazi Germany. Although almost all of these countries adopted constitutions, it was doubtful whether they still were states that served the nation and were subject to its will.

During the nineteenth century, socialists had argued that liberal constitutions effected legal but not social equality. Behind a façade of rights and liberties, parliamentary regimes in fact represented the interests of the ruling bourgeoisie. After gaining power, the Russian Bolsheviks wanted a "true" democracy that represented the class interests of the large majority of the population. Lenin hoped to achieve this by conferring power to soviets of workers, soldiers, and peasants while doing away with private ownership of the means of production. However, in the context of a raging civil war, a "communist dictatorship of the proletariat" was imposed, while state institutions were controlled by a centralized Communist Party. Initially, many members of the old regime, such as officials, clerics, and large property owners, were excluded from the suffrage, and the 1918 constitution of the Russian Soviet Federative Socialist Republic clearly favored the industrial working classes by conferring on urban workers one deputy per 25,000 electors, while the inhabitants of the countryside received only one per 125,000 electors. New Soviet republics such as Ukraine and Georgia were incorporated by signing bilateral treaties. Although they nominally retained the right to self-determination and received considerable cultural autonomy, they committed themselves to forming a close military and economic union with the other republics. The 1924 constitution of the new Union of Soviet Socialist Republics established both a Council of the Union—representing the entire population—and a Council of Nationalities, in which each republic had the same number of representatives, implicitly guaranteeing the equality of all titular nations. Nonetheless, ethnic communities were subordinated to a proletarian *demos*. The All-Union Communist Party supposedly safeguarded the common interests of all workers and peasants. Moreover, the new multinational state could potentially expand beyond the borders of the old tsarist empire.[30]

Whereas the Soviet Union was a revolutionary one-party dictatorship, in many nation-states more conservative authoritarian regimes came to power, most of which were fiercely nationalist. Dictators were not a new phenomenon—the concept originated in classical antiquity. But the most famous nineteenth-century examples, Napoleon I and Napoleon III of France and Mexico's president Porfirio Díaz, had maintained a constitutional façade and continued to organize elections. Toward the end of the nineteenth century, extreme right-wing intellectuals such as Julius Langbehn and Maurice Barrès and movements such as French Action and the Italian Nationalist Association increasingly rejected the notion that the state had to serve the nation and that the will of citizens had to be expressed by political parties competing for individuals' votes. Influenced by a social Darwinist view of the international arena, they argued that a strong state was needed for the nation to prevail. Parliamentary rule led to endless discussions, weak compromises, and political instability, and as a result, it tended to undermine national unity and debilitate the state. Hierarchy, efficiency, and order could be achieved by a more authoritarian setup. Accordingly, vigorous leaders with a clear view of the nation's interests should lead the regeneration of the state.[31]

After the First World War these ideas became more mainstream, and numerous authoritarian regimes came to power in Latin America and in Southern and Eastern Europe. Sometimes these regimes were led by a monarch, as was the case with King Zog in Albania, King Alexander in Yugoslavia, Tsar Boris of Bulgaria, and King Carol in Romania, or by high military officers such as Admiral Miklos Horthy in Hungary, Marshal Józef Piłsudski in Poland, General Miguel Primo de Rivera and Generalissimo Francisco Franco in Spain, General Ioannis Metaxas in Greece, General Mustafa Kemal in Turkey, General José Uriburu in Argentina, and General Maximiliano Hernández Martínez in El Salvador. Other authoritarian regimes were headed by civilians, including Antonio de Oliveira Salazar in Portugal, Engelbert Dolfuss in Austria, Antanas Smetona in Lithuania, Karlis Ulmanis in Latvia, Konstantin Päts in Estonia, and Getúlio Vargas in Brazil. Most of these regimes restricted the electoral participation of opposition parties—mostly those on the left or those representing ethnic minorities—and curtailed civil liberties. Many dictators tried to install a dominant regime party, which in several countries was the only party permitted. These dominant regime parties included the Nonpartisan Bloc for Cooperation with the Government in Poland, the Unity Party in Hungary, and the Imperial Rule Assistance Association in wartime Japan. Political representation was monopolized by the Patriotic Union in Spain, the National Union in Portugal, the Fatherland Front in Austria, the Fatherland League in Estonia, and the Front of National Rebirth in Romania. Many of these parties also had a militia and a uniformed youth movement, and some regimes also adopted other paraphernalia of the Fascist movements.[32]

Most authoritarian regimes adopted corporatist ideals, which had been developed by Catholic authors in the late nineteenth century. In the encyclical *Rerum Novarum* of 1891, Pope Leo XIII officially endorsed a corporatist reordering of society. To avoid both the individualism of liberal capitalism and the class struggle preached by socialists, Catholics should establish corporations—modeled after an idealized image of the medieval guilds—that would bring together workers and employers from each economic branch to defend their common interests while creating harmonious relations at the workplace. These ideas were quickly taken up by other right-wing authors and movements, who also applied them to the political sphere, calling for an organic, corporatist organization of the state. Such a structure was first adopted in Spain by Primo de Rivera, who, after a military coup in 1923, tried to institute a more permanent regime by creating a single party and a parliament in which professional groups and members selected by the party would get seats. However, he stepped down seven years later, before he could fully implement his plans. In neighboring Portugal, Salazar also created a single party, and in 1933 he introduced a directly elected parliament and a consultative corporatist chamber. Similar institutional frameworks were introduced in Austria and Brazil, and most of the other authoritarian regimes in Europe, Latin America, and Asia adopted various corporatist elements. Although its proponents argued that corporatism allowed for a more truly and organic expression of the nation's interests, in fact, power was centralized in the hands of the dictator. Therefore, it is debatable whether many of these states still can be defined as full-fledged nation-states.[33]

Corporatist elements were also adopted by Fascist regimes, especially by forcing trade unions and employers to collaborate with the state to determine production goals and working conditions. However, the Fascist parties in Italy and Germany were truly mass movements led by charismatic leaders. Benito Mussolini and Adolf Hitler gained power by being appointed prime minister of a coalition cabinet and then installing a one-party dictatorship. Whereas right-wing authoritarian dictators mostly aimed to maintain the existing order and ward off external threats, the Fascist regimes actively mobilized the population and conducted an expansionist foreign policy. The nation and its resources should be put at the service of the state, which should not merely preserve the status quo but instead persecute internal enemies and create a strong imperial state.[34]

Like the Soviet Union, which for the moment was too weak to pursue world revolution, and imperial Japan, where social Darwinist conceptions of the international arena also became mainstream, Fascist Italy and Nazi Germany sought to expand their territories. In a departure from the practices of the existing European colonial empires, territorial expansion was sought closer at home in order to create Japan's Greater East Asia Co-Prosperity Sphere and to make the Mediterranean an Italian sea and Eastern Europe a German "living space." During the Second World War Italy and Germany annexed extensive territories, but they also created a number of authoritarian puppet states. Japan showed the way by creating Manchukuo in 1932, followed by, among others, the Reorganized National Government of the Republic of China, the State of Burma, and the Second Philippine Republic. Italy turned Albania, Greece, Montenegro, and Croatia into satellite states, and the Third Reich did the same with, among others, Slovakia, the Protectorate of Bohemia and Moravia, Vichy France, and Serbia. Although many collaborationist regimes also tried to expand their territories and even conducted ethnic cleansing campaigns to homogenize their populations, they were in fact politically and economically subordinate to the larger interests of the Third Reich, Fascist Italy, and imperial Japan, and all of them disappeared with them.[35] Notwithstanding their fierce nationalist rhetoric, Japan, the Third Reich, and Fascist Italy clearly favored empire over the nation-state.

Citizenship

Citizenship became more important during the interwar period, as it encompassed more people and reached into new domains. The First World War conferred novel responsibilities on belligerent states that directly affected people's lives, including levying ever-growing numbers of recruits, requisitioning supplies for the army, coordinating the war economy, taking care of war victims, and distributing scarce food supplies. This was a serious challenge for most governments. Mutinies broke out on several fronts in 1917, and strikes expressed widespread discontent. Social unrest caused by war-weariness, rising prices, shortages, and growing inequality also appeared in the colonies and even in several neutral countries, for example in Latin America.[36] In fact, many weak states were unable to meet the growing expectations of their populations. This failure surely was a major factor in the collapse of Russia, Austria-Hungary, and the Ottoman Empire.

Mass mobilization during the war, the introduction of general suffrage in most European countries immediately after its end, and the example of the Communist revolution in Russia profoundly transformed the relationship between citizens and the state. Social demands—ranging from land reform and the creation of a welfare state to a radical redistribution of wealth—were at the top of the political agenda. Moreover, in the countries that had participated in the war, the care of disabled veterans, widows, and orphans required a prolonged involvement of the state. Several new constitutions in East and Central Europe guaranteed a variety of social rights, while the left-wing constitution adopted in Mexico in 1917 even mentioned health insurance, the eight-hour day, and old-age pensions. Japan developed a system of voluntary district commissioners who functioned as effective intermediaries between the poor and local social services. However, postwar political instability and economic slump prevented states from taking a more active role in public welfare. Although the central administrations of many Western European countries were reinforced after the war, most states in Southern, Central, and Eastern Europe and Latin America had difficulty living up to the raised expectations, and this prepared the way for more authoritarian regimes.[37]

The Wall Street Crash of 1929 and the subsequent Great Depression worsened the situation, since more people depended on welfare institutions for survival and governments faced serious budget deficits. International cooperation to combat the crisis failed, and countries devalued their currencies to gain competitive advantages and raised tariffs to protect their own economies. Some regimes pursued a policy of autarky. Many administrations also experimented with a more interventionist role in economic affairs; President Franklin Delano Roosevelt's New Deal is probably the best-known example of this, although aside from restoring confidence through economic coordination and public works, it merely introduced many of the social insurance policies that were already current in Western Europe. Social Democratic governments in Scandinavia were much more interventionist, increasing public spending and extending welfare measures such as universal health care and parental leave. The most drastic measures were taken in the Soviet Union, though they were not related to the crisis in the capitalist world. In 1928, Moscow adopted its first Five-Year Plan, which set detailed targets for all sectors of the economy. This idea was copied by Nazi Germany in the form of its Four-Year Plan. Economic plans were also introduced in Belgium and Turkey in 1933, in Poland in 1936, and in a more flexible way in the Scandinavian countries; corporatist and authoritarian solutions became increasingly popular as well.[38] Naturally, state interference in the economy would become even more prominent during the Second World War. Whether the economic plans were for a capitalist or a communist system, they curtailed the economic freedom of companies, impacted the workforce, and influenced consumer choices, while at the same time increasing the economic integration within a national framework.

Female citizens also took a more public role. During the Great War, many women bore the sole responsibility for their families while substituting for men in the workplace. Toward the end of the war, they constituted one-third of the munition workers in France and more than 40 percent of the industrial workforce in Russia. After the February Revolution, the Russian army even created female battalions. Many feminists expected that after the war, women would be rewarded with the vote, which effectively happened in most European countries, thus making women full members of the nation. Ironically, the main Entente powers were mostly unmoved. Great Britain gave the vote only to single women over thirty who owned property or had a university degree, and in France the Senate rejected female suffrage out of fear that women would be controlled by the reactionary clergy. Other Catholic countries such as Italy, Spain, Portugal, and most Latin American states were also hesitant to give women the vote. And the same was true for Japan, China, and most Asian and Middle Eastern countries, with the important exception of Turkey. The Soviet Union, on the other hand, added the right to divorce and eight weeks of maternity leave, and legalized abortion.[39]

Paternalistic views were still ingrained in many family law codes. In most countries, the husband determined the nationality of the family. Many Alsatian women who had married Germans during the period when the region had been part of the German Empire were expelled after the reincorporation of Alsace into France. The growing participation of women in all kinds of professions also created legal problems. When a female German doctor contracted marriage to a Peruvian, she lost her citizenship and therefore was barred from the German Medical Association; as a consequence, she could no longer treat insured patients.[40] Thus, men's bonds to the patria trumped those of women.

Women also assumed a greater role in nationalist movements outside Europe. In Egypt, women protested against Britain's refusal to grant the country self-determination. Huda Sha'arawi, the wife of the vice president of the Wafd Party, organized a separate women's demonstration that ended in a showdown with British troops. Soon after, she founded a women's committee within the Wafd Party and the Egyptian Feminist Union. Women also participated on a massive scale in the nationalist mobilization campaigns in India, such as Gandhi's boycott of British products and a countrywide action against the British salt monopoly. In 1927, a separate All India Women's Conference was set up to improve female opportunities in the field of education.[41]

The more prominent role of women in the public sphere during the war produced a backlash. Trade unions and veterans' organizations agitated against women keeping paid jobs, and governments promoted a return to the male breadwinner model. In 1921, the British government introduced family allowances. France, which had one of the highest death tolls during the war, was particularly preoccupied with its lagging birth rate. The government outlawed abortion and introduced medals for motherhood, ranging from a bronze medal for five children and gold for ten. Mother's Day, which the United States made an official holiday in 1914, was also adopted elsewhere, beginning with France. Motherhood training courses were organized, and the Socialist city council of Vienna introduced a "social contract" with parents, supporting them to create optimal conditions for a healthy family life. The backlash against women was also visible in East Asia. In China, the forces of Chiang Kai-shek killed thousands of "modern" women for displaying un-Chinese behavior, which was thought to be a sign of communist sympathies.[42]

There was also a growing preoccupation with public health, particularly because of the damaging effects of the Spanish flu pandemic, tuberculosis, venereal diseases, and alcohol. The National Prohibition Act was adopted in the United States in 1919, and both Great Britain and France set up a Ministry of Health. Public housing was organized in many parts of Europe to improve the living conditions of the poor. Some governments adopted eugenic measures, which could be expressed as increased attention to physical exercise, fresh air, and healthy nutrition, but also as sterilization of mentally ill persons, which occurred in the United States, Scandinavian countries, and above all, Nazi Germany.[43]

The more intrusive role of the state also made possible a more thorough assimilation of the population. This was partly an indirect consequence of the democratization process. Political parties and social and cultural associations had been increasingly organized along ethnic or religious lines, and this received a massive boost during the First World War. Whereas before 1914, most nationalist movements had striven for cultural autonomy or home rule, by the end of the war an independent and preferably ethnically homogeneous nation-state had become the goal. This, however, made ethnic minorities a problem.

With hundreds of thousands of stateless refugees and rampant ethnic violence in East-Central Europe and Asia Minor, the Paris Peace Conference had to find a solution to guarantee that the new states would abide by "civilized" standards. Since Jews were particularly targeted, their organizations actively lobbied the main participants at the peace conference. One of the solutions proposed was the recognition of a Jewish nation within each of the new European states; they would get separate parliaments and even a seat in the League of Nations. But this idea of collective representation at both the national and the international levels was rejected because it would undermine the sovereignty of the new nation-states. In the end, individual treaties for the protection of ethnic and religious minorities were signed with eighteen states in Eastern Europe and the Middle East. They guaranteed to minorities equality before the law, freedom of religion, and the right to create social and cultural institutions, but there was no obligation to fund education in minority languages. Although similar treaties had been signed before, especially at the Berlin Conference of 1878, they had referred primarily to religious groups. Now they were extended to include ethnic minorities, albeit only those in defeated countries or new nation-states. The treaties would be supervised by the League of Nations, but it had no means to enforce them. As Eric Weitz has argued, the new system of international relations devised in Paris implied that unlike what happened later with the introduction of human rights, individuals deserved these special rights only as members of a recognized ethnic or religious community. The minority treaties also suggested that the ethnically homogenous nation-state had become the norm, and in fact, minorities had been turned into anomalies.[44]

The imposition of minority treaties was seen as unfair by politicians and intellectuals from the new countries. Queen Marie of Romania asked Wilson whether similar minority protection measures would apply to Blacks in the United States and to Irish in the United Kingdom. A similar double standard led to the rejection of the Japanese proposal to include racial equality in the covenant of the League of Nations. Apart from retaining the territories it had conquered from Germany, including the racial equality clause was Japan's major objective during the negotiations. Having been treated differently by the great powers until the abrogation of the extraterritorial rights for foreigners, the Japanese were very sensitive to discriminatory practices, which many still experienced when traveling to Western countries. The barring of Asian immigrants from most American countries and British dominions, discriminatory measures such as excluding Japanese from buying land or attending school in several U.S. states, and outcries about the "yellow peril" in many Western news outlets were a thorn in the side of the Japanese. However, the plea for racial equality met with fierce opposition from Australia and New Zealand, who feared that it would threaten their restrictive immigration policies. Wilson and Lloyd George were not very enthusiastic either. Wilson argued that the League of Nations would be based on the equality of nations and that the Japanese should not worry too much about racial prejudices.[45]

A different way of dealing with a multiethnic population was devised by Vladimir Lenin and Joseph Stalin in the Soviet Union. Although national self-determination officially was recognized, a parting of ways was not an option, and the construction of a socialist society was the first priority. Nevertheless, ethnically defined nations were seen as a historical reality, and in order to encourage support for the communist cause, the construction and development of national cultures, even of the tiniest minorities, was actively promoted from 1923, a policy that Rogers Brubaker has defined as ethnoterritorial federalism. This was also done to encourage irredentism in neighboring countries, where related ethnic groups still lived under capitalist oppression. As a result, minority languages were codified, and newspapers, movies, folklore, and museums were created for each ethnic group in the Soviet Union. This meant that many people were made aware of their "national identity" for the first time. Larger "peoples" received their own republics, while minor ethnic groups were awarded national districts or even smaller territorial units where they were the "titular nationality" that determined the official language used in schools and by the administration. A crucial element of this "indigenization" policy was that within their territory, members of the "titular nationality" held leadership positions in the government and the Communist Party. In this "affirmative action empire"—a concept coined by Terry Martin—rights were awarded collectively to ethnic groups living in their supposed homelands. Moreover, in the context of the collectivization of agriculture and the regulation of migration flows, the state introduced an internal passport system that legally codified nationality based on ethnic descent. Thus, although the Soviet Union characterized itself as internationalist, the state in fact nationalized both its territories and citizens. Inhabitants had both an ethnic substate nationality and a supranational Soviet identity.[46]

Another "solution" to the "minority problem"—population exchange—was also tried in the immediate postwar era. During the Russo-Turkish Wars and the wars in the Balkans, many Muslims had fled to the Ottoman Empire, while smaller numbers of Orthodox Christians had moved in the opposite direction. After the victory of Turkish forces in Anatolia, many argued that the rights of Greeks and Turks could be guaranteed only in their own nation-states. Thus, the Greek and Turkish leadership agreed on an obligatory population exchange. The agreement was brokered by Fridtjof Nansen, the High Commissioner for Refugees of the League of Nations, and endorsed by the great powers in the Treaty of Lausanne. In total, around one million Greek Orthodox—many of whom did not speak Greek—fled or were expelled from Anatolia and Thrace to Greece, and approximately 350,000 Muslims were forced out of Greece.[47]

Although many ethnic minorities were now officially protected by treaties, most states implemented an active nation-building policy. Assimilation was pursued first through education. In most Eastern European and Middle Eastern states minority schools were discouraged, and when they survived, they were mostly obliged to teach the language and history of the dominant nation. Often, the state administration used only the national language, and members of ethnic minorities were underrepresented in the civil service. Resettlement programs made many original inhabitants into small minorities, including the Ruthenes in Eastern Galicia and Slavic-speaking Macedonians and Jews in Greek Macedonia, while discriminatory measures in land reform, religious policies, political patronage, and schooling induced members of ethnic and religious minorities to emigrate. Sometimes they were even explicitly encouraged to leave, by state officials and by hostile actions of the dominant ethnic group. Thus, instead of encouraging integration, these policies often had contrary effects. Tensions grew even in countries that had brought together groups with similar ethnic backgrounds and languages but different kingdoms or empires of origin. Slovaks resented the ascendancy of Czechs, and in Yugoslavia Croats and others grudgingly accepted the dominance of the Serbs. Often these frictions were exacerbated by religious cleavages. Groups that were not easily integrated, such as Jews and Sinti and Roma, were openly excluded and stigmatized, and antisemitic pogroms occurred in various parts of Eastern Europe. Similar developments also occurred outside of Europe. Attempts by Assyrian Christians to obtain autonomy in the new Kingdom of Iraq were met with brutal violence by the army.[48]

Discriminatory measures in the Americas such as the Jim Crow laws in the United States and the severe curtailment or banning of Chinese and Japanese immigration remained in place or were reinforced. In the United States a new act adopted in February 1917 prohibited immigration from an "Asiatic Barred Zone," which now included almost all parts of South Asia, and a quota system introduced a few years later favored emigrants from Northwestern Europe. White dominions tried to exclude Indians, ignoring their rights as British subjects to migrate freely within the empire. In later decades, similar restrictive measures for immigrants from Asia were adopted in Canada, Mexico, Peru, and Brazil. Most Latin American countries favored immigration from Europe, with the explicit goal of "whitening" the population.[49]

Latin America's Indigenous populations also continued to be treated as second-rate citizens. Most of their communal land holdings had been privatized, and they were subjected to policies of cultural assimilation. In Mexico, an uprising of Yaqui Indians in 1896 had been brutally repressed, and many of those who survived were deported or practically enslaved. The arrival of mass politics, on the other hand, increased the significance of Indigenous and mestizo support. In 1910, Brazil set up the Service for the Protection of the Indians, which aimed to protect their land titles and enhance their education. This example was followed in the next few decades by Peru and Mexico. The new revolutionary authorities in Mexico were particularly active, opening a large number of rural and Indigenous schools, which were also used for craft workshops, agrarian reform, and political mobilization. In 1923, José Vasconcelos, the minister of education, created cultural missions by sending groups of urban intellectuals to the countryside to educate the population and show them the benefits of modern secular civilization. This example would be copied in the 1930s by Peru, and similar attempts to nationalize the countryside could also be found further afield, such as the Pedagogical Missions in the Spanish Second Republic and the Village Institutes in Turkey. In the 1930s some Mexican intellectuals even recommended applying the Soviet model by recognizing Native communities as submerged nationalities that should be granted autonomy.[50]

The United States and several British dominions had established more intrusive assimilationist policies targeting Indigenous minorities beginning in the late nineteenth century. Arguing that children were more malleable than adults and that it was appropriate to separate them from their "barbarous," "disorderly," and "superstitious" environments, the state took many of them away from their families and sent them to boarding schools. They were forbidden to speak their mother tongues and practice traditional lifestyles, their hair was shaved, and they had to wear modern school uniforms. A strict regime of education, religious teachings—many Canadian boarding schools were run by Christian congregations—and domestic and manual labor should turn them into "civilized" and diligent citizens. A new curriculum in the U.S. boarding schools from 1916 included "military and gymnastic drills." Native Americans were drafted into the army, both in Canada and in the United States, which finally led to granting of American citizenship to all Native Americans in 1924. At about the same time, the expectation make them fully "civilized" Americans dwindled, and education in the United States for Native American children began to focus more on vocational training, preparing the boys for simple manual trades or agricultural labor and teaching the girls mainly cooking, sewing, and housekeeping. Similar programs were devised for Indigenous communities in the northern islands of Japan. In Australia, officials recommended removing Aboriginal children from their parents at a very young age. Some even hoped to absorb them into the "white race"; especially "half-caste Aboriginal girls" could be matched to white males to "breed out the color." Thus, forceful assimilation policies were not the sole preserve of totalitarian countries.[51]

Most ethnic minorities did not accept their fate passively—they created nationwide emancipatory associations. In the United States, the National Association for the Advancement of Colored People was set up in 1909, followed by the Society for American Indians. In Canada, too, Native Americans became more assertive, and the Six Nations Council of the Iroquois claimed that they retained sovereignty within Canada. When the British government refused to recognize this, they presented their case to the League of Nations in 1923. However, major concessions were out of the question.[52]

The Fascist regimes of Italy and Germany were also very intrusive as they aimed to put an ethnically or racially defined nation at the service of the state. Before the March on Rome, Mussolini's Fascist militia were extraordinarily violent toward the "internal enemies" of the nation such as the socialists—this "Russian army" on Italian soil—and the Slovene minority. It was only after consolidating his regime that Mussolini began to focus on strengthening the state. One way to do this was to increase the number of Italians. Thus, abortion and birth control were prohibited, and women were encouraged to be good and productive mothers. The National Agency for Maternal and Infant Welfare professionalized the care for pregnant women and young children, while family allowances and a bachelor's tax encouraged couples to get married and procreate. The regime also tried to mobilize society with a whole range of Fascist mass societies, including a youth movement, the national leisure organization After Work, university groups, and women's sections. Nonetheless, because the regime functioned only due to the tacit support of the monarchy, the army, big business, large landowners, and the Catholic Church, its power to turn Italians into dedicated Fascists was relatively limited.[53]

The National Socialist regime that came to power in Germany in 1933 was more radical. Almost immediately, existing professional and voluntary associations were forced to merge into new umbrella organizations under strict Nazi supervision. Concentration camps were created for social deviants, petty criminals, and members of the opposition. The rest of the population—at least those of supposed Aryan descent—was mobilized in mass organizations such as party militias, the Hitler Youth, the Labor Front, and Strength through Joy, the national leisure organization. People were fed propaganda, but they could also go to a holiday camp or participate in a savings scheme for a Volkswagen. House purchases were subsidized and marriage loans were made available. Women were encouraged to become productive mothers and good housewives. Maternity homes were created for "racially pure" single mothers, and their children were given to "healthy" Nazi families for adoption. Eugenic measures focused on the fitness of the German "race" were implemented by promoting sports and physical exercise. The health of the national community also had to be "safeguarded," so in the first years of the regime the Nazis forcefully sterilized hundreds of thousands of mentally ill persons, beggars, Roma, and prostitutes. The Reich Central Office for the Combating of Homosexuality and Abortion actively persecuted tens of thousands of homosexuals, many of whom were castrated, and shortly before the start of the Second World War the regime "finished off" almost one hundred thousand "unworthy lives" in clinics and asylums.[54]

At the same time, Hitler's racial and antisemitic ideas were translated into practical measures. Jews, who according to the Nazis undermined the strength of the German nation, were banned from civil service and professional organizations in 1933. The Nuremberg laws made Jewish citizens and opponents of the regime "subjects of the state," with obligations but no rights. In 1938, in retaliation for the murder of a Nazi diplomat in Paris by a Jewish student, a nationwide pogrom was unleashed in Kristallnacht (Night of Broken Glass). The German Jews were collectively made responsible for paying a huge fine and the costs for clearing up the mess, and insurance payments for the damage were confiscated by the state.[55]

Many Fascists and ultranationalists argued that the state, which embodied the nation, had to be as strong as possible. This did not mean just reinforcing the nation internally, but also expanding its role in the internal arena. In the protectionist climate of the 1930s, this implied acquiring primary materials, land, and other resources by occupying and monopolizing access to new territories. A strong nation needed an empire, preferably close at home. This led to a new round of imperial conquests, initiated by Japan's occupation of Manchuria in 1931. Italy and Germany soon followed with their own invasions. The populations of the conquered areas were subjugated and the economies were made subservient to the metropole's interests, while any sign of resistance was brutally suppressed.[56] A similar radicalization was also visible in the Soviet Union, where international tensions and Stalin's own suspicions led to violent purges. The forced collectivization of agriculture, combined with fears of nationalist rumblings and aggressive grain requisition campaigns, led to the starvation of millions of Ukrainian peasants in 1932 to 1933. In later years, Stalin began to emphasize the leading role of the Russian people, while ethnic minorities who were perceived as a threat—Volga Germans, Poles, Finns, Koreans, and Japanese—fell victim to the Great Purge in disproportionate numbers. After the Molotov-Ribbentrop Pact, the Soviet Union invaded eastern Poland, killing tens of thousands of Polish officers and intellectuals in Katyn; turned the Baltic countries into puppet states; and attempted to conquer Finland. During the Second World War this was followed by the large-scale deportation of suspected minorities, including Chechens and Crimean Tatars.[57]

In Nazi Germany, not only did the population have to serve the state, but people were also moved around on a massive scale to create the new German living space in the East. The areas in Eastern Europe that were conquered in the early stages of the Second World War had to be prepared for fresh German settlers, while the local Slavic population was categorized to see who could be "re-Germanized." The rest either served as a kind of permanent underclass for the new German overlords, were sent to work camps, or could in the future be resettled in Siberia. Ethnic Germans from Russia, East European allies, and Italy could move to Germany or get a farm in the newly occupied territories. Prisoners of war, particularly "racially inferior" Russians, were used for forced labor and sometimes were worked to death, whereas Jews, who were at the bottom of the Nazi racial hierarchy, were resettled in the General Government in southeastern Poland or killed immediately. Those who survived deportation were eventually sent to extermination camps, where millions were gassed to death. Paradoxically, in order to combat the growing labor shortages in the Third Reich, millions of foreign workers were brought into Germany proper, converting many villages and towns into truly multinational laboratories.[58]

National Awareness

Possessing full citizenship rights was more consequential in most European and American countries, where the growth of national awareness was almost inevitable. The nation-state had become omnipresent in daily life, be it through conscription, education, law enforcement, or a welfare system. Newspapers and radio widened the national public sphere, and the extension of the suffrage opened new opportunities for political participation. This process was reinforced by the First World War, which mobilized not just soldiers but also the home front, and this was repeated on an even larger scale during the Second

World War, which also affected larger parts of Asia, Africa, and the Pacific. After 1918, individuals were supposed to be integral members of the dominant nationality or to identify with a specific ethnic minority. Both old and new nation-states intensified their nation-building policies, while associations and parties representing specific minorities did their best to mobilize their rank and file. In addition, the economic depression of the 1930s gave the state a larger role in society, and in many cases it promoted various forms of economic nationalism ranging from mild forms of protectionism to autarky. As a result, both the identification with the nation-state and the awareness of one's own ethnic identity increased substantially during this period.

An indifferent attitude was harder to sustain, but it had not disappeared. Many Native Americans in the United States preferred to ignore "white society" and the institutions of the nation-state as much as possible. The Indian Reorganization Act of 1934 aimed to strengthen the position of the Native American tribes, but they were required to adopt a constitution and elect officials— instead of following their traditional selection methods to choose a chief. The proposal was rejected by 78 of the 252 tribes. Another fascinating example can be found in the ethnically mixed eastern provinces of Poland, where during the 1921 census about forty thousand people identified themselves as "people from here," a label invented by experts for persons who did not fit any of the existing national categories. Ten years later, seven hundred thousand people answered that they spoke "the language from here" in response to a question about their mother tongue. For many peasants, social and religious identifications continued to be more important than ethnicity or nationality, and they defined themselves as, for instance, "simple people," who were fundamentally different from nobles, Jews, and modern town-dwellers.[59]

In other ethnically diverse areas in East-Central Europe, many people tried to avoid hard choices, or to approach the nationality question from an instrumental angle. In the formerly Hungarian region of Transylvania, many Romanian, Hungarian, and German speakers opted to celebrate a shared Transylvanian identity. In Moldavia, on the other side of Romania, Csangos, a Roman Catholic community that mostly spoke Hungarian dialects, opposed a plan in the early 1940s to expatriate them to Hungary, by arguing that their blood groups were more in line with the Romanians' and thus they were of Romanian stock. Inhabitants of Upper Silesia and Bohemia, many of whom were bilingual, used opportunities that national governments or nationalist movements offered them, such as schooling, as they saw fit. Some changed their national adscriptions when it seemed opportune, for example, becoming German when Hitler conquered Bohemia or adopting the opposite option after Nazi Germany lost the war. Some even switched sides several times.[60]

In any case, national awareness increased rapidly, outside of Europe, too. The World Wars mobilized millions of people around the world as soldiers or laborers. Direct foreign military threats or occupations enhanced the national consciousness of the population, while economic dislocations and shortages made farmers and consumers aware that their lot was connected to the outcome of the conflict. Many people became accustomed to dividing the world into different nation-states and colonies, although it is unlikely that many also internalized a more historicist interpretation of national identities, each with its own heritage and peculiarities. Few of the tens of thousands of Moroccan soldiers who participated in the Spanish Civil War on the side of General Franco would have cherished the ideas that propagandists of the Francoist cause disseminated about a shared medieval past, embodied by the magnificent monuments of Al-Andalus, or about the supposed racial affinities between them and the Spaniards.[61]

Protests and uprisings in favor of national self-determination mobilized large sectors of society in, for instance, Egypt, Syria, Iraq, India, Korea, and China. In India, Gandhi succeeded in rallying the masses in various campaigns against the colonial authorities, becoming a source of inspiration for nationalist activists elsewhere in the colonial world. Opposing a common enemy—the "foreign oppressor"—made it easier to overcome internal religious, ethnic, and ideological differences in order to unify the population behind a shared program of national independence. Thus, the Indian National Congress and the Muslim League made a pact to collaborate in order to obtain concessions from the British. In China, Chiang Kai-shek's Guomindang and Mao Zedong's Communist Party worked together in a United Front during a military campaign, first against the northern warlords from 1923 to 1927 and later against Japan from 1937 to 1941.[62]

There were also more structural reasons for the greater national awareness. As education levels increased, more people learned to read. In urban areas, newspapers became more widely available, keeping people informed about major events throughout the world, especially in times of war. The invention and rapid dissemination of film and radio made it easier to reach broad strata of the population, including the illiterate. Cinema became enormously popular; in 1934, the average Briton saw twenty-two films. Newsreels, which had been introduced in France in 1908, brought a weekly update of political developments, sports, natural disasters, and society events to a rapidly growing audience. Although international items were covered as well, a strong focus on domestic news made the public familiar with their country's geography, politics, celebrities, and major sporting events. Dictatorial regimes such as Fascist Italy used the newsreels for political propaganda, but most newsreels were made by film companies. Although they attempted to adopt a neutral tone, they usually provided a pro-government perspective. Because weekly newsreels were expensive to produce, smaller countries depended on foreign film companies, though these often included locally shot items. The one-man Flandria Film enterprise had difficulty entering the predominantly French-language cinemas in Belgium and therefore catered mostly to the alternative market of Flemish nationalist organizations; its commercial successes consisted mainly of documentaries of Flemish sporting (cycle) events. The dominant position of international firms could cause friction and, in fact, could have an indirect nationalizing effect. Irish audiences sometimes booed the British who appeared onscreen, and Canadian spectators complained about the patriotic coverage of U.S. war exploits.[63]

Radio broadcasting, which equally framed the world in national terms, was introduced in the early 1920s, and with the availability of ever-more affordable radio sets, it quickly became a highly influential mass medium. In the United States and several other countries, commercial stations dominated the airwaves, focusing primarily on entertainment and music. In most parts of Europe and Japan, national broadcasting organizations received a monopoly; they generally paid more attention to elite culture and educational programs. They were either neutral public service organizations, like the British Broadcasting Corporation (BBC), or state-controlled institutions that mostly reflected the views of the incumbent government. The radio quickly strengthened the imagined community of the nation, as millions of listeners could simultaneously experience the same event. In 1926, millions of Japanese were captivated by frequent updates on the final illness of their emperor. Politicians also discovered the power of the medium, and Adolf Hitler's mass rallies, Roosevelt's fireside chats, and the British king's Christmas addresses reached a broad nationwide audience. Sporting events such as the Oxford-Cambridge Boat Race and the Wimbledon tennis tournament were broadcast live, and in the United States the frequent reports on baseball made Babe Ruth a national superstar. International sporting contests such as the Olympic Games and the football World Cup encouraged sports commentators to abandon journalistic objectivity and become national cheerleaders, provoking patriotic feelings among the audience. Radio broadcasts, finally, had a crucial role in standardizing and nationalizing cultural practices. In the 1930s the Mexican government decreed that all radio stations had to include 25 percent "typical" national music in their broadcasts. By adopting vernacular traditions stripped of their most disorderly aspects, they created a respectable national musical heritage that could compete with "vile" foreign rhythms such as jazz. As the BBC made clear, radio broadcasts could also have a huge impact on the standardization of the national language—even the "right" pronunciation—by diffusing it to the far corners of the country, to the detriment of dialects and minority languages.[64]

Nationalization of Culture

The period between the beginning of the First and the end of the Second World War was a time of conflicting tendencies. The hope for a better world with a spirit of cooperation was expressed in Wilson's and Roosevelt's claim to be fighting to "make the world safe for democracy," in the founding of the League of Nations, and in the "spirit of Locarno." Others were encouraged by the Russian and Mexican Revolutions, while inhabitants of new nation-states such as Poland, Turkey, and China hoped for national rebirth. In the Western world, after an initial postwar crisis, the Roaring Twenties brought back an atmosphere of optimism. On the other hand, a more aggressive and pessimistic worldview was expressed in the rise of Fascism, Nazism, numerous authoritarian regimes, the drive for protectionism, and autarky that began to dominate the international arena after the Wall Street Crash, and in the racism, xenophobia, and imperialist mentality that became more pronounced in the 1930s and early 1940s. Both the open, cosmopolitan, optimistic mood and the more closed, aggressive, imperialist mentality were visible in the humanities, the social sciences, and the arts. In general, the German-speaking world, which had been cut off from Western scientific and intellectual developments during the First World War, tilted toward a more closed and exclusionary view—although there were important exceptions, such as Bauhaus—while in most Western European countries and the United States, internationalist ideas found a more fertile breeding ground. At the same time, the earlier attempts to ground the nation more firmly in natural factors such as race or geography continued, which also meant that territorial units both smaller and larger than the nation-state continued to be relevant. Some authors rejected these almost deterministic views in favor of a more social or cultural approach, while taking ethnic communities or nation-states as their main unit of analysis. Although they pretended to conduct objective empirical research, they implicitly reified national societies and cultures.

Racial ideas influenced many scientists, especially in the field of physical anthropology, where measurements and classifications of corporal traits continued to be in vogue. Many assumed that not just many diseases but also traits such as manual dexterity, intellectual capacity, "wander instincts," and homosexuality were heritable; biological factors even largely determined the cultural characteristics of entire nations and races. The discovery of blood groups elicited a new fascination with the potential connections between blood and race. Many scholars actively promoted eugenic measures to improve the racial makeup of the nation, which in fact were applied in many countries. In the German-speaking world, physical anthropology became more prominent after the First World War, and nationalist and racial views were widespread. Many physical anthropologists actively contributed to the Nazi regime's eugenic and racial policies by giving advice on cases regarding racial ancestry and sterilization, on settlement plans for the newly conquered areas in Eastern Europe, or on finding a "solution" to the Jewish question.[65]

On the other side of the Atlantic, the anthropologist Franz Boas dismissed the evolutionary and racial assumptions that had dominated the discipline, in favor of a more cultural approach. From his chair at Columbia University, he rejected as simplistic the notion that humanity was divided into stages. Even before 1914, he argued that the character of a tribe or society was determined not by its stage on the evolutionary ladder, but by the way it interacted with its specific geographical and historical context. He also maintained that a society's level of civilization or an individual's health was not determined primarily by racial factors. This idea was reinforced by a major research project he conducted, measuring the statures and cranial features of European immigrants and their U.S.-born offspring, which showed that major changes could not be explained by racial or biological factors, but were due in large part to the change of environment. As a consequence, he rejected notions of racial superiority and encouraged the empirical study of individual tribes and societies. He argued that each language and culture should be studied on its own terms, which could be seen as a plea for cultural relativism. According to Boas—who had many prominent disciples, including Ruth Benedict and Margaret Mead—each tribe, ethnic community, and nation had its own unique culture that had been created over time, in interaction with its specific natural environment. During the 1920s, Bronislaw Malinowski and Alfred Reginald Radcliffe-Brown laid the foundation for the British school of social anthropology. Although they were less interested in historical developments, their research was also characterized by systematic fieldwork, a holistic approach to individual societies, and the rejection of evolutionary and racial ideas. Ethnography also received a boost in the Soviet Union, as its practitioners were deployed in support of the new "indigenization" policy to study the cultural attributes of all Soviet nationalities and ethnic groups, which in fact contributed to a reification of nationally defined "societies" and "cultures."[66]

Determinist views continued to be popular among some geographers, while others preferred a more pragmatic, empirical approach. Some scholars, such as Yale professor Ellsworth Huntington, believed race to be a crucial component in determining the character of a certain area or population—praising, for instance, the superior qualities of the "Teutons"—but most geographers concentrated on climatic, geological, and natural factors. Some, especially followers of Paul Vidal de la Blache, conducted detailed regional case studies in which they examined the land use, habits, and mentality that were the result of the interaction of the natural environment and the inhabitants over time.

They mostly studied agricultural regions and largely ignored the urbanization, industrialization, and modernization processes that had begun to erode regional differences. Others continued the geopolitical approach. Russian émigrés such as Petr Savitskii argued that Eurasia constituted a geographical and cultural unity of its own, which was fundamentally different from both Europe and Asia. In Japan and Nazi Germany, expansionist theories had the upper hand. Based on the argument that German settlers had disseminated their culture to many parts of Eastern Europe, geographers claimed these areas for Germany, while ex-general Karl Haushofer radicalized Ratzel's concept of "living space." Other scholars took a less overtly ideological approach by conducting empirical studies of the geographical characteristics of a specific area or landscape, while mostly taking for granted the existing boundaries of the nation-state. In Germany, Alfred Hettner propagated the systematic analysis of the geological, geographic, economic, and demographic characteristics of specific substate territories. In the United States, Carl Otwin Sauer adopted a similar method and added an outspoken historical dimension. Like many anthropologists, he advised his students to conduct prolonged field studies.[67]

Whereas anthropologists and geographers examined a variety of geographic and demographic units, most social scientists took the existing international order as their starting point, conducting practical investigations within one national context. This was certainly true of economics, which had been institutionalized as a separate discipline only in the late nineteenth century. Since Adam Smith's *The Wealth of Nations* (1776), economic thinking had been concerned primarily with the functioning of (national) markets and the advantages of (international) free trade. However, as a consequence of the rise of protectionist measures and the introduction of welfare measures, discussions increasingly focused on the role of the (nation-) state. This tendency was reinforced during the interwar years by the challenges posed by the collectivist model of the Soviet Union, the autarkic ideals of Fascist Italy and Nazi Germany, and the corporatist practices of authoritarian regimes. Many scholars defended the measures taken to protect national economies. Even in democratic countries, planning and "economic nationalism" became fashionable. This led to a reorientation of liberal economic thought, which was led by John Maynard Keynes. In response to the worldwide economic crisis of the 1930s, he began to argue for state intervention and some form of insulation from international free trade. In his article "National Self-Sufficiency," he argued for "homespun" goods, and claimed that finance should be national. This led to the publication of his seminal *General Theory of Employment, Interest and Money* (1936), in which he advocated for activist national governments, focusing primarily on budgetary and monetary policies, to mitigate the conjunctural fluctuations of their economies.[68]

Historians continued to study the past mostly through a national lens, as they had done since the Romantic era. This was particularly true in East-Central Europe, where the new states wholeheartedly promoted the construction and dissemination of new national master narratives. Even in a small country like Latvia, new chairs and historical journals were created; archaeological, historical, and folkloric research received generous funding; extensive source editions were published; and a national historical and an open-air museum were established. In Turkey, Mustafa Kemal was aware of the need for a new national story. Earlier histories had focused on the Ottoman Empire or, eventually, the ethnic origins of the Turks in Central Asia. In a thirty-six-hour speech at the party congress of 1927, the Turkish president gave his own interpretation of the recent "heroic" struggle for independence, which became the basis for subsequent historical narratives. He also strongly encouraged the construction of a new, nationalist interpretation of the more distant past and endorsed the sun language theory, which held that Turkish had been the original language of humanity. Historians also maintained that the Turks were Aryans and that the Hittites and Sumerians—and their glorious ancient civilizations—were ethnically related to the Turks. Thus, the Turkish presence in Anatolia dated from the mist of times, and views that portrayed Turks as foreign invaders should be dismissed.[69]

Outside of Europe, nationalist interpretations of the past were constructed in new countries such as Australia, Syria, and Iraq, while the creation of Hebrew University in Jerusalem by Zionists laid the foundation for the Jewish reinterpretation of the history of Palestine. Western authors also framed the history of colonial territories increasingly in national terms and assigned the inhabitants more agency in assimilating foreign influences and developing their own "national" cultural peculiarities. Many Asian scholars adopted a similar teleological view. In Siam, Prince Damrong wrote a book on "our wars with the Burmese," in which he reframed the dynastic conflicts of the past as national wars between Thai and Burmese. Others wrote biographies of heroic figures from the past who had challenged foreign rule. Abdul Hadi published a *History of the Malay World*, in which he refashioned the development of the various principalities in British Malaya and parts of the Dutch Indies as the history of the Malay people, thus anticipating the creation of a Malaysian nation-state.[70]

The polarization between ethnic or even racially informed hypernationalist history writing and more cosmopolitan approaches can also be detected. The first tendency was clearly present in Germany. Historians published extensive diplomatic source editions proving that Germany was not solely responsible for the outbreak of the First World War. During the Third Reich, many historians concentrated on racial issues, examining. for instance, the "Jewish question." In Western Europe, most historians professed a profound admiration for the German historical tradition, but some had turned their backs on it after the First World War. This was true of the Belgian historian Henri Pirenne, who had been deported to Germany. After the war, he eliminated any reference to race or ethnic nationalism from his publications and adopted a more comparative or transnational socioeconomic perspective, focusing on cities and classes. In France, a younger generation of scholars led by Marc Bloch and Lucien Febvre founded the influential journal *Annales*, which prioritized long-term socioeconomic factors over nationality and a strong interdisciplinary approach. Meanwhile, Black historians, including W.E.B. Du Bois, began to combat the negative, racially framed assessments of the role of African Americans in the history of the United States.[71]

In art history, similar developments could be identified, although here, many of the innovative approaches originated in the German-speaking world. In the late nineteenth century, art historians such as Heinrich Wölfflin and Alois Riegl had distanced themselves from the traditional historicist interpretation by developing a formal approach that focused on composition and style, rather than on the message or meaning of an artwork. At about the same time, Aby Warburg began to systematize the study of iconography. In both approaches, national aspects were of secondary importance. The First World War had a notable impact on art historical debates. In 1916, as a belated response to the German bombing of the Gothic cathedral of Reims, Émile Mâle published a series of essays on German art, claiming in his opening statement that "in the sphere of arts, Germany has invented nothing." This understandably led to an angry response from German and Austrian scholars, and although tempers calmed after the war, the hatchet was not entirely buried. Strzygowski radicalized his earlier views on the separate development of northern and southern Europe, arguing that the Nordic, Germanic, and Aryan artistic inclinations of the Germans were incompatible with those of the Latin peoples, and French authors such as Mâle and Henri Focillon ignored possible Germanic influences in the rise of medieval art, declaring that Romanesque and Gothic art were primarily products of the urban middle classes of Western Europe.[72]

The First World War also heavily influenced wider intellectual debates. Many prominent German intellectuals defended their national "culture" as authentic and spiritual, as well as focused on ethical values and community, whereas Western "civilization" was superficial, materialistic, hypocritical, and atomistic. The famous novelist Thomas Mann asserted that Germany was "a morally oriented nation" of "metaphysics, pedagogy, and music." But this spiritualist interpretation of a country's national identity was not unique to Germany. The preceding decades had already seen a strong reaction against the optimistic belief in material progress. Intellectuals such as Charles Maurras and Maurice Barrès in France urged their compatriots to take their spiritual—in this case, Catholic—heritage more seriously. Others like Leo Tolstoy in Russia, William Butler Yeats in Ireland, and Miguel de Unamuno in Spain proclaimed the essentially spiritual characters of their own nations.[73]

The rejection of a materialist West could also be found in many parts of Asia, Latin America, and Africa. Around the turn of the century, authors such as Okakura, Tagore, and Rodó had characterized their own countries or continents as gifted with a more spiritual disposition. Such ideas would become more widespread after 1918 through the writings and activities of figures like José Vasconcelos, Mahatma Gandhi, and Léopold Senghor. In his book *The Cosmic Race* (1925), Vasconcelos argued that the future civilization would be led by Latin America. Because of widespread miscegenation, the continent combined the best elements of European and Indigenous populations in their new "mestizo race," making it ideally suited to overcome the focus on the material needs and rational order of the dominant "civilization of the whites." By focusing on feeling and imagination, this new "cosmic race" could lead humanity into a more spiritual and aesthetic period. In contrast, Gandhi's emphasis on spirituality was based not on racial theories, but on a combination of Hindu traditions and modern reform ideas related to the arts and crafts movement, Madame Blavatsky's theosophism, pacifism, and vegetarianism. In his 1909 book *Hind Swaraj* (*Indian Home Rule*), he rejected not only British rule in India but also the dominance of Western civilization. An inner "soul force," which could only be acquired through self-knowledge, was necessary for his campaigns of nonviolent resistance. However, he did not oppose just Western materialism, but also trains, modern medicine, and Western dress, in favor of traditional modes of transport, dietary reform, abstinence, and homespun clothing. In the 1930s, Senghor—in close collaboration with Aimé Césaire—developed the notion of *négritude* (Blackness), countering European analytical reason, individualism, and materialism with the emotion and intuition of Black Africans. In several lectures and publications, he vindicated the contributions of Blacks to human civilization by emphasizing their sense of community, their spiritual values and empathy, and the harmony that existed between humans, God, and nature.[74]

A cosmopolitan modernism began to dominate the cultural realm, though it was not uncontested. After 1914 the artistic scene was dominated by the avant-garde, which aimed to overcome the shackles of past traditions. In 1909, Filippo Marinetti's *Futurist Manifesto* had called for the demolition of museums and libraries, "those cemeteries of wasted effort." In 1921, the painter Amédée Ozenfant and the architect Le Corbusier similarly asked themselves whether the Louvre should be set on fire. Marcel Duchamp exhibited a signed urinal as "ready-made art," radically questioning the concept of art itself. The function-alist design and buildings promulgated by Bauhaus obviated both fine arts aestheticism and artisanal traditions. In 1925, Le Corbusier proposed demol-ishing large parts of Paris and replacing historically grown neighborhoods with a symmetrical grid of identical skyscrapers in a park landscape. New York's new Museum of Modern Art showed the rise of the artistic avant-garde—for instance in the seminal *Cubism and Abstract Art* exhibition—as a quick succession of -isms that were defined solely by formal and stylistic criteria. Nationality and geographical background seemed to have become irrelevant.[75]

However, at the same time, there was a distinct return to order after the First World War. Even the groundbreaking cubist Pablo Picasso adopted a classicizing style. Nationalist influences continued to thrive, even among the most radical avant-garde artists. Thus, in his manifesto, Marinetti also glorified war, militarism, and patriotism. During the First World War he embraced an exalted form of nationalism, and in the early 1920s he became one of the lead-ers of the Italian Fascists. In the 1930s, Le Corbusier flirted with Italian Fascism and soon put himself at the service of the Vichy regime, hoping that an authoritarian state could realize some of his audacious plans. Some French authors began to classify the rise of the avant-garde as an essentially French *affaire*, and in 1937, when plans for a Parisian museum of modern art became concrete, it was clear that the history of the avant-garde would be presented as the continuation of a long and innovative French artistic tradition. On the left, avant-garde artists such as Diego Rivera put his work at the service of the Mexican revolutionary nation-building project, while he and his wife Frida Kahlo incorporated many Indigenous motifs in their paintings.[76]

Like Marinetti and Le Corbusier, composers such as Arnold Schönberg and Albin Berg broke with the existing musical traditions by developing atonal music and later devising a totally new twelve-tone technique. Another revolu-tion had its origins in the United States, where Black musicians from New Orleans developed jazz music, using a wide variety of vernacular and classical sources of inspiration. Jazz broke with the harmonious, rational order, in which the audience listened silently and the musicians faithfully followed the guidelines of the composers. Instead, the performers spontaneously articu-lated their feelings in rapturous melodies, while the listeners could participate by clapping their hands and dancing. It was mostly frowned on by the estab-lishment, but stars such as Louis Armstrong, Benny Goodman, and Duke El-lington quickly spread jazz to the rest of the world, where younger generations of musicians and listeners embraced the freedom of expression. Even in Nazi Germany it was impossible to totally suppress this "inferior" and "degenerate" art form.[77]

Meanwhile, nationalist influences did not disappear, as striking vernacular music continued to be standardized and codified. Radio broadcasting enabled the quick dissemination of popular tunes. New specialized exhibitions, such as the 1927 Music in the Life of the Peoples exposition in Frankfurt and the First International Congress of Popular Arts, held in Prague with support from the League of Nations' International Institute on Intellectual Cooperation, offered a platform to present each nation's "characteristic" musical highlights. New national traditions were also created. In the Americas, Native and African American vernacular traditions became more popular and were fused with transnational influences. In Rio de Janeiro, carnival groups were regularized in more formal samba schools. During the populist Getúlio Vargas regime, they were supposed to stage historical or patriotic themes; this model was subsequently exported to other parts of Brazil, making samba the national musical tradition. In Mexico, the mariachi music from Jalisco was standardized through recordings, radio performances, and appearances in film, becoming an essential part of the national repertoire. Local elites often had difficulties accepting the "scandalous" practices connected to popular music, such as the "lascivious" dance connected to the tango and the licentious taverns or caves where flamenco performances were held. Thus, the tango became an Argentinian national emblem only after it had become popular in Europe, whereas the flamenco, which was sought-after by foreign visitors to Andalusia and at world's fairs, began to improve its reputation only after intellectuals like Manuel de Falla and Federico García Lorca organized a festival to present it as an original and authentic Spanish art form.[78]

In the literary realm, modernist authors consciously broke with literary conventions and traditional modes of representation. Some of the pioneering works had already been produced before 1914, and authors such as Marcel Proust, James Joyce, Virginia Woolf, Karel Čapek, Fernando Pessoa, F. Scott Fitzgerald, Jorge Luis Borges, and Akutagawa Ryūnosuke continued to dominate the literary scene in the interwar years. Their writings dealt with individual experiences and questioned the nature of reality; the national frame was largely absent from their texts. At about the same time, a much more place-bound regionalist literature quickly became popular. Many authors, including many women, depicted everyday life in particular regions, using dialects, typical customs, and specific landscapes to give their stories local flavor. In Germany this type of writing was known as *Heimat* literature, but it also flourished elsewhere in Europe and the Americas. Some authors wrote sentimental feel-good stories and were famous only in their own regions; others wrote works with more literary qualities and appealed to a broad national audience; and a few such as William Faulkner and John Steinbeck gained international fame. Although some of these stories were quite nostalgic, with reactionary undertones, many were more open and tolerant. Most authors depicted the idiosyncratic regions of their stories as integral parts of the fatherland, which they implicitly presented as an organically grown ensemble of unique land-scapes, cultural traditions, and types of people. Although most stories were set in the countryside, some authors focused on traditional life in immigrant, Black, or Indigenous communities.[79]

Developments in film were somewhat different, partly because of its capital-intensive nature. Film was invented in the late nineteenth century and rapidly reached broad audiences. Like music and painting, film—especially in its early silent form—was potentially a very international art form, but like the rest of high culture, it was quickly nationalized. During the First World War the large studios in Hollywood professionalized their businesses, while the nascent film industries in Europe faltered as they were largely cut off from foreign markets. As a consequence, the more professional U.S. silent films became the main box-office hits, making global audiences familiar with the American way of life—that is, immigrant life, self-made men, gangsters, and cowboys, while generally ignoring African, Asian, and Native Americans—and with American landscapes, particularly through the genre of the Western. In some instances, stereotypical Westerns were even more popular abroad than at home, and some were produced explicitly for export.[80]

The hegemony of Hollywood triggered reactions from European intellectu-als and filmmakers who opposed the invasion of American popular culture, which they deemed vulgar and superficial. In response, they hoped to revive their national film industries, arguing that movies should explore national top-ics and traditions while reflecting the nation's "spirit." Filmmakers should also develop a recognizable cinematographic style. From the late 1920s various European governments began to adopt protectionist measures by imposing quotas for foreign films. In 1937, Japan went so far as to impose a total ban on U.S. films. The Weimar Republic stipulated that films qualified as German only when most of the cast, crew, and scriptwriters were Germans. In this way, truly national film industries were created throughout Europe and in various parts of Asia and Latin America. Nazi Germany and Fascist Italy also centralized their film production. The combination of economic and cultural incentives produced national film industries that were defined in national terms. This was done by focusing on specific genres, such as comedies and aristocratic cos-tume films in the United Kingdom, or by thematizing the Roman Empire in Italy, bullfights in Spain, or the tension between Paris and the provinces in France. The introduction of sound in the late 1920s provided another incentive for national film industries. Together with the radio, this had a particularly strong effect in countries like Italy, where the use of a standardized national language was intensely promoted by the Fascist regime.[81]

Nationalization of Physical Environment and Everyday Life

Although globalization processes such as the rapid advance of industrial products, modern architecture, and mass-produced Western clothes seemed to flatten out territorial differences, the nationalization of the physical environment advanced considerably in the period from 1914 to 1945, becoming almost inevitable in myriad domains of everyday life. Many nineteenth-century trends carried on during the interwar period. Statues to national heroes continued to be built, historical monuments were protected and restored, new museums were created to display the highlights of the nation's cultural patrimony, all kinds of buildings were erected in a recognizable national or regional style, and the growing tourism industry encouraged countries and regions to emphasize their most distinctive characteristics. But there were also some important changes. As a consequence of the carnage of the First World War, thousands of war memorials were erected in villages and towns of the participating countries, and instead of honoring generals, statesmen, or exceptional heroes, they were dedicated to the ordinary soldiers who had sacrificed their lives for the fatherland. Indeed, spontaneous shrines were already being erected by ordinary citizens during the early stages of the war. In addition, a "thriving industry of wartime kitsch"—as Jay Winter frames it—massproduced commemorative objects and images, which ended up in millions of households. Annual commemorations made it possible for people to mourn their loved ones while at the same time honoring the national community. Commemorative poppies, which were introduced in Great Britain in 1921, became a national symbol of remembrance in both the private and public spheres. Poppies were also worn in the British dominions, where the memory of the war reinforced the national communities of Australian, New Zealander, and Canadian citizens as well as their intimate bond with Great Britain. War memorials were also built in the colonies, honoring the colonial soldiers who had lost their lives, but with the rise of nationalist movements, particularly in India, loyalty to the British crown was increasingly seen in a negative light.[82]

During the First World War, many European countries began to make plans for rebuilding the devastated areas. In most cases, architects and officials advocated the use of local materials and vernacular building techniques and stressed the importance of fresh air and green spaces, promoting both the physical and psychological well-being of the population and their attachment to the motherland. Nonetheless, the challenges of the difficult postwar years and the enormous housing shortage led to the mass production of small apartments and the use of cheap materials that had no national associations, such as steel and concrete. The federal war housing project in the United States pioneered the serial construction of workers' settlements by using standardized

FIGURE 6.1 Henri Maclaine Pont, *Bandung Institute of Technology*, 1918–1919, Bandung. The Dutch architect was born on Java, and after studying architecture in Delft, he returned to the East Indies, where he extensively studied local building traditions. By combining natural materials, artisanal construction techniques, and modern, hygienic ideas, he contributed to the creation of a typically Indonesian neo-vernacular style.

building materials.[83] In the 1920s and 1930s, avant-garde movements such as Bauhaus and Le Corbusier's International Congresses of Modern Architecture rapidly gained influence as they propagated a cosmopolitan functionalist style and the use of glass, steel, and concrete. But modern architecture could also be used to give a country a progressive, future-oriented image: this was explicitly done in the national pavilions at world's fairs by the United States, by new regimes such as the Soviet Union and the Weimar Republic, and by new countries such as Poland, Czechoslovakia, and Turkey.[84]

Still, neo-vernacular styles continued to thrive, especially in the suburbs and tourist areas. In Latin America new national styles were developed, sometimes inspired by the Indigenous heritage, as in the neo-Mayan style in Mexico, and sometimes mixing Indigenous with colonial elements to create a "mestizo" style, as in Peru, for instance. World's fairs also played a crucial role in defining new national styles in Asia, many of which had origins in the colonial period. Although Indigenous architects played a role, most signature buildings were designed by Western architects, such as Henri Maclaine Pont's Bandung Institute of Technology (1918–1919) in the Dutch Indies (figure 6.1)

FIGURE 6.2 Edwin Lutyens, *Viceroy's House* (now Presidential Palace), 1912–1929, New Delhi. The architect combined classic forms with a dome, overhanging eaves, and decorative elements that were clearly inspired by traditional Indian examples. Moreover, by using local sandstone, he gave the building a distinctive national flavor.

and Ernest Hébard's French School of the Far East (1928–1932) in Hanoi.[85] A nation's identity could also be expressed in a very different way by emphasizing its greatness with awe-inspiring classicist buildings, which was the style favored by most Fascist dictators, exemplified by the Foro Italico (1928–1938) in Rome and Albert Speer's grandiose reconstruction plans for Germania, the new capital of the Third Reich. The British also favored a grandiose classicist style for many of the new colonial capitals such as Lusaka, Nairobi, and Kampala, but Edwin Lutyens's magnificent designs for New Delhi are the best known (figure 6.2). With his use of the local red and cream sandstone and Indian architectural elements in the Viceroy's House and other state buildings, the city became the emblematic capital of the nation.[86]

The preservation of ancient buildings became more important in the interwar period, and there was a clear tendency to focus on the most characteristic features. In Fascist Rome, the classical heritage was made more visible by demolishing adjacent buildings and constructing the grandiose Via dell'Impero (Imperial Avenue), which revealed the fora of the Roman Empire while connecting the huge monument to King Victor Emmanuel II to the Roman Colosseum. In

Tuscany, preservation efforts emphasized the golden age of the city-states. In cities like Florence and Arezzo, monuments, plazas, and entire cityscapes were restored in an idealized medieval or Renaissance form, which meant removing later additions and adding characteristic Tuscan towers. By also reinventing medieval festivals, these cities became more typically Tuscan than they had ever been. Elsewhere, the restoration of the Barcelona city center reinforced its Gothic character, which helped distinguish Catalonia from the rest of Spain, where Gothic architecture was rare. The iconic bridge over the Carrer del Bisbe (figure 6.3) was added in 1928. At about the same time, the French seaside resort Deauville was turned into a rustic fantasy in which not just hotels and villas but also the market and the train station were built in a neo-Norman style.[87]

Tourism also became more important, particularly because more people had the means and time to make an excursion or go on vacation. During the Great War, the French government made plans to attract foreign visitors to help enable the economic recovery of the country and its colonies. Private associations and enterprises contributed to the effort, too. In 1921 the French Touring Club launched an annual contest for pleasant villages in bloom, and the Michelin tire company published guidebooks of major battlefields, which were aimed at American tourists in particular. The Danish Touring Club closely collaborated with Ford's automobile factory in Copenhagen to encourage trips to all of the most attractive parts of the country. In the United States, the government was surprisingly committed to tourism. Railway companies and boosters had already promoted tourism with the slogan "See America First!," presenting it as a patriotic duty to discover the country's natural highlights. In 1916 the Wilson administration created the National Park Service, which would help acquaint Americans with the nation's geology, flora, and fauna while promoting the construction of roads. The Federal Writers' Project of the New Deal produced the American Guide Series to help stimulate the economy and to promote the national awareness of domestic tourists.[88]

A very important development in the democratization of tourism practices was paid vacation time for ordinary workers, which was introduced first in the Soviet Union in 1922. But the two weeks off were not just a reward for hard-working proletarians; vacations and excursions were organized by the authorities s to make workers into exemplary Soviet citizens. In addition to trips to industrial enterprises and agricultural cooperatives, regional tours were also part of the program, and the trips to Crimea and the Caucasus were especially popular. They were meant to acquaint the population with the history, landscapes, and social life of the different parts of the communist fatherland. In Germany, the Nazi leisure organization Strength through Joy also encouraged

FIGURE 6.3 Joan Rubió i Bellver, *Neo-Gothic Bridge over the Carrer del Bisbe,*
1928, Barcelona. During the restoration of the city center of Barcelona, Gothic
elements were strongly emphasized, setting Catalonia apart from the rest of
Spain, where this style was relatively rare. This iconic bridge in the "Gothic
Quarter" was added in the late 1920s. A clear example of the invention of a
national tradition.

travel to various national highlights, but like in the Soviet Union, domestic tourism served mainly to bind the majority population to the regime. Ordinary Germans could go on a cruise or visit the beach at the four-kilometer-long Nazi
resort at Prora Bay. More conservative authoritarian regimes prioritized the
nation-building aspects of tourism. Both the Horthy dictatorship in Hungary
and the Ulmanis regime in Latvia encouraged their citizens to visit the provinces
to get to know their natural beauty, cultural highlights, and authentic
traditions.[89]

FIGURE 6.4 *German Tourists in Kruger National Park, South Africa*, 1931–1932. Like in the United States, national parks in Africa primarily served to show nature in its pristine state. Obviously, big game, such as the giraffes that are crossing the road, had to be protected, especially from Indigenous "poachers."

Nature conservation was high on the agenda, and the number of natural reserves and national parks increased rapidly. In Europe, characteristic natural monuments received the most attention, but some national parks were connected to history, such as Covadonga, the mountainous area where the medieval reconquest of Spain against the Arabs began. In French Algeria, reforestation was used to create a Mediterranean landscape that evoked the glorious memories of the Roman Empire—thus it referred to a shared heritage while obliterating the Arab past. In other parts of Africa, national parks served to protect big game and the "last vestiges of flora in their natural state" (figure 6.4). Natural highlights had to made accessible as well. Scenic tourist routes were built in the French Alps and on the Côte d'Azur, while the United States pioneered the construction of parkways. The long and winding Blue Ridge Parkway was built as a project of the New Deal. In Nazi Germany, engineers blended most of the autobahns into the scenery by positioning them around mountains and hills, which also made for beautiful vistas.[90]

Sometimes nature was manipulated with the explicit aim of making landscapes more distinctive. In Southern California, the planting of palm trees and cacti was encouraged to distinguish the region from the rest of the United States. Elsewhere, landscapes were adapted to make them more natural and thus more national. The German landscape architect Willy Lange promulgated the "nature garden," which should fit into the surrounding landscape, containing artistically arranged "native" plants; the "unnatural" cutting of shrubs and hedges—a distinct feature of "un-Nordic" formal gardens—was banned. Using insights from the new science of ecology or "plant sociology," garden designers like Lange rejected "exotic" plants. In the U.S. Midwest, Wilhelm Miller and Jens Jensen developed a prairie-style garden by rejecting European models and emphasizing horizontal lines, local colors, and native plants. Similarly, the botanist Edith Roberts and the landscape architect Elsa Rehmann promoted "naturalistic planting" in their *American Plants for American Gardens* (1929). During the Third Reich, landscape architects such as Alwin Seifert, who was responsible for embedding the new autobahns into the landscape, proscribed the use of "non-German" shrubs and trees. Some even argued for the "extermination" of "foreign intruders" and the revival of "original plant communities." Similar ideas were applied to the animal world. For the 1936 Olympics, Lutz Heck, the director of the Berlin Zoo, created a special Teutonic Zoo, dedicated exclusively to autochthonous animals, with the Wolf Rock as main attraction. He also attempted to "breed back" animals to their "primordial purity," and some of them, such as the wisent, were reintroduced into German forests.[91]

Nature also had to be made productive. In order to compensate for the loss of the last colonies in 1898, Spanish politicians and intellectuals developed an obsession with hydraulic projects in order to combat drought, improve the quality of the soil, and increase agricultural output. In the 1920s, the dictatorship of General Primo de Rivera was particularly active in constructing new barrages and irrigation canals. The Franco dictatorship would continue this policy after 1939, while building about three hundred new villages on reclaimed land. Other examples could be found in the United States, where the Tennessee Valley Authority pursued similar goals of agricultural regeneration and community development. The Netherlands and Fascist Italy undertook ambitious wetland reclamation projects with the goal of expanding cultivation and providing work. Settlers would live in new harmonious rural communities, without class struggle and population loss through emigration. Although the draining of marshes and the construction of polders were large-scale, very modern engineering projects, references to national history abounded in the names of new villages and towns. The newly reclaimed Italian settlements adopted a geometric street plan inspired by the Roman Empire, and spacious layouts and the use of neo-vernacular architecture gave the villages in the new Dutch polders a traditional look. During the Second World War, ideas about reclamation, colonization, and racial hierarchies became enmeshed in a very radical way in the Nazi project to drain the wetlands of the Pripet River in occupied Eastern Europe. There, forced laborers of supposedly inferior races— Slavs and Jews—were worked to death to create new farmland for racially pure German settlers.[92]

During the interwar era, as nature became more national, so did its products. Before the First World War, manufacturers of agricultural products such as cheese, wine, and other alcoholic beverages had begun to protect their wares, marketing them as organically connected to the soil, climate, and artisanal traditions of a particularly territory. French villages and regions such as Roquefort, Champagne, Bourgogne, and Cognac quickly became famous trademarks. In 1919, these regional products received legal protection with the introduction of the "controlled designation of origin." This French innovation was quickly adopted elsewhere, and as a consequence, almost all "artisanal" agricultural products are now linked to a specific territory, forming an integral part of a nation's patrimony.[93]

At about the same time, the nationalization of cooking practices received a boost, especially with the rapid growth of the tourism industry. The famous culinary author Curnonsky began to publish a series, Gastronomic France, which consisted of more than twenty regional culinary guides. Michelin included restaurants in its guidebooks and ranked them with stars. The Spanish Tourism Board and the Italian Touring Club followed, publishing guides to highlight the regional specialties of their countries. Similarly, cookbooks not only promoted the recently invented national cuisines but also defined a rapidly growing number of regional dishes and local specialties, while restaurants increasingly offered regional fare. In the United States this encouraged the standardization of the culinary traditions of the South in particular.[94]

Culinary nationalism affected people's everyday lives, and not just when they went on a trip, visited a restaurant, or used a national cookbook. Many governments pressed their populations to adopt more rational diets, preferably with national products. In the first decades of the twentieth century the Japanese government launched campaigns to encourage diligence and thrift. Small European countries such as Switzerland, Denmark, and the Netherlands had active buy national organizations. Fascist Italy encouraged "alimentary sovereignty" with the Battle for Grain and other campaigns to consume national products such as rice and grapes; the goal was both economic autarky and the strengthening of the "Italian race." After the Wall Street Crash in 1929, more countries tried to stimulate agricultural production. Spain introduced a national rice day and promoted the domestic consumption of oranges. The Third Reich endorsed one-pot Sundays and the consumption of "patriotic grain" by eating rye bread, and the preparation of quark from leftover milk was presented as a patriotic duty for German housewives. During the Second World War, ethnic German women who "returned" to the Reich were taught "German ways" of cleaning and housekeeping in order to safeguard their new fatherland.[95]

Fascist regimes also tried to loosen the grip of foreign (read: Parisian) dictates in the domain of fashion by creating national fashion agencies and encouraging women to wear traditional costumes such as the dirndl. Nonetheless, their main innovation in the field of sartorial nationalism was the widespread use of uniforms. During the late nineteenth century, youth movements such as Baden-Powell's scouts and German hiking groups had already adopted uniforms for their members. After the First World War, Fascist militias did the same. Mussolini's Blackshirts were the most influential model, but after taking power, the Italian Fascists created a host of other uniformed organizations. The uniform had distinct egalitarian connotations, and marches, mass meetings, and theatrical rituals conveyed an image of national unity and strength, while emphasizing virile and military values for men and a more supportive role for women.[96]

National folkloric dresses had been defined during the nineteenth century in Europe, and now this was also happening elsewhere. In Latin America, richly colored and elegant indigenous costumes for special occasions became national symbols. In the 1920s in Mexico, even middle-class women like Frida Kahlo began wearing the embroidered *tehuana* dress (figure 6.5). At the same time, typical white masculine characters such as the American cowboy, the Argentinian or Brazilian *gaucho*, and the Chilean *huaso* became national icons.[97]

In Asia, Western clothing was radically different from indigenous garments, and initially it was adopted by only a few people. In independent countries such as Japan and Siam, Western dress was worn in public by reformist elites, including the king and emperor, for whom this was an integral part of their nationalist modernization program. School children, soldiers, and modern professionals donned Western uniforms or costumes, while growing groups of well-to-do women followed the latest fashions from Europe. Many people were not dogmatic in their choices and wore indigenous and Western attires for different occasions, or combined various elements from both. In colonies such as the Philippines and the Dutch East Indies, and in various parts of Africa, educated elites also adopted Western clothing styles to appear "modern." Sometimes, there were very practical incentives to do so: in the Dutch East Indies, men in traditional clothing were expected to sit on the floor, whereas those who wore Western suits were given a chair. In other colonies, such as Ceylon and Burma, nationalists began to reject Western clothing and promoted indigenous garments that were typical or connected to the country's history. Clothing should uphold an image of modesty and decency, which was particularly important for women. In India, Gandhi set new standards not just

FIGURE 6.5 *Frida Kahlo in Typical Tehuana Dress*, 1943. In the photo she sits before her self-portrait, in which she is also wearing a *tehuana* dress. The painting is titled *Thinking of Diego*; she had painted a small portrait of her husband, the famous Mexican muralist Diego Rivera, on her forehead. Both artists represented this traditional dress frequently in their work.

by wearing very simple peasant clothes, but also by requiring them to be homespun, which provoked strong reactions. In 1931, Winston Churchill called Gandhi a "half-naked fakir," consciously disqualifying him as uncivilized.[98]

Some nationalist regimes rejected traditional dress by steering a radical modernization course that implied adopting Western costumes, hairstyles, and etiquette. Chinese nationalists had already opted for Western clothing styles and rejected the queue as a foreign, Manchu import. One of the first measures of the new Chinese Republic was banning this traditional hairstyle and the "backward" tradition of foot-binding. Western costumes became obligatory for officials, and some local authorities required all civil servants to wear a suit, leather shoes, and a hat. Western greeting styles such as doffing the hat and shaking hands were also adopted, and many women cut their hair short. Western dress was also strongly encouraged in Siam during the dictatorship of Marshall Phibun Songkhram. His semi-Fascist regime also enforced the use of forks and spoons and orderly queuing—foreigners should understand that Siam was a civilized country.[99]

The most radical reforms to nationalize and "civilize" the population were undertaken in Afghanistan, Persia, and Turkey, where King Amanullah, Reza Shah, and Mustafa Kemal (Atatürk) tried to turn their traditional Muslim countries into modern nation-states. King Amanullah required men to wear suits and hats in the government premises in Kabul, and he even tried to abolish the veil for women, but his reforms were cut short when an uprising forced him out in 1929. In Persia, to foster national unity, Reza Shah obliged all men to abandon tribal clothes and wear trousers, a coat, and a hat. They were encouraged to shave their beards, and only modest moustaches were acceptable. The dictatorial regime also encouraged the unveiling of women. The Muslim calendar was replaced by a solar calendar that started with the ancient Persian New Year and adopted Zoroastrian names for the months, giving it a national flavor. Moreover, Reza Shah changed the name of the country to Iran, in reference to the supposed place of origin of the ancient Aryans. The Turkish Republic banned the fez and discouraged the use of the veil. Religious attire was allowed only for ceremonial use. Atatürk's regime also adopted the metric system and the Western calendar, and made Sunday the official rest day. Religious schools were abolished, and Western civil and penal codes replaced shari'a. Another radical measure was the introduction of the Latin alphabet, while the Turkish language was purified by eliminating Arabic and Persian terms.[100]

Industrial products were nationalized as well, which made the "Made in Germany" label, in particular, into a national emblem. National designations for industrial products had been introduced with the British Merchandise Marks Act of 1887, which aimed to ban cheap and inferior foreign products that falsely claimed to be produced in the United Kingdom, many of which actually came from the German Empire. Around the turn of the century, the German government and German professionals undertook concerted action to improve the quality of artisanal products. The German Werkbund, which was established in 1907 as a kind of national umbrella organization by artists, architects, and workshop owners, also involved industrial companies such as AEG, Bosch, Siemens, and Mercedes Benz. Over time, the emphasis shifted from high-quality handwork to functionalist industrial design, and after the First World War this was further encouraged by the international success of Bauhaus artists, designers, and architects. In the end, "Made in Germany" came to stand for reliable, high-quality, and functional industry products.[101]

A very different type of modernization could be seen in the reformist policies to promote the physical strength of the nation, especially its boys and men. Physical exercise at school and modern sports were encouraged by nationalists in Japan, China, Persia, and Turkey. Japan, the Ottoman Empire, and Egypt had already participated at the 1912 Olympics in Stockholm. The Turkish Republic was willing to take drastic measures to overcome its image as the "sick man of Europe," so in 1938, the government introduced a law, written by Carl Diem, the organizer of the Berlin Olympics, that obliged men between twelve and forty-five and women between twelve and thirty to exercise their bodies in their spare time. The one-party state supervised the execution of the law, and local People's Houses taught gymnastics, wrestling, team sports, and national folk dances.[102]

Meanwhile, modern sports had become popular in the colonies, and some sports became connected with their national identities. This happened with cricket in the West Indies, baseball in the Philippines, and soccer in most French possessions. Initially, Indigenous players were mostly excluded, but they rapidly created their own clubs. National leagues were set up. The Indian Football Association dates from 1893, and in Ceylon, a cricket school league was created in 1897. Indigenous elites saw sports as an opportunity to combat allegations of effeminacy. Victories of Indigenous teams over British squads were celebrated as "beating them at their own game." Thus, when the barefooted players of Mohun Bagan won the Indian soccer final against the East Yorkshire Regiment in 1911, this was widely celebrated as a "national" victory. Sometimes, traditional games were transformed into modern sports; in late nineteenth-century Japan, martial arts forms were turned into judo. However, even in highly nationalist Japan, Western sports like baseball became very popular. Indeed, they were promoted by the authorities because they could help the country to gain international respect.[103]

Sports became more important in the 1920s and 1930s. More people were members of clubs, more people watched games, and more people followed their favorite teams through the media. In many countries there were now specialized sports newspapers and magazines, and most newspapers had dedicated sports pages. The coverage of sporting events by new media such as the radio and newsreels proved crucial. The Olympic Games of Los Angeles in 1932 and the Nazi Olympic Games of 1936 attracted large crowds and extensive media coverage. The same was true for the football World Cup, the first of which was hosted by Uruguay in 1930. New Olympic traditions, such as the victory ceremony with national anthems and flags and the Olympic Village, where national teams were housed together, reinforced the inter-*national* framework of the games. Clubs sometimes received nationalist names. Thus, in the United States, many baseball teams were named after Native American tribes, such as the Boston Braves and the Cleveland Indians. The name of the Glasgow football club Celtic referred to the ethnic background of many of its Irish members. In the Americas and Australia, many clubs were founded by immigrant communities and their names often contained references to their home countries or native regions.[104]

Barbara Keys makes clear that even countries that were averse to "foreign" or "bourgeois" games ended up embracing modern sports and its emphasis on (international) competition. This was the case with the Soviet Union. Initially it promoted hygiene, health, and premilitary training through its own proletarian organizations as well as athletic meetings of workers throughout the world. The focus on individualism, excellence, and records was rejected in favor of collectivism and disciplined physical exercise. There were even attempts to prohibit football and boxing. In the 1930s these policies were reversed in order to strengthen support at home, to impress foreign countries, and to be a more attractive model for working classes around the globe. Modern sports and their internationally standardized rules were now supported. The goal was to "bring worldwide glory to Soviet sport," and the regime even argued that "all world sports records should belong to the USSR." This meant that international matches were encouraged, foreign trainers were hired, and innovative training methods were adopted. Although the Soviet Union did not yet participate in the Olympic Games, it made overtures to join international sports federations. Soviet officials also emulated the Olympic rhetoric, declaring that international competitions should "strengthen peace and friendship among peoples."[105]

The Nazis also favored collective exercises and paramilitary training. At first, modern sports were seen as liberal and pacifist, and the employment of foreign coaches was rejected, as was competing with members of "inferior races." But when the Nazis gained power, they quickly realized that sports was already immensely popular and that it would be better to use the 1936 Olympic Games in Berlin for propagandistic purposes. The government accepted the rules of the International Olympic Committee, toned down repressive measures, and did its utmost to make the Olympic Games a success. In this way, the regime transmitted a positive image to foreign visitors and international sports fans, and as German athletes topped the ranks in international medals, it also boosted its popularity at home. In order to avoid a boycott by the United States, the German authorities included two "half-Jews" on their Olympic team. However, their goal that sports should show the "innate superiority" of the Aryan race was not fully achieved, as Jesse Owens, an African American athlete, became the star of the games. But racial discrimination in sports was not an issue in Nazi Germany alone. Great Britain prohibited interracial boxing in 1910 in order to prevent a match between a white British boxer and the Black American heavyweight champion John Johnson, who also upset the color line by courting white women. In the United States, many sports banned African Americans. Nevertheless, in 1938 many Americans would cheer the knockout of Max Schmeling, a model of Nordic manhood celebrated by the Nazis, by Joe Louis, an African American boxer who secured the world heavyweight title. To boost a nation's prestige on the international stage, it was advisable to use the talents of the entire population. Thus, sports encouraged the loyalty of the inhabitants to the nation-state by inducing audiences to cheer for its best national representatives in international competitions.[106]

Conclusion

Many new nation-states were created after the First World War, primarily in East-Central Europe. Only a few British protectorates in the Middle East became independent during the interwar period. Political activists outside of Europe, nonetheless, still felt the allure of the nation-state model. Meanwhile, in many parts of Europe and Latin America, the liberal nation-state was on the defensive as Communists, Fascists, and corporatist regimes increasingly preferred an authoritarian or even totalitarian alternative, which aimed to strengthen the state instead of empowering the nation. Citizenship rights were extended as a consequence of the First World War, while states took over more responsibilities in the social domain. Even so, the situation worsened for many people around the world. Women were still excluded from voting rights in many parts of the world, and female emancipation was actively opposed by many regimes. Minorities in most new nation-states were put under pressure to assimilate; this also happened, often even more forcefully, with Indigenous populations in North America, Australia, and Japan. Sometimes eugenic measures were taken to prevent the procreation of "undesirable" populations. During the First and Second World Wars these exclusionary tendencies led to forced population transfers, ethnic-cleansing campaigns, and genocides.

Nationalism continued to have a widespread and multifarious impact on the arts, the humanities, and the social sciences. Although various avant-garde artists adopted a cosmopolitan modernism that aimed to radically break with the past and national boundaries, most scholars and artists continued to take for granted the national framework. Racial factors, geographical determinism, and vernacular influences continued to play important roles. Some artists and scholars actively supported imperial expansion or the radical exclusion of ethnic outsiders from the national community. Nationalism also became more omnipresent in the physical environment and everyday life. Myriad war memorials reminded the people of the sacrifices made by millions of ordinary soldiers. Picturesque landscapes, newly reclaimed lands, and even plants and animals were nationalized, as were foods and beverages. Many nationalists in Europe, the Americas, and the colonies encouraged the wearing of traditional costumes, especially by women. Several modernizing regimes in Asia, on the other hand, encouraged the adoption of European clothing and habits in order to gain respect as a "civilized" country. Sports were promoted as a means to strengthen the national body, and also increasingly to mobilize national feelings and to achieve international acclaim.

7

Modernizing Nation-States,
1945–1979

THE DEFEAT OF Nazi Germany and the end of the Second World War was a
real watershed moment. Exalted nationalism and exclusivist racial theories
were rejected because of their association with the wars of aggression and
genocidal policies of the Nazis and their allies. However, by condemning the
imperial expansion of the Axis powers and their rapacious occupation regimes,
the Allies also implicitly undermined the legitimacy of the remaining colonial
empires. As a consequence, the postwar era saw a rapid process of decolonization. A partition along ethnic or religious lines had previously been seen as a
solution for some troubled colonies, but the divisions of India and Palestine
in 1947 and 1948 were not successful. As a consequence, partition was no longer
a viable option when other colonies became independent. Even though many
borders were highly artificial, they were respected almost without exception.
Nonetheless, in the late 1950s and early 1960s there were many attempts to
create larger federal units, and it was only when these projects failed that the
nation-state became the indisputable norm for independent statehood. In fact,
respect for the territorial boundaries of new and existing nation-states became
one of the pillars of the new international order. This implied that states could
ignore demands for independence from ethnic minorities, and sometimes they
received active support from the international community to suppress secessionist movements. Territorial expansion was equally repudiated, and in the
few cases where annexations did occur—when Morocco occupied the Western Sahara, for instance—they were not officially recognized.

The same paradoxical combination of a widespread aversion to open expressions of ethnic nationalism and the self-evident status of the nation-state
was visible in the cultural realm. Racial theories were banned from academia,
and the nation-state was taken for granted as the logical geographical unit for
studying historical, social, economic, and cultural developments. High culture
was dominated by an optimistic modernization paradigm that pretended to

be cosmopolitan, though in fact, it very much propagated Western standards. Nationalism, at the same time, was primarily focused on the nation-state, and now it became increasingly banal, associating even cars with specific countries, while nationalist strife was increasingly channeled through trivial events such as international sporting competitions and beauty contests.

The Impact of the Second World War

The rise of a large number of new nation-states after the Second World War, making the nation-state the hegemonic form of statehood, was not a foregone conclusion. The war raised the expectations of anti-imperial activists. The consequences of the war were not immediately visible, as they had been in 1918; instead, they took several decades to fully materialize, resulting in a long, drawn-out process of decolonization. Although the independent nation-state became the norm, various alternatives were tried.

Contrary to what had happened during the First World War, the warring parties stirred up very little nationalist unrest in enemy territories. Although the Axis Powers were all fiercely nationalist, they did not have a nationalist understanding of international politics. Instead, they viewed international relations as a kind of social Darwinian imperial struggle for regional dominance. Fascist Italy, Nazi Germany, and imperial Japan each envisioned their own sphere of influence as a mix of occupied territories, protectorates, and nominally independent states.[1] In almost all their occupied territories they worked with local collaborators, most of whom were local Fascists, right-wing authoritarians, or opportunists. Many nationalists, too, actively collaborated with the Axis Powers. The Nazi occupation forces, for instance, cooperated with Flemish and Breton nationalists, while Slovakia became a satellite state governed by Jozef Tiso's right-wing nationalist Slovak People's Party. Italy set up a puppet regime in Croatia led by the extreme nationalist Ante Pavelić of Ustaše. Japan also found many willing collaborators among nationalists in the colonies they had conquered from the Western powers. Many of these nationalists hoped for independence or at least a significant amount of political autonomy within the new Fascist world order, but their interests remained totally subordinate to those of the occupiers. Thus, even though Burma, the Philippines, Cambodia, and the Empire of Vietnam became nominally independent during the last years of the war, they were in fact puppet states within Japan's Greater East Asia Co-Prosperity Sphere.[2]

Once the odds were stacked against them, the Axis powers began to actively recruit soldiers among foreign sympathizers and nationalists. Nazi Germany had some success in territories where abhorrence of the Soviets was an important incentive. Many volunteers came from the Baltic countries and Ukraine, where the resurrection of an independent nation-state, even in a subordinate role, was a widely shared dream. The German governor of Galicia gave permission for the formation of a Ukrainian National Committee, and the Wehrmacht created separate legions for Georgians, Armenians, Caucasian Muslims, and Turkestanis. In the spring of 1943, the Nazis even established a Russian Army of Liberation, consisting of both prisoners of war and anti-communist volunteers. Toward the end of the war, Alfred Rosenberg, the minister of the Occupied Eastern Territories, organized meetings of national committees of Tatars, Azerbaijanis, Turkestanis, and Caucasians. Yet, the independence of peoples the Nazis essentially viewed as "subhuman races" was never an objective. Mark Mazower concludes that these nationalist recruits merely served as German cannon fodder.[3]

Nor did the Axis powers put much effort into encouraging nationalist activities in areas beyond the reach of their armies, to undermine the dominant position of Great Britain in the Middle East and Asia, for instance. Even though Germany could count on considerable sympathy in the Arab world, the Nazis did not encourage a nationalist uprising in the Middle East or North Africa. Hitler preferred to stand by his allies, and he respected both the colonial interests of Vichy France and the territorial ambitions of Fascist Italy. He was reticent even when his assistance was sought by nationalists under British rule. In the autumn of 1940, from his exile in Bagdad, the grand mufti of Jerusalem, Mohammed Amin al-Husayni, requested Italian and German aid in achieving the independence of the Arab states and in dealing with the "Jewish question" in Palestine, but he did not receive significant support. In the spring of 1941, the Nazis made some belated attempts to send some armaments to Rashid Ali al-Gaylani's short-lived nationalist regime in Iraq, primarily because it was a good opportunity to subvert British interests in the region.[4]

Japan also was reluctant to provide material support to independence movements in Western colonies. In the summer of 1941 the military authorities merely gave some military training to "thirty comrades" from Burma, one of whom was the young nationalist Bogyoke Aung San. Japan's objective was not to help them liberate their fatherland from the British yoke, but to disrupt the supply lines to the Guomindang stronghold in Western China. When Japan finally decided to invade Burma, Aung San and his comrades became the core of the Burma Independence Army, which had a mostly auxiliary role.[5]

Germany and Japan did not make sustained efforts to sap British rule even in India. The Nazis did allow Subhas Chandra Bose, a prominent Indian nationalist who had fled to Berlin, to recruit prisoners of war in order to create an Indian legion within the Wehrmacht. However, in 1943, when German support for the liberation of India failed to materialize, he left for Japan. Indian nationalists in Southeast Asia had created the somewhat more impressive

Indian National Army, which largely consisted of soldiers who had been taken prisoner after the fall of Singapore. The Imperial General Headquarters never envisaged the incorporation of India into the Japanese Empire, and it was only after the deterioration of Japan's military situation and the arrival of the charismatic Bose that they decided to revitalize the Indian National Army and use it for a small-scale offensive in Eastern India. Again, the main objective was disruption of the communications between nationalist China and the Western Allies, not the "liberation" of India.[6]

The Allied powers shared a nationalist view of the international order, with some restrictions. This became clear in their joint effort to create a successor to the League of Nations. In the Atlantic Charter of August 1941, the United States and Great Britain had already declared that they did not seek territorial expansion, that they aimed to establish a "permanent system of general security," that they favored freedom of trade, and that they were determined to respect "the right of all peoples to choose the form of government under which they will live." President Franklin Roosevelt and Prime Minister Winston Churchill also added that they wished "to see the sovereign rights and self-government restored to those who have been forcibly deprived of them." In October 1943, the Western allies renewed their pledges together with the Soviet Union and the Republic of China, declaring that the new international organization would be based on the "sovereign equality of all peace-loving states."[7] The primary objective of the Allied powers, therefore, was to liberate the territories that had been conquered by Germany, Italy, and Japan. The British government accommodated governments in exile, such as those of the Netherlands, Poland, and Greece. Charles de Gaulle and his Free French forces also found shelter in London. Resistance movements could count on sympathy and possibly material support from the Allies, although the Soviet Union's open obstruction of the non-Communist Polish underground was a clear exception. Independent countries that were under threat or partially occupied by the army of one of the Axis powers mostly received assistance. This was the case with the beleaguered Guomindang regime in China; not only did it receive military and financial aid, but Great Britain and the United States abrogated the unequal treaties and territorial concessions that were still in place.[8]

Supporting nationalist movements that threatened the status quo ante, however, was not in their interests. Consequently, the Allies' view on colonies was more ambivalent. Both the United States and the Soviet Union preferred the dissolution of the colonial empires, but in general, they refrained from making concrete promises. In 1941, Roosevelt had told Churchill that he was in favor of a regime of international trusteeship, which would gradually prepare all colonies for independence. In the end, though, the United Nations formed the Trusteeship Council that was responsible only for League of

Nations mandates and for the colonies of the defeated powers. For strategic reasons, moreover, the United States decided to retain the Mariana, Caroline, and Marshall Islands—which had been a Japanese mandate—as United Nations trust territories without developing plans for independence in the immediate future. The Soviets continued the anti-imperialist stance that they had adopted since the Revolution. In international fora the Soviet Union became a staunch advocate for decolonization and the right to self-determination. Nevertheless, after the war they did not hesitate to re-annex the Baltic states and add slices of Poland, Czechoslovakia, and Romania. Moreover, they quickly turned the "liberated" Eastern European countries into Communist satellite states.[9]

During the war, the Allies' support for even recently colonized countries was limited. Although Mussolini's invasion of Ethiopia in 1935 provoked an international outcry, nobody came to the rescue of Haile Selassie's independent empire. It was only after Italy entered the Second World War on the side of Nazi Germany that the British helped the emperor and a small force of Ethiopian refugees to reconquer the country. Although the British officially recognized the independence of Ethiopia, in fact they treated it as an occupied territory, and in 1942 Haile Selassie was forced to sign an agreement that practically made his country a vassal state. Even after the war, British interests prevailed. The hesitancy with respect to colonies was even more obvious in the case of Korea, which had been governed by Japan since 1910. The Guomindang regime sustained a tiny Korean Liberation Army, and other Koreans fought with the Chinese Communists or the Red Army. But no major effort was made to create a unified fighting force. Moreover, none of the Allied powers was willing to recognize Syngman Rhee's Provisional Government of the Republic of Korea. In December 1943 the United States, Great Britain, and the Republic of China declared that Korea would become independent in "due course," as supposedly it was not yet ready to govern itself. After the defeat of Japan, a kind of trusteeship was installed; the Soviet Union and the United States each administered one half of the country. Only three years later, a North Korean people's republic and a South Korean republic became independent, but both were effectively client states of the new superpowers, and they quickly became enmeshed in the Korean War, the first conflict in which the Cold War became hot.[10]

The Dissolution of Colonial Empires

After 1945, the European colonial powers were not very eager to wind up their empires. The contributions of the colonies, in both manpower and resources, had been crucial to the war effort, and close economic bonds between metropole and colonies were seen as indispensable for the postwar economic recovery. Overseas territories, moreover, were needed to preserve the metropole's international standing. Finally, even progressive politicians argued that most colonial societies were not yet ready to stand on their own feet; a European presence was required to guide these societies and bring them into contact with modern civilization. Yet, political leaders were also aware that reforms were needed. Racial discrimination should be avoided in favor of cooperation between equals, which suggested that more opportunities for political participation and social advancement should be offered. Economic development of the colonies also was moved up on the agenda.[11]

But the plans for a continued imperial presence clashed with the raised expectations among inhabitants of the colonies. This was already visible in India. The decision that India would enter the war on the side of Great Britain had been made in London without consulting local parties or provincial governments. To appease the nationalists, the British authorities vowed that India would eventually get dominion status. In March 1942, they even promised to convene a constitutional assembly after the war. Although most Indians continued to collaborate with the colonial authorities, the Indian National Congress rejected the proposal. Gandhi had already started a campaign of civil disobedience, and now he called for an immediate withdrawal of the British. The resultant "Quit India" resolution led to widespread strikes and violent attacks against official buildings, and the British responded with mass arrests and repression.[12]

Anticolonial nationalism was on the rise elsewhere as well. The military defeats against Germany and Japan during the early stages of the war damaged the prestige of most colonial powers. The war caused economic hardship; many colonies made huge contributions to the Allied victory, while others suffered under Axis occupation. As a consequence, nationalist claims were expressed with renewed vigor at the end of the war. The collapse of the Japanese Empire led Sukarno to declare the independence of the Republic of Indonesia, and Ho Chi Minh did the same for the Democratic Republic of Vietnam. But both leaders lacked the power to have their way. In Algeria, there were well-attended demonstrations for independence; one of them, in Sétif, ended in a bloodbath, with several thousand casualties. Nationalism also gained ground in Madagascar, leading to a mass uprising in 1947 with tens of thousands of victims. Even in colonies where mass unrest and uprisings failed to appear right away, it was clear that a return to colonial normalcy was out of the question.[13]

Promises made before or during the war had to be honored. Sometimes this went quite smoothly, as when the United States relinquished power in the Philippines. In other cases there was a tug-of-war between the former colonial power and the new authorities, which is what happened in Syria and Lebanon. Both territories had been promised independence when the Free French took the reins from the Vichy regime. Mass demonstrations occurred when the French vainly tried to stall steps toward complete independence. The British had already given independence to the mandate of Iraq before the war, and Transjordan now followed. Ceylon and Burma, which had been granted some measure of self-government, became independent in 1948. In all of these cases, independence meant becoming a nation-state, with a constitution and an elected parliament, while respecting the existing territorial borders.[14]

Over time, international pressure rose. At the Bandung Conference of 1955, twenty-nine African and Asian states and colonies proclaimed the right to self-determination, revealing a more assertive "Third World." Five years later, the growing number of former colonies in the General Assembly of the United Nations succeeded in passing a resolution condemning colonialism as a crime against international law. The resistance against colonial occupation also increased, and the fierce repression that was necessary for the occupiers to remain in control meant growing financial costs as well as moral indignation. Toward the end of the 1950s many European leaders realized that granting independence to most colonies would save them money and trouble. Providing foreign aid to maintain good relations with the former colonies was a much more flexible and cheaper option than bearing the responsibility for the economic well-being and public order in a faraway territory.[15] The main challenge was to find a trustworthy partner to whom they could hand over power.

In many cases the decolonization process was not a straightforward transition from colonial empire to independent nation-state. In fact, almost all of the European colonial powers first tried to transform their hierarchical empires into more egalitarian unions or commonwealths. When this proved difficult, many imperial governments and colonial politicians attempted to cluster various neighboring territories into federations; the idea was that this would increase their stability and economic viability. Authors such as Michael Collins and Frederick Cooper have argued that after 1945 there was a clear "federal moment" that lasted until the early 1960s, during which serious attempts were made to create larger political units.[16]

In fact, however, this was part of a broader federal moment that had begun much earlier. By the nineteenth century, many pan movements, such as those among Slavs, Germans, Celts, and Turks, aimed at the cooperation or even fusion of several ethnically related populations or states. Before 1945 there had also been several attempts to overcome the economic, social, and political limitations of the nation-state by focusing on pragmatic cooperation between neighboring states. The Pan American Union had been founded in 1890, and

in Europe, Count Richard Coudenhove-Kalergi had been an indefatigable
propagandist of a pan-European federation. During the Great Depression
there were initiatives to reduce trade barriers between several small European
countries. After the Second World War, many intellectuals and politicians had
become wary of the vulnerability of most new nation-states, whose situation
was now denounced as *Kleinstaaterei*, a German term that referred to the many
statelets that had existed before the German unification, or as "balkanization,"
an also pejorative term that referred to the situation in Southeast Europe,
where the Habsburg and Ottoman Empires had been dissolved into many
small units. In order to survive, nation-states needed to cooperate or even pool
their resources. Instead of isolationism and protectionism, international cooperation was the new watchword.[17]

It was in the Balkans where the first steps toward a multinational federation
were taken. In the immediate postwar years, Josip Broz Tito, the leader of the
new Socialist Federal Republic of Yugoslavia, strengthened its relationships
with the neighboring Communist states of Bulgaria and Albania in an attempt
to create a Balkan federation that could potentially also include Greece.
However, Stalin—afraid of losing his grip on Eastern Europe—openly opposed the initiative, and in June 1948 this led to the expulsion of Yugoslavia
from the Cominform, the new Moscow-led international organization of the
communist movement. In the same period, other projects with federal characteristics that did survive were the Organization of American States, the Ben-
elux Union, the Nordic Council, and most importantly, the European Coal and
Steel Community. In 1957, the latter was transformed into the European Economic Community, and although power would remain largely in the hands of
the member states, the organization would become a resounding success.[18]

The British Empire was profoundly affected by the Second World War, and
federalist ideas played a vital role in its postwar transformation. Although
Churchill had signed the Atlantic Charter, he had no intention of liquidating
the empire. He was willing to make some concessions to the overseas territories, such as turning the British Commonwealth of Nations, in which Great
Britain cooperated with the dominions, into a more coherent body. When the
British parliamentary elections of July 1945 were won by the Labour Party, an
about-turn looked possible. But the new government, too, was unwilling to
dissolve the empire. Instead, they hoped to develop a fruitful political partnership with both the dominions and the colonies. Social advancement of the
colonies should go hand in hand with improving trade relations and the economic recovery of Great Britain. In the end, a more unified and powerful
Commonwealth, led by a prosperous United Kingdom, would serve as a kind
of "third force" in an international arena dominated by the United States and
the Soviet Union.[19]

The Labour government was also confronted with a few conundrums for which there were no easy solutions. In the Mandate for Palestine communal tensions between the large Arab majority and a Jewish community that was rapidly growing through Zionist immigration had already boiled over before the Second World War. The British had presented a partition plan and a proposal for independence in ten years under a joint Arab and Jewish government. Violence—especially Jewish attacks against the British "occupiers"—did not subside during the Second World War, and in 1947 the British government requested the assistance of the United Nations. An international commission drew up a new partition plan, awarding about 55 percent of the former mandate territories to the state of Israel, which was adopted by the UN General Assembly. Although this did not calm the situation, the British withdrew in the spring of 1948, which led first to a civil war between a well-organized Jewish community and an Arab population that pinned its hopes on the support of neighboring states, and then to an Arab-Israeli war. When the Jewish forces prevailed, Israel expanded its borders. About three-quarters of a million Palestinians fled, while the West Bank was annexed by Transjordan and the Gaza Strip became an Egyptian trusteeship.[20] The conflict was not solved, and in later years it would lead to more rounds of violence.

The partition of India was not peaceful either. Although the dominant Indian National Congress aimed to maintain the territorial integrity of the colony by being a catchall movement, political mobilization occurred largely along religious lines. In 1909, the colonial authorities had promoted this implicitly by awarding a number of reserved seats in the Central Legislative Council to the Muslim minority. The Indian National Congress, moreover, fiercely opposed the British wartime promise that provinces and princely states would be allowed to opt out of a future independent state, as this would lead to discord and "balkanization." The Muslim League, on the other hand, feared to losing leverage in a unitary state. During the war, its leader, Muhammad Ali Jinnah, began to redefine India's Muslims as a "nation" with the right to self-determination, while espousing the idea of Pakistan ("land of the pure") as a Muslim homeland, first as part of a larger federation and finally as an independent nation-state. After the end of the war, the British government wanted to withdraw from India as quickly as possible, whereas the Indian National Congress began to support the idea of a limited partition in which the Muslim-majority districts in the west and east would be allowed to go their own way. The partition, which took place when India and Pakistan became independent in August 1947, was marked by widespread bloodshed. Several hundred thousand people lost their lives in a population exchange in which about twelve million people left their homes amid scenes of violence. Moreover, the status of Kashmir became a permanent bone of contention.[21]

Both countries remained within the British Commonwealth. In 1931 the dominions had become independent, but within the British Commonwealth of Nations they continued to closely cooperate with the United Kingdom in the fields of defense, international relations, and trade. In fact, this cooperation had deepened as a consequence of the Great Depression and the Second World War. There still were some vestiges of the older bonds, as the dominions recognized the British monarch as their head of state and the inhabitants continued to be British subjects, and as such, they owed allegiance to the Crown. The whole constellation changed when India and Pakistan gained independence as dominions, which was a solution that made possible a speedier withdrawal of the British. In the end, India decided to become a republic, although the leadership preferred to remain within the Commonwealth. In order to accommodate the new republic, the Commonwealth had to be transformed, making the British king a mere "symbol of a free association." Thus, a Commonwealth citizenship was created. On achieving independence, most former colonies decided to become a member of this reformed Commonwealth of Nations ("British" was dropped from the name). But as the Commonwealth gained more Asian, African, and Caribbean members, its coordinating role was weakened. This had become clear halfway through the 1950s when the Indian prime minister Jawaharlal Nehru began to steer an independent course by becoming one of the leaders of the new Non-Aligned Movement, and when Great Britain did not consult the other members of the Commonwealth before its attack on Egypt during the Suez Crisis.[22]

Great Britain, nonetheless, had some success in pooling various territories in federations. The British assembled a patchwork of protectorates with some of the British Straits Settlements into a Malayan Union, which in 1948 was transformed into the Federation of Malaya. This move meant that all inhabitants, including the very substantial Chinese and Indian immigrant communities, received Malayan citizenship. The three major ethnic political parties formed an alliance in 1955 and quickly negotiated independence with London, which was obtained two years later. Within the next few years, more territories joined the federation. The leaders of Singapore—which had become a self-governing British colony in 1959—thought that independence would not be a viable solution for the city-state and wanted a merger with Malaya. In order not to upset the delicate ethnic balance, the government of Malaya also managed to include the British colonies of North Borneo and Sarawak, creating the Federal State of Malaysia in 1963.[23]

In the British West Indies, too, London applied the federal formula. Trade unions and welfare organizations had begun to mobilize the populations in the early twentieth century, but it was only during the Second World War that colonial assemblies were created. The British subsequently launched plans for a West Indies Federation, which in time would become independent. Most local politicians also favored such a solution. They were aware that most islands were too small to be feasible nation-states, whereas a federation would give them some international leverage. In 1958 they adopted a constitution that provided for a weak central government; the federation did not even constitute a customs union. The more affluent islands, such as Jamaica, feared they would have to subsidize the poorer ones. Moreover, none of the prominent political leaders wanted to become president of the federation because a prolonged absence could endanger their power base at home. Since the federation did not gain independence immediately, many Jamaicans became impatient, and in 1961 they voted for secession. The next year, both Jamaica and Trinidad and Tobago became independent, leaving the other islands without federation in British hands.[24]

The timetable for independence of the British sub-Saharan colonies and protectorates was less concrete, but federal solutions were also tried there (map 7.1). Colonial assemblies were only partially elected, and whenever white settlers were present, they tended to dominate these bodies, which is what happened in Southern Rhodesia and Kenya. In Southern Rhodesia, the franchise was very restricted, effectively excluding Blacks for not meeting the property qualifications. In 1953, a Central African Federation was established after Roy Welensky, the leader of the Northern Rhodesian whites, proposed the merger of Northern and Southern Rhodesia, both for economic reasons and to safeguard the leading role of the settlers. The British government, however, insisted on adding the protectorate of Nyasaland—where almost no Europeans lived— in order to encourage the cooperation between Blacks and whites. The subsequent elections in the protectorate were won by the Nyasaland African Congress of Hastings Kamuzu Banda, who was in favor of independence. Although the British governor tried to undo the election results, this backfired. Soon after, Kenneth Kaunda's United National Independence Party won the elections in Northern Rhodesia. By now it was obvious that the large majority of the population did not want to live in a federation dominated by white settlers. The British, as a consequence, decided to dissolve the federation, and Nyasaland became independent as Malawi. Northern Rhodesia followed in 1965, taking the name Zambia, while Southern Rhodesia—where the settlers remained in the driver's seat—unilaterally declared independence.[25]

In East Africa, too, the British promoted plans for a federation, both to overcome ethnic tensions and to create an economically viable state. In Kenya the relatively small number of white settlers still received one-third of the seats in the colonial assembly at the height of the Mau Mau's massive armed struggle for independence, whereas another third was reserved for the more numerous Indian immigrant community; only (the last) one-third represented the

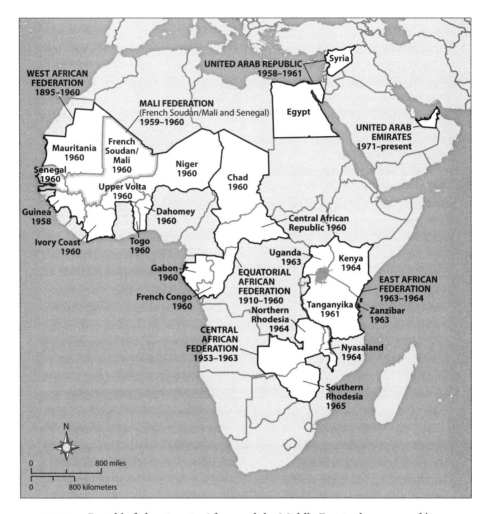

MAP 7.1 Possible federations in Africa and the Middle East in the 1950s and '60s. The British helped create the Central African Federation (nowadays Zimbabwe, Zambia, and Malawi), the East African Federation (Tanzania, Kenya, and Uganda), and the United Arab Emirates. The French founded the Equatorial African Federation and the West African Federation, while African leaders created the Mali Federation (nowadays Senegal and Mali). Egypt and Syria merged to form the United Arab Republic. Indicated are the dates of each federation and the date of independence of the respective colonies.

overwhelming Black majority. It became increasingly clear that blocking majority rule was untenable. As a result, the British relaunched their plans for a federation, but these gained substance only in June 1963, when Jomo Kenyatta, Julius Nyerere, and Milton Obote, the Black leaders of Kenya, Tanganyika, and Uganda, respectively, announced the establishment of an East African

Federation by the end of the year, also enabling the speeding up of Kenya's independence. They hoped that a centralized federation would create a strong state and a stable environment for rapid economic development. At the same time, it could cement their own domestic power bases ahead of divisive "tribalist" forces. Many opposition parties also embraced the idea of federalism, advocating a decentralized state with extensive autonomy for regions and traditional kingdoms. In the end, though, agreement could not be reached on fundamental issues such as international borrowing rights, the powers of the federal president, the official language (Swahili would put Ugandans at a disadvantage), and representation on the international stage. Giving up sovereign powers that had already been attained proved too difficult.[26]

The Netherlands was another colonial power that aimed to transform the relationship with its colonies by setting up a kind of commonwealth. During the Second World War, the government in exile had declared that the demand for equality and political participation from the colonies could not be ignored any longer. In 1945, a new Dutch coalition government consisting of Social Democrats and Catholics proposed the creation of a United States of Indonesia—one of which would be Sukarno's already proclaimed republic—as an integral part of a new Dutch-Indonesian Union. However, this diplomatic solution was rejected by hardliners on both sides. A subsequent Dutch military intervention—euphemistically called "police actions"—encountered massive resistance and provoked condemnation by the United Nations. Since the republic demonstrated no communist inclinations, the Truman administration pressed the Dutch government to grant independence to Indonesia, which finally became a reality in 1949. At the same time, the Netherlands-Indonesian Union—which also encompassed Suriname and the Dutch Antilles—was instated to encourage mutual cooperation. However, after years of violent conflict, the union largely remained an empty shell.[27]

The French authorities had similar ideas in mind. In January 1944, at a conference in Brazzaville, Charles de Gaulle had made significant concessions to the inhabitants of the colonies, promising equal citizenship in a new union, political participation through territorial assemblies, and some form of representation in the National Assembly. The founders of the Fourth Republic—Christian Democrats, Socialists, and Communists—largely adopted his course of colonial reform. With the constitution of October 1946, they conferred citizenship of a new French Union on the inhabitants of the colonies, which meant that they could vote for territorial assemblies and that forced labor and repressive Indigenous law codes were abolished. Nonetheless, in order to avoid France becoming "the colony of its former colonies"—as former prime minister Edouard Herriot phrased it during the constitutional debates—power remained firmly in the hands of the French National Assembly, in which the overseas territories and colonies received only a limited number of representatives.[28]

The situation in Indochina at the end of the war was very similar to that of the Dutch Indies, and so were the solutions proposed by the French. Indochina was transformed into a federation of associate states, which together would be part of the French Union. Cambodia and Laos became associate kingdoms, while Ho Chi Minh's Democratic Republic of Vietnam was offered the status of autonomous free state. However, many on both sides opposed a compromise, and at the end of 1946 the French began a major offensive against Ho's Vietminh. In this case, however, the Cold War had a negative impact on the decolonization process. As the Vietminh was dominated by the Communists, the United States backed the French military efforts to reestablish control in Vietnam, and U.S. support became more substantial after the proclamation of the Communist People's Republic of China in 1949 and the start of the Korean War. Another communist victory had to be avoided at all costs. In 1953, Paris decided to give independence to Laos and Cambodia, but the French were not prepared to give up Vietnam. Nonetheless, after the defeat at Dien Bien Phu in 1954, the French government had no option but to grant independence to both North and South Vietnam; the former was dominated by the Communists, the latter effectively became a client state of the United States. The conflict between North and South Vietnam would flare up again, and it finally came to an end with the victory of the Communists in 1975.[29]

In Africa, the French also faced serious obstacles in their aim to turn the empire into a sort of French commonwealth. Although the inhabitants of the colonies had become citizens of the French Union, voting occurred through two electoral colleges—one for the small group of inhabitants with French civil status and one for the rest of the population. This was most problematic in Algeria, which officially was part of France and where European settlers elected half of the members of the new Algerian assembly. Inspired by developments in Vietnam, a newly created National Liberation Front started an uprising in 1954. Although the French troops suppressed the revolt in most parts of the country, the National Liberation Front succeeded in putting the issue on the international agenda. The war, moreover, proved to be very costly. Most conscripts were not eager to serve in Algeria, and the extensive use of torture severely damaged the moral authority of the French government. Most settlers and high officers fiercely opposed a negotiated solution, and in 1958 they prompted the fall of the Fourth Republic and the return of General de Gaulle as president. He promised to make Algeria "fully French," meaning that all inhabitants would receive the same rights, while an ambitious program of industrialization, land reform, and schooling would improve living standards. But this did not really change the situation, and in 1962 he conceded independence, leading to an exodus of European settlers and Algerian Muslims enlisted in the French armed forces.[30]

The Algerian War of Independence greatly affected the situations of the French colonies elsewhere in Africa. In 1946, both the West African Federation and the Equatorial African Federation had become part of the French Union and received elected assemblies with advisory roles (map 7.1). Nationalist movements, nevertheless, demanded investments and full democratic rights. In 1956, France granted independence to Morocco and Tunisia, avoiding the escalation of the tense situation in these protectorates. At the same time, the French cabinet awarded self-government to the remaining African colonies and abolished the separate electoral colleges; they also became responsible for their own expenses, relieving the French treasury. Meanwhile, France became one of the founding members of the European Economic Community, which implied that the African territories—except for Algeria—were excluded from the European Common Market; in fact, this ruled out a more thorough integration of the French Union. The French government clearly preferred Europe over Africa.[31]

The Fifth Republic came with a new constitution, and the French Union became the French Community. De Gaulle hoped to transform it into a strong, centralized federation that would be responsible for defense, foreign affairs, and economic coordination. African leaders, many of whom had been members of the National Assembly or even ministers in a French cabinet, preferred a federation of equals. Some African politicians, including Léopold Sédar Senghor, proposed an intermediate solution. Senghor feared that a growing role for the individual territories would lead to a "balkanization" of Africa. The Senegalese intellectual-cum-politician argued that all great civilizations had been the product of cultural and biological mixing, pointing to the United States, the Soviet Union, India, and China as good examples. He hoped that a revitalized West African Federation could play a middling role between the individual territories and the French Union, effectively dividing sovereignty between three different levels.[32]

In the end, however, the French Community would be dominated by the metropole; it would be headed by the French president, and the ministries in Paris would coordinate policies. The constitution had to be approved by all "member states," and on a trip to various African capitals, De Gaulle made it clear that a "no" in the referendum would prompt the immediate withdrawal of the French. This happened only in Guinea, where Ahmed Sékou Touré—who favored an equal partnership—told De Gaulle that "we prefer poverty in freedom to wealth in slavery." The other African leaders preferred to stay within the French Community. Nevertheless, they quickly tried to increase the competences of their administrations. Senghor, for instance, made concrete steps toward reinventing the West African Federation, but in 1959 only Senegal and French Sudan (now Mali) became part of the federation, which adopted the name of the ancient empire of Mali. As with the West Indies Federation, the richest colonies opposed the idea of a federation because it would probably involve a heavy financial burden This was the case with Ivory Coast in West Africa, and Gabon was the principal opponent of a federal restructuring of French Equatorial Africa.[33]

Both the Mali Federation and the French Community soon ended in failure. In December 1959 the leaders of the new Mali Federation requested a transfer of competences, which would make it effectively independent without leaving the French Community, making its relationship to France a more egalitarian union, similar to the Commonwealth of Nations. Their request was accepted by De Gaulle, and negotiations between France and the Federation of Mali led to independence the next summer. Félix Houphouët-Boigny, the leader of Ivory Coast, was indignant: the French Community had been transformed without the other member states having been consulted. Now he, too, claimed independence, and he achieved it, as the Malians had done, through bilateral talks with France. The other African leaders followed his lead, and within a year, the French Community had become largely meaningless.[34]

Surprisingly, the Mali Federation also collapsed within two months. Although its leaders were truly dedicated to the federal project, the differences between the two parts and their principal leaders were problematic. French Sudan had a larger population, but Senegal was wealthier. The Sudanese, led by Modibo Keita, were in favor of a unitary state; the Senegalese preferred a more federalist solution. Sudan's leaders were more radical in "Africanizing" the bureaucracy, and they opposed Senghor's presidential candidacy because he was too French, not a Muslim, and married to a white woman. Eventually, Prime Minister Keita attempted to oust his Senegalese rivals, but they succeeded in expelling him from Dakar and proclaiming the independence of Senegal. France refused to intervene, to Keita's disappointment. Thus, in the end, the plans to create meaningful federations within the French Empire failed. Cooper argues that this can be explained by the fact that political power was already entrenched at the territorial level. Since 1945, the individual territories had become electoral districts, which led to political parties based on territories. This process was institutionalized in 1956 by awarding each territory its own government. Politicians therefore had a strong power base in their own territory, which they put at stake in a federation, as the case of Senghor proved.[35] In fact, this was also a major obstacle in most colonial federations within the British Empire.

In addition to forming federations and unions, there was another option to preserve the colonies: making them an integral part of the metropole. In 1946 most of France's old colonies, including French Guiana, Guadeloupe, and Réunion, became overseas departments, and most of these small territories are still part of France.[36] In the 1950s this model was also adopted by Portugal and

Spain, as it helped to shield them from criticism from the international community. Both countries had semi-Fascist authoritarian regimes, so it was not problematic to confer citizenship on the inhabitants of the colonies because there were no free democratic elections, and no costly social welfare system either. Beginning in the early 1960s, however, they were confronted with independence movements that used guerrilla tactics. For Spain this was not much of a threat, because its remaining colonies were small and sparsely inhabited, but it was very different for Portugal. In the end, the colonial wars in Angola and Mozambique sowed profound discontent among the army and the public, resulting in the overthrow of the Portuguese dictatorial regime in April 1974. This led to the independence of the remaining colonies, and soon after, Morocco pressured the ailing Franco dictatorship to give up the Province of the Sahara.[37] By this time, it was no longer acceptable for a modern European country to cling to its empire by employing violence on a massive scale.

Pan movements also flared up. The most successful, at least for a short period, was the pan-Arab movement. Pan-Arabism had already been a driving force of Sharif Hussein bin Ali's attempt to carve out an Arab state during the First World War. A unified Arab nation-state also was the explicit goal of the Arab Renaissance Party—the Ba'ath Party—which was founded in Syria in 1947; other branches appeared in Iraq, Lebanon, and Jordan. The common opposition of the Arab countries to the establishment of the state of Israel was another unifying factor. The pan-Arab movement received a boost when Gamal Abdel Nasser took power in Egypt in 1952 as leader of a coup by the Free Officers. He pursued an assertive international policy and became one of the leaders of the Non-Aligned Movement. The nationalization of the Suez Canal Company in 1956 provoked a concerted attack by Israel, the United Kingdom, and France, who were forced to withdraw under heavy pressure from the United States and the Soviet Union. Nasser's moral victory increased his prestige in the Arab world, which he used in calls for Arab solidarity and concerted action.[38]

An opportunity to realize some of his pan-Arab ideals was handed to Nasser on a silver platter by Syrian officers. Syria had already been politically unstable for several years, and both the Ba'ath Party and the Communists had approached him with proposals for the unification of Syria and Egypt, either as a merger or a federation. In 1958, the army leadership decided to take matters into their own hands—they flew to Cairo and negotiated a union with the Egyptian president. Nasser imposed conditions that led to the creation of a centralized United Arab Republic, ruled from Cairo through the existing Egyptian institutions (map 7.1). This set off an unexpected chain of events, as Nasserists in Jordan, Iraq, and Lebanon also wanted to join the new republic. These hopes were impeded by a short-lived federal Arab Union between Jordan and Iraq, a military coup in Iraq, and the Lebanese and Jordan authorities' requests for military support, which were granted by the United States and Great Britain, respectively. The United Arab Republic did not last very long. The main reason for the collapse was Syrian frustration with Egyptian domination. Socialist reforms, which affected large landowners and the business community, caused further discontent. In 1961 a military coup in Syria dissolved the union and expelled all Egyptians.[39]

Pan-African ideas gained traction at about the same time. Pan-Africanism had its origins among Black intellectuals in the Americas, such as W.E.B. Du Bois in the United States, Marcus Garvey in Jamaica, and Eric Williams in Trinidad. The aim was to promote the unity of all Africans, including those in the diaspora, and to claim full political rights. Kwame Nkrumah, the president of Ghana, the first sub-Saharan colony to become independent in 1957, was a staunch defender of pan-Africanism, not just to combat discrimination but also to encourage economic cooperation and increase the political leverage of Africa in the international arena. One year after Ghana's independence, he convened a meeting in Accra of independent African countries and representatives of nationalist movements and labor unions from the rest of the continent. He hoped to create a United States of Africa, but profound divisions soon came to the surface and the initiative slipped away from Nkrumah. Five years later, at a conference in Addis Ababa, Ghana proposed the creation of an African federation with a free trade area, a defense force, and a continental government that would coordinate economic development while ensuring a prominent place for Africa in world politics. In the end, though, thirty-two African countries embraced the more modest Ethiopian plan to create the Organisation of African Unity, which was merely an intergovernmental body for mutual cooperation without major supranational ambitions.[40]

More lasting than many of the large-scale federations were some minor mergers of territories: Eritrea joined Ethiopia in 1950; British Togoland merged with Gold Coast to become independent as Ghana in 1957; British Somaliland and Italian Somaliland were merged in 1960; British Cameroon was split up in 1961, with one part joining Nigeria and the other Cameroon; and in 1964 Zanzibar merged with Tanganyika to form the United Republic of Tanzania. In 1971 seven small states in the Persian Gulf became independent as the United Arab Emirates. Nevertheless, most territories that became independent after 1960— the Year of Africa—became nation-states while respecting the existing borders.[41] A few years later, most of the ambitious projects to create larger federations and unions had foundered. The French Community, the Netherlands-Indonesian Union, and the Commonwealth of Nations had become largely obsolete; Nkrumah's United States of Africa and the East African Federation had proven to be no more than beautiful dreams; and the West Indies Federation, the Central African Federation, the Mali Federation, and the United Arab

Republic had collapsed. So the federal moment was over, and from this time on, the trend was toward further territorial fragmentation. During the next decades, the number of member states of the United Nations increased rapidly, primarily because many island states became independent.[42]

There were some other attempts to change the arbitrary borders of the colonial empires—not by creating large, heterogenous federations, but by forming more homogenous nation-states. Some politicians tried to make ancient kingdoms into independent nation-states, others hoped to secede from a larger unit, while in some cases irredenta were claimed. Almost all of these attempts failed, confirming the hegemonic position of the nation-state and the inviolability of existing borders. A good example of the first type was the Kingdom of Buganda in Uganda. The British governed Uganda mostly via indirect rule, and they had signed a treaty with Buganda in 1900. The king rapidly modernized his realm, turning the advisory council into a modern parliament, reorganizing agriculture on a commercial basis, and converting to Christianity. People from Buganda also dominated the colonial administration, but when British governors aimed to prepare Uganda for independence in the 1950s, a statewide legislature was created. King Mutesa II hoped to achieve independence for Buganda, and the monarchical party therefore boycotted the national elections of 1961. At independence, a federal state model respected the autonomy of Buganda, appointing Mutesa as ceremonial president of Uganda, but politics was dominated by Prime Minister Milton Obote, who within a few years succeeded in sidelining the king and even dismantling the autonomous position of Buganda. Elsewhere, the traditional Ashanti and Bakongo kingdoms suffered a similar fate.[43]

There were also ethnic groups who sought to create their own nation-states. In 1946, educated elites of the Ewe, a people who lived in French and British Togoland and the easternmost parts of Gold Coast, created an All-Ewe Conference with the goal of unifying all Ewe in one state. In the end they were outsmarted by Nkrumah, as the majority of the population of British Togoland voted for the integration of their United Nations trust territory with Gold Coast. Nkrumah had promised that French Togoland could merge with the new state of Ghana as well, but the country opted for independence. Many ordinary Ewe, moreover, were not in favor of doing away with the existing states and the borders between them. Instead of pinning their hopes on a theoretical construct, they directed their demands to the existing states, first to the colonial authorities and then to the independent nation-states of Ghana and Togo. According to Paul Nugent, the border was a "theatre of opportunity" for profitable cross-border trade and smuggling, and it could also serve to protect people fleeing to the other side. Thus, the Ewe did not have very strong incentives to embark on a risky adventure by breaking with the existing states.[44]

Most secession attempts failed, as demonstrated by the example of Congo. The colony had barely been prepared for independence—proposals to create a Belgian Union after the French model did not bear fruit—when Belgium hastily handed over power in June 1960. The new state rapidly descended into chaos, leading to the proclamation of independence by the rich mining province of Katanga and a Belgian military intervention to protect its citizens. It was clear that the secessionists had received the backing of foreign mining companies and the Belgian state. In response, President Joseph Kasavubu and Prime Minister Patrice Lumumba secured military assistance from the United Nations. Shortly afterward, the Mining State of South Kasai also claimed independent statehood. When it became clear that the UN forces would not actively combat the secessionist movements, Lumumba—who would soon be murdered—sought military support from the Soviet Union. In order to prevent Congo from becoming a site for neocolonial experiments or another proxy war between the superpowers, African and Asian leaders pressured the United Nations to take decisive action. As a result, a resolution was passed by the Security Council that allowed the use of force to restore order. The new secretary-general U Thant pursued a more vigorous course, and UN troops defeated the secessionist forces of both Katanga and South Kasai by 1963.[45]

The international community also took decisive action to prevent the secession of Biafra from Nigeria. The constitution of 1954 had turned Nigeria into a federation consisting of three autonomous regions. This led to fierce competition between various largely ethnically based political parties, each of which sought to monopolize power primarily in its own region. The instability was aggravated after independence. A military putsch that was perceived as an eastern Igbo conspiracy and the subsequent attempt to create a unitary state by abolishing the regions led to the widespread killings of Igbos in the north and a countercoup. The new regime was not accepted in the Eastern Region, and in 1967 its military governor, Lieutenant-Colonel Odumegwu Ojukwu, proclaimed the independence of the region as the Republic of Biafra. Ojukwu anticipated the dissolution of the federation and hoped to profit from the booming oil industry, which was located primarily in his region. This new variant of "nationalism of the rich"—which had also been an obstacle in the creation of many federations—led to a violent conflict between the secessionist region and the Nigerian government. Although the Biafran authorities succeeded in appealing to international humanitarian sentiments, portraying themselves as a Christian minority suffering persecution and starvation at the hands of the Muslim majority, they failed to secure substantial external assistance. The multinational oil companies refused to pay revenues to the secessionist government, and the Organisation of African Unity and the United Nations actively supported the territorial integrity of Nigeria. Without financial resources, major weapons deliveries, and international recognition, the secessionist army was defeated four years later.[46]

Secessions succeeded only in very exceptional cases. The case of Singapore was singular, as the city-state was expelled from the Federal State of Malaysia. Shortly after its creation, both the governing United Malays National Organisation and the People's Action Party—the main political force in Singapore, dominated by ethnic Chinese—tried to gain an electoral foothold in the other's territories. This led to communal riots in Singapore, with dozens of casualties. After first considering the option of a looser federation, in 1965 the Malaysian government decided that a complete separation would be the best solution, and this was reluctantly accepted by Singapore. The secession of Bangladesh in 1971 was a much more violent affair. Although East Pakistan had a larger population than the western part of the country, its people suffered from pervasive discrimination. After the fall of the Ayub Khan military dictatorship, the pro-autonomist Awami League won a landslide victory in East Pakistan, securing an absolute majority in the legislative assembly. However, the president, General Yahya Khan, and the Pakistan People's Party, which had won a majority in West Pakistan, refused to accept the new government. In March 1970, the president ordered the army to suppress Bengali nationalism, and they did so with extreme brutality. The Awami League set up a government in exile in India, while a resistance movement took up arms. The conflict created about twenty million internally displaced persons, and about ten million people fled to India. The international community was divided over the issue, so no decisive action was taken by the United Nations. In the end, India sent troops and the Pakistan army in the east surrendered within a matter of weeks, thus creating the new state of Bangladesh.[47]

In other areas, irredentism was an issue, including in Somalia. The country was ethnically relatively homogenous, but the mostly nomadic Somali clans also lived in the north of Kenya, in Djibouti, and in Ogaden, which was part of Ethiopia. Thus, at independence, the idea of a Greater Somalia was quite popular. In 1962, feeble attempts to support an armed insurrection in northern Kenya were met by unwavering British and Kenyan authorities, and the new Organisation of African Unity explicitly sanctioned the existing borders. In Ogaden, too, local Somalis revolted, and they received military support from Mogadishu. The first Somali-Ethiopian war was a relatively minor affair, but the second, which started in 1977, involved more troops. However, the new Marxist regime in Ethiopia received massive military aid from the Soviet Union. As a consequence, this attempt to create a Greater Somalia also fell flat.[48]

There were other attempts to change international borders or create new states, but almost all of them failed utterly. There were many secessionist movements, some of which resorted to guerrilla or terrorist strategies. These include the Karen in eastern Myanmar, South Sudan, the Spanish Basque Country, Quebec, Eritrea, Northern Ireland, Bangsamoro in the Philippines, the Tamil regions of Sri Lanka, Turkish Kurdistan, and Assam in India, but none of these movements achieved their goals during the Cold War era.[49] There were also some futile attempts to annex foreign territory. In 1977 Egypt briefly conquered some oil fields in eastern Libya, and the next year, Idi Amin's Uganda tried to annex Tanzania's Kagera Region. Although in some instances secessionist movements or foreign aggressors did receive some support from abroad, in general, the international community tried to block weapons deliveries while calling for negotiated settlements that respected the territorial integrity of existing states. In cases where a powerful aggressor had its way— Israel conquered the Palestinian territories and the Golan Heights in 1967, Turkey occupied Northern Cyprus in 1974, Indonesia invaded East Timor in 1975, and Morocco occupied the Western Sahara in 1975—the international community refused to recognize the situation, leading to frozen conflicts.[50]

After the negative experiences of the partitions of India and Palestine and as a consequence of the failures of most federations and secessionist and irredentist movements, existing borders became sacrosanct. Even though most new states were not ethnically, linguistically, religiously, and culturally homogeneous, they all adopted the template of the nation-state, with a constitution, an elected parliament, legal equality for all citizens, a flag, an anthem, and a national holiday. However, this process of global isomorphism, supported by a host of international organizations such as the United Nations, the World Bank, UNESCO, and the World Health Organization, also entailed adopting a cabinet, more or less uniform ministries, a standardized provincial and municipal administration, secular education, modern security forces, and a centralized health care system. Through global processes of mimesis and professionalization, even accounting systems, scientific research, and the definition of diseases became standardized.[51] Nonetheless, behind a constitutional façade and modern state bureaucracy, many dictators wielded great personal power, but only mavericks such as Colonel Muammar al-Gaddafi in Libya openly refused to live up to some of the growing exigencies of world society.[52]

Citizenship

The relationship between citizens and the state underwent a profound transformation during the postwar era, weakening the nation-in-arms as the strength of the armies was no longer determined by the number of draftees. Whereas during the First World War the number of recruits had still been crucial to the outcome of the war, the Second World War was decided primarily by industrial capacity and military technology. Battleships, submarines, airplanes, tanks, and atomic bombs fundamentally changed the nature of warfare by prioritizing the contributions of highly trained professionals over conscripts. Wars also became less heroic. During the Second World War, most victims were civilians, and they were killed during genocidal ethnic-cleansing campaigns, in massive air raids, or in retaliation for acts of resistance. After 1945, the lack of heroism was due to not only the brutality of the fighting, but also the hollowness of the patriotic rhetoric used to mobilize the citizenry. Wars of national defense had become rare; most wars were proxy wars between Communism and the "free world," or wars of decolonization, such as those in Indonesia, Algeria, and Angola. Although colonial resistance fighters still became national heroes or martyrs after independence, among imperial powers the opposition to warfare became louder. Most conscripts were not eager to go to distant lands to fight in a "senseless" struggle, and in the increasingly risk-averse societies, the public's attention shifted from patriotic sacrifice to inhumane suffering, while ordinary soldiers were seen as victims.[53] As a consequence, the focus shifted from land and demography—*Lebensraum* and eugenics—to economic growth and technological modernization.

As the figure of the citizen-soldier lost relevance, the male entitlement to a privileged role in the nation's affairs was undermined. This was accompanied by the emancipation of female citizens. After 1945, voting rights were rapidly extended in the colonies, which in almost all cases included suffrage for women. Moreover, the countries in Europe, Latin America, and Asia that had hesitated to confer political rights on women also began to grant them the vote. In some exceptional cases, such as Switzerland and Jordan, female suffrage would have to wait until the early 1970s. Although women now had the right to vote, there were few female politicians and even fewer high-ranking officials and ministers. Nonetheless, women slowly made progress and reached top positions. In Asia, Sirimavo Bandaranaike, the widow of a prominent politician, and Indira Gandhi, the daughter of Nehru, became prime ministers of Sri Lanka and India, respectively, in the 1960s, and Isabel Perón succeeded her deceased husband as president of Argentina in 1974. Golda Meir had a political career of her own and became Israel's prime minister in 1969.[54]

Female emancipation did not progress in linear fashion. During the Second World War and the decolonization process, women had taken active roles in the war industry and resistance movements. In the immediate postwar era, however, there was a backlash, just as there had been after 1918, and the progress women had made in the job market was largely undone. Assertive women and single mothers were widely seen as a threat to moral decency, and the same applied to gay men and lesbians. Same-sex acts were still persecuted in many countries in both the Eastern and Western blocs, and at height of McCarthyism the U.S. administration discharged hundreds of employees accused of having "homosexual proclivities."[55] Single mothers were not persecuted by the state, but in Catholic areas "fallen women" were often confined in workhouses, such as Irish Magdalene laundries, where they had to perform long hours of unpaid labor. In addition, many unmarried women were pressured to give up their babies to be adopted by "decent" families, sometimes even abroad. In Spain and the Netherlands, many single mothers were falsely told that their babies were stillborn, and these practices continued into the 1980s.[56]

Although in many countries women officially received equal rights, many legal obstacles were still in place. In France, married women continued to be regarded as "legal minors" until 1965, and in Austria husbands could forbid their wives to work outside the home until 1976. In many former colonies customary or religious law codes remained in place after independence, relegating women to a subordinate position. The 1960s was a clear turning point, as a younger generation of women—inspired by Simone de Beauvoir's *The Second Sex* (1949) and Betty Friedan's *The Feminine Mystique* (1963) and helped by the introduction of "the pill"—began to demand equal rights, free childcare, access to birth control, the right to abortion, and even the end of patriarchy. The United Nations played an encouraging role by declaring 1975 the International Women's Year, and four years later it adopted the Convention on the Elimination of All Forms of Discrimination against Women.[57]

Since political citizenship of both the male and female populations was increasingly taken for granted, the state assumed a more prominent role in protecting the well-being of its citizens. Most independent East Asian countries massively increased spending on education, health care, and housing, but for other benefits they continued to rely primarily on informal networks and social insurance schemes provided by companies. In Western Europe and North America, the welfare state tied citizens more closely to the state. The first social insurance systems had been in place since the late nineteenth century, and in the Nordic countries the social democratic welfare state had been developed during the Great Depression. In Western Europe, rivalry with the totalitarian regimes motivated states to take a more activist approach. Thus, after 1945, the Labour government in Great Britain introduced a comprehensive social security system that included unemployment and retirement benefits. The government also guaranteed a uniform standard of care by nationalizing the health sector, creating the National Health Service. Most Western European countries took similar measures—often also nationalizing basic necessities such as water and energy supply, as well as airlines—and in many cases redistributed more resources to the needy. At the same time, spending on social housing multiplied and access to secondary and higher education quickly expanded.[58]

The emancipation of the colonies also raised the expectations of the population. While the main imperial powers tried to create a more egalitarian relationship with their overseas territories, many inhabitants of the colonies—especially in Africa and the Caribbean—hoped to be treated equally and get access to the benefits of the new metropolitan welfare states. According to Cooper, this incentivized the imperial powers to dissolve their colonial empires as they became increasingly aware that it would be very costly to fully honor the demands for social citizenship.[59] After independence, most African governments took up the challenge by making considerable efforts to provide their citizens with health care, education, and economic opportunities. Nkrumah accordingly asserted that the first objective of his government was to abolish "poverty, ignorance and disease." Botswana set up village development committees, invested heavily in education and health facilities, and created a drought relief program.[60]

In communist countries, the state was particularly intrusive. The number of Communist regimes had expanded greatly. The Soviet model was imposed in many parts of Eastern Europe, but communist parties also gained power in Mongolia, North Korea, China, North Vietnam, Cuba, Cambodia, and Laos. They adopted a system of comprehensive planning and full employment and provided free access to education and health care. Nevertheless, individual interests were subordinate to the collective goal of strengthening the state and enhancing economic production. The Soviet Union already had an internal passport system to coordinate labor supply and control migration, and other communist countries deployed similar means. The People's Republic of China adopted a system of household registration that enabled food rationing and the reallocation of workers. Moreover, ruthless social engineering projects, such as China's Great Leap Forward, were undertaken to create a modern, egalitarian society, but in China and Cambodia they resulted in millions of deaths.[61]

The nation's progress sometimes was used to justify radical measures to ensure the healthy development of the population. Canada and the Scandinavian countries, for example, continued to sterilize "feeble minded" people until the 1970s, while Bangladesh and India conducted mass sterilization programs to avoid overpopulation. China decided to ruthlessly enforce a one-child policy in 1980 after less invasive measures to curb population growth did not yield the desired results.[62]

In order to pay for the new welfare measures, high tax receipts were needed, and the best way to achieve this was through economic growth. Many governments had experimented with economic planning during the Great Depression and the Second World War. The Marshall Plan, adopted in 1948, provided a much-needed kick start for Western Europe, and in the context of the Cold War, President Truman announced that the United States was willing to provide technical assistance to the "underdeveloped areas" in the rest of the world, arguing that "greater production is the key to prosperity and peace." The

United States and other Western governments collaborated with new international institutions such as the World Bank, the Food and Agriculture Organization (FAO), the World Health Organization (WHO) and the United Nations Educational, Scientific and Cultural Organization (UNESCO) to provide loans for ambitious infrastructural projects, improve agricultural output, eradicate disease, and extend schooling. Although the Soviet Union provided development aid to Communist regimes, it stepped up its support to left-leaning regimes in Africa and Asia only in the 1960s. Development became the new hallmark, and this applied to the democratic countries of the West, where Keynesian policies became commonplace, the Communist countries in the East, and the increasingly assertive "Third World."[63]

Development would have to operate through national channels. Territorial imbalances had to be redressed by the state through subsidies and regional planning initiatives. Even in the Communist world, the national level predominated. Notwithstanding the rhetoric about international solidarity, in practice, each state set its own economic priorities. This idea of making the nation-state responsible for its own social and economic development was institutionalized through the adoption of the International Covenant on Economic, Social and Cultural Rights by the United Nations in 1966. The covenant contained a long list of social rights, including the right to work, education, and an adequate standard of living. The list started with the right to self-determination, which suggested that each "people" could freely determine their own socioeconomic policy and dispose of their own natural resources. As a result, nation-states were made responsible for implementing the covenant and guaranteeing the well-being of their citizens, which also suggested that imperial powers had no formal obligation to assist their former subjects and that the international community bore no collective responsibility.[64]

The activist economic policies created more cohesive national markets while increasingly nationalizing the socioeconomic realm. Economic regulations, tariffs, and credit were all organized on a national level, national industries were protected, and the mobility of capital was heavily restricted, although the protectionist excesses of the 1930s were avoided. India under Prime Minister Jawaharlal Nehru, for instance, actively pursued a policy to become economically independent. This entailed establishing a central planning commission, creating an active redistribution policy to reduce income disparities, strengthening the industry to replace foreign imports, and most importantly, creating India's own heavy industry, which would provide steel, vehicles, and weapons for the army. Because of vested interests, land reform was not pursued with the same vigor. Most of these elements, such as economic planning and the emphasis on import substitution, were included in the policies of most former colonies. Generally, the native population was favored through land reform and preferential access to positions in the army and the civil service, and in some cases, former colonial officials were expelled. Many regimes pursued a more socialist course by creating state industries and nationalizing foreign companies and natural resources, further strengthening the control of the state over the economy.[65]

With this focus on economic development, many regimes also emphasized national unity. In many instances this led to the institution of single-party regimes. Sometimes these allowed open debate and contested elections with multiple candidates, as in Tanzania. In other countries, the party was a pliable instrument in the hands of the ruler, as in Nkrumah's Ghana. While many single-party regimes were very autocratic, other regimes achieved dominance without explicitly prohibiting other political parties. The main avenue to regime change in such cases was a military coup, which happened mainly when economic progress was disappointing, or when politicians squandered state resources or were perceived as ineffective and divisive. The new military leaders generally justified their deeds by arguing that they merely served the national interest. Military coups took place in Asia mostly in the 1950s and 1960s, and in Africa in the 1960s and 1970s. In Latin America, where the ascent to power of Fidel Castro in Cuba inspired many left-wing insurgencies, concerns about national security were invoked during military coups in the 1960s and 1970s, leading to military dictatorships in Brazil, Uruguay, Chile, and Argentina.[66]

Both economic development policies and authoritarian regimes were defended with nationalist arguments, arguing that the situation required measures that befitted the nation. Thus, in Indonesia a new, national Pancasila ideology was invented, and elsewhere in Asia, a Filipino-first policy and "Thai democracy" were created. Many countries introduced a national version of socialism, such as "Buddhist socialism" in Burma, "Arab socialism" in Egypt, and "African socialism" in Tanzania. Even semi-Fascist regimes reinvented themselves, as "justicialism" in Argentina and "organic democracies" in Spain and Portugal. These new national ideologies mostly meant that economic development had the highest priority and that self-sufficiency and social justice were emphasized. Even Communist countries developed their unique, national brands, such as Maoism in China and *Juche* (self-reliance) in North Korea.[67] That these nationalist ideologies were often nothing more than a fig leaf was nowhere more obvious than in Congo, where President Mobutu Sese Seko introduced an "authenticity" campaign renaming the country Zaire, conducted a policy of Zairianisation, and devised his own ideology of "Mobutism," which had to be taught in schools. National unity should reign supreme. In fact, however, his dictatorial regime was characterized by ethnic favoritism and personal enrichment. Mobutu relied mostly on people from his home region, and in the end, his personal fortune was larger than the national debt.[68]

Connecting nationalist rhetoric with economic growth was not limited to the Second and Third Worlds. In the immediate postwar years, Great Britain conducted savings campaigns under the motto "Export and thrive," encouraging the population to save money to finance the reconstruction of the country. Japan and South Korea developed an explicit "growth nationalism," appealing to the patriotic sentiments of the inhabitants to avoid overspending so that the country could invest more in heavy industry and export-driven growth. Very similar was the emphasis on technological modernization, national grandeur, and rapid economic growth in France—especially during the "Glorious Thirty" years—and the pride in the "economic miracle" and the strength of the national currency in West Germany.[69]

Together with the rising importance of the nation-state, ethnic and racial factors lost some of their sharp edges. After the wave of mass population transfers in the immediate postwar years—the expulsion of ethnic Germans from Eastern Europe, the deportation of various ethnic minorities to Siberia, the population exchange between India and Pakistan, and the expulsion of Palestinians from Israel—ethnic-cleansing campaigns became rare. The decolonization wave in Africa, moreover, coincided with measures to curb racially motivated exclusion in the Western world. In Latin America, questions about race were removed from national censuses after 1945, as most state authorities now focused on national integration, converting Indians into peasants. In the United States, the civil rights movement mounted mass protests to end the racial segregation policies that were still in place in the South. New federal laws in the 1960s banned racial discrimination in public places and protected the voting rights of minorities. The civil rights movement also provided a stimulus for the emancipation of Native Americans. In Canada, for instance, they finally received voting rights in 1960. At about the same time, the racially based restrictions on the immigration of Asians to the United States and Australia were abolished, and in the early 1970s the White Australia policy was officially abandoned.[70]

There was one clear exception to this trend: the apartheid systems in South West Africa (Namibia), Rhodesia, and above all, South Africa. In order to maintain its political dominance, the white minority in South Africa decided to designate "tribal homelands" for the Black population in 1948, most of which were presumably self-governing. These "Bantustans" were puppet states and did not receive international recognition. Meanwhile, Blacks did not have citizenship rights in South Africa and could be expelled if they lost their jobs. Within South Africa, the strict system of racial segregation even made interracial sexual relations a crime. These measures almost immediately led to resistance, primarily from the African National Congress. The apartheid system also became a prime target of criticism, sanctions, and boycotts by the international community, demonstrating that blatant racism had become an anomaly.[71]

The decline of racial categorizations and policies did not mean that states were more interested in cultural diversity. In line with modernization theory, it was widely thought that in the long term, internal cultural and ethnic differences were bound to disappear. Samora Machel, the Marxist freedom fighter who became the first president of Mozambique, proclaimed that "for the nation to live, the tribe must die." Thus, until the 1970s, most countries offered education only in the national language. Immigrants, ethnic minorities, and Indigenous populations were supposed to assimilate, and no special programs existed to defend their cultural heritage, beyond a harmless folkloric fringe. In Western Europe there were almost no measures to protect minority languages; colonial immigrants were supposed to merge into the wider population, and the rapidly growing number of guest workers did not receive citizenship. Latin American states also focused on nation-building policies by inducing Indigenous communities to adopt the language, behavior, and cultural attributes of the dominant group. In the Mexican census, racial categories were abolished, but the anthropologist Manuel Gamio defended the inclusion of cultural questions—about going barefoot or wearing shoes, for example—as useful tools in developing measures to eradicate "primitive" behavior. In the United States, Canada, Australia, and the Scandinavian countries, drastic policies to assimilate Indigenous populations (e.g., forcefully removing children from their parents and placing them in boarding schools) remained in place until the late 1960s or early 1970s. With the notable exception of the federally organized India, most Asian governments, too, were highly assimilationist and were not inclined to grant any cultural rights to ethnic minorities, Indigenous populations, or immigrants.[72]

However, the governments of many new countries also understood that national unity could be achieved only by avoiding ethnic polarization. Communist China, for instance, adopted the nationality policy of the Soviet Union, which meant that fifty-five ethnic minorities were recognized. Larger communities such as the Tibetans, the Mongolians, and the Uighurs were given autonomous republics; smaller ones received autonomous prefectures or counties. Self-government included education in their own language, but excluded the right to secede. Nonetheless, the pressure to assimilate into the large Han majority was considerable, and especially during the Cultural Revolution many traditional cultural and religious practices were repressed. Meanwhile, simplified Chinese—which had been invented in 1932 and was based on the Mandarin dialect of Beijing—was widely adopted as a result of the expanding education system and the active propagation by the Communist regime.[73]

Former colonies that adopted parliamentary democracy similarly steered an inclusive course. Many of the larger multiethnic states such as India, Pakistan, and Nigeria became federal states, with a considerable amount of regional autonomy. Instead of adopting a language that was spoken by a dominant group and thus putting the rest of the population at a disadvantage, many governments decided to adopt a widely used lingua franca as national language. Indonesia adopted Malay, the traditional language of commerce, which was used throughout the archipelago, rather than Javanese, which was spoken by the overwhelming majority of the inhabitants of the central island of Java. In India, Hindi, which was spoken mostly in the north of the country, became the official language at the federal level, but English also received official status for fifteen years, which later was extended indefinitely. Moreover, another fourteen regional languages gained official status at the state or territorial level, and the list was gradually expanded, but there are still a large number of smaller languages and dialects without such a privileged position. Many African countries decided to use either English, French, or Portuguese (the languages of the former colonial regimes) as a lingua franca, and in many cases these have official status.[74]

In various multiethnic states, explicit power-sharing arrangements were introduced, some of which aimed to find a balance between various communities and others which clearly favored one community over the others. In some plantation societies with a large number of indentured laborers from India, such as Fiji, arrangements were made to ensure the political dominance of the Indigenous population. In Malaysia, a new policy of preferential treatment for the "sons of the soil" in terms of education, employment, housing, and business was introduced in 1970, excluding Malaysians with Indian or Chinese roots, who together constituted about one-third of the population. More egalitarian power-sharing arrangements were introduced in Lebanon, where an unwritten pact was concluded between the country's largest religious communities in 1943. Accordingly, the president had to be a Maronite Christian, the prime minister a Sunni Muslim, the speaker of parliament a Shi'i Muslim, the deputy prime minister Greek Orthodox, and the chief of staff a Druze. Palestinian refugees were largely excluded from citizenship. The shifting demographic balance and the presence of Palestinian forces, however, destabilized the equilibrium, and in 1975 a civil war broke out that would last for twenty-five years.[75]

A more informal way to keep the nation together was political patronage. By prioritizing individual favors over the general good, political patronage in theory went against the national interest. Nevertheless, patronage networks operated within the boundaries of the nation-state, linking important segments of the population more directly to the state. Although in weak states, such as in sub-Saharan Africa, political leaders tended to favor clients from their own kin, region, or ethnicity, in most instances these patronage networks covered the entire national territory and included most ethnic groups. Skillful political leaders such as Houphouët-Boigny, Senghor, and Nyerere made sure that political favors landed among a geographically wide and ethnically diverse constituency, thus preventing the formation of powerful coalitions of outsiders that could threaten their positions.[76] Political patronage was not limited to poor states in Africa; it also played a crucial role in middle-income countries such as Mexico and Asian tigers like Singapore, Taiwan, and Japan. There, the strategic use of state resources and the support of business communities enabled dominant parties such as Japan's Liberal Democratic Party and Mexico's Institutional Revolutionary Party to remain in power for decades. Although clientelism, corruption, and pork-barrel practices was less widespread in multi-party democracies in Western Europe and North America, party patronage— that is, providing jobs to party supporters—became more important, especially in Italy, Austria, and Belgium.[77] Critics tended to use nationalist arguments to expose either their own exclusion from the benefits of the system or the system's corrupt nature, but the fierce national debates that ensued tended to naturalize the nation-state as the paramount political arena.

National Awareness

National indifference must have been widespread in many parts of the world, especially in newly independent nation-states. There, identification with religious or ethnic communities often trumped feelings of loyalty to the nation. In several cases, however, national awareness was fostered by a protracted and violent struggle for independence. But even in these cases, many people in peripheral areas—for instance, in the Indonesian archipelago—were not aware of or did not actively identify with the new nation-state.[78]

Nonetheless, the state became much more intrusive in this period. New nation-states generally tried to connect the different parts of the country by improving the infrastructure, extending the education system, and introducing some welfare provisions. The identification with the nation-state tended to lose its sharp edges after independence, and as a consequence, it became largely banal.[79] The Cold War determined the main political fault lines, and in most countries, ethnic or national differences were not stirred up. Moreover, in many parts of the world, politics was primarily a matter of direct personal contacts and favors, while the business of governments was presented as a mostly technocratic affair. This led to political apathy among wide sections of the population.

After independence, most regimes invested heavily in primary education, and so did countries that had never been colonized. Literacy rates in the colonies had generally been very low, from 5 percent in Senegal and Mauretania to 14 percent in Pakistan and 25 percent in Nigeria. In Asian or African countries that had remained independent, the situation was not much different. Around the Second World War, Nepal's literacy rate was below 5 percent, China stood at 20 percent, and Thailand reached 30 percent. There were many serious impediments to improving the situation. Financial constraints and traditional practices (which affected girls more than boys) did not favor schooling. Moreover, most countries were linguistically very diverse. As a consequence, many pupils had to learn reading and writing in a standardized national language that was very different from their mother tongue. Nonetheless, literacy rates advanced substantially during the Cold War period. In 1990, in some countries such as Sierra Leone and Burkina Faso, literacy remained at a very low level of about 20 percent; Pakistan and Bangladesh stood at 35 percent; and in African countries such as Ghana, Nigeria, and Ivory Coast more than half of the population could read and write. Several Asian countries, including the Philippines, Vietnam, and Thailand, reached literacy rates of about 90 percent.[80]

With lagging literacy rates and a weak infrastructure, the circulation of written media was very low in many parts of Africa and also in Asia and Latin America. Whereas in the late 1980s more than four hundred newspapers were sold per one thousand inhabitants in the Federal Republic of Germany, the circulation number was only thirty-seven per thousand in Ghana, and in Chad and Niger it was less than one per thousand. Radio reached a much broader audience. The Second World War incentivized radio broadcasting, as governments were eager to present the "right" information to the population and listeners were interested in the latest developments at the front lines. The authorities of new states understood the value of radio broadcasting for putting across their messages, unifying the country, and promoting national development. Radios became more affordable in the 1960s and 1970s, and the new transistor radio meant people could listen wherever they went. Ghana even set up a hire-purchase scheme to enable more people to buy a radio, while radio sets for communal listening were accessible in public buildings in poor rural areas. The radio thus had a strong nation-building effect. News bulletins, educational programs, and talk shows targeted and implicitly created national audiences. The radio turned the national anthem into a familiar hymn, and most broadcasts disseminated knowledge of the national language. From the late 1950s, for instance, a standardized and accessible Beijing dialect became the new "common speech" in the People's Republic of China. Regional languages were used primarily in special radio programs for rural audiences, providing information on public health and agriculture in Ghana, for example.[81]

Television would have even more profound nation-building effects. Broadcasts had started in a few countries in the 1930s, but television developed into a mass medium only in the 1950s, first in the United States and then in the rest of the world. This leading position gave the three U.S. networks an important advantage, and many of their programs were imported or copied elsewhere in the world. Television broadcasting largely built on the infrastructure that had been developed for radio transmission. Thus, the United States and large parts of Latin America and Asia opted for commercial stations, while Northwestern European countries generally preferred a public service model. Other countries, including those in the Communist bloc, had national broadcasting organizations that were directed by the state. The number of television sets increased very rapidly, but until the 1970s there were very few channels and broadcasting was largely limited to the evening hours. As a result, television really created a national audience, with families sitting together watching the same events and programs. Since television was an expensive medium, national broadcasters from smaller countries acquired many U.S. programs and series, which not only were cheap and sophisticated but also were seen as representing modernity. This was the case even in many Communist countries in Eastern Europe. Large countries with a strong cinematic tradition also became important regional providers, such as Brazil for Latin America, Egypt for the Arab world, and India in Asia.[82]

But most television programs were national productions. This generally was the case with news bulletins, dramas, historical documentaries, and sports broadcasts. Drama series such as *Coronation Street* in Great Britain and *I'm Checking Out* in Nigeria became huge successes by reflecting the everyday reality of many viewers. National events such as royal weddings, natural disasters, and air crashes glued many people to the television, while international matches, world championships (especially for football), and the Olympic Games united viewers behind their national athletes or teams. Most channels also contributed to the nationalization of local and regional traditions by popularizing typical customs, folk music, and traditional sports. Like the radio, television also contributed hugely to the diffusion of the national language and the standardization of its pronunciation. The Beijing dialect could be heard on a daily basis on Chinese television, but the use of subtitles in characters— which had been in use for all dialects and languages in the People's Republic— meant that it was more easily understood. In Korea, where high culture had been dominated by Chinese classics and script, the adoption of the language of the common people and a Korean alphabet significantly contributed to the creation of a truly Korean national culture. Since broadcast companies were mostly licensed or even controlled by the government, television programs mostly adopted a state-centered perspective.[83]

The Cold War era thus became the heyday of national mass media. Radio and television created national routines of simultaneous listening or watching the news in the evening or a favorite broadcast at a specific hour in the week. The most successful programs became a source of everyday conversations, creating a national public sphere. Presenters became national celebrities, while leading politicians, famous singers, and sports heroes became familiar faces, providing a shared national order of things that provided stability and continuity. This was reinforced by the broadcasting of specific events such as national holiday festivities, commemorations, and sporting matches. The collective outpouring of emotions during these events created shared rituals of celebration and mourning. Michael Skey argues that mass media, by representing and reinterpreting the nation on a daily basis, presented the nation as a solid entity, which moreover existed in a world inhabited by other nations, each with their own identity and characteristics. This banal "mediation of nationhood" was particularly pronounced on television, where each nation-state had its own statesmen, iconic buildings (such as the White House and the Kremlin), particular landscapes, and characteristic traditions, which regularly featured in news items, series, and documentaries.[84]

Nationalization of Culture

After 1945, racial and geographic determinism quickly became anathema in academic discourse. They had been prominent in the social sciences and humanities, but now they were associated with the excesses of Fascism and Nazism. Instead, the nation-state was taken for granted and forms of methodological nationalism could be detected in almost all branches of the social sciences and humanities. The quick decline of racial and determinist views was very clear in the field of anthropology, where physical anthropology almost vanished and the culturist view became dominant. Anthropologists such as Ruth Benedict and Margaret Mead further developed Boas's holistic cultural approach by studying the "ethos" or collective personality of individual societies. Although some anthropologists began to conduct studies in urban neighborhoods, mining districts, or migrant communities, the large majority continued to do fieldwork among a single people or tribe in order to dissect its "authentic" culture. This focus on the supposedly unique social structure and cultural particularities of a single ethnic group can be understood as a form of methodological nationalism. From the 1960s onward, however, some scholars began to pay more attention to comparative approaches—with (national) societies as the main unit of comparison—or even universal aspects of culture. Claude Lévi-Strauss, for instance, examined the universal structures of kinship and myths.[85]

In the field of linguistics, authors such as Ferdinand de Saussure and Roman Jakobson had already redirected the discipline's previous strong historical orientation—scrutinizing the historical and often also racial roots of language families—to the synchronic study of languages during the early decades of the twentieth century. Franz Boas also had a major impact. In his *Handbook of North American Indian Languages* (1911) he had explored the linguistic structures and mental worlds of a broad variety of Native American languages, without taking "civilized" European languages and their grammatical categories as a benchmark. However, his broad comparative approach also had strong culturalist implications. Edward Sapir and Benjamin Whorf radicalized Boas's cultural relativism, arguing that each language determined how one experiences and understands the world. Linguistics blossomed in the postwar period, and although the historicist approach had largely become obsolete, the discipline continued to be strongly influenced by various forms of methodological nationalism. Standardized national languages were analyzed as closed systems—with only one "correct" form set by elite "native speakers"—which eventually needed to be purified of "foreign" elements. Monolingualism was taken as the norm, and widespread practices such as speaking dialects, mixing languages, and code-switching were considered "backward" anomalies. Languages, in fact, were seen as stable, so change needed to be explained. National languages were thus reified and "normalized"; minority languages and dialects were seen as subordinate varieties. Languages of immigrants were mostly denied official status because they were not "native." In the 1960s the focus on individual languages shifted to more structural approaches, particularly influenced by the work of Noam Chomsky, who focused primarily on syntax and argued that there was a universal "generative grammar." According to Chomsky, children were not socialized in a language by a difficult process of trial and error, but instead quickly learned to form well-structured sentences. Nevertheless, even in structuralist approaches, national languages remained the self-evident starting point.[86]

In the Anglo-Saxon philosophical world, logical positivism, as developed by Ludwig Wittgenstein and the Vienna Circle, became dominant after 1945. It also had a major impact on the postwar reorientation of the social sciences, in which academics from the United States played a leading role. Logical positivists rejected metaphysical concepts and holistic explanations that could not be verified by empirical research or analytical reasoning. This led to a fundamental change in the discipline of geography, for instance, where historical and environmental factors had been very prominent. Like their colleagues in anthropology and linguistics, scholars in geography increasingly abandoned the search for origins. In *The Nature of Geography* (1939) Richard Hartshorne had rejected widely used anatomical, organic, and musical metaphors with which geographers had routinely presented regions as harmonious organisms. Instead, he proposed the detailed study of particular geographical elements and their specific purposes, without presupposing any fixed territories or landscapes with a clear essence or character. The German exile Fred Schaefer went further, rejecting Hartshorne's preference for discrete facts, since this would merely lead to a descriptive method and a focus on the unique. Instead, the discipline should be oriented in the natural sciences and search for patterns and general laws. This challenge was taken up by a younger generation of geographers who started to conduct spatial analysis with a more quantitative approach, using statistics, graphs, models, maps, and diagrams. Moreover, they largely shifted the focus from the natural and rural areas that had been the preferred topic of research in the interwar period to urban, industrial areas and economic modernization.[87]

An emphasis on universalist theories, quantitative data, and modeling and a focus on modernization can also be detected in other social sciences. This also implied that they turned the nation-state into the dominant unit of analysis, which was quite logical because statistics were gathered primarily at a national level, as were surveys and polls. In economics, the separation between domestic and international developments was already taken for granted, and this was now also applied to the realm of politics, where political science and international relations became two separate branches. Political scientists mainly investigated forms of mass politics for which the older traditions of political philosophy and constitutional law were not very relevant. Empirical research and quantitative methods were increasingly employed to study the actual functioning of the democratic system, while the focus was on political parties, public opinion, electoral behavior, and pressure groups. This behavioralism became the dominant approach in political science until the late 1960s. Aggregate data, from both surveys and governmental statistics, were also widely used in the subfield of comparative politics, in which the almost exclusive unit of comparison was the nation-state. Behavioralism also influenced the field of international relations, which systematically examined the relations between (nation-) states. Studies with a more historical, legal, or philosophical approach continued to be produced, but they too took the (nation-) state as their starting point.[88]

Apart from the fundamental distinction between domestic and foreign, there was another important spatial divide: between "the West" and "the rest," or between the "developed" and the "underdeveloped" worlds. Modern Western societies were the domain of sociology, economics, and political science, whereas "the rest" was studied primarily by historians, anthropologists, and scholars from the new field of area studies, which focused on clusters of nation-states such as Latin America, the Middle East, and Southeast Asia.[89] This was not just a pragmatic division of labor; it also reflected the quick rise of modernization theory. Whereas in the period between 1890 and 1945 social change had been explained by a wide variety of factors ranging from geography to race, national character, culture, and history, now the transition from traditional to modern societies was thought to develop along a linear path of modernization, which consisted of various interconnected processes such as urbanization, industrialization, secularization, bureaucratization, and democratization. Sociologists such as Talcott Parsons and Edward Shils explored the values that distinguished "advanced" from "primitive" societies, while the economist Walt Rostow—in *The Stages of Economic Growth: A Non-Communist Manifesto* (1960)—examined the conditions under which economic modernization reached "take-off," leading to an "age of high mass consumption." The basic unit of their analysis was the nation-state. The theoretical insights gained from these sociological, statistical, economic, and demographic studies could then be applied to developing countries, enabling them to catch up. Many social scientists provided practical advice on how to accelerate the transition to modernity. Rostow, for instance, worked as a national security advisor for both the Kennedy and Johnson administrations, using his position to successfully advocate for a substantial increase in development aid to the "Third World."[90]

The Communist countries had their own, equally universalist and encompassing theory of modernization. Although the mechanics (dialectical materialism instead of unilinear growth) and methods (planned economy versus free market) were different, there was a similar emphasis on scientific knowledge, economic growth, and technocratic solutions. The definition of the modernist end goal also differed, as communists strove for an egalitarian socialist utopia, whereas liberal democracy constituted the final stage in the "free world," but both consisted of secular, industrial nation-states.[91]

Strikingly, cultural differences between nation-states were not emphasized; the main divide existed between the "developed" and the "underdeveloped" worlds, or between the Communist bloc and the "free world." At colleges in the United States, courses in Western civilization—ironically characterized as "Plato to NATO"—dealt with Europe and eventually North America, whereas "the rest" was relegated to area studies. Widely used handbooks such as R. R. Palmer's *A History of the Modern World* and Ernst Gombrich's *The Story of Art*, both published in 1950, presented a triumphant picture of the rise of the "modern," developed world. Palmer's overview started with ancient Greece and Rome but quickly turned to the crucial transformations that occurred during the Renaissance, the Scientific Revolution, the Enlightenment, the Atlantic Revolutions, and the Industrial Revolution. The non-European world entered the story only when it was discovered, conquered, or "opened" by Europeans. Gombrich was even more blatantly Eurocentric. Although he also dealt with the "strange beginnings" of prehistoric art, the story basically began with the "great awakening" that occurred in ancient Greece. Before turning to the European Middle Ages, he paid some attention to China, the Islamic world, and Byzantium, but contrary to the immobile East, the West "was always restless, groping for new solutions and new ideas." As a consequence, he focused on the innovations of successive generations of artists in Western Europe, and in the twentieth century the United States entered the stage. Even Scandinavia and Eastern Europe were largely excluded from the story. Thus, both Palmer and Gombrich presented the history of the West as a coherent story, in which (nation-) states were the main geographic units and in which "the rest" was irrelevant. Although in many chapters they discussed developments by country, national differences were clearly subordinated to the overall course of the modernization process.[92]

Within this broad framework of the progress of human civilization—which spread from the West to "the rest"—most (art) historians continued to write case studies in which the national framework was taken for granted, embracing the historicist logic that in order to understand a society, one had to study its past. This suggests that transnational influences, foreign actors, and transborder transfers were largely ignored, and as a consequence, most authors succumbed to a form of methodological nationalism. In Communist countries, Marxism-Leninism had to be integrated into the story, but otherwise the historical narratives remained quite conventional and adopted the national framework. In Germany, Italy, and Japan, scholars had to come to terms with the recent history of the rise of Fascism and the horrors of the Second World War. Most historians depicted the Fascist era as an exception or aberration in the nation's evolution, and it took several decades before more critical accounts were published. History writing in newly independent countries was generally explicitly nationalistic, not just in denouncing foreign invaders and lionizing the struggle for independence, but also in searching for the ancient roots of their own civilization. In 1954 the Senegalese historian Cheikh Ante Diop argued that ancient Egyptians had been Black and that the Egyptian culture from antiquity had spread to Western Africa, thus implicitly presenting modern Senegal as Egypt's spiritual descendant. Over time, many ethnic groups—in Nigeria, for instance—began to produce their own nationally framed histories to demand recognition of their prominent roles in the past, while emphasizing their unique characters.[93]

The 1960s and 1970s saw the rise of new critical currents, such as feminist approaches and neo-Marxist theories. Another innovative trend was the rise of poststructuralism, exemplified especially by the work of Michel Foucault and Jacques Derrida. Their groundbreaking views on the disciplining power of discourse and the deconstruction of texts fundamentally questioned the basic rationalist assumptions of the social sciences and humanities while also exposing their crucial Western bias. They also argued that the way people perceived and understood social reality was fundamentally shaped by dominant discourses and hegemonic relations. The social scientist Peter Berger and Thomas Luckmann presented a similar argument in *The Social Construction of Reality* (1966), arguing that over time, beliefs, mental representations, and symbols have become institutionalized and thus they largely determine the way human beings perceive reality. Nevertheless, since most of these scholars focused on text and discourse, they—like the neo-Marxists and the feminists—did not really challenge the nation-state as the basic geographical unit of humanity.[94]

The swift disappearance of openly racist views, the focus on modernization, and the downplaying of national differences also was manifested in the cultural realm, where the naturalization of the nation-state as the basic division of humanity was equally prominent. Avant-garde culture generally was presented as cosmopolitan, whereas commercial culture was more focused on national realities. Modernism, which had already become dominant in the interwar period, achieved almost complete hegemony in the art world after 1945. Whereas many artists in the previous decades had flirted with various forms of exalted nationalism or Fascism, this had become unacceptable after the Second World War. The idea that artists should create pure forms independent of place and time, unhindered by academic conventions, was widely taken for granted. The only exception was the Communist countries, where socialist realism became the official style whereby the political message and the glorification of "the people" was packaged in an easily recognizable pictorial language. Elsewhere, many artists also continued to produce realist or traditional works of art to meet local demand, but generally it was not taken seriously as "fine art." In galleries and museums, art was usually displayed in a context-free "white cube." In the 1960s and 1970s the ideal of "sitelessness" began to be criticized, sometimes by assertive inhabitants who complained about insensitive public art works that had been "dropped" into their living spaces, or by followers of the new land art movement that tried to incorporate art works more harmoniously within the landscape.[95]

Notwithstanding the cosmopolitanism and placelessness of modern art, one of the first characteristics mentioned in discussing artists was their nationality. Moreover, many exhibitions featured the art of a specific country, as if the artists from one country shared a certain aesthetic outlook. This happened even in the Communist bloc countries. Various avant-garde movements such as the School of Paris, U.S. pop art, and Italian arte povera were associated with a specific nationality or city.[96] Many artists, too, depicted national symbols, regional traditions, or particular landscapes in an idiosyncratic modern style. Throughout her long career, Georgia O'Keeffe painted a large number of landscapes, flowers, and other motifs from New Mexico, while Jasper Johns began to produce his famous paintings of the U.S. flag in 1954.

The attention on the national context was more prominent in newly independent countries. Sometimes, state authorities played a crucial role. At independence, President Senghor created a Senegalese art academy in which the "free section" was supposed to translate the "authentic" character of Black Africans into contemporary art forms. This meant that artists mostly depicted the country's flora, fauna, and folkloric traditions while creating a highly personal modern style, which preferably had a certain African or Senegalese flavor. The artists who graduated from the academy, including Ibou Diouf and Ousmane Faye, were presented to the outside world as a coherent group. At the first World Exhibition of Black Art, organized in Senegal in 1966, Senghor praised the combination of tradition and modernity of the "Dakar School." Later, the state also sponsored exhibitions abroad, such as an ambitious Senegalese contemporary art exhibition in the Parisian Grand Palais. In Nigeria, it was students at the Nigerian College of Arts, Science, and Technology in Zaria who, shortly before independence, took the initiative to establish a Nigerian Art Society. Young artists such as Uche Okeke and Demas Nwoko aimed to create a natural synthesis by studying the country's folklore in order to translate traditional forms into a modern artistic idiom. While Okeke focused on the traditional curvilinear Uli designs of his native Igboland, Nwoko drew inspiration from traditional potters from various parts of the country for his own terracotta sculptures. So in both Nigeria and Senegal there was a conscious attempt to create a new national art that was both contemporary and inspired by the country's "authentic" traditions. Moreover, in order to attract foreign attention—especially in the European and American art centers—a certain "ethnic" flavor was almost indispensable.[97]

In literature, the gap between high and low forms was more conspicuous than in the arts. Many avant-garde writers, including absurd playwrights like Samuel Beckett and Eugène Ionesco and postmodern writers such as William S. Burroughs, Jorge Luis Borges, and Italo Calvino, produced literary texts that hardly referred to a specific time and place, focusing instead on the human condition or on formal experiments.[98] But generally, literature was written in a national standard language and mostly continued to refer to a world of nation-states, each with its own specific geographical and social environment. In 1960 Harper Lee published *To Kill a Mockingbird*, which dealt with the Deep South of her own youth, characterized by its blatant racial inequality. Soon after, Philip Roth's novel *Portnoy's Complaint* caused a stir with its explicit treatment of the sexual frustration of his protagonist, who, like the author, had grown up in a Jewish milieu in New Jersey. In the Soviet Union, Aleksandr Solzhenitsyn profited from the thaw under Khrushchev to publish his controversial *One Day in the Life of Ivan Denisovich* (1962), about an ordinary prisoner in a Soviet labor camp. South American magical realists also often referred to their own life worlds, although in many instances they chose to portray them as fictitious locations, as Gabriel García Márquez did in his portrayal of the provincial life in Macondo in *One Hundred Years of Solitude* (1969). The tendency to depict the everyday reality of the nation was probably even more pronounced in newly independent countries, as demonstrated by the impressive oeuvres of Egypt's Naguib Mahfouz and Nigeria's Chinua Achebe.

Ignored by literary magazines and critics, the large majority of popular fiction generally adopted a more nationalist tone. This was particularly the case with comics, which had begun to appear in newspapers in the nineteenth century. In the early twentieth century they also featured prominently in children's magazines. The nationalist content became more explicit in times of war. Even before the United States entered the Second World War, the new superhero Captain America punched Hitler in the face on the cover of the first, best-selling issue. During the war more superheroes were created, including some female ones such as Superwoman in the United States and Nelvana of the Northern Lights in Canada. In the 1970s various new nationalist superheroes were invented, such as Captain Canuck in Canada and Captain Britain. But generally, after 1945 the tone of most comics was less exultant and they mostly focused on romance, horror, and crime. Nonetheless, many comics—especially in Europe—portrayed a world divided into nation-states, each with its own unique, often quite stereotypical character. This was obvious in Hergé's *The Adventures of Tintin*, the young Belgian reporter who traveled the world. Another extraordinarily successful series was René Goscinny and Albert Uderzo's *Asterix*, which tells the history of two unlikely superheroes from the only village in Gaul not occupied by the Roman Empire. It clearly plays on the trope of the French resistance in the Second World War while mockingly using many contemporary stereotypes of various regions of France and the countries visited by Asterix and Obelix. Japan also became a very productive center for the publication of comics—known as manga—which were increasingly translated, creating a unique brand with a distinctive national aesthetics.[99]

In music, the gap between popular music and the formal music tradition of the West—which continued the modernist experiments, such as atonal music, developed during the early twentieth century—was even wider than in art and literature. Although classical music still reached broad audiences, avant-gardist contemporary music was mostly confined to a small elite. Popular music in the forms of both updated regional or indigenous traditions and modern genres such as rock and roll, soul, and disco dominated the air waves and record shops. Pop groups and performers were routinely referred to by their nationalities, and many musical styles were also closely connected to a particular nation or nation-state. In many countries there were various rival regional or urban centers, sometimes with a clear specialization, such as country music in Nashville and the Mersey beat from Liverpool; abroad, however, these performers and bands were generally seen as American or British. In Europe, there were various national traditions for sentimental songs, such as the German *Schlager* and the French *chanson*. Sometimes, successful innovative artists created a new genre that became associated with a particular country, like Bob Marley's reggae from Jamaica. In other cases, active state involvement helped to create a national style that achieved international acclaim. For example, because Mobutu favored Indigenous traditions, Kinshasa developed a thriving music scene where Franco Luambo became an international star. Although in most Communist countries popular music was tightly controlled, Fidel Castro's regime in Cuba was more relaxed about the dance music that already prospered on the island. The government heavily subsidized bands, concerts, and tours, and with this support, Cuban salsa became very popular abroad.[100]

Because of its commercial nature, film was probably one of the most nationalist art forms of this period. Most movies reflected national reality, either as the everyday setting for an entertaining story or in a more critical vein by highlighting social abuses. Film was profoundly affected by the rise of television. The great Hollywood studios responded to the declining numbers of cinema goers by adopting widescreen formats and switching to color. New opportunities were provided by the conquest of foreign markets, the release of films for television screening, and the production of tv series. In this way, formulaic studio movies continued to dominate the global markets, presenting the American dream to an ever-widening audience. Nevertheless, not all movies depicted American society as rosy. Nicholas Ray's *Rebel without a Cause* (1955), about the difficult coming of age of suburban teenagers, and Francis Ford Coppola's story of a New York mafia boss in *The Godfather* (1972) became modern classics. During the postwar era, many film directors had a strong social awareness and employed innovative methods to document (national) reality. In Italy, neorealist filmmakers such as Roberto Rossellini and Vittorio De Sica expressed the difficult everyday life of ordinary people. Films such as *Rome, Open City* (1945) and *Bicycle Thieves* (1948) were shot largely on location with nonprofessional actors. From about 1960, portable cameras made it easier to directly film everyday reality. This was reflected in documentaries like *Hour of the Furnaces* (1969) by Fernando Solanas and Octavio Getino, which denounced the neocolonial economic and cultural exploitation of Argentina by the Western powers. Handheld cameras were also used by French New Wave directors such as Jean-Luc Godard, who in movies such as *Breathless* (1960) broke with many aesthetic conventions while providing a more direct sense of French reality. In Communist Eastern Europe, filmmakers such as Miloš Forman and Krzysztof Kieślowski began their careers by making documentaries, and many of their films examined a specific segment of society. In *The Fireman's Ball* (1967) Forman mocked the petty corruption in a small Czechoslovak town.[101]

Studios and film companies that were fortunate enough to have a big domestic market produced most of the cinematographic output. In smaller countries, state support allowed some filmmakers to prosper, which happened, for instance, in Communist Cuba. In smaller production centers there was frequent cross-fertilization with other art forms, particularly literature. Thus, influential novelists like Tadeusz Konwicki in Poland, Sembene Ousmane in Senegal, and Assia Djebar in Algeria directed several movies. The nationalist content was often more obvious in historical dramas than in films focusing on everyday reality. This could have a celebratory tone, as in Mehboob Khan's *Mother India* (1957), or it could be conveyed by representing typical aspects of the national past, as in Kurosawa Akira's *Seven Samurai* (1954).[102]

Nationalization of the Physical Environment

The nationalization of the physical environment suffered a setback during this period. Only relatively few exalted expressions of nationalism were added in the decades after 1945, and they commemorated either the victory during the Second World War or the country's independence. Two such examples are the huge, fifty-two-meter-high monument to the motherland to celebrate the Soviet victory at Stalingrad, and the oversized obelisk at the enormous Independence Square in Jakarta, representing an Indonesian pestle and mortar crowned with a golden flame (figure 7.1). The new obsession with development and modernization translated into a near hegemony of modernist architecture styles for buildings and monuments, with almost no references to national particularities, which is what happened in Ghana, for instance (figure 7.2).[103] A technocratic approach could also be detected in tourism and nature conservation, where national differences were clearly downplayed. At the same time, aided by the decolonization process, a world divided into nation-states, each with its own characteristics and representatives, was increasingly taken for granted.

The rebuilding of bombed cities and devastated areas after 1945 was a daunting task. Public opinion was mostly in favor of rebuilding important monuments and historic city centers, but this happened only in exceptional cases such as Warsaw's Old Town. Many architects and urban planners, on the other hand, saw a great opportunity to start afresh, either by bulldozing the rubble and starting from scratch or abandoning the ruins and building smaller and healthier cities elsewhere. As a consequence, many new functional settlements were built, but only a few existing cities, such as Coventry and Rotterdam, opted for a radical transformation. These cities introduced the pedestrianized shopping street as an important innovation. Many ambitious reconstruction plans did not get off the ground because it proved too difficult to fundamentally alter existing street plans and disregard property rights. A dearth of finance and building materials, moreover, meant that pragmatism was the order of the day. In the end, only the most important monuments were rebuilt, and standardized housing, mostly in functional apartment blocks, became the norm. As a consequence, a placeless modernism quickly became the dominant architectural style. The widespread use of concrete, glass, and steel suited the

FIGURE 7.1 Friedrich Silaban and Soedarsono, *National Monument at the Merdeka Square*, 1961–1976, Jakarta. This 132-meter-high obelisk, clad in Italian marble, at the immense Independence Square represents a traditional rice pestle and mortar and is crowned with a flame. Even though the symbolism is national, the obelisk and the abstracted forms could have been built anywhere.

new emphasis on technology and industrial development. New monumental buildings appeared primarily in Eastern Europe, such as the Stalinist wedding-cake skyscrapers in Moscow and Warsaw, but these celebrated the achievements of communism rather than the nation, although the monumental Stalinallee in East Berlin combined the Soviet model with neoclassicist motifs that referred back to the glory days of Prussia.[104]

Most new states aimed to present themselves as taking part in international modernity, and so they adopted architectural modernism. After its partition, India had to house millions of refugees, and this was done partly by building over one hundred new towns, including Chandigarh, the capital of Punjab, which was named after a local Hindu temple. President Nehru argued that the building of a new city had the advantage of doing away with the "existing encumbrances of old towns and old traditions." The "newly earned freedom" would be translated into up-to-date new cities, for which the best foreign architects were invited. Thus, in 1951 Le Corbusier took charge of the planning

FIGURE 7.2 Theodore S. Clerk, *Black Star Square with the Independence Arch*, 1961, Accra. Ghana's first President Kwame Nkrumah commissioned a monumental arch on a giant square with seating capacity for thirty thousand visitors. It is used for parades on National Independence Day. The concrete buildings had very few national particularities and were primarily meant to show that the country had become part of international modernity.

of Chandigarh and the design of its monumental government buildings. Although he slightly adapted his designs to the climate by using brise-soleils and shell-vaults, the geometrical structures in raw concrete could have been located almost anywhere. In the end, the city itself was not filled with the high-rise buildings he had planned. Boxlike houses in local brick and stone, designed mostly by Le Corbusier's assistants, provided modern homes to all government workers without separating them by caste or religion, creating an egalitarian community divided only by meritocratic principles.[105]

The construction of Brasilia, which began a few years later, was a similar utopian venture. The initiative was taken by Brazil's Social Democratic president Juscelino Kubitschek, who had campaigned with the slogan "Fifty years of progress in five." The transfer of the capital from Rio de Janeiro, with its strong colonial legacy, to the heart of the country was conceived as a decisive step in the settling of the interior. Two of the country's most prominent

FIGURE 7.3 *Superblocks in Brasilia*, late 1950s. Several countries built new
modern capitals. Brasilia had a symmetrical plan with two monumental
axes and was designed by Brazil's most prominent modernist architects.
All functionalist buildings, such as the six-story apartment buildings of the
photo—where all inhabitants, regardless of race or class, should reside—were
built in concrete and contained no references to national particularities.

modernist architects, Lúcio Costa and Oscar Niemeyer, made a symmetrical
plan for the city with two monumental axes and designed most of the impressive government buildings. Although the architects took into account the location of the city in the tropical rainforest and also included some rather abstract
references to the country's history and traditions, the overall impression was
one of international modernity. Like in Chandigarh, the objective was to create
an egalitarian community where regardless of racial or social background, people
would intermingle, living in large six-story apartment buildings (figure 7.3).[106]
Although the names of these new capital cities had national significance, the
geometrical sectors or quarters were numbered and thus did not contain any
reference to the past or geography

In Ghana, President Nkrumah also embarked on an ambitious modernization program, which aimed to increase the country's economic independence.
The construction of a hydroelectric dam on the Volta River would create the

largest artificial lake in the world and provide electricity for an aluminum smelter, water for irrigation, and new opportunities for fishing and tourism. Although the project originated in the colonial period, it was pursued with more vigor after independence. It involved the construction of a new port town and the transfer of about eighty thousand people to new settlements. Nkrumah employed experienced modernist architects such as Jane Drew and Maxwell Fry—who had worked with Le Corbusier in Chandigarh—and Constantinos Doxiadis, who had already designed a plan for the modernization of Baghdad and later would be responsible for the layout of Islamabad, the new capital of Pakistan. Although the architects bore in mind that many farmers and fishermen were not yet willing up to give their traditional lifestyles—providing, for instance, open-compound houses with gardens for poultry—these were seen as transitory measures. The middle classes were already housed in modern apartments in a parklike landscape and well-ordered grid. Drew and Fry detailed some of the lessons they had drawn from their activities in West Africa and India in *Village Housing in the Tropics* (1947) and *Tropical Architecture in the Humid Zone* (1956). Traditional building practices, according to them, were too primitive and unhygienic, but climatic conditions had to be taken into consideration in order to provide well-lit and ventilated homes. Thus, their modernist buildings could largely ignore local and national particularities by finding modern solutions to the tropical conditions in large parts of Africa and Asia.[107] However, as air conditioners became cheaper, the need to take tropical conditions into account decreased. Slick modernist buildings quickly became the norm in countries such as Nigeria, where energy was cheap, and Singapore, where land scarcity necessitated high-rise buildings.[108]

After 1945, a technocratic view of nature also replaced the organic and metaphysical interpretations that assumed an intimate bond between the nation and its soil, and which had been very popular since the late nineteenth century. The focus on productivity, which had already begun in the interwar era, became dominant in the 1950s and 1960s. This led to not only new reclamation projects and the construction of gigantic hydroelectric dams but also the so-called green revolution, which began in Mexico. Radical land reforms under President Lázaro Cárdenas in the late 1930s had a negative impact on agricultural output, and his more moderate successor, Manuel Ávila Camacho, sought the assistance of the Rockefeller Foundation to improve productivity. Systematic experiments with plant breeding led to improved varieties of wheat, beans, maize, and other crops; the biologist Norman Borlaug even bred a new "miracle wheat." Innovations from the highly commercial agricultural sector in the United States such as mechanization, specialization, and the use of chemical fertilizers and pesticides were also implemented. The program was adopted in many other "developing" countries, such as India and the Philippines, where improved rice strains substantially increased harvest yields. Scaling up through land consolidation in Western Europe and collectivization projects in Communist countries, together with a shared preference for technocratic solutions and functionalist buildings, also thoroughly modernized the countryside in the First and Second Worlds. National or regional differences largely disappeared, while biodiversity was also seriously affected. Several radical collectivization programs—which in China were combined with the Four Pests campaign, meant to eliminate rats, mosquitos, flies, and sparrows—had counterproductive effects and sometimes even led to disastrous famines.[109]

Although urban and rural areas throughout the world became more homogenous, many individual objects became associated with specific nations. The role of commercial actors was crucial; apparently, it was profitable to associate products with nations. Marketing commodities by connecting them with their country of origin was already a trend, dating from the late nineteenth century, but it had been limited mainly to agricultural and artisanal products; now it also began to impact the fashion industry. New trends for women's fashion traditionally had been set in Paris, while London was important for men's clothing. After the Second World War the Parisian haute couture firms increasingly faced competition from mass-produced garments from the United States. Following the example of Christian Dior, haute couture companies reinvented themselves as luxury brands, not only producing high-fashion designs but also selling ready-to-wear collections, perfumes, and accessories under their own name. In this way, they managed to prosper while continuing to associate French fashion with luxury and distinction. Elsewhere, nationalist marketing strategies were even more pronounced. Italy, for instance, already had some well-known designers, but the marketing of Italian fashion as high-quality design began only in the 1950s. Giovanni Giorgini organized the first Italian high-fashion show in Florence, mainly targeting American buyers and fashion reporters. He encouraged Italian designers to avoid "French influences" while taking into consideration American preferences for more practical, casual clothing. The catwalk was located in a beautiful Renaissance palace, while models were photographed in the city's aristocratic mansions and gardens, explicitly associating the elegant designs with the country's long artistic history, plentiful nature, and traditional elegance. Although Milan would later replace Florence as the country's fashion center, Giorgini's efforts to market Italian fashion collectively abroad—combined with relatively affordable prices—proved to be a huge success.[110]

Other forms of sartorial nationalism continued to prosper as well. From the late nineteenth century, nationalists in various parts of Asia had promoted the adoption of Western clothing styles as a sign of modernity, while others had rejected them explicitly in favor of indigenous traditions. Both responses could still be found after 1945. The most radical modernizing course could be found in China, where political leaders in the interwar period had already shown their preference for a simple Western-style military uniform known as the "Sun Yat-sen suit." After the Communist takeover, it was rebaptized the "Mao suit" and became the standard dress for both men and women, symbolizing the modern egalitarian ethos of the party. In Indonesia, President Sukarno promoted Western suits, though he kept the *peci*, a black cap originally inspired by the fez, as a secular national headdress that could be adopted throughout the archipelago. Women, on the other hand, were supposed to embody national traditions by wearing the *kain kebaya*, an elegant sarong with blouse. In the Philippines, Ramon Magsaysay presented himself in the presidential campaign as a man of the masses, wearing a traditional long-sleeved embroidered shirt, the *barong tagalog*. The shirt was further popularized— after a makeover by French designer Pierre Cardin—during the dictatorship of Ferdinand Marcos; thus, surprisingly, men became the "bearers of the nation." In Zaire, Mobutu favored a policy of authenticity, but he decided to prescribe a version of the Mao uniform—called *abacost*—for officials, while he himself wore it with a leopard-skin cap. National dresses also became fashionable for airline crews, with Japan Airlines taking the lead by cladding their air hostesses in kimonos. At the Miss Universe beauty pageant, which was invented in the 1950s, participants also had to don a "national costume," thus obliging all participating countries to select, develop, or invent a spectacular traditional dress that would impress a global audience.[111]

Nation-building also occurred in the culinary field. Cookbooks, menus in restaurants, and recipes in journals and newspapers standardized local cooking practices by constructing national cuisines in almost all countries of the world. In most cases, a handful of signature dishes or foods were singled out, such as the hamburger for the United States, pizza and pasta for Italy, sushi for Japan, pad thai for Thailand, and tacos for Mexico. Some dishes, such as kebabs in the Middle East and couscous in North Africa, were shared or contested by various countries. In addition, specific regional kitchens achieved national prominence, such as Punjab cooking in India. Some characteristic dishes were created abroad, such as chop suey, which was invented in Chinese restaurants in the United States, and chicken tikka masala, which originated in Great Britain. Typical dishes were also attractive to foreign tourists, and international hotel chains such as Hilton began to offer local specialties. Migrant communities, including the Chinese, had already created their own eating houses during the late nineteenth century. In the United States, where Chinese migrants were increasingly excluded from other jobs, the service sector was one of the few niches that remained open to them. Thus, many migrant restaurants began to cater to a broader public, adapting their food to Western preferences. By

profusely decorating their locales, they turned them into exotic objects of cu-
riosity. This also happened a bit later in European port cities such as London,
Rotterdam, and Hamburg. But it was only with the rising living standards of
the 1960s that eating out became a more common habit, making Chinese and
Italian restaurants a regular feature in most European and American cities.
Other migrant communities—such as Indians in Great Britain, Turks in Germany, and Mexicans in the United States—quickly followed their lead.[112]

The marketing of products by associating them with a nation was now also
applied to rather interchangeable manufactured objects—most strikingly, automobiles. Although they were built by multinational companies, cars became
closely identified with a particular country such as the United States, Germany, Japan, or Czechoslovakia. Many models received iconic status, such as
the Volkswagen Beetle, the Citroën 2CV, and the Mini Cooper. The stretch
limousine became a powerful image of American excess, while the Rolls Royce
came to symbolize British luxury. Driving was also associated with national
landscapes and practices, such as the German autobahn in a rolling landscape
where no speed limit had to be obeyed, the U.S. interstate routes with their
characteristic motels, roadside cafés, and drive-in cinemas, and the noisy and
busy Indian roads where cars mingled with rickshaws. These images, moreover, were widely disseminated through film and television series.[113]

Tourism was also highly affected by the postwar modernization wave. Rising living standards and the introduction of cheap charter flights and tourist-
class airfares led to the rise of modern mass tourism, which during the 1950s
and 1960s was characterized mainly by standardized forms. The beach became
the preferred destination, and the number of foreign visitors to Spain, for example, grew from about four million in 1959 to thirty-four million in 1973.
Sleepy fishing villages such as Benidorm and Cancún were rapidly turned into
hedonistic beach resorts with high-rise tourist accommodations. Package
deals were the norm, and holiday camps such Butlin's in Great Britain—
brilliantly parodied in the BBC television series Hi-de-Hi in the 1980s—and
the vacation villages of France's Club Méditerranée became very popular. Excursions to a typical village, buying local souvenirs, and taking in a folkloric
show became side dishes of a generic beach vacation that revolved around sun,
sea, and sand. Amusement was also the main objective of a day trip to a theme
park. Only a few attractions had a national flavor, such as the sanitized version
of the American past in Disneyland's Main Street or Frontierland.[114]

With the demise of Fordist forms of tourism in the 1970s, national influences gained more prominence. Individual preferences were becoming more
important and diverse. Growing car ownership made it easier to get off
the beaten track and discover the natural beauty and cultural patrimony of the
fatherland or neighboring countries. Although most campsites and apartments

were still located at the beach, the more attractive parts of the countryside now became dotted with vacation homes, creating national vacation cultures around the Russian dacha, the Yugoslav *vikendica*, and the Swedish *stuga*. The car also enabled a rapid growth in day trips. Thus, in 1967, Beaulieu Palace House, the historic country house of an enterprising baron in the south of England, had already received over half a million visitors. The number of heritage sites increased rapidly, and many added toilet buildings, parking lots, and other services to accommodate the masses. The new cultural climate of the 1960s also sparked interest in individual self-cultivation, authentic traditions, and handicrafts, leading to the growth of rural tourism and the invention of ecotourism, while new annual folk festivals were established in, for instance, Newport in the United States and Kaustinen in Finland.[115]

Several developments simultaneously encouraged countries and areas to become more typical. Many governments saw tourism as a way to stimulate the economy and earn hard currency. Ireland organized an ambitious Ireland at Home Festival in 1954, encouraging Irish emigrants and their descendants to return "home" for a vacation. The Irish population was encouraged to remove eyesores and spruce up their homes. Four years later, this gave rise to the Tidy Towns and Villages Campaign, in which people were encouraged to clean up their neighborhoods, paint their houses in bright colors, and decorate their gardens with flowers, making Ireland Irish, as Eric Zuelow put it. Similar beautification contests were organized elsewhere on the Old Continent, and in 1975 they were even internationalized in the Entente Florale Europe.[116]

Many Latin American, Asian, and African countries also hoped to attract more tourists in order to boost their economies. Ethiopia was particularly active. In its five-year plan of 1962, the government reserved funds to restore ancient monuments, establish game reserves and national parks, build hotels, and organize tourist information centers. Ethiopian Airlines promoted the country as the biblical "Land of Queen Sheba," while the Ethiopian Tourism Organization opened duty-free shops—called "King Solomon's Mines"—that sold traditional handicrafts. Experts from UNESCO advised the authorities to improve the tourist services and build hotels with entertainment facilities such as swimming pools and miniature golf. Elsewhere, UNESCO consultants encouraged the preservation of cultural and natural highlights in order to boost tourist revenues, recommending, for instance, the prohibition of modern developments in the historic city center of Isfahan and a ban on farming in Bolivia's national park. Monuments also deserved to be seen, so signposts and floodlights were installed and parking lots were built at the Taj Mahal. Farmers around Angkor Wat received subsidies to preserve their traditional lifestyle in order to enhance the image of a bucolic idyll. As a consequence, the use of these sites in everyday life and their meanings—which were generally

connected to local myths and often had religious connotations—were profoundly altered as they now became part of a secular natural or cultural heritage that belonged primarily to the nation.[117]

Sports probably had the strongest nationalizing impact during the Cold War
era. After 1945 the association of sports with military preparedness, racial
health, and national prowess largely disappeared. Sports now was increasingly
focused on competition, individual achievement, and a modern lifestyle. More
people practiced a sport, went to matches, and followed sporting events
through the media. Radio broadcasts of sporting events conveyed a great sense
of immediacy unmatched by the written press, and this was further enhanced
by television. Not only could the public listen to the inspired reports of specialized commentators, now they could watch the matches. Zoom lenses enabled
cameras to focus on individual players or athletes, contributing to the worshipping of national heroes. Since television was organized nationally, it created
national audiences while following a national calendar of sporting highlights,
such as the Superbowl in the United States and the FA Cup Final in Great
Britain. International sporting contests allowed reporters to abandon their professional objectivity and focus on fellow nationals, praising their performances
in a blatantly patriotic tone and thus heating up the nationalist atmosphere in
many living rooms. Although this nationalism usually dissipated quickly after
the match, glorious victories or heroic defeats became part of the collective
memory of the nation.[118] During the postwar era sports became more standardized as they were played in official competitions organized by national associations according to the rules of international federations, and they increasingly
displaced traditional pastimes and indigenous sports. World championships and
international matches became popular among global audiences and had an isomorphic effect. Achieving national independence now implied having not only
a head of state, a national flag, and an anthem, but also a national team. This
suggested that national movements without a state were hardly visible in the
sporting arena. The main exceptions were Scotland and Wales, which for historical reasons had their own teams in several sports. Nonetheless, popular clubs
such as FC Barcelona in Catalonia and Athletic de Bilbao in the Basque Country
could become focal points for substate national sentiments.[119]

Nationalism could easily become heated, and Communist countries such
as the Soviet Union and the German Democratic Republic did their utmost—
including paying amateur athletes and providing illegal performance drugs—
to overtake the capitalist powers. They succeeded in dominating the medal
rankings of most Olympic Games, but they also encouraged their Cold War
opponents such as the United States and West Germany to step up their efforts. As a result, the unexpected victory of the amateur ice hockey players of
the United States over the team of the Soviet Union at the Winter Olympic

FIGURE 7.4 Lance Wyman and Peter Murdoch, *Emblem of the Olympic Games in Mexico*, 1968. For the Olympic Games of 1968, Mexico built modernist sports venues and adopted a highly modern, psychedelic emblem, designed by two young artists. In this way, the organizers emphasized the country's modernity.

Games in Lake Placid in 1980 was widely celebrated as the "miracle on ice." Other national rivalries between neighbors or archenemies, for instance between India and Pakistan in cricket, led to feverish nationalist feelings on both sides. In July 1969 El Salvador and Honduras even fought a short football war after existing tensions escalated at a qualification match. National identities could also be strengthened and recalibrated in more subtle ways. The hosting of a major sporting event was frequently used to present a positive image of the country. This was the case with the 1968 Olympic Games in Mexico City, where the new sporting venues and the psychedelic emblem (figure 7.4) emphasized the country's modernity. Many countries also showed a preference for a specific sport, sometimes for historical or climatological reasons, or to continue international successes won in the past. As a consequence, baseball became the national sport in the United States, skiing in Norway, table tennis in China, and badminton in Indonesia. Playing styles, particularly in football, were also defined in national terms, thus the creative and playful style of the Brazilian national team was defined as "samba football," while the passionate, ruthless defensive style of many Italian squads came to be seen as characteristic of the entire nation.[120] Hence, the nationalizing effects of sports were greatly enhanced during this era.

Conclusion

During the postwar period nationalism became less visible, but paradoxically, an international order consisting of independent nation-states was increasingly taken for granted. Because empires had become tainted after the Second World War, the nation-state became the hegemonic model of statehood during the Cold War era. However, this happened only after alternative solutions had been tried. Most imperial powers did their best to transform their possessions into a union or commonwealth, but as they were reluctant to admit their colonial partners as full equals, these attempts ended in failure by 1960. Federal projects were another alternative. Many political leaders, both in the metropole and the colonies, had doubts about the economic and political viability of the new independent nation-states, and several federations were established during the 1950s and early 1960s. Since richer territories were apprehensive of having to foot the bill, and smaller territories feared being dominated by larger ones, creating a well-functioning federation was quite a challenge. Moreover, politicians continued to depend on their national electorate and so it was difficult to make concessions in favor of federal unity. Only the relatively modest Federal State of Malaysia and the United Arab Emirates survived. The only ambitious project with federal aspirations that became a success was the European Economic Community. Nevertheless, a supranational framework of European directives and regulations would come into being only in the 1980s. Meanwhile, almost all secessionist attempts and irredentist projects—based primarily on ethnic arguments—ran ashore as well. Only some minor mergers of territories in Africa were accepted. In general, existing boundaries became sacrosanct and were guaranteed by the international community, which toward the end of the 1970s consisted almost exclusively of independent nation-states.

Meanwhile, the national framework became more important in everyday life. The period between 1945 and 1979 saw the rise of new emancipatory movements, connecting more people to the state. Women gained voting rights, even in nation-states where they had been refused during the interwar period, and measures were taken to abolish racial segregation. As changes in warfare diminished the role of the male citizen-soldier in favor of the productive citizen, states began to focus more on economic development and developing a welfare state. As a consequence, states became more intrusive, which was particularly clear in Communist countries. Many governments emphasized national unity by creating one-party states and installing dictatorial regimes or even a supposedly unique national ideology. Ethnic diversity was downplayed, and many countries pragmatically adopted a lingua franca as their national language. At the same time, the identification of the population with the nation-state increased substantially with the extension of education systems, which now reached a majority of the world's population, while new mass media such as radio and television enormously broadened the reach of a national public sphere and a standardized national language.

Whereas in the preceding period scholars had studied a variety of territorial units, now the nation-state was taken for granted as the starting point of almost all research. Scholars rejected metaphysical concepts and a holistic search for origins in favor of hard data and empirical analysis, but methodological nationalism was more dominant than ever. Racial and geographic determinism were replaced by a strong focus on the economic and technocratic modernization of nationally defined societies. Transnational influences and internal ethnic and cultural differences were disregarded; more emphasis was put on the gap between the West and "the rest." Nationalism also had a profound impact on cultural life around the globe. Remarkably, fine art, modernist music, and avant-garde literature mostly presented itself as time- and placeless. Nonetheless, their makers were routinely referred to by their nationalities, and many artistic currents were defined in national terms. The nationalist content was much more pronounced in commercial mass culture such as pop music, comics, and film, although exultant expressions of nationalism were relatively rare. Most films, songs, and novels documented national reality while portraying the world as naturally divided into nation-states.

A cosmopolitan modernism profoundly transformed the earth's surface in both urban and rural environments. Functionalist buildings dominated this era of reconstruction and most new capitals were built in a rather interchangeable modernist style in which national differences had almost no place. This affected even the tourist sector, where parking lots, swimming pools, concrete hotels, and apartment buildings focused more on efficiency and comfort than on the unique characters of specific locations. The drive for modernization also shaped the natural world, as large hydroelectric dams were constructed and agriculture became an almost industrial activity with extensive monoculture fields. In other areas, the nationalization of the physical environment had more impact. Regional beverages and dishes were turned into standardized national cuisines, and the same happened with some local clothing traditions. Sports, whose organization closely matched the international organization of states, was the area where short-lived national emotions could most easily find an outlet. Radio and television broadcasted international matches and World Cups to a global audience, making the peaceful competition between nation-states a fact of everyday life and further contributing to the naturalization of a world consisting of independent nation-states.

8

Neoliberalism and Identity Politics, 1979 to the Present

THE 1970S AND 1980S WERE a period of transition. In the first postwar decades, the emphasis had been very much on modernization and technocratic planning, but many former colonies did not rapidly catch up. The oil crisis of the 1970s, moreover, caused economic stagnation in both the "free world" and the Communist bloc. Budget deficits, growing debts, unemployment, rising inflation, and environmental pollution posed challenges almost everywhere. Existing ideologies such as communism and Keynesian welfare policies no longer seemed to work. Although various solutions were tried, in the end, two major responses would become dominant: neoliberalism and identity politics. Both of them were presented as logical. Whereas state intervention failed to ensure sustained growth, neoliberals argued that the economy should be regulated by the disciplining but supposedly neutral forces of the global market, which would allocate resources in a much more efficient way. The British prime minister Margaret Thatcher famously argued that there was "no alternative," presenting her neoliberal policies as the only conceivable solution. There also was a new search for roots and a renewed emphasis on national differences, while identity politics made a strong comeback. Peoples and communities, accordingly, should follow their natural inclinations and find political solutions that fitted with their cultural and religious traditions. The strong focus on the future, thus, was replaced by a growing attention for the past, especially in the form of cultural heritage, collective memory, and the long-lasting impacts of traumatic events such as national humiliations, slavery, colonization, and genocides.[1] Surprisingly, neoliberalism and identity politics would often go hand in hand as states began to retreat from the economic domain, while political debates shifted from economic modernization and social justice to identity issues.

Neoliberalism was inspired primarily by the ideas of the economist and philosopher Friedrich Hayek. In 1944 he had published *The Road to Serfdom*, in which he argued that state planning should be opposed because it threatened the freedom of the individual and the regulatory powers of the market. The breakthrough of neoliberal solutions came in 1979. In May, Thatcher's Conservative Party won the elections in Great Britain. Like the dictatorial regime of Augusto Pinochet had done slightly earlier in Chile, she adopted the neoliberal formula by privatizing state-run companies, imposing budgetary discipline to combat inflation, and attacking trade unions. She also liberalized international trade and the financial sector. The goal was to create a business-friendly climate. In November 1980, the Republican Ronald Reagan was elected president of the United States, and his administration abolished business regulations, drastically cut taxes—especially on higher incomes—and undermined union rights in order to make labor more flexible and the economy more competitive. These neoliberal tactics were quickly exported to the rest of the world, often with the help of the International Monetary Fund and the World Bank.[2]

Almost simultaneously, the two most important Communist powers embarked on a course of reform that would eventually dismantle the collectivist planned economy. In 1979, Deng Xiaoping, who had emerged as the new Chinese leader, designated four special zones in the south to experiment with market reforms, allowing foreign investment while focusing on the production of export goods. Meanwhile, farmers were permitted to return to household farming and sell surpluses on the market, and agricultural communes were quickly abolished. At the same time, township and village companies were allowed to produce for the global market, and they rapidly became the most dynamic sector of the economy, with growth rates of over 30 percent per year. Since central planning, price controls, and state enterprises persisted as well, China developed a dual-track economy that was abandoned only in the 1990s. With the appointment of Mikhail Gorbachev as general secretary of the Communist Party in 1985, the Soviet Union also embarked on a course of reform by encouraging "transparency" and "restructuring," meaning the introduction of market reforms. But the economic reforms were less successful than in China, leading to the collapse of Communism in Eastern Europe, and with the fall of the Soviet Union in 1991, the planned economy simply disappeared.[3]

At first, identity politics was expressed primarily as a religious revival—or more precisely, as a global tendency of staunch believers to make politics subservient to religion—which was best visible in the Islamic world. Discontent with secular regimes that had pursued modernization had grown over the years. Calls to obey Islamic rules in private life but also to apply them to the realm of politics, from Islamists such as Sayyid Qutb of the Egyptian Muslim Brotherhood and Ayatollah Ruhollah Khomeini, an exiled Shi'i scholar from Iran, began to appeal to more and more Muslims. In January 1979, Khomeini's Council of the Islamic Revolution took power in Iran after mass protests had ousted Muhammad Reza Shah. After adopting a new constitution,

Khomeini became the supreme leader, while a Council of Guardians, consisting mostly of Shi'i clerics, would oversee the actions of parliament and the government. The religious revival also profoundly affected the Sunni world. At the end of 1979, armed Islamists occupied the Grand Mosque in the holy city of Mecca, vainly trying to overthrow the Saudi monarchy and institute a theocratic regime. Nonetheless, after the mosque was retaken, Saudi Arabia decided to enforce shari'a more strictly, while supporting the export of their purist Wahhabi strand of Islam. Finally, in the same watershed year of 1979, the Soviet Union backed up the faltering Communist regime in Afghanistan with an armed invasion. In subsequent years, mujahideen from around the Islamic world flocked to the country to combat the atheist regime in Kabul. In all cases, Islamists argued that both the Western and Soviet modernization policies did not suit their country because they did not respect the religious and cultural traditions of the population. A return to the origins of the Muslim faith by installing an Islamic regime—which in fact was a novel idea—would remedy the situation.[4]

A similar reaction against the materialism of modern society and in favor of traditional values could be found outside the Muslim world. In 1979 the American Baptist minister Jerry Falwell created the Moral Majority, a lobby organization to politically mobilize conservative Christians—mostly evangelicals—and seek broad support for their agenda, which he summarized as "pro-life, pro-traditional family, pro-moral, and pro-American." Meanwhile, in 1978 the Catholic Church elected the conservative Polish cardinal Karol Wojtyła as Pope John Paul II. He strongly opposed abortion and favored traditional family values. The new pope was also openly hostile to communism, and his visit to his native Poland in June 1979, where he was cheered by large crowds, seriously undermined the position of communism in Poland and elsewhere in Eastern Europe. At about the same time, Hindu nationalists became more active in India as their new political party, the Indian People's Party (BJP), began a campaign to rebuild a temple at the alleged birthplace of the god Ram in Ayodhya, which had been replaced by a mosque. They argued that the secular policies of the Indian National Congress effectively turned Hindus into second-rate citizens. In 1992 Hindu extremists demolished the mosque, asserting that India was in fact a Hindu country.[5] In almost all cases, these religious revival movements accepted the framework of the nation-state and most of them were even openly nationalist.

Nationalism was another response to the decline of modernizing ideologies, and surprisingly, it was intimately connected with the rise of neoliberalism. At first glance, the neoliberal emphasis on individualism, global free trade, and the rolling back of the welfare state seemed to be incompatible with nationalism, but the contrary was true. By enabling the mobility of capital, companies, and people across borders, neoliberals forced countries to compete with each other and to present themselves as attractive places for foreign investments, international business, and young talents. Over time, many neoliberals also began to emphasize national sovereignty in order to protect the nation-state from having to adopt multilateral agreements concerning tax regimes, social standards, or environmental protection.[6] Strikingly, neoliberal politicians such as Thatcher and Reagan frequently used nationalist rhetoric to sell their drastic reform policies. Thus, Ronald Reagan was not just a fierce anti-communist who aimed to restore the military strength of the United States; he also claimed that the country's best days lay ahead. He believed in American exceptionalism and presented the United States as God's chosen country. By emphasizing conservative values—which according to him were threatened by the permissiveness of the 1960s and the subsequent decline of the family— he actively sought the support of religious conservatives. He argued that a return to the cherished values of hard work, freedom, and moral discipline would quickly restore America's greatness. Possibly inspired by Reagan's landslide victory, Thatcher also explicitly justified her neoliberal policies during her second election campaign by adopting a nationalist tone. She argued that during the preceding decades, Great Britain had entered a period of decline characterized by a "permissive society" in "which the old virtues of discipline and self-restraint were denigrated." Her aim was to restore the "very best of the British character to its former preeminence" by promoting quintessential British virtues such as freedom, thrift, and responsibility. After two terms in office, the crisis of British identity had been largely resolved, according to her, and as a consequence, the Conservative Party adopted the slogan "Britain is great again" for the elections of 1987.[7]

Interestingly, nationalism was also on the rise in the Communist world. Thus, Deng defined his reform policies explicitly as "socialism with Chinese characteristics." Communist regimes in Europe often also pursued nationalist policies. Most remarkable were the initiatives of Lyudmila Zhivkova, the daughter of Bulgaria's party leader Todor Zhivkov. During the 1970s, her main activities focused on disseminating a new interpretation of the country's past that hardly conformed to communist orthodoxy. She organized numerous international exhibitions on the Thracians, the medieval Bulgarian Empire, and its religious heritage. This culminated in 1981 in a grand celebration of the 1,300th anniversary of the foundation of the Bulgarian state. The implication was that the Bulgarians had ancient roots and that the country had been a center of Orthodox religion and Slavic culture long before Russia.[8]

Thanks in part to the rise of neoliberalism and identity politics, the decades after 1979 would see fundamental changes as the international order was upset by new wars of conquest and ethnic violence. In 1980 Iraq's president Saddam

Hussein hoped to profit from the chaos caused by the Islamic Revolution in Iran by annexing oil fields in disputed border areas, leading to an all-out war. Ten years later he conquered Kuwait, but was quickly repelled by an international coalition led by the United States. In 1982, another dictatorial regime tried to boost its popularity as Argentina made a vain attempt to conquer the British Falkland Islands. Ethnic violence was on the rise as well, with Hussein's genocidal campaign against the Iraqi Kurds and an aggressive assimilation program targeting ethnic Turks in Zhivkov's Bulgaria.[9] More impactful would be the dissolution of both the Soviet Union and Yugoslavia and the widespread ethnic violence in Africa's Great Lakes region.

During the post-1979 period, citizenship was affected primarily by the retreat of the welfare state and a new emphasis on human rights. This strengthened the legal position of several minorities but weakened socioeconomic rights in most parts of the world. In academia and the cultural realm, contradictory tendencies could be seen. Many scholars fundamentally questioned the role of nationalism, while several new disciplines, such as memory studies and intercultural communication, implicitly endorsed its basic principles. Moreover, nationalism was on the rise in commercial art forms such as music and cinema. The nationalization of the physical environment also reached new heights. Global competition prompted authorities to create spectacular landmark buildings to brand their countries. The introduction of UNESCO's world heritage and the growth of tourism encouraged countries to become more typical than they had ever been. Although the internet at first seemed to blur boundaries, social media in fact had a strong polarizing effect, encouraging culture wars and the hardening of national identities, and thus nationalizing cyberspace, too. Little wonder that in the twenty-first century, populist politicians who appealed to national sentiments could boost their electoral support, even in well-established democracies such as the United States, Great Britain, Brazil, and India.

New Nation-States

The fall of Communism would lead to many new states, which generally adopted existing (internal) boundaries, although the post-1989 period would also see a significant increase in ethnic violence. The pillars of the existing international order were slowly undermined by the oil crisis of the 1970s and the subsequent ideological readjustments, and then the fall of the Berlin Wall quite suddenly opened a window of opportunity for new nation-states to arise.

The Communist bloc had serious difficulties adapting to the new economic realities. Instead of innovating and changing course, as China hesitantly did, most Communist countries experienced growing debts and economic stagnation. Gorbachev's reforms in the Soviet Union did not succeed in finding a way out. Nonetheless, in December 1988 he took a crucial step by announcing that the Soviet Union would not interfere in the internal affairs of its Eastern European satellite states. After the Polish Communist Party suffered a humiliating defeat in the first free elections, he even urged the Polish authorities to respect the outcome. In November 1989, responding to growing pressure from the population, the Communist leadership of East Germany opened the border to the West. As crowds of East Germans immediately seized the opportunity, using their bare hands to bring down the Berlin Wall, people understood that communism had become a thing of the past. As a result, all Communist regimes in Eastern Europe collapsed within a few months' time.[10] The Soviet Union followed in 1991, while the Communist regimes in Indochina mimicked China's path of gradual reform.

The first major change in the international system made possible by the fall of the Berlin Wall would be the reunification of Germany. In March 1990, at the first free elections in East Germany, the Christian Democratic Alliance for Germany won almost half of the votes with reunification as its main electoral promise. Helmut Kohl, the Christian Democratic chancellor of West Germany, immediately proposed a treaty of unification that implied that the German Democratic Republic would be absorbed by West Germany. Meanwhile, Kohl had secured the fiat of both the United States and the Soviet Union, but many European leaders were fearful of a strong, unified German state. Urged by the French president François Mitterrand, the German government therefore promised to embed the new country in a further integrated Europe. As a consequence, the member states of the European Community signed the Maastricht Treaty, which deepened their collaboration and changed the name of the community to the European Union. At the same time, it was decided that the euro would replace the national currencies, including the cherished deutsche mark. Formerly neutral countries such as Sweden, Finland, and Austria now also joined the European Union. Many former Communist countries in East-Central Europe would follow in 2004 and 2007, creating a powerful political and economic union of twenty-seven nation-states.[11]

Another consequence of the fall of Communism was the dissolution the Soviet Union, Czechoslovakia, and Yugoslavia. Communist nationalities' policies—which had given ethnic minorities their own autonomous republics or provinces—backfired in various parts of Eastern Europe and Central Asia. Under the Communist dictatorship they had functioned quite well, appeasing nationalist discontent by leaving activists ample room for cultivating their separate identities. This meant that over time, ethnic and national identities had become much more pronounced. At the same time, the policies that ensured loyalty to the state had become associated with the now discredited Communist regime. This created an ideological void that was easily filled by nationalist intellectuals and politicians. Since the Soviet Union, Yugoslavia, and Czechoslovakia had already been organized along ethnic lines, strong nationalist mobilization was not required to bring down the federation; determined local leaders could simply proclaim the sovereignty of their republic or province by appealing to the principle of national self-determination.

The first cracks in the state structure of Soviet Union had already begun to appear shortly before 1989. The Baltic republics took the lead. There, awareness that things were better in the West was very widespread. In addition, there were important historical grievances. The Baltic states had been independent in the interwar era, and this had been brought to an end by the Molotov-Ribbentrop Pact between the Soviet Union and Nazi Germany. The integration into the Soviet Union had caused a massive inflow of Russian professionals. Moreover, many inhabitants of Lithuania, Latvia, and Estonia had been (temporarily) deported to Siberia. When civic protests became possible thanks to the reforms of Gorbachev, they had a nationalist tone right away. Nationalist coalitions or "popular fronts" won the first free elections for the republican Supreme Councils of March 1990. Subsequently, the Lithuanian parliament decided to "restore" the independence of the country. Although Gorbachev responded with only an economic boycott, independence was suspended, leaving the outcome undecided.[12]

At about the same time, nationalist violence erupted in the Caucasian Soviet republics. In 1988 Armenians and Azeris had clashed over Nagorno-Karabakh, a region that officially belonged to Azerbaijan, but where Armenians constituted the majority of the population. In April 1989, nationalist protests in Georgia were suppressed by the Red Army, resulting in twenty casualties. Meanwhile, "popular fronts" appeared in other Soviet republics such as Ukraine and Belarus, but in the elections of March 1990 they gained majorities only in the Baltic states and Moldova. Elsewhere, local Communists took matters into their own hands by proclaiming the sovereignty—but not yet independence—of their own republics during the summer of 1990. Surprisingly, this also happened in Russia, where Boris Yeltsin emerged as the new strongman, first as chair of the Russian Supreme Soviet, then in July 1991 as the elected president of the Russian Soviet Republic.[13]

In January 1991, after much hesitation, Gorbachev ordered troops to force Lithuania and Latvia back into the Union. This led to widespread protests elsewhere in the Soviet Union, while Yeltsin's Russia recognized the sovereignty of the Baltic republics. Gorbachev hoped to save the union by adopting a new federal constitution that included the right of secession as a compromise with the republics. For most reformers this was too little too late, while for Communist hardliners this was more than they could swallow. In July the new constitution was adopted, but the next month, conservative officers staged a coup.

MAP 8.1 The dissolution of the Soviet Union in 1991. A leading role in disbanding the Soviet Union was taken by the Russian Federation under President Yeltsin. Other newly independent states were Estonia, Latvia, Lithuania, Belarus, Ukraine, Moldova, Georgia, Armenia, Azerbaijan, Kazakhstan, Uzbekistan, Turkmenistan, Kyrgyzstan, and Tajikistan. All were former Soviet republics.

The plotters, however, did not have the support of the majority of the armed forces, and Yeltsin, sporting a Russian flag, successfully mobilized the population in Moscow to save democracy. After three days, the coup ended in failure. Instead of preserving the Soviet Union, the putschists had hastened its dissolution. Within days, Ukraine declared independence, and most other republics followed suit. In December 1991 the Russian president met the leaders of Ukraine and Belarus and they decided to disband the Soviet Union (map 8.1), definitively confirming the independence of fifteen new states. The Russian Federation would be the main successor state of the Soviet Union, inheriting its army, ministries, and the permanent seat on the Security Council of the United Nations. As a replacement for the Soviet Union the three leaders created the Commonwealth of Independent States, a loose intergovernmental organization of former Soviet republics.[14]

Soon after, Czechoslovakia was also dissolved peacefully along existing internal boundaries. The state had been created after the fall of the Habsburg

Empire, but the differences between the highly industrialized Czech lands and Slovakia, which had been a peripheral rural part of the Hungarian half, did not disappear. The different parts had considerable cultural autonomy and in 1968 the country even received a federal constitution. After the fall of Communism, what put an end to the state was not so much nationalist mobilization but the determination of regional leaders. In June 1992 Václav Klaus of the new Civic Democratic Party won the elections in Czech lands, while Vladimir Mečiar's Movement for a Democratic Slovakia won almost 40 percent of the vote in Slovak districts. Their political ideals were almost diametrically opposed, as Klaus preferred a neoliberal shock therapy, whereas Mečiar opposed privatization plans. As prime ministers of the Czech and Slovak lands, they agreed to split the country by January 1993, thus gaining full power by abolishing the federal level, as Yeltsin and his colleagues from Ukraine and Belarus had done with the Soviet Union.[15]

Yugoslavia was the third Communist state that was dissolved along existing borders. The state had come into being after the First World War by uniting territories that had belonged to the Ottoman and Habsburg Empires around a Serbian core that had been independent since 1878. After the Second World War, Yugoslavia became a Communist federation of nationally defined republics. Their autonomy was increased by the adoption of a new constitution in 1974, and the death of the charismatic President Tito further weakened the position of the central government. Economic differences between a relatively affluent north—Slovenia and Croatia—and an underdeveloped south were exacerbated over time. Moreover, the economic situation significantly worsened during the 1980s. Influenced by Gorbachev's reform policies, the power monopoly of the Communist Party was increasingly criticized, and the dismantling of the Communist system began in 1988 when socialist property laws and Yugoslavia's unique workers' self-management of companies were abolished. However, it was only after the fall of the Berlin Wall that it became clear that one-party rule was doomed. In January 1990 the ruling League of Communists fell apart, and the subsequent free elections were won by new nationalist parties or by Communist leaders turned nationalists such as the Serbian president Slobodan Milošević.[16]

The demise of Yugoslavia would be a very violent affair. Nationalist leaders and their followers in Slovenia, Croatia, and Bosnia were determined to take advantage of the new situation. But the main reason for the bloody civil war was that Milošević wanted to protect the interests of the many Serbs living outside of Serbia—particularly in Croatia and Bosnia—at all costs. In March 1989 Milošević had abolished the autonomous status of the Serbian provinces of Vojvodina and Kosovo, heightening fears of Serbian domination in the other republics. When Slovenia and Croatia declared independence in

June 1991, the Yugoslav People's Army, which closely collaborated with Milošević, intervened. Although the Slovenian cause was abandoned after ten days of fighting, this was not the case with Croatia. The army and Serbian paramilitary forces conquered considerable parts of Croatia and expelled most non-Serbian inhabitants. This first phase of the war ended in January 1992 with a ceasefire under the auspices of the United Nations.[17]

In 1991 Macedonia was allowed to peacefully secede from Yugoslavia, but ethnically mixed Bosnia-Herzegovina quickly became a new battleground. Local Serbs, Croats, and Muslims created their own armed militias. In March 1992 a majority of the population voted in favor of independence, but most Serb inhabitants boycotted the referendum. This led to an all-out civil war in which Bosnian Serbs received covert aid of both the People's Army and a Yugoslav rump state, both dominated by Serbia. Thousands of civilians were killed in ethnic-cleansing campaigns that culminated in the executions of about eight thousand Bosnian Muslim men from Srebrenica by Serbian militias. At this point, NATO intervened by bombarding Serbian positions. Croatia used the opportunity to reconquer the separatist Serb areas within its own territory and expel most of the remaining inhabitants. The Dayton Accords, signed under pressure from the international community in 1995, restored the territorial integrity of both Croatia and Bosnia-Herzegovina, although the latter was split between a Serb republic and a Croat-Muslim federation.[18]

The Dayton Accords offered no solution to the dire situation of Albanian Kosovars—who had lost their autonomy, their cultural rights, and in many cases, their jobs in 1989—and so the Kosovo Liberation Army became more active. In response, Milošević stepped up the repression, expelling more than two hundred thousand Kosovars. In March 1999, when the Serbian president refused to accept a deal brokered by the international community that included self-government for Kosovo, NATO began to attack positions in Serbia. As China and Russia opposed the intervention, it did not receive the approval of the Security Council of the United Nations. More than eight hundred thousand Kosovars fled their homes before NATO bombardments forced the Serbian government to accept a provisional United Nations administration of Kosovo. In revenge, the Kosovo Liberation Army expelled tens of thousands of Serbs from the province. It was only in 2008 that the Kosovar parliament proclaimed independence. Two years before that, Montenegro also had seceded—peacefully—from Yugoslavia, so the country finally fell apart into seven new nation-states.[19]

The situation of Russia was not unlike Serbia's. Both had been the historical core of a federal state that had just disappeared. Moreover, Russians and Serbians had been the dominant ethnic groups of those states. In many Soviet republics there were large numbers of ethnic Russians, and during the

Communist era, migration, education, social mobility, and mixed marriages had further increased the number of Russians and Russian speakers. As a consequence, in 1989 almost thirty million Russians lived outside of Russa proper. Another parallel was that neither Russia nor Serbia was ethnically homogeneous: Serbia had two autonomous regions, and the Russian Federation has twenty-two autonomous republics and ethnic minorities represent about 20 percent of the population. Surprisingly, in the Russian Federation this did not lead to violence at the same levels seen in Yugoslavia, at least during the dissolution of the Soviet Union. Whereas Serbia used the rump of Yugoslavia for its own purposes, the Russian Federation under Yeltsin mostly opposed the Soviet Union. Although many ethnic Russians suffered from discrimination in several successor states, they successfully rebelled only in Transnistria, a largely Russian-speaking border area of Moldova. After the failed coup in August 1991, Moldova declared itself independent and Transnistria decided to secede and become a sovereign state. The Russian Federation recognized the independence of Moldova within its existing borders and handed over several units of the Red Army to the new state. Many members of the military, on the other hand, supported the rebels. In 1992 the fighting ended in a stalemate. Although Transnistria continues to function as an independent state, it is not recognized by the international community; not even by the Russian Federation.[20]

In subsequent years Russia got enmeshed in ethnic conflicts both outside and inside its borders, first in Georgia, where the formerly autonomous regions of Abkhazia and South Ossetia tried to secede. Yeltsin's government and many Russian democrats recognized the existing borders, but conservative officials offered covert support to the secessionists. Although Georgian authorities aimed to create a strong centralized state, Zviad Gamsakhurdia and Eduard Shevardnadze, the former minister of foreign affairs of the Soviet Union, got enmeshed in a yearlong power struggle. Within this unstable political context, violent clashes between Georgian and South Ossetian activists escalated in January 1992 after South Ossetia held a referendum on secession. The goal was the incorporation of South Ossetia into the Russian Federation, where it could join the autonomous region of North Ossetia. In June 1992 Shevardnadze and Yeltsin agreed to "freeze" the situation by sending international peacekeeping forces under the banner of Organization for the Security and Co-operation in Europe, consisting of Russian, North Ossetian, and Georgian troops. After ending the conflict with South Ossetia, Shevardnadze sent his army to Abkhazia to regain control of the rebellious region. Although the Georgian troops initially advanced rapidly, Abkhazia received aid from other nationalist movements from the North Caucasus, including five thousand Chechen fighters. Moreover, many Russian inhabitants of the region actively supported the Abkhazian cause, and furtive assistance was received from

Russian secret services. The Abkhazian authorities eventually expelled both the Georgian army and more than two hundred thousand ethnic Georgians. The Commonwealth of Independent States promised to send in peacekeepers to safeguard a ceasefire. In the end, however, only the Russian Federation sent troops, which effectively continue to protect the independence of another unrecognized state.[21]

Because various autonomous republics and regions within the Russian Federation also sought independent statehood, the Yeltsin administration was not eager to openly encourage separatist movements in neighboring countries. In the autumn of 1991 Jokhar Dudayev, the newly elected Chechen president, had proclaimed the independence of the Republic of Chechnya, which was part of the Russian Federation, and his example was soon followed by others. Yeltsin tackled the relationship between the central government and the autonomous territories by drafting a new constitution. In the end, all regional governments with the exception of Chechnya formally returned to the Russian Federation. Yeltsin now mounted a full-scale attack on the rebellious republic, but the war proved to be a disaster and the Russian army withdrew in 1996. Three years later, another Chechen war started after armed forces from the rebellious republic invaded the neighboring Russian republic of Dagestan. Under the newly appointed prime minister Vladimir Putin, who in 2000 also became Yeltsin's successor as president of the Russian Federation, the war was conducted with utmost brutality. Chechens retaliated with spectacular terrorist attacks in Moscow and Beslan, but to no avail. The Russian army conquered most of the region, and Ahmad Kadyrov, the new head of the Chechen Republic, had free rein to reestablish order.[22]

Unlike what happened with the Serbian province of Kosovo, Chechnya did not succeed in attracting significant international support, let alone an international military intervention. Dudayev had profiled Chechnya as an independent Muslim state, which played into Western fears of political Islam. Dudayev also failed to win active support from Islamic countries or from other nationalist movements in the Caucasus. Moreover, no one seriously considered intervening militarily in the internal affairs of an atomic power like the Russian Federation. As a result, the international community mostly looked for ways to mediate between the warring parties or to ameliorate the human rights situation, with little success.[23]

Although the consequences for the state system were less substantial than in East-Central Europe and the Caucasus, ethnic tensions also increased elsewhere in the world. This was most clearly visible in Africa's Great Lakes region, where the genocide in Rwanda and the related military conflicts in neighboring countries resulted in the deaths of millions of people. Rwanda had been a semifeudal kingdom where a small Tutsi aristocracy of pastoralists ruled a large majority of Hutu peasants. The kingdom became a colony of Germany and then a mandate administered by Belgium. Both colonial powers ruled through the existing state structure while defining the differences between the two ethnicities in racial terms. As independence was nearing, tensions escalated. Tutsi chiefs clung to their privileges, and a new generation of Hutu activists framed the Tutsis as foreign intruders. The Belgian authorities replaced the existing Tutsi authorities with Hutu leaders, to no avail. Independence was accompanied by widespread violence, and more than one hundred thousand Tutsis fled the country. A military coup by General Juvénal Habyarimana in 1973 brought significant changes. Although he did not fully abrogate the quota system that was meant to undo the privileged position of the Tutsis, he recognized them as an Indigenous ethnic group. In 1989, as part of a global democratization wave, Habyarimana introduced freedom of the press, and a new constitution enabled multiparty elections. However, as in Yugoslavia, the demise of the one-party dictatorship led to escalating ethnic tensions. Radical Hutus founded chauvinist political parties, while experienced Tutsi fighters created the Rwandan Patriotic Front, which aimed to invade the country from their bases in Uganda. In this neighboring country, Tutsi refugees had participated in the successful rebellion of Yoweri Museveni's National Resistance Army, and now they embraced the idea of a return to their native land. They received the backing of Museveni's regime, but on the condition that they would leave Uganda.[24]

Led by Paul Kagame, the Rwandan Patriotic Front invaded Rwanda in October 1990. Instead of being welcomed as liberators, masses of Hutu peasants fled the border area, and Hutu radicals began to arm themselves and perpetrated several massacres against Tutsis. Habyarimana pursued a policy of reconciliation, forming a coalition government and entering into negotiations with Kagame. In August 1993, they agreed a peace deal that entailed the integration of the Rwandan Patriotic Front into the army and government assistance for returning refugees. Hutu militants tried to block the implementation of the accords. The situation got completely out of hand in April 1994 when the presidential aircraft was hit by a missile, killing Habyarimana onboard. Hutu radicals immediately responded by killing huge numbers of Tutsis and moderate Hutus, who, like the perished president, favored reconciliation. Ordinary Hutus in the countryside, fearing they would lose their land and maybe their lives at the hands of the Rwanda Patriotic Front, participated in the mass killings, which continued for over three months. Meanwhile, the rebel fighters conquered most of the country, finally ending the mass killings. In the end, more than over half a million people had died.[25]

The ethnic violence in Rwanda spilled over to neighboring Burundi and Zaire. In Burundi, a minority of Tutsis had successfully remained in power after independence, but in the 1980s radicals from the Hutu majority founded armed rebel groups. As a consequence of the democratization wave of the early 1990s, the Tutsi president Pierre Buyoya appointed a Hutu prime minister. However, in the first free elections, in June 1993, Buyoya's party suffered defeat. Four months later—shortly after an accord had been signed between the two warring factions in Rwanda—Tutsi officers staged a coup, killing the new Hutu president. This set off a violent civil war, primarily between Hutu militias and the army, which was still dominated by Tutsis. The civil war would continue until 2005, when a peace agreement was negotiated between the government and the main rebel groups.[26]

The conflicts in Rwanda and Burundi were clearly linked, but this was even more evident with respect to the violence that erupted in eastern Zaire. After the final victory of the Rwanda Patriotic Front in the summer of 1994, about one million Hutu refugees fled into neighboring provinces in Zaire, including many perpetrators of the genocide. They quickly set up their own army and carved out their own territory while killing local Tutsis, thus effectively splitting Hutus and Tutsis in the eastern provinces. Since Hutus and Tutsis spoke the same language, in Zaire they had been regarded as one minority group and they had naturally banded together to improve their situation. Now, other ethnic groups created armed militias, too. As a consequence, the situation quickly deteriorated and violence became endemic. Tutsi militias received support from Kagame's regime, and in October 1996 Rwanda invaded eastern Zaire. Subsequently, Tutsi militias allied with Laurent Kabila, an opposition leader who capitalized on the declining popularity of the Mobutu regime, while their Hutu opponents supported Mobutu. In May 1997 the opposition forces conquered Kinshasa, Kabila became president, and he renamed the country Congo. The new regime proved to be a harsh dictatorship, and when Kabila ordered the Rwandan troops to leave the country, Tutsi militias began a new rebellion, which quickly received the support of Rwanda and Uganda. The new Congolese regime received military assistance from Angola, Namibia, Zimbabwe, and Chad, turning the conflict into a full-scale war, with millions of victims. The war officially ended in 2003, but the eastern provinces remain unstable and the conflict between Hutus and Tutsis continues to play a significant role.[27]

Ethnic conflicts are not inevitable. During the Cold War they mostly remained muted, and when identity politics became more important in the 1980s and 90s, conflicts did not necessarily follow ethnic lines, and when they did, they often were not stoked up or they were solved by peaceful means. Indeed, the Yugoslav wars and the eruption of widespread violence in the Great Lakes region in Africa were exceptions. What was striking, moreover, was that these conflicts occurred in areas where ethnic differences were relatively minor. In the case of Yugoslavia, the large majority of the population consisted of South Slavs, who spoke mutually intelligible dialects. Halfway through the nineteenth century, Croat and Serb intellectuals had decided to adopt a shared standardized Serbo-Croatian language that was written in both the Cyrillic alphabet in use in Orthodox areas and the Latin script of the Catholics. Under Austrian rule, the Latin alphabet was also introduced in Bosnia-Herzegovina. During the interwar era the new Yugoslav state even tried to institute an official Serbo-Croato-Slovenian language that was imposed from Slovenia in the north to Macedonia in the south. In 1945, the Communist regime established Slovenian and Macedonian as separate languages, while the fundamentally different languages of the Hungarian and Albanian minorities received recognition. Nonetheless, in Croatia and Bosnia-Herzegovina, where most of the bloodshed took place, only minor differences in pronunciation and lexicon can be detected, and schools taught both the Cyrillic and Latin alphabets.[28]

Thus, in Yugoslavia, the main differences were not linguistic, but religious and historic, as Serbians traditionally were Orthodox, Croats were Catholic, and many Bosnians were Muslim. But under Communism, religion was actively discouraged and secularism made large inroads. As a result, in 1968 over half of the Yugoslavs declared they were not religious and in 1990, only 37 percent of the Bosnian Muslim population considered themselves devout. Moreover, a growing segment of the population of Yugoslavia identified themselves as Yugoslavs instead of Croats, Serbs, or another group, and many marriages were mixed. In Bosnia-Herzegovina, for instance, more than 20 percent of married couples were in mixed marriages in the early 1980s. International cultural trends and fashions, such as blue jeans and short skirts, were adopted by teenagers not just in the cities but also in rural areas. Nonetheless, especially in the countryside, religious differences continued to play a role. Many people still had religious names or used traditional greetings or expressions such as the Arabic *inshallah*, or wore traditional hats and caps that distinguished ethno-religious communities from each other. Historical grievances, especially those related to the ethnic-cleansing campaigns during the Second World War, continued to exist and were revived in various historical controversies during the 1980s. Nonetheless, those who did the actual fighting were far too young to have a living memory of the atrocities perpetrated against "their" ethnic communities in the 1940s.[29]

The situation in Rwanda was not very different, as Mahmood Mamdani has convincingly argued. Hutus and Tutsis spoke the same language, and in Uganda and Zaire they were even known as one ethnic group, the Banyarwanda. Moreover, they largely shared the same cultural traditions, most of them were Christians, and intermarriages were common. Ethnicity was determined by one's father, thus many people had a mother, grandparents, or cousins who belonged to the other ethnic group. This also meant that possible physical differences between Hutus and Tutsis—who presumably came from different parts of Africa—became blurred over time. So the main differences were social: most Tutsis were pastoralists, while most Hutus were small-scale farmers. The ethnic classifications still were quite fluid until the Belgian colonial authorities racialized these differences and recorded them in the census. As a consequence, ethnic boundaries became harder, and they were noted on identity cards. These fixed ethnic identities continued to play a crucial role after independence, culminating in the genocide of 1994.[30] Like in Yugoslavia, there were important historical grievances (e.g., unequal access to privileged positions, the hardships of refugee life), but very few guerrillas of the Rwanda Patriotic Front, nor many of the Hutu radicals, had experienced the ethnic violence of the early 1960s firsthand.

Thus, ethnic violence is not inevitable, nor is it a logical outcome of ancient hatreds. Rogers Brubaker convincingly argues that ethnicities and nations are not "things-in-the-world," but rather "perspectives on the world." Concepts simplify reality, and by using terms like "Hutus" and "Serbs," we frame them as internally homogenous groups that operate together. However, ethnic categories are social constructs that change over time. Most of the time, these categories hardly play a role in everyday life, and only in very exceptional circumstances—of political mobilization, invasions, or civil war—can a category turn into a group, but even these moments of "high levels of groupness" are generally short-lived and usually they do not affect everyone in the same manner. Discussing the case of Kosovo, Brubaker even argues that "group crystallization" was "the result of violence, not the cause." Thus, by explaining wars in terms of clashes between Serbs, Croats, and Muslims or between Hutus and Tutsis, we tend to take for granted the reality of these ethnic groups. Instead, Brubaker argues, we should see collective identities not as a substance, but as mosaics of different layers and hues, which are in constant flux.[31] The issue with identity politics, however, is that its leaders, activists, and followers take group identities very seriously. They think that differences between groups are more important than differences within groups, and that people tend to feel loyal to their group and that they are even morally obliged to do so.

The rise of identity politics and the growing aversion to heavy-handed assimilationist policies led to hostilities elsewhere in the world, too. Tensions occurred not so much where ethnic differences were pronounced, but where territories of different colonial empires had been merged or where religious differences were prominent. In Cameroon, friction between the large French-speaking areas and the western provinces that had been part of British Empire grew from the early 1990s, while the largely Arabic Muslim population on the island of Zanzibar increasingly felt marginalized by the Tanzanian mainland with which it had merged. In 1991, when state authority in Somalia almost completely collapsed with the fall of the dictator Siad Barre, the former British colonial territories declared themselves independent as the Republic of Somaliland. Although Somaliland continues to function as a de facto state, it is not recognized by the international community. A somewhat peculiar case is Palestine. The Palestine Liberation Organization declared independence in 1988, and five years later, an agreement with Israel led to the creation of a Palestinian National Authority. Even though Palestine currently is recognized by more than 130 states, because of Israeli obstruction, its sovereignty remains a sham. In total, there were only three negotiated secessions that did receive international backing, which demonstrates that the sacredness of borders, which had been established in the 1950s and 1960s, continued to be largely respected. The first exception that proves the rule was the former Italian colony of Eritrea. In 1950 Eritrea had merged with Ethiopia, but the autonomy it secured within the federal state structure was later abolished. In 1991 a coalition of rebel forces, including the Eritrean People's Liberation Front, succeeded in overthrowing the oppressive, Marxist Derg regime. Two years later, a massive victory in a referendum led to the peaceful secession of Eritrea. The former Portuguese colony of East Timor, which had been annexed by Indonesia in 1975, profited from the fall of the Suharto dictatorship in 1998. The transitional government in Jakarta allowed the territory to organize a referendum that led to independence. The Christian and animistic South Sudan also suffered long-term brutal repression, by the Arab-speaking Islamic north. After a civil war lasting several decades, a peace agreement was reached in 2005, leading to independence in 2011. Thus, secession on ethnic grounds remains extremely rare, so it should come as no surprise that the unilateral plebiscites in favor of independence organized in 2017 by the nationalist authorities of the autonomous region of Catalonia and Iraqi Kurdistan ended in failure because of a lack of international support.[32]

Variations on the Nation-State

After the fall of Communism and the end of the Cold War, the liberal democratic nation-state seemed to be the only viable model of statehood left. This continued to be a dominant view well into the twenty-first century. However, there were also new developments, some of which sought to broaden democratic practices, while others seemed to undermine the hegemony of the constitutional nation-state. The democratization wave had already begun several decades before the fall of the Berlin Wall, tumbling authoritarian regimes and military dictatorships in Southern Europe, Latin America, and various parts of Asia. The inspiration provided by the collapse of the totalitarian regimes in East-Central

Europe and the growing pressure of Western donors also led to a democratization process in Africa, resulting in free elections in countries such as Cape
Verde, Benin, Niger, Zambia, Malawi, and both Rwanda and Burundi. In February 1990, even South Africa legalized Nelson Mandela's African National Congress and began to dismantle its discriminatory apartheid regime.[33]

At the same time, many established democracies began to introduce more
responsive forms of governance by devolving power to regional assemblies. This
process was most pronounced in Europe. Paradoxically, European integration
reinforced the position of the regions. In 1975 the European Economic Community had introduced the European Regional Development Fund, which was
meant to improve the economies of the poorer regions. Since the funds had to
be requested and administered by the regions, even centralized states—such as
France—had to create meaningful regional political-administrative units in
order to receive European subsidies. Beginning in the 1970s, some countries also
consciously gave more autonomy to the regions. As a response to rising Flemish
demands, Belgium took the lead. In successive reform waves, the government
divided the country into three regions: Flanders, Wallonia, and Brussels-Capital
Region. Both Flanders and Wallonia became officially monolingual, and as a
consequence, political parties split into Flemish and Walloon variants, seriously
weakening the cohesion of the Belgian nation-state. In Spain, regional autonomy
was introduced soon after. Its primarily goal was to give cultural autonomy to
Catalonia and the Basque Country, which each had its own standardized language and a strong nationalist movement. However, other regions demanded
similar forms of self-government. As a result, the country ended up with a "coffee for all" model with seventeen autonomous regions. The United Kingdom
joined this trend in the late 1990s as Scotland and Northern Ireland received
their own assemblies, followed by Wales in 2011.[34]

Meanwhile, identity policies also affected the substate level. Regional authorities began to brand their own territories, emphasizing their unique and
most attractive characteristics in order to attract investments and tourists.
Politicians increasingly appealed to regional sentiments, arguing that policies
had to be adapted to the area's particular situation. Substate nationalist movements in Flanders, Northern Italy, Scotland. and Catalonia, for instance, became more assertive as well. They were not underprivileged regions, and in
their pleas for fiscal autonomy or even independence, some of them began to
use neoliberal arguments against an inefficient central state, which, according
to their version of "nationalism of the rich," heavily subsidized less dynamic
parts of the country and their masses of undeserving poor.[35]

Devolution was also on the agenda in some African countries, including
Ethiopia, the most prominent example. After the Derg regime was ousted by a
coalition of five ethnically based rebel movements (of which the Tigray People's

Liberation Front was the strongest), Ethiopia became an ethno-federal state. Now all "nations, nationalities, and peoples" received the right to self-determination, implying the right to regional autonomy and even secession. The country was divided into nine autonomous regions. The governing Ethiopian People's Revolutionary Democratic Front was also organized along ethnic lines, as it was based—after the peaceful secession of Eritrea—on the four remaining former rebel movements. Although each of them governed their "home" region, the party exerted strong centralized control, and by co-opting activists from other regions, it effectively prevented smaller ethnic groups from claiming autonomous regions. But ethnic tensions became stronger and escalated in 2018 when the new prime minister, Abiy Ahmed, decided to liberalize the political situation. The Sidama, an ethnic group living in the Southern Region, now also claimed autonomy, which led to interethnic violence and similar claims for special rights from other "nationalities." In an attempt to regain control and to promote Ethiopian national unity, Abiy Ahmed created a new governing party, a move that was openly rejected by Tigray leaders. The government also postponed the 2020 elections due to the Covid-19 pandemic, but this was repudiated by the regional government of Tigray, which continued with its own elections. Notwithstanding the prime minister's attempt to encourage a pan-Ethiopian national sentiment, political mobilization now occurred mainly along ethnic lines, and in November 2020 it led to a full-scale civil war with the "rebellious" Tigray region that included episodes of ethnic cleansing.[36]

Another major development in the post-1979 period was the growing role of religion in politics, which was most visible in the rise of Islamism, which to some extent can be interpreted as a form of both democratization and identity politics. Most Islamist regimes basically worked within the international order without challenging existing borders. This is quite logical for movements such as the Turkish Justice and Development Party of Recep Tayyip Erdoğan, but is equally true of the Islamic Revolution in Iran. Even though Khomeini's regime initially tried to export its revolution to the rest of the Muslim world, it quickly focused on supporting Shi'i groups—creating powerful militant movements such as Hezbollah in Lebanon—which undermined the internal stability of some of their neighbors and implicitly fanned sectarian strife throughout the Islamic world. However, Khomeini's principal objective was the consolidation of his own regime.[37]

Although they might appeal to Muslims all around the world, most Islamic movements accepted the existing national framework. Thus, the transnational Muslim Brotherhood mainly operated through national branches that give priority to their own domestic agendas. More violent groups focused primarily on one national context, be it Afghanistan, Algeria, Palestine, Kashmir, or Chechnya. However, after the withdrawal of the Soviet troops from

Afghanistan, a generation of professional jihadists began to travel from one conflict to another. A group of these transnational fighters, led by Osama bin Laden, created Al-Qaeda in 1988. At first, they targeted mainly the "impious" regimes in various Muslim countries, by attempting to kill Egyptian president Hosni Mubarak, for instance. The stationing of U.S. troops in Bin Laden's native Saudi Arabia as a result of the First Gulf War was interpreted as an "occupation," and in response, Bin Laden shifted his attention from the "near" to the "far enemy": the United States. This culminated in the spectacular terrorist attacks of September 11, 2001, when hijacked passenger airplanes were flown into the Pentagon outside Washington, D.C., and the Twin Towers of the World Trade Center in New York City. The subsequent U.S. attack on the Taliban regime in Afghanistan, which had hosted Al-Qaeda's leadership, demolished the centralized command structure of the movement, but also led to a splintering of its activities organized by local sympathizers throughout the world. However, they again mostly chose domestic targets. Although the ultimate aim of Al-Qaeda's terror campaign was the reestablishment of the caliphate, it did not even bring about regime change at a national level. Only Daesh, an even more violent terrorist organization, succeeded in effectively creating a substantial Islamic state, on the border of Syria and Iraq between 2014 and 2019. Its leader, Abu Bakr al-Baghdadi, was proclaimed caliph, and Daesh effectively aimed to transcend existing borders and national loyalties.[38]

Identity politics was also on the rise outside the Islamic world. The end of the Cold War initially led to widespread optimism, but quite soon, in many parts of the world, discontent with the functioning of the democratic system began to grow. The endless parliamentary debates, the growing role of party politics, the lack of moral leadership, and the ineffectiveness of elected governments were increasingly criticized. Economic insecurity, the growing gap between rich and poor, lack of opportunities, and the consequences of mass migration were urgent problems that remained largely unsolved, partly because after the neoliberal adjustments, governments had less institutional power and financial means to take effective measures. Moreover, since economic policies hardly triggered ideological controversy and the traditional left-right spectrum began to lose most of its relevance, identity issues like family values, immigration, and the threat of globalization began to take a more central role in political debates. Compromises over identity and values are difficult because they are related to deeply felt convictions, so pragmatic solutions were hard to find or did not last, leading to frustration and further political polarization. As a consequence, moderate political parties had difficulty preserving their electoral bases, creating a void that was increasingly filled by populist movements and authoritarian leaders. They embraced identity issues, and claimed that they defended the national interests of the large mass of population.

Populism was not a new phenomenon. In the nineteenth century, various populist movements, politicians, and political strategies could already be found in Europe and the United States. During the 1920s and 1930s, Mussolini and Hitler gained power with a populist message, while populism also made headway in Latin America, with Brazil's Getúlio Vargas and the Argentinian presidential couple Juan and Eva Perón being the most important representatives. The postwar economic boom and the creation of a welfare state left little room for populist politicians, and it was only in the 1990s that populism made a strong comeback, starting in Latin America. Around 1990, the outsiders Carlos Menem and Alberto Fujimori won elections in Argentina and Peru, respectively. Both argued that the oligarchic elites were out of touch with reality and that the corporatist solutions of the past had led to economic stagnation, political chaos, and widespread corruption. They adopted neoliberal shock treatments, opened up closed markets, privatized state companies, and brought inflation down. Shortly afterward, a new wave of populists gained power with a very different left-wing message that emphasized national sovereignty in the face of rampant globalization. The most radical were Hugo Chávez in Venezuela, Evo Morales in Bolivia, and Rafael Correa in Ecuador. They agitated against corrupt political elites who had surrendered their countries to multinational companies, the interests of the United States, and the disastrous neoliberal formulas of the International Monetary Fund and the World Bank. Once in power, they organized constituent assemblies to draft more inclusive constitutions, strengthened the governments, introduced new forms of direct democracy, nationalized natural resources, and used the revenues to boost social spending.[39]

Although some left-wing populist presidents, such as Brazil's Luiz Inácio Lula da Silva, largely respected the rule of law and existing institutions, others were less patient and used authoritarian means to rapidly increase social justice and strengthen the country's international position. This was most particularly the case in Venezuela. The new constitution of 1999 had centralized power in the hands of the president, but subsequently, the parliament authorized Chávez to govern by decree in order to implement urgent measures. "Disrespectful" behavior was punishable by several laws that could be arbitrarily applied to members of the opposition and other critical voices, especially after Chávez packed the courts with sympathetic judges. The government also increasingly controlled the media by creating state-owned newspapers and television channels and by inducing other outlets to refrain from open criticism. Elections were manipulated to ensure that Chávez's United Socialist Party of Venezuela (PSUV) stayed in power. The repressive tendencies became even more pronounced under Chávez's successor, Nicolás Maduro.[40]

Left-wing populists could also be found elsewhere. Good examples are for-mer presidential candidate Bernie Sanders in the United States, Podemos in Spain, and Syriza in Greece—a party that gained power in 2015, at a critical moment in the country's sovereign debt crisis. Nonetheless, in most countries right-wing populists dominated the scene with a clear nationalist agenda. Before the 1990s, right-wing populist parties were rather marginal in Europe; most embraced a neoliberal agenda of lower taxes and conservative morals, which was the case with Jean-Marie Le Pen's National Front (FN) in France and the Danish Progress Party. In the 1990s, immigration became an important issue, and many new populist parties were founded. When Jörg Haider's Austrian Freedom Party (FPÖ) entered a government coalition in 2000, this provoked large-scale demonstrations and international calls for a boycott. The terrorist attacks of September 2001, the global financial crisis of 2008, and the arrival of around one million Syrian refugees in Europe in 2015 helped right-wing popu-lists to broaden their electoral bases, and this was not limited to Europe and the United States. Many populist parties also entered into tacit alliances with religious groups that claimed to represent the traditional values of the majority population, such as Catholics in Poland and Italy, evangelical Protestants in the United States, Orthodox Christians in Russia and Serbia, Sunnis in Turkey, and Hindus in India. As a consequence, populist parties gained more influ-ence. They not only gave parliamentary support to minority governments, as in Denmark and the Netherlands, or entered coalition governments, as in Aus-tria, Italy, Bulgaria, and Israel, but also, in many cases, governed on their own, as in Hungary, Poland, Turkey, and India. Moreover, populist politicians such as Rodrigo Duterte, Donald Trump, Jair Bolsonaro, and Javier Milei won presi-dential elections in the Philippines, the United States, Brazil, and Argentina, respectively.[41]

Both left- and right-wing populist regimes sought to strengthen national sovereignty by increasing their control over borders and natural resources and by disengaging from international commitments. They also opposed oligarchic elites and claimed that they themselves embodied the will of the people. But whereas the left-wing populists in Latin America aimed to emancipate the poor masses, especially those with Indigenous or African American backgrounds, right-wing populists wanted to protect the majority population against foreign immigration and assertive minorities. The authoritarian inclinations of some of the Latin American populists could also be encountered elsewhere. First, most populists preferred direct democracy, such as plebiscites, over represen-tative forms. Moreover, they did not always respect the separation of powers and the rule of law when this put obstacles in the way of what they perceived to be the will of the majority. Many populist regimes nominated sympathizers to judgeships in courts of law and top positions at semi-official bodies. They often rejected oppositional views as foreign or illegitimate and impeded the work of nongovernmental organizations and the free press. Sometimes this was done quite subtly, by having sympathetic businessmen buy up newspapers and television channels, for instance; in other cases, critical media outlets were banned outright or their licenses were withdrawn. Under these circumstances, the populist regimes of Viktor Orbán in Hungary, Law and Justice in Poland, and Erdoğan in Turkey can barely be classified as free democracies in which the rule of law is respected, and thus they implicitly make the nation subservient to the state or their personal rule.[42]

Outright authoritarian states continued to exist as well, and after the turn of the century, China and Russia became influential models of this type. China's fabulous economic growth, based on a strongly centralized Communist state, was difficult to copy in a time when not even the Chinese believed in Marxism anymore. Easier to follow was Russia's "guided" or "managed democracy" as it developed under Putin. Guided democracies are based not so much on personal charisma or populist politics, but on the skillful use of state institutions, while using nationalist rhetoric to justify measures taken. Guided democracies were not new—in nineteenth-century France, Napoleon III ensured that elections always resulted in a friendly majority, while in the twentieth century many authoritarian leaders upheld a façade of democracy to mask their personal rule. Russia had adopted a democratic constitution, but under Yeltsin, the state apparatus was already being used to favor friendly oligarchs and manipulate elections. After the political chaos and profound economic downturn in the late 1990s, Putin brought stability. Rising energy prices gave him the resources to buy off the population and specific interest groups. The new president was obsessed with stability, and he particularly focused on eliminating the uncertainty of competitive elections. He therefore co-opted the main opposition parties and harassed those that were not willing to cooperate. If necessary, political opponents were excluded from the electoral lists, persecuted, or even physically eliminated. What happened in 2008 was a typical example of Putin's feigning acceptance of constitutional rule. As his second term as president had finished (his final term, per the constitution), he stepped down in favor of Dmitry Medvedev, who then appointed him prime minister, and he continued to act as a spider in the web, making all the main decisions. Putin was especially hostile to the "color revolutions," such as those in Ukraine and Georgia. After he was reelected president in 2012, widespread protests against voting fraud were harshly suppressed. Several repressive measures were introduced, including a "foreign agents" law, which was used to strictly monitor or close down civil society associations. Although independent media outlets continued to exist until the 2022 full-scale invasion of Ukraine, the main television stations became nationalist propaganda channels for the regime. Over the years, Putin also enhanced his power by creating new unofficial bodies such as the State Council, the Nashi youth organization, and the Wagner group, a private military organization. He could employ these at will, which further undermined the sovereignty of the community of citizens. Thus he has been able to stay in power for more than two decades without facing major internal threats.[43]

Citizenship

Citizens' leverage with the state diminished after the late 1970s. The end of the Cold War meant that conscription was abolished in many parts of the world. During the first few decades after the fall of the Berlin Wall, interstate warfare became rare, and when it occurred, during the U.S.-led invasion of Iraq in 2003, for example, high-tech arms made all the difference. Civil wars happened more frequently, but whereas previously they had been fought mostly for ideological reasons—by Marxist guerrilla movements, for instance—now a main driving force was control over resources. So wars were not very heroic anymore, and the growing individualism and consumerism further undermined the ideal of the citizen-in-arms.[44]

In addition, citizens' leverage was undermined by the weakening of trade unions. Neoliberal economists such as Milton Friedman argued that state intervention and the strong bargaining power of trade unions had led to inflationary pressures. In order to increase a country's competitiveness in an ever more interdependent world, economic policies should be insulated from societal and political pressures. Guided by these ideas, central banks became more independent and focused primarily on price stability, while governments curtailed the power of the unions. With the liberalization of world trade, production was easily outsourced, and many employers preferred cheap migrant workers who had more difficulty vindicating their rights. As a result, traditional workers' strongholds such as heavy industry and coal mining largely disappeared from the Western world, while they prospered in parts of the world, such as China, where labor rights were minimal. The exploration of other fossil fuels such as oil and gas and the quickly expanding renewable energies relied primarily on a small number of well-paid technicians who rarely took a leading role in defending civic rights.[45]

Another factor was the partial dismantling of the welfare state. From the late 1970s, neoliberal governments took measures to dismantle or seriously restrict the welfare state in order to encourage private initiative, individual responsibility, and international competitivity. Many state agencies were converted into lean service providers, turning citizens into customers. Structural adjustment programs were imposed on many countries in Latin America, Africa, and Asia. As a consequence, nongovernmental organizations took over many functions of the state, weakening the role of citizens. Neoliberal princi-ples continued to dominate economic thinking, and after 1989 they were ap-plied quite ruthlessly—often as shock therapy—to most former Communist states. As a consequence, the safety net of the "nanny state" was increasingly removed in the West, the East, and the Global South. The opening of national markets and the liberalization of finance also caused profound dislocations, especially through the deep financial crises of 1997 to 1998 and 2008. The re-location of labor-intensive industries to low-income countries turned formerly prosperous industrial regions such as the U.S. Midwest and Germany's Ruhr into rustbelts. Elsewhere, particularly in East Asia, hundreds of millions of people escaped poverty, but many did so only by moving to new urban areas or to faraway lands and working long hours in often dismal conditions.[46]

Until the 1980s, state planning for the future of the nation had resulted in ideologically charged public debates on long-term priorities and the re-distribution of collective wealth. Now, this was increasingly abandoned in favor of the market, which based its choices primarily on individual gain. This also meant that political debates became more focused on the present: Where do we stand? Who are we? What rights to we have? Thus, identity issues and individual rights replaced ideological questions. This led not just to a religious revival and populist nationalism but also to movements that claimed the ex-tension of civil rights to minorities such as Indigenous populations and the LGBTQ+ community.

The weakening of the welfare state and the declining effectiveness of social demands brought a shift in the relations between state and civil society. New social movements increasingly appealed to human rights in order to reinforce their claims. At first, the focus was on basic freedoms—the right of political participation and equal access to social services such as education and health care. The civil rights movement in the United States had a pioneering role. As a response to mass protests, the Kennedy administration began implementing affirmative action programs. Sometimes these included quotas to redress racial injustices, but after this was prohibited by the Supreme Court in 1978, the pri-mary goal of most programs became diversity and inclusion. At about the same time, various groups demanded that the state recognize the collective rights of cultural communities. In this way, a younger generation of civil rights activists began to defend racial pride and Black power. Indigenous groups and recent immigrants—especially Hispanics—also more actively tried to "pre-serve" their own culture, traditions, and heritage. Dissolving in the melting pot—which in fact meant assimilation into the dominant Anglo-Saxon middle classes—had lost its attraction. Activists increasingly demanded bilingual edu-cation and the reform of curricula and textbooks to take into account the cul-tural diversity of the population. In 1968 the Black Student Union, in collaboration with the so-called Third World Liberation Front, had succeeded in reforming the curriculum at San Francisco State University. Other universities and colleges quickly followed, and many also established ethnic studies departments.[47] Protests against discrimination and racial inequality continued to flare up in the United States, leading to, for instance, the founding of the Black Lives Matter movement in 2013.

The Canadian government tackled diversity issues more actively than its counterpart in Washington, and its focus was on Quebec, immigrants, and Indigenous groups. In response to rising demands for political autonomy in French-speaking Quebec, the government installed the Royal Commission on Bilingualism and Biculturalism in Canada and adopted its advice to give official language status to both English and French. The commission also acknowledged the cultural contribution of Indigenous and immigrant communities, and in 1971 the Liberal government of Pierre Trudeau officially adopted a multicultural policy that aimed not only to assist immigrants in learning English or French, but also to help "cultural groups to retain and foster their identity." In 1988, these policies were further extended and institutionalized with the Multiculturalism Act, and after the turn of the century the country began to celebrate a Canadian Multiculturalism Day.[48]

Both the civil rights movement in the United States and the introduction of multicultural policies in Canada would have a great impact on the emancipation of Native Americans. Protests against the appropriation of sacred grounds, the use of caricatural mascots by sports teams, and the display and sale of cultural artefacts, religious objects, and human remains by museums and art dealers mobilized Indigenous groups, who convinced judges and governmental bodies to take action. In Canada, the government and religious congregations offered apologies and financial compensation for the abuses suffered at boarding schools, which had isolated children from their communities in order to assimilate them. In the United States, judges recognized the right of the Seminole tribe—based on their right to govern themselves—to open bingo halls and casinos on their reservations. Their example was quickly followed by hundreds of other Native American communities. In Canada, there were serious plans to recognize the right to self-government of the so-called First Nations, but in the end, they were voted down. However, in 1999, as a concession to the eastern Inuit—who did not have their own reserve—the new province of Nuvanut was created in the Far North.[49]

Multicultural policies would also have a strong impact on Latin America. There, many Indigenous and "Afro-descendant" activists became more assertive. During the 1960s and 1970s they primarily used class-based organizations such as trade unions and peasant associations to put their demands forward. Their position changed fundamentally in the 1980s when the corporate structures that had been prominent in Latin America were dismantled. New social movements appealed directly to both the public and the authorities to denounce abuses or to protest against the worsening of their socioeconomic position. One strategy was to call for individual rights to be upheld, the other was to advocate for the protection of minority rights. This second strategy received a boost with the establishment of a United Nations Working Group on Indigenous Populations in 1981, and in the 1990s many Latin American governments ratified the Indigenous and Tribal Peoples Convention that had been adopted by the International Labour Organization. With it, they pledged not only to respect the language and cultural and religious traditions of their Indigenous communities, but also to give them collective land rights, their own political institutions, control over natural resources, and the right to apply customary law. Several governments introduced constitutional reforms granting collective rights to Indigenous communities, and sometimes also to groups of African Americans, mostly descendants of runaway slaves living in rural communities. The official adoption of multiculturalism, which constituted a clear break with earlier assimilationist policies, strongly reinforced the position of Indigenous communities, but in a sense, they also imprisoned individuals within their ethnic groups, as it tended to essentialize their identity.[50]

The most radical implementation of multicultural policies in Latin America occurred in Bolivia. The Movement for Socialism (Movimiento al Socialismo, MAS)—a coalition of Indigenous movements, peasant organizations, and trade unions—won the elections in 2005, and its charismatic leader, Evo Morales, became the country's first Indigenous president. He quickly convened a Constituent Assembly. Representatives of various grassroots organizations asserted that the new constitution should recognize Indigenous and peasant communities as "nations" with a right to self-determination. In the end, the new constitution proclaimed Bolivia to be a "plurinational state," and Indigenous cultural and legal traditions received broad recognition. Moreover, thirty-six Indigenous languages—some of which still had to be standardized—received official status and were now also used in schools. However, it was not easy for Indigenous communities to get autonomy, and it did not include veto rights on vital issues regarding their territory. Another priority of Morales's left-wing populist government was to recover Bolivian sovereignty over natural resources. Thus, he nationalized the country's hydrocarbon resources, using the revenues to pay for new welfare programs for the underprivileged classes. The focus on economic development, however, was not always compatible with the demands for territorial self-determination by Indigenous groups. When the government tried to press ahead with the construction of a highway through an Indigenous territory–cum–national park, there were several large-scale protest marches and the project was halted, demonstrating the resilience and power of the Indigenous social movements and the new autonomous authorities.[51]

Multiculturalism would make considerable progress in subsequent decades, and not just in the Americas. In the 1990s, prominent authors such as the Canadians Charles Taylor and Will Kymlicka wrote extensive theoretical tracts to defend a "politics of recognition" and a new model of "multicultural citizenship." About the same time, multicultural ideals were adopted by international organizations. The convention of the International Labour Organization was quickly followed by a Declaration on the Rights of Persons Belonging to National or Ethnic, Religious or Linguistic Minorities from the United Nations. In these proclamations a clear hierarchy among minorities could be discerned. Indigenous peoples had a strong position and could appeal for international support for their claims on land, the right to self-government, and the use of customary law. For ethnic minorities, these proclamations could be used to demand primary education in their mother tongue, but they did not provide a legal basis to claim official language status or regional autonomy. But immigrant communities—because they were not "native"—could not develop any collective (cultural) claims on the basis of these international conventions.[52]

Australia was inspired by the Canadian developments, but there was more opposition to recognizing the collective rights of Indigenous groups. Historically, Australia had refused to give citizenship and voting rights to Aboriginals and Torres Strait Islanders, and many children had been removed from their families to institutions where they were thoroughly assimilated. In 1973 the Labor government reversed the assimilationist policies, and sixteen years later, multiculturalism was adopted. However, it was only the celebration of the International Year of the World's Indigenous People in 1993 that induced a new Labor government to officially apologize for the injustices of the past. Soon after, an official report concluded that the forcible removal of more than one hundred thousand Indigenous children had been a "gross violation of human rights" that could even be characterized as "genocide." The report argued that reparations were needed, but this was rejected by the government. In the meantime, the Supreme Court had acknowledged Indigenous land rights, but only if communities could prove their continuous connection to the land, which in many cases was impossible. The author Damien Short argues that by not recognizing Indigenous peoples as a nation—which in fact also applies to Canadian multiculturalism—the Australian "settler state" continues to withhold sovereign rights from the Aboriginals.[53]

The Saami, an Indigenous group living in the polar areas of Northern Europe, began their emancipation more or less at the same time as the Native Americans. Assimilationist policies were abandoned in the 1970s, while Norwegian plans to construct a huge hydroelectric dam that would flood large areas used for reindeer grazing provoked mass protests. As a result, in the 1980s the collective rights of the Saami began to receive recognition and they got their own parliament in both Norway and Sweden. In 2000 a transnational Saami Council was created that also included communities in Finland and the Russian Federation.[54]

Some West European countries also adopted multicultural policies that targeted immigrant communities. At the start, immigration from the colonies and the arrival of guest workers led to some modest measures to curtail immigration. In the 1970s and 1980s it became clear that most guest workers would not return to their home countries and that not all people from the former colonies would easily integrate into society. The Dutch government developed new policies to reduce the cultural and socioeconomic deprivation of immigrant groups after radical young Moluccans—whose fathers had been Dutch colonial soldiers—committed several terrorist acts. Margaret Thatcher, whose policies had been quite detrimental to most immigrant communities, introduced a youth training scheme and spent more on the Urban Aid Programme as a response to massive race riots in Brixton.[55]

Most African and Asian countries—except for federal states such as India, Nigeria, and Ethiopia—were not very inclined to make concessions to minority groups. Indigenous populations such as the Ainu in Japan, the hill tribes in Thailand, the Formosans in Taiwan, the "isolated peoples" in Indonesia, and the San in Botswana were generally seen as "backward people" who would benefit from economic development and adopting more "civilized" manners. Assimilationist pressure was great, and even the constitutional democracy of Japan recognized the Ainu as an "indigenous people" only in 2019. Ethnic minorities such as the Tamils in Sri Lanka, the Karen in Myanmar, the Tibetans and Uighurs in China, and the non-Arabic population of Sudan did not get collective recognition either, and they, too, suffered under harsh assimilationist policies. In many cases, they were even considered a security threat that should be dealt with forcefully. Migrants, especially construction workers and domestic servants, were generally barred from citizenship. Middle Eastern countries such as Qatar and the United Arab Emirates are still notorious in this respect, but it also applies to Singapore and many African countries. Even long-standing communities have had difficulty acquiring citizenship. Koreans who arrived in Japan when their country still was a colony were treated as "aliens" and could acquire citizenship only with difficulty and only by adopting a Japanese name; the official policies with regard to this substantial group became more conciliatory only in the 1990s.[56] In Myanmar, the Muslim Rohingya minority was considered foreign, and in 1982 they even lost their citizenship. In 2017, the army intervened in the escalating ethnic tensions in the Rakhine region by effectively driving hundreds of thousands of Rohingya over the borders.

The United Nations played an important role in the emancipation of other groups, declaring 1981 the International Year of Disabled Persons, and a few years before that, adopting the Convention on the Elimination of All Forms of Discrimination against Women. By then, the position of female citizens had already improved substantially. Legal equality of men and women was by now recognized in most countries. The democratization wave increased the role of women in politics; several countries even introduced electoral quotas. New constitutions paid specific attention to the needs of female citizens mostly by adding clauses related to labor rights and gender-based violence. Nonetheless, the glass ceiling was still in place in most areas of life. In sports, for instance, equal pay for men and women—at tournaments and on national teams— advanced only very slowly. As a consequence, nongovernmental organizations continued to draw attention to subtle forms of discrimination against women at home, in the workplace, and in society.[57] More recently, the Me Too movement, driven by American actresses denouncing perpetrators of sexual assault and harassment, had ripple effects around the world.

The LGBTQ+ community is another group that made limited progress. The International Gay and Lesbian Association had mounted campaigns during the Cold War era to denounce violence against gay and lesbian persons and call for equal rights. The AIDS pandemic of the 1980s provided a strong incentive to more actively protest failing health care policies and negative stereotypes. Renewed activism helped to decriminalize consensual same-sex relationships in a growing number of countries, and in various Western European countries civil unions for same-sex couples were legalized. In 1990, the World Health Organization finally removed "homosexuality" from its international classification of diseases. In 2001 a major step was taken when the Netherlands legalized same-sex marriage. This example was quickly followed by dozens of countries, mostly in Europe and the Americas. International organizations also began to defend the rights of the LGBTQ+ persons. In 2003, the member states of the European Union explicitly prohibited discrimination on the basis of sexual orientation, and the United Nations Human Rights Council adopted a similar resolution soon after. Finally, the rights of transgender and nonbinary persons began to receive protection, and in 2012 Argentina was the first country to allow its citizens to easily change their gender on official documents.[58]

In the new millennium, however, there was a distinct backlash against the growing rights and public roles of minorities, women, and LGBTQ+ persons, leading to open culture wars in many parts of the world. Many conservatives, orthodox religious communities, and authoritarian regimes had not been in favor of the expansion of rights for women and the LGBTQ+ community. In the twenty-first century, they were joined by many right-wing populist movements, which rejected these rights as a project of liberal cosmopolitan elites that threatened the moral integrity of the nation. In 2014, Nigeria and Uganda adopted laws that criminalized same-sex relations. From 2015, pride parades in Turkey were banned, and at about the same time, Russia prohibited exposing minors to "propaganda of nontraditional sexual relations." Similar policies were introduced in Brazil under Bolsonaro. In Poland, Jaroslaw Kaczyński, the populist leader of the governing Law and Justice Party, argued that the "LGBT ideology" constituted a "threat to Polish identity, to our na-tion . . . and thus to the Polish state." Various local governments officially pro-claimed their areas to be "LGBT-free zones," and the Russian autonomous region of Chechnya even had detention camps for gay men. Right-wing popu-lists generally favored traditional gender roles: men should be strong and take on the role of breadwinner, while the primary task of women was to ensure the survival of the nation by taking care of the family. Marriage, therefore, should be reserved for unions between men and women. Orbán's government even closed down the gender studies programs in Hungary, arguing that "people are born either male or female."[59]

Populists also restricted the rights of other groups of citizens. Most populist regimes were tough on crime, and often they were willing to circumvent exist-ing legal procedures. An extreme example was provided by President Duterte, who encouraged Philippine citizens and police forces to kill drug dealers and addicts. Almost all populist governments took anti-immigration measures, such as Trump's attempt to build a wall on the border with Mexico. Populist politicians such as Nigel Farage and Boris Johnson successfully used the "Take back control" slogan during the Brexit referendum, promising to severely cur-tail immigration into the United Kingdom in order to protect British national identity. But citizenship was also ethnicized in many parts of Africa, restricting it to the autochthonous population. Measures were frequently taken against Muslims as well, usually masked as counterterrorism actions. President Trump banned citizens of various Muslim countries from entering the United States, while Modi's government in India took discriminatory measures against Mus-lim refugees and long-established Muslim immigrants. Populists also cracked down on minority rights. In 2018, Benjamin Netanyahu's government declared Israel to be the "national home of the Jewish people," further marginalizing Israeli citizens with Arab backgrounds. The rights of Indigenous populations were also violated, especially in the service of the exploitation of raw materials such as tropical timber or oil. Bolsonaro proclaimed that he would "never cede a centimeter to the Indians," and during his tenure, farmers and mining com-panies were given free rein in many of Brazil's Indigenous Territories. Another option was to "reinforce" the majority population. Many populist regimes adopted natalist policies to strengthen the nation. Hungary even tried to partly undo the loss of territories after the First World War, by allowing ethnic Hungarians from neighboring countries to acquire Hungarian nationality. As a consequence, about one million people received Hungarian citizenship, which included the right to vote.[60]

National Awareness

With the advance of education and mass media, the vast majority of the world's inhabitants were aware of their nationality. Moreover, the division of the world into nation-states was taken for granted. Only in extremely remote areas were people still unaware of the boon of the nation-state. Nonetheless, the rise of satellite television and the invention of the internet, social media, and the smartphone had an enormous impact on the way nation-states and national identities were framed. Satellite television and the internet, in fact, deterritorialized the mass media, which before then had been connected to the nation-state by the distribution networks of newspapers and radio and television transmitters, creating national audiences for nationally organized media. Cable television had already broadened the offer of commercial channels, which often also included a number of regional and foreign channels. During the 1980s broadcasters using the regional language were created in Wales, the Basque Country, and Catalonia. Satellite television and the internet, however, easily cross national borders, allowing emigrant populations to maintain close contacts with their homelands by watching television programs, following websites, and staying connected with family and friends through social media and video calls. Sometimes this led to open forms of "long-distance nationalism" in which not just sports teams but also struggles for national liberation were actively supported. Satellite television and the internet also allowed ethnic minorities and stateless nations such as the Kurds and the Tamils to create their own media outlets that could be accessed throughout the world.[61]

A major innovation of the internet and social media was that the public could talk back—not just by leaving comments on news sites or forums, but also by creating websites and online communities. As a consequence, it became harder for state authorities and traditional media to control the narrative on policy priorities or the nation's identity, for instance. This democratization of the public sphere also led to fragmentation, creating niches for every ideological hue and minority group. But the internet also enabled the creation of truly transnational communities—mostly using English as the lingua franca—often around celebrities, sports teams, or computer games.[62] This had fundamental consequences especially for the Arab world, where new media reignited a kind of pan-Arabism. The new satellite news channel Al Jazeera provided an Arab perspective on crucial events such as the Second Gulf War and the

Second Palestinian Intifada with live footage, largely turning Middle Eastern audiences away from U.S., British, and French media outlets. During the Arab Spring, which began in Tunisia in 2010, the public closely followed what happened in different parts of North Africa and the Middle East through television and social media, while activists throughout the Arab world found inspiration for their own protest campaigns. Reality shows such as *Arab Idol* and *Arabs Got Talent* connected millions of people who could actively participate by voting for their favorite candidates and posting comments on social media. These shows created a transnational public sphere, but in many ways, they also confirmed national boundaries because people mostly supported their national representatives, while ethnic minorities such as the Kurds could gain visibility.[63]

New media also explicitly reinforced national frameworks. Most websites and email addresses have a national domain name, so cyberspace largely reproduces the territorial layout of the real world. Most hyperlinks refer to websites from the same country. Search engines and social media prioritize references to the national environment of the user, while their algorithms reproduce existing national and ethnic biases. By playing on emotions and prioritizing shocking images and extreme opinions, social media seem to encourage nationalist feelings. Various countries, moreover, tried to create their own national digital ecosystems. China is the best example; it enforces strict political censorship of content and search terms, it also established its own platforms in Baidu, Weibo, and WeChat. Elsewhere, the U.S. multinationals Google, Facebook, and Amazon have largely taken over. But many websites and applications for news or for finding old school comrades or buying houses, for instance, continue to be organized nationally. Political events, national holidays, sporting victories, and natural disasters continue to spark essentially national debates on the World Wide Web.[64]

Culture

Although collective identities and clearly bounded cultures were increasingly taken for granted in public debates, in academia they were generally interpreted as social constructs. This was visible in the study of nationalism, where in the early 1980s scholars like Benedict Anderson and Eric Hobsbawm famously interpreted nations as social constructs, as "imagined communities" that were largely based on "invented traditions."[65] Under the impact of rising levels of globalization and the introduction of the internet, scholars in the humanities and social sciences also increasingly argued that nation-states and national societies should not be studied as isolated units, but as nodes in transnational networks that connected all parts of the globe. Nonetheless, other academics focused on the legacy of the (national) past, which could be defined in cultural, ethnic, or even genetic terms.

In the social sciences and humanities there was a distinct reaction against the emphasis on quantitative methods, structures, and discourse of the previous era and the habitual use of (national) societies as the undisputed main unit of analysis. Many scholars now focused on individual agency, with a clear preference for the role of ordinary people and everyday life. This can be seen in the writings of the Marxist philosopher Henri Lefebvre and the Jesuit Michel de Certeau. In the 1970s and 1980s they rejected Foucault's strong focus on the disciplinary power of discourse in favor of mundane forms of resistance. Instead of examining the strategies used by governments, institutions, and intellectual elites to influence the behavior of the population on a national scale, they preferred to study concrete social spaces and everyday practices in order to explore how individuals adapted the immediate environment to their own preferences. At about the same time, the Subaltern Studies Group—which originated in South Asia—analyzed the agency of ordinary peasants, showing that local communities were not passive pawns in the hands of powerful capitalist forces and (post-) colonial authorities, while implicitly situating a small area within a transnational or even global context.[66]

In the discipline of geography, authors such as Edward Soja, David Harvey, and Doreen Massey also brought human agency back into the discussion by focusing on space as a continuously changing social construct. Although most geographers acknowledge that spaces have their own materiality that delimits their use, these scholars argued that spaces were not just objective entities that could be measured and arranged rationally; they were made, reproduced, and transformed in everyday life. According to this "spatial turn," space was no longer understood as an abstract, empty entity, but as a place that was used and perceived differently by each individual, which implied that spaces were historicized. Spatial identities were not fixed; they changed over time and varied depending on the user. Massey, moreover, argued that places were not static and isolated, but should be seen as dynamic meeting places, consisting of networks of social relations. The focus on lived spaces also meant that the nation-state as the primary unit of analysis lost some of its relevance, while its borders were now increasingly seen as porous.[67]

Comparable developments occurred in the field of anthropology. The traditional focus on societies and cultures as discrete, bounded entities, each with its own unique set of values and practices that could be studied in a neutral, objective manner, was increasingly criticized. Empirical research had already shown that individuals mostly engaged with a variety of social networks and that the distributional patterns for different cultural practices generally did not overlap, which challenged the notion of clearly bounded cultural communities.

Moreover, in *Orientalism* (1978) the literary scholar Edward Said argued that scientific studies had created a reified and static representation of the "Orient" by "othering" their object of study. This work exerted a strong influence on anthropological debates. Scholars were conscious that the classical anthropological studies, which generally had given a holistic, synchronic description of one tribe or society, basically portrayed their objects of study as passive and changeless bearers of an impersonal culture. As a consequence, the discipline became extremely self-reflective, as authors like Ulf Hannerz, Arjun Appadurai, and Marc Augé shifted the focus to the impact of globalization, transnational flows, and processes of hybridization, studying societies as dispersed, overlapping networks. This implied that they also paid more attention to the agency and creativity of local actors.[68]

The same trends were visible in other disciplines. Social scientists began to put more emphasis on transnational networks; well-known examples of this are Bruno Latour's actor-network theory and Manuel Castells's ambitious *Information Age* (1996–1998). Migration and borderland studies became new interdisciplinary fields of research. Some scholars now denounced the largely unconscious "methodological nationalism" that had been dominant in the social sciences and humanities. In 2002, Andreas Wimmer and Nina Glick Schiller argued that classical social theory had not seen nationalism as an important topic of research, and at the same time it took for granted a world consisting of nation-states. For most sociologists, society was equated with national society, nation-states were the dominant territorial unit for analyzing developments, and everything that extended over the boundaries of the nation-state was excluded. Britta Schneider criticized methodological nationalism in the field of linguistics, where monolingualism had been the norm and bilingualism, dialects, and minority languages were mostly ignored.[69]

Similarly, Stefan Berger censured historians for having researched, narrated, and interpreted the past primarily through a national lens. The dominant historicist approach—which suggested that a society can be understood by studying its historical roots—meant that the nation-state was projected into the distant past and was taken as a closed container, largely isolated from the outside world. Berger was not alone in his critique; in fact, many of his insights had been anticipated in the new fields of global and transnational history, which explored the circulation of goods, ideas, and people across borders by examining the roles of transnational networks, cosmopolitan nodes, and intellectual transfers. Nonetheless, popular history books and many scientific case studies continue to take the nation-state as their main frame of reference. New nation-states, such as Croatia and Belarus, tended to invest heavily in producing a national master narrative. Many authoritarian states also actively propagated a "positive" interpretation of the national past in an attempt to legitimize the regime. Especially after Xi Jinping's rise to power, China not only prohibited "distorted" views on the Communist past, but also actively combatted "historical nihilism." This meant that those approaches that undermined the centrality of the nation-state, such as microhistory, gender history, and transnational perspectives, were rejected as a Western threat—not just to the discipline, but to the "well-being of the people."[70]

However, whereas most academics became increasingly critical of the traditional understanding of ethnic communities, national societies, and cultures as discrete, internally homogenous, and clearly bounded entities with their own peculiar values and characteristics, nationalism and identity politics were on the rise in everyday life. Throughout the world, nationalists, right-wing populists, Indigenous communities, and ethnic minorities, in fact, adopted the now-outdated classical anthropological understanding of culture.[71]

There were also new scientific trends that consciously or unconsciously reinforced this culturalist view of the world. First, the new interdisciplinary fields of memory studies and heritage studies mostly took national or ethnic communities as their main frame of reference. The 1980s saw the publication of a few seminal works that stood at the head of the memory and heritage boom, such as Pierre Nora's *Realms of Memory* (1984–1992) and David Lowenthal's *The Past Is a Foreign Country* (1985). Both employed a critical perspective, showing how collective memory and cultural heritage had been constructed over time, but both studied memory and heritage primarily within a national context. This was most obvious in the case of Nora's multiauthored project, which resulted in seven illustrated volumes on France's most important "sites of memory." These publications sparked a wave of case studies that investigated specific aspects of a collective memory or cultural heritage. Mostly, the authors also explored how heritage and collective memory were connected to the identity formation of a particular national or ethnic community, while implicitly defining its boundaries. Transnational approaches are only recently getting more attention from heritage and memory scholars.[72]

A new discipline that even tended to reify national cultures was the multidisciplinary field of intercultural communication. A pioneering study was Geert Hofstede's *Culture's Consequences* (1980), which was based on questionnaires on work-related values completed by tens of thousands of employees of IBM in fifty countries. Hofstede distinguished six different value orientations in order to "uncover the secrets of entire national cultures." His goal was to overcome obstacles in interpersonal communication, and the results of his quantitative study would enable professionals to take into account substantial cultural differences among their employees and customers. His book sparked a wave of other investigations, the creation of new university chairs for intercultural communication throughout the world, and the application of its findings not just in business but also in public health, the military, and other domains where people from different cultural backgrounds meet. Although scholars within the field have added nuance to many of Hofstede's views and put more emphasis on intercultural sensitivity and multicultural diversity as an asset, they still perceive national cultures as clearly bounded, homogeneous entities—with an almost unchanging core—that largely determine an individual's behavior.[73]

More surprising than the survival of culturalist views in some scientific domains was the return of biology. In the field of statistics, for instance, there was a new focus on ethnicity and identity, and this was particularly clear in Latin America. In the 1980s and 1990s grassroots organizations began to call for including questions on ethnicity and race in population censuses to help combat discrimination. To assess the impact of specific measures to improve the situations of Indigenous and African American communities, they had to be visible in the statistical records. Their cause was helped by international pressure. The Ford Foundation introduced a racial impact statement in its international grant applications, for which solid data on the ethnic composition of the local population was needed. Various international organizations began to pay more attention to the impact of racial and ethnic factors in explaining disparate socioeconomic development, and in the early 2000s the World Bank organized technical workshops to discuss how ethnic and cultural diversity could be included in censuses. As a consequence, almost all Latin American countries decided to make ethnic and cultural diversity visible in their population statistics. Contrary to what had happened in the early twentieth century, when censuses were based on supposedly objective criteria such as skin color and racial characteristics, respondents had to declare their own membership of an ethnic or racial community. Sometimes questions about descent or language were added. This suggests that the melting pot ideal had been abandoned in favor of a multicultural, multiethnic, and multiracial statistical representation of the nation, in which ethnic and racial categories were converted into clearly bounded entities.[74]

In biomedicine, a similar effort to reduce disparities induced researchers to investigate whether biological differences were medically significant. With this goal in mind, health authorities in the United States required that women and members of racial and ethnic minorities be included in clinical trials. The new focus on race and ethnicity was strengthened by the unravelling of the human genome around the turn of the century. Scholars began to examine whether certain ethnic groups were more prone to getting specific diseases and whether they responded differently to medicines. Although in most cases it was unclear whether the differences that were found were related to social and environmental factors—poverty, lifestyle, unhealthy neighborhoods—or to biological causes, this type of research tended to naturalize ethnic and racial categories. These categories, which were based on the patients' possibly dubious self-identifications, have become associated with certain genetic variants that are considered medically relevant. As a consequence, rather vague racial and ethnic categories have become institutionalized and "grounded in biological differences." Because it is still difficult to test patients for all known relevant genetic variants—which would enable personalized medicine with individually tailored treatments—rather doubtful racial and ethnic categories continue to be used and are naturalized in the process.[75]

The growing use of DNA testing—which is increasingly popular for finding out more about one's ancestors—has led to comparable outcomes in other disciplines. Even though genetic variation is greater within communities than between communities, researchers tend to associate specific genetic variants with particular ethnic groups. In the field of archaeology, individual genetic samples from archaeological sites were taken as representative of a specific ethnic group and a clearly bounded culture. But the attachment of an ethnic label to an individual sample implies that social or cultural groups were understood as being genetically homogenous. Moreover, in many studies, this ethnic label was then associated with particular burial practices and aspects of material culture, creating bounded, homogeneous, enduring groups that are biologically grounded. Other studies based on Y-chromosome sequences—limited to male lineages—related the resulting migration patterns to mobile war bands of young men, even though the authors had no actual data about women.[76]

These essentialist interpretations can also be found in the field of sociobiology, where authors such as Edward Osborne Wilson, Paul Shaw, Yuwa Wong, and Azar Gat argued that social behavior has evolutionary roots. According to them, people of close kin show solidarity to each other because they share a considerable amount of their genes. The evolutionary drive toward self-reproduction therefore also operates on a collective level. As a consequence, these scholars interpreted war as a means to maximize one's reproductive success by violently expanding one's domination over people, territories, and resources; thus they largely ignored the roles of ideology, political institutions, social organizations, and technology, while interpreting ethnic communities as clearly bounded, enduring, and cohesive biological and cultural groups. In *Nations* (2013), Azar Gat even asserted that political ethnicity and nationalism are rooted in these innate sociobiological dispositions of humankind.[77]

In the cultural realm, the emancipation of the Global South and the rise of postmodernism undermined the hegemonic position of Western high culture, whereas the liberalization of the economy, the fall of Communism, and the quick rise of the internet prompted questions about national rootedness in a globalized world. Instead of debates about the differences between high and low culture, issues related to globalization began to draw the attention. This meant that migrant experiences were often thematized, but in general, national identities were taken for granted and often were even reinforced. That high culture could no longer be equated with the Western tradition became clear in the critical reception of the exhibition *Primitivism in Twentieth-Century Art: Affinity of the Tribal and the Modern* at the Museum of Modern Art in New York City in 1984. The aim was to show how "primitive" tribal art had inspired Western avant-garde artists such as Paul Gauguin and Pablo Picasso, but this implied a hierarchical ordering of the two types of art, which raised the question whether the distinction between ethnographic and artistic exhibits should not be entirely abolished. Five years later, as a kind of response, the Centre Pompidou in Paris organized the *Magicians of the Earth* exhibition and invited more than one hundred contemporary artists to participate, half from the West and half from "the rest." However, non-Western artists were selected primarily as representatives of a foreign (exotic) culture, whereas the Western artists were implicitly presented as representing of a placeless modernity. In subsequent decades, non-Western artists had more opportunities to exhibit in European and North American galleries, but usually their works were selected because they were "authentic" representations of their national backgrounds; rootedness was almost a prerequisite for success. This was the case with the *Indian Highway* exhibition that was mounted in London in 2008 and then went on tour to other European art venues. African artists living in the West also felt inclined to incorporate the "hybridity" of their identity as cosmopolitan Africans in their work.[78]

In more commercial media such as film and music, nationalist influences were more pronounced. In cinema, historical melodramas with a strong nationalist tone became increasingly fashionable. Many of these films portray national heroes defending their fatherlands against foreign aggression; a perfect example is the blockbuster *Braveheart* (1995), about the medieval hero William Wallace who bravely fought the English forces to liberate Scotland. This Hollywood movie provided a strong external stimulus for Scottish nationalism. Most nationalist films were produced for a domestic audience, and Russia under Putin very actively promoted the production of nationalist epics. In 2010 the government overtly subsidized "films of historical, military and patriotic content, developing a sense of pride in one's country," and after the annexation of Crimea, the Ministry of Culture prioritized films on "Crimea and Ukraine in the thousand-year history of the Russian state." Supposedly incorrect depictions of the past were publicly denounced or even banned. In the more commercially oriented Indian film industry, national sentiments were also foregrounded, albeit in a less muscular form. Bollywood films, with their typical songs and dances, increasingly depicted an all-Indian modernity grounded in Hinduism and traditional family values. This also applied to films about the large Indian diaspora, another favorite topic, as demonstrated by *The Brave Hearted Will Take the Bride* (1995), a love story about two second generation Indian immigrants who have to navigate the romantic traditions of both India and the United Kingdom. Certainly, there was a lot of overlap with television productions. Television costume dramas generally presented a nostalgic picture of the past, as in the feel-good series *Downton Abbey* (2010–2015), with its Yorkshire country estates and high tea with scones. Joep Leerssen argues that such celebrations of Englishness and the flurry of films on Great Britain's role in the Second World War ("England's finest hour," according to Churchill) contributed to Brexit.[79]

Internet-based video on demand offers the possibility, in theory, to create a borderless realm for film and television series. Several U.S. companies, including Netflix, aim to become such a global player. Netflix embarked on a global expansion strategy in 2016. Although this has been a success in terms of growing the number of countries where the streaming service is available, the company remains a niche player in many parts of Asia, where subscriptions are limited mainly to cosmopolitan elites. Moreover, copyright issues and government regulations (e.g., imposing quotas to protect the national language and/or media) have resulted in nationally divided catalogs. In order to remedy this, Netflix invested heavily in its own productions, collaborating with production companies throughout the world. However, these productions still tend to reinforce national identities, not just by using national languages and actors, but also through national storylines and settings.[80]

The music industry underwent profound changes during this era. New sound storage media appeared—first cheap audio cassettes, then the compact disc in the 1980s. The rise of music videos, which were popularized particularly through new television channels focused entirely on music such as MTV, increased the costs of launching new artists. The business model of the music industry was further upset by new formats for digital audio, which enabled mass illegal downloads via the internet. In 2005 the introduction of YouTube enabled artists to upload music videos themselves, which could catapult them to instant fame. In this rapidly changing environment, nationalism continued to be expressed through music. In new countries such as Kazakhstan, there was a strong incentive to emphasize the nation's identity both in musical styles and in the accompanying video clips. Thus, many of the country's pop singers and rock bands not only adopted the Kazakh language but also used traditional instruments and typical melodies. Videos often showed a nostalgic image of the national past, with horses, warriors, yurts, and beautiful landscapes, most of it associated with an ancient nomadic lifestyle. Autocratic countries also keenly promoted patriotic music. Although the early 2000s saw a rapid liberalization of the music industry in China, the Communist Party continued to control television networks. State television promoted patriotic songs by presenting annual awards, commemorating important events from the national past, and employing successful artists for the annual Spring Festival Gala. Independent artists, too, willingly adopted patriotic themes in lyrics, music, and videos, although many of them expressed themselves in the global musical idioms of rock or rap.[81]

In democratic countries, nationalizing tendencies were equally prominent. A strong incentive was provided by the Anglo-American domination of the music industry. While new genres from the United States such as hip hop, house, and R&B were rapidly picked up throughout the world, many pop artists began to sing in their own languages and to include national aspects in their productions. In 1993 several record companies challenged MTV's hegemony in the German market by launching Viva, a German music television channel where about 40 percent of the videos were German. Jingoism was avoided because of the tainted memory of the Second World War, but various German artists playfully referred to German national identity in their music. The entertainer Stefan Raab represented Germany at the 1998 Eurovision song contest with a highly ironic song featuring the old-fashioned schlager artist Guildo Horn. A very different reshaping of German national traditions became the signature style of Rammstein, a bombastic heavy-metal band that gained international fame by incorporating ironic references to the Nazi's into its music, lyrics, and stage performance. The internet and the lowering of trade barriers also enabled Korean bands to conquer the world. Since South Korea did not have a very strong independent music scene, when producers decided to enter the market they were focused on exporting their acts. They selected the best local talents, trained them thoroughly, and used experienced composers, stylists, and choreographers to create bands with polished, good-looking singers. By avoiding sex, violence, and deviant behavior and using catchy tunes and simple dance routines, Korean groups such as BTS captured a global audience. Even though K-pop is ultramodern, international, and contains few if any traditional features, it instills pride in South Koreans because it associates their country with creativity and coolness.[82]

Nationalization of the Physical Environment

In the previous era, nationalist elements in the physical environment had been largely downplayed in favor of large-scale modernization projects and functionalist architecture. In the 1970s, nationalism made a strong comeback. Postmodernists such as Aldo Rossi, Roberto Venturi, and Charles Jencks rejected the grand narratives of progress that had led to a placeless uniformity. Many architects responded by favoring fragmentation, variety, and eclecticism to reflect the ambiguity and messiness of reality. Venturi, for instance, advocated a cheerful, decorative architecture, provocatively presenting Las Vegas as a shining example. Charles Moore's Piazza d'Italia in New Orleans became a prototype of postmodern references to the past. The circular piazza was surrounded by a colorful collage of Italian Renaissance architectural fragments and contained a basin with a large map of Italy. Instead of a structurally honest building or a truthful historicist reconstruction, this was a playful recollection of Italian elements in an American city. In the 1980s Kenneth Frampton rejected both the placelessness of modernist architecture and the banal use of arbitrary historical references by postmodernists, calling for a new "critical regionalism." The critic argued that architects should take into consideration the specific characteristics of a location—such as climate, natural light, and topography—when designing buildings and choosing materials. Ecological motives were important as well, due to the oil crisis and rising concerns about resource depletion and environmental pollution. This did not mean that architects should revert to neo-vernacular sentimentalism; modern materials and techniques required modern solutions. Frampton himself praised the sensitive designs of Alvar Aalto, Jørn Utzon, and Alvaro Siza, and his ideas resonated widely, sparking a new interest in national and regional building traditions and natural materials.[83]

At about the same time, city planners promoted a "new urbanism" as an alternative to the monotonous high-rise public-housing projects and the insipid suburban sprawl. The aim was to construct attractive communities with a strong sense of place. This was done by planning densely built neighborhoods with a clear center, narrow pedestrian-oriented streets, good public transportation, and a mix of commercial, residential, and green zones. Several of these new neighborhoods were given contemporary designs in Europe, but most were built in historical or vernacular architectural styles, renationalizing the built environment. One of the earliest examples was Seaside in Florida, which followed the theories of Léon Krier, the main propagandist of traditional European cities and classical architecture. Seaside had a geometric layout, a center with shops and civic buildings, small lots, narrow streets focused on pedestrians, and a shared access to the beach. All buildings were done in a picturesque Southern style, and the commercial development became a popular community with quickly rising real estate prices. Other well-known and somewhat kitschy examples are Celebration, built by the Disney Corporation, near Orlando, Florida, and Poundbury village, in Dorset, England, an initiative of Krier and Prince Charles, who also fervently advocated traditional building styles. Although only a few projects followed all of the prescripts of new urbanism, many of its aspects were widely adopted. Since the 2000s, the strong emphasis on sustainability, environmental protection, and smart growth helped foster these ideas among urban planners and local politicians. As a consequence, regional and national identities were strengthened as many new neighborhoods were given village-like layouts. They projected hominess and mostly were decorated with characteristic details, often by reverting to a quite generic rural or traditional style.[84]

Another development that encouraged the nationalization of the physical environment was city and nation branding. As a consequence of the growing globalization of the economy, cities and countries increasingly emphasized their particular identities in order to attract foreign investments, talent, and tourists. This was done either by constructing conspicuous ultramodern buildings and ensembles or by accentuating traditional elements. Another option was to produce a spectacular design in which modernity and tradition were combined. A first example of a sensational building was the Centre Pompidou in Paris, a large public library and modern art museum that opened its doors in 1977. The ultramodern design by Richard Rogers and Renzo Piano was an inside-out building: all the brightly colored structural elements such as staircases, plumbing, and climate control, were located on the exterior. Although the building vividly contrasted with the historical architecture of the city, it was an instant success and it helped to revitalize the decrepit Beaubourg district, while underlining the city's pretension to be a world leading cultural center.[85]

After the end of the Franco dictatorship in France's southern neighbor, both the Social Democratic government and ambitious local authorities aimed to rebrand Spain as a modern European country. This was particularly visible in the periphery. Barcelona's infrastructure was updated for the 1992 Olympic Games by reconnecting the inner city with the harbor and reconverting a dilapidated industrial area into a fashionable Olympic Village with a port and beach. Spectacular futuristic buildings by star architects, such as a new airport terminal by Ricardo Bofill and a communication tower by Santiago Calatrava, as well as a huge goldfish sculpture by Frank Gehry, boosted Barcelona's reputation as a city of innovative art and design. But the most radical transformation happened in Bilbao, where the run-down industrial zone was redeveloped. Norman Foster was employed to build the subway stations, and Calatrava designed a futuristic bridge. The cherry on the cake was the Guggenheim Museum, an innovative computer-designed building by Frank Gehry with a shining organic form of undulating titanium petals, on the banks of the Nervión. The inauguration of the museum in 1997 made the formerly dull Basque city a trendy tourist destination.[86]

The "Bilbao effect" reinforced the trend to rebrand cities by constructing iconic buildings. Cities, regions, and countries increasingly competed with each other, leading to an avalanche of spectacular buildings, mostly museums but also public offices and corporate buildings, and mostly designed by a select group of international star architects. By also upgrading the surrounding neighborhoods, local authorities hoped to increase the attractiveness of their cities. Various countries also competed to construct the tallest building in the world. In 1998 Malaysia built the 451-meter-high Petronas Towers in Kuala Lumpur, but within a few years it was surpassed by the Taipei 101 and the Shanghai World Financial Center. Most star architects used enigmatic forms and suggestive references that defied unequivocal interpretations, turning spectacular buildings into self-referential icons. However, many of these buildings also subtly referred to historical traditions or even to the natural environment. Thus, the Taipei 101 echoed the tiered buildup of traditional pagodas, and in the Petronas Towers the cross-section was based on the Islamic star and its architect, César Pelli, pointed out that the reflection of the sun created a mixture of deep shadows and dazzling brightness that was reminiscent of the country's tropical forests. In Singapore, architects combined the tall buildings craze with the local garden city tradition. Moshe Shafdie connected the three skyscrapers of the Marina Bay Sands—an ultramodern hotel and convention center—by creating a sky park with hundreds of trees and a panoramic view. Another tall building, the Ecological Design in the Tropics, ingeniously incorporated street life, gardens and green façades using only indigenous plants in a twenty-six-story building.[87]

The most striking example of international city-branding through iconic projects could be found in Dubai, the capital of one of the United Arab Emirates. In order to make the economy less dependent on oil, the ruling Al Maktoum dynasty decided to turn Dubai into a major service center and tourist hub. The first step was the founding of the Emirates airline in 1985, which was quickly followed by the Dubai Shopping Festival and the Burj Al Arab, the world's first seven-star hotel. This tallest hotel in the world was built on a small island and was loosely modeled on the traditional dhow (figure 8.1). Like other ambitious local and national governments of the time, the emirate adopted a neoliberal entrepreneurial model, based on cheap migrant labor and iconic buildings that appealed to well-to-do consumers. In the early 2000s, the artificial Palm Islands were developed to attract the world's rich and famous to Dubai, providing them with a beautiful location for a beach villa in a secure environment. The city also built several ultramodern, air-conditioned shopping malls, one of which was named after the famous fourteenth-century traveler Ibn Battuta, with different sections styled after areas that he had visited, thus providing an overview of the stereotypical architectural highlights of most of the Islamic world. The branding of Dubai as a glamorous destination culminated in the opening of the Burj Khalifa in 2010, the tallest building of the

FIGURE 8.1 Tom Wright, *Burj Al Arab Hotel*, 1999, Dubai. Neoliberal globalization encouraged international competition for talents, tourists, and investments. The United Arab Emirates were very active in this, constructing several iconic buildings designed by international star architects. A good example is this extremely luxurious hotel, which at the time was the tallest in the world. It is a slick, futuristic building, loosely modeled on a traditional dhow.

world at the time. Adrian Smith's design incorporated various references to the Islamic architecture of the area, while the base of the astonishing 828-meter-high tower was inspired by a typical desert flower.[88]

Similar tendencies could be found in new countries, which often refurbished their capital cities. This implied a conscious reformulation of the country's collective identity, which usually was presented as both modern and rooted in tradition. An effusive example was Skopje, the capital of North Macedonia. In 2010 the right-wing government decided to transform the inner city with about twenty new buildings and dozens of new monuments and statues. The goal was to give Skopje a more antique and European look and to reclaim the heritage of ancient Macedonia. Thus, a thirty-three-meter-high statue of Alexander the Great was erected in the central Macedonia Square. As Alexander's legacy was also claimed by Greece—which had fiercely opposed the country's decision to name itself Macedonia—the statue officially was named "Warrior." The new buildings in the city center were executed in a mixture of updated European architectural styles such as Renaissance, baroque, and neoclassic, which all referred to classical antiquity and which, in

fact, had almost no connection to the country's strong Byzantine and Ottoman heritage. Dozens of other buildings received new exuberant façades, effectively erasing the memory of Communist Yugoslavia.[89]

In Berlin, the capital of a reunified Germany, local authorities also aimed
to break with the Communist past by removing almost all vestiges of the Berlin Wall, demolishing the Palace of the Republic, and filling in the open spaces
that had been used for parades. Star architect Norman Foster crowned the
Reichstag with a marvelous glass dome, but the suggestion to use the opportunity to turn Berlin's inner city into an exuberant postmodern fairytale was
rejected. The goal was to create a "European city" with small plots, pedestrian-
friendly streets, and historical buildings. This could best be done by returning
to Berlin's historic tradition, which essentially meant the long nineteenth
century. In a long, tedious process, the historic street plan was largely restored.
Architects were encouraged to use natural building materials such as brick and
stone and restrained, classic forms. After much debate, the former Royal
Palace—which had been demolished after the Second World War—was faithfully reconstructed with one modern façade. This building in the heart of the
old city did not openly glorify the Prussian or German past; instead, it became
the Humboldt Forum, a cosmopolitan cultural center that also exhibited Berlin's ethnographic and Asian art collections.[90]

The construction of a new capital offered even better opportunities to rebrand a country's image. New capitals were constructed in Kazakhstan, Malaysia, and Myanmar, and projects are underway in Egypt and Indonesia. One of
the objectives was to locate the capital in the center of the country, but there was
also a clear wish to create an ordered environment away from the overcrowded
old capital city, with its unruly masses, eternal traffic jams, and pollution. An
additional goal was to break with the recent colonial past while providing a new,
closely circumscribed interpretation of the nation's collective identity. Most of
these new capitals were the pet projects of authoritarian rulers who presented
themselves as benevolent, modernizing statesmen. In Malaysia, the development of a new administrative capital, Putrajaya, was driven mostly by domestic
concerns. In 1995 the prime minister, Mahathir Mohamad, who would remain
in office for more than two decades, started the project, which was meant to
demonstrate that Malaysia was an efficient, modern country. Mahathir also
aimed to show that the country could successfully accomplish such a mega-
project, and unlike what had happened with the Petronas Towers, all the work
was done exclusively by domestic firms. The main civic buildings, including
the Prime Minister's Office (figure 8.2), were clustered along a monumental
central axis, while an artificial lake and parks should provide a healthy environment. Surprisingly, the architectural designs were not inspired by national
building traditions, but instead had an updated, eclectic Islamic style with

FIGURE 8.2 Ahmad Rozi Abd Wahab, *Perdana Putra*, 1999, Putrajaya. Various new capital cities were built around 2000. The aim was to redefine the country's national identity by constructing a tidy and monumental capital in the heart of the country. Most official buildings in Malaysia's new capital, such as the Prime Minister's Office, were built in an eclectic Islamic style, with oriental domes and arches.

lavishly decorated domes and arches. The inspiration was drawn from Islamic monuments from Moorish Spain to Northern India, presenting Malaysia as modern, cosmopolitan Muslim country. This was in line with the government's policy to favor the indigenous, largely Muslim Malays while at the same time undercutting the fundamentalist Islamic opposition.[91]

The transfer of Myanmar's capital from Yangon to Naypyidaw followed similar lines. In 2005, the military strongman Than Shwe decided to construct a new capital in the Upper Burmese heartland of the country, which was strategically located to combat secessionist movements in the periphery. The city's layout was grandiose, with broad avenues in a well-manicured, parklike landscape. Most of the low-rise buildings were executed in an austere, modern style. However, all symbolic elements referred to the Buddhist traditions of the majority Bamar ethnic group. The town hall and the gigantic parliamentary buildings all have traditional tiered roofs, the military parade ground is decorated with three imposing statues of Burmese warrior kings, and the most impressive landmark of the city is the gilded Uppatasanti Pagoda, a copy of the country's most famous Buddhist temple.[92]

The 1997 decision by Kazakhstan's first president, Nursultan Nazarbayev, to relocate the capital from Almaty to the more centrally located Astana was also strategic, as he hoped it would restore the ethnic balance in an area with a large Russian population. The president also aimed to boost the international reputation of Kazakhstan, which he presented as linking East and West. Thus, Nazarbayev employed international star architects such as Kisho Kurokawa, who designed a monumental city plan with broad avenues. Most signature buildings were done in a "Eurasian" style, mixing ultramodern glass façades with colorful Eastern domes. In order to underline the Kazakh character of the city, some national elements were added too, such as the Baytarak Tower (2002), symbolizing a mythical tree of life, and Norman Foster's Khan Shatyr Entertainment Center (2006), which consisted of a gigantic yurt construction with a 150-meter spire.[93] Nazarbayev's international ambitions became clear when his new capital hosted Expo 2017 and in 2007 when the National Welfare Fund sponsored an Astana bicycle team that still participates in the world's major cycling contests.

In response to the globalization of the economy, positive associations with a country of origin were also increasingly used for marketing purposes by commercial companies. A good example is the Swedish furniture producer Ikea. In 1958 Ingvar Kamprad opened a furniture store in his native region of Småland and found success with his cheap, flat-packed products that had to be transported and assembled at home by the customer. In the 1970s Ikea expanded to dozens of countries, and instead of promoting itself as functionalist, it presented itself as quintessentially Swedish. This was done by appealing both to modern, democratic principles, and to the artisanal and rural values of Småland. The company explicitly appealed to the social democratic values of the Swedish welfare state by producing simple, well-designed products that were affordable for everyone—in essence, bringing a beautiful home within reach of the masses. The practical and light furniture—mostly made with Nordic timber variants such as birch and pine—was designed according to functionalist "Scandinavian" principles. The names of the products—with recognizable Nordic diacritical marks—were left untranslated. The company's logo, stores, uniforms, and bags were even more explicitly nationalist as they displayed the colors of the Swedish flag. In addition, Ikea's home region provided the traditional dishes and products that were sold in the stores' restaurants and food shops.[94]

The branding of culinary practices and food items as belonging to a specific area also increased substantially from the final decades of the twentieth century. Ethnic foods became widely available in supermarkets, not just in specialized shops. A broad variety of ethnic restaurants could now be found in any major city in the world. Catering services regularly put geographical labels on their products—such as French onion soup, Moroccan tagine, and Greek-style lamb—in order to diversify their menus with supposedly "authentic" dishes. Several governments even turned to active "gastrodiplomacy" to boost the presence of their national cuisine abroad. Probably the most successful of these initiatives was the 2002 Global Thai program, which aimed to substantially increase the number of Thai restaurants around the world by providing loans, training for cooks, and standardized dishes. Restaurants were encouraged to obtain the Thai Select label, which meant that not only the food but also the décor, music, and staff uniforms presented an appealing—and homogenized—image of the country. The European Union, too, was very active in protecting local, regional, or national products like French champagne, Irish whiskey, and Greek feta by awarding special labels, such as protected designation of origin. In order to protect food security, now even very ordinary food items such as oranges and coffee, have a country-of-origin label and thus are nationalized. This trend to root food products in the terroir and value local or regional traditions only increased as ecological concerns led to a new emphasis on home cooking, local produce, unprocessed foods, and artisanal production processes.[95]

The rising demand for organic food was accompanied by a growing rejection of the ruthless exploitation of nature, in favor of a new interest in biological farming, environmental protection, and nature preservation. However, preservation often implied restoring nature to a supposedly pristine state, before the arrival of European settlers, as happened in New Zealand. Untouched and visually appealing landscapes were seen as more worthy of preserving, implicitly strengthening a country's unique identity. In 1993, the United Nations also became active in this field by adopting the Convention on Biological Diversity. The signatories promised to protect their endangered habitats and ecosystems in order to conserve the earth's biodiversity. "Alien" or "non-native" species— especially those that threatened the interests of agriculture or forestry—were combatted. In fact, "invasion biology" became a major field of research, and scholars often advocated the "extermination" of "alien" or "exotic" species that threatened the equilibrium of "native" ecosystems, which often coincided with the boundaries of the nation-state. Some far-right parties in Europe even claimed that only native inhabitants really cared for the nation's natural treasures. They frequently characterized immigrants as causing overpopulation, building illegal settlements in green spaces, littering the landscape, being cruel to animals—ritual slaughter was particularly attacked as a barbarous practice—and harming protected species.[96]

Not just the natural patrimony of the nation had to be preserved; the same was true of its cultural heritage. A crucial step in the nationalization of spaces, buildings, and objects was the adoption of UNESCO's World Heritage List in

1975. Sixteen years before, the Egyptian government had requested UNES-CO's help to save the monuments of the ancient Nubian civilization that was under threat from the building of the hydroelectric Aswan Dam. The subsequent international campaign salvaged about twenty ancient temple complexes by tacitly converting them into patrimony of humanity. Encouraged by this success, UNESCO decided to create a list of both natural and cultural world heritage sites. As a consequence of the decolonization process and a new, more critical view on Eurocentrism, UNESCO tried to do justice to the world's broad cultural diversity. Among the earliest sites were the ruins of Palmyra, the Taj Mahal, the old city of Dubrovnik, the Galapagos Islands, and the Grand Canyon National Park. Inclusion meant that a site received legal protection, that funds were available for conservation purposes, and that more visitors could be expected. However, because UNESCO was an international organization, only member states could nominate heritage sites. This meant that ethnic minorities or regional governments had no voice, and that transnational sites were only very rarely included on the list. Thus, by turning local or regional gems into national patrimony validated by the international community, the World Heritage List in fact supports both the nation-branding and the nation-building processes of its member states.[97]

In 2003 UNESCO decided to also include intangible cultural heritage. The original list had been criticized for adopting a static, object-based, Western view of heritage, focusing only on historical monuments and artistic treasures. Australian activists argued that the existing criteria excluded the cultural legacy of the Aboriginals. Others worried about Marrakesh's Jemaa-el-Fna square, arguing that it was not so much the buildings that were in need of protection, but the traditional practices performed by storytellers, snake charmers, dancers, and others. As a result, oral traditions, performing arts, social practices, and traditional crafts that had been transmitted "from generation to generation" were now deemed worthy of international protection as well. But again, as with the original list, examples of intangible heritage had to be nominated by member states. The most extraordinary traditions, particularly those that were spectacular and colorful, had the best chances of being included. In the culinary field, these included the gastronomic meal of the French, traditional Mexican cuisine, and Turkish coffee culture. Local and transnational traditions were "nationalized" in the process. Although UNESCO encouraged countries to nominate shared intangible heritages—such as skills related to the cultivation of date palms, which were claimed by fourteen countries—some governments clashed over ownership of specific traditions. Azerbaijan, for instance, contested Armenia's proposal to include their bard tradition and their typical flatbread in the list, arguing that these also existed in their territory. In the end, a compromise was reached for flatbread by defining its preparation "as an expression of culture in Armenia." One of Italy's entries on the list was the Festival of the Lilies, celebrated in the Southern Italian city of Nola. Although similar processions of huge papier-mâché lilies were also organized in neighboring towns and by Italian immigrant communities in the United States, only the "original" festivity has become part of the nation's cultural heritage and is now protected by UNESCO.[98]

With the growing status of heritage, the question of ownership led to heated debates that had a variety of outcomes. Indigenous peoples in the Americas, South Africa, Australia, and New Zealand began reclaiming sacred objects that had ended up in numerous museum collections around the world. An important turning point was the United States' adoption of the Native American Graves Protection and Repatriation Act of 1990, which stipulated that even objects that had been acquired legally had to be returned and that no requirements for their later use or preservation could be made. In most cases, however, only officially recognized Indigenous communities could reclaim objects. "Urban people" were often ignored, as they lacked a direct "historical connection" or an unbroken commitment to their ancestral traditions. This meant that implicitly, Indigenous communities were "ossified" in a static past.[99]

Valuable objects seized by the Nazis and by imperial Japan received renewed attention as well. After the Second World War they had been returned to the national authorities of the formerly occupied territories, and most of them ended up in public museums. However, in Europe, many of these objects had belonged to Jews, who began to reclaim their rightful property. In 1998, over forty countries subscribed to the Washington Conference Principles on Nazi-Confiscated Art. Artistic objects looted by the Nazis did not belong to the nation, but had to be returned to the individual owners or their heirs. The growing interest in the "repatriation" of indigenous artefacts and looted art inspired many countries to repeat earlier requests to restitute colonial art, such as Nigeria's Benin Bronzes. In 2017, French president Emmanuel Macron announced a new generous restitution policy during his state visit to Burkina Faso. This was a game changer, as Germany, the Netherlands, and Belgium quickly made similar promises to return looted art from the colonies. Nonetheless, one of the vital issues that remains to be solved is to whom these objects should be returned. Do they belong to the colonial successor states, to traditional kingdoms and sultanates from which they were taken, to local communities, or to the individual owners and their heirs? As public museums and state authorities tend to favor national interlocutors, the colonial successor states seem to be in the best position to become the new owners, which is in marked contrast with current practices concerning artistic objects confiscated by the Nazis in Europe.[100]

It was not just "real" heritage that received more attention in this period. As a consequence of the new "experience economy," myriad "fake" national environments were created in consumer and tourist spaces, including the best-known example, the Strip in Las Vegas. However, banal displays of a world divided into discrete nation-states, each with their own unique identities, could be found around the globe. A fascinating mix of new urbanism and postmodern "theming" could be found in Shanghai, where in the first decade of the twenty-first century nine thematic suburbs were planned, each modeled on the typical architecture of a Western country; thus, Thames Town included Tudor and Victorian villas, a neo-Gothic church, a fake castle, an English pub, and statues of Churchill and Princess Diana. Shopping malls also introduced themed sections referring to iconic places from both the past and the present. The exuberant Trafford Centre in Manchester has sections related to the United States, China, and ancient Rome, while the Festival Village resembles a traditional English market. Mega-hotels have adopted themes as well. In the Turkish beach resort Antalya, the Topkapi Palace Hotel—mimicking the Ottoman sultan's dwellings in Istanbul—inaugurated a whole series of theme hotels, such as the Venezia and Kremlin Palace Hotels (figure 8.3); the Orange County Resort Hotel was modeled after Amsterdam's rich architectural heritage and included kitschy references to the Dutch fishing village of Volendam.[101]

Attracting tourists and day trippers was a primary motive in such theming initiatives. Tourism was one of the fastest-growing sectors of the global economy. The dropping of the Iron Curtain opened up new markets. More people could afford to go on vacation, and growing car ownership, low-cost airlines, and high-speed trains made travel easier. As a result, the number of international arrivals increased fourfold between 1980 and 2013, encouraging the creation of new heritage sites. In the late 1980s, the United Kingdom, an established tourist destination, had 1,750 museums, whereas the United States had 37,000 registered historic places, and these numbers have only increased since then. The rising numbers of travelers also meant that myriad tourist spaces around the world, including bars, restaurants, hotels, vacation homes, urban districts, and souvenir shops were decorated in typical styles. New types of tourism developed as well. Many old coal mines, industrial plants, and dockyards were converted into industrial heritage sites, and Germany even created the Industrial Heritage Route in the Ruhr area. Dark tourism was no longer confined to the concentration camps of the Second World War; it included new iconic sites such as Robben Island in South Africa and Ground Zero in New York. Roots tourism expanded beyond Western Europe and came to include many parts of the world, such as West African countries, which primarily targeted descendants of slaves from the United States, thus emphasizing very particular aspects of a nation's patrimony.[102]

Tourism also affected the people working in the sector. Many of them had to put on folkloric dresses, while others performed traditional activities for an audience of tourists. Flamenco shows could be found in most Spanish beach

FIGURE 8.3 *The Kremlin Palace Hotel*, 2002, Antalya. Theme hotels became very popular, and this is a great example from a Turkish beach resort. The hotel offers tourists the opportunity to sleep in the ancient residence of the Russian tsars, and a replica of the Saint Basil's Cathedral overlooks the swimming pool.

resorts, while belly dances were performed in many Egyptian hotels. Artisans such as glassblowers in Murano, Mexican potters in Tonalá, and wood-carvers in Bali opened their workshops to tourists. Many survived only by adapting their wares to the demands of this new international clientele. Indigenous people also realized that their "exoticness" could be sold to foreign visitors. In

Mali, for instance, the Dogon adapted their funeral rites—which included dances, mock battles, and beautiful masks—to a new audience.[103] There were also more regulated spaces, such as historical theme parks. In France, the Puy du Fou theme park is based on the history of the Vendée region, while in South Korea, the Yongin Daejanggeum Park was developed from a film set into a theme park, with villages and buildings from various of the country's historic kingdoms.

Several territories affiliated themselves with a mythical (national) hero in order to attract visitors. Nottinghamshire in England introduced a Robin Hood itinerary that leads visitors to various places associated with the legendary outlaw. Romania associated itself with a fictional vampire, Count Dracula, and there are various castles that claim to be the original residence of Bram Stoker's character. Visitors can also experience famous film locations by themselves. Many people walk around New York looking for the places seen in U.S. television series such as *Friends* and *Sex and the City*. The Visit Britain website has a list of famous films with links to the actual locations where crucial scenes were shot; the Harry Potter films top the list. But one can also experience typical activities by doing them yourself. In Buenos Aires there are various schools that offer tango lessons to visitors, and in northern Finland one can take a reindeer sleigh ride. Tourists can also immerse themselves in various iconic historical periods. The Viking Ship Museum in Roskilde, Denmark, offers the chance to step on board a reconstructed historical ship while clad as a Viking. Historical reenactments became increasingly popular, too. They tend to focus on the most salient parts of the (national) past. The Swedish town of Visby organizes an annual medieval week, and in 1998, the 135th anniversary of the U.S. Civil War battle at Gettysburg was commemorated with a huge reenactment with tens of thousands of participants.[104]

Another way to attract visitors and put a country on the map, was to organize a mega-event. World's fairs had been the most important mega-event until the 1930s, but that role was taken over by the Olympic Games and FIFA World Cups. Radio and television brought these tournaments directly into the homes of hundreds of millions of people around the globe. Since they bring large audiences together, even in the current fragmented media landscape, their importance has only increased. Moreover, they generally spread positive vibes and therefore are excellent occasions for enhancing a country's reputation or soft power. Although many of these mega-events continued to be organized in major Western countries, emerging powers like Brazil, China, and Russia have become particularly active as hosts. There were also a few newcomers, such as South Africa and Qatar, which organized the football World Cups of 2010 and 2022, respectively. A similar globalization of sports can be detected in the Formula I Championship, with new races in China, Malaysia,

Singapore, Russia, Azerbaijan, Abu Dhabi, Saudi Arabia, and Qatar. For many of these events, spectacular buildings were erected. For the Beijing Summer Olympics, star architect Rem Koolhaas designed the new headquarters of China Central Television, whereas the iconic Bird's Nest Stadium was the result of a collaboration between Ai Weiwei and Herzog & de Meuron.[105]

Attracting the attention of the world by organizing such a mega-event, could also put a spotlight on negative aspects such as crime, pollution, exploitation of migrant workers, and human right abuses, which could damage a host country's reputation. But there were other methods to boost a country's prestige, such as organizing state support for national top athletes, thus increasing the chances of scoring major victories, a practice that was already widespread during the Cold War. A more subtle option, which was used mostly by rich oil-producing countries, was to create a positive brand by sponsoring a famous club or team, especially a football team. Azerbaijan sponsored Atlético de Madrid, promoting itself with a "Land of Fire" shirt logo. More effective were several Gulf states that used their national airlines as sponsor vehicles and targeted top-tier teams. Dubai's Emirates airline supported, among others, Real Madrid, Arsenal, and AC Milan. The neighboring emirate of Abu Dhabi acquired Manchester City and promoted Etihad Airways on the club's jerseys. Qatar Sports Investments bought Paris Saint-Germain, while Saudi Arabia acquired Newcastle United. Many of these clubs pay astronomical salaries for major international stars, increasing their chances to win the national league or the European Champions League. Although occasionally these moves are criticized as "sportswashing," many of the millions of global followers of these clubs now associate these countries with their favorite squads.[106]

Sporting events also brought people together in a less cynical way. After abolishing apartheid, South Africa organized the 1995 Rugby World Cup, which turned out to be a moment of festive reconciliation. The national "Springboks" team, which still consisted primarily of whites, was supported almost unanimously, and after the final victory of South Africa, President Nelson Mandela, wearing a Springbok jersey, handed the cup to the team captain. Three years later, the victory of the French national team in the FIFA World Cup, hosted by France itself, led to a similar outburst of euphoria, particularly because the players were a faithful representation of the country's diversity, including all major immigrant communities. Sometimes, international federations lent a helping hand. FIFA obliged Japan and South Korea, who both wanted to host the World Cup of 2002, to organize the tournament together. This worked out very well and brought closer together the two neighbors with a complicated history of conquest and colonization. Both national teams performed better than expected, leading to ecstatic outbursts of "feel-good nationalism." This was quite new in Japan, which bore the burden of the Second

World War, but the cheerful atmosphere pierced the image of the Japanese as being very reserved. Something similar happened with the World Cup in Germany four years later. Not only did the German public throw off its generally restrained attitude by embracing a new, openly expressed "feel-good nationalism," but the national team also adopted an "un-German" creative and attractive playing style. In the host cities, fans from all over the world fraternized in a playful celebration of the "greatest show on earth."[107]

Sports and the way it related to national identities also changed profoundly in the neoliberal era, and this was particularly true for football. The rise of commercial television, the new freedom of movement of players, and the growing role of marketing turned football into big business. In order to increase safety, football stadiums with free-standing terraces—which had been the preserve of working-class fans—were turned into fully seated theaters. Stadiums were upgraded and became more woman- and family-friendly, and as a result, male hooliganism became marginal. Scholars began to speak of "post-fandom," as supporters increasingly are dispersed around the globe and follow specific celebrity players. Fandom has become a fluid and highly commodified activity, with replica shirts as its primary badge. Support for national teams, especially at major tournaments, also became an almost postmodern, playful happening. In the 1970s football fans wore national scarves and waved flags, but in the 1980s supporters began to dress up for the game, putting on the national jersey or typical garments such as a Scottish kilt. Major tournaments became festive, carnivalesque occasions where attendees wore fanciful outfits based on national stereotypes. Still, most fans acquired merchandised items in the national colors, making them an individualist consumer choice for one evening and creating what Zygmunt Bauman has called "cloakroom communities"—a synchronized, highly emotive but temporary experience.[108] These festive expressions of "feel-good nationalism" occur at other international competitions such as the Olympic Games and the Davis Cup in tennis, and they now are increasingly seen at women's sports tournaments as well.

Not only the physical environment but also cyberspace was nationalized. Although national borders do not matter in most online games, some video games clearly reproduce both national stereotypes and a self-evident division of the world into nation-states, each with its own unique characteristics. This is the case with the historical video game *Civilization*. Most civilizations in the game are actual nation-states, although ancient empires such as Babylon and Rome are also included. Nevertheless, each "civilization" is designed according to the nation-state model, with a distinct homogenous identity and clear borders, and it operates in an international environment of similar states. The player chooses a civilization and guides its development through six thousand years of history, but each civilization has certain characteristics that predetermine the optimal playing strategy. Each has a starting bias, meaning that it is adapted to a specific terrain, of which it takes advantage. Players can get bonuses adapted to their civilization; thus, Russia's Cossacks constitute a strong cavalry, while English ships of line are faster than other vessels. The output also depends on a country's characteristics, so only Morocco can build a kasbah, which protects it against foreign invaders. As a consequence, participants are strongly encouraged to play according to the "intrinsic nature" of their chosen civilization, which implicitly interiorizes an international order consisting of discrete nation-states.[109]

Nationalism is also omnipresent in content-based social media such as Facebook, YouTube, and X. Even on a visually oriented social medium such as Instagram, references to a person's territorial identity abound. Investigators found that in a large set of randomly collected selfies, more than 12 percent contained a tag that referred to an ethnic or national identity. Moreover, about 7 percent of the selfies could be related to travel, and most showed the user in a clearly recognizable location such as the Rialto Bridge in Venice, thus presenting the globe as a world of nation-states, each with its own natural and cultural highlights. These images of iconic monuments, landscapes, and events not only attract viewers, they also inspire others to put them on their bucket lists. By using geotags, images can easily be linked to specific locations, whereas comments tend to be seen as trusted recommendations. In this way, Instagram reinforces the already existing focus on stereotypical national highlights.[110] Nonetheless, most images on Instagram represent everyday spaces. These pictures often provide a familiar, homey feeling, which is enhanced as users generally portray themselves as immersed in the scene, or if photographed from afar, they tend to act as a kind of personal narrator telling a story to intimate friends. The emphasis on home often is accompanied by implicit or explicit references to a hometown, native land, or nation. Migrants in a very similar way fashion their identity around their original nationality, presenting themselves as, for instance, a "Scottish girl in London," or writing extensive blogs when visiting the "homeland."[111]

Social media do not just reinforce national frameworks, they also tend to encourage nationalist feelings. This was already visible in other commercial media. Radio and television companies generally pay more attention to national news, national showbiz celebrities, and national heroes than public broadcasters do. To encourage the audience to stay tuned, they tend to simplify problems, dramatize conflicts, appeal to emotions, focus on spectacular events, and employ a subjective tone. This is even more the case with digital media. Clickbait, dramatic images, and hyperbolic language are used to draw visitors. Extreme views tend to get more attention, and without the gatekeeper function of the traditional media, many internet forums have become havens for hotheaded nationalism, xenophobia, and racism. Emotions and individual expression have replaced rational arguments and the public interest. Over the last few decades, intolerant attitudes seem to have become more common, both on the left, where many argue that only those who suffer certain injustices themselves can speak out for "their community," and on the right, where nativism, ethnonationalism, racism, and misogyny have become widespread. This tendency is strengthened by the fact that social media creates "filter bubbles" or "echo chambers" in which users are constantly fed with (fake) news and opinions that confirm their views. Instead of becoming a harmonious global village, cyberspace has become crowded with national hatred and xenophobia.[112] As a result, the existence of groups, such as ethnic communities and clearly bounded nations, is very much taken for granted and individuals are expected to be loyal to their "own" group.

Conclusion

Nationalism has been on the rise since the late 1970s. Neoliberalism and identity politics often went hand in hand, and both put a greater emphasis on ethnicity, culture, and religion. This could have strong polarizing effects. After 1989, the formerly Communist states of Yugoslavia, Czechoslovakia, and the Soviet Union fell apart. They were federal states that under Communism had already been organized along ethnic lines, but like what happened almost everywhere else, ethnic boundaries did not fully coincide with existing territorial divisions. In some cases, this led to violent ethnic conflicts, mostly between closely related communities. Nonetheless, in the end, existing internal borders determined the shape of the new independent republics. Liberalization and democratization also led to the secessions of Eritrea, East Timor, and South Sudan. But these cases were really exceptional, and like had happened during the decolonization process, the international community ensured that existing administrative boundaries were used to create new nation-states.

As neoliberal formulas were embraced around the globe, identity issues replaced the economy and modernization as the main topics for political debates. Although the leverage of citizens diminished substantially during this period, existing processes of emancipation and democratization deepened and affected more people, such as women, Indigenous communities, and other minority groups. Devolution had already begun in the 1970s, and was encouraged both to combat economic backwardness and to protect regions with a distinct identity, such as Quebec, Flanders, Catalonia, Wales, and Scotland. In Latin America, many Indigenous communities received some form of political autonomy. Measures were also taken, especially in Europe and the Americas, to improve the rights of members of the LGBTQ+ community. However, in recent years a distinct backlash can be detected as many authoritarian regimes and right-wing populists have launched a counteroffensive appealing to the supposedly threatened collective identity of the majority group, to conservative family values, and to religious beliefs. Political polarization and chauvinist attitudes, moreover, were facilitated by the rise of commercial television, talk radio, and above all, social media.

Nationalism seems to be on the rise, and not just in public discourse, commercial media, and internet forums, but also in cultural domains such as movies, in the field of heritage, and in the physical appearance of new capitals and many suburban neighborhoods. But there are also trends that oppose this tendency to essentialize national identities. Most scholars no longer see nation-states and national cultures as unique and isolated entities, but rather as social constructs with porous borders that are embedded within social and cultural networks that span the globe. Moreover, a postmodern, playful attitude toward national identities has become ubiquitous in nation-branding, in sports events, and in the tourism sector. Nation-states compete against each other with iconic buildings with some vague references to the nation's cultural or natural heritage, while people dress up in fanciful costumes that good-naturedly reference national stereotypes during international matches. In addition, they happily spend their leisure time in theme hotels, ethnic restaurants, and traditional bars, where national identities are performed for money. The question now is whether this playfulness actually implies ironic detachment, or whether this helps naturalize national identities.

Conclusion

THE MANY FACES OF NATIONALISM

THE RISE OF nationalism was not a linear story leading to the final victory of the nation-state. There were many twists and turns, and the natures of both nation-states and nationalism changed profoundly over time. Although no story can do justice to the sheer variety of experiences and developments around the globe, several distinct patterns can be detected. Here I will present some general reflections, then outline the most important findings for each of the topics that have been examined in this book: first, the rise of new nation-states; next, the evolution of citizenship; and last, the nationalization of the cultural sphere and the physical realm, which will be discussed together because they were heavily influenced by the same intellectual trends. Finally, I will briefly reflect on what the future might bring.

General Reflections

At first glance, *Nationalism: A World History* clearly aligns with the dominant modernist approach. Nation-states and nationalism came into existence only in the late eighteenth century, and their diffusion is related to modernization processes such as state-building, economic progress, and isomorphic processes, in both the political and the cultural realms. However, this was not a linear process. In fact, it looked more like a random zigzag course. The major turning points were defined primarily by shifts in mentality after the shattering of collective dreams, such as the disillusionment with the French Revolution around 1815, with Romantic nationalism in 1848, with positivist optimism around 1885, with racial ideas in 1945, and with technocratic development policies around 1979. The question now is, when will the frustration with neoliberalism and identity politics definitively set in, and where will the world be heading next?

Capitalism—a crucial ingredient of modernity—seems to have a deep but variegated bond with nationalism, in terms of both nation-states and national identity construction. In the early modern era, print capitalism helped to standardize national languages, while commercial actors were crucial to creating a national cultural sphere for an audience of anonymous consumers. Nation-states and modernizing empires encouraged capitalism—especially in the countryside—so that taxes could be raised to strengthen the state.[1] Moreover, the nation sells well. Food items, tourist experiences, and even many industrial products are marketed by associating them with a country of origin, while commercial mass media such as newspapers, international exhibitions, cinema, talk radio, private television channels, and social media not only present a world divided into discrete nation-states as self-evident, but also openly encourage nationalist feelings.

Another fascinating issue is the relationship between nationalism and religion. Religious cleavages were instrumentalized several times to create new nation-states, as in the Balkans and on the Indian subcontinent. Since the 1970s, religions have acquired a more prominent political role. Although religions easily transcend national boundaries, in most cases, politically active religious movements operate within the framework of existing states. This is the case with most forms of political Islam for instance. The notorious exception is Daesh, but it is unlikely that its radical and utterly violent, borderless religious dictatorship will serve as an attractive alternative in the future.[2] Outside of the Islamic world, the religious revival seems to strengthen the existing international order. Many authoritarian regimes and right-wing populists appeal to religious values to reinforce their legitimacy, which is the case with, for example, Hindu nationalists in India, Myanmar's military regime and Buddhism, Putin's Russia and the Orthodox Church, the Polish Law and Justice Party and Catholicism, and Donald Trump's alliance with evangelicals. Even Communist China increasingly propagates traditional Confucian ideas. As Rogers Brubaker has made clear, it seems that language has lost some of its mobilizing potential in favor of religion.[3]

Another conclusion that can be drawn is that nationalism was much more connected to the state than to ethnic or cultural communities. Because of their institutions, legal frameworks, taxation, armies, and borders, states have more leverage and fixity than ethnic or cultural communities. This can be detected both in the creation and evolution of nation-states and in the construction of national identities. All nation-states engaged in nation-building activities, whether explicitly through education and national holidays, or implicitly by creating a national public sphere. Most new nation-states adopted existing (internal) borders, and only in very rare cases were the latter redrawn according to ethnic or linguistic criteria. In the scholarly realm, most scientists took existing nation-states as their main unit of analysis, while both high and popular culture tended to take for granted the existing international order. The nation-state also was the main driver of the nationalization of the physical realm, often functioning as an assumed framework in, for instance, heritage preservation and the construction of "ethnic foods" (a clear misnomer).

A crucial lesson that we might draw from *Nationalism: A World History* is that we should not take for granted the nation, the nation-state, and nationalism. They are not natural phenomena, but the products of history. Nonetheless, in everyday life, nations and nation-states are often naturalized. Maps, for instance, are simplifications, and by giving countries their own colors, they efface internal differences while assuming that every country is fundamentally different from its neighbors. Terms like "the people" or "the nation"—except in certain legal contexts—are similarly simplifications, aside from the frequent but incorrect use of "nation" as a synonym for "state" or "country." By designating the inhabitants of a country as the "people," the "French," or the "Mexicans," we imply that that they form one homogenous national community, with one culture and language, and we erase the complex patchwork of Indigenous groups, ethnic minorities, immigrant populations, and "mixed offspring," while at the same time assuming fundamental differences with neighboring areas across the border. So we should be careful when using this terminology. In addition, we should be aware of the dangers of methodological, terminological, and normative nationalism: we should not presume that the nation-state or national society is the natural unit of analysis; we should be careful when using concepts that apply to only one particular national case and assume that it is unique; and we should not understand the nation-state as the logical final stage of human history and automatically condemn all other forms of statehood as outdated anomalies.

The Rise of New Nation-States

There are also more detailed findings that are worth mentioning. The analysis of the rise and evolution of the nation-state has shown that three major phases can be distinguished: the invention of the nation-state during the age of revolutions, the dissemination of the nation-state model during the nineteenth and early twentieth centuries, and its hegemony from the 1960s onward.

The nation-state did not appear out of thin air. Even though vague national identities of the *ethnos* type already existed before the end of the eighteenth century, they did not play a major role in the creation of new nation-states during the age of revolutions, which were based on the community of citizens, or *demos*. The rise of a secular worldview and the quick expansion of literacy thanks to the printing press were important developments that undermined existing social hierarchies, the sacred nature of ancient texts, and monarchical authority. Traditional state models were further eroded by the growing popularity of new Enlightenment ideas on liberty and equality. Another crucial prerequisite was the state-building process during the seventeenth and eighteenth centuries that was driven by the need to finance ever more costly wars. Fiscal crises and subsequent attempts to contest existing privileges and tax exemptions triggered both the American and the French Revolutions, which led to the invention of the nation-state; thus, it was primarily the product of a conflict over political legitimacy. Consequently, the new revolutionary authorities adopted a written constitution based on the sovereignty of the nation and the equality of all citizens before the law.

The nation-state quickly proved to be a success. By abolishing feudal privileges and treating inhabitants as citizens, nation-states could tap more resources than traditional states and build stronger conscripted armies. The nation-state and its rule of law also provided a fertile framework for economic growth. As a consequence, the new model for statehood was quickly emulated elsewhere. This process of dissemination has generally been described as the consequence of a process of political modernization in which traditional empires were replaced by modern nation-states. Accordingly, nationalist ideas were transmitted primarily within an imperial context, while the driving force was nationalist movements that strove for independence.[4] However, new nation-states mostly came in waves. Nationalist activists generally were not strong enough to create a nation-state on their own; they needed a "window of opportunity," such as a broad geopolitical crisis, the collapse of existing empires, or outside intervention.

Nation-states and empires, moreover, were not mutually exclusive forms of statehood; they were thoroughly entangled, both as nationalizing empires and imperial nation-states. Adopting this perspective, a very different dynamic becomes visible: an intricate interplay between a global process of emulation and a succession of imperial crises. In fact, three different responses to the rise of the nation-state can be detected. The first is dismissal: many traditional rulers and elites rejected the new model of statehood as a heterodox, foreign threat. In the long run, such a reaction was not very effective. Other elite groups in traditional states realized that certain aspects of the nation-state model could be judiciously adopted to reinforce the state. This mostly led to authoritarian reform policies that aimed to strengthen the army and raise more taxes. During the nineteenth and early twentieth centuries this strategy of gradual change was adopted by many traditional rulers. Members of the middle classes mostly advocated a third response: the wholesale adoption of the nation-state model, including liberal constitutionalism. They were attracted primarily by the prospect of political participation, legal equality, and economic modernization. However, they mostly lacked the means to impose their views and had to await their opportunity.

This provides a very different picture of the rise of new nation-states. During the age of revolutions it was not strong nationalist movements that liberated countries from traditional monarchs or colonial oppression, but imperial crises that created power vacuums that were quickly filled by the aspiring middle classes. This pattern would be repeated in the Balkans and Eastern Europe, where Christian minorities received outside support in their struggles against the Ottoman Empire, while the First World War occasioned the collapse of the Habsburg, the tsarist, and the Ottoman Empires, yielding the floor to nationalist activists. The post-1945 decolonization process, too, was prompted primarily by the retreat of colonial empires.

But imperial collapse was not the only route for nation-state creation. The nation-state model advanced mostly thanks to ambitious monarchs who embarked on authoritarian courses of reform to strengthen their realms. This usually occurred after a humiliating defeat that made them acutely aware that the nation-state model had made Western countries more powerful. The Habsburg, Romanov, and Ottoman Empires adopted various aspects of that model after losing wars against Western powers. During the long nineteenth century, the same happened in Persia, China, and Japan. Ambitious smaller states such as Mysore, Egypt, Madagascar, Siam, and Ethiopia also pursued authoritarian reform policies.

In these states, a process of isomorphism can be detected. In order to strengthen the army, they felt compelled to adopt ever more interrelated aspects of the new nation-state model. The first of these was conscription and modern military equipment. In order to pay for this, they had to raise the tax revenue. This was done by introducing direct taxation, for which a cadastre and a census were required. They generally also stimulated the economy by abolishing traditional privileges and the remnants of feudalism, thus freeing land and labor for a market-oriented economy. This required more legal security, which could be achieved by codifying laws and creating an independent judiciary. These new tasks had to be performed by a centralized government and a rational bureaucracy based on meritocracy. Modern education, in turn, was needed to train officers, doctors, and officials and to raise the literacy of broader strata of the population. However, a better educated population that paid higher taxes and served in the army tended to claim legal equality and political participation. A Western-style criminal code and penal system, moreover, were needed to get rid of extraterritorial rights. These modernizing monarchies did not adopt the nation-state model at once, but in order to avoid lagging behind they mostly ended up accepting the entire package. As the initiative for these reforms generally came from the ruler, political participation was postponed as long as possible, and when a constitution and a parliamentary system were finally introduced, most of these states looked to the

German Empire for inspiration, as its constitution warranted a strong and relatively independent executive.

Many of the policies adopted by these modernizing monarchies were also implemented in overseas colonies. European empires sought to raise tax revenues through economic and administrative reforms. They were not in favor of granting political participation, and generally they gave in only when the pressure from native elites and their followers could no longer be ignored. Nationalist activists in the colonies felt inspired by reformist monarchies, especially Japan, admiring how they modernized their societies on their own initiative. Thus, the nation-state model was attractive for two different reasons: it could strengthen the state through reforms, enabling it to prosper in the international arena, and it could make the nation sovereign, giving power to the people, which could be achieved either by overthrowing the existing regime or by becoming independent. Nationalist rhetoric, hence, was used both by the authorities of reforming states and by aspiring middle classes.

Because they focus only on nationalist activists and movements, most existing explanations for the rise and rapid dissemination of nationalism are seriously flawed. The emphasis on cultural continuity between early modern ethnic communities and modern nation-states by anti-modernist authors such as Anthony Smith and Azar Gat ignores the fact that most new nation-states were not ethnically or culturally homogenic. Moreover, the rise of the nation-state was driven primarily by political motives and geopolitical crises. Modernists like Ernest Gellner put the emphasis on socioeconomic factors, arguing that nationalism arose as a consequence of the transition from an agricultural to an industrial society, which required the education of the masses. In fact, however, a global process of emulation produced the dissemination of the nation-state model. Capitalism, not industrialization, was a crucial aspect of this process, and it was promoted primarily by reformist regimes that aimed to strengthen the state, rather than by an enterprising bourgeois class. Mass education, moreover, was necessary not so much for factory work, but to provide well-educated officials for the bureaucracy and literate soldiers for the army. So state-building was much more important than economic developments. Benedict Anderson convincingly argues that by the early nineteenth century, the "model" of the nation-state was "available for pirating." He also asserts that this model contained a number of aspects that were indissolubly attached to it, such as state institutions, national citizenship, popular sovereignty, national anthems, and flags. Brubaker in a similar way asserts that the "organizational model of nation, state, citizenship, and popular sovereignty" was a package with a clear common core.[5]

It might seem that the triumph of the nation-state was inevitable, and President Wilson's proclamation of the right to self-determination is usually presented as a crucial turning point. However, the British and French Empires reached their greatest extents only after the First World War. Moreover, the United States became an imperial power by annexing the Philippines. The 1930s and early 1940s can even be defined as a new imperial apex, as Fascist Italy, Nazi Germany, and imperial Japan conquered large swaths of territory in Asia, Africa, and Europe. The decolonization process, which most scholars define as a watershed moment, did accelerate after 1945, but as we have seen, many small and vulnerable colonies or nation-states attempted to create larger federations. It was only in the late 1960s, after most of these federations ended in failure, that the nation-state became the uncontested, hegemonic model of statehood.

Citizenship

In the field of nationalism studies, the meaning and content of citizenship has barely been thematized. Many studies deal with recent periods and therefore take citizenship for granted. Scholars focusing on earlier periods sometimes briefly mention voting restrictions, but in general they do not regard citizenship as a very relevant issue. Nonetheless, this topic has been studied in various other, largely disconnected research traditions. In Europe, scholars have focused on the democratization process, the rise of the welfare state, and various emancipation processes. In the Americas, the exclusion of people of color and Indigenous people has been investigated extensively. In Asia and Africa, scholars have examined discrimination against native populations in colonial or semicolonial contexts. However, these studies have not been related systematically to the rise of nationalism and the dissemination of the nation-state model.[6]

Nationalism: A World History has made clear that the invention of the nation-state had profound implications for the inhabitants, and just as the nation-state changed greatly over time, this also happened with the scope and content of citizenship. The age of revolutions began with high hopes and aspirations. The new revolutionary regimes put an end to monarchical absolutism, local privileges, and obsolete hierarchies by introducing legal equality and political participation, thus creating a nation of citizens. This had immediate consequences, such as the emancipation of religious minorities, like the Jews, who received citizenship in France. In practice, however, there were many limitations. Initially, suffrage was quite extensive both in the United States and in revolutionary France, but minors, women, servants, and vagabonds were excluded from active citizenship. After the French Revolution, the government, like other more or less liberal regimes in Europe, restricted voting rights to male owners of substantial properties. However, more serious cleavages can be detected in the Americas. In general, slaves, Indigenous people, and free people of color were excluded from citizenship, and the same happened in Europe's overseas colonies, where native populations became subjects of "special regimes." Thus, the introduction of the nation-state in many instances deepened the chasm between men and women, between whites and people of color, and between the inhabitants of the metropole and those of the colonies, by erecting hard legal boundaries.

In many new nation-states, citizenship constituted a privilege for the few and a burden for the many. Whereas only few men obtained voting rights, the large majority of the population had to pay higher taxes and young males had to serve in the army, while traditional social safety nets were abolished. As a consequence, after the initial enthusiasm about the abolition of feudal remnants and the recognition of equal rights, the nation-state was not very popular among broad strata of the population. For the same reasons, the reform policies conducted by modernizing rulers in East-Central Europe and parts of Asia and Africa met with widespread opposition, and not just from traditional elites, but also from large sections of the population.

The nation-state model was generally welcomed by the well-educated, urban middle classes. Many disadvantaged groups also appealed to the ideals of the revolutionary era in order to be recognized as equals. This led to a broad succession of emancipatory movements. The working classes campaigned for voting rights, and toward the end of the nineteenth century, universal male suffrage began to be the norm. Women also demanded the vote, which was mostly conceded after the First or Second World War.

Awarding political rights to inhabitants was not popular among ruling elites in modernizing empires. In general, they were introduced only at the end of long series of reforms. The Ottoman Empire briefly had a general assembly in the late 1870s and then again after 1908. Japan followed in 1890, and Russia in 1905. Most of these parliaments had limited powers. In liberal nation-states, most governing parties feared that introducing general suffrage would lead to not just a political but also a social revolution and communism. As a consequence, many regimes tried other solutions, mitigating or even obstructing the expression of the popular will in fair elections. Dictatorships had existed before, but in the twentieth century authoritarian regimes became quite common, and many of them experimented with forms of corporate representation, one-party rule, or Fascism. After 1945, most new nation-states adopted a democratic or communist system. A solution that was embraced across the board was the welfare state, which bound citizens more closely to the state. The nationalizing of poor relief had already begun during the late nineteenth century, when Bismarck introduced social insurance, state pensions, and unemployment benefits. After 1918 and particularly after 1945, the welfare state would be rolled out throughout most of the world. Because global migration flows were relatively limited during the Cold War era, efforts to actively exclude poor immigrants were slow to develop.

The oil crisis of the 1970s caused high inflation and economic stagnation, and as response, neoliberal governments began to roll back the welfare state, while trade unions and social movements lost leverage. At the same time, there was a growing emphasis on human rights, which combined well with the rise of identity politics. This expressed itself in the civil rights movement in the United States and it enabled the emancipation of Indigenous populations in many parts of the Americas. Meanwhile, various minority regions in Europe received political autonomy. LGBTQ+ rights also made considerable progress, and in the new millennium a growing group of countries, mostly in Europe and the Americas, legalized same-sex marriage. Today, various activists and small political parties call for extending civil rights not just to humans, but also to "other animals." It is clear that once certain supposedly universal rights are given to some, it is difficult to deny them to others. As a result, the period since the age of revolutions can be seen as a succession of emancipatory movements.

Many advances provoked backlash. Rights were often denied in practice, particularly by authoritarian regimes. They generally have constitutions that recognize a broad diversity of civil rights, but in everyday life these are ignored or openly violated. Thus, there is a continuous struggle between claims from civil society and the state authorities' desire to control the population. Sometimes citizens succeed in increasing their leverage, for instance by serving as indispensable conscripted soldiers, by paying a large share of the state's budget in the form of taxes, or by putting pressure on the government through mass protests and strikes. Some states are too weak to guarantee the rights and welfare of their citizens, and as a consequence, politicians and officials tend to hand them out as individual favors to their "clients." Other states prefer to tightly control the population, and this is made easier when citizens do not have many options for pressuring the government, or when political, economic, and military establishments are so thoroughly interwoven that significant concessions are perceived as a fundamental threat to the entire political system. Nevertheless, the now universally accepted logic of the nation-state model means that citizens expect protection, rights, and services, and even the most repressive regimes need to address these demands in order to survive. How the balance between the leverage of citizens in a globalized world and the controlling power of the state develops in the future, particularly in light of new methods of digital surveillance, remains an open question.

The Nationalization of Culture

The impact of nationalism on the cultural domain has been studied only in a fragmentary way. For Europe, there are a few historical overviews. Initially they had a narrow history-of-ideas approach, and more recently, the focus has been primarily on cultural expressions of dedicated nationalists during the long nineteenth century. Another research tradition, initiated by Michael Billig, deals with expressions of banal and everyday nationalism from the 1960s onward.[7] But in general, the field is dominated by case studies that mostly focus on one country or one particular aspect.

The chapters of this book have shown that the impact of nationalism on both the cultural realm and the physical environment has changed even more profoundly than its political role. Although vague national identities existed before the age of revolutions, more closely defined national cultures were created only during the Romantic era, and in later periods they would pervade ever more domains of everyday life. Moreover, from the early nineteenth century on, a pendulum movement can be detected: about every forty to fifty years, a major crisis brought on by widespread disillusionment with existing views created a major shift from openly expressed exalted nationalism to more subdued forms, and back again.

Many nationalists argue that a nation is defined primarily by having its own language and culture. However, national cultures and monolingual territories came into existence only in modern times. Certainly in Western Europe, vernacular languages were standardized during the early modern era. This was not due to print capitalism only; it had already begun during the late Middle Ages, when state administrations began to use vernacular languages. However, it was only from the Enlightenment era that initiatives were taken to impose a standardized spelling and grammar. Nonetheless, even on the eve of the age of revolutions, linguistic pluralism continued to be the norm and language use was determined primarily by social group or professional domain. Territorial borders were largely irrelevant, as within a sea of dialects, various prestigious languages were used for religious, literary, scholarly, or mercantile purposes. Outside of Europe, it was not very different.

Within Europe, the Church, the monarchy, and the aristocracy were the main patrons of artists and writers. The French court set the tone in architecture, fine arts, music, and manners, and French was the main vehicle of communication for aristocratic and intellectual elites. Popular culture was expressed mostly in dialect and consisted of an irregular patchwork of regional forms and local traditions. It was only in the main urban centers that commercial actors created a national market for cultural products in a standardized vernacular language, such as novels and plays. Again, we see a relationship between capitalism and nationalism, which at this stage involved a limited number of customers in the major Western European countries and some parts of Asia, such as Japan.

In addition, until the eighteenth century there were no concepts to distinguish an autonomous domain of human creativity. Artistic objects, for instance, had a practical, decorative, or religious function, and in Europe they were not ordered geographically or chronologically, but rather as part of an eternal cosmological order. During the Enlightenment, with the awareness that contemporary scholarship and arts had surpassed those of antiquity, existing concepts such as civilization and culture received a new meaning and began to be used to distinguish a separate sphere of human achievements. A new, more rational outlook also inspired scholars to take a more detached interest in history and geography, preparing the ground for a nationalist reinterpretation of the cultural sphere.

State-oriented initiatives also contributed to a reinterpretation of the cultural past along national lines. In various European countries, steps were taken to encourage domestic artistic production for the market. Unintentionally, this process advanced during the French Revolution. Even though most revolutionary activists had universalist aspirations and preferred classical art, they in fact invented the concept of "national heritage." Confiscated artistic treasures were made publicly accessible in new "national" museums, which did not mean that they represented the *ethnos*, but that they belonged to the *demos*. Many older works of art glorified the pillars of the ancien régime and therefore had to be rearranged in a new "rational" order in which the focus was on aesthetic development, creating chronologically ordered national schools. This enabled the viewer to comprehend the progress of the arts attained by the principal (European) nations.

The Revolutionary era ended in disillusionment. Various scholars had already begun to question the universalist pretentions of the revolutionaries. After 1815, a rapidly growing group of Romantic authors began to focus on differences, the legacy of the past, and organic growth. According to them, every linguistically or ethnically defined "people" had adapted to the particular geographical circumstances of their territory, which over time resulted in a specific national character or "spirit." As a consequence, every people or nation had its own unique culture and was now redefined as *ethnos*. Scholars therefore focused on folk stories and history in order understand the nation's authentic character.

The Romantic view of the nation became a self-fulfilling prophecy. Authors, musicians, and artists now adopted the national language and focused on national topics, thus, in fact, creating a national high culture. Many of their traditional patrons had disappeared, so they had to rely on the state or the market. In order to reach a broad public of anonymous consumers, they adopted a didactic tone while showing themselves to be committed to the national cause. Many historical novels, poems, history paintings, and operas even openly glorified the nation.

This new cultural nationalism also manifested itself in the physical realm. Before the age of revolutions, most landmarks and striking buildings were connected to the Church, the monarchy, the nobility, or local communities.

Only in exceptional cases did places refer to popular myths or heroes with a countrywide significance. This changed fundamentally in the late eighteenth century. During the French Revolution royal collections were nationalized and housed in a new national museum, a national library, and a national archive. Most other European and American states created similar institutions, as well as lavishly decorated national theaters. Public monuments memorializing the nation's most important heroes or victories followed during the early nineteenth century. Moreover, impressive historical buildings now were seen as testimonies to the nation's glorious past, and this national heritage deserved to be preserved. As a consequence, national cultures were projected into the distant past and institutionalized in the present.

However, in practice, not all languages and cultures were equal. Only languages that were recognized as "civilized" and had a sufficient number of speakers were considered a viable basis for a national community. This is what Eric Hobsbawm has defined as the "threshold principle." Thus, minority languages in Europe were not recognized as sufficient to build a national community, nor were indigenous languages in the Americas. The idea was that these languages, like dialects, would slowly disappear, and the ideal of one nation, one language, one culture would prevail. Gellner therefore has concluded that the nationalist ideology inverts reality: "It claims to defend folk culture while in fact it is forging a high culture; it claims to protect an old folk society while in fact helping to build up an anonymous mass society. . . . It preaches and defends cultural diversity, when in fact it imposes homogeneity."[8]

Accordingly, in Western Europe and the Americas, the nation was largely defined as coinciding with existing borders. Historians focused mostly on the rise and evolution of the existing state, creating a rather finalistic national master narrative. This also happened in many modernizing monarchies in Asia, such as Japan, China, and Siam. However, educated elites of various minority communities—first in East-Central Europe and later also in the Americas, Asia, and Africa—started a process of national emancipation, standardizing their own vernacular language and producing a national high culture. Historians studied their own "national past" while tracing the continuity with earlier forms of statehood. Sometimes these attempts found widespread resonance, but often they met with indifference or even incomprehension.

After the failure of the Revolutions of 1848, when Romantic ideals clashed with hard power, the exalted nationalist tone in the cultural sphere became more subdued or even largely disappeared. The folk tales, hero worshipping, and talk about national "souls" gave way to a new focus on the present, systematic research, and hard facts. Academic investigations, statistics offices, and scientific methods would provide a more objective examination of social reality. However, reality was clearly framed in national terms, as nation-states and their "societies" became the basic unit of research. Artists and writers also explored national reality in their plein-air paintings and realist novels. These developments were not limited to Europe and the Americas; they could also be found in many modernizing states and European colonies in Asia and Africa, where they often had to compete with more traditional, religiously colored interpretations.

In many parts of Europe and the Americas the nation-state was becoming a fact of life, and as a result, the national awareness of the population increased substantially. This was a logical consequence of modernization processes such as the growth of the state and the improvement of infrastructure. The dissemination of a self-evident image of a world consisting of nation-states, each with its unique culture and identity, was also helped by rising literacy numbers and the rapid growth of the press. Technical inventions enabled the cheap reproduction of illustrations in magazines and newspapers, familiarizing readers with images of myriad individual countries.

From about the 1870s, national governments also pursued active nation-building policies. First, the socialization of future citizens was taken more seriously. By extending the school system, more pupils learned the nation's language, history, and geography, and gymnastics would strengthen their bodies. In this way, as Eugen Weber has argued, peasants were turned in Frenchmen, while many ethnic and linguistic minorities were assimilated.[9] Policies toward Indigenous populations were often forceful and included removing children from their families for adoption or education at boarding schools. State authorities also put much effort into strengthening the loyalty of the masses by beautifying their capital cities, constructing impressive state buildings, erecting statues, and organizing large-scale commemorations. Maybe even more important was the role of world's fairs, where countries learned to present their national identities in a favorable light. At these occasions states tended to show the most attractive and extraordinary aspects of their national heritage, leading to what Joep Leerssen has called the "typicality effect."[10]

As a consequence, a process of isomorphism can also be encountered in the area of culture. In order to be taken seriously on the international stage, countries needed not only a national flag and an anthem, but also a system of higher education, scientific institutions, national museums, a thriving literature in the national language, a secular interpretation of the national past, and artists who provided a realist depiction of the nation. In addition, every country needed to have a unique national heritage, characteristic landscapes, typical building styles, traditional costumes, artisanal products, folkloric traditions, and typical songs, dances, dishes, and drinks. Ideally, a country also had a few globally known national icons, which could be old, like the Taj Mahal, or new, like the Eiffel Tower. In most cases, national cultures were created by existing states and within their boundaries.

The optimistic, forward-looking mood disappeared toward the turn of the century. There was no clear turning point, but the agrarian crisis, the rise of socialism, modern imperialism, social Darwinism, and new philosophical currents all undermined the trust in free trade, liberalism, positivist science, and rational progress. As a consequence, many scholars hoped to ground the nation more firmly in the past by shifting the focus from language to race and the impact of geography. Although the period from about 1885 to 1945 is known for its nationalist extremism, as exemplified by the aggressive nationalist policies and megalomanic buildings of the Fascist regimes, scholars in fact relativized the role of the nation-state as the main unit of analysis. Many geographers, philologists, physical anthropologists, and art historians focused on larger regions such as Eurasia, or on larger population groups such as Aryans, Celts, or pan-Africans. Other scholars preferred a smaller scale, distinguishing between various landscape types, geographical regions, or ancient tribes within existing countries. Racial theories entered the works of many authors, but in novels it was more common to evoke the "spirit" of a particular small region. Musicians, painters, and architects developed a fascination for vernacular traditions, and the same happened with filmmakers, resulting in the global success of the American western, for instance. Tourism strongly encouraged the preservation of local heritage and characteristic landscapes, as well as the sale of typical handicrafts and regional dishes. Although territorial identities became more diversified as nations now were often presented as a unity in diversity or as part of a larger racial group, nationalism began to pervade more areas of everyday life, affecting even clothing, gardening, and pets. Sports became a mass phenomenon and not only strengthened the national body, but also encouraged national feelings.

Within a few decades, however, some scholars began to reject racial, biological, and geographical determinism and the frequent use of holistic concepts such as spirit or organic unity in favor of a more objective, empirical analysis of social and cultural reality. This implied that they took existing (national) societies anew as their starting point, while generally ignoring both substate regions and larger territorial units. Some anthropologists explicitly rejected racial theories in favor of a detailed analysis of the culture of individual societies or tribes on their own terms—thus, in fact, reifying them. This reaction gained pace after the First World War and would become hegemonic after 1945. Social scientists relied more on statistics and modeling to present an "objective" portrayal of social developments. Much emphasis was put on the linear modernization of "society." However, this implied a division of tasks: economics, sociology, political science, and art history dealt with developed Western societies, while "the rest" was relegated to anthropology and area studies. Thus, methodological nationalism and Eurocentrism went hand in hand.

The focus on international modernity was also visible in the rise of avant-garde art, modern architecture, and functionalist design, all of which originated in the early twentieth century but only achieved global hegemony after the Second World War. Radical modernization policies, such as Atatürk's thorough Westernization of Turkey or the ambitious wetland reclamation projects in several countries, had already begun in the interwar era, but they would dominate in the 1950s and 1960s. Thus, Brazil constructed a new modernist capital, Ghana built the huge Volta Dam, and the green revolution transformed the countryside across the world. In the tourist sector, the picturesque and the romantic were subordinated to efficiency; most new hotels were high-rise concrete buildings. Even sports was used to show a country's participation in international modernity, as demonstrated by the modernist venues of the 1968 Olympics in Mexico City and the large number of medals won by the Eastern bloc countries, which supposedly were physical proof of the progress made by communist societies. A strong emphasis on national peculiarities was largely limited to commercial popular culture, such as comics and film.

The late 1970s brought profound changes as the focus on state-led modernization and technocratic planning did not produce easy solutions for the oil crisis and the lagging economic growth in the Global South. A new belief in the disciplining force of the market led to the quick implementation of neoliberal solutions such as the opening up of protected (national) markets. Globalization did not lead to a decline in national feelings. In fact, national differences were underlined as countries became brands in order to attract foreign investments, tourists, and talents. Moreover, as ideological and class differences lost most of their relevance, identity politics advanced rapidly in the form of a greater assertiveness among ethnic minorities, the emancipation of the LGTBQ+ community, and a religious revival, but it also expressed itself increasingly in chauvinist attitudes, populist nationalism, and xenophobia.

Since the late 1970s, two conflicting tendencies can be detected in academia—one openly questioning national identities and the other naturalizing them. The rise of postmodernism and the growing interconnectedness of the world inspired scholars to present national identities as social constructs, or even to question the dominance of the national framework by focusing on transnational flows and networks. In other academic fields, however, nationally defined cultures are taken very seriously. Various new disciplines, such as intercultural communication and memory studies, take the nation-state as their starting point. Other scholars tried to ground racial, ethnic, and cultural identities in biology through the study of genetics.

At the same time, a new interest in bottom-up perspectives challenged both the strong state-oriented focus of academia and the cultural hegemony of the West. The emancipation of the Global South was visible in the introduction of UNESCO's World Heritage List and in efforts to restitute colonial and Indigenous art, which in fact reinforce existing national identities by converting individual objects and sites into the historical patrimony of the nation. Nationalism also made a strong comeback in the physical environment, but now with an almost ironic playfulness in the construction of spectacular, iconic buildings, neotraditional suburbs, and new capital cities. Cheerful performances for tourists, historical reenactments, and nationally themed spaces in hotels, restaurants, and shopping malls have made national identities increasingly banal. In the end, a world divided into nation-states has become taken for granted as the natural order of things, and even entering cyberspace. Instead of leading to a global village, the internet has fanned nationalist feelings. Since the algorithms of social media prioritize messages with emotional content, exalted nationalism, xenophobia, and hate speech increasingly infiltrate the "cloud." Filter bubbles and echo chambers lead to chauvinism and polarization, stirred up on many occasions by populist politicians and nationalist activists. It remains to be seen whether this tendency will deepen in the coming years, or whether citizens will become fed up with identity politics, realizing that this will only pit people against each other, while the urgent problems of the future such as climate change, sustainability, and the growing gap between rich and poor remain unresolved. In the end, we can conclude that over the last two centuries people around the globe have become nationalized. As ever-more aspects of everyday life have become associated with specific nations or nation-states, national identities became "thicker" over time. On the other hand, the identification with the nation has become banal, and it heats up primarily in particular situations such as during World Cup matches—or in times of crisis.[11]

Outlook

But what will the future bring? It is extremely difficult to think of a world beyond the nation-state or to predict which direction nationalism will take. At the moment, three relatively recent developments come to mind that seem to undermine the current hegemony of the nation-state model: regional cooperation, the resurgence of empire, and the climate crisis.

The first process, which has its roots in the immediate postwar era, is the growing role of regional organizations such as the Association of Southeast Asian Nations, the Arab League, and the African Union. However, at this stage, only the European Union has evolved into a meaningful and mighty transnational organization. Although the soft power of the EU is very considerable, setting technological and ecological standards globally, it remains a geopolitical dwarf that for hard military power still depends on the armies of its larger member states and—through NATO—on the assistance of the United States. Although an unstable geopolitical constellation would require a unified response, power within the European Union continues to be in the hands of the European Council. Unlike the European Commission, which is a kind of European government with a clear leader, the European Council consists of the heads of state and prime ministers of the member states. So in the end, the twenty-seven nation-states still determine the fate of the European Union.[12]

Another development is the resurgence of empire. One could argue that imperial tendencies have never completely disappeared. From the perspective of ethnic minorities and Indigenous communities, most existing nation-states still are multinational empires in which inhabitants with a different mother tongue are effectively treated as second-rate citizens. Even if we accept that most existing states adhere to the nation-state model, this does not rule out the existence of imperial tendencies. Even though the United States pretends to uphold the existing rights-based international order, consisting of equal sovereign nation-states, in some aspects its foreign policy can be interpreted as imperial. Thus, Washington's military interventions—without the approval of the Security Council of the United Nations—in Kosovo, Iraq, and Libya have been widely criticized as violating international law. France, another prominent Western country, not only strongly promotes French culture throughout the world but also maintains close relations with many of its former colonies, leading even to military interventions in various parts of Africa. Other powers have also flexed their muscles. In the Middle East, Saudi Arabia, Egypt, Iran, and Israel vie for power and influence, and this is even more true of Turkey. The Turkish government has recently occupied parts of Syria, intervened in the Libyan civil war, and actively supported Azerbaijan in the Second Nagorno-Karabakh War against Armenia. One could argue that all of these foreign interventions mentioned so far are not aiming to permanently occupy new territories. It seems the same cannot be said for Russia and China. Russia already supported the nonrecognized states of Transnistria, Abkhazia, and South Ossetia, but in 2014 it also annexed Crimea from Ukraine and supported fake secessionist movements in Eastern Ukraine, and in 2022 it embarked on a full-scale invasion of its southwestern neighbor. China has effectively abolished the autonomy of Hong Kong, strives for a "peaceful reunification" with Taiwan, and has substantially extended its claims to territorial waters in the South China Sea by building new islands. Moreover, with the recent Belt and Road Initiative and by creating its own international institutions such as the Shanghai Cooperation Organization and the Asian Infrastructure Investment Bank, Beijing seems to be establishing its own international system, centered on China and based on authority, hierarchy, and deference. While increasingly treating their citizens as mere subjects, Russia and China both propagate their imperial ambitions at home by appealing to nationalist sentiments.[13] So it seems that the intricate and ever-evolving relationship between empire and nation-state is taking another unexpected turn.

A final issue is the worsening condition of the planet. Climate change, environmental pollution, degrading ecosystems, and a rapid decline in biodiversity require a fundamental change of course, such as a rapid transition to renewable sources of energy and a sustainable economy. This is a global problem that clearly transcends national boundaries. Unified action is urgently needed. Various scholars argue that we have to not only change our policies, but also rethink our fundamental categories. Should we not overcome the dichotomies between human beings and "other animals" and between society and nature? Civilization has traditionally been defined—at least in the post-Enlightenment Western world—as the capacity of human societies to transform the external world, which implied that nature has been treated as a cheap resource that could be exploited at will. Not only we have reached the limits of what nature can sustain, but we are already revising our understanding of "civilized" behavior. Successive emancipation waves have undermined the limited view on human civilization: men's productive work should no longer be privileged over women's reproductive labor, the able-bodied should not be privileged over people with disabilities, and a growth-oriented market economy should not be privileged over "barbarous" subsistence farming. Surprisingly, the ecological crisis has not yet led to a widely supported plea to fundamentally reform the existing international order. Green parties, ecological movements, and the new animal advocacy parties—which have gained parliamentary seats in several European countries—still operate primarily through the existing national framework, attempting to introduce new legislation in individual nation-states or pressuring their governments to be more active on the international stage. Will Kymlicka and Sue Donaldson even argue that we should integrate the animal world into the existing international system by giving national citizenship rights to domesticated animals—even though, like children and some intellectually disabled persons, they cannot speak for themselves—and by recognizing wild animal species as sovereign nations with territorial rights.[14] So, confronted with the enormous challenge of the current climate crisis, the organizational power of the existing nation-states still prevails, as even for radical environmentalists, the nation-state model has not yet lost its allure. The question now is whether the international community will effectively join hands. If not, the climate catastrophe may result in chaos. In a situation of everyone for themselves, politicians may feel tempted to stir up the nationalist feelings of the population, but without a well-functioning international order, this would only lead to a revival of imperial tendencies, with powerful countries resorting to the principle of might is right.

NOTES

Introduction

1. Bea Vidacs, "Banal Nationalism, Football, and Discourse Community in Africa," *Studies in Ethnicity and Nationalism* 11, no. 1 (2011): 25–41; Steve Bloomfield, *Africa United: Soccer, Passion, Politics, and the First World Cup in Africa* (New York: Harper Perennial, 2010). The term "feel-good nationalism" is used by Jeff Kingston, *Nationalism in Asia: A History since 1945* (Chichester: Wiley, 2017), 138.

2. Bloomfield, *Africa United*, 188–99.

3. Vidacs, "Football in Africa"; Emilio Depetris-Chauvin, Ruben Durante, and Filipe Campante, "Building Nations through Shared Experiences: Evidence from African Football," *American Economic Review* 110, no. 5 (May 2020): 1572–602.

4. Alejandro Quiroga and Fernando Molina, "National Deadlock: Hot Nationalism, Dual Identities and Catalan Independence (2008–2019)," *Genealogy* 4, no. 1 (2020): 15; Dylan O'Driscoll and Bahar Baser, "Referendums as a Political Party Gamble: A Critical Analysis of the Kurdish Referendum for Independence," *International Political Science Review* 41, no. 5 (2020): 652–66.

5. FIFA has 211 member states; David M. Eberhard, Gary F. Simons, and Charles D. Fennig, eds., *Ethnologue: Languages of the World*, 25th ed. (Dallas: SIL, 2022); Ernest Gellner, *Nations and Nationalism* (Ithaca, NY: Cornell University Press, 1983), 43–45; Pietro Bortone, *Language and Nationality: Social Inferences, Cultural Differences and Linguistic Misconceptions* (London: Bloomsbury, 2022), 145–230; Walker Connor, *Ethnonationalism: The Quest for Understanding* (Princeton, NJ: Princeton University Press, 1994), xi–xii, 76–81, 89–118.

6. Andreas Wimmer, *Waves of War: Nationalism, State Formation, and Ethnic Exclusion in the Modern World* (Cambridge: Cambridge University Press, 2013), 37–107, 237–41, 256; Siniša Malešević, *Nation-States and Nationalisms: Organization, Ideology and Solidarity* (Cambridge: Polity Press, 2013); Pascal Ory, *Qu'est-ce qu'une nation?: Une histoire mondiale* (Paris: Gallimard, 2020), 77–78.

7. Umut Özkirimli, *Contemporary Debates on Nationalism: A Critical Engagement* (Basingstoke, UK: Palgrave Macmillan, 2005); Stefan Berger and Eric Storm, eds., *Writing the History of Nationalism* (London: Bloomsbury Academic, 2019); Florian Bieber, *Debating Nationalism: The Global Spread of Nations* (London: Bloomsbury Academic, 2020).

8. Aviel Roshwald, "Nations Are (Occasionally) Forever: Alternatives to the Modernist Perspective," in Berger and Storm, *Writing the History of Nationalism*, 83–105.

9. Anderson, however, also pays attention to Latin America, where language was not an issue. Benedict Anderson, *Imagined Communities: Reflections on the Origin and Spread of Nationalism* (London: Verso, 1991), 5–67; Gellner, *Nations and Nationalism*.

10. Wimmer, *Waves of War*, 73–108.

11. Eric J. Hobsbawm, *Nations and Nationalism since 1780: Programme, Myth, Reality* (Cambridge: Cambridge University Press, 1990); John Breuilly, ed., *The Oxford Handbook of the History of Nationalism* (Oxford: Oxford University Press, 2013); Ory, *Une nation*.

12. Wimmer, *Waves of War*.

13. David Armitage, *The Declaration of Independence: A Global History* (Cambridge, MA: Harvard University Press, 2007); Janet Polasky, *Revolutions without Borders: The Call to Liberty in the Atlantic World* (New Haven, CT: Yale University Press, 2015); Sujit Sivasundaram, *Waves across the South: A New History of Revolution and Empire* (London: William Collins, 2020); Linda Colley, *The Gun, the Ship, and the Pen: Warfare, Constitutions, and the Making of the Modern World* (London: Profile, 2021).

14. Gary Wilder, *The French Imperial Nation-State: Negritude and Colonial Humanism between the Two World Wars* (Chicago: University of Chicago Press, 2005); Stefan Berger and Alexei Miller, eds., *Nationalizing Empires* (Budapest: Central European University Press, 2015); Josep Maria Fradera, *The Imperial Nation: Citizens and Subjects in the British, French, Spanish, and American Empires* (Princeton, NJ: Princeton University Press, 2018); Siniša Malešević, "Empires and Nation-States: Beyond the Dichotomy," *Thesis Eleven* 139, no. 1 (2017): 3–10.

15. Xosé-Manoel Núñez, "Nations and Territorial Identities in Europe: Transnational Reflections," *European History Quarterly* 40, no. 4 (2010): 669–84; John Breuilly, "Nationalism as Global History," in *Nationalism and Globalisation: Conflicting of Complementary?*, ed. Daphne Halikiopoulou and Sofia Vasilopoulou (London: Routledge, 2011), 65–84.

16. Andreas Wimmer and Nina Glick Schiller, "Methodological Nationalism and Beyond: Nation-State Building, Migration and the Social Sciences," *Global Networks* 2, no. 4 (2002): 301–34; Stefan Berger, *The Past as History: National Identity and Historical Consciousness in Modern Europe* (Basingstoke, UK: Palgrave Macmillan, 2014).

17. Joep Leerssen, *National Thought in Europe: A Cultural History* (Amsterdam: Amsterdam University Press, 2006); Lloyd S. Kramer, *Nationalism in Europe and America: Politics, Cultures, and Identities since 1775* (Chapel Hill: University of North Carolina Press, 2011); Derek Hastings, *Nationalism in Modern Europe: Politics, Identity and Belonging since the French Revolution* (London: Bloomsbury, 2019); Kingston, *Nationalism in Asia*; James F. Siekmeier, *Latin American Nationalism: Identity in a Globalizing World* (London: Bloomsbury, 2017).

18. Dated are John Breuilly, *Nationalism and the State* (Manchester: Manchester University Press, 1982), and Hobsbawm, *Nations and Nationalism since 1780* (1990). Recently, two multi-authored volumes have been published: Breuilly, *The Oxford Handbook of the History of Nationalism* (2013), and Cathie Carmichael, Matthew D'Auria, and Aviel Roshwald, eds., *The Cambridge History of Nationhood and Nationalism*, 2 vols. (Cambridge: Cambridge University Press, 2023). Quite traditional are Azar Gat, *Nations: The Long History and Deep Roots of Political Ethnicity and Nationalism* (Cambridge: Cambridge University Press, 2013), and Ory, *Une nation*.

19. This concept referring to equal (iso) forms comes from sociological institutionalism. See Paul J. DiMaggio and Walter W. Powell, "The Iron Cage Revisited: Institutional Isomorphism and Collective Rationality in Organizational Fields," *American Sociological Review* 48, no. 2 (1983): 147–60.

Chapter 1

1. Anderson, *Imagined Communities*, 5–46.

2. Gellner, *Nations and Nationalism*.

3. Hobsbawm, *Nations and Nationalism since 1780*, 1–13.

4. Ernest Gellner and Anthony D. Smith, "The Nation: Real or Imagined? The Warwick Debates on Nationalism," *Nations and Nationalism* 2, no. 3 (1996): 357–88. See also Steven Grosby, Joep Leerssen, and Caspar Hirschi, "Continuities and Shifting Paradigms: A Debate on Caspar Hirschi's *The Origins of Nationalism*," *Studies on National Movements* 2, no. 1 (2014): 1–48; John Hutchinson et al., "Debate on Azar Gat's *Nations: The Long History and Deep Roots of Political Ethnicity and Nationalism*," *Nations and Nationalism* 21, no. 3 (2015): 383–402.

5. Caspar Hirschi, *The Origins of Nationalism: An Alternative History from Ancient Rome to Early Modern Germany* (Cambridge: Cambridge University Press, 2012), 34. The author himself locates the roots of nationalism in Renaissance humanism.

6. See, respectively, Gat, *Nations*; Steven Grosby, *Nations and Nationalism in World History* (New York: Routledge, 2022); Anthony D. Smith, *The Ethnic Origins of Nations* (Oxford: Blackwell, 1986).

7. Liah Greenfeld, *Nationalism: Five Roads to Modernity* (Cambridge, MA: Harvard University Press, 1992); Philip S. Gorski, "The Mosaic Moment: An Early Modernist Critique of Modernist Theories of Nationalism," *American Journal of Sociology* 105, no. 5 (2000): 1428–68.

8. Susan Reynolds, "The Idea of the Kingdom as a Political Community," in *Power and the Nation in European History*, ed. Len Scales and Oliver Zimmer (Cambridge: Cambridge University Press, 2005), 54–67; Adrian Hastings, *The Construction of Nationhood Ethnicity, Religion and Nationalism* (Cambridge: Cambridge University Press, 1997); Hirschi, *Origins of Nationalism*.

9. Steven Grosby, *Biblical Ideas of Nationality: Ancient and Modern* (Winona Lake, IN: Eisenbrauns, 2002); Aviel Roshwald, *The Endurance of Nationalism: Ancient Roots and Modern Dilemmas* (Cambridge: Cambridge University Press, 2006).

10. Gat, *Nations*.

11. Krishan Kumar, *The Making of English National Identity* (Cambridge: Cambridge University Press, 2003), 39–121.

12. Victor B. Lieberman, *Strange Parallels: Southeast Asia in Global Context, c. 800–1830*, 2 vols. (Cambridge: Cambridge University Press, 2009); John Darwin, *After Tamerlane: The Rise and Fall of Global Empires, 1400–2000* (London: Penguin, 2008), 118–37.

13. Lieberman, *Strange Parallels*, 1:37–44, 2:897–98.

14. Darwin, *After Tamerlane*, 72–93; Toby Green, *A Fistful of Shells: West Africa from the Rise of the Slave Trade to the Age of Revolution* (London: Allen Lane, 2019), 307–33.

15. Claire Weeda, *Ethnicity in Medieval Europe, 950–1250: Medicine, Power and Religion* (York: York Medieval Press, 2021), 41–62; Anthony D. Smith, *Chosen Peoples: Sacred Sources of National Identity* (Oxford: Oxford University Press, 2004).

16. Hirschi, *Origins of Nationalism*, 36–62; Arnold Labrie, "Van patriotisme tot nationalisme: Patria en natio voor 1815," in *Nationalisme, naties en staten: Europa vanaf circa 1800 tot heden*, ed. Leo H. M. Wessels and Toon Bosch (Nijmegen: Vantilt, 2012), 108–11.

17. Weeda, *Ethnicity in Medieval Europe*, 41–230.

18. Hagen Schulze, *Staat und Nation in der europäischen Geschichte* (Munich: Beck, 1995), 118–19.

19. Peter Burke, *Languages and Communities in Early Modern Europe* (Cambridge: Cambridge University Press, 2004), 161; Hirschi, *Origins of Nationalism*, 78–88.

20. Hirschi, *Origins of Nationalism*, 35–44.

21. Adrian Brisku, *Political Reform in the Ottoman and Russian Empires: A Comparative Approach* (London: Bloomsbury, 2019), 66–69; Henrietta Harrison, *China: Inventing the Nation* (London: Bloomsbury, 2011), 55–56.

22. Robert Ross, *Clothing: A Global History: Or, the Imperialists' New Clothes* (Cambridge: Polity, 2008), 12–25; Paul Freedman, *Images of the Medieval Peasant* (Stanford, CA: Stanford University Press, 1999).

23. Michael Mann, *The Sources of Social Power*, vol. 1, *A History of Power from the Beginning to AD 1760* (Cambridge: Cambridge University Press, 1986), 416–63; Charles Tilly, *Coercion, Capital, and European States, AD 990–1990* (Cambridge: Blackwell, 1990).

24. Mann, *Sources of Social Power*, 1:463–75; Tilly, *Coercion, Capital*, 91–95; Colley, *Gun, Ship*, 25–34.

25. Charles S. Maier, *Once within Borders: Territories of Power, Wealth, and Belonging since 1500* (Cambridge, MA: Belknap, 2016), 50–82.

26. Michael J. Braddick, *State Formation in Early Modern England, c. 1550–1700* (Cambridge: Cambridge University Press, 2000); Peter Sahlins, *Boundaries: The Making of France and Spain in the Pyrenees* (Berkeley: University of California Press, 1989), 9, 25–167.

27. Annie Jourdan, "France, patrie, nation: Figures de lutte et discours national (XVIème–XIXème siècles)," *European Review of History* 21, no. 1 (2014): 38–39; Chimène I. Keitner, *The Paradoxes of Nationalism: The French Revolution and Its Meaning for Contemporary Nation Building* (Albany: State University of New York Press, 2007), 31–43.

28. Hirschi, *Origins of Nationalism*, 59–62, 124–42; Labrie, "Patriotisme," 123–26; Annelien de Dijn, *Freedom: An Unruly History* (Cambridge, MA: Harvard University Press, 2020), 127–84.

29. Hirschi, *Origins of Nationalism*, 120–42.

30. Berger, *Past as History*, 28–35; Hirschi, *Origins of Nationalism*; Jaime E. Rodríguez O., *The Independence of Spanish America* (Cambridge: Cambridge University Press, 1998), 13–19.

31. Martin van Gelderen and Quentin Skinner, eds., *Republicanism: A Shared European Heritage* (Cambridge: Cambridge University Press, 2002).

32. Berger, *Past as History*, 36–43; Leerssen, *National Thought*, 36–70; Martin Thom, *Republics, Nations and Tribes* (London: Verso, 1995), 212–40.

33. Peter Burke, "Nationalisms and Vernaculars, 1500–1800," in Breuilly, *Oxford Handbook of Nationalism*, 30–31; David A. Bell, *The Cult of the Nation in France: Inventing Nationalism, 1680–1800* (Cambridge, MA: Harvard University Press, 2001), 112–14; Uffe Østergård, "Nation-Building and Nationalism in the Oldenburg Empire," in Berger and Miller, *Nationalizing Empires*, 474–75.

34. Raúl Moreno Almendral, "Nationhood as Practice and the Modernity of Nations: A Conceptual Proposal," *Nationalities Papers* 49, no. 1 (2020): 16–18; Raúl Moreno Almendral, *Relatos de vida, conceptos de nación: Reino Unido, Francia, España y Portugal (1780–1840)* (Valencia: Publicacions de la Universitat de València, 2021), 54–57; Leerssen, *National Thought*, 25–82; Lotte Jensen, ed., *The Roots of Nationalism: National Identity Formation in Early Modern Europe, 1600–1815* (Amsterdam: Amsterdam University Press, 2016).

35. Joachim Bahlcke, "Adelsnation," in *Enzyklopädie der Neuzeit*, ed. Friedrich Jaeger (Stuttgart: Metzler, 2005), 1:70–73; Schulze, *Staat und Nation*, 116–18.

36. Hirschi, *Origins of Nationalism*, 66–67, 181–82.

37. Jasper van der Steen, "Remembering the Revolt of the Low Countries: Historical Canon Formation in the Dutch Republic and Habsburg Netherlands, 1566–1621," *Sixteenth Century Journal* 49, no. 3 (Fall 2018): 713–42; Judith Pollmann, *Memory in Early Modern Europe, 1500–1800* (Oxford: Oxford University Press, 2017), 94–119.

38. Andreas Fahrmeir, *Citizenship: The Rise and Fall of a Modern Concept* (New Haven, CT: Yale University Press, 2007), 9–26; Pollmann, *Memory*, 74–94; Tamar Herzog, *Defining Nations: Immigrants and Citizens in Early Modern Spain and Spanish America* (New Haven, CT: Yale University Press, 2003); Peter Sahlins, "The Eighteenth-Century Citizenship Revolution in France," in *Migration Control in the North Atlantic World: The Evolution of State Practices in Europe and the United States from the French Revolution to the Inter-war Period*, ed. Andreas Fahrmeir, Olivier Faron, and Patrick Weil (New York: Berghahn, 2003), 11–25.

39. Braddick, *State Formation*, 11–27; Mann, *Sources of Social Power*, 1:458–61.

40. Kumar, *English National Identity*, 48–130; Mann, *Sources of Social Power*, 1:461–70; R. A. Houston, "People, Space, and Law in Late Medieval and Early Modern Britain and Ireland," *Past and Present* 230, no. 1 (2016): 47–89.

41. Burke, *Languages and Communities*, 43–60, 85–88, 127–29, 154; Tomasz Kamusella, *The Politics of Language and Nationalism in Modern Central Europe* (Basingstoke, UK: Palgrave Macmillan, 2009), 90, 139–40.

42. Kamusella, *Politics of Language*, 40–41, 81, 89–90.

43. Burke, *Languages and Communities*, 54, 91–110; Anderson, *Imagined Communities*, 37–46. For the Dutch case, see Gijsbert Rutten, *Language Planning as Nation Building: Ideology, Policy and Implementation in the Netherlands, 1750–1850* (Amsterdam: John Benjamins, 2019).

44. Kamusella, *Politics of Language*, 89; Burke, *Languages and Communities*, 49, 55; R. A. Houston, *Literacy in Early Modern Europe: Culture and Education 1500–1800* (Abingdon, UK: Routledge, 2002), 37–60.

45. Burke, *Languages and Communities*, 46–47, 52–60.

46. Lieberman, *Strange Parallels*, 2:355–61, 441–44, 471–75; Linda Colley, *Britons: Forging the Nation, 1707–1837* (New Haven, CT: Yale University Press, 1992), 11–12, 117–32, 147–77.

47. Graham Robb, *The Discovery of France: A Historical Geography from the Revolution to the First World War* (New York: W. W. Norton, 2007), 19–49; Pollmann, *Memory*, 94–119; Peter Burke, *Popular Culture in Early Modern Europe* (New York: Harper & Row, 1978), 244–81.

48. Burke, *Languages and Communities*, 61–78; Joachim Küpper, "The Early Modern European Drama and the Cultural Net: Some Basic Hypotheses," in *Theatre Cultures within Globalising Empires*, ed. Joachim Küpper and Leonie Pawlita (Berlin: De Gruyter, 2018), 1–12; Leerssen, *National Thought*, 95–97.

49. Lieberman, *Strange Parallels*, 2:308–12, 473–81; Orlando Figes, *Natasha's Dance: A Cultural History of Russia* (London: Penguin, 2003), 49–51.

50. Maarten Prak, "Guilds and the Development of the Art Market during the Dutch Golden Age," *Simiolus* 30, no. 3/4 (2003): 236–51; Rachel Laudan, *Cuisine and Empire: Cooking in World History* (Berkeley: University of California Press, 2013), 225–38.

51. Anderson, *Imagined Communities*, 12–36.

52. David Lowenthal, *The Past Is a Foreign Country* (Cambridge: Cambridge University Press, 2006), 74–125; Berger, *Past as History*, 28–68.

53. Jörg Fisch, "Zivilisation, Kultur," in *Geschichtliche Grundbegriffe: Historisches Lexikon zur politisch-sozialen Sprache in Deutschland*, ed. Otto Brunner, Werner Conze, and Reinhardt Koselleck (Stuttgart: Klett-Cotta, 1992), 7:679–89; Larry Shiner, *The Invention of Art: A Cultural History* (Chicago: University of Chicago Press, 2001), 19–56; John Hale, *The Civilization of Europe in the Renaissance* (London: Fontana, 1994), 355–413.

54. Shiner, *Invention of Art*, 79–140; Oskar Bätschmann, *Ausstellungskünstler: Kult und Karriere im modernen Kunstsystem* (Cologne: DuMont, 1997).

55. Fisch, "Zivilisation, Kultur," 679–740; Raymonde Monnier, "The Concept of Civilisation from Enlightenment to Revolution: An Ambiguous Transfer," *Contributions to the History of Concepts* 4, no. 1 (2008): 106–36.

56. Shiner, *Invention of Art*; Giuseppe Olmi, "Italiaanse verzamelingen van de late middeleeuwen tot het einde van de zeventiende eeuw," in *Verzamelen: Van rariteitenkabinet tot kunstmuseum*, ed. Ellinoor Bergvelt, Debora J. Meijers, and Mieke Rijnders (Heerlen, Netherlands: Open Universiteit, 1993), 93–122.

57. Debora J. Meijers, "Naar een systematische presentatie," in Bergvelt, Meijers, and Rijnders, *Verzamelen*, 225–44; Bätschmann, *Ausstellungskünstler*, 12–17.

58. Thomas DaCosta Kaufmann, *Toward a Geography of Art* (Chicago: University of Chicago Press, 2004), 26–35; Meijers, "Systematische presentatie"; Colley, *Britons*, 85–98, 177–83.

59. Bell, *Cult of the Nation*, 107–39; László Marácz, "The Roots of Modern Hungarian Nationalism: A Case Study and Research Agenda," in Jensen, *Roots of Nationalism*, 243; Eric Storm, *The Discovery of El Greco: The Nationalization of Culture versus the Rise of Modern Art (1860–1914)* (Brighton: Sussex Academic Press, 2016), 9–11.

60. David N. Livingstone, *The Geographical Tradition: Episodes in the History of a Contested Enterprise* (Oxford: Blackwell, 1992), 63–155.

61. Berger, *Past as History*, 29–51; François Hartog, *Regimes of Historicity: Presentism and Experiences of Time* (New York: Columbia University Press, 2015), 55–79.

62. Anderson, *Imagined Communities*, 21.

63. Lars Behrisch, "Statistics and Politics in the 18th Century," *Historical Social Research* 41, no. 2 (2016): 238–57; Philip Bobbitt, *The Shield of Achilles: War, Peace and the Course of History* (London: Penguin, 2002), 118–43.

64. Maier, *Once within Borders*, 82–132; John H. Elliott, *Empires of the Atlantic World: Britain and Spain in America, 1492–1830* (New Haven, CT: Yale University Press, 2006), 292–325; Darwin, *After Tamerlane*, 125–37; Mann, *Sources of Social Power*, 1:483–85.

65. Marvin Perry, *An Intellectual History of Modern Europe* (Boston: Houghton Mifflin, 1993), 121–70; Jonathan I. Israel, *A Revolution of the Mind: Radical Enlightenment and the Intellectual Origins of Modern Democracy* (Princeton, NJ: Princeton University Press, 2010).

66. Alain Blum and Jacques Houdaille, "L'alphabétisation aux XVIIIe et XIXe siècles: L'illusion parisienne?," *Population* (French ed.) 40, no. 6 (1985): 944–51.

67. Jürgen Habermas, *The Structural Transformation of the Public Sphere: An Inquiry into a Category of Bourgeois Society* (Cambridge, MA: MIT Press, 1989).

68. Colley, *Britons*, 40–43, 209–10; Jill Lepore, *These Truths: A History of the United States* (New York: W. W. Norton, 2018), 59; Michael Mann, *The Sources of Social Power*, vol. 2, *The Rise*

of Classes and Nation-States, 1760–1914 (Cambridge: Cambridge University Press, 1993), 102–7; Robert Darnton, *The Forbidden Best-Sellers of Pre-Revolutionary France* (New York: W. W. Norton, 1995).

69. Bell, *Cult of the Nation*, 50–107; J. H. Shennan, "The Rise of Patriotism in 18th-Century Europe," *History of European Ideas* 13, no. 6 (1991): 689–710.

70. Colley, *Gun, Ship*, 17–25, 57–92; Matthew Levinger, *Enlightened Nationalism: The Transformation of Prussian Political Culture, 1806–1848* (Oxford: Oxford University Press, 2002), 20–21.

Chapter 2

1. Colley, *Gun, Ship*, 1–14; C. A. Bayly, *The Birth of the Modern World, 1780–1914: Global Connections and Comparisons* (Malden, MA: Blackwell, 2004), 86–106; Lieberman, *Strange Parallels*, 1:30, 2:303–6, 340–55; Sebastian Conrad, "Enlightenment in Global History: A Historiographical Critique," *American Historical Review* 117, no. 4 (2012): 999–1027.

2. Mann, *Sources of Social Power*, 2:137–48; Lepore, *These Truths*, 55–91; Colley, *Britons*, 133–45.

3. T. H. Breen, "Ideology and Nationalism on the Eve of the American Revolution: Revisions Once More in Need of Revising," *Journal of American History* 84, no. 1 (1997): 19–23, 27–34; Keith Michael Baker, "Revolutionizing Revolution," in *Scripting Revolution: A Historical Approach to the Comparative Study of Revolutions*, ed. Keith Michael Baker and Dan Edelstein (Stanford, CA: Stanford University Press, 2015), 71–103.

4. Jack P. Greene, "State and National Identities in the Era of the American Revolution," in *Nationalism in the New World*, ed. Don H. Doyle and Marco Antonio Pamplona (Athens: University of Georgia Press, 2006), 61–80; Mann, *Sources of Social Power*, 2:149–55.

5. Jasper M. Trautsch, "The Origins and Nature of American Nationalism," *National Identities* 18, no. 3 (2015): 294–95; Thomas Bender, *A Nation among Nations: America's Place in World History* (New York: Hill and Wang, 2006), 88, 102–5; Lepore, *These Truths*, 109–49; David C. Hendrickson, *Peace Pact: The Lost World of the American Founding* (Lawrence: University Press of Kansas, 2006).

6. William Doyle, *The Oxford History of the French Revolution* (Oxford: Oxford University Press, 2018), 97–105.

7. Doyle, *French Revolution*, 86–120; Nigel Aston, *The French Revolution, 1789–1804: Authority, Liberty and the Search for Stability* (Basingstoke, UK: Palgrave Macmillan, 2004), 9–31.

8. Aston, *French Revolution, 1789–1804*, 27–73; Michael Rowe, "The French Revolution, Napoleon, and Nationalism in Europe," in Breuilly, *Oxford Handbook Nationalism*, 131–48.

9. Decree quoted in Michael Howard, *War in European History* (Oxford: Oxford University Press, 2009), 80; Charles J. Esdaile, *The Wars of the French Revolution, 1792–1801* (London: Routledge, 2018), 63–92; Timothy C. W. Blanning, *The French Revolutionary Wars: 1787–1802* (London: Arnold, 1996), 82–105.

10. Quoted in Kramer, *Nationalism in Europe and America*, 44.

11. Howard, *War in European History*, 75–86; Blanning, *Revolutionary Wars*, 116–28; David A. Bell, *The First Total War: Napoleon's Europe and the Birth of Modern Warfare* (London: Bloomsbury, 2008); Michael Broers, "The Concept of 'Total War' in the Revolutionary-Napoleonic Period," *War in History* 15, no. 3 (2008): 247–68.

12. Polasky, *Revolutions without Borders*; Sivasundaram, *Waves*; Ian Coller, "The French Revolution and the Islamic World of the Middle East and North Africa," in *The Routledge Companion to the French Revolution in World History*, ed. Alan Forrest and Matthias Middell (Abingdon, UK: Routledge, 2016), 127; Conrad, "Enlightenment in Global History," 1013; Green, *Fistful of Shells*, 392–96, 428.

13. Annie Jourdan, "The Netherlands in the Constellation of the Eighteenth-Century Western Revolutions," *European Review of History* 18, no. 2 (2011): 199–225; Jane C. Judge, *The United States of Belgium: The Story of the First Belgian Revolution* (Leuven: Leuven University Press, 2018); Doyle, *French Revolution*, 165–66, 198, 342–44.

14. Blanning, *Revolutionary Wars*, 91–92. See also Keitner, *Paradoxes of Nationalism*, 87–120.

15. Franz Dumont, "The Rhineland," in *Nationalism in the Age of the French Revolution*, ed. Otto Dann (London: Bloomsbury, 1988), 157–71; Doyle, *French Revolution*, 197–219; Jourdan, "Netherlands"; Cirilo Chico Comerón, "Actitudes políticas en Guipúzcoa durante la Guerra de la Convención (1793–1795)" (PhD diss., Universidad Nacional de Educación a Distancia, Madrid, 2012), 33–56.

16. Michael Broers, Peter Hicks, and Agustín Guimerá Ravina, eds., *The Napoleonic Empire and the New European Political Culture* (Basingstoke, UK: Palgrave Macmillan, 2012).

17. Pieter M. Judson, *The Habsburg Empire: A New History* (Cambridge, MA: Belknap, 2016), 52, 92–93.

18. Levinger, *Enlightened Nationalism*, 47–63; Christopher Clark, *Iron Kingdom: The Rise and Downfall of Prussia, 1600–1947* (London: Allen Lane, 2006), 312–45.

19. Sivasundaram, *Waves*, 79–97; Polasky, *Revolutions without Borders*, 75–111.

20. Sivasundaram, *Waves*, 97–110; Jeremy Adelman, *Sovereignty and Revolution in the Iberian Atlantic* (Princeton, NJ: Princeton University Press, 2006); Tomás Pérez Vejo, "Nuevos enfoques teóricos en torno a las guerras de independencia," in *De colonias a estados nacionales: Independencias y descolonización en América y el mundo en los siglos XIX y XX*, ed. Enrique Ayala Mora (Buenos Aires: Corrigedor, 2019), 91–123.

21. Laurent Dubois, *Avengers of the New World: The Story of the Haitian Revolution* (Cambridge, MA: Belknap Press, 2005); Philippe R. Girard, *Paradise Lost: Haiti's Tumultuous Journey from Pearl of the Caribbean to Third World Hot Spot* (New York: Palgrave Macmillan, 2005), 31–58; Frédéric Régent, "Revolution in France, Revolution in the Caribbean," in Forrest and Middell, *Routledge Companion to the French Revolution*, 61–77.

22. Michael Zeuske, "The French Revolution in Spanish America," in Forrest and Middell, *Routledge Companion to the French Revolution*, 77–96; Brian R. Hamnett, *The End of Iberian Rule on the American Continent, 1770–1830* (Cambridge: Cambridge University Press, 2017), 107–10, 115–19.

23. Rodríguez O., *Independence of Spanish America*, 75–107; Natalia Sobrevilla Perea, "Nation-Making and Nationalism," in *The Andean World*, ed. Linda J. Seligmann and Kathleen S. Fine-Dare (Abingdon, UK: Routledge, 2019), 303; Pérez Vejo, "Nuevos enfoques."

24. Rodríguez O., *Independence of Spanish America*, 36–169; Hamnett, *End of Iberian Rule*, 119–44, 176–208; Roberto Breña, "The Emancipation Process in New Spain and the Cádiz Constitution: New Historiographical Paths regarding the Revoluciones Hispánicas," in *The Rise of Constitutional Government in the Iberian Atlantic World: The Impact of the Cádiz Constitution of*

1812, ed. Scott Eastman and Natalia Sobrevilla Perea (Tuscaloosa: Alabama University Press, 2015), 38–51; Sobrevilla Perea, "Nation-Making and Nationalism."

25. Hamnett, *End of Iberian Rule*, 209–304; Adelman, *Sovereignty and Revolution*, 258–308, 344–94; Elliott, *Empires of the Atlantic World*, 325–403.

26. Fahrmeir, *Citizenship*, 41–42.

27. Rodríguez O., *Independence of Spanish America*, 130–44, 202–46; Sobrevilla Perea, "Nation-Making and Nationalism"; Girard, *Paradise Lost*, 60–67.

28. Fidel J. Tavárez, "Building Nation-Empires in the Eighteenth-Century Iberian Atlantic," in Carmichael, D'Auria, and Roshwald, *Cambridge History of Nationhood*, 2:5; Hamnett, *End of Iberian Rule*, 72–104; Fradera, *Imperial Nation*, 61–71.

29. Dumont, "Rhineland," 163; Doyle, *French Revolution*, 360; Christopher Duggan, *The Force of Destiny: A History of Italy since 1796* (London: Penguin, 2008), 26–27; Mart Rutjes, *Door gelijkheid gegrepen: Democratie, burgerschap en staat in Nederland 1795–1801* (Nijmegen: Vantilt, 2012), 29–57.

30. Levinger, *Enlightened Nationalism*, 50–51, 62, 66–68; Judson, *Habsburg Empire*, 95–96.

31. Pierre Rosanvallon, *Le sacre du citoyen: Histoire du suffrage universel en France* (Paris: Gallimard, 1992), 11–195; Michael Graetz, *The Jews in Nineteenth-Century France: From the French Revolution to the Alliance Israelite Universelle* (Stanford, CA: Stanford University Press, 1996), 17–41.

32. R. R. Palmer, *The Age of the Democratic Revolution: A Political History of Europe and America, 1760–1800*, updated ed. (Princeton, NJ: Princeton University Press, 2014), 629–35; Antonio Feros, *Speaking of Spain: The Evolution of Race and Nation in the Hispanic World* (Cambridge, MA: Harvard University Press, 2017), 253–56.

33. Fradera, *Imperial Nation*, 57–59; Fahrmeir, *Citizenship*, 28–37; Sivasundaram, *Waves*, 87–92, 97–103, 110.

34. Fradera, *Imperial Nation*, 65–71; Hamnett, *End of Iberian Rule*, 225, 258, 283, 287, 301, 308; Adelman, *Sovereignty and Revolution*, 366–72.

35. Fradera, *Imperial Nation*, 61–64, 82–88, 233–42; Bender, *Nation among Nations*, 98.

36. Moreno Almendral, *Relatos de vida, conceptos de nación*, 91–105, 173–88, 218–36, 249–61; Keitner, *Paradoxes of Nationalism*, 93, 107; Scott Eastman, *Preaching Spanish Nationalism across the Hispanic Atlantic, 1759–1823* (Baton Rouge: Louisiana State University Press, 2012), 73–93; Rebecca A. Earle, *The Return of the Native: Indians and Myth-Making in Spanish America, 1810–1930* (Durham, NC: Duke University Press, 2007), 47–79.

37. Shennan, "Rise of Patriotism"; Javier Fernández Sebastián, "From Patriotism to Liberalism: Political Concepts in Revolution," in *The Routledge Companion to Iberian Studies*, ed. Javier Múñoz Basols, Laura Lonsdale, and Manuel Delgado (London: Routledge, 2019), 305–19; Bernard Manin, *The Principles of Representative Government* (Cambridge: Cambridge University Press, 1997), 67–93.

38. Rosanvallon, *Le sacre du citoyen*, 194; Alan I. Forrest, *Conscripts and Deserters: The Army and French Society during the Revolution and Empire* (New York: Oxford University Press, 2001); Doyle, *French Revolution*, 228–46.

39. Michael Broers, *Napoleon's Other War: Bandits, Rebels and Their Pursuers in the Age of Revolutions* (Oxford: Peter Lang, 2010), xi–xii; Doyle, *French Revolution*, 224–26, 308–18, 342–43, 350–70; Duggan, *Force of Destiny*, 53–57; Hamnett, *End of Iberian Rule*, 145–76.

40. Doyle, *French Revolution*, 317–18; John Lawrence Tone, *La guerrilla española y la derrota de Napoleón* (Madrid: Alianza Editorial, 1999), 77–85; Ute Planert, "Wann beginnt der 'moderne' deutsche Nationalismus? Plädoyer für eine nationale Sattelzeit," in *Die Politik der Nation: Deutscher Nationalismus in Krieg und Krisen 1760 bis 1960*, ed. Jörg Echternkamp and Sven O. Müller (Berlin: De Gruyter, 2002), 55–56.

41. Charles J. Esdaile, *Spain in the Liberal Age: From Constitution to Civil War, 1808–1939* (Oxford: Blackwell, 2000), 37; Hamnett, *End of Iberian Rule*, 150, 171–73, 284–85; Eric Van Young, "Revolution and Imagined Community in Mexico, 1810–21," in Doyle and Pamplona, *Nationalism in the New World*, 192–98.

42. Broers, *Napoleon's Other War*, xi–xiv; Michael Broers, "The First Napoleonic Empire, 1799–1815," in Berger and Miller, *Nationalizing Empires*, 127–32; Bell, *Cult of the Nation*, 169–97, esp. 175.

43. Jourdan, "France, Patrie, Nation," 45; Aston, *French Revolution, 1789–1804*, 106–8; Palmer, *Age of the Democratic Revolution*, 623–34; Jürgen Osterhammel, *The Transformation of the World: A Global History of the Nineteenth Century* (Princeton, NJ: Princeton University Press, 2014), 105.

44. Barry Bergdoll, *European Architecture: 1750–1980* (Oxford: Oxford University Press, 2000), 105–7.

45. Lynn Hunt, *Politics, Culture, and Class in the French Revolution* (Berkeley: University of California Press, 2004), 52–87; Leora Auslander, *Cultural Revolutions: Everyday Life and Politics in Britain, North America, and France* (Berkeley: University of California Press, 2009), 113–49.

46. Hunt, *Politics, Culture, and Class*, 19–119; Charles Sowerwine, "Revising the Sexual Contract: Women's Citizenship and Republicanism in France, 1789–1944," in *Confronting Modernity in Fin-de-Siècle France: Bodies, Minds and Gender*, ed. Christopher E. Forth and Elinor Accampo (Basingstoke, UK: Palgrave Macmillan, 2010), 19–43; Auslander, *Cultural Revolutions*, 142–48, and for the United States, see 102–3.

47. Aston, *French Revolution, 1789–1804*, 86–88; Laura Mason, *Singing the French Revolution: Popular Culture and Politics, 1787–1799* (Ithaca, NY: Cornell University Press, 1996).

48. Astrid Swenson, *The Rise of Heritage: Preserving the Past in France, Germany and England, 1789–1914* (Cambridge: Cambridge University Press, 2013); Shiner, *Invention of Art*.

49. Andrew McClellan, *Inventing the Louvre: Art, Politics, and the Origins of the Modern Museum in Eighteenth-Century Paris* (Cambridge: Cambridge University Press, 1994), 13–124; François Loyer, *Histoire de l'architecture française*, vol. 3, *De la Révolution à nos jours* (Paris: Editions du Patrimoine, 1999), 24–27.

50. Swenson, *Rise of Heritage*, 31–33; François Souchal, *Le vandalisme de la Révolution* (Paris: Nouvelles Éditions Latines, 1993), 247–50. For the David quote, see McClellan, *Inventing the Louvre*, 106.

51. McClellan, *Inventing the Louvre*, 109–13, quote at 113; Shiner, *Invention of Art*, 180–86.

52. McClellan, *Inventing the Louvre*, 131–48.

53. McClellan, 155–98; Swenson, *Rise of Heritage*, 32–35.

54. Swenson, *Rise of Heritage*, 25–31; McClellan, *Inventing the Louvre*, 99–102.

55. McClellan, *Inventing the Louvre*, 114–23, 130–31; Swenson, *Rise of Heritage*, 37–41; Hartog, *Regimes of Historicity*, 170–76.

56. McClellan, *Inventing the Louvre*, 119, 131–54.

57. Hunt, *Politics, Culture, and Class*, 19–51; Beatrice F. Hyslop, "The Theater during a Crisis: The Parisian Theater during the Reign of Terror," *Journal of Modern History* 17, no. 4 (1945): 332–55; Hugh Honour, *Neo-Classicism: Style and Civilization* (Harmondsworth, UK: Penguin, 1968); Auslander, *Cultural Revolutions*, 92, 109, 141; Niek C. F. van Sas, *De metamorfose van Nederland: Van oude orde naar moderniteit, 1750–1900* (Amsterdam: Amsterdam University Press, 2004), 129–45.

58. Quoted in McClellan, *Inventing the Louvre*, 103.

59. Warren Roberts, *Jacques-Louis David, Revolutionary Artist: Art, Politics, and the French Revolution* (Chapel Hill: University of North Carolina Press, 2011).

60. Bergdoll, *European Architecture*, 105–17, 127–29, 134–35; Loyer, *Histoire de l'architecture française*, 3:17–23, quote at 22.

Chapter 3

1. Levinger, *Enlightened Nationalism*, 97–108; Leerssen, *National Thought*, 105–14.

2. Patrick Griffin et al., eds., *Between Sovereignty and Anarchy: The Politics of Violence in the American Revolutionary Era* (Charlottesville: University of Virginia Press, 2015); Girard, *Paradise Lost*, 55–56; John Lawrence Tone, *The Fatal Knot: The Guerrilla War in Navarre and the Defeat of Napoleon in Spain* (Chapell Hill: University of North Carolina Press, 1994), 53; Hamnett, *End of Iberian Rule*, 152–57.

3. Gat, *Nations*.

4. Thom, *Republics, Nations and Tribes*.

5. Johann Gottlieb Fichte, *Addresses to the German Nation* (Chicago: Open Court, 1922), 152–87; Arash Abizadeh, "Was Fichte an Ethnic Nationalist? On Cultural Nationalism and Its Double," *History of Political Thought* 26, no. 2 (2005): 340–58; Hans Kohn, "The Paradox of Fichte's Nationalism," *Journal of the History of Ideas* 10, no. 3 (1949): 333–40.

6. Leerssen, *National Thought*, 95–101; Anne-Marie Thiesse, *La création des identités nationales: Europe XVIIIe–XXe siècle* (Paris: Seuil, 1999), 34–43; Isaiah Berlin, *Vico and Herder: Two Studies in the History of Ideas* (London: Hogarth Press, 1976).

7. Thiesse, *Identités nationales*, 23–34; Leerssen, *National Thought*, 82.

8. Joep Leerssen, "Language Interest," in *Encyclopedia of Romantic Nationalism in Europe*, ed. Joep Leerssen (Amsterdam: Amsterdam University Press, 2018), 59–63; Kamusella, *Politics of Language*, 47, 370–73.

9. Krisztina Lajosi and Andreas Stynen, introduction to *Choral Societies and Nationalism in Europe*, ed. Krisztina Lajosi and Andreas Stynen (Leiden: Brill, 2015), 1–13; Krisztina Lajosi and Andreas Stynen, eds., *The Matica and Beyond: Cultural Associations and Nationalism in Europe* (Leiden: Brill, 2020).

10. Kamusella, *Politics of Language*, 368–81, 489–95.

11. Leerssen, "Language Interest"; see also Leerssen, *Encyclopedia of Romantic Nationalism*, 377–78, 387–390. Bálint Varga, "The Habsburg Monarchy," in Carmichael, D'Auria, and Roshwald, *Cambridge History of Nationhood*, 2:64–88.

12. Kamusella, *Politics of Language*, 407, 1129–40, 488–89, 531–67, 259–64; Paul Landau, "Language," in *Missions and Empire*, ed. Norman Etheringhthon, Oxford History of the British Empire Companion Series (Oxford: Oxford University Press, 2005), 194–216; Serhii Plokhy, *Lost*

Kingdom: A History of Russian Nationalism from Ivan the Great to Vladimir Putin (London: Allen Lane, 2017), 108–19, 148–51; Leerssen, *Encyclopedia of Romantic Nationalism*, 211, 1207–8.

13. Leerssen, "Language Interest"; see also entries on "language interest," in Leerssen, *Encyclopedia of Romantic Nationalism*.

14. Samuel E. Finer, *The History of Government from the Earliest Times*, vol. 3, *Empires, Monarchies, and the Modern State* (Oxford: Oxford University Press, 1999), 1434–38, 1572–83.

15. Luis Díez del Corral, *El liberalismo doctrinario* (Madrid: Instituto de Estudios Políticos, 1956).

16. Kramer, *Nationalism in Europe and America*, 48–49; Levinger, *Enlightened Nationalism*, 71–97, 127–91; Brian E. Vick, *The Congress of Vienna: Power and Politics after Napoleon* (Cambridge, MA: Harvard University Press, 2014), 266–74; John Edward Toews, *Becoming Historical: Cultural Reformation and Public Memory in Early Nineteenth-Century Berlin* (Cambridge: Cambridge University Press, 2004), 19–67.

17. Marie-Pierre Le Hir, *The National Habitus: Ways of Feeling French, 1789–1870* (Berlin: De Gruyter, 2014), 72–121; Geoffrey Hosking, *Russia: People and Empire, 1552–1917* (London: Harper Collins, 1997), 146–47; Duggan, *Force of Destiny*, 155–62.

18. Clark, *Iron Kingdom*, 350; José Alvarez Junco, "La invención de la Guerra de la Independencia," *Studia Historica. Historia Contemporánea* 12 (1994): 82; Plokhy, *Lost Kingdom*, 75; Karen Hagemann, *"Mannlicher Muth und teutsche Ehre": Nation, Militär und Geschlecht zur Zeit der antinapoleonischen Kriege Preußens* (Paderborn: Schöningh, 2002), 394–427.

19. Adam Zamoyski, *Rites of Peace: The Fall of Napoleon and the Congress of Vienna* (London: Harper Perennial, 2008), 386–87 and passim.

20. Brisku, *Political Reform*, 17–51; Zamoyski, *Rites of Peace*, 535–49.

21. Robert Tombs, *France, 1814–1914* (London: Longman, 1996), 330–33; Robert Gildea, *Children of the Revolution: The French, 1799–1914* (London: Penguin, 2009), 38–45.

22. Vick, *Congress of Vienna*, 240–58; Brisku, *Political Reform*, 17–20, 52–60; Alexei Miller, "The Romanov Empire and the Russian Nation," in Berger and Miller, *Nationalizing Empires*, 318–20.

23. Finer, *History of Government*, 1567–94.

24. John Breuilly, "Nationalism and National Unification in Nineteenth-Century Europe," in Breuilly, *Oxford Handbook of Nationalism*, 149–75.

25. Duggan, *Force of Destiny*, 57–68, 82–89, 122–24.

26. Duggan, 125–34; C. A. Bayly and Eugenio F. Biagini, eds., *Giuseppe Mazzini and the Globalization of Democratic Nationalism, 1830–1920* (Oxford: Oxford University Press, 2008).

27. Ishita Banerjee-Dube, *A History of Modern India* (Delhi: Cambridge University Press, 2015), 24–26, 67–69; Sivasundaram, *Waves*, 104–11.

28. Sivasundaram, *Waves*, 50–78.

29. Colley, *Gun, Ship*, 284–305.

30. Solofo Randrianja and Stephen Ellis, *Madagascar: A Short History* (London: Hurst, 2009), 112–57.

31. Banu Turnaoğlu, *The Formation of Turkish Republicanism* (Princeton, NJ: Princeton University Press, 2017), 29–49; Ali Yaycioglu, *Partners of the Empire: The Crisis of the Ottoman Order in the Age of Revolutions* (Stanford, CA: Stanford University Press, 2016).

32. Frederick F. Anscombe, *State, Faith, and Nation in Ottoman and Post-Ottoman Lands* (Cambridge: Cambridge University Press, 2014).

33. Jan Lucassen and Erik Jan Zürcher, "Introduction: Conscription and Resistance. The Historical Context," in *Arming the State: Military Conscription in the Middle East and East Asia 1775–1925*, ed. Erik J. Zürcher (London: Tauris, 1999), 8. See also Virginia Aksan, "Ottoman Military Recruitment Strategies in the Late Eighteenth Century," in Zürcher, *Arming the State*, 21–28.

34. M. Şükrü Hanioğlu, *A Brief History of the Late Ottoman Empire* (Princeton, NJ: Princeton University Press, 2008), 42–54; Anscombe, *State, Faith*, 33–60.

35. Afaf Lutfi Sayyid-Marsot, *A History of Egypt: From the Arab Conquest to the Present* (Cambridge: Cambridge University Press, 2007), 61–70; Kalid Mahmud Fahmi, *All the Pasha's Men: Mehmed Ali, His Army and the Making of Modern Egypt* (Cambridge: Cambridge University Press, 1997), 239–78.

36. Paschális M. Kitromilídis, *Enlightenment and Revolution: The Making of Modern Greece* (Cambridge, MA; Harvard University Press, 2013), 21–62, 200–230; Marie-Janine Calic, *The Great Cauldron: A History of Southeastern Europe* (Cambridge, MA: Harvard University Press, 2019), 150–63; Umut Özkirimli and Spyros A. Sofos, *Tormented by History: Nationalism in Greece and Turkey* (New York: Columbia University Press, 2008), 15–27; Kamusella, *Politics of Language*, 255–59.

37. Stevan K. Pavlowitch, *A History of the Balkans 1804–1945* (London: Routledge, 2014), 27–31; Stevan K. Pavlowitch, *Serbia: The History of an Idea* (New York: New York University Press, 2002), 26–39.

38. Anscombe, *State, Faith*, 68–69; Pavlowitch, *Balkans*, 31–37; Eric D. Weitz, *A World Divided: The Global Struggle for Human Rights in the Age of Nation-States* (Princeton, NJ: Princeton University Press, 2019), 72–73; Michalis Sotiropoulos and Antonis Hadjikyriacou, "Patris, Ethnos, and Demos: Representation and Political Participation in the Greek World," in *Re-imagining Democracy in the Mediterranean, 1780–1860*, ed. Joanna Innis and Mark Philp (Oxford: Oxford University Press, 2018), 99–127.

39. Pavlowitch, *Balkans*, 30, 35, 38–40; Weitz, *World Divided*, 56–76; Davide Rodogno, *Against Massacre: Humanitarian Interventions in the Ottoman Empire, 1815–1914* (Princeton, NJ: Princeton University Press, 2012), 63–90.

40. Hanioğlu, *Late Ottoman Empire*, 58–64; Pavlowitch, *Balkans*, 30, 35; Erik Jan Zürcher, *Turkey: A Modern History* (London: Tauris, 1997), 38–48.

41. Fahmī, *All the Pasha's Men*, 38–75, 285–304; Kalid Mahmud Fahmi, *Mehmed Ali: From Ottoman Governor to Ruler of Egypt* (Oxford: Oneworld, 2008), 82–99; Sayyid-Marsot, *History of Egypt*, 71–77; Rodogno, *Against Massacre*, 63–90.

42. Brisku, *Political Reform*, 61–98; Anscombe, *State, Faith*, 87–102; Ross, *Clothing*, 113.

43. Rosanvallon, *Le sacre du citoyen*, 209–49; Tombs, *France, 1814–1914*, 68–69; Díez del Corral, *El liberalismo doctrinario*.

44. Fahrmeir, *Citizenship*, 37–88.

45. Joan B. Landes, *Women and the Public Sphere in the Age of the French Revolution* (Ithaca, NY: Cornell University Press, 1988), 139–51, 201–6; Karen Offen, *The Woman Question in France, 1400–1870* (Cambridge: Cambridge University Press, 2017), 46–82; Colley, *Gun, Ship*, 261–75; Berger, *Past as History*, 125–27, 181; Gildea, *Children of the Revolution*, 141–67.

46. David Sorkin, *Jewish Emancipation: A History across Five Centuries* (Princeton, NJ: Princeton University Press, 2019), 118–28, 141–62.

47. Sorkin, 142, 211–12.

48. Mara Loveman, *National Colors: Racial Classification and the State in Latin America* (Oxford: Oxford University Press, 2014), 77–83; John Seh David, *The American Colonization Society and the Founding of the First African Republic* (Bloomington, IN: iUniverse, 2014).

49. Bender, *Nation among Nations*, 192–99; Fradera, *Imperial Nation*, 162–72.

50. Brisku, *Political Reform*, 41–52, 55, 66; Fahmī, *All the Pasha's Men*, 282; Adam Mestyan, *Arab Patriotism: The Ideology and Culture of Power in Late Ottoman Egypt* (Princeton, NJ: Princeton University Press, 2017), 71; Marie Tyler-McGraw, *An African Republic: Black and White Virginians in the Making of Liberia* (Chapel Hill: University of North Carolina Press, 2007), 179; Christine Whyte, "Between Empire and Colony: American Imperialism and Pan-African Colonialism in Liberia, 1810–2003," *National Identities* 18, no. 1 (2016): 77–80.

51. "Le Sacre de Charles X," Promenade en France, 2017, http://promenade34.free.fr/Documents/nostal52.htm.

52. Thomas Nipperdey, *Deutsche Geschichte, 1800–1866: Bürgerwelt und starker Staat* (Munich: Beck, 1983), 610–11.

53. Duggan, *Force of Destiny*, 84–86; Ernst H. Kossmann, *De Lage Landen 1780–1940: Anderhalve eeuw Nederland en België* (Amsterdam: Elsevier, 1984), 91–108; Siniša Malešević, *Grounded Nationalisms: A Sociological Analysis* (Cambridge: Cambridge University Press, 2019), 193–98; Anscombe, *State, Faith*, 68–69; Dennis P. Hupchick, *The Balkans: From Constantinopole to Communism* (Basingstoke, UK: Palgrave Macmillan, 2002), 221–22.

54. Keely Stauter-Halsted, *The Nation in the Village: The Genesis of Peasant National Identity in Austrian Poland, 1848–1914* (Ithaca, NY: Cornell University Press, 2004), 1–2; Judson, *Habsburg Empire*, 157–59.

55. Fisch, "Zivilisation, Kultur," 705–16, 724–30; Andrea Wulf, *Magnificent Rebels: The First Romantics and the Invention of the Self* (London: Murray, 2022).

56. Berger, *Past as History*, 80–82.

57. Andrea Wulf, *The Invention of Nature: Alexander von Humboldt's New World* (London: Murray, 2015); Livingstone, *Geographical Tradition*, 119–89; William Whewell, *A History of the Inductive Sciences* (Cambridge: Cambridge University Press, 2010), 519–27.

58. Berger, *Past as History*, 81, 101–2, 120–23.

59. Toews, *Becoming Historical*, 281–372; Matti Bunzl, "Franz Boas and the Humboldtian Tradition: From Volksgeist and Nationalcharakter to an Anthropological Concept of Culture," in *Volksgeist as Method and Ethic: Essays on Boasian Ethnography and the German Anthropological Tradition*, ed. George W. Stocking (Madison: University of Wisconsin Press, 1996), 19–36.

60. Lyle Campbell, "The History of Linguistics," in *The Handbook of Linguistics*, ed. Mark Aronoff and Janie Rees-Miller (Oxford: Blackwell, 2001), 87–90; Thom, *Republics, Nations and Tribes*, 221–28; Kamusella, *Politics of Language*, 84.

61. Leerssen, *Encyclopedia of Romantic Nationalism*; Berger, *Past as History*, 129–36.

62. Berger, *Past as History*, 83, 100–128, 137–39.

63. Thom, *Republics, Nations and Tribes*, 227–30.

64. Berger, *Past as History*, 98–100, 106–13, 120; Toews, *Becoming Historical*, 372–419.

65. Eliana de Freitas Dutra, "The Mirror of History and Images of the Nation: The Invention of a National Identity in Brazil and Its Contrasts with Similar Enterprises in Mexico and Argentina," in *Writing the Nation: A Global Perspective*, ed. Stefan Berger (Basingstoke, UK: Palgrave

Macmillan, 2007), 84–103; Gérard Bouchard, *The Making of the Nations and Cultures of the New World: An Essay in Comparative History* (Montreal: McGill-Queen's University Press, 2008), 290–99, 309–32.

66. Berger, *Past as History*, 93–95; Margarita Díaz-Andreu García, *A World History of Nineteenth-Century Archaeology: Nationalism, Colonialism, and the Past* (Oxford: Oxford University Press, 2007); Timothy Baycroft and David M. Hopkin, eds., *Folklore and Nationalism in Europe during the Long Nineteenth Century* (Leiden: Brill, 2012); Eric Storm, "Art History," in *European Regions and Boundaries: A Conceptual History*, ed. Diana Mishkova and Balázs Trencsényi (New York: Berghahn, 2017), 372–94.

67. Wulf, *Magnificent Rebels*, 163–70; Thiesse, *Identités nationales*, 114–17; Joep Leerssen, "Patriotic Poetry and Verse," in Leerssen, *Encyclopedia of Romantic Nationalism*, 109–11.

68. Joep Leerssen, "Romanticism, Music, Nationalism," *Nations and Nationalism* 20, no. 4 (2014): 606–27; Leerssen, "Patriotic Poetry."

69. Thiesse, *Identités nationales*, 133–39; Ann Rigney, "The Historical Novel," in Leerssen, *Encyclopedia of Romantic Nationalism*, 114–16.

70. Monika Flacke, ed., *Mythen der Nationen: Ein europäisches Panorama* (Munich: Koehler & Amelang, 1998); William Vaughan, *Romantic Art* (London: Thames and Hudson, 1988), 55–222.

71. Berger, *Past as History*, 151–54; Kamusella, *Politics of Language*, 437.

72. Gabriella Elgenius and Peter Aronsson, eds., *Building National Museums in Europe 1750–2010* (Linköping: Linköping University Electronic Press, 2011); Stefan Berger, Peter Aronsson, and Gabriella Elgenius, "National Museums in between Nationalism, Imperialism and Regionalism, 1750–1915," in *National Museums and Nation-Building in Europe 1750–1920: Mobilization and Legitimacy, Continuity and Change*, ed. Peter Aronsson and Gabriella Elgenius (London: Routledge, 2015), 13–33; Donald Malcolm Reid, *Whose Pharaohs? Archaeology, Museums, and Egyptian National Identity from Napoleon to World War I* (Berkeley: University of California Press, 2002), 54–56; Elsa van Wezel, "Het Alte Museum te Berlijn: Wijzigingen in het museumconcept omstreeks 1800," in *Verzamelen: Van rariteitenkabinet tot kunstmuseum*, ed. Ellinoor Bergvelt, Debora J. Meijers, and Mieke Rijnders (Heerlen, Netherlands: Open Universiteit, 1993), 317–32.

73. Bätschmann, *Ausstellungskünstler*, 21, 36; Emma McEvoy, *Gothic Tourism* (London: Palgrave Macmillan, 2016), 57–60; Aude Déruelle, "Galerie des Batailles et histoire-bataille," *Romantisme* 169, no. 2 (2015): 55–68.

74. Swenson, *Rise of Heritage*, 46–65; Thomas Nipperdey, "Der Kölner Dom als Nationaldenkmal," in *Nachdenken über die deutsche Geschichte* (Munich: DTV, 1986), 189–208; Loyer, *Histoire de l'architecture française*, 121–24.

75. Eveline Bouwers, *Public Pantheons in Revolutionary Europe: Comparing Cultures of Remembrance, c. 1790–1840* (Basingstoke, UK: Palgrave Macmillan, 2012).

76. Christian Demange, *El dos de mayo: Mito y fiesta nacional, 1808–1958* (Madrid: Marcial Pons, 2004), 107–8, 135–59.

77. Joep Leerssen, "Collective Memories, Embodied Communities, Festivals and Commemorations," in Leerssen, *Encyclopedia of Romantic Nationalism*, 149–51; Toews, *Becoming Historical*, 120–41.

78. Joy M. Giguere, *Characteristically American Memorial Architecture, National Identity, and the Egyptian Revival* (Knoxville: University of Tennessee Press, 2014), 163–68; Rodrigo

Gutiérrez Viñuales, *Monumento conmemorativo y espacio público en Iberoamérica* (Madrid: Cátedra, 2004), 507–663.

79. Bergdoll, *European Architecture*, 139–70; Udo Kultermann, "Histoire de l'art et identité nationale," in *Histoire de l'histoire de l'art*, ed. Edouard Pommier (Paris: Musée du Louvre, 1997), 2:230–40.

80. Nadia Urbinati, "The Legacy of Kant: Giuseppe Mazzini's Cosmopolitanism of Nations," in Bayly and Biagini, *Giuseppe Mazzini*, 11–37.

81. Jonathan Sperber, *The European Revolutions, 1848–1851* (Cambridge: Cambridge University Press, 2005), 109–56; Gildea, *Children of the Revolution*, 53–61.

82. Sperber, *European Revolutions*; Hastings, *Nationalism in Modern Europe*, 80–81, 87–88.

83. Sperber, *European Revolutions*, 136–37; Nipperdey, *Deutsche Geschichte, 1800–1866*, 624–26.

84. Sperber, *European Revolutions*, 135–36; Nipperdey, *Deutsche Geschichte, 1800–1866*, 626–28.

85. Sperber, *European Revolutions*, 138–40; Judson, *Habsburg Empire*, 172–212; Nipperdey, "Kölner Dom," 628–29.

86. Sperber, *European Revolutions*, 142–47; Judson, *Habsburg Empire*, 162–67, 184–90, 199–201, 215–16; Calic, *Great Cauldron*, 289–93.

87. Sivasundaram, *Waves*, 312–21; Osterhammel, *Transformation of the World*, 547.

88. Sperber, *European Revolutions*, 241–46; Nipperdey, *Deutsche Geschichte, 1800–1866*, 651, 660–61.

Chapter 4

1. Nipperdey, *Deutsche Geschichte, 1800–1866*, 358–61.

2. Tombs, *France, 1814–1914*, 403–6.

3. Duggan, *Force of Destiny*, 188–211; David Laven, "Italy: The Idea of the Nation in the Risorgimento and Liberal Eras," in *What Is a Nation? Europe 1789–1914*, ed. Timothy Baycroft and Mark Hewitson (Oxford: Oxford University Press, 2006), 255–72.

4. Nipperdey, *Deutsche Geschichte, 1800–1866*, 749–805; Thomas Nipperdey, *Deutsche Geschichte, 1866–1918, vol. 2, Machtstaat vor der Demokratie* (Munich: Beck, 1992), 11–85.

5. Hobsbawm, *Nations and Nationalism since 1780*, 30–38.

6. Hugo Hantsch, "Pan-Slavism, Austro-Slavism, Neo-Slavism: The All-Slav Congresses and the Nationality Problems of Austria-Hungary," *Austrian History Yearbook* 1 (1965): 23–37; Berger, *Past as History*, 217–22; Leerssen, *National Thought*, 154–58.

7. José Antonio Rocamora Rocamora, "Un nacionalismo fracasado: El iberismo," *Espacio, tiempo y forma, series 5, Historia contemporánea* 2 (1989): 29–56.

8. Ruth Hemstad, "Scandinavianism," *Contributions to the History of Concepts* 13, no. 1 (2018): 1–21; Eric Helleiner, *The Making of National Money: Territorial Currencies in Historical Perspective* (Ithaca, NY: Cornell University Press, 2003), 135–36.

9. Margaret Conrad, *A Concise History of Canada* (Cambridge: Cambridge University Press, 2011), 134–38, 143–52.

10. Pavlowitch, *Balkans*, 108–14; Hupchick, *Balkans*, 255–67.

11. Jens Beckert, "Institutional Isomorphism Revisited: Convergence and Divergence in Institutional Change," *Sociological Theory* 28, no. 2 (2010): 150–66.

12. Judson, *Habsburg Empire*, 218–33, 248–57; Sorkin, *Jewish Emancipation*, 183–86; Peter Haslinger, "How to Run a Multilingual Society: Statehood, Administration and Regional Dynamics in Austria-Hungary, 1867–1914," in *Region and State in Nineteenth-Century Europe: Nation-Building, Regional Identities and Separatism*, ed. Joost Augusteijn and Eric Storm (Basingstoke, UK: Palgrave Macmillan, 2012), 111–31.

13. Brisku, *Political Reform*, 105–19; Hosking, *Russia*, 270–77, 315–20; Plokhy, *Lost Kingdom*, 121–22.

14. Hosking, *Russia*, 194–97, 315–44; Brisku, *Political Reform*, 115–37.

15. Howard Eisenstat, "Modernization, Imperial Nationalism, and the Ethnicization of Confessional Identity in the Late Ottoman Empire," in Berger and Miller, *Nationalizing Empires*, 434–45; Mehmet Hacisalihoğlu, "Inclusion and Exclusion: Conscription in the Ottoman Empire," *Journal of Modern European History* 5, no. 2 (2007): 265–75; Zürcher, *Turkey*, 67–74; Anscombe, *State, Faith*, 92–96.

16. Brisku, *Political Reform*, 149–88; Zürcher, *Turkey*, 58–85.

17. Fahmī, *All the Pasha's Men*, 285–305; Sayyid-Marsot, *History of Egypt*, 71–89; Mestyan, *Arab Patriotism*, 44–45, 69–73, 170–72, 184–97.

18. Klaus Mühlhahn, *Making China Modern: From the Great Qing to Xi Jinping.* (Cambridge, MA: Harvard University Press, 2019), 35–44, 76–81; P. F. Kornicki, "A Transnational Approach to East-Asian Book History," in *New World Order: Transnational Themes in Book History*, ed. Swapan Chakravorty and Abhijit Gupta (Delhi: Worldview, 2011), 35–44, 76–81.

19. Mühlhahn, *Making China Modern*, 85–94, 120–34; Pär Kristoffer Cassel, *Grounds of Judgment: Extraterritoriality and Imperial Power in Nineteenth-Century China and Japan* (New York: Oxford University Press, 2012), 46–55.

20. Mühlhahn, *Making China Modern*, 94–106; Cassel, *Grounds of Judgment*, 57–61; Harrison, *China*, 55–64.

21. Mühlhahn, *Making China Modern*, 101–4, 131–34, 153–69; Harrison, *China*, 63–68.

22. Mühlhahn, *Making China Modern*, 170–75; Harrison, *China*, 74–75.

23. M. C. Ricklefs et al., *A New History of Southeast Asia* (Basingstoke, UK: Palgrave Macmillan, 2010), 168–75.

24. Chris Baker and Pasuk Phongpaichit, *A History of Thailand* (Cambridge: Cambridge University Press, 2009), 44–80; Ricklefs et al., *Southeast Asia*, 137–42, 227–37.

25. Marius B. Jansen, *The Making of Modern Japan* (Cambridge, MA: Belknap, 2002), 257–86; Milton W. Meyer, *Japan: A Concise History* (Lanham, MD: Rowman & Littlefield, 2012), 125–30.

26. Jansen, *Modern Japan*, 286–317; Meyer, *Japan*, 130–35.

27. Jansen, *Modern Japan*, 307–70; Meyer, *Japan*, 141–44.

28. Jansen, *Modern Japan*, 371–77.

29. Berger and Miller, *Nationalizing Empires*; James L. MacClain, *Japan: A Modern History* (New York: Norton, 2002), 179–81, 256–59; Carol Gluck, *Japan's Modern Myths: Ideology in the Late Meiji Period* (Princeton, NJ: Princeton University Press, 1985), 42–73; Tessa Morris-Suzuki, *Re-inventing Japan: Time, Space, Nation* (Armonk, NY: M. E. Sharpe, 1998), 187–92.

30. Banerjee-Dube, *Modern India*, 83–87, 160–69; Henk L. Wesseling, *The European Colonial Empires, 1815–1919* (Harlow, UK: Longman, 2004), 105–9.

31. Banerjee-Dube, *Modern India*, 43–147.

32. Frédéric Bon, *Les élections en France: Histoire et sociologie* (Paris: Seuil, 1978), 28–43; Miguel A. Centeno and Agustin E. Ferraro, "Republics of the Possible," in *State and Nation Making in Latin America and Spain: Republics of the Possible*, ed. Miguel A. Centeno and Agustin E. Ferraro (Cambridge: Cambridge University Press, 2013), 3–24; Gabriele Ranzato, "Le elezioni nei sistemi liberali italiano e spagnolo," *Rivista di storia contemporanea*, no. 2 (1989): 244–63; Javier Moreno Luzón, "Political Clientelism, Elites, and Caciquismo in Restoration Spain (1875–1923)," *European History Quarterly* 37, no. 3 (2007): 417–41.

33. Sylvia Paletschek and Bianka Pietrow-Ennker, eds., *Women's Emancipation Movements in the Nineteenth Century: A European Perspective* (Stanford, CA: Stanford University Press, 2004); Kramer, *Nationalism in Europe and America*, 102–15.

34. John C. Torpey, *The Invention of the Passport: Surveillance, Citizenship and the State* (Cambridge: Cambridge University Press, 2000), 91–113.

35. Maier, *Once within Borders*, 195–205, 210–12, 218–19; Eric Vanhaute, *Peasants in World History* (New York: Routledge, 2021), 87–103.

36. Anthony Arblaster, *The Rise and Decline of Western Liberalism* (Oxford: Blackwell, 1989); Dieter Langewiesche, ed., *Liberalismus im 19. Jahrhundert: Deutschland im europäischen Vergleich* (Göttingen: Vandenhoeck & Ruprecht, 1988).

37. Osterhammel, *Transformation of the World*, 322–68, 376–82; Maier, *Once within Borders*, 204–5; Brett L. Walker, *A Concise History of Japan* (Cambridge: Cambridge University Press, 2015), 201–5; Banerjee-Dube, *Modern India*, 106–16; Guillermo de la Peña, "Social and Cultural Policies towards Indigenous Peoples: Perspectives from Latin America," *Annual Review of Anthropology* 34 (2005): 719–23.

38. Bender, *Nation among Nations*, 160–75; Fradera, *Imperial Nation*, 172–75; Nancy P. Appelbaum, "Envisioning the Nation: The Mid-Nineteenth-Century Colombian Chorographic Commission," in Centeno and Ferraro, *State and Nation Making*, 388–89.

39. Fradera, *Imperial Nation*, 94–110, 128–42, 199–204; Catherine Hall, *Civilising Subjects: Metropole and Colony in the English Imagination, 1830–1867* (Cambridge: Polity, 2002).

40. Fradera, *Imperial Nation*, 118–26; James McDougall, *A History of Algeria* (Cambridge: Cambridge University Press, 2017), 89–128; Judith Surkis, *Sex, Law, and Sovereignty in French Algeria, 1830–1930* (Ithaca, NY: Cornell University Press, 2019), 90–118.

41. Eugen Weber, *Peasants into Frenchmen: The Modernization of Rural France, 1870–1914* (Stanford, CA: Stanford University Press, 1976), 193–375.

42. Anderson, *Imagined Communities*, 44–46, 61–67, 77–82; Weber, *Peasants into Frenchmen*, 452–71.

43. Michael Billig, *Banal Nationalism* (London: Sage, 1995), 93–128.

44. Thomas Smits, *The European Illustrated Press and the Emergence of a Transnational Visual Culture of the News, 1842–1870* (London: Routledge, 2020).

45. Miroslav Hroch, *Social Preconditions of National Revival in Europe: A Comparative Analysis of the Social Composition of Patriotist Groups among the Smaller European Nations* (New York: Columbia University Press, 2000).

46. Jeremy King, *Budweisers into Czechs and Germans: A Local History of Bohemian Politics, 1848–1948* (Princeton, NJ: Princeton University Press, 2002), 48–80; Judson, *Habsburg Empire*, 269–332; Paul Bew, *Ireland: The Politics of Enmity, 1789–2006* (Oxford: Oxford University Press, 2007), 302–60.

47. Weber, *Peasants into Frenchmen*; Charles Sowerwine, *France since 1870: Culture, Politics and Society* (Basingstoke, UK: Palgrave, 2001), 27–38.

48. Weber, *Peasants into Frenchmen*, 303–39, 485–97; Tombs, *France, 1814–1914*, 302–25.

49. Miguel Cabo and Fernando Molina, "The Long and Winding Road of Nationalization: Eugen Weber's *Peasants into Frenchmen* in Modern European History (1976–2006)," *European History Quarterly* 39, no. 2 (2009): 264–86; Timothy Baycroft and Mark Hewitson, eds., *What Is a Nation? Europe 1789–1914* (Oxford: Oxford University Press, 2006); Fernando Reimers, "Education and Social Progress," in *The Cambridge Economic History of Latin America*, vol. 2, *The Long Twentieth Century*, ed. Victor Bulmer-Thomas, John Coatsworth, and Robert Cortes-Conde (Cambridge: Cambridge University Press, 2006), 427–80; Nicola Miller, *Republics of Knowledge: Nations of the Future in Latin America* (Princeton, NJ: Princeton University Press, 2021), 200–203.

50. Hans-Ulrich Wehler, "Bismarck's Imperialism 1862–1890," *Past and Present*, no. 48 (1970): 119–55; Nipperdey, *Deutsche Geschichte, 1866–1918*, 2:359–426.

51. Stuart Woolf, "Statistics and the Modern State," *Comparative Studies in Society and History* 31, no. 3 (1989): 588–604; Loveman, *National Colors*, 93–113.

52. Kamusella, *Politics of Language*, 43–44, 49, 399; Judson, *Habsburg Empire*, 309–12.

53. Nira Wickramasinghe, *Sri Lanka in the Modern Age: A History* (Oxford: Oxford University Press, 2015), 48–54; Banerjee-Dube, *Modern India*, 141–54.

54. Wimmer and Schiller, "Methodological Nationalism and Beyond."

55. Berger, *Past as History*, 140–226; Stefan Berger, ed., *Writing the Nation: A Global Perspective* (Basingstoke, UK: Palgrave Macmillan, 2007).

56. Plokhy, *Lost Kingdom*, 83–84; Brisku, *Political Reform*, 84–85, 176; Mestyan, *Arab Patriotism*, 28–31, 44–46, 162–63; Ervand Abrahamian, *A History of Modern Iran* (Cambridge: Cambridge University Press, 2008), 35–36; Ami Ayalon, *Language and Change in the Arab Middle East: The Evolution of Modern Arabic Political Discourse* (Oxford: Oxford University Press, 1987); Weigui Fang, *Modern Notions of Civilization and Culture in China* (Singapore: Palgrave Macmillan, 2019).

57. Usman Ahmedani, "History-Writing and Historicism in Late-Ottoman Turkey," in Leerssen, *Encyclopedia of Romantic Nationalism*, 1447–48; Reid, *Whose Pharaohs?*, 108–12, 146–48, 172–212; Mestyan, *Arab Patriotism*, 41, 73–77, 149–52.

58. Q. Edward Wang, "Between Myth and History: The Construction of the National Past in Modern East Asia," in Berger, *Writing the Nation*, 126–34.

59. Jansen, *Modern Japan*, 320–21; Christopher L. Hill, *National History and the World of Nations: Capital, State, and the Rhetoric of History in Japan, France and the United States* (Durham, NC: Duke University Press, 2009), 1–4, 52–61; Wang, "Myth and History," 128–30; Fang, *Notions of Civilization*, 41–44.

60. Wang, "Myth and History," 134–46; Xiaobing Tang, *Global Space and the Nationalist Discourse of Modernity: The Historical Thinking of Liang Qichao* (Stanford, CA: Stanford University Press, 1996), 11–116.

61. Storm, "Art History," 373–77; Kaufmann, *Toward a Geography of Art*, 43–51; Udo Kultermann, *Geschichte der Kunstgeschichte: Der Weg einer Wissenschaft* (Munich: Prestel, 1990), 104–29; Partha Mitter, *Art and Nationalism in Colonial India, 1850–1922: Occidental Orientations* (Cambridge: Cambridge University Press, 1994), 221–28.

62. Kaufmann, *Toward a Geography of Art*, 107–54; Storm, *Discovery of El Greco*, 7–45.

63. Nina Lübbren, *Rural Artists' Colonies in Europe, 1870–1910* (Manchester: Manchester University Press, 2001); John House, ed., *Landscapes of France: Impressionism and Its Rivals* (London: Hayward Gallery, 1995).

64. Robert Jensen, *Marketing Modernism in Fin-de-Siècle Europe* (Princeton, NJ: Princeton University Press, 1994); Tricia Cusack, *Riverscapes and National Identities* (Syracuse, NY: Syracuse University Press, 2019).

65. Mitter, *Art and Nationalism*, 179–219.

66. See individual entries in Leerssen, *Encyclopedia of Romantic Nationalism*; Chetan Bhatt, *Hindu Nationalism: Origins, Ideologies and Modern Myths* (Oxford: Berg, 2001), 26–31.

67. Leerssen, "Romanticism, Music, Nationalism"; see also Leerssen, *Encyclopedia of Romantic Nationalism*.

68. Leerssen, "Romanticism, Music, Nationalism," 619–20; Mestyan, *Arab Patriotism*, 84–120; Lou Charnon-Deutsch, *The Spanish Gypsy: The History of a European Obsession* (University Park: Pennsylvania State University Press, 2004).

69. Michiel Wagenaar, *Stedebouw en burgerlijke vrijheid: De contrasterende carrières van zes Europese hoofdsteden* (Bussum, Netherlands: Thoth, 1998); Mestyan, *Arab Patriotism*, 85–89.

70. Eric Hobsbawm, "Mass-Producing Traditions: Europe, 1870–1914," in *The Invention of Tradition*, ed. Eric Hobsbawm and Terence Ranger (Cambridge: Canto, 1992), 263–309; Pierre Nora, ed., *Les lieux de mémoire*, 3 vols. (Paris: Gallimard, 1984); Maoz Azaryahu, "The Power of Commemorative Street Names," *Environment and Planning D: Society and Space* 14, no. 3 (1996): 311–30; Gutiérrez Viñuales, *Monumento conmemorativo y espacio público en Iberoamérica*.

71. Swenson, *Rise of Heritage*, 66–144.

72. Mark David Spence, *Dispossessing the Wilderness: Indian Removal and the Making of the National Parks* (New York: Oxford University Press, 2000); Patrick Kupper, *Creating Wilderness: A Transnational History of the Swiss National Park* (New York: Berghahn, 2014), 15–21.

73. Roland Quinault, "The Cult of the Centenary, c. 1784–1914," *Historical Research* 71, no. 176 (1998): 303–23; Joep Leerssen and Ann Rigney, eds., *Commemorating Writers in Nineteenth-Century Europe: Nation-Building and Centenary Fever* (Basingstoke, UK: Palgrave Macmillan, 2014); Avner Ben-Amos, "Les funérailles de Victor Hugo: Apothéose de l'événement spectacle," in *Les lieux de mémoire*, vol. 1, *La république*, ed. Pierre Nora, e (Paris: Gallimard, 1984), 473–523.

74. James Heintze, "When in the Course of Human Events It Became Necessary to Celebrate July 4th," *Phi Kappa Phi Forum* 89, no. 2 (2009): 4–6; Hendrik Kraay, *Days of National Festivity in Rio de Janeiro, Brazil, 1823–1889* (Stanford, CA: Stanford University Press, 2013); Gabriella Elgenius, *Symbols of Nations and Nationalism: Celebrating Nationhood* (Basingstoke, UK: Palgrave Macmillan, 2019); Demange, *El dos de mayo*; Alon Confino, *The Nation as a Local Metaphor: Württemberg, Imperial Germany, and National Memory, 1871–1918* (Chapel Hill: University of North Carolina Press, 1997), 27–97.

75. Christian Amalvi, "Le 14-juillet. Du Dies Irae à jour de fête," in Nora, *Les lieux de mémoire*, 1:421–73; Maurice Agulhon, *Marianne au pouvoir: L'imagerie et la symbolique républicaines de 1880 à 1914* (Paris: Flammarion, 1989); Elgenius, *Symbols*, 27–38, 41–45, 104–9, 141–44.

76. Elgenius, *Symbols*, 96–101, 112–22; Henk te Velde, *Gemeenschapszin en plichtsbesef: Liberalisme en nationalisme in Nederland, 1870–1918* (The Hague: SDU, 1992), 123–48; David

Cannadine, "The Context, Performance and Meaning of Ritual: The British Monarchy and the 'Invention of Tradition,' c. 1820–1977," in Hobsbawm and Ranger, *Invention of Tradition*, 101–65; Michael Cronin and Daryl Adair, *The Wearing of the Green: A History of St. Patrick's Day* (London: Routledge, 2002), 51–103.

77. Paul Greenhalgh, *Fair World: A History of World's Fairs and Expositions, from London to Shanghai, 1851–2010* (Winterbourne, UK: Papadakis, 2011); Marta Filipová, ed., *Cultures of International Exhibitions 1840–1940: Great Exhibitions in the Margins* (Farnham, UK: Routledge, 2015); Joep Leerssen and Eric Storm, eds., *World Fairs and the Global Moulding of National Identities: International Exhibitions as Cultural Platforms, 1851–1958* (Leiden: Brill, 2022).

78. Greenhalgh, *Fair World*; Martin Wörner, *Vergnügung und Belehrung: Volkskultur auf den Weltausstellungen 1851–1900* (Münster: Waxmann, 1999); Eric Storm, "The Transnational Construction of National Identities: A Classification of National Pavilions at World Fairs," in Leerssen and Storm, *World Fairs and National Identities*, 71–75.

79. Sven Schuster, *Die Inszenierung der Nation: Das Kaiserreich Brasilien im Zeitalter der Weltausstellungen* (Frankfurt: Peter Lang, 2015), 112, 135–37; Mauricio Tenorio-Trillo, *Mexico at the World's Fairs: Crafting a Modern Nation* (Berkeley: University of California Press, 1996), 65–77.

80. Reid, *Whose Pharaohs?*, 128–29; Abigail McGowan, *Crafting the Nation in Colonial India* (New York: Palgrave Macmillan, 2009), 27–65, 104–48; Joep Leerssen, "Type, Typicality," in *Imagology: The Cultural Construction and Literary Representation of National Characters: A Critical Survey*, ed. Manfred Beller and Joep Leerssen (Amsterdam: Rodopi, 2007), 450–51.

81. Daniel Hedinger, *Im Wettstreit mit dem Westen: Japans Zeitalter der Ausstellungen 1854–1941* (Frankfurt: Campus Verlag, 2011), 65–98; Caroline A. Jones, *The Global Work of Art: World's Fairs, Biennials, and the Aesthetics of Experience* (Chicago: Chicago University Press, 2016), 54; Taka Oshikiri, "Selling Tea as Japanese History: Culture, Consumption and International Expositions, 1873–1910," in Leerssen and Storm, *World Fairs and National Identities*, 193–217.

Chapter 5

1. Eric Hobsbawm, *The Age of Empire, 1875–1914* (New York: Vintage, 1989), 34–40.

2. Darwin, *After Tamerlane*, 304–18; Maier, *Once within Borders*, 214–29.

3. Richard Bellamy, *Liberalism and Modern Society: An Historical Argument* (Cambridge: Polity, 1992); Hobsbawm, *Age of Empire, 1875–1914*, 112–41; Kevin Repp, *Reformers, Critics, and the Paths of German Modernity: Anti-politics and the Search for Alternatives, 1890–1914* (Cambridge, MA: Harvard University Press, 2000), 22–25.

4. Steven E. Aschheim, *The Nietzsche Legacy in Germany, 1890–1990* (Berkeley: University of California Press, 1992); H. Stuart Hughes, *Consciousness and Society: The Reorientation of European Social Thought, 1890–1930* (New York: Vintage Books, 1961); Eric Storm, *La perspectiva del progreso: Pensamiento político en la España del cambio de siglo (1890–1914)* (Madrid: Biblioteca Nueva, 2001).

5. Mike Hawkins, *Social Darwinism in European and American Thought, 1860–1945: Nature as Model and Nature as Threat* (Cambridge: Cambridge University Press, 2003); Daniel Pick, *Faces of Degeneration: A European Disorder, c. 1848–c. 1918* (Cambridge: Cambridge University Press, 1989).

6. Duggan, *Force of Destiny*, 374–80; Nipperdey, *Deutsche Geschichte, 1866–1918*, 2:602–6; Aviel Roshwald, *Ethnic Nationalism and the Fall of Empires: Central Europe, Russia and the Middle East, 1914–1923* (London: Routledge, 2001), 62–63; Özkirimli and Sofos, *Tormented by History*, 108–16.

7. Joseph W. Esherick, "How the Qing Became China," in *Empire to Nation: Historical Perspectives on the Making of the Modern World*, ed. Joseph W. Esherick, Hasan Kayali, and Eric Van Young (Lanham, MD: Rowman & Littlefield, 2006), 237.

8. Raymond E. Lindgren, *Norway-Sweden Union, Disunion, and Scandinavian Integration* (Princeton, NJ: Princeton University Press, 1959).

9. Joseph Smith, *The Spanish-American War: Conflict in the Caribbean and the Pacific, 1895–1902* (London: Longman, 1994), 1–28, 188–226; Thomas M. Leonard, *Central America and the United States: The Search for Stability* (Athens: University of Georgia Press, 1991), 47–54.

10. Sebastian Balfour, *The End of the Spanish Empire, 1898–1923* (Oxford: Clarendon Press, 1997), 49–91, 132–63; Xosé Manoel Núñez Seixas, *Los nacionalismos en la España contemporánea (siglos XIX y XX)* (Barcelona: Hipòtesi, 1999), 31–73.

11. John Darwin, *The Empire Project: The Rise and Fall of the British World-System, 1830–1970* (Cambridge: Cambridge University Press, 2009), 114–79, 217–54.

12. Joost Augusteijn, "Irish Nationalism and Unionism between State, Region and Nation," in Augusteijn and Storm, *Region and State in Nineteenth-Century Europe*, 192–209; Andrew G. Newby, "'A Mere Geographical Expression'? Scotland and Scottish Identity, c. 1890–1914," in Augusteijn and Storm, *Region and State in Nineteenth-Century Europe*, 149–72; Alvin Jackson, "'Prison of the Nations?' Union and Nationality in the United Kingdom, 1870–1925," in *Sovereignty, Nationalism, and the Quest for Homogeneity in Interwar Europe*, ed. Emmanuel Dalle Mulle, Davide Rodogno, and Mona Bieling (London: Bloomsbury, 2023), 39–60.

13. Sayyid-Marsot, *History of Egypt*, 81–90; Banerjee-Dube, *Modern India*, 204–55; Darwin, *Empire Project*, 233–54.

14. Judson, *Habsburg Empire*, 282, 302–6, 315–16, 329–32, 363–66; James Shedel, "Emperor, Church, and People: Religion and Dynastic Loyalty during the Golden Jubilee of Franz Joseph," *Catholic Historical Review* 76, no. 1 (1990): 71–92; Daniel L. Unowsky, *The Pomp and Politics of Patriotism: Imperial Celebrations in Habsburg Austria, 1848–1916* (West Lafayette, IN: Purdue University Press, 2005); Pieter M. Judson, "Making Minorities and Majorities: National Indifference and National Self-Determination in Habsburg Central Europe," in Dalle Mulle, Rodogno, and Bieling, *Sovereignty, Nationalism*, 21–38.

15. Judson, *Habsburg Empire*, 266–68, 302–9, 344–45, 363–70; Kamusella, *Politics of Language*, 442–72; Pavlowitch, *Balkans*, 119–22.

16. Stefan Berger and Alexei Miller, "Introduction: Building Nations in and with Empires—a Reassessment," in *Nationalizing Empires*, 4–7.

17. Hosking, *Russia*, 390–97, 424–49; Sorkin, *Jewish Emancipation*, 202–7.

18. Hosking, *Russia*, 367–97, 402; Theodore R. Weeks, "Russification: Word and Practice 1863–1914," *Proceedings of the American Philosophical Society* 148, no. 4 (2004): 471–89; Aneta Pavlenko, "Linguistic Russification in the Russian Empire: Peasants into Russians?," *Russian Linguistics* 35, no. 3 (2011): 331–50; Miller, "Romanov Empire," 347–62; Plokhy, *Lost Kingdom*, 85–101, 121–53.

19. Zürcher, *Turkey*, 76–111; Eisenstat, "Late Ottoman Empire," 447–56; Murat R. Sivilolu, *The Emergence of Public Opinion: State and Society in the Late Ottoman Empire* (Cambridge: Cambridge University Press, 2018), 174–75.

20. Eisenstat, "Late Ottoman Empire," 440–59; Zürcher, *Turkey*, 76.

21. Rodogno, *Against Massacre*, 185–247; Ronald Grigor Suny, *"They Can Live in the Desert but Nowhere Else": A History of the Armenian Genocide* (Princeton, NJ: Princeton University Press, 2015), 64–140; Hosking, *Russia*, 386–88; Nader Sohrabi, "Reluctant Nationalists, Imperial Nation-State, and Neo-Ottomanism: Turks, Albanians, and the Antinomies of the End of Empire," *Social Science History* 42, no. 4 (2018): 386–88; Roshwald, *Ethnic Nationalism*, 63–67.

22. Abrahamian, *History of Modern Iran*, 8–62; Nader Sohrabi, *Revolution and Constitutionalism in the Ottoman Empire and Iran* (Cambridge: Cambridge University Press, 2011), 287–426.

23. Mühlhahn, *Making China Modern*, 154–86; Harrison, *China*, 65–87.

24. Mühlhahn, *Making China Modern*, 209–55.

25. Andreas Wimmer, *Nation Building: Why Some Countries Come Together While Others Fall Apart* (Princeton, NJ: Princeton University Press, 2018), 113–40; Esherick, "How the Qing"; Harrison, *China*, 36–44, 132–49.

26. Jansen, *Modern Japan*, 402–11, 423–41, 445–55; Gluck, *Japan's Modern Myths*, 104–56.

27. Cassel, *Grounds of Judgment*, 3–55, 149–60; Jansen, *Modern Japan*, 423–29.

28. Ricklefs et al., *Southeast Asia*, 172–80, 186–92, 198–204, 208–10; Wesseling, *European Colonial Empires*, 206–20.

29. Ricklefs et al., *Southeast Asia*, 180–86, 204–8, 217–20; Wesseling, *European Colonial Empires*, 192–206.

30. Ricklefs et al., *Southeast Asia*, 250–55, 283–91.

31. Wesseling, *European Colonial Empires*, 147–91.

32. Randrianja and Ellis, *Madagascar*, 112–57.

33. Bahru Zewde, *A History of Modern Ethiopia, 1855–1991* (Oxford: James Currey, 2001), 23–150; Harold G. Marcus, *A History of Ethiopia* (Berkeley: University of California Press, 2002), 63–130.

34. Greg Eghigian, *Making Security Social: Disability, Insurance, and the Birth of the Social Entitlement State in Germany* (Ann Arbor: University of Michigan Press, 2000), 25–66; Peter Hall, *Cities of Tomorrow: An Intellectual History of Urban Planning and Design in the Twentieth Century* (Oxford: Blackwell, 2002), 13–48; Bernard Harris, *The Origins of the British Welfare State: Society, State, and Social Welfare in England and Wales, 1800–1945* (Basingstoke, UK: Palgrave Macmillan, 2004), 150–66.

35. Bender, *Nation among Nations*, 246–96; Victoria C. Hattam, *Labor Visions and State Power: The Origins of Business Unionism in the United States* (Princeton, NJ: Princeton University Press, 1993); Ezequiel Gallo, "Argentina: Society and Politics, 1880–1916," in *The Cambridge History of Latin America*, vol. 5, *c. 1870 to 1930*, ed. Leslie Bethell (Cambridge: Cambridge University Press, 1986), 359–92; Sheldon M. Garon, *Molding Japanese Minds: The State in Everyday Life* (Princeton, NJ: Princeton University Press, 1997), 32–49.

36. Karen M. Offen, *European Feminisms, 1700–1950: A Political History* (Stanford, CA: Stanford University Press, 2000), 182–250; Karen M. Offen, ed., *Globalizing Feminisms, 1789–1945* (London: Routledge, 2010).

37. Robert A. Nye, *Crime, Madness, and Politics in Modern France: The Medical Concept of National Decline* (Princeton, NJ: Princeton University Press, 1984); Pick, *Faces of Degeneration*.

38. Sebastian Conrad, "Globalization Effects: Mobility and Nation in Imperial Germany, 1880–1914," *Journal of Global History* 3, no. 1 (2008): 43–66; Stefan Berger, "Building the Nation among Visions of German Empire," in Berger and Miller, *Nationalizing Empires*, 247–309.

39. Eric Steven Yellin, *Racism in the Nation's Service: Government Workers and the Color Line in Woodrow Wilson's America* (Chapel Hill: University of North Carolina Press, 2013); Erika Lee, "The 'Yellow Peril' and Asian Exclusion in the Americas," *Pacific Historical Review* 76, no. 4 (2007): 537–62; Loveman, *National Colors*, 144–47.

40. Hobsbawm, *Nations and Nationalism since 1780*, 1990, 101–30; Schulze, *Staat und Nation in der europäischen Geschichte*, 243–78; Hastings, *Nationalism in Modern Europe*, 124–32.

41. Reid, *Whose Pharaohs?*, 258, 277; Sven Schuster, "Colombia in the Age of Exhibitions: Envisioning the Nation in a Global Context, 1892–1929," in Leerssen and Storm, *World Fairs and National Identities*, 237–64.

42. Richard M. Dorson, "Folklore in the Modern World," in *Folklore in the Modern World*, ed. Richard M. Dorson (The Hague: Mouton, 1978), 18–19; Eric Storm, *The Culture of Regionalism: Art, Architecture and International Exhibitions in France, Germany and Spain, 1890–1939* (Manchester: Manchester University Press, 2011), 124.

43. Tchavdar Marinov, "Famous Macedonia, the Land of Alexander: Macedonian Identity at the Crossroads of Greek, Bulgarian and Serbian Nationalism," in *Entangled Histories of the Balkans*, vol. 1, *National Ideologies and Language Policies*, ed. Roumen Daskalov and Tchavdar Marinov (Leiden: Brill, 2013), 273–331; Zürcher, *Turkey*, 82; Pavlowitch, *Balkans*, 146–47, 196–202.

44. Augusteijn and Storm, *Region and State in Nineteenth-Century Europe*.

45. Tara Zahra, "Imagined Noncommunities: National Indifference as a Category of Analysis," *Slavic Review* 69, no. 1 (2010): 93–119; Maarten Van Ginderachter and Jon E. Fox, eds., *National Indifference and the History of Nationalism in Modern Europe* (Abingdon, UK: Routledge, 2019); Cyril Robelin, "La plus petite communauté imaginée du monde: Le territoire neutre de Moresnet," *Language, Discourse and Society* 5 (2017): 71–89.

46. Chris Manias, *Race, Science, and the Nation: Reconstructing the Ancient Past in Britain, France and Germany* (London: Routledge, 2013), 103–7, 202–22.

47. Bhatt, *Hindu Nationalism*, 7–40; Romila Thapar, "The Theory of Aryan Race and India: History and Politics," *Social Scientist* 24, no. 1/3 (1996): 3–10; Crispin Bates, "Race, Caste and Tribe in Central India: The Early Origins of Indian Anthropometry," in *The Concept of Race in South Asia*, ed. Peter Robb (Oxford: Oxford University Press, 1995), 219–59; Banerjee-Dube, *Modern India*, 145–50.

48. Livingstone, *Geographical Tradition*, 177–215; Maier, *Once within Borders*, 233–47; Virginie Mamadouh and Martin Müller, "Politcal Geography and Geopolitics," in Mishkova and Trencsényi, *European Regions and Boundaries*, 261–65.

49. Livingstone, *Geographical Tradition*, 260–90; Guy Mercier, "The Region and the State according to Friedrich Ratzel and Paul Vidal de la Blanche," *Annales de géographie* 104, no. 583 (1995): 211–35.

50. Joachim Wolschke-Bulmahn, "Landscape Design and the Natural Sciences in Germany and the United States in the Early Twentieth Century: 'Reactionary Modernism?,'" in *Gardens, Knowledge and the Sciences in the Early Modern Period*, ed. Hubertus Fischer, Volker R. Remmert, and Joachim Wolschke-Bulmahn (Cham, Switzerland: Birkhäuser, 2016), 345–65; Marco Antonsich, "Natives and Aliens: Who and What Belongs in Nature and in the Nation?," *Area* 53, no. 2 (June 2021): 303–10.

51. David M. Hopkin, "Regionalism and Folklore," in *Regionalism and Modern Europe: Identity Construction and Movements from 1890 to the Present Day*, ed. Xosé Manoel Núñez Seixas and Eric Storm (London: Bloomsbury, 2019), 43–50; Manias, *Race, Science, and the Nation*, 221–29; Earle,

Return of the Native; Regina Bendix, *In Search of Authenticity: The Formation of Folklore Studies* (Madison: University of Wisconsin Press, 1997), 119–53; Gluck, *Japan's Modern Myths*, 180–83.

52. Fritz Stern, *The Politics of Cultural Despair* (Berkeley: University of California Press, 1961), 97–183; Eric Storm, "The Birth of Regionalism and the Crisis of Reason: France, Germany and Spain," in Augusteijn and Storm, *Region and State in Nineteenth-Century Europe*, 36–57; Magdalena Bushart, *Der Geist der Gotik und die expressionistische Kunst: Kunstgeschichte und Kunsttheorie, 1911–1925* (Munich: Schreiber, 1990); Vojtěch Jirat-Wasiutyński, ed., *Modern Art and the Idea of the Mediterranean* (Toronto: University of Toronto Press, 2007); Figes, *Natasha's Dance*, 355–431; Mitter, *Art and Nationalism*, 234–375.

53. Nicola Miller, *In the Shadow of the State: Intellectuals and the Quest for National Identity in Twentieth-Century Spanish America* (London: Verso, 1999), 174–77; Peter Van der Veer, "Spirituality in Modern Society," *Social Research* 76, no. 4 (2009): 1107–14; Carolien Stolte and Harald Fischer-Tiné, "Imagining Asia in India: Nationalism and Internationalism (ca. 1905–1940)," *Comparative Studies in Society and History* 54, no. 1 (2012): 76–82.

54. Suzanne L. Marchand, "The Rhetoric of Artifacts and the Decline of Classical Humanism: The Case of Josef Strzygowski," *History and Theory* 33, no. 4 (1994): 106–30; Julio Ignacio Arrechea Miguel, "Focilllón y Strzygowski o la lejana raíz del arte occidental," *Espacio, tiempo y forma*, series 7, *Historia del arte*, no. 6 (1993): 559–606.

55. Berger, *Past as History*, 186, 200–204, 215–17; Allan Smith, "Seven Narratives in North American History: Thinking the Nation in Canada, Quebec and the United States," in Berger, *Writing the Nation*, 67–68; Anthony D. Smith, "Nationalism and Classic Social Theory," *British Journal of Sociology* 34, no. 1 (1983): 19–38; Daniel Chernilo, "Classical Sociology and the Nation-State: A Re-interpretation," *Journal of Classical Sociology* 8, no. 1 (2008): 27–43.

56. Martti Koskenniemi, *The Gentle Civilizer of Nations: The Rise and Fall of International Law, 1870–1960* (Cambridge: Cambridge University Press, 2002), 11–166; Mark Mazower, *Governing the World: The History of an Idea* (London: Penguin, 2012), 65–81; Harald Kleinschmidt, "Plädoyer für eine kritische Historisierung des Nationenbegriffs," *Geschichte und Gesellschaft* 47, no. 3 (2021): 506–22.

57. Michelle Facos, *Nationalism and the Nordic Imagination: Swedish Art of the 1890s* (Berkeley: University of California Press, 1998); Claus Pese, ed., *Künstlerkolonien in Europa: Im Zeichen der Ebene und des Himmels* (Nuremberg: Germanisches Nationalmuseum, 2001).

58. Storm, *Culture of Regionalism*, 21–73.

59. Sharon L. Hirsh, "Swiss Art and National Identity at the Turn of the Twentieth Century," in *Art, Culture and National Identity in Fin-de-Siècle Europe*, ed. Michelle Facos and Sharon L. Hirsh (Cambridge: Cambridge University Press, 2003), 250–87; Sofía Barrón and Isabel Justo, eds., *Sorolla: Visión de España: Colección de la Hispanic Society of America* (Valencia: Fundación Bancaja, 2007); Erin Dusza, "Pan-Slavism in Alphonse Mucha's *Slav Epic*," *Nineteenth-Century Art Worldwide* 13, no. 1 (2014): n.p.; Janne Gallen-Kallela-Siren, "Axel Gallén and the Constructed Nation: Art and Nationalism in Young Finland, 1880–1900" (PhD diss., New York University, 2001).

60. Hans Kraan, *Dromen van Holland: Buitenlandse kunstenaars schilderen Holland, 1800–1914* (Zwolle, Netherlands: Waanders, 2002), 224–62.

61. Mitter, *Art and Nationalism in Colonial India, 1850–1922*, 27–120, 219–34, 262–66, 283–302; Tapati Guha-Thakurta, *Monuments, Objects, Histories: Institutions of Art in Colonial and Postcolonial India* (New York: Columbia University Press, 2004).

62. Charles Harrison, Francis Frascina, and Gillian Perry, *Primitivism, Cubism, Abstraction: The Early Twentieth Century* (New Haven, CT: Yale University Press, 1993); Modris Eksteins, *Rites of Spring: The Great War and the Birth of the Modern Age* (New York: Doubleday, 1989), 9–55; Bushart, *Der Geist der Gotik*, 18–120.

63. Leerssen, "Romanticism, Music, Nationalism," 615–20; individual entries in Leerssen, *Encyclopedia of Romantic Nationalism*; Jim Samson, "Music and Nationalism: Five Historical Moments," in *Nationalism and Ethnosymbolism: History, Culture and Ethnicity in the Formation of Nations*, ed. Steven Grosby and Athena S. Leoussi (Edinburgh: Edinburgh University Press, 2007), 55–68; Sandie Holguín, "Music and Spanish Nationalism," in *Metaphors of Spain: Representations of Spanish National Identity in the Twentieth Century*, ed. Javier Moreno Luzón and Xosé M. Núñez Seixas (New York: Berghahn, 2017), 225–27.

64. Bob van der Linden, "Non-Western National Music and Empire in Global History: Interactions, Uniformities, and Comparisons," *Journal of Global History* 10, no. 3 (2015): 431–56; Pamela Moro, "Constructions of Nation and the Classicisation of Music: Comparative Perspectives from Southeast and South Asia," *Journal of Southeast Asian Studies* 35, no. 2 (2004): 187–211.

65. Anne-Marie Thiesse, *Écrire la France: Le mouvement littéraire régionaliste de langue française entre la Belle Époque et la Libération* (Paris: Presses Universitaires de France, 1991); Robert L. Dorman, *Revolt of the Provinces: The Regionalist Movement in America, 1920–1945* (Chapel Hill: University of North Carolina Press, 2003); Elizabeth Boa and Rachel Palfreyman, *Heimat—A German Dream: Regional Loyalties and National Identity in German Culture 1890–1990* (Oxford: Oxford University Press, 2011).

66. Zeev Sternhell, *Maurice Barrès et le nationalisme français*, (Paris: Fayard, 2000); Storm, "Birth of Regionalism."

67. Celia Applegate, *A Nation of Provincials: The German Idea of Heimat* (Berkeley: University of California Press, 1990); Thiesse, *Écrire la France*; Xosé Manoel Núñez Seixas and Eric Storm, eds., *Regionalism and Modern Europe: Identity Construction and Movements from 1890 to the Present Day* (London: Bloomsbury, 2019); Rudy Koshar, *Germany's Transient Pasts: Preservation and National Memory in the Twentieth Century* (Chapel Hill: University of North Carolina Press, 1998), 1–75; Joshua Hagen, *Preservation, Tourism and Nationalism: The Jewel of the German Past* (Aldershot, UK: Ashgate, 2006).

68. Michael Falser, *Angkor Wat: A Transcultural History of Heritage* (Berlin: De Gruyter, 2019); Marieke Bloembergen and Martijn Eickhoff, *The Politics of Heritage in Indonesia: A Cultural History* (Cambridge: Cambridge University Press, 2020); Charlotte Jelidi, "Le transfert intra-maghrébin d'une politique patrimoniale en contexte colonial: Le baron d'Erlanger, Sidi Bou Saïd et la préservation de l'architecture dite 'arabe' en Tunisie (1910–1932)," in *Villes maghrébines en situations coloniales*, ed. Charlotte Jelidi (Paris: Karthala, 2014), 269–95.

69. Danny Trom, "Natur und nationale Identität: Der Streit um den Schutz der 'Natur' um die Jahrhundertwende in Deutschland und Frankreich," in *Nation und Emotion: Deutschland und Frankreich im Vergleich 19. und 20. Jahrhundert*, ed. Etienne Francois, Hannes Siegrist, and Jakob Vogel (Göttingen: Vandenhoeck & Ruprecht, 1995), 147–68; Caroline Ford, *Natural Interests: The Contest over Environment in Modern France* (Cambridge, MA: Harvard University Press, 2016), 114–37; Aline Demay, *Tourism and Colonization in Indochina (1898–1939)* (Newcastle: Cambridge Scholars, 2015), 106–14; Jane Carruthers, *The Kruger National Park: A Social and Political History* (Pietermaritzburg: University of Natal Press, 1995).

70. Daniel Alan Degroff, "Artur Hazelius and the Ethnographic Display of the Scandinavian Peasantry: A Study in Context and Appropriation," *European Review of History* 19, no. 2 (2012): 229–48; Ad de Jong, *De dirigenten van de herinnering: Musealisering en nationalisering van de volkscultuur in Nederland 1815–1940* (Nijmegen: SUN, 2001).

71. Hirsh, "Swiss Art"; Terri Switzer, "Hungarian Self-Representation in an International Context: The Magyar Exhibited at International Expositions and World's Fairs," in Facos and Hirsh, *Art, Culture, and National Identity*, 160–86; Todd Courtenay, "The 1911 International Exposition in Rome: Architecture, Archaeology, and National Identity," *Journal of Historical Geography* 37, no. 4 (2011): 440–59; Robert W Rydell, *All the World's a Fair: Visions of Empire at American International Expositions, 1876–1916* (Chicago: University of Chicago Press, 1984).

72. Wörner, *Vergnügung und Belehrung*, 72–82; Hirsh, "Swiss Art"; Shona Kallestrup, "Romanian 'National Style' and the 1906 Bucharest Jubilee Exhibition," *Journal of Design History* 15, no. 3 (2002): 147–62; Marta Filipová, "Peasants on Display: The Czechoslavic Ethnographic Exhibition of 1895," *Journal of Design History* 24, no. 1 (2011): 15–36.

73. Caroline R. Malloy, "Exhibiting Ireland: Irish Villages, Pavilions, Cottages, and Castles at International Exhibitions, 1853–1939" (PhD diss., University of Wisconsin–Madison, 2013), 119–75; Robert W. Rydell and Rob Kroes, *Buffalo Bill in Bologna: The Americanization of the World, 1869–1922* (Chicago: University of Chicago Press, 2005); Nicolas Bancel, Pascal Blanchard, and Gilles Boëtsch, eds., *Zoos humains: Au temps des exhibitions humaines* (Paris: La Découverte, 2004).

74. Eric Storm, "Tourism and the Construction of Regional Identities," in Núñez Seixas and Storm, *Regionalism and Modern Europe*, 99–119.

75. Catherine Bertho Lavenir, *La roue et le stylo: Comment nous sommes devenus touristes* (Paris: Odile Jacob, 1999); Eric G. E. Zuelow, *A History of Modern Tourism* (London: Palgrave Macmillan, 2016); Stephen L. Harp, *Marketing Michelin: Advertising and Cultural Identity in Twentieth-Century France* (Baltimore: Johns Hopkins University Press, 2001); Akira Soshiroda, "Inbound Tourism Policies in Japan from 1859 to 2003," *Annals of Tourism Research* 32, no. 4 (2005): 1100–1120; Demay, *Tourism and Colonization*, 88–94.

76. Patrick Young, *Enacting Brittany: Tourism and Culture in Provincial France, 1871–1939* (Farnham, UK: Ashgate, 2012); Storm, "Tourism."

77. Adrian Vickers, *Bali: A Paradise Created* (Hong Kong: Periplus, 1989); Michel Picard, *Bali: Cultural Tourism and Touristic Culture* (Singapore: Archipelago, 1996).

78. Bayly, *Birth of the Modern World, 1780–1914*, 325–65; Gluck, *Japan's Modern Myths*, 127–46; Banerjee-Dube, *Modern India*, 99–106.

79. Barbara Miller Lane, *National Romanticism and Modern Architecture in Germany and the Scandinavian Countries* (Cambridge: Cambridge University Press, 2000); François Loyer and Bernard Toulier, eds., *Le régionalisme, architecture, et identité* (Paris: Éditions du Patrimoine, 2001); Storm, *Culture of Regionalism*; Rodrigo Gutiérrez Viñuales, "Arquitectura historicista de raíces prehispánicas," *Goya*, no. 289–290 (2002): 267–86; Rodrigo Gutiérrez Viñuales, "Arquitectura de raíces hispanas: Entre los 'estilos californianos' y el neocolonial (1880–1940)," in *Baja California: Herencia, memoria e identidad patrimonial*, ed. Miguel Angel Sorroche Cuerva (Granada: Atrio, 2014), 281–307.

80. Lane, *National Romanticism*; Matthew F. Bokovoy, *The San Diego World's Fairs and Southwestern Memory, 1880–1940* (Albuquerque: University of New Mexico Press, 2005); Chris

Wilson, *The Myth of Santa Fe: Creating a Modern Regional Tradition* (Albuquerque: University of New Mexico Press, 1997); Storm, *Culture of Regionalism*, 98–101, 126–36, 171–74.

81. Elizabeth Cumming and Wendy Kaplan, *The Arts and Crafts Movement* (London: Thames and Hudson, 2004); Javier Gimeno Martínez, *Design and National Identity* (London: Bloomsbury, 2016), 51–64; Anne-Marie Thiesse, *The Transnational Creation of National Arts and Crafts in 19th-Century Europe* (Antwerp: Nise, 2013); Bokovoy, *San Diego World's Fairs*, 114–23.

82. Laudan, *Cuisine and Empire*, 248–306; Eric Storm, "The Nationalisation of the Domestic Sphere," *Nations and Nationalism* 23, no. 1 (2017): 173–93; Jeffrey M. Pilcher, *¡Que Vivan Los Tamales! Food and the Making of Mexican Identity* (Albuquerque: University of New Mexico Press, 2008); Katarzyna J. Cwiertka, *Modern Japanese Cuisine: Food, Power and National Identity* (London: Reaktion Books, 2014).

83. Eric Storm, "When Did Nationalism Become Banal? The Nationalization of the Domestic Sphere in Spain," *European History Quarterly* 50, no. 2 (2020): 204–25; Anne Helmreich, *The English Garden and National Identity: The Competing Styles of Garden Design, 1870–1914* (Cambridge: Cambridge University Press, 2002); Nancy R. Reagin, *Sweeping the German Nation: Domesticity and National Identity in Germany, 1870–1945* (New York: Cambridge University Press, 2009).

84. Michael Worboys, Julie-Marie Strange, and Neil Pemberton, *Invention of the Modern Dog: Breed and Blood in Victorian Britain* (Baltimore: Johns Hopkins University Press, 2018); Kathleen Kete, *The Beast in the Boudoir: Petkeeping in Nineteenth-Century Paris* (Berkeley: University of California Press, 1997).

85. Barbara J. Keys, *Globalizing Sport: National Rivalry and International Community in the 1930s* (Cambridge, MA: Harvard University Press, 2013), 6–24; Marjet Derks, "Sports, Pastimes: Introductory Survey Essay," in Leerssen, *Encyclopedia of Romantic Nationalism*, 72–75; Marjet Derks and Joep Leerssen, "Sports/Athletics Associations: Survey Article," in Leerssen, *Encyclopedia of Romantic Nationalism*, 142–43; Alan Bairner, *Sport, Nationalism, and Globalization: European and North American Perspectives* (Albany: State University of New York Press, 2001), 103–4.

86. Keys, *Globalizing Sport*, 6–24, 43–45, 51, 58; Derks and Leerssen, "Sports/Athletics Associations," 143; Bairner, *Sport, Nationalism, and Globalization*, 95–100; Mahfoud Amara, "The Middle East and North Africa," in *Routledge Companion to Sports History*, ed. Steven W. Pope and John R. Nauright (London: Routledge, 2009), 503–4.

87. Grant Jarvie, "Highland Gatherings, Balmorality, and the Glamour of Backwardness," *Sociology of Sport Journal* 9, no. 2 (1992): 167–78; Marjory Brewster, Joanne Connell, and Stephen J. Page, "The Scottish Highland Games: Evolution, Development and Role as a Community Event," *Current Issues in Tourism* 12, no. 3 (2009): 271–93; Bairner, *Sport, Nationalism, and Globalization*, 69–98; Eugen Weber, *France, Fin de Siècle* (Cambridge, MA: Belknap, 1986), 209–12; Niels Kaiser Nielsen, "Nordic Countries," in Pope and Nauright, *Routledge Companion to Sports History*, 535.

88. Keys, *Globalizing Sport*, 17–63.

Chapter 6

1. Eksteins, *Rites of Spring*; Niall Ferguson, *The Pity of War: 1914–1918* (London: Penguin, 1998), 174–98.

2. Margaret MacMillan, *The War That Ended Peace: How Europe Abandoned Peace for the First World War* (London: Profile, 2014), 378–411; Christopher M. Clark, *The Sleepwalkers: How Europe Went to War in 1914* (London: Penguin Books, 2013), 451–70.

3. Ferguson, *Pity of War*, 168–73, 282–90.

4. Jörn Leonhard, *Pandora's Box: A History of World War I.* (Cambridge, MA: Harvard University Press, 2018), 268–75 and 419–21.

5. Erez Manela, *The Wilsonian Moment: Self-Determination and the International Origins of Anticolonial Nationalism* (Oxford: Oxford University Press, 2007).

6. Leonhard, *Pandora's Box*, 385–875, 891–911.

7. Peter Gatrell, *The Making of the Modern Refugee* (Oxford: University Press, 2013), 41–46; Roshwald, *Ethnic Nationalism*, 75–77, 84–86, 91–92, 108–12; Miller, "Romanov Empire," 364–65; Christoph Mick, "Legality, Ethnicity and Violence in Austrian Galicia, 1890–1920," *European Review of History* 26, no. 5 (2019): 766–68; Tara Zahra, "'Condemned to Rootlessness and Unable to Budge': Roma, Migration Panics, and Internment in the Habsburg Empire," *American Historical Review* 122, no. 3 (2017): 722–24.

8. Zürcher, *Turkey*, 107–17; Suny, *"They Can Live in the Desert,"* 208–327, 350–65.

9. Roshwald, *Ethnic Nationalism*, 118–25; Lode Wils, "Het aandeel van de 'Flamenpolitik' in de Vlaamse natievorming," *Belgisch Tijdschrift voor Nieuwste Geschiedenis* 45 (2015): 216–37.

10. Duggan, *Force of Destiny*, 387–89; Pavlowitch, *Balkans*, 210–19.

11. Leonhard, *Pandora's Box*, 202–3, 442–44, 478–80, 586–87, 620; Andreas Kappeler, *The Russian Empire: A Multiethnic History* (New York: Routledge, 2013), 348–49; Roshwald, *Ethnic Nationalism*, 128.

12. Erik-Jan Zürcher, ed., *Jihad and Islam in World War I: Studies on the Ottoman Jihad at the Centenary of Snouck Hurgronje's "Holy War Made in Germany"* (Leiden: Leiden University Press, 2016); Roshwald, *Ethnic Nationalism*, 105–8, 146–47; Andrew T. Jarboe, "The Long Road Home: Britain, Germany and the Repatriation of Indian Prisoners of War after the First World War," in *Colonial Soldiers in Europe, 1914–1945: "Aliens in Uniform" in Wartime Societies*, ed. Eric Storm and Ali Al Tuma (London: Routledge, 2016), 143–47.

13. Roshwald, *Ethnic Nationalism*, 128–55; Andrea Carteny, "All against One: The Congress of Oppressed Nationalities of Austria-Hungary (1918)" (Working paper 67, Department of Communication, University of Teramo, 2010).

14. Leonhard, *Pandora's Box*, 490–606; Kappeler, *Russian Empire*, 353–61.

15. Leonhard, *Pandora's Box*, 606–15, 732–39; Kappeler, *Russian Empire*, 361–72.

16. Judson, *Habsburg Empire*, 391–441; Leonhard, *Pandora's Box*, 674–75, 799–811; Judson, "Making Minorities."

17. Leonhard, *Pandora's Box*, 434–38, 856–59; Zürcher, *Turkey*, 133–65; Margaret MacMillan, *Peacemakers: The Paris Conference of 1919 and Its Attempts to End War* (London: John Murray, 2001), 377–92, 438–69.

18. MacMillan, *Peacemakers*, 392–438; Roshwald, *Ethnic Nationalism*, 187–97.

19. MacMillan, *Peacemakers*, 11–34; Eric D. Weitz, "Self-Determination: How a German Enlightenment Idea Became the Slogan of National Liberation and a Human Right," *American Historical Review* 120, no. 2 (2015): 462–96; Xosé M. Núñez Seixas, "Wilson's Unexpected Friends: The Transnational Impact of the First World War on Western European Nationalist Movements," in *The First World War and the Nationality Question in Europe: Global Impact and Local Dynamics*, ed. Xosé M. Núñez Seixas (Leiden: Brill, 2021), 37–65.

20. Judson, "Making Minorities," 31–32; Núñez Seixas, "Wilson's Unexpected Friends," 44–45; Martina Steber, *Ethnische Gewissheiten: Die Ordnung des Regionalen im bayerischen*

Schwaben vom Kaiserreich bis zum NS-Regime (Göttingen: Vandenhoeck & Ruprecht, 2010), 198–206.

21. Roshwald, *Ethnic Nationalism*, 86–88, 156–71; MacMillan, *Peacemakers*, 119–34, 217–54, 265–81.

22. MacMillan, *Peacemakers*, 402; Eugene Rogan, *The Arabs: A History* (London: Penguin, 2018), 195–205, 213–18, 234–36.

23. Rogan, *Arabs*, 205–12; Manela, *Wilsonian Moment*, 63–77, 141–57.

24. Manela, *Wilsonian Moment*, 77–99, 159–77; Banerjee-Dube, *Modern India*, 272–88.

25. Manela, *Wilsonian Moment*, 99–137, 177–215; Mühlhahn, *Making China Modern*, 230–47.

26. Martin O'Donoghue, "'Ireland's Independence Day': The 1918 Election Campaign in Ireland and the Wilsonian Moment," *European Review of History* 26, no. 5 (September 3, 2019): 834–54; Bew, *Ireland*, 374–444.

27. Rogan, *Arabs*, 211–12, 234–42; Darwin, *Empire Project*, 375–410, 449–69; Wickramasinghe, *Sri Lanka in the Modern Age*, 148–53; Ricklefs et al., *Southeast Asia*, 266; Banerjee-Dube, *Modern India*, 329–80.

28. Rogan, *Arabs*, 266–312; Jonathan Wyrtzen, "Colonial War and the Production of Territorialized State Space in North Africa," in *Rethinking the Colonial State*, ed. Søren Rud and Søren Ivarsson (Bingley, UK: Emerald, 2017), 151–75; William L. Cleveland, *A History of the Modern Middle East* (London: Routledge, 2018), 206–16.

29. Mühlhahn, *Making China Modern*, 264–73; Zewde, *Modern Ethiopia*, 140–43; Ricklefs et al., *Southeast Asia*, 255–62.

30. Lewis H. Siegelbaum, *Soviet State and Society between Revolutions, 1918–1929* (Cambridge: Cambridge University Press, 1992), 6–25, 117–26.

31. Stern, *Politics of Cultural Despair*; Zeev Sternhell, *La droite révolutionnaire, 1888–1914: Les origines françaises du fascisme* (Paris: Seuil, 1978); Stanley G. Payne, *A History of Fascism, 1914–1945* (Madison: University of Wisconsin Press, 1995), 23–71.

32. Payne, *History of Fascism*, 129–47, 245–349; Stephen J. Lee, *European Dictatorships, 1918–1945* (Abingdon, UK: Routledge, 2008).

33. António Costa Pinto, "Fascism, Corporatism and the Crafting of Authoritarian Institutions in Inter-war European Dictatorships," in *Rethinking Fascism and Dictatorship in Europe*, ed. António Costa Pinto and Aristotle Kallis (Basingstoke, UK: Palgrave Macmillan, 2014), 87–117; António Costa Pinto, "Authoritarianism and Corporatism in Latin America: The First Wave," in *Authoritarianism and Corporatism in Europe and Latin America: Crossing Borders*, ed. António Costa Pinto and Federico Finchelstein (London: Routledge, 2018), 110–42.

34. Payne, *History of Fascism*, 80–129, 147–245; Robert O. Paxton, *The Anatomy of Fascism* (New York: Knopf, 2004).

35. Mark Mazower, *Hitler's Empire: How the Nazis Ruled Europe* (New York: Penguin Books, 2009); Davide Rodogno, "Wartime Occupation by Italy," in *The Cambridge History of the Second World War*, vol. 2, *Politics and Ideology*, ed. Joseph Maiolo and Richard Bosworth (Cambridge: Cambridge University Press, 2015), 436–60; Calic, *Great Cauldron*, 452–60; Prasenjit Duara, *The Global and Regional in China's Nation-Formation* (London: Routledge, 2008), 40–60; Jeremy A. Yellen, *The Greater East Asia Co-prosperity Sphere: When Total Empire Met Total War* (Ithaca, NY: Cornell University Press, 2019), 76–103.

36. Leonhard, *Pandora's Box*, 567–81, 631–77; Stefan Rinke, *Latin America and the First World War* (Cambridge: Cambridge University Press, 2017), 177–84.

37. Leonhard, *Pandora's Box*, 893–901; Mark Mazower, *Dark Continent: Europe's Twentieth Century* (London: Penguin Books, 1998), 6–8, 12–20; Paul Lewis, *Authoritarian Regimes in Latin America: Dictators, Despots, and Tyrants* (Lanham, MD: Rowman & Littlefield, 2006), 101–4; Garon, *Molding Japanese Minds*, 49–59; Calic, *Great Cauldron*, 402–13.

38. Mazower, *Dark Continent*, 106–41, 190–92; Bender, *Nation among Nations*, 263–95; António Costa Pinto and Federico Finchelstein, eds., *Authoritarianism and Corporatism in Europe and Latin America: Crossing Borders* (London: Routledge, 2019); Zürcher, *Turkey*, 195–98.

39. Leonhard, *Pandora's Box*, 692–701; Offen, *European Feminisms*, 257–72.

40. Elizabeth Vlossak, *Marianne or Germania? Nationalizing Women in Alsace, 1870–1946* (Oxford: Oxford University Press, 2011), 210–19; Fahrmeir, *Citizenship*, 126–28.

41. Rogan, *Arabs*, 208–14; Banerjee-Dube, *Modern India*, 292–98, 329–36.

42. Offen, *European Feminisms*, 272–76; Mazower, *Dark Continent*, 77–90; Duara, *Global and Regional*, 117–30.

43. Mazower, *Dark Continent*, 88–106; Véronique Mottier, "Eugenics and the State: Policy-Making in Comparative Perspective," in *The Oxford Handbook of the History of Eugenics*, ed. Alison Bashford and Philippa Levine (Oxford: Oxford University Press, 2010), 135–51.

44. Roshwald, *Ethnic Nationalism*, 164–71; Weitz, *World Divided*, 163–85.

45. MacMillan, *Peacemakers*, 496–97, 315–31.

46. Rogers Brubaker, *Nationalism Reframed: Nationhood and the National Question in the New Europe* (Cambridge: Cambridge University Press, 2009), 23–40; Weitz, *World Divided*, 281–92; Terry Martin, *The Affirmative Action Empire: Nations and Nationalism in the Soviet Union, 1923–1939* (Ithaca, NY: Cornell University Press, 2001).

47. Weitz, *World Divided*, 185–90, 203–5; Umut Özsu, "Fabricating Fidelity: Nation-Building, International Law, and the Greek–Turkish Population Exchange," *Leiden Journal of International Law* 24, no. 4 (2011): 823–47; Erol Ülker, "Nationalism, Religion, and Minorities from the Ottoman Empire to the Republic of Turkey," in Dalle Mulle, Rodogno, and Bieling, *Sovereignty, Nationalism*, 61–82.

48. Roshwald, *Ethnic Nationalism*, 198–217; Brubaker, *Nationalism Reframed*, 79–106; Mazower, *Dark Continent*, 54–63; Oliver Zimmer, *Nationalism in Europe: 1890–1940* (Basingstoke, UK: Palgrave Macmillan, 2003), 59–79.

49. Lee, "Yellow Peril and Asian Exclusion"; Aristide R. Zolberg, *A Nation by Design: Immigration Policy in the Fashioning of America* (New York: Russell Sage, 2006), 199–293; Frederick Cooper, *Citizenship, Inequality, and Difference: Historical Perspectives* (Princeton, NJ: Princeton University Press, 2018), 96–98; Peter Wade, *Race and Ethnicity in Latin America* (London: Pluto, 2015), 30–35.

50. De la Peña, "Social and Cultural Policies," 720–28; Wade, *Race and Ethnicity*, 32–33; Alan Knight, "Racism, Revolution, and Indigenismo: Mexico, 1910–1940," in *The Idea of Race in Latin America, 1870–1940*, ed. Richard Graham (Austin: University of Texas Press, 1990), 76–87.

51. Christina Firpo and Margaret Jacobs, "Taking Children, Ruling Colonies: Child Removal and Colonial Subjugation in Australia, Canada, French Indochina, and the United States, 1870–1950s," *Journal of World History* 29, no. 4 (2018): 529–62; Roger L. Nichols, *Indians in the United States and Canada: A Comparative History* (Lincoln: University of Nebraska Press, 2018), 285–310; Frederick E. Hoxie, *A Final Promise: The Campaign to Assimilate the Indians, 1880–1920* (Lincoln: University of Nebraska Press, 2001), 189–210; Tessa Morris-Suzuki, "Becoming

Japanese: Imperial Expansion and Identity Crises in the Early Twentieth Century," in *Japan's Competing Modernities: Issues in Culture and Democracy, 1900–1930*, ed. Sharon A. Minichiello (Honolulu: University of Hawai'i Press, 1998), 163–67.

52. Nichols, *Indians*, 312–27; Kyle T. Mays, "Transnational Progressivism: African Americans, Native Americans, and the Universal Races Congress of 1911," *American Indian Quarterly* 37, no. 3 (2013): 243–61.

53. Richard J. B. Bosworth, *Mussolini* (London: Arnold, 2002), 123–287.

54. Richard J. Evans, *The Third Reich in Power, 1933–1939* (New York: Penguin, 2005), 1–536; Laura A. Belmonte, *The International LGBT Rights Movement: A History* (London: Bloomsbury, 2021), 62–67.

55. Evans, *Third Reich*, 536–602.

56. Rodogno, "Wartime Occupation by Italy"; Yellen, *Co-prosperity Sphere*.

57. Martin, *Affirmative Action Empire*, 273–462; Plokhy, *Lost Kingdom*, 238–77; Theodore R. Weeks, "Separatist Nationalism in the Romanov and Soviet Empires," in Breuilly, *Oxford Handbook Nationalism*, 209–11.

58. Mazower, *Hitler's Empire*, 78–256, 294–328, 368–416; Helena Waddy, *Oberammergau in the Nazi Era: The Fate of a Catholic Village in Hitler's Germany* (Oxford: Oxford University Press, 2010), 189–253.

59. Nichols, *Indians*, 312–13, 327–31; Morgane Labbé, "National Indifference, Statistics and the Constructivist Paradigm: The Case of the Tutejsi ('the People from Here') in Interwar Polish Censuses," in *National Indifference and the History of Nationalism in Modern Europe*, ed. Maarten Van Ginderachter and Jon E. Fox (London: Routledge, 2019), 161–80; Olga Linkiewicz, "Nationalism and Vernacular Cosmologies: Revisiting the Concept of National Indifference and the Limits of Nationalization in the Second Polish Republic," in Dalle Mulle, Rodogno, and Bieling, *Sovereignty, Nationalism*, 171–90.

60. Irina Livezeanu and Petru Negura, "Borderlands, Provinces, Regionalisms, and Culture in East-Central Europe," in Núñez Seixas and Storm, *Regionalism in Modern Europe*, 253–57; John Davis, "Rescue and Recovery: The Biopolitics and Ethnogenealogy of Moldavian Catholics in 1940s Romania," in *Local and Transnational Csángó Lifeworlds*, ed. Sándor Ilyés, Lehel Peti, and Ferenc Pozsony (Cluj-Napoca: Kriza János Ethnographical Society, 2008), 95–113; King, *Budweisers into Czechs*, 177–211; Brendan Karch, "Instrumental Nationalism in Upper Silesia," in Van Ginderachter and Fox, *National Indifference in Modern Europe*, 180–204.

61. Eric Storm and Ali al Tuma, eds., *Colonial Soldiers in Europe, 1914–1945: "Aliens in Uniform" in Wartime Societies* (London: Routledge, 2015); Ali al Tuma, *Guns, Culture and Moors: Racial Perceptions, Cultural Impact and the Moroccan Participation in the Spanish Civil War (1936–1939)* (Abingdon, UK: Routledge, 2018), 203–9.

62. Banerjee-Dube, *Modern India*, 272–88; Mühlhahn, *Making China Modern*, 255–64, 298–339.

63. Federico Caprotti, "Information Management and Fascist Identity: Newsreels in Fascist Italy," *Media History* 11, no. 3 (2005): 177–91; Ciara Chambers, "'British for the British—Irish Events for the Irish': Indigenous Newsreel Production in Ireland," *Historical Journal of Film, Radio, and Television* 32, no. 3 (2012): 361–77; Rosemary Bergeron, "A History of the Newsreel in Canada: A Struggle for Screen Time," *Moving Image* 7, no. 2 (2007): 25–54; Roel Vande

Winkel and Daniel Biltereyst, "Filmed News and Nationalism in Belgium: Flemish Events at the Crossroads of Politics, Culture and Commerce (1929–1942)," *Historical Journal of Film, Radio, and Television* 32, no. 3 (2012): 379–99.

64. Suzanne Lommers, *Europe—On Air: Interwar Projects for Radio Broadcasting* (Amsterdam: Amsterdam University Press, 2013), 41–71; Tim Crook, *International Radio Journalism: History, Theory and Practice* (London: Routledge, 1998), 57–90; Andres Crisell, *An Introductory History of British Broadcasting* (London: Routledge, 1997), 28–43; Kerim Yasar, *Electrified Voices: How the Telephone, Phonograph, and Radio Shaped Modern Japan, 1868–1945* (New York: Columbia University Press, 2018), 114–44; Joy Hayes, "'Touching the Sentiments of Everyone': Nationalism and State Broadcasting in Thirties Mexico," *Communication Review* 1, no. 4 (1996): 411–39; Jürg Rainer Schwyter, *Dictating to the Mob: The History of the BBC Advisory Committee on Spoken English* (Oxford: Oxford University Press, 2016).

65. Marius Turda, "Race, Science, and Eugenics in the Twentieth Century," in Bashford and Levine, *Oxford Handbook of Eugenics*, 63–75; Andre Gingrich, "After the Great War: National Reconfigurations of Anthropology in Late Colonial Times," in *Doing Anthropology in Wartime and Warzones: World War I and the Cultural Sciences in Europe*, ed. Reinhard Johler, Christian Marchetti, and Monique Scheer (Bielefeld, Germany: Transcript Verlag, 2010), 355–80; Robert Procter, "From Anthropologie to Rassenkunde in the German Anthropological Tradition," in *Bones, Bodies, and Behavior: Essays in Behavioral Anthropology*, ed. George W. Stocking (Madison: University of Wisconsin Press, 1988), 138–16.

66. Bunzl, "Boas and the Humboldtian Tradition," 52–73; John S. Allen, "Franz Boas's Physical Anthropology: The Critique of Racial Formalism Revisited," *Current Anthropology* 30, no. 1 (1989): 79–84; Turda, "Race, Science, and Eugenics," 71–72; Thomas Hylland Eriksen and Finn Sivert Nielsen, *A History of Anthropology* (London: Pluto, 2013), 46–83; Francine Hirsch, *Empire of Nations: Ethnographic Knowledge and the Making of the Soviet Union* (Ithaca, NY: Cornell University Press, 2005).

67. Ben de Pater and Herman van der Wusten, *Het geografische huis: De opbouw van een wetenschap* (Bussum, Netherlands: Coutinho, 1996), 66–98, 109–23, 131–33; Mark Bassin, "Eurasia," in Mishkova and Trencsényi, *European Regions and Boundaries*, 215–17; Keiichi Takeuchi, "Japanese Geopolitics in the 1930s and 1940s," in *Geopolitics: An Introductory Reader*, ed. Jason Dittmer and Joanna Sharp (London: Routledge, 2014), 67–75; Guntram Henrik Herb, *Under the Map of Germany: Nationalism and Propaganda, 1918–1945* (London: Routledge, 1997), 49–68, 119–50.

68. Alessandro Roncaglia, *The Wealth of Ideas: A History of Economic Thought* (Cambridge: Cambridge University Press, 2005), 278–416; Thomas Fetzer, "Nationalism in Political Economy Scholarship," in *Nationalism and the Economy: Explorations into a Neglected Relationship*, ed. Stefan Berger and Thomas Fetzer (Budapest: Central European University Press, 2019), 43–48; Hagen Schulz-Forberg, "Embedding the Social Question into International Order: Economic Thought and the Origins of Neoliberalism in the 1930s," in Berger and Fetzer, *Nationalism and the Economy*, 249–69.

69. Berger, *Past as History*, 238–45; Hans-Lukas Kieser, "Die Herausbildung des nationalistischen Geschichtsdiskurses in der Türkei (spätes 19.–Mitte 20. Jahrhundert)," in *Beruf und Berufung: Geschichtswissenschaft und Nationsbildung in Ostmittel—und Südosteuropa im 19. und 20. Jahrhundert*, ed. Markus Krzoska and Hans-Christian Maner (Münster: Lit, 2005), 59–98; Zürcher, *Turkey*, 174–75, 190–91.

70. Berger, *Past as History*, 244–45; Berger, *Writing the Nation*, 105–11, 182–87; Anthony Milner, "South East Asian Historical Writing," in *The Oxford History of Historical Writing*, vol. 4, *1800–1945*, ed. Stuart Macintyre, Juan Maiguashca, and Attila Pók (Oxford: Oxford University Press, 2011), 552–56; Cheah Boon Kheng, "Writing Indigenous History in Malaysia: A Survey on Approaches and Problems," *Crossroads: An Interdisciplinary Journal of Southeast Asian Studies* 10, no. 2 (1996): 33–81.

71. Berger, *Past as History*, 226–38, 259–60; Peter Schötter, "After the Deluge: The Impact of the Two World Wars on the Historical Work of Henri Pirenne and Marc Bloch," in *Nationalizing the Past: Historians as Nation-Builders in Modern Europe*, ed. Stefan Berger and Chris Lorenz (Basingstoke, UK: Palgrave Macmillan, 2010), 404–26; Thomas Bender, "Writing American History, 1789–1945," in Macintyre, Maiguashca, and Pók, *Oxford History of Historical Writing*, 4:382–87.

72. Kultermann, *Geschichte der Kunstgeschichte*, 149–216; Matthew Rampley, *The Vienna School of Art History: Empire and the Politics of Scholarship, 1847–1918* (University Park: Pennsylvania State University Press, 2013), 31–52; Michela Passini, *La fabrique de l'art national: Le nationalisme et les origines de l'histoire de l'art en France et en Allemagne 1870–1933* (Paris: Maison des sciences de l'homme, 2012), 147–57, 228–50; Storm, "Art History," 379–83.

73. Leonhard, *Pandora's Box*, 210–23, Mann quotes at 219; Eksteins, *Rites of Spring*, 76–94; Storm, *La perspectiva del progreso*, 212–39.

74. Ilan Stavans, *José Vasconcelos: The Prophet of Race* (New Brunswick, NJ: Rutgers University Press, 2011); Knight, "Racism, Revolution," 78–98; Banerjee-Dube, *Modern India*, 290–98; Carolien Stolte, "Orienting India: Interwar Internationalism in an Asian Inflection, 1917–1937" (PhD diss., Leiden University, 2013), 75–83; Janet G. Vaillant, *Black, French, and African: A Life of Léopold Sédar Senghor* (Cambridge, MA: Harvard University Press, 1990), 87–117, 243–72.

75. Eric Hobsbawm, *The Age of Extremes: A History of the World, 1914–1991* (New York: Vintage Books, 1996), 178–99; Daniele Conversi, "Art, Nationalism, and War: Political Futurism in Italy (1909–1944)," *Sociology Compass* 3, no. 1 (2009): 94–96; Chara Kolokytha, "The Debate over the Creation of a Museum of Modern Art in Paris between the Wars and the Shaping of an Evolutionary Narrative for French Art," *Il capitale culturale*, no. 14 (2016): 200; Hall, *Cities of Tomorrow*, 219–25; Susan Noyes Platt, "Modernism, Formalism, and Politics: The 'Cubism and Abstract Art' Exhibition of 1936 at the Museum of Modern Art," *Art Journal* 47, no. 4 (1988): 284–95; Astrit Schmidt Burkhardt, "Shaping Modernism: Alfred Barr's Genealogy of Art," *Word and Image* 16, no. 4 (2000): 387–400.

76. Kenneth E. Silver, *Esprit de Corps: The Art of the Parisian Avant-Garde and the First World War, 1914–1925* (Princeton, NJ: Princeton University Press, 1989); Conversi, "Art"; Hall, *Cities of Tomorrow*, 225–27; Kolokytha, "Museum of Art in Paris"; Stephanie J. Smith, *The Power and Politics of Art in Postrevolutionary Mexico* (Chapel Hill: University of North Carolina Press, 2017).

77. William R. Everdell, *The First Moderns: Profiles in the Origins of Twentieth-Century Thought* (Chicago: University of Chicago Press, 1997), 265–83; Lawrence W. Levine, "Jazz and American Culture," *Journal of American Folklore* 102, no. 403 (1989): 6–22; Michael H. Kater, "Forbidden Fruit? Jazz in the Third Reich," *American Historical Review* 94, no. 1 (1989): 11–43.

78. Van der Linden, "Non-Western National Music"; Daniel Laqua, "Exhibiting, Encountering and Studying Music in Interwar Europe: Between National and International Community," in *European Encounters: Intellectual Exchange and the Rethinking of Europe, 1914–1945*, ed. Carlos

Reijnen and Marleen Rensen (Amsterdam: Rodopi, 2014), 207–23; Thomas Turino, "Nationalism and Latin American Music: Selected Case Studies and Theoretical Considerations," *Latin American Music Review* 24, no. 2 (2003): 169–209; María Susana Azzi, "The Tango, Peronism, and Astor Piazzola in the 1940s and 50s," in *From Tejano to Tango: Essays on Latin American Popular Music*, ed. Walter Aaron Clark (New York: Routledge, 2002), 25–40; Sandie Holguín, *Flamenco Nation: The Construction of Spanish National Identity* (Madison: University of Wisconsin Pres, 2019), 144–77.

79. Gregory Castle, ed., *A History of the Modernist Novel* (Cambridge: Cambridge University Press, 2015); Thiesse, *Écrire la France*; Dorman, *Revolt of the Provinces*; Boa and Palfreyman, *Heimat*; Carlos J. Alonso, "The Criollista Novel," in *The Cambridge History of Latin American Literature*, vol. 2, *The Twentieth Century*, ed. Roberto Gonzalez Echevarría and Enrique Pupo-Walker (Cambridge: Cambridge University Press, 1996), 195–212.

80. Paula Marantz Cohen, *Silent Film and the Triumph of the American Myth* (Oxford: Oxford University Press, 2001); Gerben Bakker, *Entertainment Industrialised: The Emergence of the International Film Industry, 1890–1940* (Cambridge: Cambridge University Press, 2008), 264–68; Victoria De Grazia, "Mass Culture and Sovereignty: The American Challenge to European Cinemas, 1920–1960," *Journal of Modern History* 61, no. 1 (1989): 53–87.

81. De Grazia, "Mass Culture"; Patrick Merziger, "Americanised, Europeanised or Nationalised? The Film Industry in Europe under the Influence of Hollywood, 1927–1968," *European Review of History* 20, no. 5 (2013): 793–813; Marta García Carrión, "Cine y nacionalización en la Europa de entreguerras: El caso español en perspectiva comparada," in *Nación y nacionalización: Una perspectiva europea comparada*, ed. Ferran Archilés, Marta García Carrión, and Ismael Saz (Valencia: Publicacions Universitat de Valencia, 2013), 155–70; Christophe Gauthier, "Le cinéma des nations: Invention des écoles nationales et patriotisme cinématographique (années 10–années 30)," *Revue d'histoire moderne et contemporaine*, 51, no. 4 (2004): 58–77; Yuji Tosaka, "The Discourse of Anti-Americanism and Hollywood Movies: Film Import Controls in Japan, 1937–1941," *Journal of American–East Asian Relations* 12, no. 1–2 (2003): 59–80; Geoffrey Nowell-Smith, ed., *The Oxford History of World Cinema* (Oxford: Oxford University Press, 1999).

82. Jay Winter, *Sites of Memory, Sites of Mourning: The Great War in European Cultural History* (Cambridge: Cambridge University Press, 1995), 78–117; Jennifer Iles, "In Remembrance: The Flanders Poppy," *Mortality* 13, no. 3 (2008): 201–21; David Omissi, "The Indian Army in Europe, 1914–1918," in Storm and al Tuma, *Colonial Soldiers in Europe*, 133–35.

83. Hugh Clout, *After the Ruins: Restoring the Countryside of Northern France after the Great War* (Exeter: University of Exeter Press, 1996); Lane, *National Romanticism*, 27–28, 41–69, 125–28; Nicholas Bullock and James Read, *The Movement for Housing Reform in Germany and France, 1840–1914* (Cambridge: Cambridge University Press, 1985), 532–34; Storm, *Culture of Regionalism*, 111–14, 144–53.

84. Sibel Bozdoğan, *Modernism and Nation Building: Turkish Architectural Culture in the Early Republic* (Seattle: University of Washington Press, 2001); Martin Kohlrausch, *Brokers of Modernity: East Central Europe and the Rise of Modernist Architects, 1910–1950* (Leuven: Leuven University Press, 2019); Storm, "Construction of National Identities."

85. Gutiérrez Viñuales, "Arquitectura historicista"; Huib Akihary, *Architectuur en stedebouw in Indonesie 1870–1970* (Zutphen, Netherlands: Walburg, 1990), 43–54; Caroline Herbelin, *Architectures du Vietnam colonial: Repenser le métissage* (Paris: CTHS-INHA, 2016).

86. Richard A. Etlin, *Modernism in Italian Architecture, 1890–1940* (Cambridge, MA: MIT Press, 1991), 391–431; Léon Krier, *Albert Speer: Architecture, 1932–1942* (New York: Monacelli, 2013); Jane Ridley, "Edwin Lutyens, New Delhi, and the Architecture of Imperialism," *Journal of Imperial and Commonwealth History* 26, no. 2 (1998): 67–83; John M. MacKenzie, *The British Empire through Buildings: Structure, Function, Meaning* (Manchester: Manchester University Press, 2020), 244–53.

87. Aristotle A. Kallis, *The Third Rome, 1922–1943: The Making of the Fascist Capital* (Basingstoke, UK: Palgrave Macmillan, 2014), 42–106; D. Medina Lasansky, *The Renaissance Perfected: Architecture, Spectacle, and Tourism in Fascist Italy* (University Park: Pennsylvania State University Press, 2004); Agustín Cócola Gant, "El Barrio Gótico de Barcelona: De símbolo nacional a parque temático," *Scripta Nova*, no. 15 (2011); Storm, *Culture of Regionalism*, 151–52.

88. Harp, *Marketing Michelin*, 89–126; Demay, *Tourism and Colonization*, 88–94; Michael Frederik Wagner, "The Rise of Autotourism in Danish Leisure, 1910–1970," *Journal of Tourism History* 5, no. 3 (2013): 265–86; Marguerite S. Shaffer, *See America First: Tourism and National Identity, 1880–1940* (Washington, DC: Smithsonian Institution Press, 2002).

89. Diana P. Koenker, *Club Red: Vacation Travel and the Soviet Dream* (Ithaca, NY: Cornell University Press, 2013); Rudy Koshar, *German Travel Cultures* (Oxford: Berg Publishers, 2000), 115–61; Andrew Behrendt, "Educating Apostles of the Homeland: Tourism and 'Honismeret' in Interwar Hungary," *Hungarian Cultural Studies* 7 (2015): 159–76; Aldis Purs, "'One Breath for Every Two Strides': The State's Attempt to Construct Tourism and Identity in Interwar Latvia," in *Turizm: The Russian and East European Tourist under Capitalism and Socialism*, ed. Anne E. Gorsuch and Diana P. Koenker (Ithaca, NY: Cornell University Press, 2006), 97–115.

90. Bernhard Gissibl, Sabine Höhler, and Patrick Kupper, eds., *Civilizing Nature: National Parks in Global Historical Perspective* (New York: Berghahn, 2015); Jacobo García Álvarez, "Paisaje, memoria histórica e identidad nacional en los inicios de la política de conservación de la naturaleza en España: De Covadonga a San Juan de La Peña," *Hispania* 73, no. 244 (2013): 409–38; Ford, *Natural Interests*, 114–63; Zuelow, *History of Tourism*, 120–25; Young, *Enacting Brittany*, 239–41; Thomas Zeller, "'The Landscape's Crown': Landscape, Perceptions, and Modernizing Effects of the German Autobahn System, 1934 to 1941," in *Technologies of Landscape: From Reaping to Recycling*, ed. David E. Nye (Amherst: University of Massachusetts Press, 1999), 218–38.

91. Kevin Starr, *Material Dreams: Southern California through the 1920s* (New York: Oxford University Press, 1990), 184–87; Gert Gröning and Joachim Wolschke-Bulmahn, "The Native Plant Enthusiasm: Ecological Panacea or Xenophobia?," *Landscape Research* 28, no. 1 (2003): 75–88; Wolschke-Bulmahn, "Landscape Design"; Zeller, "Landscape Crown," 227–29; Sandra Swart, "The Other Citizens: Nationalism and Animals," in *The Routledge Companion to Animal-Human History*, ed. Hilda Kean and Philip Howell (London: Routledge, 2018), 38–40.

92. Erik Swyngedouw, *Liquid Power: Contested Hydro-Modernities in Twentieth-Century Spain, 1898–2010* (Cambridge: MIT Press, 2015), 39–99; Jean-François Lejeune, "Built Utopias in the Countryside: The Rural and the Modern in Franco's Spain" (PhD diss., Delft University of Technology, 2019); Hall, *Cities of Tomorrow*, 169–78; Hans Renes and Stefano Piastra, "Polders and Politics: New Agricultural Landscapes in Italian and Dutch Wetlands, 1920s to 1950s," *Landscapes* 12, no. 1 (May 1, 2011): 24–41; Ben de Pater, "Conflicting Images of the Zuider Zee around 1900: Nation-Building and the Struggle against Water," *Journal of Historical Geography* 37, no. 1 (2011): 82–94; David Blackbourn, *The Conquest of Nature: Water, Landscape and the Making of Modern Germany* (London: Cape, 2006), 239–97.

93. Kolleen M. Guy, "Regional Foods," in Núñez Seixas and Storm, *Regionalism and Modern Europe*, 83–99; Kolleen M. Guy, *When Champagne Became French: Wine and the Making of a National Identity* (Baltimore: Johns Hopkins University Press, 2003).

94. Storm, "Domestic Sphere"; Harp, *Marketing Michelin*, 225–69; Angela Jill Cooley, *To Live and Dine in Dixie: The Evolution of Urban Food Culture in the Jim Crow South* (Athens: The University of Georgia Press, 2015).

95. Sheldon Garon, "Fashioning a Culture of Diligence and Thrift: Savings and Frugality Campaigns in Japan, 1900–1931," in Minichiello, *Japan's Competing Modernities*, 312–34; Oliver Kühschelm, "Buy National Campaigns: Patriotic Shopping and the Capitalist Nation State," *Journal of Modern European History* 18, no. 1 (2020): 79–95; Carol Helstosky, "Fascist Food Politics: Mussolini's Policy of Alimentary Sovereignty," *Journal of Modern Italian Studies* 9, no. 1 (2004): 1–26; Lara Anderson, *Cooking Up the Nation: Spanish Culinary Texts and Culinary Nationalization in the Late Nineteenth and Early Twentieth Century* (Woodbridge, UK: Tamesis, 2013), 139–44; Reagin, *Sweeping the German Nation*, 95–98, 217; Evans, *Third Reich*, 487, 521–23.

96. Perry Willson, "The Nation in Uniform? Fascist Italy, 1919–43," *Past and Present* 221, no. 1 (2013): 239–72.

97. Francie Chassen-López, "The Traje de Tehuana as National Icon: Gender, Ethnicity, and Fashion in Mexico," *The Americas* 71, no. 2 (2014): 281–314; Ruben George Oliven, *Tradition Matters: Modern Gaúcho Identity in Brazil* (New York: Columbia University Press, 1996); Rebecca Earle, "Nationalism and National Dress in Spanish America," in *The Politics of Dress in Asia and the Americas*, ed. Mina Roces and Louise P. Edwards (Eastbourne, UK: Sussex Academic Press, 2007), 171–73.

98. Wickramasinghe, *Sri Lanka in the Modern Age*, 97–104; Mina Roces and Louise P. Edwards, eds., *The Politics of Dress in Asia and the Americas* (Eastbourne, UK: Sussex Academic Press, 2007), 19–42, 65–139; Ross, *Clothing*, 119–38.

99. Harrison, *China*, 2011, 134–40, 150–66; Maurizio Peleggi, "Refashioning Civilization: Dress and Bodily Practice in Thai Nation-Building," in Roces and Edwards, *Politics of Dress*, 65–81; Baker and Phongpaichit, *History of Thailand*, 131–35.

100. Thomas Barfield, *Afghanistan: A Cultural and Political History* (Princeton, NJ: Princeton University Press, 2010), 181–95; Abrahamian, *History of Modern Iran*, 77–88; Zürcher, *Turkey*, 186–90; Ross, *Clothing*, 103–18.

101. Maiken Umbach, "Made in Germany," in *Deutsche Erinnerungsorte*, ed. Etienne Francois and Hagen Schulze (Munich: Beck, 2001), 2:405–19.

102. Keys, *Globalizing Sport*, 26–27; Birgit Krawietz, "Sport and Nationalism in the Republic of Turkey," *International Journal of the History of Sport* 31, no. 3 (2014): 336–46; Sait Tarakçıoğlu, "A Failed Project in Turkey's Sports History: The Law on Physical Education of 1938," *International Journal of the History of Sport* 31, no. 14 (2014): 1807–19.

103. Chris Valiotis, "South Asia," in Pope and Nauright, *Routledge Companion to Sports History*, 571–86; Richard L. Light, "Japan," in Pope and Nauright, *Routledge Companion to Sports History*, 472–87; Keys, *Globalizing Sport*, 27.

104. Keys, *Globalizing Sport*, 42–43, 52–54, 69–70, 90–158; Bairner, *Sport, Nationalism, and Globalization*, 54–57, 146; J. Gordon Hylton, "Before the Redskins Were the Redskins: The Use of Native American Team Names in the Formative Era of American Sports, 1857–1933," *North Dakota Law Review* 86, no. 4 (2010): 879–904; Daryl Adair, "Australia," in Pope and Nauright, *Routledge Companion to Sports History*, 339.

105. Keys, *Globalizing Sport*, 158–80.

106. Keys, 115–58.

Chapter 7

1. Mazower, *Hitler's Empire*, 245–48; Davide Rodogno, "Wartime Occupation by Italy," in Maiolo and Bosworth, *Cambridge History of the Second World War*, 2:436–41; Yellen, *Co-prosperity Sphere*, 83–86.

2. Els Witte, Alain Meynen, and Dirk Luyten, *Politieke geschiedenis van België: Van 1830 tot heden* (Antwerp: Manteau, 2016), 231–59; Ludger Mees, "The Völkisch Appeal: Nazi Germany, the Basques, and the Bretons," in *War, Exile, Justice and Everyday Life, 1936–1946*, ed. Sandra Ott (Reno: Centre for Basque Studies, 2011), 251–85; Mazower, *Hitler's Empire*, 342–49; Ricklefs et al., *Southeast Asia*, 300–316.

3. Mazower, *Hitler's Empire*, 454–70.

4. Francis R. Nicosia, *Nazi Germany and the Arab World* (Cambridge: Cambridge University Press, 2014), 135–79, 222–63.

5. Yellen, *Co-prosperity Sphere*, 124–37.

6. Banerjee-Dube, *Modern India*, 403–5; Joyce C. Lebra, *The Indian National Army and Japan* (Singapore: Institute of South East Asian Studies, 2008).

7. Dietmar Rothermund, *The Routledge Companion to Decolonization* (London: Routledge, 2006), 50–51; Gerry J. Simpson, *Great Powers and Outlaw States: Unequal Sovereigns in the International Legal Order* (Cambridge: Cambridge University Press, 2004), 175–76, 264–66.

8. Mühlhahn, *Making China Modern*, 333–38.

9. Rothermund, *Decolonization*, 51–52, 239–40; Weitz, *World Divided*, 295–302; Anne Applebaum, *Iron Curtain: The Crushing of Eastern Europe, 1944–1956* (London: Allen Lane, 2012).

10. Marcus, *History of Ethiopia*, 140–56; Zewde, *Modern Ethiopia*, 178–81; David P. Fields, *Foreign Friends: Syngman Rhee, American Exceptionalism, and the Division of Korea* (Lexington: University Press of Kentucky, 2019), 136–74.

11. Jane Burbank and Frederick Cooper, *Empires in World History: Power and the Politics of Difference* (Princeton, NJ: Princeton University Press, 2010), 413–22; Wim van der Doel, *Zo ver de wereld strekt: De geschiedenis van Nederland overzee vanaf 1800* (Amsterdam: Bert Bakker, 2011), 341–43.

12. Banerjee-Dube, *Modern India*, 387–402.

13. Ricklefs et al., *Southeast Asia*, 312–13, 338–40; McDougall, *Algeria*, 179–95; Randrianja and Ellis, *Madagascar*, 173–77.

14. Ricklefs et al., *Southeast Asia*, 321–27; Rogan, *Arabs*, 239–40, 304–12, 322; Wickramasinghe, *Sri Lanka in the Modern Age*, 154–61.

15. Jan C. Jansen and Jürgen Osterhammel, *Decolonization: A Short History* (Princeton, NJ: Princeton University Press, 2017), 12–13; Adom Getachew, *Worldmaking after Empire: The Rise and Fall of Self-Determination* (Princeton, NJ: Princeton University Press, 2019), 71–107; Cooper, *Citizenship, Inequality*, 138–39.

16. Michael Collins, "Decolonisation and the 'Federal Moment,'" *Diplomacy and Statecraft* 24, no. 1 (2013): 21–40; Frederick Cooper, *Citizenship between Empire and Nation: Remaking France and French Africa, 1945–1960* (Princeton, NJ: Princeton University Press, 2014).

17. Tom Long, "Historical Antecedents and Post–World War II Regionalism in the Americas," *World Politics* 72, no. 2 (2020): 214–53; Anne-Isabelle Richard, "A Global Perspective on European Cooperation and Integration since 1918," in *The Cambridge History of the European Union*, ed. Mathieu Segers and Steven Van Hecke (Cambridge: Cambridge University Press, 2023), 2:459–80; Wim van Meurs et al., *The Unfinished History of European Integration* (Amsterdam: Amsterdam University Press, 2018), 21–28; Benyamin Neuberger, "The African Concept of Balkanisation," *Journal of Modern African Studies* 14, no. 3 (1976): 523–29.

18. Marie-Janine Calic, *A History of Yugoslavia* (West Lafayette, IN: Purdue University Press, 2019), 176–77; Long, "Historical Antecedents"; Meurs et al., *Unfinished History*, 28–43; Kiran Klaus Patel, *Project Europe: Myths and Realities of European Integration* (Cambridge: Cambridge University Press, 2020), 176–208.

19. Rothermund, *Decolonization*, 51; Darwin, *Empire Project*, 492–565.

20. Rogan, *Arabs*, 247–61, 313–40.

21. Banerjee-Dube, *Modern India*, 220–55, 304–14, 339–40, 369–73, 386–92, 408–44; Joya Chatterji, "Nationalism in India, 1857–1947," in Breuilly, *Oxford Handbook of Nationalism*, 242–63.

22. W. David MacIntyre, *The Commonwealth of Nations: Origins and Impact, 1869–1971* (Minneapolis: University of Minnesota Press, 1977), 181–93, 318–64; Darwin, *Empire Project*, 553–55.

23. Ricklefs et al., *Southeast Asia*, 327–38; Rothermund, *Decolonization*, 90–93.

24. Rothermund, *Decolonization*, 210–16; Getachew, *Worldmaking after Empire*, 107–31.

25. Collins, "Federal Moment"; Rothermund, *Decolonization*, 188–92; Darwin, *Empire Project*, 578, 619–21, 626–32.

26. Darwin, *Empire Project*, 570–71, 616–19, 621–26; Chris Vaughan, "The Politics of Regionalism and Federation in East Africa, 1958–1964," *Historical Journal* 62, no. 2 (June 2019): 519–40.

27. Doel, *Zo ver de wereld strekt*, 323–73; Ricklefs et al., *Southeast Asia*, 338–45; Jennifer L. Foray, "A Unified Empire of Equal Parts: The Dutch Commonwealth Schemes of the 1920s–40s," *Journal of Imperial and Commonwealth History* 41, no. 2 (2013): 259–84.

28. Alice L. Conklin, Sarah Fishman, and Robert Zaretsky, *France and Its Empire since 1870* (Oxford: Oxford University Press, 2011), 242–69; Cooper, *Empire and Nation*, 26–165; Clive J. Christie, *A Modern History of Southeast Asia: Decolonization, Nationalism and Separatism* (London: Tauris, 1996), 88–95.

29. Ricklefs et al., *Southeast Asia*, 310–13, 346–52; Rothermund, *Decolonization*, 81–87.

30. Cooper, *Empire and Nation*, 127–47; Rogan, *Arabs*, 406–18; McDougall, *Algeria*, 182–235.

31. Rothermund, *Decolonization*, 128–29, 137–39; Cooper, *Empire and Nation*, 124–278.

32. Cooper, *Empire and Nation*, 261–62, 279–326, 341.

33. Cooper, 306–40, 388, quote at 315; Rothermund, *Decolonization*, 137–41.

34. Cooper, *Empire and Nation*, 342–88.

35. Cooper, 388–413; Paul Nugent, *Africa since Independence: A Comparative History* (Basingstoke, UK: Palgrave Macmillan, 2012), 79.

36. Emmanuelle Saada, "France: The Longue Durée of French Decolonization," in *The Oxford Handbook of the Ends of Empire* (Oxford: Oxford University Press, 2018), 85–102.

37. Rothermund, *Decolonization*, 222–38; Nugent, *Africa*, 265–75; Filipe Ribeiro de Meneses, "The Idea of Empire in Portuguese and Spanish Life, 1890 to 1975," in *The Routledge Companion to Iberian Studies* (London: Routledge, 2017), 401–12.

38. Rogan, *Arabs*, 188–98, 361–87; James P. Jankowski, *Nasser's Egypt, Arab Nationalism, and the United Arab Republic* (Boulder, CO: Lynne Rienner, 2002), 14–41, 54–88.

39. Rogan, *Arabs*, 386–405; Jankowski, *Nasser's Egypt*, 91–179.

40. Keith Somerville, *Africa's Long Road since Independence: The Many Histories of a Continent* (London: Penguin, 2017), 52–56; Getachew, *Worldmaking after Empire*, 131–41; Klaas van Walraven, *Dreams of Power: The Role of the Organization of African Unity in the Politics of Africa 1963–1993* (Aldershot, UK: Ashgate, 1999), 84–153.

41. Rothermund, *Decolonization*, 118–19, 127–32, 142, 149–51, 157–61, 167–71; Nugent, *Africa*, 73–79.

42. Rothermund, *Decolonization*, 210, 218–22, 239–43; Mazower, *Governing the World*, 268–70.

43. Rothermund, *Decolonization*, 132–33, 161–64; Nugent, *Africa*, 32–35, 126–30; Somerville, *Africa's Long Road*, 27–28, 41.

44. Nugent, *Africa*, 76–77; Paul Nugent, *Smugglers, Secessionists and Loyal Citizens on the Ghana-Togo Frontier: The Life of the Borderlands since 1914* (Oxford: James Currey, 2002), 147–275.

45. Nugent, *Africa*, 52–55, 86–91; Alanna O'Malley, *The Diplomacy of Decolonisation: America, Britain and the United Nations during the Congo Crisis 1960–64* (Manchester: Manchester University Press, 2018).

46. Nugent, *Africa*, 91–99; John J. Stremlau, *The International Politics of the Nigerian Civil War, 1967–1970* (Princeton, NJ: Princeton University Press, 1977). For "nationalism of the rich," see Emmanuel Dalle Mulle, *The Nationalism of the Rich: Discourses and Strategies of Separatist Parties in Catalonia, Flanders, Northern Italy and Scotland* (London: Routledge, 2019).

47. Ricklefs et al., *Southeast Asia*, 338; Matthew Jones, *Conflict and Confrontation in South East Asia, 1961–1965: Britain, the United States, and the Creation of Malaysia* (Cambridge: Cambridge University Press, 2001), 268–75; M. Rafiqul Islam, "Secessionist Self-Determination: Some Lessons from Katanga, Biafra, and Bangladesh," *Journal of Peace Research* 22, no. 3 (1985): 211–21; Willem van Schendel, *A History of Bangladesh* (Cambridge: Cambridge University Press, 2009), 107–30, 159–82.

48. Nugent, *Africa*, 80–83; Somerville, *Africa's Long Road*, 83–86; Marco Zoppi, "Greater Somalia, the Never-Ending Dream? Contested Somali Borders: The Power of Tradition vs. the Tradition of Power," *Journal of African History, Politics and Society* 1, no. 1 (2015): 43–64.

49. Damien Kingsbury, *Separatism and the State* (London: Routledge, 2021); Christie, *Southeast Asia*.

50. Somerville, *Africa's Long Road*, 135–38; Rogan, *Arabs*, 488–91; Magdalena Dembinska and Aurélie Campana, "Frozen Conflicts and Internal Dynamics of De Facto States: Perspectives and Directions for Research," *International Studies Review* 19, no. 2 (2017): 254–78.

51. John W. Meyer et al., "World Society and the Nation-State," *American Journal of Sociology* 103, no. 1 (1997): 144–81; Beckert, "Institutional Isomorphism Revisited."

52. Dirk J. Vandewalle, *A History of Modern Libya* (Cambridge: Cambridge University Press, 2012), 96–137.

53. Howard, *War in European History*, 116–44; John Hutchinson, *Nationalism and War* (Oxford: Oxford University Press, 2017), 125–38; Sibylle Scheipers, ed., *Heroism and the Changing Character of War: Toward Post-heroic Warfare?* (Basingstoke, UK: Palgrave Macmillan, 2014).

54. Francisco O. Ramirez, Yasemin Soysal, and Suzanne Shanahan, "The Changing Logic of Political Citizenship: Cross-National Acquisition of Women's Suffrage Rights, 1890 to 1990," *American Sociological Review* 62, no. 5 (1997): 735–45; Marlene LeGates, *In Their Time: A History of Feminism in Western Society* (New York: Routledge, 2011), 333–35; Gretchen Bauer and Manon Tremblay, eds., *Women in Executive Power: A Global Overview* (Abingdon, UK: Routledge, 2011).

55. Martin Conway, *Western Europe's Democratic Age: 1945–1968* (Princeton, NJ: Princeton University Press, 2020), 108–11, 235–44; Belmonte, *International LGBT Rights Movement*, 71–108.

56. LeGates, *Their Time*, 327–35; Marta Trenado Díaz, "The Cases of 'Stolen Children' in Spain and Ireland—Curtailing the Most Suitable Legal Framework on the Fight for 'Real' Identities," *ICL Journal* 9, no. 2 (2015); Jan Kok, *Beklemd in de scharnieren van de tijd: Beleid, praktijk en ervaringen van afstand ter adoptie door niet-gehuwde moeders in Nederland tussen 1956 en 1984* (The Hague: WODC, 2017).

57. LeGates, *Their Time*, 335–67; Louise P. Edwards and Mina Roces, eds., *Women's Movements in Asia: Feminisms and Transnational Activism* (Abingdon, UK: Routledge, 2010); Kaden Paulson-Smith and Aili Mari Tripp, "Women's Rights and Critical Junctures in Constitutional Reform in Africa (1951–2019)," *African Affairs* 120, no. 480 (2021): 365–89.

58. Fancis G. Castles et al., eds., *The Oxford Handbook of the Welfare State* (Oxford: Oxford University Press, 2010); Charles Webster, *The National Health Service: A Political History* (Oxford: Oxford University Press, 2002).

59. Cooper, *Citizenship, Inequality*, 138–39; Cooper, *Empire and Nation*, 218–26. See also Darwin, *Empire Project*, 618.

60. Samuel Moyn, *Not Enough: Human Rights in an Unequal World* (Cambridge, MA: Belknap Press of Harvard University Press, 2018), 100–102, quoting Nkrumah at 101; Nugent, *Africa*, 141–207; Wimmer, *Nation Building*, 77–82.

61. Mazower, *Dark Continent*, 269–86; Mühlhahn, *Making China Modern*, 408–11, 437–47; Ricklefs et al., *Southeast Asia*, 397–98.

62. Tony Judt, *Postwar: A History of Europe since 1945* (New York: Penguin, 2005), 368–69; Matthew Connelly, "Population Control in India: Prologue to the Emergency Period," *Population and Development Review* 32, no. 4 (2006): 629–67; Mühlhahn, *Making China Modern*, 573–75.

63. Conway, *Western Europe*, 137–42, 192–96, 209–19; Mazower, *Governing the World*, 273–99; Christopher Heurlin, "Authoritarian Aid and Regime Durability: Soviet Aid to the Developing World and Donor-Recipient Institutional Complementarity and Capacity," *International Studies Quarterly* 64, no. 1 (2020): 968–79; Frederick Cooper and Randall M. Packard, eds., *International Development and the Social Sciences: Essays on the History and Politics of Knowledge* (Berkeley: University of California Press, 1997); Valeska Huber, "Introduction: Global Histories of Social Planning," *Journal of Contemporary History* 52, no. 1 (2017): 3–15.

64. Michael Keating, *Rescaling the European State: The Making of Territory and the Rise of the Meso* (Oxford: Oxford University Press, 2013), 43–44, 55–56; Moyn, *Not Enough*, 89–113.

65. Mazower, *Governing the World*, 348–50; Kingston, *Nationalism in Asia*, 59–75; Arvind Panagariya, *India: The Emerging Giant* (New York: Oxford University Press, 2008), 22–47; Ricklefs et al., *Southeast Asia*, 363–97; Nugent, *Africa*, 147–207.

66. Nugent, *Africa*, 148–49, 154–56, 175–76, 207–64; Benjamin Smith, "Life of the Party: The Origins of Regime Breakdown and Persistence under Single-Party Rule," *World Politics* 57, no. 3 (2005): 421–51; Kenneth F. Greene, "The Political Economy of Authoritarian Single-Party Dominance," *Comparative Political Studies* 43, no. 7 (2010): 807–34; Ricklefs et al., *Southeast Asia*, 363–400; Lewis, *Authoritarian Regimes in Latin America*, 209–31.

67. Ricklefs et al., *Southeast Asia*, 363–93; Rogan, *Arabs*, 405–6; Nugent, *Africa*, 141–56, 253–60; Lewis, *Authoritarian Regimes in Latin America*, 144–52; Carlos Domper Lasús, "Ni liberales ni comunistas: La 'democracia orgánica' y la integración del Franquismo y el Estado Novo en la Europa posterior a 1945," *Espacio, tiempo y forma*, series 5, *Historia contemporánea*, no. 31 (2019): 151–72; Mühlhahn, *Making China Modern*, 430–37, 454–60; Grace Lee, "The Political Philosophy of Juche," *Stanford Journal of East Asian Affairs* 3, no. 1 (2003): 105–13.

68. Nugent, *Africa*, 235–42.

69. Sheldon Garon, "Saving for 'My Own Good and the Good of the Nation': Economic Nationalism in Modern Japan," in *Nation and Nationalism in Japan*, ed. Sandra Wilson (Abingdon, UK: Routledge, 2013), 97–115; Aaron William Moore, "Nationalism in Northeast Asia since 1945," in Breuilly, *Oxford Handbook of Nationalism*, , 453–72; Sowerwine, *France since 1870*, 319–27; Harold James, "Die D-Mark," in François and Schulze, *Deutsche Erinnerungsorte*, 2:434–50.

70. Philipp Ther, "Ethnic Cleansing," in *The Oxford Handbook of Postwar European History*, ed. Dan Stone (Oxford: Oxford University Press, 2012), 155–58; Loveman, *National Colors*, 207–49; Deborah J. Yashar, "Democracy, Indigenous Movements, and Postliberal Challenge in Latin America," *World Politics* 52, no. 1 (1999): 88–90; Adam Fairclough, *Better Day Coming: Blacks and Equality, 1890–2000* (New York: Viking, 2001), 203–95; Nichols, *Indians*, 339–97; Zolberg, *A Nation by Design: Immigration Policy in the Fashioning of America*, 293–337; Peter McDonald, "Migration to Australia: From Asian Exclusion to Asian Predominance," *Revue européenne des migrations internationales* 35, no. 1 (2019): 88–89.

71. Robert Ross, *A Concise History of South Africa* (Cambridge: Cambridge University Press, 2008), 122–53, 174–97.

72. Bruce Berman, Dickson Eyoh, and Will Kymlicka, "Ethnicity and the Politics of Democratic Nation-Building in Africa," in *Ethnicity and Democracy in Africa*, ed. Bruce Berman, Dickson Eyoh, and Will Kymlicka (Oxford: James Currey, 2004), 8–9; Loveman, *National Colors*, 207–49; Will Kymlicka, "Liberal Multiculturalism: Western Models, Global Trends, and Asian Debates," in *Multiculturalism in Asia*, ed. Will Kymlicka and Baogang He (Oxford: Oxford University Press, 2005), 23–55.

73. Mühlhahn, *Making China Modern*, 414–15, 583–87; Harrison, *China*, 234–37, 242–45; Qingsheng Zhou, *Ethnic Minority Languages in China: Policy and Practice* (Boston: De Gruyter, 2020), 66–77.

74. Gilbert Ansre, "Four Rationalisations for Maintaining the European Languages in Education in Africa," *Kiswahili* 47, no. 2 (1977): 55–62; H. Ekkehard Wolff, *Language and Development in Africa: Perceptions, Ideologies and Challenges* (Cambridge: Cambridge University Press, 2016), 172–237.

75. Rothermund, *Decolonization*, 178–88, 207–9; Ricklefs et al., *Southeast Asia*, 393–96; Rogan, *Arabs*, 305–7, 392–95, 479–88.

76. Bruce Berman, "Ethnicity, Patronage and the African State: The Politics of Uncivil Nationalism," *African Affairs* 97 (1998): 305–41; Leonardo R. Arriola, "Patronage and Political Stability in Africa," *Comparative Political Studies* 42, no. 10 (2009): 1339–62; Nugent, *Africa*, 141–207.

77. Greene, "Single-Party Dominance"; Ethan Scheiner, "Pipelines of Pork: Japanese Politics and a Model of Local Opposition Party Failure," *Comparative Political Studies* 38, no. 7 (2005): 799–823; Petr Kopecký and Gerardo Scherlis, "Party Patronage in Contemporary Europe," *European Review* 16, no. 3 (2008): 355–71; Conway, *Western Europe*, 216–19.

78. Basil Davidson, *Africa in Modern History: The Search for a New Society.* (Harmondsworth, UK: Penguin, 1978), 341–57, 372–84; Christie, *Southeast Asia*; Stefani Nugroho, *The Divergent Nation of Indonesia: Heterogeneous Imaginings in Jakarta, Kupang, and Banda Aceh* (Singapore: Springer, 2020), 127–45.

79. Billig, *Banal Nationalism*.

80. Hubert Oswald Quist, "Illiteracy, Education and National Development in Postcolonial West Africa: A Re-appraisal," *Africa Development/Afrique et développement* 19, no. 4 (1994): 127–45; Chander J. Daswani, "Literacy and Development in South-East Asia," in *Functional Literacy: Theoretical Issues and Educational Implications*, ed. Ludo Th. Verhoeven (Philadelphia: John Benjamins, 1994), 279–91.

81. Quist, "Illiteracy," 139–40; Crook, *International Radio Journalism*, 179–221; Gilbert K. M. Tietaah, Margaret I. Amoakohene, and Marquita S. Smith, "Continuity in Change: A History of Radio for National Development," *Radio Journal* 17, no. 2 (2019): 217–34; Harrison, *China*, 235–36.

82. Jonathan Bignell and Andreas Fickers, eds., *A European Television History* (Malden, MA: Wiley-Blackwell, 2009), 55–101, 154–83; Anthony Smith, ed., *Television: An International History* (Oxford: Oxford University Press, 1995), 13–62, 309–18.

83. Bignell and Fickers, *European Television History*, 101–45, 184–205; Smith, *Television*, 148–69, 318–28, 358–80.

84. Michael Skey, "The Mediation of Nationhood: Communicating the World as a World of Nations," *Communication Theory* 24, no. 1 (2014): 1–20.

85. Eriksen and Nielsen, *History of Anthropology*, 77–197; David N. Gellner, "Uncomfortable Antinomies: Going beyond Methodological Nationalism in Social and Cultural Anthropology," in *Beyond Methodological Nationalism: Research Methodologies for Cross-Border Studies*, ed. Anna Amelina et al. (New York: Routledge, 2012), 111–29.

86. Campbell, "History of Linguistics," 95–104; Britta Schneider, "Methodological Nationalism in Linguistics," *Language Sciences* 76 (November 2019); Bortone, *Language and Nationality*, 105–23, 183–223.

87. Livingstone, *Geographical Tradition*, 304–28; Pater and Wusten, *Het geografische huis*, 149–75.

88. James Farr, "Political Science," in *The Cambridge History of Science*, vol. 7, *The Modern Social Sciences*, ed. Theodore M. Porter and Dorothy Ross (Cambridge: Cambridge University Press, 2003), 306–29; Robert Adcock and Mark Bevir, "Political Science," in *The History of the Social Sciences since 1945*, ed. Roger E. Backhouse and Philippe Fontaine (Cambridge:

Cambridge University Press, 2010), 71–101; Brian C. Schmidt, "On the History and Historiography of International Relations," in *Handbook of International Relations*, ed. Walter Carlsnaes, Thomas Risse, and Beth A. Simmons (London: Sage, 2013), 3–29.

89. Cooper and Packard, *International Development*, 16; Vicente L. Rafael, "The Cultures of Area Studies in the United States," *Social Text* 41, no. 41 (1994): 91–111.

90. Michael Latham, "Modernization," in Porter and Ross, *Cambridge History of Science*, 7:721–34; Mazower, *Governing the World*, 278–99.

91. Johann P. Arnason, "Communism and Modernity," *Daedalus* 129, no. 1 (2000): 61–90; Elizabeth A. Weinberg, *Sociology in the Soviet Union and Beyond: Social Enquiry and Social Change* (London: Routledge, 2017).

92. Matthias Middell and Katja Naumann, "Global History and the Spatial Turn: From the Impact of Area Studies to the Study of Critical Junctures of Globalization," *Journal of Global History* 5, no. 1 (2010): 149–58; John Layton Harvey, "Robert Roswell Palmer: A Transatlantic Journey of American Liberalism," *Historical Reflections* 37, no. 3 (2011): 1–17; Storm, "Art History," 384–86.

93. Berger, *Past as History*, 285–318; Wang, "Myth and History," 146–49; Kingston, *Nationalism in Asia*, 196–205; Toyin Falola, "Nationalism and African Historiography," in *Turning Points in Historiography: A Cross-Cultural Perspective*, ed. Q. Edward Wang and Georg G. Iggers (Rochester, NY: University of Rochester Press, 2002), 209–31.

94. Eriksen and Nielsen, *History of Anthropology*, 138–92; Arthur Marwick, *The Sixties: Cultural Revolution in Britain, France, Italy, and the United States, 1958–1974* (Oxford: Oxford University Press., 1998), 288–316; Berger and Storm, *Writing the History of Nationalism*, 131–71.

95. Dario Gamboni, "'Independent of Time and Place': On the Rise and Decline of the Modernist Ideal," in *Time and Place: The Geohistory of Art*, ed. Thomas DaCosta Kaufmann and Elizabeth Pilliod (Aldershot, UK: Ashgate, 2005), 173–203.

96. Piotr Piotrowski, "Nationalizing Modernism: Exhibitions of Hungarian and Czechoslovakian Avant-Garde in Warsaw," in *Art beyond Borders: Artistic Exchange in Communist Europe (1945–1989)*, ed. Jerome Bazin, Pascal Dubourg Glatigny, and Piotr Piotrowski (Budapest: Central European University Press, 2016), 209–24.

97. Joanna Grabski, "Painting Fictions/Painting History: Modernist Pioneers at Senegal's École des Arts," *African Arts* 39, no. 1 (2006): 38–94; Chika Okeke-Agulu, "Nationalism and the Rhetoric of Modernism in Nigeria: The Art of Uche Okeke and Demas Nwoko, 1960–1968," *African Arts* 39, no. 1 (2006): 26–93; Per Bäckström, Benedikt Hjartarson, and Aart Jan Bergshoeff, eds., *Decentring the Avant-Garde* (Amsterdam: Rodopi, 2014).

98. Matthew Schneider-Mayerson, "Popular Fiction Studies: The Advantages of a New Field," *Studies in Popular Culture* 33, no. 1 (2010): 21–35; Marwick, *Sixties*, 340–59.

99. Jason Dittmer, *Captain America and the Nationalist Superhero: Metaphors, Narratives, and Geopolitics* (Philadelphia: Temple University Press, 2013); Nicolas Rouvière, "Astérix, oeuvre gaullienne ?," in *Le tour du monde d'Astérix*, ed. Bertrand Richet (Paris: Presses Sorbonne Nouvelle, 2018), 73–86; Pascal Lefèvre, "The Construction of National and Foreign Identities in French and Belgian Postwar Comics (1939–1970)," *Comicalités*, May 2012; Craig Norris, "Manga, Anime and Visual Art Culture," in *The Cambridge Companion to Modern Japanese Culture*, ed. Yoshio Sugimoto (Cambridge: Cambridge University Press, 2009), 236–60.

100. Marwick, *Sixties*, 329–34; Nugent, *Africa*, 241; Peter Manuel, "Marxism, Nationalism and Popular Music in Revolutionary Cuba," *Popular Music* 6, no. 2 (1987): 161–79.

101. Nowell-Smith, *Oxford History of World Cinema*, 436–60, 527–37, 576–86, 632–39.

102. Nowell-Smith, 576–750.

103. Sergiusz Michalski, *Public Monuments: Art in Political Bondage, 1870–1997* (London: Reaktion Books, 1998), 125–48, 194–200.

104. Jeffry M. Diefendorf, ed., *Rebuilding Europe's Bombed Cities* (Basingstoke, UK: Macmillan, 1990); Jeffry M. Diefendorf, *In the Wake of War: The Reconstruction of German Cities after World War II* (Oxford: Oxford University Press, 1993); Carola Hein, Jeffry M. Diefendorf, and Yorifusa Ishida, eds., *Rebuilding Urban Japan after 1945* (Basingstoke, UK: Palgrave Macmillan, 2003); Liane Lefaivre and Alexander Tzonis, *Architecture of Regionalism in the Age of Globalization: Peaks and Valleys in the Flat World* (London: Routledge, 2012), 112–28.

105. Annapurna Shaw, "Town Planning in Postcolonial India, 1947–1965: Chandigarh Re-examined," *Urban Geography* 30, no. 8 (2009): 857–78; Lefaivre and Tzonis, *Architecture of Regionalism*, 150–55.

106. Martino Stierli, "Building No Place: Oscar Niemeyer and the Utopias of Brasília," *Journal of Architectural Education* 67, no. 1 (2013): 8–16; Hall, *Cities of Tomorrow*, 230–34.

107. Laura B. Johnson, Jordan P. Howell, and Kyle T. Evered, "'Where Nothing Was Before': (Re)Producing Population and Place in Ghana's Volta River Project," *Journal of Cultural Geography* 32, no. 2 (2015): 195–213; Viviana d'Auria and Bruno De Meulder, "Unsettling Landscapes: The Volta River Project," *Oase*, no. 82 (2010): 116–38; Antoni S. Folkers and Belinda A. C. van Buiten, *Modern Architecture in Africa: Practical Encounters with Intricate African Modernity* (Cham, Switzerland: Springer, 2019), 136–42.

108. Lefaivre and Tzonis, *Architecture of Regionalism*, 170–73; Ola Uduku, "Modernist Architecture and 'the Tropical' in West Africa: The Tropical Architecture Movement in West Africa, 1948–1970," *Habitat International* 30, no. 3 (2006): 396–411; Johannes Widodo, "Modernism in Singapore," *Docomomo*, no. 29 (2003): 54–60.

109. Raj Patel, "The Long Green Revolution," *Journal of Peasant Studies* 40, no. 1 (2013): 1–63; Vanhaute, *Peasants in World History*, 103–11; Stevan Harrell, "The Four Horsemen of the Ecopocalypse: The Agricultural Ecology of the Great Leap Forward," *Human Ecology* 49, no. 1 (2021): 7–18.

110. Veronique Pouillard, "Keeping Designs and Brands Authentic: The Resurgence of the Post-war French Fashion Business under the Challenge of US Mass Production," *European Review of History* 20, no. 5 (2013): 815–31; Valeria Pinchera and Diego Rinallo, "The Emergence of Italy as a Fashion Country: Nation Branding and Collective Meaning Creation at Florence's Fashion Shows (1951–1965)," *Business History* 62, no. 1 (2020): 151–78.

111. Roces and Edwards, *Politics of Dress*, 19–65, 101–21, 175–76; Nugent, *Africa*, 238; Yoshiko Nakano, "'Wings of the New Japan': Kamikaze, Kimonos, and Airline Branding in Postwar Japan," *Verge: Studies in Global Asias* 4, no. 1 (2018): 160–86; Sarah Banet-Weiser, *The Most Beautiful Girl in the World: Beauty Pageants and National Identity* (Berkeley: University of California Press, 1999), 181–205.

112. Laudan, *Cuisine and Empire: Cooking in World History*, 308–34; Yong Chen, *Chop Suey, USA: The Story of Chinese Food in America* (New York: Columbia University Press, 2014), 92–102; Lars Amenda, "Food and Otherness: Chinese Restaurants in West European Cities in the 20th Century," *Food and History* 7, no. 2 (2009): 157–79; Patrick Bernhard, "Pädagogische Pizza: Ernährung, Erziehung und der Boom der italienische Küche in der Spätmoderne," *ZeitRäume*, 2016, 82–91.

113. Tim Edensor, *National Identity, Popular Culture and Everyday Life* (Oxford: Berg, 2002), 118–37; Tim Edensor, "Automobility and National Identity: Representation, Geography and Driving Practice," *Theory, Culture and Society* 21, no. 4–5 (2004): 101–20.

114. Orvar Löfgren, *On Holiday: A History of Vacationing* (Berkeley: University of California Press, 1999), 109–283; Zuelow, *History of Tourism*, 149–80; Ellen Furlough, "Packaging Pleasures: Club Méditerranée and French Consumer Culture, 1950–1968," *French Historical Studies* 18, no. 1 (1993): 65; Sasha D. Pack, *Tourism and Dictatorship: Europe's Peaceful Invasion of Franco's Spain* (New York: Palgrave Macmillan, 2006).

115. Löfgren, *On Holiday*, 122–55; Karin Taylor, "My Own Vikendica: Holiday Cottages as Idyll and Investment," in *Yugoslavia's Sunny Side: A History of Tourism in Socialism (1950s–1980s)*, ed. Hannes Grandits and Karin Taylor (Budapest: Central European University Press, 2010), 171–210; Sean Nixon, "Trouble at the National Trust: Post-war Recreation, the Benson Report and the Rebuilding of a Conservation Organization in the 1960s," *Twentieth Century British History* 26, no. 4 (2015): 529–50; Hopkin, "Regionalism and Folklore."

116. Eric G. E. Zuelow, *Making Ireland Irish: Tourism and National Identity since the Irish Civil War* (Syracuse, NY: Syracuse University Press, 2009); Zuelow, *History of Tourism*, 174–76.

117. Marie Huber, "Creating Destinations for a Better Tomorrow: UN Development Aid for Cultural Tourism in the 1960s," *Journal of Contemporary History* 57, no. 2 (2021): 317–40.

118. Raymond Boyle, *Power Play: Sport, the Media and Popular Culture* (Edinburgh: Edinburgh University Press, 2009), 19–42; Matti Goksøyr, "Nationalism," in Pope and Nauright, *Routledge Companion to Sports History*, 288–90.

119. Barbara Keys, "International Relations," in Pope and Nauright, *Routledge Companion to Sports History*, 255–56; Rothermund, *Decolonization*, 256; Alejandro Quiroga, "Football and Nation: F. C. Barcelona and Athletic de Bilbao during the Franco Dictatorship (1937–1977)," *Journal of Iberian and Latin-American Studies* 26, no. 1 (2020): 65–82.

120. James Riordan, "Russia/Soviet Union," in Pope and Nauright, *Routledge Companion to Sports History*, 547–50; Goksøyr, "Nationalism"; Keys, "International Relations," 255–59.

Chapter 8

1. David Harvey, *A Brief History of Neoliberalism* (Oxford: Oxford University Press, 2005), 1–4, 39–42, 64–78; Hartog, *Regimes of Historicity*, 101–27, 180–91.

2. Harvey, *Brief History of Neoliberalism*, 7–31, 51–63, 87–199; Christian Caryl, *Strange Rebels: 1979 and the Birth of the 21st Century* (New York: Basic Books, 2013).

3. Mühlhahn, *Making China Modern*, 487–514; Harvey, *Brief History of Neoliberalism*, 120–51; Judt, *Postwar*, 594–605.

4. Rogan, *Arabs*, 500–552; Caryl, *Strange Rebels*, 83–93, 137–54, 211–28, 239–42, 261–74, 289–311.

5. Harvey, *Brief History of Neoliberalism*, 48–52; Lepore, *These Truths*, 662–68; Judt, *Postwar*, 374–76, 585–87, 605; Caryl, *Strange Rebels*, 73–81, 197–209, 275–88; Christophe Jaffrelot, *Modi's India: Hindu Nationalism and the Rise of Ethnic Democracy* (Princeton, NJ: Princeton University Press, 2021), 11–22.

6. Adam Harmes, "The Rise of Neoliberal Nationalism," *Review of International Political Economy* 19, no. 1 (February 1, 2012): 59–86; Melissa Aronczyk, *Branding the Nation: The Global*

Business of National Identity (New York: Oxford University Press, 2013); Somogy Varga, "The Politics of Nation Branding: Collective Identity and Public Sphere in the Neoliberal State," *Philosophy and Social Criticism* 39, no. 8 (2013): 825–45.

7. Gary Gerstle, *American Crucible: Race and Nation in the Twentieth Century* (Princeton, NJ: Princeton University Press, 2017), 357–65; Yanek Mieczkowski, "Reagan Runs: His Campaigns for the Presidency, 1976, 1980 and 1984," in *A Companion to Ronald Reagan*, ed. Andrew L. Johns (Malden, MA: Wiley, 2015), 54–71; Lilia Fernandez and Andrew L. Johns, "Reagan, Religion, and the Culture Wars of the 1980s," in Johns, *Companion to Ronald Reagan*, 204–20; Antony Mullen, "Spectres of Thatcher: Narratives of National Identity in Contemporary Britain" (PhD diss., Durham University, 2018), quotes at 44, 46; Caryl, *Strange Rebels*, 159–61; Florence Sutcliffe-Braithwaite, "Neo-liberalism and Morality in the Making of Thatcherite Social Policy," *Historical Journal* 55, no. 2 (2012): 497–520.

8. Mühlhahn, *Making China Modern*, 502, 518–26, 541–49; Caryl, *Strange Rebels*, 327–37; Ivanka Nedeva Atanasova, "Lyudmila Zhivkova and the Paradox of Ideology and Identity in Communist Bulgaria," *East European Politics and Societies* 18, no. 2 (2004): 278–315.

9. Rogan, *Arabs*, 520–21; Lewis, *Authoritarian Regimes in Latin America*, 226–27; Ofra Bengio, *Kurds of Iraq: Building a State within a State* (Boulder, CO: Lynne Rienner, 2012), 169–97; Lilia Petkova, "The Ethnic Turks in Bulgaria: Social Integration and Impact on Bulgarian-Turkish Relations, 1947–2000," *Global Review of Ethnopolitics* 1, no. 4 (2002): 42–59.

10. Judt, *Postwar*, 585–633.

11. Judt, 638–43, 713–23.

12. Jörg Hackmann, "Baltic and Polish Regionalism(s): Concepts, Dimensions and Trajectories," in Núñez Seixas and Storm, *Regionalism and Modern Europe*, 298–300; Judt, *Postwar*, 644–46.

13. Judt, *Postwar*, 646–54; Mark R. Beissinger, "Nationalism and the Collapse of Soviet Communism," *Contemporary European History* 18, no. 3 (2009): 331–47.

14. Judt, *Postwar*, 647, 654–59; Plokhy, *Lost Kingdom*, 308–13.

15. Judt, *Postwar*, 659–64; Kamusella, *Politics of Language*, 714–905.

16. Calic, *Great Cauldron*, 467–80, 509–14, 522–258; Sabine Rutar, "Nationalism in Southeastern Europe, 1970–2000," in Breuilly, *Oxford Handbook of Nationalism*, 522–26; Catherine Baker, *The Yugoslav Wars of the 1990s* (London: Palgrave Macmillan, 2015), 7–43.

17. Brubaker, *Nationalism Reframed*, 69–76; Baker, *Yugoslav Wars*, 33–53.

18. Baker, *Yugoslav Wars*, 57–77; Calic, *Great Cauldron*, 529–34.

19. Baker, *Yugoslav Wars*, 78–88; Rutar, "Nationalism in Southeastern Europe," 528–29.

20. Brubaker, *Nationalism Reframed*, 26–54; Anna Batta, *The Russian Minorities in the Former Soviet Republics: Secession, Integration, and Homeland* (London: Routledge, 2021); Andrei A. Kazantsev et al., "Russia's Policy in the 'Frozen Conflicts' of the Post-Soviet Space: From Ethno-Politics to Geopolitics," *Caucasus Survey* 8, no. 2 (2020): 142–62.

21. Kazantsev et al., "Russia's Policy"; Sergey Markedonov and David Matsaberidze, "Georgia vs. Abkhazia and Southern Ossetia," in *"Frozen Conflicts" in Europe*, ed. Anton Bebler (Opladen, Germany: Barbara Budrich, 2015), 71–93, 107–19.

22. Michael McFaul, "The Russian Federation," in *The Cambridge History of Russia*, vol. 3, *The Twentieth Century*, ed. Ronald Grigor Suny (Cambridge: Cambridge University Press, 2006), 361–80.

23. Tracey C. German, *Russia's Chechen War* (London: Routledge, 2003), 65–67, 138, 151–53, 161–63; Alexander Cherkasov and Dmitry Grushkin, "The Chechen Wars and Human Rights in Russia," in *Chechnya: From Past to Future*, ed. Richard Sakwa (London: Anthem, 2012), 131–57.

24. Mahmood Mamdani, *When Victims Become Killers: Colonialism, Nativism, and the Genocide in Rwanda* (Princeton, NJ: Princeton University Press, 2020), 41–184; Filip Reyntjens, "Understanding Rwandan Politics through the Longue Durée: From the Precolonial to the Post-genocide Era," *Journal of Eastern African Studies* 12, no. 3 (2018): 514–20; Nugent, *Africa*, 55–57.

25. Mamdani, *When Victims Become Killers*, 185–234; Nugent, *Africa*, 469–73.

26. Nugent, *Africa*, 470–75.

27. Nugent, 475–82; Mamdani, *When Victims Become Killers*, 234–63.

28. Kamusella, *Politics of Language*, 217–40.

29. Calic, *History of Yugoslavia*, 173–75, 202–12, 269–73; Dejan Jovic, "The Disintegration of Yugoslavia: A Critical Review of Explanatory Approaches," *European Journal of Social Theory* 4, no. 1 (2001): 107–10; Calic, *Great Cauldron*, 517–19.

30. Mamdani, *When Victims Become Killers*, 41–102.

31. Rogers Brubaker, "Ethnicity without Groups," *European Journal of Sociology* 43, no. 2 (2002): 163–89; Harris Mylonas and Maya Tudor, *Varieties of Nationalism: Communities, Narratives, Identities* (Cambridge: Cambridge University Press, 2023), 49–51.

32. Nugent, *Africa*, 448–63; Wimmer, *Nation Building*, 93–112; Kingston, *Nationalism in Asia*, 239–42; Quiroga and Molina, "National Deadlock"; O'Driscoll and Baser, "Referendums as a Political Party Gamble."

33. Samuel P. Huntington, *The Third Wave: Democratization in the Late Twentieth Century* (Norman: University of Oklahoma Press, 1991), 3–31; Nugent, *Africa*, 376–447.

34. Daniele Petrosino, "Democracy and Regionalism in Western Europe," in Núñez Seixas and Storm, *Regionalism in Modern Europe*, 151–69; Witte, Meynen, and Luyten, *Politieke geschiedenis van België*, 387–450; Omar Guillermo Encarnación, *Spanish Politics: Democracy after Dictatorship* (Cambridge: Polity, 2008), 91–111.

35. Storm, "Tourism"; Dalle Mulle, *Nationalism of the Rich*.

36. Christophe Van der Beken, "External and Internal Secession in Ethiopia's Multinational Federation," *International Journal on Minority and Group Rights* 28, no. 5 (2021): 944–71; Lovise Aalen, "Ethiopia: The Interplay between Federalism and Dominant Party Rule and the Sidama's Quest for Statehood," *International Journal on Minority and Group Rights* 28, no. 5 (2021): 972–92; Mehdi Labzaé and Sabine Planel, "La république fédérale démocratique en guerre: Mobilisations nationalistes, ordre martial et renouveaux partisans en Éthiopie," *Politique africaine* 164, no. 4 (2021): 141–64.

37. Jeffrey Mankoff, *Empires of Eurasia: How Imperial Legacies Shape International Security* (New Haven, CT: Yale University Press, 2022), 81–207.

38. Katerina Dalacoura, *Islamist Terrorism and Democracy in the Middle East* (Cambridge: Cambridge University Press, 2011), 40–65; Olivier Roy, "The Failure of Political Islam Revisited," in *Pathways to Contemporary Islam: New Trends in Critical Engagement*, ed. Mohamed Nawab Mohamed Osman (Amsterdam: Amsterdam University Press, 2020), 167–80.

39. Carlos de la Torre, "Populism in Latin America," in *The Oxford Handbook of Populism*, ed. Cristóbal Rovira Kaltwasser et al. (Oxford: Oxford University Press, 2017), 195–213; Cas Mudde and Cristóbal Rovira Kaltwasser, "Exclusionary vs. Inclusionary Populism: Comparing

Contemporary Europe and Latin America," *Government and Opposition* 48, no. 2 (2013): 147–74.

40. Javier Corrales, "Autocratic Legalism in Venezuela," *Journal of Democracy* 26, no. 2 (2015): 37–51.

41. Cas Mudde, *The Far Right Today* (Cambridge: Polity, 2020), 1–21; Ángel Rivero, "Populism and Democracy in Europe," in *Routledge Handbook of Global Populism*, ed. Carlos de la Torre (London: Routledge, 2018), 281–95.

42. Jan-Werner Müller, *What Is Populism?* (Philadelphia: University of Pennsylvania Press, 2016), 41–75.

43. Richard Sakwa, *The Putin Paradox* (London: Tauris, 2020), 23–84; Lilia Shevtsova, "Forward to the Past in Russia," in *Authoritarianism Goes Global: The Challenge to Democracy*, ed. Larry Diamond, Marc F. Plattner, and Christopher Walker (Baltimore: Johns Hopkins University Press, 2016), 40–57.

44. Hutchinson, *Nationalism and War*, 130–38.

45. Charles S. Maier, "'Malaise': The Crisis of Capitalism in the 1970s," in *The Shock of the Global: The 1970s in Perspective*, ed. Niall Ferguson et al. (Cambridge: Belknap, 2010), 25–49; Timothy Mitchell, *Carbon Democracy: Political Power in the Age of Oil* (London: Verso, 2011).

46. Mazower, *Governing the World*, 347–66; Fahrmeir, *Citizenship*, 221–25; Jonathan Holslag, *World Politics since 1989* (Cambridge: Polity, 2021), 23–31, 116–68, 221–48; Ian Kershaw, *The Global Age: Europe, 1950–2017* (New York: Viking, 2018), 459–74.

47. Amaka Okechukwu, *To Fulfill These Rights: Political Struggle over Affirmative Action and Open Admissions* (New York: Columbia University Press, 2019), 29–67; Rita C.-K. Chin, *The Crisis of Multiculturalism in Europe: A History* (Princeton, NJ: Princeton University Press, 2017), 8–19; Yashar, "Democracy, Indigenous Movements" 76–88.

48. Shibao Guo and Lloyd Wong, *Revisiting Multiculturalism in Canada: Theories, Policies and Debates*, Transnational Migration and Education (Rotterdam: Sense, 2015), 1–4.

49. Nichols, *Indians*, 397–420.

50. Yashar, "Democracy, Indigenous Movements"; Loveman, *National Colors*, 250–300; Wade, *Race and Ethnicity*, 112–50.

51. Nancy Postero, "'El Pueblo Boliviano, de Composición Plural': A Look at Plurinationalism in Bolivia," in *The Promise and Perils of Populism: Global Perspectives*, ed. Carlos de la Torre (Lexington: University Press of Kentucky, 2015), 395–431; Anna F. Laing, "Re-producing Territory: Between Resource Nationalism and Indigenous Self-Determination in Bolivia," *Geoforum* 108 (2020): 28–38; Soledad Valdivia Rivera, "The Indigenous State: Progress and Limitations in the Promotion of the 'Indigenous' in Contemporary Bolivia," in *The Many Voices of Indigenous Latin America: Reconstruction, Describing, and Preserving Cultural and Linguistic Diversity*, ed. M. Françozo, R. van Gijn, and M. Bruil (Leiden: Brill, forthcoming)

52. Kymlicka, "Liberal Multiculturalism," 23–32; Rogers Brubaker, *Grounds for Difference* (Cambridge, MA: Harvard University Press, 2017), 131–44.

53. Bouchard, *Making of the Nations*, 234–42; Damien Short, "When Sorry Isn't Good Enough: Official Remembrance and Reconciliation in Australia," *Memory Studies* 3, no. 5 (2012): 293–304.

54. Eva Josefsen, Ulf Mörkenstam, and Jo Saglie, "Different Institutions within Similar States: The Norwegian and Swedish Sámediggis," *Ethnopolitics* 14, no. 1 (2015): 32–51.

55. Chin, *Crisis of Multiculturalism*, 80–112; Will Kymlicka, "Neoliberal Multiculturalism?," in *Social Resilience in the Neoliberal Era*, ed. Michèle Lamont and Peter A. Hall (Cambridge: Cambridge University Press, 2013), 99–126.

56. Will Kymlicka and Baogang He, eds., *Multiculturalism in Asia* (Oxford: Oxford University Press, 2005); Berman, Eyoh, and Kymlicka, "Politics of Democratic Nation-Building"; Will Kymlicka, "Nation-Building and Minority Rights: Comparing Africa and the West," in Berman, Eyoh, and Kymlicka, *Ethnicity and Democracy in Africa*, 54–71.

57. Paul van Trigt, "Farewell to Social Europe? An Entangled Perspective on European Disability Policies in the 1980s and 1990s," in *Marginalized Groups, Inequalities and the Post-war Welfare State*, ed. Monika Baár and Paul van Trigt (London: Routledge, 2019), 69–80; Mina Roces, "Asian Feminisms: Women's Movements from the Asian Perspective," in Edwards and Roces, *Women's Movements in Asia*, 1–21; Paulson-Smith and Tripp, "Women's Rights"; Cheryl Cooky and Michael A. Messner, eds., *No Slam Dunk: Gender, Sport and the Unevenness of Social Change* (New Brunswick, NJ: Rutgers University Press, 2018).

58. Belmonte, *International LGBT Rights Movement*, 145–86.

59. Belmonte, 186–93; Mudde, *Far Right*, 147–62; Rogers Brubaker, "Why Populism?," *Theory and Society* 46, no. 5 (2017): 372–73.

60. Mudde, *Far Right*, 24–49, 113–28; Bruce Berman, "Nationalism in Post-colonial Africa," in Breuilly, *Oxford Handbook of Nationalism*, 369–72; Jaffrelot, *Modi's India*, 188–201, 360–445; François-Michel Le Tourneau, "O governo Bolsonaro contra os Povos Indígenas: As garantias constitucionais postas à prova," *Confins*, no. 501 (2019); Magdalena Lesińska and Dominik Héjj, "Pragmatic Trans-border Nationalism: A Comparative Analysis of Poland's and Hungary's Policies towards Kin-Minorities in the Twenty-First Century," *Ethnopolitics* 20, no. 1 (2021): 53–66.

61. Thomas Hylland Eriksen, "Nationalism and the Internet," *Nations and Nationalism* 13, no. 1 (2007): 1–17; Bignell and Fickers, *European Television History*, 145–51; Benedict Anderson, *Long-Distance Nationalism: World Capitalism and the Rise of Identity Politics* (Amsterdam: CASA, 1992).

62. Sabina Mihelj and César Jiménez-Martínez, "Digital Nationalism: Understanding the Role of Digital Media in the Rise of 'New' Nationalism," *Nations and Nationalism*, no. 27 (2021): 337–39.

63. Ratiba Hadj-Moussa, *The Public Sphere and Satellite Television in North Africa: Gender, Identity, Critique* (Newcastle, UK: Cambridge Scholars, 2018), 94–130; Noureddine Miladi, "Transformative Pan-Arab TV: National and Cultural Expression on Reality TV Programmes," *Journal of Arab and Muslim Media Research* 8, no. 2 (2015): 99–115.

64. Mihelj and Jiménez-Martínez, "Digital Nationalism," 335–37.

65. Christian Wicke, "Constructivism in the History of Nationalism since 1945," in Berger and Storm, *Writing the History of Nationalism*, 131–55.

66. Berger and Storm, *Writing the History of Nationalism*, 173–78, 216–18.

67. Barney Warf and Santa Arias, eds., *The Spatial Turn: Interdisciplinary Perspectives* (London: Routledge, 2008); Jörg Döring and Tristan Thielmann, *Spatial Turn: Das Raumparadigma in den Kultur- und Sozialwissenschaften* (Bielefeld, Germany: Transcript Verlag, 2008).

68. Eriksen and Nielsen, *History of Anthropology*, 166–220; Gary M. Feinman and Jill E. Neitzel, "Excising Culture History from Contemporary Archaeology," *Journal of Anthropological*

Archaeology 60 (2020); Jean-François Bayart, *The Illusion of Cultural Identity* (London: Hurst, 2005), 1–122.

69. Wimmer and Schiller, "Methodological Nationalism and Beyond"; Schneider, "Methodological Nationalism in Linguistics."

70. Berger, *Past as History*, 318–79; Maria Framke and Andreas Weiß, "Forum: Nation: The Role of the Nation in History Writing in the 21st Century," *H-Soz-Kult*, September 27, 2021; Marc Matten, "Forum: Nation: Fighting for the Nation? The Campaign against Historical Nihilism in Contemporary China," *H-Soz-Kult*, September 13, 2021.

71. Thomas Hylland Eriksen, "Between Universalism and Relativism: A Critique of the UNESCO Concept of Culture," in *Culture and Rights: Anthropological Perspectives*, ed. Jane K. Cowan, Marie-Bénédicte Dembour, and Richard A. Wilson (Cambridge: Cambridge University Press, 2001), 127–48.

72. Chiara de Cesari and Ann Rigney, introduction to *Transnational Memory: Circulation, Articulation, Scales*, ed. Chiara de Cesari and Ann Rigney (Berlin: De Gruyter, 2014), 1–26; Stephen Legg, "Contesting and Surviving Memory: Space, Nation, and Nostalgia in *Les lieux de mémoire*," *Environment and Planning D: Society and Space* 23, no. 4 (2005): 481–504; John Carman and Marie Louise Stig Sørensen, "Heritage Studies: An Outline," in *Heritage Studies: Methods and Approaches*, ed. Marie Louise Stig Sørensen and John Carman (London: Routledge, 2009), 11–29.

73. Joana Breidenbach and Pál Nyíri, *Seeing Culture Everywhere: From Genocide to Consumer Habits* (Seattle: University of Washington Press, 2009), 262–327; Pál Nyíri and Joana Breidenbach, "Intercultural Communication: An Anthropological Perspective," in *International Encyclopedia of the Social and Behavioral Sciences*, ed. James D. Wright (Amsterdam: Elsevier, 2015), 12:357–61.

74. Loveman, *National Colors*, 250–300.

75. Brubaker, *Grounds for Difference*, 48–61.

76. Brubaker, 50–52; Susanne E. Hakenbeck, "Genetics, Archaeology and the Far Right: An Unholy Trinity," *World Archaeology* 51, no. 4 (2019): 517–27; Feinman and Neitzel, "Excising Culture."

77. Siniša Malešević, *The Sociology of War and Violence* (Cambridge: Cambridge University Press, 2010), 50–58.

78. Wilfried van Damme and Kitty Zijlmans, "Art History in a Global Frame: World Art Studies," in *Art History and Visual Studies in Europe*, ed. Matthew Rampley et al. (Leiden: Brill, 2012), 217–29; Catherine Bublatzky, "The Display of Indian Contemporary Art in Western Museums and the Question of 'Othering,'" in *Global Studies: Mapping Contemporary Art and Culture*, ed. Hans Belting et al. (Ostfildern, Germany: Hatje Cantz, 2011), 298–314; Salah M. Hassan, "Contemporary African Art as a Paradox," *NKA Journal of Contemporary African Art*, no. 46 (2020): 8–26.

79. Joep Leerssen, *Hiding in the Popcorn: How Romantic Nationalism Survived into the 21st Century* (Amsterdam: University of Amsterdam, 2022); Mariëlle Wijermars, *Memory Politics in Contemporary Russia: Television, Cinema and the State* (London: Routledge, 2018), 12, 221, and passim; Rini Bhattacharya Mehta, *Unruly Cinema: History, Politics, and Bollywood* (Urbana: University of Illinois Press, 2020), 141–77.

80. Ramon Lobato, *Netflix Nations: The Geography of Digital Distribution* (New York: New York University Press, 2019).

81. Megan Rancier, "Resurrecting the Nomads: Historical Nostalgia and Modern National-ism in Contemporary Kazakh Popular Music Videos," *Popular Music and Society* 32, no. 3 (2009): 387–405; Zhihong Gao, "When Nationalism Goes to the Market: The Case of Chinese Patriotic Songs," *Journal of Macromarketing* 35, no. 4 (2015): 473–88.

82. Ulrich Adelt, "'Ich bin der Rock'n'Roll-Übermensch': Globalization and Localization in German Music Television," *Popular Music and Society* 28, no. 3 (2005): 279–95; John Lie, "What Is the K in K-Pop? South Korean Popular Music, the Culture Industry, and National Identity," *Korea Observer* 43, no. 3 (2012): 339–63.

83. David Harvey, *The Condition of Postmodernity: An Enquiry into the Origins of Cultural Change* (Oxford: Blackwell, 1989), 66–99; Marine Urbain, "The Critical Reconstruction of Criti-cal Regionalism (1971–1983)," *Oase*, no. 103 (2019): 41–49; Vincent B. Canizaro, ed., *Architectural Regionalism: Collected Writings on Place, Identity, Modernity and Tradition* (New York: Princeton Architectural Press, 2007).

84. Douglas S. Kelbaugh, *Repairing the American Metropolis: Common Place Revisited* (Seattle: University of Washington Press, 2002), 52–93, 133–80; Jill Grant, *Planning the Good Community: New Urbanism in Theory and Practice* (London: Routledge, 2006), 81–130.

85. Joan Ockman, "New Politics of the Spectacle: 'Bilbao' and the Global Imagination," in *Architecture and Tourism: Perception, Performance and Place*, ed. D. Medina Lasansky and Brian McLaren (Oxford: Berg, 2004), 227–28.

86. Carmelo Adagio, "Il PSOE e la gestione dei grandi eventi del 1992," *Spagna contempora-nea*, no. 25 (2004): 69–99; Ockman, "New Politics of the Spectacle."

87. Gregory Ashworth, "The Instruments of Place Branding: How Is It Done?," *European Spatial Research and Policy* 16, no. 1 (2009): 9–22; Charles Jencks, *The Story of Post-modernism: Five Decades of the Ironic, Iconic and Critical in Architecture* (Chichester, UK: Wiley, 2011), 200–248; Tim Bunnell, "Views from Above and Below: The Petronas Twin Towers and/in Contesting Visions of Development in Contemporary Malaysia," *Singapore Journal of Tropical Geography* 20, no. 1 (1999): 1–23; Mir M. Ali and Kheir Al-Kodmany, "Tall Buildings and Urban Habitat of the 21st Century: A Global Perspective," *Buildings*, no. 2 (2012): 384–423.

88. Christian Steiner, "From Heritage to Hyper-Reality? Tourism Destination Development in the Middle East between Petra and the Palm," *Journal of Tourism and Cultural Change* 8, no. 4 (2010): 240–53; Ali and Al-Kodmany, "Tall Buildings"; Natalie Koch, *The Geopolitics of Spectacle: Space, Synecdoche, and the New Capitals of Asia* (Ithaca, NY: Cornell University Press, 2018), 124–34.

89. Andrew Graan, "Counterfeiting the Nation? Skopje 2014 and the Politics of Nation Branding in Macedonia," *Cultural Anthropology* 28, no. 1 (2013): 161–79; Leonora Grcheva, "The Birth of a Nationalistic Planning Doctrine: The 'Skopje 2014' Project," *International Planning Studies* 24, no. 2 (2019): 140–55.

90. Mary Dellenbaugh-Losse, *Inventing Berlin: Architecture, Politics and Cultural Memory in the New/Old German Capital Post-1989* (Cham, Switzerland: Springer, 2020).

91. Sarah Moser, "Putrajaya: Malaysia's New Federal Administrative Capital," *Cities* 27, no. 4 (2010): 285–97.

92. Donald M. Seekins, "'Runaway Chickens' and Myanmar Identity: Relocating Burma's Capital," *City* 13, no. 1 (2009): 63–70; Koch, *Spectacle*, 140–44.

93. Koch, *Spectacle*; Natalie Koch, "The Monumental and the Miniature: Imagining 'Moder-nity' in Astana," *Social and Cultural Geography* 11, no. 8 (2010): 769–87.

94. Sara Kristoffersson, *Design by IKEA: A Cultural History* (London: Bloomsbury, 2014), 15–79; Ursula Lindqvist, "The Cultural Archive of the IKEA Store," *Space and Culture* 12, no. 1 (2009): 43–62.

95. Atsuko Ichijo and Ronald Ranta, *Food, National Identity and Nationalism: From Everyday to Global Politics* (Basingstoke, UK: Palgrave Macmillan, 2016), 61–72, 147–63; Laudan, *Cuisine and Empire*, 350–53.

96. Franklin Ginn, "Extension, Subversion, Containment: Eco-nationalism and (Post)Colonial Nature in Aotearoa New Zealand," *Transactions of the Institute of British Geographers* 33, no. 3 (2008): 335–53; Antonsich, "Natives and Aliens"; Joe Turner and Dan Bailey, "'Ecobordering': Casting Immigration Control as Environmental Protection," *Environmental Politics* 31, no. 1 (2022): 110–31.

97. Andrea Rehling, "Universalismen und Partikularismen im Widerstreit: Zur Genese des UNESCO-Welterbes," *Zeithistorische Forschungen* 8, no. 3 (2011): 414–36; Huber, "Creating Destinations," 8–14, 21–23.

98. Chiara Bortolotto, "From Objects to Processes: UNESCO'S 'Intangible Cultural Heritage,'" *Journal of Museum Ethnography*, no. 19 (2007): 21–33; Chiara Bortolotto, "Placing Intangible Cultural Heritage, Owning a Tradition, Affirming Sovereignty: The Role of Spatiality in the Practice of the 2003 Convention," in *The Routledge Companion to Intangible Cultural Heritage*, ed. Michelle Stefano and Peter Davis (London: Routledge, 2016), 70–82.

99. Laetitia La Follette, "Looted Antiquities, Art Museums and Restitution in the United States since 1970," *Journal of Contemporary History* 52, no. 3 (2017): 669–87; Piotr Bienkowski, "Authority and the Power of Place: Exploring the Legitimacy of Authorized and Alternative Voices in the Restitution Discourse," in *Museums and Restitution: New Practices, New Approaches*, ed. Louise Tythacott and Kostas Arvanitis (Farnham, UK: Routledge, 2014), 37–55.

100. Bianca Gaudenzi and Astrid Swenson, "Looted Art and Restitution in the Twentieth Century—Towards a Global Perspective," *Journal of Contemporary History* 52, no. 3 (2017): 491–518; Jos Beurden, *Inconvenient Heritage: Colonial Collections and Restitution in the Netherlands and Belgium* (Amsterdam: Amsterdam University Press, 2022), 206–24.

101. Jie Shen and Fulong Wu, "The Development of Master-Planned Communities in Chinese Suburbs: A Case Study of Shanghai's Thames Town," *Urban Geography* 33, no. 2 (2012): 183–203; John Urry and Jonas Larsen, *The Tourist Gaze 3.0* (London: Sage, 2011), 119–35; S. Banu Garip and Ervin Garip, "Copying the Identity through Tourism Architecture: 'Theme Hotels' in Antalya," *Academic Research International* 6, no. 4 (2015): 24–36.

102. Zuelow, *History of Tourism*, 172–81; Urry and Larsen, *Tourist Gaze 3.0*, 135–49; Cheryl Finley, "Authenticating Dungeons, Whitewashing Castles: The Former Sites of the Slave Trade on the Ghanaian Coast," in Lasansky and McLaren, *Architecture and Tourism*, 109–29; Gert-Jan Hospers, "Industrial Heritage Tourism and Regional Restructuring in the European Union," *European Planning Studies* 10, no. 3 (2002): 397–404.

103. Urry and Larsen, *Tourist Gaze 3.0*, 149–51; Erve Chambers, *Native Tours: The Anthropology of Travel and Tourism* (Long Grove, IL: Waveland, 2010), 80–84, 111–16; Walter van Beek, "To Dance or Not to Dance: Dogon Masks as a Tourist Arena," in *African Hosts and Their Guests: Cultural Dynamics of Tourism*, ed. Walter van Beek and Annette Schmidt (Woodbridge, UK: James Currey, 2012), 37–57.

104. Urry and Larsen, *Tourist Gaze 3.0*, 115–18, 125–26, 150–52; Vanessa Agnew, "Introduction: What Is Reenactment?," *Criticism* 46, no. 3 (2004): 327–39.

105. John Horne, "Sports Mega-Events," in *Research Handbook on Sports and Society*, ed. Elizabeth Pike (Northampton, UK: Elgar, 2021), 128–42; Jencks, *Story of Post-modernism*, 227–39.

106. Michael Skey, "Sportswashing: Media Headline or Analytic Concept?," *International Review for the Sociology of Sport* 58, no. 5 (2022): 749–64; John S. Krzyzaniak, "The Soft Power Strategy of Soccer Sponsorships," *Soccer and Society* 19, no. 4 (2018): 498–515.

107. Goksøyr, "Nationalism," 282–88; Kingston, *Nationalism in Asia*, 137–40; Roy Hay and Tony Joel, "Football's World Cup and Its Fans—Reflections on National Styles: A Photo Essay on Germany 2006," *Soccer and Society* 8, no. 1 (2007): 1–32.

108. Leon Davis, "Football Fandom and Authenticity: A Critical Discussion of Historical and Contemporary Perspectives," *Soccer and Society* 16, no. 2–3 (2015): 422–36; Hay and Joel, "World Cup"; Kim Toffoletti, "Sexy Women Sports Fans: Femininity, Sexuality, and the Global Sport Spectacle," *Feminist Media Studies* 17, no. 3 (2017): 457–72; Zygmunt Bauman, *Liquid Modernity* (Cambridge: Polity, 2000), 199–201.

109. Andrés Bijsterveld Muñoz, "National Identity in Historical Video Games: An Analysis of How Civilization V Represents the Past," *Nations and Nationalism* 28, no. 4 (2022): 1311–25.

110. Julia Deeb-Swihart et al., "Selfie-Presentation in Everyday Life: A Large-Scale Characterization of Selfie Contexts on Instagram," in *Proceedings of the Eleventh International AAAI Conference on Web and Social Media* (Palo Alto, CA: AAAI Press, 2017), 42–51; Luca Rossi, Eric Boscaro, and Andrea Torsello, "Venice through the Lens of Instagram: A Visual Narrative of Tourism in Venice," in *Companion Proceedings of the Web Conference 2018* (Geneva: IW3C2, 2018), 1190–97; Megasari Noer Fatanti and I. Wayan Suyadnya, "Beyond User Gaze: How Instagram Creates Tourism Destination Brand," *Procedia—Social and Behavioral Sciences* 211 (2015): 1089–95; Sean P. Smith, "Landscapes for 'Likes': Capitalizing on Travel with Instagram," *Social Semiotics* 31, no. 4 (2021): 604–24.

111. Lev Manovich, *Instagram and Contemporary Image* (Online, 2016), 90–95, 125–26, http:// manovich.net/index.php/projects/instagram-and-contemporary-image; Madeleine Marcella-Hood, "Scottish Style: The Construction of National Identity and Place amongst Scottish Fashion Influencers on Instagram," in *Proceedings of 21st International Foundation of Fashion Technology Institute* (Manchester: IFFTI, 2019), 350–61.

112. Mihelj and Jiménez-Martínez, "Digital Nationalism," 339–40; Michael Skey, "Nationalism and Media," *Nationalities Papers*, 2022, 1–11; Brubaker, "Why Populism?," 370; Lepore, *These Truths*, 666–68, 701–18, 724–38, 769–72, 779–82.

Conclusion

1. See also Eirik Magnus Fuglestad, "Nationalism and Private Property," *The State of Nationalism*, 2021, https://stateofnationalism.eu/article/nationalism-and-private-property/.

2. Colin P. Clarke, *After the Caliphate: The Islamic State and the Future of the Terrorist Diaspora* (Medford, MA: Polity Press, 2019).

3. Brubaker, *Grounds for Difference*, 85–119.

4. Breuilly, *Nationalism and the State*; Hobsbawm, *Nations and Nationalism since 1780*, 1990; Ory, *Une nation*.

5. Anderson, *Imagined Communities*, 80–82, 135; Brubaker, *Grounds for Difference*, 145–57.

6. Partial exceptions are Fradera, *Imperial Nation* and Cooper, *Citizenship*.

7. Thiesse, *Identités nationales*; Leerssen, *Encyclopedia of Romantic Nationalism*; Billig, *Banal Nationalism*; Edensor, *National Identity*.

8. Hobsbawm, *Nations and Nationalism since 1780*, 30–43; Gellner, *Nations and Nationalism*, 124–25.

9. Cabo and Molina, "Long and Winding Road."

10. Leerssen, "Type, Typicality."

11. Mylonas and Tudor, *Varieties of Nationalism*, 42–49; Brubaker, "Ethnicity without Groups."

12. Luuk van Middelaar, *Alarums and Excursions: Improvising Politics on the European Stage* (Newcastle upon Tyne, UK: Agenda, 2019).

13. Mankoff, *Empires of Eurasia*; Holslag, *World Politics since 1989*.

14. Jason W. Moore, ed., *Anthropocene or Capitalocene? Nature, History, and the Crisis of Capitalism* (Oakland, CA: PM Press, 2016); Will Kymlicka and Sue Donaldson, "Animal Rights, Multiculturalism, and the Left," *Journal of Social Philosophy* 45, no. 1 (2014): 116–35; William A. Edmundson, "Do Animals Need Citizenship?," *International Journal of Constitutional Law* 13, no. 3 (2015): 749–65.

BIBLIOGRAPHY

Aalen, Lovise. "Ethiopia: The Interplay between Federalism and Dominant Party Rule and the Sidama's Quest for Statehood." *International Journal on Minority and Group Rights* 28, no. 5 (2021): 972–92.

Abizadeh, Arash. "Was Fichte an Ethnic Nationalist? On Cultural Nationalism and Its Double." *History of Political Thought* 26, no. 2 (2005): 334–59.

Abrahamian, Ervand. *A History of Modern Iran*. Cambridge: Cambridge University Press, 2008.

Adagio, Carmelo. "Il PSOE e la gestione dei grandi eventi del 1992." *Spagna contemporanea* no. 25 (2004): 69–99.

Adair, Daryl. "Australia." In *Routledge Companion to Sports History*, edited by Steven W. Pope and John R. Nauright, 330–49. London: Routledge, 2009.

Adcock, Robert, and Mark Bevir. "Political Science." In *The History of the Social Sciences since 1945*, edited by Roger E. Backhouse and Philippe Fontaine, 71–101. Cambridge: Cambridge University Press, 2010.

Adelman, Jeremy. *Sovereignty and Revolution in the Iberian Atlantic*. Princeton, NJ: Princeton University Press, 2006.

Adelt, Ulrich. "'Ich bin der Rock'n'Roll-Übermensch': Globalization and Localization in German Music Television." *Popular Music and Society* 28, no. 3 (2005): 279–95.

Agnew, Vanessa. "Introduction: What Is Reenactment?" *Criticism* 46, no. 3 (2004): 327–39.

Agulhon, Maurice. *Marianne au pouvoir: L'imagerie et la symbolique républicaines de 1880 à 1914*. Paris: Flammarion, 1989.

Ahmedani, Usman. "History-Writing and Historicism in Late-Ottoman Turkey." In *Encyclopedia of Romantic Nationalism in Europe*, edited by Joep Leerssen, 1447–48. Amsterdam: Amsterdam University Press, 2018.

Akihary, Huib. *Architectuur en stedebouw in Indonesie 1870–1970*. Zutphen, Netherlands: Walburg, 1990.

Aksan, Virginia. "Ottoman Military Recruitment Strategies in the Late Eighteenth Century." In *Arming the State: Military Conscription in the Middle East and East Asia 1775–1925*, edited by Erik J. Zürcher, 21–41. London: Tauris, 1999.

Ali, Mir M., and Kheir Al-Kodmany. "Tall Buildings and Urban Habitat of the 21st Century: A Global Perspective." *Buildings*, no. 2 (2012): 384–423.

Allen, John S. "Franz Boas's Physical Anthropology: The Critique of Racial Formalism Revisited." *Current Anthropology* 30, no. 1 (1989): 79–84.

Alonso, Carlos J. "The Criollista Novel." In *The Cambridge History of Latin American Literature*, vol. 2, *The Twentieth Century*, edited by Roberto Gonzalez Echevarría and Enrique Pupo-Walker, 195–212. Cambridge: Cambridge University Press, 1996.

Alvarez Junco, José. "La invención de la Guerra de la Iindependencia." *Studia historica. Historia contemporánea* 12 (1994): 75–99.

Amalvi, Christian. "Le 14 Juillet: Du Dies Irae à jour de fête." In *Les lieux des mémoire*, vol. 1, *La république*, edited by Pierre Nora, 421–73. Paris: Gallimard, 1984.

Amara, Mahfoud. "The Middle East and North Africa." In *Routledge Companion to Sports History*, edited by Steven W. Pope and John R. Nauright, 498–510. London: Routledge, 2009.

Amenda, Lars. "Food and Otherness: Chinese Restaurants in West European Cities in the 20th Century." *Food and History* 7, no. 2 (2009): 157–79.

Anderson, Benedict. *Imagined Communities: Reflections on the Origin and Spread of Nationalism.* London: Verso, 1991.

———. *Long-Distance Nationalism: World Capitalism and the Rise of Identity Politics.* Amsterdam: CASA, 1992.

Anderson, Lara. *Cooking Up the Nation: Spanish Culinary Texts and Culinary Nationalization in the Late Nineteenth and Early Twentieth Century.* Woodbridge, UK: Tamesis, 2013.

Anscombe, Frederick F. *State, Faith, and Nation in Ottoman and Post-Ottoman Lands.* Cambridge: Cambridge University Press, 2014.

Ansre, Gilbert. "Four Rationalisations for Maintaining the European Languages in Education in Africa." *Kiswahili* 47, no. 2 (1977): 55–62.

Antonsich, Marco. "Natives and Aliens: Who and What Belongs in Nature and in the Nation?" *Area* 53, no. 2 (June 2021): 303–10.

Appelbaum, Nancy P. "Envisioning the Nation: The Mid-Nineteenth-Century Colombian Chorographic Commission." In *State and Nation Making in Latin America and Spain: Republics of the Possible*, edited by Miguel A. Centeno and Agustin E. Ferraro, 375–96. Cambridge: Cambridge University Press, 2013.

Applebaum, Anne. *Iron Curtain: The Crushing of Eastern Europe, 1944–1956.* London: Allen Lane, 2012.

Applegate, Celia. *A Nation of Provincials: The German Idea of Heimat.* Berkeley: University of California Press, 1990.

Arblaster, Anthony. *The Rise and Decline of Western Liberalism.* Oxford: Blackwell, 1989.

Armitage, David. *The Declaration of Independence: A Global History.* Cambridge, MA: Harvard University Press, 2007.

Arnason, Johann P. "Communism and Modernity." *Daedalus* 129, no. 1 (2000): 61–90.

Aronczyk, Melissa. *Branding the Nation: The Global Business of National Identity.* New York: Oxford University Press, 2013.

Arrechea Miguel, Julio Ignacio. "Focilllón y Strzygowski o la lejana raíz del arte occidental." *Espacio, tiempo y forma.* Series 7, *Historia del arte*, no. 6 (1993): 559–606.

Arriola, Leonardo R. "Patronage and Political Stability in Africa." *Comparative Political Studies* 42, no. 10 (2009): 1339–62.

Aschheim, Steven E. *The Nietzsche Legacy in Germany, 1890–1990.* Berkeley: University of California Press, 1992.

Ashworth, Gregory. "The Instruments of Place Branding: How Is It Done?" *European Spatial Research and Policy* 16, no. 1 (2009): 9–22.

Aston, Nigel. *The French Revolution, 1789–1804: Authority, Liberty and the Search for Stability.* Basingstoke, UK: Palgrave Macmillan, 2004.

Atanasova, Ivanka Nedeva. "Lyudmila Zhivkova and the Paradox of Ideology and Identity in Communist Bulgaria." *East European Politics and Societies* 18, no. 2 (2004): 278–315.

Augusteijn, Joost. "Irish Nationalism and Unionism between State, Region and Nation." In *Region and State in Nineteenth-Century Europe: Nation-Building, Regional Identities and Separatism*, edited by Joost Augusteijn and Eric Storm, 192–209. Basingstoke, UK: Palgrave Macmillan, 2012.

Augusteijn, Joost, and Eric Storm, eds. *Region and State in Nineteenth-Century Europe: Nation-Building, Regional Identities and Separatism*. Basingstoke, UK: Palgrave Macmillan, 2012.

Auslander, Leora. *Cultural Revolutions: Everyday Life and Politics in Britain, North America, and France*. Berkeley: University of California Press, 2009.

Ayalon, Ami. *Language and Change in the Arab Middle East: The Evolution of Modern Arabic Political Discourse*. Oxford: Oxford University Press, 1987.

Azaryahu, Maoz. "The Power of Commemorative Street Names." *Environment and Planning D: Society and Space* 14, no. 3 (1996): 311–30.

Azzi, María Susana. "The Tango, Peronism, and Astor Piazzola in the 1940s and 50s." In *From Tejano to Tango: Essays on Latin American Popular Music*, edited by Walter Aaron Clark, 25–40. New York: Routledge, 2002.

Bäckström, Per, Benedikt Hjartarson, and Aart Jan Bergshoeff, eds. *Decentring the Avant-Garde*. Amsterdam: Rodopi, 2014.

Bahlcke, Joachim. "Adelsnation." In *Enzyklopädie der Neuzeit*, edited by Friedrich Jaeger, 1:70–73. Stuttgart: Metzler, 2005.

Bairner, Alan. *Sport, Nationalism, and Globalization: European and North American Perspectives*. Albany: State University of New York Press, 2001.

Baker, Catherine. *The Yugoslav Wars of the 1990s*. London: Palgrave Macmillan, 2015.

Baker, Chris, and Pasuk Phongpaichit. *A History of Thailand*. Cambridge: Cambridge University Press, 2009.

Baker, Keith Michael. "Revolutionizing Revolution." In *Scripting Revolution: A Historical Approach to the Comparative Study of Revolutions*, edited by Keith Michael Baker and Dan Edelstein, 71–103. Stanford, CA: Stanford University Press, 2015.

Bakker, Gerben. *Entertainment Industrialised: The Emergence of the International Film Industry, 1890–1940*. Cambridge: Cambridge University Press, 2008.

Balfour, Sebastian. *The End of the Spanish Empire, 1898–1923*. Oxford: Clarendon Press, 1997.

Bancel, Nicolas, Pascal Blanchard, and Gilles Boëtsch, eds. *Zoos humains: Au temps des exhibitions humaines*. Paris: La Découverte, 2004.

Banerjee-Dube, Ishita. *A History of Modern India*. Delhi: Cambridge University Press, 2015.

Banet-Weiser, Sarah. *The Most Beautiful Girl in the World: Beauty Pageants and National Identity*. Berkeley: University of California Press, 1999.

Barfield, Thomas. *Afghanistan: A Cultural and Political History*. Princeton, NJ: Princeton University Press, 2010.

Barrón, Sofía, and Isabel Justo, eds. *Sorolla: Visión de España: Colección de la Hispanic Society of America*. Valencia: Fundación Bancaja, 2007.

Bassin, Mark. "Eurasia." In *European Regions and Boundaries: A Conceptual History*, edited by Diana Mishkova and Balázs Trencsényi, 210–33. New York: Berghahn, 2017.

Bates, Crispin. "Race, Caste and Tribe in Central India: The Early Origins of Indian Anthropometry." In *The Concept of Race in South Asia*, edited by Peter Robb, 219–59. Oxford: Oxford University Press, 1995.

Bätschmann, Oskar. *Ausstellungskünstler: Kult und Karriere im modernen Kunstsystem*. Cologne: DuMont, 1997.

Batta, Anna. *The Russian Minorities in the Former Soviet Republics: Secession, Integration, and Homeland*. London: Routledge, 2021.

Bauer, Gretchen, and Manon Tremblay, eds. *Women in Executive Power: A Global Overview*. Abingdon, UK: Routledge, 2011.

Bauman, Zygmunt. *Liquid Modernity*. Cambridge: Polity, 2000.

Bayart, Jean-François. *The Illusion of Cultural Identity*. London: Hurst, 2005.

Baycroft, Timothy, and Mark Hewitson, eds. *What Is a Nation? Europe 1789–1914*. Oxford: Oxford University Press, 2006.

Baycroft, Timothy, and David M. Hopkin, eds. *Folklore and Nationalism in Europe during the Long Nineteenth Century*. Leiden: Brill, 2012.

Bayly, C. A. *The Birth of the Modern World, 1780–1914: Global Connections and Comparisons*. Malden, MA: Blackwell, 2004.

Bayly, C. A., and Eugenio F. Biagini, eds. *Giuseppe Mazzini and the Globalization of Democratic Nationalism, 1830–1920*. Oxford: Oxford University Press, 2008.

Beckert, Jens. "Institutional Isomorphism Revisited: Convergence and Divergence in Institutional Change." *Sociological Theory* 28, no. 2 (2010): 150–66.

Beek, Walter van. "To Dance or Not to Dance: Dogon Masks as a Tourist Arena." In *African Hosts and Their Guests: Cultural Dynamics of Tourism*, edited by Walter van Beek and Annette Schmidt, 37–57. Woodbridge, UK: James Currey, 2012.

Behrendt, Andrew. "Educating Apostles of the Homeland: Tourism and 'Honismeret' in Interwar Hungary." *Hungarian Cultural Studies* 7 (2015): 159–76.

Behrisch, Lars. "Statistics and Politics in the 18th Century." *Historical Social Research* 41, no. 2 (2016): 238–57.

Beissinger, Mark R. "Nationalism and the Collapse of Soviet Communism." *Contemporary European History* 18, no. 3 (2009): 331–47.

Bell, David A. *The Cult of the Nation in France: Inventing Nationalism, 1680–1800*. Cambridge, MA: Harvard University Press, 2001.

———. *The First Total War: Napoleon's Europe and the Birth of Modern Warfare*. London: Bloomsbury, 2008.

Bellamy, Richard. *Liberalism and Modern Society: An Historical Argument*. Cambridge: Polity, 1992.

Belmonte, Laura A. *The International LGBT Rights Movement: A History*. London: Bloomsbury, 2021.

Ben-Amos, Avner. "Les funérailles de Victor Hugo: Apothéose de l'événement spectacle." In *Les lieux de mémoire*, vol. 1, *La république*, edited by Pierre Nora, 473–523. Paris: Gallimard, 1984.

Bender, Thomas. *A Nation among Nations: America's Place in World History*. New York: Hill and Wang, 2006.

———. "Writing American History, 1789–1945." In *The Oxford History of Historical Writing*, vol. 4, *1800–1945*, edited by Stuart Macintyre, Juan Maiguashca, and Attila Pók, 369–90. Oxford: Oxford University Press, 2011.

Bendix, Regina. *In Search of Authenticity: The Formation of Folklore Studies.* Madison: University of Wisconsin Press, 1997.

Bengio, Ofra. *Kurds of Iraq: Building a State within a State.* Boulder, CO: Lynne Rienner, 2012.

Bergdoll, Barry. *European Architecture: 1750–1980.* Oxford: Oxford University Press, 2000.

Berger, Stefan. "Building the Nation among Visions of German Empire." In *Nationalizing Empires,* edited by Stefan Berger and Alexei Miller, 247–309. Budapest: Central European University Press, 2015.

———. *The Past as History: National Identity and Historical Consciousness in Modern Europe.* Basingstoke, UK: Palgrave Macmillan, 2014.

———, ed. *Writing the Nation: A Global Perspective.* Basingstoke, UK: Palgrave Macmillan, 2007.

Berger, Stefan, Peter Aronsson, and Gabriella Elgenius. "National Museums in between Nationalism, Imperialism and Regionalism, 1750–1915." In *National Museums and Nation-Building in Europe 1750–1920: Mobilization and Legitimacy, Continuity and Change,* edited by Peter Aronsson and Gabriella Elgenius, 13–33. London: Routledge, 2015.

Berger, Stefan, and Alexei Miller. "Introduction: Building Nations in and with Empires—a Reassessment." In *Nationalizing Empires,* edited by Stefan Berger and Alexei Miller, 1–31. Budapest: Central European University Press, 2015.

———, eds. *Nationalizing Empires.* Budapest: Central European University Press, 2015.

Berger, Stefan, and Eric Storm, eds. *Writing the History of Nationalism.* London: Bloomsbury Academic, 2019.

Bergeron, Rosemary. "A History of the Newsreel in Canada: A Struggle for Screen Time." *Moving Image* 7, no. 2 (2007): 25–54.

Berlin, Isaiah. *Vico and Herder: Two Studies in the History of Ideas.* London: Hogarth Press, 1976.

Berman, Bruce. "Ethnicity, Patronage and the African State: The Politics of Uncivil Nationalism." *African Affairs* 97 (1998): 305–41.

———. "Nationalism in Post-colonial Africa." In *The Oxford Handbook of the History of Nationalism,* edited by John Breuilly, 359–77. Oxford: Oxford University Press, 2013.

Berman, Bruce, Dickson Eyoh, and Will Kymlicka. "Ethnicity and the Politics of Democratic Nation-Building in Africa." In *Ethnicity and Democracy in Africa,* edited by Bruce Berman, Dickson Eyoh, and Will Kymlicka, 1–22. Oxford: James Currey, 2004.

Bernhard, Patrick. "Pädagogische Pizza: Ernährung, Erziehung und der Boom der italienische Küche in der Spätmoderne." *ZeitRäume,* 2016, 82–91.

Bew, Paul. *Ireland: The Politics of Enmity, 1789–2006.* Oxford: Oxford University Press, 2007.

Bhatt, Chetan. *Hindu Nationalism: Origins, Ideologies and Modern Myths.* Oxford: Berg, 2001.

Bieber, Florian. *Debating Nationalism: The Global Spread of Nations.* London: Bloomsbury Academic, 2020.

Bienkowski, Piotr. "Authority and the Power of Place: Exploring the Legitimacy of Authorized and Alternative Voices in the Restitution Discourse." In *Museums and Restitution: New Practices, New Approaches,* edited by Louise Tythacott and Kostas Arvanitis, 37–55. Farnham, UK: Routledge, 2014.

Bignell, Jonathan, and Andreas Fickers, eds. *A European Television History.* Malden, MA: Wiley-Blackwell, 2009.

Bijsterveld Muñoz, Andrés. "National Identity in Historical Video Games: An Analysis of How Civilization V Represents the Past." *Nations and Nationalism* 28, no. 4 (2022): 1311–25.

Billig, Michael. *Banal Nationalism*. London: Sage, 1995.

Blackbourn, David. *The Conquest of Nature: Water, Landscape and the Making of Modern Germany*. London: Cape, 2006.

Blanning, Timothy C. W. *The French Revolutionary Wars: 1787–1802*. London: Arnold, 1996.

Bloembergen, Marieke, and Martijn Eickhoff. *The Politics of Heritage in Indonesia: A Cultural History*. Cambridge: Cambridge University Press, 2020.

Bloomfield, Steve. *Africa United: Soccer, Passion, Politics, and the First World Cup in Africa*. New York: Harper Perennial, 2010.

Blum, Alain, and Jacques Houdaille. "L'alphabétisation aux XVIIIe et XIXe siècles: L'illusion parisienne?" *Population* (French ed.) 40, no. 6 (1985): 944–51.

Boa, Elizabeth, and Rachel Palfreyman. *Heimat—A German Dream: Regional Loyalties and National Identity in German Culture 1890–1990*. Oxford: Oxford University Press, 2011.

Bobbitt, Philip. *The Shield of Achilles: War, Peace and the Course of History*. London: Penguin, 2002.

Bokovoy, Matthew F. *The San Diego World's Fairs and Southwestern Memory, 1880–1940*. Albuquerque: University of New Mexico Press, 2005.

Bon, Frédéric. *Les élections en France: Histoire et sociologie*. Paris: Seuil, 1978.

Bortolotto, Chiara. "From Objects to Processes: UNESCO's 'Intangible Cultural Heritage.'" *Journal of Museum Ethnography*, no. 19 (2007): 21–33.

———. "Placing Intangible Cultural Heritage, Owning a Tradition, Affirming Sovereignty: The Role of Spatiality in the Practice of the 2003 Convention." In *The Routledge Companion to Intangible Cultural Heritage*, edited by Michelle Stefano and Peter Davis, 70–82. London: Routledge, 2016.

Bortone, Pietro. *Language and Nationality: Social Inferences, Cultural Differences and Linguistic Misconceptions*. London: Bloomsbury, 2022.

Bosworth, Richard J. B. *Mussolini*. London: Arnold, 2002.

Bouchard, Gérard. *The Making of the Nations and Cultures of the New World: An Essay in Comparative History*. Montreal: McGill-Queen's University Press, 2008.

Bouwers, Eveline. *Public Pantheons in Revolutionary Europe: Comparing Cultures of Remembrance, c. 1790–1840*. Basingstoke, UK: Palgrave Macmillan, 2012.

Boyle, Raymond. *Power Play: Sport, the Media and Popular Culture*. Edinburgh: Edinburgh University Press, 2009.

Bozdoğan, Sibel. *Modernism and Nation Building: Turkish Architectural Culture in the Early Republic*. Seattle: University of Washington Press, 2001.

Braddick, Michael J. *State Formation in Early Modern England, c. 1550–1700*. Cambridge: Cambridge University Press, 2000.

Breen, T. H. "Ideology and Nationalism on the Eve of the American Revolution: Revisions Once More in Need of Revising." *Journal of American History* 84, no. 1 (1997): 13–39.

Breidenbach, Joana, and Pál Nyíri. *Seeing Culture Everywhere: From Genocide to Consumer Habits*. Seattle: University of Washington Press, 2009.

Breña, Roberto. "The Emancipation Process in New Spain and the Cádiz Constitution: New Historiographical Paths regarding the Revoluciones Hispánicas." In *The Rise of Constitutional Government in the Iberian Atlantic World: The Impact of the Cádiz Constitution of 1812*, edited by Scott Eastman and Natalia Sobrevilla Perea, 38–51. Tuscaloosa: Alabama University Press, 2015.

Breuilly, John. "Nationalism and National Unification in Nineteenth-Century Europe." In *The Oxford Handbook of the History of Nationalism*, edited by John Breuilly, 149–75. Oxford: Oxford University Press, 2013.

———. *Nationalism and the State*. Manchester: Manchester University Press, 1982.

———. "Nationalism as Global History." In *Nationalism and Globalisation: Conflicting or Complementary?*, edited by Daphne Halikiopoulou and Sofia Vasilopoulou, 65–84. London: Routledge, 2011.

———, ed. *The Oxford Handbook of the History of Nationalism*. Oxford: Oxford University Press, 2013.

Brewster, Marjory, Joanne Connell, and Stephen J. Page. "The Scottish Highland Games: Evolution, Development and Role as a Community Event." *Current Issues in Tourism* 12, no. 3 (2009): 271–93.

Brisku, Adrian. *Political Reform in the Ottoman and Russian Empires: A Comparative Approach*. London: Bloomsbury, 2019.

Broers, Michael. "The Concept of 'Total War' in the Revolutionary-Napoleonic Period." *War in History* 15, no. 3 (2008): 247–68.

———. "The First Napoleonic Empire, 1799–1815." In *Nationalizing Empires*, edited by Stefan Berger and Alexei Miller, 99–134. Budapest: Central European University Press, 2015.

———. *Napoleon's Other War: Bandits, Rebels and Their Pursuers in the Age of Revolutions*. Oxford: Peter Lang, 2010.

Broers, Michael, Peter Hicks, and Agustín Guimerá Ravina, eds. *The Napoleonic Empire and the New European Political Culture*. Basingstoke, UK: Palgrave Macmillan, 2012.

Brubaker, Rogers. "Ethnicity without Groups." *European Journal of Sociology* 43, no. 2 (2002): 163–89.

———. *Grounds for Difference*. Cambridge, MA: Harvard University Press, 2017.

———. *Nationalism Reframed: Nationhood and the National Question in the New Europe*. Cambridge: Cambridge University Press, 2009.

———. "Why Populism?" *Theory and Society* 46, no. 5 (2017): 357–85.

Bublatzky, Catherine. "The Display of Indian Contemporary Art in Western Museums and the Question of 'Othering.'" In *Global Studies: Mapping Contemporary Art and Culture*, edited by Hans Belting, Jacob Birken, Andrea Buddensieg, and Peter Weibel, 298–314. Ostfildern, Germany: Hatje Cantz, 2011.

Bullock, Nicholas, and James Read. *The Movement for Housing Reform in Germany and France, 1840–1914*. Cambridge: Cambridge University Press, 1985.

Bunnell, Tim. "Views from Above and Below: The Petronas Twin Towers and/in Contesting Visions of Development in Contemporary Malaysia." *Singapore Journal of Tropical Geography* 20, no. 1 (1999): 1–23.

Bunzl, Matti. "Franz Boas and the Humboldtian Tradition: From Volksgeist and Nationalcharakter to an Anthropological Concept of Culture." In *Volksgeist as Method and Ethic: Essays on Boasian Ethnography and the German Anthropological Tradition*, edited by George W. Stocking, 17–97. Madison: University of Wisconsin Press, 1996.

Burbank, Jane, and Frederick Cooper. *Empires in World History: Power and the Politics of Difference*. Princeton, NJ: Princeton University Press, 2010.

Burke, Peter. *Languages and Communities in Early Modern Europe*. Cambridge: Cambridge University Press, 2004.

———. "Nationalisms and Vernaculars, 1500–1800." In *The Oxford Handbook of the History of Nationalism*, edited by John Breuilly, 21–36. Oxford: Oxford University Press, 2013.

———. *Popular Culture in Early Modern Europe*. New York: Harper & Row, 1978.

Bushart, Magdalena. *Der Geist der Gotik und die expressionistische Kunst: Kunstgeschichte und Kunsttheorie, 1911–1925*. Munich: Schreiber, 1990.

Cabo, Miguel, and Fernando Molina. "The Long and Winding Road of Nationalization: Eugen Weber's *Peasants into Frenchmen* in Modern European History (1976–2006)." *European History Quarterly* 39, no. 2 (2009): 264–86.

Calic, Marie-Janine. *The Great Cauldron: A History of Southeastern Europe*. Cambridge, MA: Harvard University Press, 2019.

———. *A History of Yugoslavia*. West Lafayette, IN: Purdue University Press, 2019.

Campbell, Lyle. "The History of Linguistics." In *The Handbook of Linguistics*, edited by Mark Aronoff and Janie Rees-Miller, 81–105. Oxford: Blackwell, 2001.

Canizaro, Vincent B., ed. *Architectural Regionalism: Collected Writings on Place, Identity, Modernity, and Tradition*. New York: Princeton Architectural Press, 2007.

Cannadine, David. "The Context, Performance and Meaning of Ritual: The British Monarchy and the 'Invention of Tradition,' c. 1820–1977." In *The Invention of Tradition*, edited by Eric Hobsbawm and Terence Ranger, 101–65. Cambridge: Canto, 1983.

Caprotti, Federico. "Information Management and Fascist Identity: Newsreels in Fascist Italy." *Media History* 11, no. 3 (2005): 177–91.

Carman, John, and Marie Louise Stig Sørensen. "Heritage Studies: An Outline." In *Heritage Studies: Methods and Approaches*, edited by Marie Louise Stig Sørensen and John Carman, 11–29. London: Routledge, 2009.

Carmichael, Cathie, Matthew D'Auria, and Aviel Roshwald, eds. *The Cambridge History of Nationhood and Nationalism*. 2 vols. Cambridge: Cambridge University Press, 2023.

Carruthers, Jane. *The Kruger National Park: A Social and Political History*. Pietermaritzburg: University of Natal Press, 1995.

Carteny, Andrea. "All against One: The Congress of Oppressed Nationalities of Austria-Hungary (1918)." Working paper 67, Department of Communication, University of Teramo, 2010.

Caryl, Christian. *Strange Rebels: 1979 and the Birth of the 21st Century*. New York: Basic Books, 2013.

Cassel, Pär Kristoffer. *Grounds of Judgment: Extraterritoriality and Imperial Power in Nineteenth-Century China and Japan*. New York: Oxford University Press, 2012.

Castle, Gregory, ed. *A History of the Modernist Novel*. Cambridge: Cambridge University Press, 2015.

Castles, Francis G., Stephan Leibfried, Herbert Obinger, Christopher Pierson, and Jane Lewis, eds. *The Oxford Handbook of the Welfare State*. Oxford: Oxford University Press, 2010.

Centeno, Miguel A., and Agustin E. Ferraro. "Republics of the Possible." In *State and Nation Making in Latin America and Spain: Republics of the Possible*, edited by Miguel A. Centeno and Agustin E. Ferraro, 3–24. Cambridge: Cambridge University Press, 2013.

Chambers, Ciara. "'British for the British—Irish Events for the Irish': Indigenous Newsreel Production in Ireland." *Historical Journal of Film, Radio, and Television* 32, no. 3 (2012): 361–77.

Chambers, Erve. *Native Tours: The Anthropology of Travel and Tourism*. Long Grove, IL: Waveland, 2010.

Charnon-Deutsch, Lou. *The Spanish Gypsy: The History of a European Obsession*. University Park: Pennsylvania State University Press, 2004.

Chassen-López, Francie. "The Traje de Tehuana as National Icon: Gender, Ethnicity, and Fashion in Mexico." *The Americas* 71, no. 2 (2014): 281–314.

Chatterji, Joya. "Nationalism in India, 1857–1947." In *The Oxford Handbook of the History of Nationalism*, edited by John Breuilly, 242–63. Oxford: Oxford University Press, 2013.

Chen, Yong. *Chop Suey, USA: The Story of Chinese Food in America*. New York: Columbia University Press, 2014.

Cherkasov, Alexander, and Dmitry Grushkin. "The Chechen Wars and Human Rights in Russia." In *Chechnya: From Past to Future*, edited by Richard Sakwa, 131–57. London: Anthem, 2012.

Chernilo, Daniel. "Classical Sociology and the Nation-State: A Re-interpretation." *Journal of Classical Sociology* 8, no. 1 (2008): 27–43.

Chico Comerón, Cirilo. "Actitudes políticas en Guipúzcoa durante la Guerra de la Convención (1793–1795)." PhD diss., Universidad Nacional de Educación a Distancia, Madrid, 2012.

Chika Okeke-Agulu. "Nationalism and the Rhetoric of Modernism in Nigeria: The Art of Uche Okeke and Demas Nwoko, 1960–1968." *African Arts* 39, no. 1 (2006): 26–93.

Chin, Rita C.-K. *The Crisis of Multiculturalism in Europe: A History*. Princeton, NJ: Princeton University Press, 2017.

Christie, Clive J. *A Modern History of Southeast Asia: Decolonization, Nationalism and Separatism*. London: Tauris, 1996.

Clark, Christopher. *Iron Kingdom: The Rise and Downfall of Prussia, 1600–1947*. London: Allen Lane, 2006.

———. *The Sleepwalkers: How Europe Went to War in 1914*. London: Penguin, 2013.

Clarke, Colin P. *After the Caliphate: The Islamic State and the Future of the Terrorist Diaspora*. Medford, MA: Polity Press, 2019.

Cleveland, William L. *A History of the Modern Middle East*. London: Routledge, 2018.

Clout, Hugh. *After the Ruins: Restoring the Countryside of Northern France after the Great War*. Exeter: University of Exeter Press, 1996.

Cócola Gant, Agustín. "El Barrio Gótico de Barcelona: De símbolo nacional a parque temático." *Scripta Nova*, no. 15 (2011).

Cohen, Paula Marantz. *Silent Film and the Triumph of the American Myth*. Oxford: Oxford University Press, 2001.

Coller, Ian. "The French Revolution and the Islamic World of the Middle East and North Africa." In *The Routledge Companion to the French Revolution in World History*, edited by Alan Forrest and Matthias Middell, 117–34. Abingdon, UK: Routledge, 2016.

Colley, Linda. *Britons: Forging the Nation, 1707–1837*. New Haven, CT: Yale University Press, 1992.

———. *The Gun, the Ship, and the Pen: Warfare, Constitutions, and the Making of the Modern World*. London: Profile, 2021.

Collins, Michael. "Decolonisation and the 'Federal Moment.'" *Diplomacy and Statecraft* 24, no. 1 (2013): 21–40.

Confino, Alon. *The Nation as a Local Metaphor: Württemberg, Imperial Germany, and National Memory, 1871–1918*. Chapel Hill: University of North Carolina Press, 1997.

Conklin, Alice L., Sarah Fishman, and Robert Zaretsky. *France and Its Empire since 1870*. Oxford: Oxford University Press, 2011.

Connelly, Matthew. "Population Control in India: Prologue to the Emergency Period." *Population and Development Review* 32, no. 4 (2006): 629–67.

Connor, Walker. *Ethnonationalism: The Quest for Understanding*. Princeton, NJ: Princeton University Press, 1994.

Conrad, Margaret. *A Concise History of Canada*. Cambridge: Cambridge University Press, 2011.

Conrad, Sebastian. "Enlightenment in Global History: A Historiographical Critique." *American Historical Review* 117, no. 4 (2012): 999–1027.

———. "Globalization Effects: Mobility and Nation in Imperial Germany, 1880–1914." *Journal of Global History* 3, no. 1 (2008): 43–66.

Conversi, Daniele. "Art, Nationalism and War: Political Futurism in Italy (1909–1944)." *Sociology Compass* 3, no. 1 (2009): 92–117.

Conway, Martin. *Western Europe's Democratic Age: 1945–1968*. Princeton, NJ: Princeton University Press, 2020.

Cooky, Cheryl, and Michael A. Messner, eds. *No Slam Dunk: Gender, Sport and the Unevenness of Social Change*. New Brunswick, NJ: Rutgers University Press, 2018.

Cooley, Angela Jill. *To Live and Dine in Dixie: The Evolution of Urban Food Culture in the Jim Crow South*. Athens: University of Georgia Press, 2015.

Cooper, Frederick. *Citizenship between Empire and Nation: Remaking France and French Africa, 1945–1960*. Princeton, NJ: Princeton University Press, 2014.

———. *Citizenship, Inequality, and Difference: Historical Perspectives*. Princeton, NJ Princeton University Press, 2018.

Cooper, Frederick, and Randall M. Packard, eds. *International Development and the Social Sciences: Essays on the History and Politics of Knowledge*. Berkeley: University of California Press, 1997.

Corrales, Javier. "Autocratic Legalism in Venezuela." *Journal of Democracy* 26, no. 2 (2015): 37–51.

Costa Pinto, António. "Authoritarianism and Corporatism in Latin America: The First Wave." In *Authoritarianism and Corporatism in Europe and Latin America: Crossing Borders*, edited by António Costa Pinto and Federico Finchelstein, 110–42. London: Routledge, 2018.

———. "Fascism, Corporatism and the Crafting of Authoritarian Institutions in Inter-war European Dictatorships." In *Rethinking Fascism and Dictatorship in Europe*, edited by António Costa Pinto and Aristotle Kallis, 87–117. Basingstoke, UK: Palgrave Macmillan, 2014.

Costa Pinto, António, and Federico Finchelstein, eds. *Authoritarianism and Corporatism in Europe and Latin America: Crossing Borders*. London: Routledge, 2019.

Courtenay, Todd. "The 1911 International Exposition in Rome: Architecture, Archaeology, and National Identity." *Journal of Historical Geography* 37, no. 4 (2011): 440–59.

Crisell, Andres. *An Introductory History of British Broadcasting*. London: Routledge, 1997.

Cronin, Michael, and Daryl Adair. *The Wearing of the Green: A History of St. Patrick's Day*. London: Routledge, 2002.

Crook, Tim. *International Radio Journalism: History, Theory and Practice*. London: Routledge, 1998.

Cumming, Elizabeth, and Wendy Kaplan. *The Arts and Crafts Movement*. London: Thames and Hudson, 2004.

Cusack, Tricia. *Riverscapes and National Identities*. Syracuse: Syracuse University Press, 2019.

Cwiertka, Katarzyna J. *Modern Japanese Cuisine: Food, Power and National Identity*. London: Reaktion Books, 2014.

Dalacoura, Katerina. *Islamist Terrorism and Democracy in the Middle East*. Cambridge: Cambridge University Press, 2011.

Dalle Mulle, Emmanuel. *The Nationalism of the Rich: Discourses and Strategies of Separatist Parties in Catalonia, Flanders, Northern Italy and Scotland*. London: Routledge, 2019.

Damme, Wilfried van, and Kitty Zijlmans. "Art History in a Global Frame: World Art Studies." In *Art History and Visual Studies in Europe*, edited by Matthew Rampley, Thierry Lenain, Charlotte Schoell-Glass, Andrea Pinotti, Hubert Locher, and Kitty Zijlmans, 217–29. Leiden: Brill, 2012.

Darnton, Robert. *The Forbidden Best-Sellers of Pre-revolutionary France*. New York: W. W. Norton, 1995.

Darwin, John. *After Tamerlane: The Rise and Fall of Global Empires, 1400–2000*. London: Penguin, 2008.

———. *The Empire Project: The Rise and Fall of the British World-System, 1830–1970*. Cambridge: Cambridge University Press, 2009.

Daswani, Chander J. "Literacy and Development in South-East Asia." In *Functional Literacy: Theoretical Issues and Educational Implications*, edited by Ludo Th. Verhoeven, 279–91. Philadelphia: John Benjamins, 1994.

D'Auria, Viviana, and Bruno De Meulder. "Unsettling Landscapes: The Volta River Project." *Oase*, no. 82 (2010): 116–38.

David, John Seh. *The American Colonization Society and the Founding of the First African Republic*. Bloomington, IN: iUniverse, 2014.

Davidson, Basil. *Africa in Modern History: The Search for a New Society*. Harmondsworth: Penguin, 1978.

Davis, John. "Rescue and Recovery: The Biopolitics and Ethnogenealogy of Moldavian Catholics in 1940s Romania." In *Local and Transnational Csángó Lifeworlds*, edited by Sándor Ilyés, Lehel Peti, and Ferenc Pozsony, 95–113. Cluj-Napoca: Kriza János Ethnographical Society, 2008.

Davis, Leon. "Football Fandom and Authenticity: A Critical Discussion of Historical and Contemporary Perspectives." *Soccer and Society* 16, no. 2–3 (2015): 422–36.

De Cesari, Chiara, and Ann Rigney. Introduction to *Transnational Memory: Circulation, Articulation, Scales*, edited by Chiara de Cesari and Ann Rigney, 1–26. Berlin: De Gruyter, 2014.

Deeb-Swihart, Julia, Christopher Polack, Eric Gilbert, and Irfan Essa. "Selfie-Presentation in Everyday Life: A Large-Scale Characterization of Selfie Contexts on Instagram." In *Proceedings of the Eleventh International AAAI Conference on Web and Social Media*, 42–51. Palo Alto, CA: AAAI Press, 2017.

De Grazia, Victoria. "Mass Culture and Sovereignty: The American Challenge to European Cinemas, 1920–1960." *Journal of Modern History* 61, no. 1 (1989): 53–87.

Degroff, Daniel Alan. "Artur Hazelius and the Ethnographic Display of the Scandinavian Peasantry: A Study in Context and Appropriation." *European Review of History* 19, no. 2 (2012): 229–48.

Dellenbaugh-Losse, Mary. *Inventing Berlin: Architecture, Politics and Cultural Memory in the New/ Old German Capital Post-1989*. Cham, Switzerland: Springer, 2020.

Demange, Christian. *El dos de mayo: Mito y fiesta nacional, 1808–1958*. Madrid: Marcial Pons, 2004.

Demay, Aline. *Tourism and Colonization in Indochina (1898–1939)*. Newcastle: Cambridge Scholars, 2015.

Dembinska, Magdalena, and Aurélie Campana. "Frozen Conflicts and Internal Dynamics of De Facto States: Perspectives and Directions for Research." *International Studies Review* 19, no. 2 (2017): 254–78.

Depetris-Chauvin, Emilio, Ruben Durante, and Filipe Campante. "Building Nations through Shared Experiences: Evidence from African Football." *American Economic Review* 110, no. 5 (May 2020): 1572–602.

Derks, Marjet. "Sports, Pastimes: Introductory Survey Essay." In *Encyclopedia of Romantic Nationalism in Europe*, edited by Joep Leerssen, 72–75. Amsterdam: Amsterdam University Press, 2018.

Derks, Marjet, and Joep Leerssen. "Sports/Athletics Associations: Survey Article." In *Encyclopedia of Romantic Nationalism in Europe*, edited by Joep Leerssen, 142–43. Amsterdam: Amsterdam University Press, 2018.

Déruelle, Aude. "Galerie des Batailles et histoire-bataille." *Romantisme* 169, no. 2 (2015): 55–68.

Díaz-Andreu García, Margarita. *A World History of Nineteenth-Century Archaeology: Nationalism, Colonialism, and the Past*. Oxford: Oxford University Press, 2007.

Diefendorf, Jeffry M. *In the Wake of War: The Reconstruction of German Cities after World War II*. Oxford: Oxford University Press, 1993.

———, ed. *Rebuilding Europe's Bombed Cities*. Basingstoke, UK: Macmillan, 1990.

Díez del Corral, Luis. *El liberalismo doctrinario*. Madrid: Instituto de Estudios Políticos, 1956.

Dijn, Annelien de. *Freedom: An Unruly History*. Cambridge, MA: Harvard University Press, 2020.

DiMaggio, Paul J., and Walter W. Powell. "The Iron Cage Revisited: Institutional Isomorphism and Collective Rationality in Organizational Fields." *American Sociological Review* 48, no. 2 (1983): 147–60.

Dittmer, Jason. *Captain America and the Nationalist Superhero: Metaphors, Narratives, and Geopolitics*. Philadelphia: Temple University Press, 2013.

Doel, Wim van der. *Zo ver de wereld strekt: De geschiedenis van Nederland overzee vanaf 1800*. Amsterdam: Bert Bakker, 2011.

Domper Lasús, Carlos. "Ni liberales ni comunistas: La 'democracia orgánica' y la integración del Franquismo y el Estado Novo en la Europa posterior a 1945." *Espacio, tiempo y forma*. Series 5, *Historia contemporánea*, no. 31 (2019): 151–72.

Döring, Jörg, and Tristan Thielmann, eds. *Spatial Turn: Das Raumparadigma in den Kultur- und Sozialwissenschaften*. Bielefeld, Germany: Transcript Verlag, 2008.

Dorman, Robert L. *Revolt of the Provinces: The Regionalist Movement in America, 1920–1945*. Chapel Hill: University of North Carolina Press, 2003.

Dorson, Richard M. "Folklore in the Modern World." In *Folklore in the Modern World*, edited by Richard M. Dorson, 11–55. The Hague: Mouton, 1978.

Doyle, William. *The Oxford History of the French Revolution*. Oxford: Oxford University Press, 2018.

Duara, Prasenjit. *The Global and Regional in China's Nation-Formation*. London: Routledge, 2008.

Dubois, Laurent. *Avengers of the New World: The Story of the Haitian Revolution*. Cambridge, MA: Belknap, 2005.

Duggan, Christopher. *The Force of Destiny: A History of Italy since 1796*. London: Penguin, 2008.

Dumont, Franz. "The Rhineland." In *Nationalism in the Age of the French Revolution*, edited by Otto Dann, 157–71. London: Bloomsbury, 1988.

Dusza, Erin. "Pan-Slavism in Alphonse Mucha's *Slav Epic*." *Nineteenth-Century Art Worldwide* 13, no. 1 (2014).

Earle, Rebecca A. "Nationalism and National Dress in Spanish America." In *The Politics of Dress in Asia and the Americas*, edited by Mina Roces and Louise P. Edwards, 163–82. Eastbourne, UK: Sussex Academic Press, 2007.

———. *The Return of the Native: Indians and Myth-Making in Spanish America, 1810–1930*. Durham, NC: Duke University Press, 2007.

Eastman, Scott. *Preaching Spanish Nationalism across the Hispanic Atlantic, 1759–1823*. Baton Rouge: Louisiana State University Press, 2012.

Eberhard, David M., Gary F. Simons, and Charles D. Fennig, eds. *Ethnologue: Languages of the World*. 25th ed. Dallas: SIL, 2022.

Edensor, Tim. "Automobility and National Identity: Representation, Geography and Driving Practice." *Theory, Culture and Society* 21, no. 4–5 (2004): 101–20.

———. *National Identity, Popular Culture and Everyday Life*. Oxford: Berg, 2002.

Edmundson, William A. "Do Animals Need Citizenship?" *International Journal of Constitutional Law* 13, no. 3 (2015): 749–65.

Edwards, Louise P., and Mina Roces, eds. *Women's Movements in Asia: Feminisms and Transnational Activism*. Abingdon, UK: Routledge, 2010.

Eghigian, Greg. *Making Security Social: Disability, Insurance, and the Birth of the Social Entitlement State in Germany*. Ann Arbor: University of Michigan Press, 2000.

Eisenstat, Howard. "Modernization, Imperial Nationalism, and the Ethnicization of Confessional Identity in the Late Ottoman Empire." In *Nationalizing Empires*, edited by Stefan Berger and Alexei Miller, 429-61. Budapest: Central European University Press, 2015.

Eksteins, Modris. *Rites of Spring: The Great War and the Birth of the Modern Age*. New York: Doubleday, 1989.

Elgenius, Gabriella. *Symbols of Nations and Nationalism: Celebrating Nationhood*. Basingstoke, UK: Palgrave Macmillan, 2019.

Elgenius, Gabriella, and Peter Aronsson, eds. *Building National Museums in Europe 1750–2010*. Linköping: Linköping University Electronic Press, 2011.

Elliott, John H. *Empires of the Atlantic World: Britain and Spain in America, 1492–1830*. New Haven, CT: Yale University Press, 2006.

Encarnación, Omar Guillermo. *Spanish Politics: Democracy after Dictatorship*. Cambridge: Polity, 2008.

Eriksen, Thomas Hylland. "Between Universalism and Relativism: A Critique of the UNESCO Concept of Culture." In *Culture and Rights: Anthropological Perspectives*, edited by

Jane K. Cowan, Marie-Bénédicte Dembour, and Richard A. Wilson, 127–48. Cambridge: Cambridge University Press, 2001.

———. "Nationalism and the Internet." *Nations and Nationalism* 13, no. 1 (2007): 1–17.

Eriksen, Thomas Hylland, and Finn Sivert Nielsen. *A History of Anthropology.* London: Pluto, 2013.

Esdaile, Charles J. *Spain in the Liberal Age: From Constitution to Civil War, 1808–1939.* Oxford: Blackwell, 2000.

———. *The Wars of the French Revolution, 1792–1801.* London: Routledge, 2018.

Esherick, Joseph W. "How the Qing Became China." In *Empire to Nation: Historical Perspectives on the Making of the Modern World*, edited by Joseph W. Esherick, Hasan Kayali, and Eric Van Young, 229–60. Lanham, MD: Rowman & Littlefield, 2006.

Etlin, Richard A. *Modernism in Italian Architecture, 1890–1940.* Cambridge, MA: MIT Press, 1991.

Evans, Richard J. *The Third Reich in Power, 1933–1939.* New York: Penguin, 2005.

Everdell, William R. *The First Moderns: Profiles in the Origins of Twentieth-Century Thought.* Chicago: University of Chicago Press, 1997.

Facos, Michelle. *Nationalism and the Nordic Imagination: Swedish Art of the 1890s.* Berkeley: University of California Press, 1998.

Fahmi, Kalid Mahmud. *All the Pasha's Men: Mehmed Ali, His Army and the Making of Modern Egypt.* Cambridge: Cambridge University Press, 1997.

———. *Mehmed Ali: From Ottoman Governor to Ruler of Egypt.* Oxford: Oneworld, 2008.

Fahrmeir, Andreas. *Citizenship: The Rise and Fall of a Modern Concept.* New Haven, CT: Yale University Press, 2007.

Fairclough, Adam. *Better Day Coming: Blacks and Equality, 1890–2000.* New York: Viking, 2001.

Falola, Toyin. "Nationalism and African Historiography." In *Turning Points in Historiography: A Cross-Cultural Perspective*, edited by Q. Edward Wang and Georg G. Iggers, 209–31. Rochester, NY: University of Rochester Press, 2002.

Falser, Michael. *Angkor Wat: A Transcultural History of Heritage.* Berlin: De Gruyter, 2019.

Fang, Weigui. *Modern Notions of Civilization and Culture in China.* Singapore: Palgrave Macmillan, 2019.

Farr, James. "Political Science." In *The Cambridge History of Science*, edited by Theodore M. Porter and Dorothy Ross, 7: The Modern Social Sciences:306–29. Cambridge: Cambridge University Press, 2003.

Fatanti, Megasari Noer, and I. Wayan Suyadnya. "Beyond User Gaze: How Instagram Creates Tourism Destination Brand." *Procedia—Social and Behavioral Sciences* 211 (2015): 1089–95.

Feinman, Gary M., and Jill E. Neitzel. "Excising Culture History from Contemporary Archaeology." *Journal of Anthropological Archaeology* 60 (2020).

Ferguson, Niall. *The Pity of War: 1914–1918.* London: Penguin, 1998.

Fernandez, Lilia, and Andrew L. Johns. "Reagan, Religion, and the Culture Wars of the 1980s." In *A Companion to Ronald Reagan*, edited by Andrew L. Johns, 204–20. Malden, MA: Wiley, 2015.

Fernández Sebastián, Javier. "From Patriotism to Liberalism: Political Concepts in Revolution." In *The Routledge Companion to Iberian Studies*, edited by Javier Múñoz Basols, Laura Lonsdale, and Manuel Delgado, 305–19. London: Routledge, 2019.

Feros, Antonio. *Speaking of Spain: The Evolution of Race and Nation in the Hispanic World.* Cambridge, MA: Harvard University Press, 2017.

Fetzer, Thomas. "Nationalism in Political Economy Scholarship." In *Nationalism and the Economy: Explorations into a Neglected Relationship*, edited by Stefan Berger and Thomas Fetzer, 43–65. Budapest: Central European University Press, 2019.

Fichte, Johann Gottlieb. *Addresses to the German Nation*. Chicago: Open Court, 1922.

Fields, David P. *Foreign Friends: Syngman Rhee, American Exceptionalism, and the Division of Korea*. Lexington: University Press of Kentucky, 2019.

Figes, Orlando. *Natasha's Dance: A Cultural History of Russia*. London: Penguin, 2003.

Filipová, Marta, ed. *Cultures of International Exhibitions 1840–1940: Great Exhibitions in the Margins*. Farnham; Burlington: Routledge, 2015.

———. "Peasants on Display: The Czechoslavic Ethnographic Exhibition of 1895." *Journal of Design History* 24, no. 1 (2011): 15–36.

Finer, Samuel E. *The History of Government from the Earliest Times. Vol. III, Empires, Monarchies, and the Modern State*. Oxford: Oxford University Press, 1999.

Finley, Cheryl. "Authenticating Dungeons, Whitewashing Castles: The Former Sites of the Slave Trade on the Ghanaian Coast." In *Architecture and Tourism: Perception, Performance and Place*, edited by D. Medina Lasansky and Brian McLaren, 109–29. Oxford: Berg, 2004.

Firpo, Christina, and Margaret Jacobs. "Taking Children, Ruling Colonies: Child Removal and Colonial Subjugation in Australia, Canada, French Indochina, and the United States, 1870–1950s." *Journal of World History* 29, no. 4 (2018): 529–62.

Fisch, Jörg. "Zivilisation, Kultur." In *Geschichtliche Grundbegriffe: Historisches Lexikon zur politisch-sozialen Sprache in Deutschland*, vol. 7, edited by Otto Brunner, Werner Conze, and Reinhardt Koselleck, 679–775. Stuttgart: Klett-Cotta, 1992.

Flacke, Monika, ed. *Mythen der Nationen: Ein europäisches Panorama*. Munich: Koehler & Amelang, 1998.

Folkers, Antoni S., and Belinda A. C. van Buiten. *Modern Architecture in Africa: Practical Encounters with Intricate African Modernity*. Cham, Switzerland: Springer, 2019.

Foray, Jennifer L. "A Unified Empire of Equal Parts: The Dutch Commonwealth Schemes of the 1920s–40s." *Journal of Imperial and Commonwealth History* 41, no. 2 (2013): 259–84.

Ford, Caroline. *Natural Interests: The Contest over Environment in Modern France*. Cambridge, MA: Harvard University Press, 2016.

Forrest, Alan I. *Conscripts and Deserters: The Army and French Society during the Revolution and Empire*. New York: Oxford University Press, 2001.

Fradera, Josep Maria. *The Imperial Nation: Citizens and Subjects in the British, French, Spanish, and American Empires*. Princeton, NJ: Princeton University Press, 2018.

Framke, Maria, and Andreas Weiß. "Forum: Nation: The Role of the Nation in History Writing in the 21st Century." *H-Soz-Kult*, September 27, 2021.

Freedman, Paul. *Images of the Medieval Peasant*. Stanford, CA: Stanford University Press, 1999.

Freitas Dutra, Eliana de. "The Mirror of History and Images of the Nation: The Invention of a National Identity in Brazil and Its Contrasts with Similar Enterprises in Mexico and Argentina." In *Writing the Nation: A Global Perspective*, edited by Stefan Berger, 84–103. Basingstoke, UK: Palgrave Macmillan, 2007.

Fuglestad, Eirik Magnus. "Nationalism and Private Property." *The State of Nationalism*, 2021. https://stateofnationalism.eu/article/nationalism-and-private-property/.

Furlough, Ellen. "Packaging Pleasures: Club Mediterranée and French Consumer Culture, 1950–1968." *French Historical Studies* 18, no. 1 (1993): 65.

Gallen-Kallela-Siren, Janne. "Axel Gallén and the Constructed Nation: Art and Nationalism in Young Finland, 1880–1900." PhD diss., New York University, 2001.

Gallo, Ezequiel. "Argentina: Society and Politics, 1880–1916." In *The Cambridge History of Latin America*, vol. 5, *c. 1870 to 1930*, edited by Leslie Bethell, 359–92. Cambridge: Cambridge University Press, 1986.

Gamboni, Dario. "'Independent of Time and Place': On the Rise and Decline of the Modernist Ideal." In *Time and Place: The Geohistory of Art*, edited by Thomas DaCosta Kaufmann and Elizabeth Pilliod, 173–203. Aldershot, UK: Ashgate, 2005.

Gao, Zhihong. "When Nationalism Goes to the Market: The Case of Chinese Patriotic Songs." *Journal of Macromarketing* 35, no. 4 (2015): 473–88.

García Álvarez, Jacobo. "Paisaje, memoria histórica e identidad nacional en los inicios de la política de conservación de la naturaleza en España: De Covadonga a San Juan de La Peña." *Hispania* 73, no. 244 (2013): 409–38.

García Carrión, Marta. "Cine y nacionalización en la Europa de entreguerras. El caso español en perspectiva comparada." In *Nación y nacionalización: una perspectiva europea comparada*, edited by Ferran Archilés, Marta García Carrión, and Ismael Saz, 155–70. Valencia: Publicaciones Universitat de Valencia, 2013.

Garip, S. Banu, and Ervin Garip. "Copying the Identity through Tourism Architecture: 'Theme Hotels' in Antalya." *Academic Research International* 6, no. 4 (2015): 24–36.

Garon, Sheldon M. "Fashioning a Culture of Diligence and Thrift: Savings and Frugality Campaigns in Japan, 1900–1931." In *Japan's Competing Modernities: Issues in Culture and Democracy, 1900–1930*, edited by Sharon Minichiello, 312–34. Honolulu: University of Hawai'i Press, 2017.

———. *Molding Japanese Minds: The State in Everyday Life*. Princeton, NJ: Princeton University Press, 1997.

———. "Saving for 'My Own Good and the Good of the Nation': Economic Nationalism in Modern Japan." In *Nation and Nationalism in Japan*, edited by Sandra Wilson, 97–115. Abingdon, UK: Routledge, 2013.

Gat, Azar. *Nations: The Long History and Deep Roots of Political Ethnicity and Nationalism*. Cambridge: Cambridge University Press, 2013.

Gatrell, Peter. *The Making of the Modern Refugee*. Oxford: University Press, 2013.

Gaudenzi, Bianca, and Astrid Swenson. "Looted Art and Restitution in the Twentieth Century—Towards a Global Perspective." *Journal of Contemporary History* 52, no. 3 (2017): 491–518.

Gauthier, Christophe. "Le cinéma des nations: Invention des écoles nationales et patriotisme cinématographique (années 10–années 30)." *Revue d'histoire moderne et contemporaine* 51, no. 4 (2004): 58–77.

Gelderen, Martin van, and Quentin Skinner, eds. *Republicanism: A Shared European Heritage*. Cambridge: Cambridge University Press, 2002.

Gellner, David N. "Uncomfortable Antinomies: Going beyond Methodological Nationalism in Social and Cultural Anthropology." In *Beyond Methodological Nationalism: Research Methodologies for Cross-Border Studies*, edited by Anna Amelina, Devrimsel D. Nergiz, Thomas Faist, and Nina Glick Schiller, 111–29. New York: Routledge, 2012.

Gellner, Ernest. *Nations and Nationalism*. Ithaca, NY: Cornell University Press, 1983.

Gellner, Ernest, and Anthony D. Smith. "The Nation: Real or Imagined? The Warwick Debates on Nationalism." *Nations and Nationalism* 2, no. 3 (1996): 357–88.

German, Tracey C. *Russia's Chechen War*. London: Routledge, 2003.

Gerstle, Gary. *American Crucible: Race and Nation in the Twentieth Century*. Princeton, NJ: Princeton University Press, 2017.

Getachew, Adom. *Worldmaking after Empire: The Rise and Fall of Self-Determination*. Princeton, NJ: Princeton University Press, 2019.

Giguere, Joy M. *Characteristically American Memorial Architecture, National Identity, and the Egyptian Revival*. Knoxville: University of Tennessee Press, 2014.

Gildea, Robert. *Children of the Revolution: The French, 1799–1914*. London: Penguin, 2009.

Gimeno Martínez, Javier. *Design and National Identity*. London: Bloomsbury, 2016.

Gingrich, Andre. "After the Great War: National Reconfigurations of Anthropology in Late Colonial Times." In *Doing Anthropology in Wartime and Warzones: World War I and the Cultural Sciences in Europe*, edited by Reinhard Johler, Christian Marchetti, and Monique Scheer, 355–80. Bielefeld, Germany: Transcript Verlag, 2010.

Ginn, Franklin. "Extension, Subversion, Containment: Eco-Nationalism and (Post)Colonial Nature in Aotearoa New Zealand." *Transactions of the Institute of British Geographers* 33, no. 3 (2008): 335–53.

Girard, Philippe R. *Paradise Lost: Haiti's Tumultuous Journey from Pearl of the Caribbean to Third World Hot Spot*. New York: Palgrave Macmillan, 2005.

Gissibl, Bernhard, Sabine Höhler, and Patrick Kupper, eds. *Civilizing Nature: National Parks in Global Historical Perspective*. New York: Berghahn, 2015.

Gluck, Carol. *Japan's Modern Myths: Ideology in the Late Meiji Period*. Princeton, NJ: Princeton University Press, 1985.

Goksøyr, Matti. "Nationalism." In *Routledge Companion to Sports History*, edited by Steven W. Pope and John R. Nauright, 268–95. London: Routledge, 2009.

Gorski, Philip S. "The Mosaic Moment: An Early Modernist Critique of Modernist Theories of Nationalism." *American Journal of Sociology* 105, no. 5 (2000): 1428–68.

Graan, Andrew. "Counterfeiting the Nation? Skopje 2014 and the Politics of Nation Branding in Macedonia." *Cultural Anthropology* 28, no. 1 (2013): 161–79.

Grabski, Joanna. "Painting Fictions/Painting History: Modernist Pioneers at Senegal's École des Arts." *African Arts* 39, no. 1 (2006): 38–94.

Graetz, Michael. *The Jews in Nineteenth-Century France: From the French Revolution to the Alliance Israelite Universelle*. Stanford, CA: Stanford University Press, 1996.

Grant, Jill. *Planning the Good Community: New Urbanism in Theory and Practice*. London: Routledge, 2006.

Grcheva, Leonora. "The Birth of a Nationalistic Planning Doctrine: The 'Skopje 2014' Project." *International Planning Studies* 24, no. 2 (2019): 140–55.

Green, Toby. *A Fistful of Shells: West Africa from the Rise of the Slave Trade to the Age of Revolution*. London: Allen Lane, 2019.

Greene, Jack P. "State and National Identities in the Era of the American Revolution." In *Nationalism in the New World*, edited by Don H. Doyle and Marco Antonio Pamplona, 61–80. Athens: University of Georgia Press, 2006.

Greene, Kenneth F. "The Political Economy of Authoritarian Single-Party Dominance." *Comparative Political Studies* 43, no. 7 (2010): 807–34.

Greenfeld, Liah. *Nationalism: Five Roads to Modernity*. Cambridge, MA: Harvard University Press, 1992.

Greenhalgh, Paul. *Fair World: A History of World's Fairs and Expositions, from London to Shanghai 1851–2010*. Winterbourne, UK: Papadakis, 2011.

Griffin, Patrick, Robert G. Ingram, Peter S. Onuf, and Brian Schoen, eds. *Between Sovereignty and Anarchy: The Politics of Violence in the American Revolutionary Era*. Charlottesville: University of Virginia Press, 2015.

Gröning, Gert, and Joachim Wolschke-Bulmahn. "The Native Plant Enthusiasm: Ecological Panacea or Xenophobia?" *Landscape Research* 28, no. 1 (2003): 75–88.

Grosby, Steven. *Biblical Ideas of Nationality: Ancient and Modern*. Winona Lake, IN: Eisenbrauns, 2002.

———. *Nations and Nationalism in World History*. New York: Routledge, 2022.

Grosby, Steven, Joep Leerssen, and Caspar Hirschi. "Continuities and Shifting Paradigms: A Debate on Caspar Hirschi's *The Origins of Nationalism*." *Studies on National Movements* 2, no. 1 (2014): 1–48.

Guha-Thakurta, Tapati. *Monuments, Objects, Histories: Institutions of Art in Colonial and Postcolonial India*. New York: Columbia University Press, 2004.

Guo, Shibao, and Lloyd Wong. *Revisiting Multiculturalism in Canada: Theories, Policies and Debates*. Transnational Migration and Education. Rotterdam: Sense, 2015.

Gutiérrez Viñuales, Rodrigo. "Arquitectura de raíces hispanas: Entre los 'estilos californianos' y el neocolonial (1880–1940)." In *Baja California: Herencia, memoria e identidad patrimonial*, edited by Miguel Angel Sorroche Cuerva, 281–307. Granada: Atrio, 2014.

———. "Arquitectura historicista de raíces prehispánicas." *Goya*, no. 289–290 (2002): 267–86.

———. *Monumento conmemorativo y espacio público en Iberoamérica*. Madrid: Cátedra, 2004.

Guy, Kolleen M. "Regional Foods." In *Regionalism and Modern Europe: Identity Construction and Movements from 1890 to the Present Day*, edited by Xosé M. Núñez Seixas and Eric Storm, 83–99. London: Bloomsbury, 2019.

———. *When Champagne Became French: Wine and the Making of a National Identity*. Baltimore: Johns Hopkins University Press, 2003.

Habermas, Jürgen. *The Structural Transformation of the Public Sphere: An Inquiry into a Category of Bourgeois Society*. Cambridge, MA: MIT Press, 1989.

Hacisalihoğlu, Mehmet. "Inclusion and Exclusion: Conscription in the Ottoman Empire." *Journal of Modern European History* 5, no. 2 (2007): 264–86.

Hackmann, Jörg. "Baltic and Polish Regionalism(s): Concepts, Dimensions and Trajectories." In *Regionalism and Modern Europe: Identity Construction and Movements from 1890 to the Present Day*, edited by Xosé M. Núñez Seixas and Eric Storm, 291–307. London: Bloomsbury, 2019.

Hadj-Moussa, Ratiba. *The Public Sphere and Satellite Television in North Africa: Gender, Identity, Critique*. Newcastle: Cambridge Scholars, 2018.

Hagemann, Karen. *"Mannlicher Muth und teutsche Ehre": Nation, Militär und Geschlecht zur Zeit der antinapoleonischen Kriege Preußens*. Paderborn: Schöningh, 2002.

Hagen, Joshua. *Preservation, Tourism and Nationalism: The Jewel of the German Past*. Aldershot, UK: Ashgate, 2006.

Hakenbeck, Susanne E. "Genetics, Archaeology and the Far Right: An Unholy Trinity." *World Archaeology* 51, no. 4 (2019): 517–27.

Hale, John. *The Civilization of Europe in the Renaissance*. London: Fontana Press, 1994.

Hall, Catherine. *Civilising Subjects: Metropole and Colony in the English Imagination, 1830–1867*. Cambridge: Polity, 2002.

Hall, Peter. *Cities of Tomorrow: An Intellectual History of Urban Planning and Design in the Twentieth Century*. Oxford: Blackwell, 2002.

Hamnett, Brian R. *The End of Iberian Rule on the American Continent, 1770–1830*. Cambridge: Cambridge University Press, 2017.

Hanioğlu, M. Şükrü. *A Brief History of the Late Ottoman Empire*. Princeton, NJ: Princeton University Press, 2008.

Hantsch, Hugo. "Pan-Slavism, Austro-Slavism, Neo-Slavism: The All-Slav Congresses and the Nationality Problems of Austria-Hungary." *Austrian History Yearbook* 1 (February 1965): 23–37.

Harmes, Adam. "The Rise of Neoliberal Nationalism." *Review of International Political Economy* 19, no. 1 (2012): 59–86.

Harp, Stephen L. *Marketing Michelin: Advertising and Cultural Identity in Twentieth-Century France*. Baltimore: Johns Hopkins University Press, 2001.

Harrell, Stevan. "The Four Horsemen of the Ecopocalypse: The Agricultural Ecology of the Great Leap Forward." *Human Ecology* 49, no. 1 (2021): 7–18.

Harris, Bernard. *The Origins of the British Welfare State: Society, State, and Social Welfare in England and Wales, 1800–1945*. Basingstoke, UK: Palgrave Macmillan, 2004.

Harrison, Charles, Francis Frascina, and Gillian Perry. *Primitivism, Cubism, Abstraction: The Early Twentieth Century*. New Haven, CT: Yale University Press, 1993.

Harrison, Henrietta. *China: Inventing the Nation*. London: Bloomsbury, 2011.

Hartog, François. *Regimes of Historicity: Presentism and Experiences of Time*. New York: Columbia University Press, 2015.

Harvey, David. *A Brief History of Neoliberalism*. Oxford: Oxford University Press, 2005.

———. *The Condition of Postmodernity: An Enquiry into the Origins of Cultural Change*. Oxford: Blackwell, 1989.

Harvey, John Layton. "Robert Roswell Palmer: A Transatlantic Journey of American Liberalism." *Historical Reflections* 37, no. 3 (2011): 1–17.

Haslinger, Peter. "How to Run a Multilingual Society: Statehood, Administration and Regional Dynamics in Austria-Hungary, 1867–1914." In *Region and State in Nineteenth-Century Europe: Nation-Building, Regional Identities and Separatism*, edited by Joost Augusteijn and Eric Storm, 111–31. Basingstoke, UK: Palgrave Macmillan, 2012.

Hassan, Salah M. "Contemporary African Art as a Paradox." *NKA Journal of Contemporary African Art*, no. 46 (2020): 8–26.

Hastings, Adrian. *The Construction of Nationhood Ethnicity, Religion and Nationalism*. Cambridge: Cambridge University Press, 1997.

Hastings, Derek. *Nationalism in Modern Europe: Politics, Identity and Belonging since the French Revolution*. London: Bloomsbury, 2019.

Hattam, Victoria C. *Labor Visions and State Power: The Origins of Business Unionism in the United States*. Princeton, NJ: Princeton University Press, 1993.

Hawkins, Mike. *Social Darwinism in European and American Thought, 1860–1945: Nature as Model and Nature as Threat.* Cambridge: Cambridge University Press, 2003.

Hay, Roy, and Tony Joel. "Football's World Cup and Its Fans—Reflections on National Styles: A Photo Essay on Germany 2006." *Soccer and Society* 8, no. 1 (2007): 1–32.

Hayes, Joy. "'Touching the Sentiments of Everyone': Nationalism and State Broadcasting in Thirties Mexico." *Communication Review* 1, no. 4 (1996): 411–39.

Hedinger, Daniel. *Im Wettstreit mit dem Westen: Japans Zeitalter der Ausstellungen 1854–1941.* Frankfurt: Campus Verlag, 2011.

Hein, Carola, Jeffry M. Diefendorf, and Yorifusa Ishida, eds. *Rebuilding Urban Japan after 1945.* Basingstoke, UK: Palgrave Macmillan, 2003.

Heintze, James. "When in the Course of Human Events It Became Necessary to Celebrate July 4th." *Phi Kappa Phi Forum* 89, no. 2 (2009): 4–6.

Helleiner, Eric. *The Making of National Money: Territorial Currencies in Historical Perspective.* Ithaca, NY: Cornell University Press, 2003.

Helmreich, Anne. *The English Garden and National Identity: The Competing Styles of Garden Design, 1870–1914.* Cambridge: Cambridge University Press, 2002.

Helstosky, Carol. "Fascist Food Politics: Mussolini's Policy of Alimentary Sovereignty." *Journal of Modern Italian Studies* 9, no. 1 (2004): 1–26.

Hemstad, Ruth. "Scandinavianism." *Contributions to the History of Concepts* 13, no. 1 (2018): 1–21.

Hendrickson, David C. *Peace Pact: The Lost World of the American Founding.* Lawrence: University Press of Kansas, 2006.

Herb, Guntram Doyle Henrik. *Under the Map of Germany: Nationalism and Propaganda, 1918–1945.* London: Routledge, 1997.

Herbelin, Caroline. *Architectures du Vietnam colonial: Repenser le métissage.* Paris: CTHS-INHA, 2016.

Herzog, Tamar. *Defining Nations: Immigrants and Citizens in Early Modern Spain and Spanish America.* New Haven, CT: Yale University Press, 2003.

Heurlin, Christopher. "Authoritarian Aid and Regime Durability: Soviet Aid to the Developing World and Donor-Recipient Institutional Complementarity and Capacity." *International Studies Quarterly* 64, no. 1 (2020): 968–79.

Hill, Christopher L. *National History and the World of Nations: Capital, State, and the Rhetoric of History in Japan, France and the United States.* Durham: Duke University Press, 2009.

Hirsch, Francine. *Empire of Nations: Ethnographic Knowledge and the Making of the Soviet Union.* Ithaca, NY: Cornell University Press, 2005.

Hirschi, Caspar. *The Origins of Nationalism: An Alternative History from Ancient Rome to Early Modern Germany.* Cambridge: Cambridge University Press, 2012.

Hirsh, Sharon L. "Swiss Art and National Identity at the Turn of the Twentieth Century." In *Art, Culture and National Identity in Fin-de-Siècle Europe*, edited by Michelle Facos and Sharon L. Hirsh, 250–87. Cambridge: Cambridge University Press, 2003.

Hobsbawm, Eric. *The Age of Empire, 1875–1914.* New York: Vintage, 1989.

———. *The Age of Extremes: A History of the World, 1914–1991.* New York: Vintage, 1996.

———. "Mass-Producing Traditions: Europe, 1870–1914." In *The Invention of Tradition*, edited by Eric Hobsbawm and Terence Ranger, 263–309. Cambridge: Canto, 1992.

———. *Nations and Nationalism since 1780: Programme, Myth, Reality.* Cambridge: Cambridge University Press, 1990.

Holguín, Sandie. *Flamenco Nation: The Construction of Spanish National Identity*. Madison: University of Wisconsin Pres, 2019.

———. "Music and Spanish Nationalism." In *Metaphors of Spain: Representations of Spanish National Identity in the Twentieth Century*, edited by Javier Moreno Luzón and Xosé M. Núñez Seixas, 219–39. New York: Berghahn, 2017.

Holslag, Jonathan. *World Politics since 1989*. Cambridge: Polity, 2021.

Honour, Hugh. *Neo-classicism: Style and Civilization*. Harmondsworth, UK: Penguin, 1968.

Hopkin, David M. "Regionalism and Folklore." In *Regionalism and Modern Europe: Identity Construction and Movements From 1890 to the Present Day*, edited by Xosé Manoel Núñez Seixas and Eric Storm, 43–65. London: Bloomsbury, 2019.

Horne, John. "Sports Mega-Events." In *Research Handbook on Sports and Society*, edited by Elizabeth Pike, 128–42. Northampton, UK: Elgar, 2021.

Hosking, Geoffrey. *Russia: People and Empire, 1552–1917*. London: HarperCollins, 1997.

Hospers, Gert-Jan. "Industrial Heritage Tourism and Regional Restructuring in the European Union." *European Planning Studies* 10, no. 3 (2002): 397–404.

House, John, ed. *Landscapes of France: Impressionism and Its Rivals*. London: Hayward Gallery, 1995.

Houston, R. A. *Literacy in Early Modern Europe: Culture and Education 1500–1800*. Abingdon, UK: Routledge, 2002.

———. "People, Space, and Law in Late Medieval and Early Modern Britain and Ireland." *Past and Present* 230, no. 1 (2016): 47–89.

Howard, Michael. *War in European History*. Oxford: Oxford University Press, 2009.

Hoxie, Frederick E. *A Final Promise: The Campaign to Assimilate the Indians, 1880–1920*. Lincoln: University of Nebraska Press, 2001.

Hroch, Miroslav. *Social Preconditions of National Revival in Europe: A Comparative Analysis of the Social Composition of Patriotist Groups among the Smaller European Nations*. New York: Columbia University Press, 2000.

Huber, Marie. "Creating Destinations for a Better Tomorrow: UN Development Aid for Cultural Tourism in the 1960s." *Journal of Contemporary History* 57, no. 2 (2021): 317–40.

Huber, Valeska. "Introduction: Global Histories of Social Planning." *Journal of Contemporary History* 52, no. 1 (2017): 3–15.

Hughes, H. Stuart. *Consciousness and Society: The Reorientation of European Social Thought, 1890–1930*. New York: Vintage Books, 1961.

Hunt, Lynn. *Politics, Culture, and Class in the French Revolution*. Berkeley: University of California Press, 2004.

Huntington, Samuel P. *The Third Wave: Democratization in the Late Twentieth Century*. Norman: University of Oklahoma Press, 1991.

Hupchick, Dennis P. *The Balkans: From Constantinople to Communism*. Basingstoke, UK: Palgrave Macmillan, 2002.

Hutchinson, John. *Nationalism and War*. Oxford: Oxford University Press, 2017.

Hutchinson, John, Chris Wickham, Bo Stråth, and Azar Gat. "Debate on Azar Gat's *Nations: The Long History and Deep Roots of Political Ethnicity and Nationalism*." *Nations and Nationalism* 21, no. 3 (2015): 383–402.

Hylton, J. Gordon. "Before the Redskins Were the Redskins: The Use of Native American Team Names in the Formative Era of American Sports, 1857–1933." *North Dakota Law Review* 86, no. 4 (2010): 879–904.

Hyslop, Beatrice F. "The Theater during a Crisis: The Parisian Theater during the Reign of Terror." *Journal of Modern History* 17, no. 4 (1945): 332–55.

Ichijo, Atsuko, and Ronald Ranta. *Food, National Identity and Nationalism: From Everyday to Global Politics*. Basingstoke, UK: Palgrave Macmillan, 2016.

Iles, Jennifer. "In Remembrance: The Flanders Poppy." *Mortality* 13, no. 3 (2008): 201–21.

Islam, M. Rafiqul. "Secessionist Self-Determination: Some Lessons from Katanga, Biafra, and Bangladesh." *Journal of Peace Research* 22, no. 3 (1985): 211–21.

Israel, Jonathan I. *A Revolution of the Mind: Radical Enlightenment and the Intellectual Origins of Modern Democracy*. Princeton, NJ: Princeton University Press, 2010.

Jackson, Alvin. "'Prison of the Nations?' Union and Nationality in the United Kingdom, 1870–1925." In *Sovereignty, Nationalism, and the Quest for Homogeneity in Interwar Europe*, edited by Emmanuel Dalle Mulle, Davide Rodogno, and Mona Bieling, 39–60. London: Bloomsbury, 2023.

Jaffrelot, Christophe. *Modi's India: Hindu Nationalism and the Rise of Ethnic Democracy*. Princeton, NJ: Princeton University Press, 2021.

James, Harold. "Die D-Mark." In *Deutsche Erinnerungsorte*, vol. 2, edited by Etienne François and Hagen Schulze, 434–50. Munich: Beck, 2001.

Jankowski, James P. *Nasser's Egypt, Arab Nationalism, and the United Arab Republic*. Boulder, CO: Lynne Rienner, 2002.

Jansen, Jan C., and Jürgen Osterhammel. *Decolonization: A Short History*. Princeton, NJ: Princeton University Press, 2017.

Jansen, Marius B. *The Making of Modern Japan*. Cambridge, MA: Belknap, 2002.

Jarboe, Andrew T. "The Long Road Home: Britain, Germany and the Repatriation of Indian Prisoners of War after the First World War." In *Colonial Soldiers in Europe, 1914–1945: "Aliens in Uniform" in Wartime Societies*, edited by Eric Storm and Ali Al Tuma, 140–61. London: Routledge, 2016.

Jarvie, Grant. "Highland Gatherings, Balmorality, and the Glamour of Backwardness." *Sociology of Sport Journal* 9, no. 2 (1992): 167–78.

Jelidi, Charlotte. "Le transfert intra-maghrébin d'une politique patrimoniale en contexte colonial: Le baron d'Erlanger, Sidi Bou Saïd et la préservation de l'architecture dite 'arabe' en Tunisie (1910–1932)." In *Villes maghrébines en situations coloniales*, edited by Charlotte Jelidi, 269–95. Paris: Karthala, 2014.

Jencks, Charles. *The Story of Post-modernism: Five Decades of the Ironic, Iconic and Critical in Architecture*. Chichester, UK: Wiley, 2011.

Jensen, Lotte, ed. *The Roots of Nationalism: National Identity Formation in Early Modern Europe, 1600–1815*. Amsterdam: Amsterdam University Press, 2016.

Jensen, Robert. *Marketing Modernism in Fin-de-Siècle Europe*. Princeton, NJ: Princeton University Press, 1994.

Jirat-Wasiutyński, Vojtěch, ed. *Modern Art and the Idea of the Mediterranean*. Toronto: University of Toronto Press, 2007.

Johnson, Laura B., Jordan P. Howell, and Kyle T. Evered. "'Where Nothing Was Before': (Re)Producing Population and Place in Ghana's Volta River Project." *Journal of Cultural Geography* 32, no. 2 (2015): 195–213.

Jones, Caroline A. *The Global Work of Art: World's Fairs, Biennials, and the Aesthetics of Experience*. Chicago: Chicago University Press, 2016.

Jones, Matthew. *Conflict and Confrontation in South East Asia, 1961–1965: Britain, the United States, and the Creation of Malaysia*. Cambridge: Cambridge University Press, 2001.

Jong, Ad de. *De dirigenten van de herinnering: Musealisering en nationalisering van de volkscultuur in Nederland 1815–1940*. Nijmegen: SUN, 2001.

Josefsen, Eva, Ulf Mörkenstam, and Jo Saglie. "Different Institutions within Similar States: The Norwegian and Swedish Sámediggis." *Ethnopolitics* 14, no. 1 (2015): 32–51.

Jourdan, Annie. "France, Patrie, Nation: Figures de lutte et discours national (XVIème–XIXème siècles)." *European Review of History* 21, no. 1 (2014): 37–57.

———. "The Netherlands in the Constellation of the Eighteenth-Century Western Revolutions." *European Review of History:* 18, no. 2 (2011): 199–225.

Jovic, Dejan. "The Disintegration of Yugoslavia: A Critical Review of Explanatory Approaches." *European Journal of Social Theory* 4, no. 1 (2001): 101–20.

Judge, Jane C. *The United States of Belgium: The Story of the First Belgian Revolution*. Leuven: Leuven University Press, 2018.

Judson, Pieter M. *The Habsburg Empire: A New History*. Cambridge, MA: Belknap Press of Harvard University Press, 2016.

———. "Making Minorities and Majorities: National Indifference and National Self-Determination in Habsburg Central Europe." In *Sovereignty, Nationalism, and the Quest for Homogeneity in Interwar Europe*, edited by Emmanuel Dalle Mulle, Davide Rodogno, and Mona Bieling, 21–38. London: Bloomsbury, 2023.

Judt, Tony. *Postwar: A History of Europe since 1945*. New York: Penguin, 2005.

Kallestrup, Shona. "Romanian 'National Style' and the 1906 Bucharest Jubilee Exhibition." *Journal of Design History* 15, no. 3 (January 1, 2002): 147–62.

Kallis, Aristotle A. *The Third Rome, 1922–1943: The Making of the Fascist Capital*. Basingstoke, UK: Palgrave Macmillan, 2014.

Kamusella, Tomasz. *The Politics of Language and Nationalism in Modern Central Europe*. Basingstoke, UK: Palgrave Macmillan, 2009.

Kappeler, Andreas. *The Russian Empire: A Multiethnic History*. New York: Routledge, 2013.

Karch, Brendan. "Instrumental Nationalism in Upper Silesia." In *National Indifference and the History of Nationalism in Modern Europe*, edited by Maarten Van Ginderachter and Jon E. Fox, 180–204. London: Routledge, 2019.

Kater, Michael H. "Forbidden Fruit? Jazz in the Third Reich." *American Historical Review* 94, no. 1 (1989): 11–43.

Kaufmann, Thomas DaCosta. *Toward a Geography of Art*. Chicago: University of Chicago Press, 2004.

Kazantscv, Andrei A., Peter Rutland, Svetlana M. Medvedeva, and Ivan A. Safranchuk. "Russia's Policy in the 'Frozen Conflicts' of the Post-Soviet Space: From Ethno-Politics to Geopolitics." *Caucasus Survey* 8, no. 2 (2020): 142–62.

Keating, Michael. *Rescaling the European State: The Making of Territory and the Rise of the Meso*. Oxford: Oxford University Press, 2013.

Keitner, Chimène I. *The Paradoxes of Nationalism: The French Revolution and Its Meaning for Contemporary Nation Building*. Albany: State University of New York Press, 2007.

Kelbaugh, Douglas S. *Repairing the American Metropolis: Common Place Revisited*. Seattle: University of Washington Press, 2002.

Kershaw, Ian. *The Global Age: Europe, 1950–2017*. New York: Viking, 2018.

Kete, Kathleen. *The Beast in the Boudoir: Petkeeping in Nineteenth-Century Paris*. Berkeley: University of California Press, 1997.

Keys, Barbara J. *Globalizing Sport: National Rivalry and International Community in the 1930s*. Cambridge, MA: Harvard University Press, 2013.

———. "International Relations." In *Routledge Companion to Sports History*, edited by Steven W. Pope and John R. Nauright, 248–68. London: Routledge, 2009.

Kheng, Cheah Boon. "Writing Indigenous History in Malaysia: A Survey on Approaches and Problems." *Crossroads: An Interdisciplinary Journal of Southeast Asian Studies* 10, no. 2 (1996): 33–81.

Kieser, Hans-Lukas. "Die Herausbildung des nationalistischen Geschichtsdiskurses in der Türkei (spätes 19.–Mitte 20. Jahrhundert)." In *Beruf und Berufung: Geschichtswissenschaft und Nationsbildung in Ostmittel- und Südosteuropa im 19. und 20. Jahrhundert*, edited by Markus Krzoska and Hans-Christian Maner, 59–98. Münster: Lit, 2005.

King, Jeremy. *Budweisers into Czechs and Germans: A Local History of Bohemian Politics, 1848–1948*. Princeton, NJ: Princeton University Press, 2002.

Kingsbury, Damien. *Separatism and the State*. London: Routledge, 2021.

Kingston, Jeff. *Nationalism in Asia: A History since 1945*. Chichester, UK: Wiley, 2017.

Kitromilídis, Paschális M. *Enlightenment and Revolution: The Making of Modern Greece*. Cambridge, MA: Harvard University Press, 2013.

Kleinschmidt, Harald. "Plädoyer für eine kritische Historisierung des Nationenbegriffs." *Geschichte und Gesellschaft* 47, no. 3 (2021): 498–524.

Knight, Alan. "Racism, Revolution, and Indigenismo: Mexico, 1910–1940." In *The Idea of Race in Latin America, 1870–1940*, edited by Richard Graham, 71–113. Austin: University of Texas Press, 1990.

Koch, Natalie. *The Geopolitics of Spectacle: Space, Synecdoche, and the New Capitals of Asia*. Ithaca, NY: Cornell University Press, 2018.

———. "The Monumental and the Miniature: Imagining 'Modernity' in Astana." *Social and Cultural Geography* 11, no. 8 (2010): 769–87.

Koenker, Diana P. *Club Red: Vacation Travel and the Soviet Dream*. Ithaca, NY: Cornell University Press, 2013.

Kohlrausch, Martin. *Brokers of Modernity: East Central Europe and the Rise of Modernist Architects, 1910–1950*. Leuven: Leuven University Press, 2019.

Kohn, Hans. "The Paradox of Fichte's Nationalism." *Journal of the History of Ideas* 10, no. 3 (1949): 319–43.

Kok, Jan. *Beklemd in de scharnieren van de tijd: Beleid, praktijk en ervaringen van afstand ter adoptie door niet-gehuwde moeders in Nederland tussen 1956 en 1984*. The Hague: WODC, 2017.

Kolokytha, Chara. "The Debate over the Creation of a Museum of Modern Art in Paris between the Wars and the Shaping of an Evolutionary Narrative for French Art." *Il capitale culturale*, no. 14 (2016): 193–222.

Kopecký, Petr, and Gerardo Scherlis. "Party Patronage in Contemporary Europe." *European Review* 16, no. 3 (2008): 355–71.

Kornicki, P. F. "A Transnational Approach to East-Asian Book History." In *New World Order: Transnational Themes in Book History*, edited by Swapan Chakravorty and Abhijit Gupta, 65–80. Delhi: Worldview, 2011.

Koshar, Rudy. *German Travel Cultures*. Oxford: Berg, 2000.

———. *Germany's Transient Pasts: Preservation and National Memory in the Twentieth Century*. Chapel Hill: University of North Carolina Press, 1998.

Koskenniemi, Martti. *The Gentle Civilizer of Nations: The Rise and Fall of International Law, 1870–1960*. Cambridge: Cambridge University Press, 2002.

Kossmann, Ernst H. *De Lage Landen 1780–1940: Anderhalve eeuw Nederland en België*. Amsterdam: Elsevier, 1984.

Kraan, Hans. *Dromen van Holland: Buitenlandse kunstenaars schilderen Holland, 1800–1914*. Zwolle, Netherlands: Waanders, 2002.

Kraay, Hendrik. *Days of National Festivity in Rio de Janeiro, Brazil, 1823–1889*. Stanford, CA: Stanford University Press, 2013.

Kramer, Lloyd S. *Nationalism in Europe and America: Politics, Cultures, and Identities since 1775*. Chapel Hill: University of North Carolina Press, 2011.

Krawietz, Birgit. "Sport and Nationalism in the Republic of Turkey." *The International Journal of the History of Sport* 31, no. 3 (2014): 336–46.

Krier, Léon. *Albert Speer: Architecture, 1932–1942*. New York: Monacelli, 2013.

Kristoffersson, Sara. *Design by IKEA: A Cultural History*. London: Bloomsbury, 2014.

Krzyzaniak, John S. "The Soft Power Strategy of Soccer Sponsorships." *Soccer and Society* 19, no. 4 (2018): 498–515.

Kühschelm, Oliver. "Buy National Campaigns: Patriotic Shopping and the Capitalist Nation State." *Journal of Modern European History* 18, no. 1 (2020): 79–95.

Kultermann, Udo. *Geschichte der Kunstgeschichte: Der Weg einer Wissenschaft*. München: Prestel, 1990.

———. "Histoire de l'art et identité nationale." In *Histoire de l'histoire de l'art*, edited by Edouard Pommier, 2:223–47. Paris: Musée du Louvre, 1997.

Kumar, Krishan. *The Making of English National Identity*. Cambridge: Cambridge University Press, 2003.

Küpper, Joachim. "The Early Modern European Drama and the Cultural Net: Some Basic Hypotheses." In *Theatre Cultures within Globalising Empires*, edited by Joachim Küpper and Leonie Pawlita, 1–12. Berlin: De Gruyter, 2018.

Kupper, Patrick. *Creating Wilderness: A Transnational History of the Swiss National Park*. New York: Berghahn, 2014.

Kymlicka, Will. "Liberal Multiculturalism: Western Models, Global Trends, and Asian Debates." In *Multiculturalism in Asia*, edited by Will Kymlicka and Baogang He, 23–55. Oxford: Oxford University Press, 2005.

———. "Nation-Building and Minority Rights: Comparing Africa and the West." In *Ethnicity and Democracy in Africa*, edited by Bruce Berman, Dickson Eyoh, and Will Kymlicka, 54–71. Oxford: James Currey, 2004.

———. "Neoliberal Multiculturalism?" In *Social Resilience in the Neoliberal Era*, edited by Michèle Lamont and Peter A. Hall, 99–126. Cambridge: Cambridge University Press, 2013.

Kymlicka, Will, and Sue Donaldson. "Animal Rights, Multiculturalism, and the Left." *Journal of Social Philosophy* 45, no. 1 (2014): 116–35.

Kymlicka, Will, and Baogang He, eds. *Multiculturalism in Asia*. Oxford: Oxford University Press, 2005.

Labbé, Morgane. "National Indifference, Statistics and the Constructivist Paradigm: The Case of the Tutejsi ('the People from Here') in Interwar Polish Censuses." In *National Indifference and the History of Nationalism in Modern Europe*, edited by Maarten Van Ginderachter and Jon E. Fox, 161–80. London: Routledge, 2019.

Labrie, Arnold. "Van patriotisme tot nationalisme: Patria en natio voor 1815." In *Nationalisme, naties en staten: Europa vanaf circa 1800 tot heden*, edited by Leo H. M. Wessels and Toon Bosch, 104–58. Nijmegen: Vantilt, 2012.

Labzaé, Mehdi, and Sabine Planel. "La République fédérale démocratique en guerre: Mobilisations nationalistes, ordre martial et renouveaux partisans en Éthiopie." *Politique africaine* 164, no. 4 (2021): 141–64.

La Follette, Laetitia. "Looted Antiquities, Art Museums and Restitution in the United States since 1970." *Journal of Contemporary History* 52, no. 3 (2017): 669–87.

Laing, Anna F. "Re-producing Territory: Between Resource Nationalism and Indigenous Self-Determination in Bolivia." *Geoforum* 108 (2020): 28–38.

Lajosi, Krisztina, and Andreas Stynen. Introduction to *Choral Societies and Nationalism in Europe*, edited by Krisztina Lajosi and Andreas Stynen, 1–13. Leiden: Brill, 2015.

———, eds. *The Matica and Beyond: Cultural Associations and Nationalism in Europe*. Leiden: Brill, 2020.

Landau, Paul. "Language." In *Missions and Empire*, edited by Norman Etherington, 194–216. Oxford History of the British Empire Companion Series. Oxford: Oxford University Press, 2005.

Landes, Joan B. *Women and the Public Sphere in the Age of the French Revolution*. Ithaca, NY: Cornell University Press, 1988.

Lane, Barbara Miller. *National Romanticism and Modern Architecture in Germany and the Scandinavian Countries*. Cambridge: Cambridge University Press, 2000.

Langewiesche, Dieter, ed. *Liberalismus im 19. Jahrhundert: Deutschland im europäischen Vergleich*. Göttingen: Vandenhoeck & Ruprecht, 1988.

Laqua, Daniel. "Exhibiting, Encountering and Studying Music in Interwar Europe: Between National and International Community." In *European Encounters: Intellectual Exchange and the Rethinking of Europe, 1914–1945*, edited by Carlos Reijnen and Marleen Rensen, 207–23. Amsterdam: Rodopi, 2014.

Lasansky, D. Medina. *The Renaissance Perfected: Architecture, Spectacle, and Tourism in Fascist Italy*. University Park: Pennsylvania State University Press, 2004.

Latham, Michael. "Modernization." In *The Cambridge History of Science*, vol. 7, *The Modern Social Sciences*, edited by Theodore M. Porter and Dorothy Ross, 721–34. Cambridge: Cambridge University Press, 2003.

Laudan, Rachel. *Cuisine and Empire: Cooking in World History*. Berkeley: University of California Press, 2013.

Laven, David. "Italy: The Idea of the Nation in the Risorgimento and Liberal Eras." In *What Is a Nation? Europe 1789–1914*, edited by Timothy Baycroft and Mark Hewitson, 255–72. Oxford: Oxford University Press, 2006.

Lavenir, Catherine Bertho. *La roue et le stylo: comment nous sommes devenus touristes*. Paris: Odile Jacob, 1999.

Lebra, Joyce C. *The Indian National Army and Japan*. Singapore: Institute of South East Asian Studies, 2008.

Lee, Erika. "The 'Yellow Peril' and Asian Exclusion in the Americas." *Pacific Historical Review* 76, no. 4 (2007): 537–62.

Lee, Grace. "The Political Philosophy of Juche." *Stanford Journal of East Asian Affairs* 3, no. 1 (2003): 105–13.

Lee, Stephen J. *European Dictatorships, 1918–1945*. Abingdon, UK: Routledge, 2008.

Leerssen, Joep. "Collective Memories, Embodied Communities, Festivals and Commemorations." In *Encyclopedia of Romantic Nationalism in Europe*, edited by Joep Leerssen, 149–51. Amsterdam: Amsterdam University Press, 2018.

———, ed. *Encyclopedia of Romantic Nationalism in Europe*. 2 vols. Amsterdam: Amsterdam University Press, 2018.

———. *Hiding in the Popcorn: How Romantic Nationalism Survived into the 21st Century*. Amsterdam: University of Amsterdam, 2022.

———. "Language Interest." In *Encyclopedia of Romantic Nationalism in Europe*, edited by Joep Leerssen, 59–63. Amsterdam: Amsterdam University Press, 2018.

———. *National Thought in Europe: A Cultural History*. Amsterdam: Amsterdam University Press, 2006.

———. "Patriotic Poetry and Verse." In *Encyclopedia of Romantic Nationalism in Europe*, edited by Joep Leerssen, 109–11. Amsterdam: Amsterdam University Press, 2018.

———. "Romanticism, Music, Nationalism." *Nations and Nationalism* 20, no. 4 (2014): 606–27.

———. "Type, Typicality." In *Imagology: The Cultural Construction and Literary Representation of National Characters: A Critical Survey*, edited by Manfred Beller and Joep Leerssen, 450–51. Amsterdam: Rodopi, 2007.

Leerssen, Joep, and Ann Rigney, eds. *Commemorating Writers in Nineteenth-Century Europe: Nation-Building and Centenary Fever*. Basingstoke, UK: Palgrave Macmillan, 2014.

Leerssen, Joep, and Eric Storm, eds. *World Fairs and the Global Moulding of National Identities: International Exhibitions as Cultural Platforms, 1851–1958*. Leiden: Brill, 2022.

Lefaivre, Liane, and Alexander Tzonis. *Architecture of Regionalism in the Age of Globalization: Peaks and Valleys in the Flat World*. London: Routledge, 2012.

Lefèvre, Pascal. "The Construction of National and Foreign Identities in French and Belgian Postwar Comics (1939–1970)." *Comicalités*, May 2012.

LeGates, Marlene. *In Their Time: A History of Feminism in Western Society*. New York: Routledge, 2011.

Legg, Stephen. "Contesting and Surviving Memory: Space, Nation, and Nostalgia in *Les lieux de mémoire*." *Environment and Planning D: Society and Space* 23, no. 4 (2005): 481–504.

Le Hir, Marie-Pierre. *The National Habitus: Ways of Feeling French, 1789–1870*. Berlin: De Gruyter, 2014.

Lejeune, Jean-François. "Built Utopias in the Countryside: The Rural and the Modern in Franco's Spain." PhD diss., Delft University of Technology, 2019.

Leonard, Thomas M. *Central America and the United States: The Search for Stability*. Athens: University of Georgia Press, 1991.

Leonhard, Jörn. *Pandora's Box: A History of World War I*. Cambridge, MA: Harvard University Press, 2018.

Lepore, Jill. *These Truths: A History of the United States*. New York: W. W. Norton, 2018.

"Le Sacre de Charles X." Promenade en France, 2017. http://promenade34.free.fr/Documents/nostal52.htm.

Lesińska, Magdalena, and Dominik Héjj. "Pragmatic Trans-Border Nationalism: A Comparative Analysis of Poland's and Hungary's Policies towards Kin-Minorities in the Twenty-First Century." *Ethnopolitics* 20, no. 1 (2021): 53–66.

Le Tourneau, François-Michel. "O governo Bolsonaro contra os Povos Indígenas: As garantias constitucionais postas à prova." *Confins*, no. 501 (2019).

Levine, Lawrence W. "Jazz and American Culture." *Journal of American Folklore* 102, no. 403 (1989): 6–22.

Levinger, Matthew. *Enlightened Nationalism: The Transformation of Prussian Political Culture, 1806–1848.* Oxford: Oxford University Press, 2002.

Lewis, Paul. *Authoritarian Regimes in Latin America: Dictators, Despots, and Tyrants.* Lanham, MD: Rowman & Littlefield, 2006.

Lie, John. "What Is the K in K-Pop? South Korean Popular Music, the Culture Industry, and National Identity." *Korea Observer* 43, no. 3 (2012): 339–63.

Lieberman, Victor B. *Strange Parallels: Southeast Asia in Global Context, c. 800–1830.* 2 vols. Cambridge: Cambridge University Press, 2009.

Light, Richard L. "Japan." In *Routledge Companion to Sports History*, edited by Steven W. Pope and John R. Nauright, 472–87. London: Routledge, 2009.

Lindgren, Raymond E. *Norway-Sweden Union, Disunion, and Scandinavian Integration.* Princeton, NJ: Princeton University Press, 1959.

Lindqvist, Ursula. "The Cultural Archive of the IKEA Store." *Space and Culture* 12, no. 1 (2009): 43–62.

Linkiewicz, Olga. "Nationalism and Vernacular Cosmologies: Revisiting the Concept of National Indifference and the Limits of Nationalization in the Second Polish Republic." In *Sovereignty, Nationalism, and the Quest for Homogeneity in Interwar Europe*, edited by Emmanuel Dalle Mulle, Davide Rodogno, and Mona Bieling, 171–90. London: Bloomsbury, 2023.

Livezeanu, Irina, and Petru Negura. "Borderlands, Provinces, Regionalisms and Culture in East-Central Europe." In *Regionalism in Modern Europe: Identity Construction and Movements from 1890 to the Present Day*, edited by Xosé M. Núñez Seixas and Eric Storm, 251–71. London: Bloomsbury, 2019.

Livingstone, David N. *The Geographical Tradition: Episodes in the History of a Contested Enterprise.* Oxford: Blackwell, 1992.

Lobato, Ramon. *Netflix Nations: The Geography of Digital Distribution.* New York: New York University Press, 2019.

Löfgren, Orvar. *On Holiday: A History of Vacationing.* Berkeley: University of California Press, 1999.

Lommers, Suzanne. *Europe—On Air: Interwar Projects for Radio Broadcasting.* Amsterdam: Amsterdam University Press, 2013.

Long, Tom. "Historical Antecedents and Post–World War II Regionalism in the Americas." *World Politics* 72, no. 2 (2020): 214–53.

Loveman, Mara. *National Colors: Racial Classification and the State in Latin America.* Oxford: Oxford University Press, 2014.

Lowenthal, David. *The Past Is a Foreign Country*. Cambridge: Cambridge University Press, 2006.

Loyer, François. *Histoire de l'architecture française*. Vol. 3, *De la Révolution à nos jours*. Paris: Éditions du patrimoine, 1999.

Loyer, François, and Bernard Toulier, eds. *Le régionalisme, architecture, et identité*. Paris: Éditions du patrimoine, 2001.

Lübbren, Nina. *Rural Artists' Colonies in Europe, 1870–1910*. Manchester: Manchester University Press, 2001.

Lucassen, Jan, and Erik Jan Zürcher. "Introduction: Conscription and Resistance. The Historical Context." In *Arming the State: Military Conscription in the Middle East and East Asia 1775–1925*, edited by Erik J. Zürcher, 1–21. London: Tauris, 1999.

MacClain, James L. *Japan: A Modern History*. New York: Norton, 2002.

MacIntyre, W. David. *The Commonwealth of Nations: Origins and Impact, 1869–1971*. Minneapolis: University of Minnesota Press, 1977.

MacKenzie, John M. *The British Empire through Buildings: Structure, Function, Meaning*. Manchester: Manchester University Press, 2020.

MacMillan, Margaret. *Peacemakers: The Paris Conference of 1919 and Its Attempts to End War*. London: John Murray, 2001.

———. *The War That Ended Peace: How Europe Abandoned Peace for the First World War*. London: Profile, 2014.

Maier, Charles S. "'Malaise': The Crisis of Capitalism in the 1970s." In *The Shock of the Global: The 1970s in Perspective*, edited by Niall Ferguson, Charles S. Maier, Erez Manela, and Daniel J. Sargent, 25–49. Cambridge, MA: Belknap, 2010.

———. *Once within Borders: Territories of Power, Wealth, and Belonging since 1500*. Cambridge, MA: Belknap Press of Harvard University Press, 2016.

Malešević, Siniša. "Empires and Nation-States: Beyond the Dichotomy." *Thesis Eleven* 139, no. 1 (2017): 3–10.

———. *Grounded Nationalisms: A Sociological Analysis*. Cambridge: Cambridge University Press, 2019.

———. *Nation-States and Nationalisms: Organization, Ideology and Solidarity*. Cambridge: Polity Press, 2013.

———. *The Sociology of War and Violence*. Cambridge: Cambridge University Press, 2010.

Malloy, Caroline R. "Exhibiting Ireland: Irish Villages, Pavilions, Cottages, and Castles at International Exhibitions, 1853–1939." PhD diss., University of Wisconsin–Madison, 2013.

Mamadouh, Virginie, and Martin Müller. "Political Geography and Geopolitics." In *European Regions and Boundaries: A Conceptual History*, edited by Diana Mishkova and Balázs Trencsényi, 258–80. New York: Berghahn, 2017.

Mamdani, Mahmood. *When Victims Become Killers: Colonialism, Nativism, and the Genocide in Rwanda*. Princeton, NJ: Princeton University Press, 2020.

Manela, Erez. *The Wilsonian Moment: Self-Determination and the International Origins of Anticolonial Nationalism*. Oxford: Oxford University Press, 2007.

Manias, Chris. *Race, Science, and the Nation: Reconstructing the Ancient Past in Britain, France and Germany*. London: Routledge, 2013.

Manin, Bernard. *The Principles of Representative Government*. Cambridge: Cambridge University Press, 1997.

Mankoff, Jeffrey. *Empires of Eurasia: How Imperial Legacies Shape International Security.* New Haven, CT: Yale University Press, 2022.

Mann, Michael. *The Sources of Social Power.* Vol. 1, *A History of Power from the Beginning to AD 1760.* Cambridge: Cambridge University Press, 1986.

———. *The Sources of Social Power.* Vol. 2, *The Rise of Classes and Nation-States, 1760–1914.* Cambridge: Cambridge University Press, 1993.

Manovich, Lev. *Instagram and Contemporary Image.* Online, 2016. http://manovich.net/index .php/projects/instagram-and-contemporary-image.

Manuel, Peter. "Marxism, Nationalism, and Popular Music in Revolutionary Cuba." *Popular Music* 6, no. 2 (1987): 161–79.

Marácz, László. "The Roots of Modern Hungarian Nationalism: A Case Study and Research Agenda." In *The Roots of Nationalism: National Identity Formation in Early Modern Europe, 1600–1815,* edited by Lotte Jensen, 235–51. Amsterdam: Amsterdam University Press, 2016.

Marcella-Hood, Madeleine. "Scottish Style: The Construction of National Identity and Place amongst Scottish Fashion Influencers on Instagram." In *Proceedings of 21st International Foundation of Fashion Technology Institute,* 350–61. Manchester: IFFTI, 2019.

Marchand, Suzanne L. "The Rhetoric of Artifacts and the Decline of Classical Humanism: The Case of Josef Strzygowski." *History and Theory* 33, no. 4 (1994): 106–30.

Marcus, Harold G. *A History of Ethiopia.* Berkeley: University of California Press, 2002.

Marinov, Tchavdar. "Famous Macedonia, the Land of Alexander: Macedonian Identity at the Crossroads of Greek, Bulgarian and Serbian Nationalism." In *Entangled Histories of the Balkans,* vol. 1, *National Ideologies and Language Policies,* edited by Roumen Daskalov and Tchavdar Marinov, 273–331. Leiden: Brill, 2013.

Markedonov, Sergey, and David Matsaberidze. "Georgia vs. Abkhazia and Southern Ossetia." In *"Frozen Conflicts" in Europe,* edited by Anton Bebler, 71–121. Opladen, Germany: Barbara Budrich, 2015.

Martin, Terry. *The Affirmative Action Empire: Nations and Nationalism in the Soviet Union, 1923–1939.* Ithaca, NY: Cornell University Press, 2001.

Marwick, Arthur. *The Sixties: Cultural Revolution in Britain, France, Italy, and the United States, 1958–1974.* Oxford: Oxford University Press., 1998.

Mason, Laura. *Singing the French Revolution: Popular Culture and Politics, 1787–1799.* Ithaca, NY: Cornell University Press, 1996.

Matten, Marc. "Forum: Nation: Fighting for the Nation? The Campaign against Historical Nihilism in Contemporary China." *H-Soz-Kult,* September 13, 2021.

Mays, Kyle T. "Transnational Progressivism: African Americans, Native Americans, and the Universal Races Congress of 1911." *American Indian Quarterly* 37, no. 3 (2013): 243–61.

Mazower, Mark. *Dark Continent: Europe's Twentieth Century.* London: Penguin, 1998.

———. *Governing the World: The History of an Idea.* London: Penguin, 2012.

———. *Hitler's Empire: How the Nazis Ruled Europe.* New York: Penguin, 2009.

McClellan, Andrew. *Inventing the Louvre: Art, Politics, and the Origins of the Modern Museum in Eighteenth-Century Paris.* Cambridge: Cambridge University Press, 1994.

McDonald, Peter. "Migration to Australia: From Asian Exclusion to Asian Predominance." *Revue Européenne des Migrations Internationales* 35, no. 1 (2019): 87–105.

McDougall, James. *A History of Algeria.* Cambridge: Cambridge University Press, 2017.

McEvoy, Emma. *Gothic Tourism*. London: Palgrave Macmillan, 2016.

McFaul, Michael. "The Russian Federation." In *The Cambridge History of Russia*, vol. 3, *The Twentieth Century*, edited by Ronald Grigor Suny, 352–80. Cambridge: Cambridge University Press, 2006.

McGowan, Abigail. *Crafting the Nation in Colonial India*. New York: Palgrave Macmillan, 2009.

Mees, Ludger. "The Völkisch Appeal: Nazi Germany, the Basques, and the Bretons." In *War, Exile, Justice and Everyday Life, 1936–1946*, edited by Sandra Ott, 251–85. Reno: Centre for Basque Studies, 2011.

Mehta, Rini Bhattacharya. *Unruly Cinema: History, Politics, and Bollywood*. Urbana: University of Illinois Press, 2020.

Meijers, Debora J. "Naar een systematische presentatie." In *Verzamelen: Van rariteitenkabinet tot kunstmuseum*, edited by Ellinoor Bergvelt, Debora J. Meijers, and Mieke Rijnders, 225–44. Heerlen, Netherlands: Open Universiteit, 1993.

Mercier, Guy. "The Region and the State according to Friedrich Ratzel and Paul Vidal de la Blanche." *Annales de géographie* 104, no. 583 (1995): 211–35.

Merziger, Patrick. "Americanised, Europeanised or Nationalised? The Film Industry in Europe under the Influence of Hollywood, 1927–1968." *European Review of History* 20, no. 5 (2013): 793–813.

Mestyan, Adam. *Arab Patriotism: The Ideology and Culture of Power in Late Ottoman Egypt*. Princeton, NJ: Princeton University Press, 2017.

Meurs, Wim van, Robin de Bruin, Liesbeth van de Grift, Carla Hoetink, Karin van Leeuwen, and Carlos Reijnen. *The Unfinished History of European Integration*. Amsterdam: Amsterdam University Press, 2018.

Meyer, John W., John Boli, George M. Thomas, and Francisco O. Ramirez. "World Society and the Nation-State." *American Journal of Sociology* 103, no. 1 (1997): 144–81.

Meyer, Milton W. *Japan: A Concise History*. Lanham, MD: Rowman & Littlefield, 2012.

Michalski, Sergiusz. *Public Monuments: Art in Political Bondage, 1870–1997*. London: Reaktion Books, 1998.

Mick, Christoph. "Legality, Ethnicity and Violence in Austrian Galicia, 1890–1920." *European Review of History* 26, no. 5 (2019): 757–82.

Middelaar, Luuk van. *Alarums and Excursions: Improvising Politics on the European Stage*. Newcastle upon Tyne: Agenda, 2019.

Middell, Matthias, and Katja Naumann. "Global History and the Spatial Turn: From the Impact of Area Studies to the Study of Critical Junctures of Globalization." *Journal of Global History* 5, no. 1 (2010): 149–70.

Mieczkowski, Yanek. "Reagan Runs: His Campaigns for the Presidency, 1976, 1980, and 1984." In *A Companion to Ronald Reagan*, edited by Andrew L. Johns, 54–71. Malden, MA: Wiley, 2015.

Mihelj, Sabina, and César Jiménez-Martínez. "Digital Nationalism: Understanding the Role of Digital Media in the Rise of 'New' Nationalism." *Nations and Nationalism*, no. 27 (2021): 331–46.

Miladi, Noureddine. "Transformative Pan-Arab TV: National and Cultural Expression on Reality TV Programmes." *Journal of Arab and Muslim Media Research* 8, no. 2 (2015): 99–115.

Miller, Alexei. "The Romanov Empire and the Russian Nation." In *Nationalizing Empires*, edited by Stefan Berger and Alexei Miller, 309–69. Budapest: Central European University Press, 2015.

Miller, Nicola. *In the Shadow of the State: Intellectuals and the Quest for National Identity in Twentieth-Century Spanish America*. London: Verso, 1999.

———. *Republics of Knowledge: Nations of the Future in Latin America*. Princeton, NJ: Princeton University Press, 2021.

Milner, Anthony. "South East Asian Historical Writing." In *The Oxford History of Historical Writing*, vol. 4, *1800–1945*, edited by Stuart Macintyre, Juan Maiguashca, and Attila Pók, 537–59. Oxford: Oxford University Press, 2011.

Mitchell, Timothy. *Carbon Democracy: Political Power in the Age of Oil*. London: Verso, 2011.

Mitter, Partha. *Art and Nationalism in Colonial India, 1850–1922: Occidental Orientations*. Cambridge: Cambridge University Press, 1994.

Monnier, Raymonde. "The Concept of Civilisation from Enlightenment to Revolution: An Ambiguous Transfer." *Contributions to the History of Concepts* 4, no. 1 (2008): 106–36.

Moore, Aaron William. "Nationalism in Northeast Asia since 1945." In *The Oxford Handbook of the History of Nationalism*, edited by John Breuilly, 453–72. Oxford: Oxford University Press, 2013.

Moore, Jason W., ed. *Anthropocene or Capitalocene? Nature, History, and the Crisis of Capitalism*. Oakland: PM Press, 2016.

Moreno Almendral, Raúl. "Nationhood as Practice and the Modernity of Nations: A Conceptual Proposal." *Nationalities Papers* 49, no. 1 (2020): 12–29.

———. *Relatos de vida, conceptos de nación: Reino Unido, Francia, España y Portugal (1780–1840)*. Valencia: Publicacions de la Universitat de València, 2021.

Moreno Luzón, Javier. "Political Clientelism, Elites, and Caciquismo in Restoration Spain (1875–1923)." *European History Quarterly* 37, no. 3 (2007): 417–41.

Moro, Pamela. "Constructions of Nation and the Classicisation of Music: Comparative Perspectives from Southeast and South Asia." *Journal of Southeast Asian Studies* 35, no. 2 (2004): 187–211.

Morris-Suzuki, Tessa. "Becoming Japanese: Imperial Expansion and Identity Crises in the Early Twentieth Century." In *Japan's Competing Modernities: Issues in Culture and Democracy, 1900–1930*, edited by Sharon A. Minichiello, 157–80. Honolulu: University of Hawai'i Press, 1998.

———. *Re-inventing Japan: Time, Space, Nation*. Armonk, NY: M. E. Sharpe, 1998.

Moser, Sarah. "Putrajaya: Malaysia's New Federal Administrative Capital." *Cities* 27, no. 4 (2010): 285–97.

Mottier, Véronique. "Eugenics and the State: Policy-Making in Comparative Perspective." In *The Oxford Handbook of the History of Eugenics*, edited by Alison Bashford and Philippa Levine, 135–51. Oxford: Oxford University Press, 2010.

Moyn, Samuel. *Not Enough: Human Rights in an Unequal World*. Cambridge, MA: Belknap Press of Harvard University Press, 2018.

Mudde, Cas. *The Far Right Today*. Cambridge: Polity, 2020.

Mudde, Cas, and Cristóbal Rovira Kaltwasser. "Exclusionary vs. Inclusionary Populism: Comparing Contemporary Europe and Latin America." *Government and Opposition* 48, no. 2 (2013): 147–74.

Mühlhahn, Klaus. *Making China Modern: From the Great Qing to Xi Jinping*. Cambridge, MA: Harvard University Press, 2019.

Mullen, Antony. "Spectres of Thatcher: Narratives of National Identity in Contemporary Britain." PhD diss., Durham University, 2018.

Müller, Jan-Werner. *What Is Populism?* Philadelphia: University of Pennsylvania Press, 2016.

Mylonas, Harris, and Maya Tudor. *Varieties of Nationalism: Communities, Narratives, Identities*. Cambridge: Cambridge University Press, 2023.

Nakano, Yoshiko. "'Wings of the New Japan': Kamikaze, Kimonos, and Airline Branding in Postwar Japan." *Verge: Studies in Global Asias* 4, no. 1 (2018): 160–86.

Neuberger, Benyamin. "The African Concept of Balkanisation." *Journal of Modern African Studies* 14, no. 3 (1976): 523–29.

Newby, Andrew G. "'A Mere Geographical Expression'? Scotland and Scottish Identity, c. 1890–1914." In *Region and State in Nineteenth-Century Europe: Nation-Building, Regional Identities and Separatism*, edited by Joost Augusteijn and Eric Storm, 149–72. Basingstoke, UK: Palgrave Macmillan, 2012.

Nichols, Roger L. *Indians in the United States and Canada: A Comparative History*. Lincoln: University of Nebraska Press, 2018.

Nicosia, Francis R. *Nazi Germany and the Arab World*. Cambridge: Cambridge University Press, 2014.

Nielsen, Niels Kaiser. "Nordic Countries." In *Routledge Companion to Sports History*, edited by Steven W. Pope and John R. Nauright, 526–41. London: Routledge, 2009.

Nipperdey, Thomas. "Der Kölner Dom als Nationaldenkmal." In *Nachdenken über die Deutsche Geschichte*, 189–208. Munich: DTV, 1986.

———. *Deutsche Geschichte, 1800–1866: Bürgerwelt und starker Staat*. Munich: Beck, 1983.

———. *Deutsche Geschichte, 1866–1918*. Vol. 2, *Machtstaat vor der Demokratie*. Munich: Beck, 1992.

Nixon, Sean. "Trouble at the National Trust: Post-war Recreation, the Benson Report and the Rebuilding of a Conservation Organization in the 1960s." *Twentieth Century British History* 26, no. 4 (2015): 529–50.

Nora, Pierre, ed. *Les lieux de mémoire*. 3 vols. Paris: Gallimard, 1984.

Norris, Craig. "Manga, Anime and Visual Art Culture." In *The Cambridge Companion to Modern Japanese Culture*, edited by Yoshio Sugimoto, 236–60. Cambridge: Cambridge University Press, 2009.

Nowell-Smith, Geoffrey, ed. *The Oxford History of World Cinema*. Oxford: Oxford University Press, 1999.

Nugent, Paul. *Africa since Independence: A Comparative History*. Basingstoke, UK: Palgrave Macmillan, 2012.

———. *Smugglers, Secessionists and Loyal Citizens on the Ghana-Togo Frontier: The Life of the Borderlands since 1914*. Oxford: James Currey, 2002.

Nugroho, Stefani. *The Divergent Nation of Indonesia: Heterogeneous Imaginings in Jakarta, Kupang, and Banda Aceh*. Singapore: Springer, 2020.

Núñez Seixas, Xosé Manoel. *Los nacionalismos en la España contemporánea (siglos XIX y XX)*. Barcelona: Hipòtesi, 1999.

———. "Nations and Territorial Identities in Europe: Transnational Reflections." *European History Quarterly* 40, no. 4 (2010): 669–84.

———. "Wilson's Unexpected Friends: The Transnational Impact of the First World War on Western European Nationalist Movements." In *The First World War and the Nationality Question in Europe: Global Impact and Local Dynamics*, edited by Xosé M. Núñez Seixas, 37–65. Leiden: Brill, 2021.

Núñez Seixas, Xosé Manoel, and Eric Storm, eds. *Regionalism and Modern Europe: Identity Construction and Movements from 1890 to the Present Day*. London: Bloomsbury, 2019.

Nye, Robert A. *Crime, Madness, and Politics in Modern France: The Medical Concept of National Decline*. Princeton, NJ: Princeton University Press, 1984.

Nyíri, Pál, and Joana Breidenbach. "Intercultural Communication: An Anthropological Perspective." In *International Encyclopedia of the Social and Behavioral Sciences*, edited by James D. Wright, 12:357–61. Amsterdam: Elsevier, 2015.

Ockman, Joan. "New Politics of the Spectacle: 'Bilbao' and the Global Imagination." In *Architecture and Tourism: Perception, Performance and Place*, edited by D. Medina Lasansky and Brian McLaren, 227–41. Oxford: Berg, 2004.

O'Donoghue, Martin. "'Ireland's Independence Day': The 1918 Election Campaign in Ireland and the Wilsonian Moment." *European Review of History* 26, no. 5 (2019): 834–54.

O'Driscoll, Dylan, and Bahar Baser. "Referendums as a Political Party Gamble: A Critical Analysis of the Kurdish Referendum for Independence." *International Political Science Review* 41, no. 5 (2020): 652–66.

Offen, Karen M. *European Feminisms, 1700–1950: A Political History*. Stanford, CA: Stanford University Press, 2000.

———, ed. *Globalizing Feminisms, 1789–1945*. London: Routledge, 2010.

———. *The Woman Question in France, 1400–1870*. Cambridge: Cambridge University Press, 2017.

Okechukwu, Amaka. *To Fulfill These Rights: Political Struggle over Affirmative Action and Open Admissions*. New York: Columbia University Press, 2019.

Oliven, Ruben George. *Tradition Matters: Modern Gaúcho Identity in Brazil*. New York: Columbia University Press, 1996.

Olmi, Giuseppe. "Italiaanse verzamelingen van de late middeleeuwen tot het einde van de zeventiende eeuw." In *Verzamelen: Van rariteitenkabinet tot kunstmuseum*, edited by Ellinoor Bergvelt, Debora J. Meijers, and Mieke Rijnders, 93–122. Heerlen, Netherlands: Open Universiteit, 1993.

O'Malley, Alanna. *The Diplomacy of Decolonisation: America, Britain and the United Nations during the Congo Crisis 1960–64*. Manchester: Manchester University Press, 2018.

Omissi, David. "The Indian Army in Europe, 1914–1918." In *Colonial Soldiers in Europe, 1914–1945: "Aliens in Uniform" in Wartime Societies*, edited by Eric Storm and Ali al Tuma, 119–40. London: Routledge, 2016.

Ory, Pascal. *Qu'est-ce qu'une nation? Une histoire mondiale*. Paris: Gallimard, 2020.

Oshikiri, Taka. "Selling Tea as Japanese History: Culture, Consumption and International Expositions, 1873–1910." In *World Fairs and the Global Moulding of National Identities: International Exhibitions as Cultural Platforms, 1851–1958*, edited by Joep Leerssen and Eric Storm, 193–217. Leiden: Brill, 2022.

Østergård, Uffe. "Nation-Building and Nationalism in the Oldenburg Empire." In *Nationalizing Empires*, edited by Stefan Berger and Alexei Miller, 461–510. Budapest: Central European University Press, 2014.

Osterhammel, Jürgen. *The Transformation of the World: A Global History of the Nineteenth Century*. Princeton, NJ: Princeton University Press, 2014.

Özkirimli, Umut. *Contemporary Debates on Nationalism: A Critical Engagement*. Basingstoke, UK: Palgrave Macmillan, 2005.

Özkirimli, Umut, and Spyros A. Sofos. *Tormented by History: Nationalism in Greece and Turkey*. New York: Columbia University Press, 2008.

Özsu, Umut. "Fabricating Fidelity: Nation-Building, International Law, and the Greek–Turkish Population Exchange." *Leiden Journal of International Law* 24, no. 4 (2011): 823–47.

Pack, Sasha D. *Tourism and Dictatorship: Europe's Peaceful Invasion of Franco's Spain*. New York: Palgrave Macmillan, 2006.

Paletschek, Sylvia, and Bianka Pietrow-Ennker, eds. *Women's Emancipation Movements in the Nineteenth Century: A European Perspective*. Stanford, CA: Stanford University Press, 2004.

Palmer, R. R. *The Age of the Democratic Revolution: A Political History of Europe and America, 1760–1800*. Updated ed. Princeton, NJ: Princeton University Press, 2014.

Panagariya, Arvind. *India: The Emerging Giant*. New York: Oxford University Press, 2008.

Passini, Michela. *La fabrique de l'art national: Le nationalisme et les origines de l'histoire de l'art en France et en Allemagne 1870–1933*. Paris: Maison des Sciences de l'Homme, 2012.

Patel, Kiran Klaus. *Project Europe: Myths and Realities of European Integration*. Cambridge: Cambridge University Press, 2020.

Patel, Raj. "The Long Green Revolution." *Journal of Peasant Studies* 40, no. 1 (2013): 1–63.

Pater, Ben de. "Conflicting Images of the Zuider Zee around 1900: Nation-Building and the Struggle against Water." *Journal of Historical Geography* 37, no. 1 (2011): 82–94.

Pater, Ben de, and Herman van der Wusten. *Het geografische huis: De opbouw van een wetenschap*. Bussum, Netherlands: Coutinho, 1996.

Paulson-Smith, Kaden, and Aili Mari Tripp. "Women's Rights and Critical Junctures in Constitutional Reform in Africa (1951–2019)." *African Affairs* 120, no. 480 (2021): 365–89.

Pavlenko, Aneta. "Linguistic Russification in the Russian Empire: Peasants into Russians?" *Russian Linguistics* 35, no. 3 (2011): 331–50.

Pavlowitch, Stevan K. *A History of the Balkans 1804–1945*. London: Routledge, 2014.

———. *Serbia: The History of an Idea*. New York: New York University Press, 2002.

Paxton, Robert O. *The Anatomy of Fascism*. New York: Knopf, 2004.

Payne, Stanley G. *A History of Fascism, 1914–1945*. Madison: University of Wisconsin Press, 1995.

Peleggi, Maurizio. "Refashioning Civilization: Dress and Bodily Practice in Thai Nation-Building." In *The Politics of Dress in Asia and the Americas*, edited by Mina Roces and Louise P. Edwards, 65–81. Brighton: Sussex Academic Press, 2010.

De la Peña, Guillermo. "Social and Cultural Policies towards Indigenous Peoples: Perspectives from Latin America." *Annual Review of Anthropology* 34 (2005): 717–39.

Pérez Vejo, Tomás. "Nuevos enfoques teóricos en torno a las guerras de independencia." In *De colonias a estados nacionales: Independencias y descolonización en América y el mundo en los siglos XIX y XX*, edited by Enrique Ayala Mora, 91–123. Buenos Aires: Corrigedor, 2019.

Perry, Marvin. *An Intellectual History of Modern Europe*. Boston: Houghton Mifflin, 1993.

Pese, Claus, ed. *Künstlerkolonien in Europa: Im Zeichen der Ebene und des Himmels*. Nuremberg: Germanisches Nationalmuseum, 2001.

Petkova, Lilia. "The Ethnic Turks in Bulgaria: Social Integration and Impact on Bulgarian-Turkish Relations, 1947–2000." *Global Review of Ethnopolitics* 1, no. 4 (2002): 42–59.

Petrosino, Daniele. "Democracy and Regionalism in Western Europe." In *Regionalism in Modern Europe: Identity Construction and Movements From 1890 to the Present Day*, edited by Xosé M. Núñez Seixas and Eric Storm, 151–69. London: Bloomsbury, 2019.

Picard, Michel. *Bali: Cultural Tourism and Touristic Culture*. Singapore: Archipelago, 1996.

Pick, Daniel. *Faces of Degeneration: A European Disorder, c. 1848–c. 1918*. Cambridge: Cambridge University Press, 1989.

Pilcher, Jeffrey M. *¡Que Vivan Los Tamales! Food and the Making of Mexican Identity*. Albuquerque: University of New Mexico Press, 2008.

Pinchera, Valeria, and Diego Rinallo. "The Emergence of Italy as a Fashion Country: Nation Branding and Collective Meaning Creation at Florence's Fashion Shows (1951–1965)." *Business History* 62, no. 1 (2020): 151–78.

Piotrowski, Piotr. "Nationalizing Modernism: Exhibitions of Hungarian and Czechoslovakian Avant-Garde in Warsaw." In *Art Beyond Borders: Artistic Exchange in Communist Europe (1945–1989)*, edited by Jerome Bazin, Pascal Dubourg Glatigny, and Piotr Piotrowski, 209–24. Budapest: Central European University Press, 2016.

Planert, Ute. "Wann beginnt der 'moderne' deutsche Nationalismus? Plädoyer für eine nationale Sattelzeit." In *Die Politik der Nation: Deutscher Nationalismus in Krieg und Krisen 1760 bis 1960*, edited by Jörg Echternkamp and Sven O. Müller, 25–61. Berlin: De Gruyter, 2002.

Platt, Susan Noyes. "Modernism, Formalism, and Politics: The 'Cubism and Abstract Art' Exhibition of 1936 at the Museum of Modern Art." *Art Journal* 47, no. 4 (1988): 284–95.

Plokhy, Serhii. *Lost Kingdom: A History of Russian Nationalism from Ivan the Great to Vladimir Putin*. London: Allen Lane, 2017.

Polasky, Janet. *Revolutions without Borders: The Call to Liberty in the Atlantic World*. New Haven, CT: Yale University Press, 2015.

Pollmann, Judith. *Memory in Early Modern Europe, 1500–1800*. Oxford: Oxford University Press, 2017.

Postero, Nancy. "'El Pueblo Boliviano, de composición plural': A Look at Plurinationalism in Bolivia." In *The Promise and Perils of Populism: Global Perspectives*, edited by Carlos de la Torre, 395–431. Lexington: University Press of Kentucky, 2015.

Pouillard, Veronique. "Keeping Designs and Brands Authentic: The Resurgence of the Post-war French Fashion Business under the Challenge of US Mass Production." *European Review of History* 20, no. 5 (2013): 815–31.

Prak, Maarten. "Guilds and the Development of the Art Market during the Dutch Golden Age." *Simiolus* 30, no. 3/4 (2003): 236–51.

Procter, Robert. "From Anthropologie to Rassenkunde in the German Anthropological Tradition." In *Bones, Bodies, and Behavior: Essays in Behavioral Anthropology*, edited by George W. Stocking, 138–80. Madison: University of Wisconsin Press, 1988.

Purs, Aldis. "'One Breath for Every Two Strides': The State's Attempt to Construct Tourism and Identity in Interwar Latvia." In *Turizm: The Russian and East European Tourist under Capitalism and Socialism*, edited by Anne E. Gorsuch and Diana P. Koenker, 97–115. Ithaca, NY: Cornell University Press, 2006.

Quinault, Roland. "The Cult of the Centenary, c.1784–1914." *Historical Research* 71, no. 176 (1998): 303–23.

Quiroga, Alejandro. "Football and Nation: F.C. Barcelona and Athletic de Bilbao during the Franco Dictatorship (1937–1977)." *Journal of Iberian and Latin-American Studies* 26, no. 1 (2020): 65–82.

Quiroga, Alejandro, and Fernando Molina. "National Deadlock. Hot Nationalism, Dual Identities and Catalan Independence (2008–2019)." *Genealogy* 4, no. 1 (2020): 15.

Quist, Hubert Oswald. "Illiteracy, Education and National Development in Postcolonial West Africa: A Re-appraisal." *Africa Development/Afrique et développement* 19, no. 4 (1994): 127–45.

Rafael, Vicente L. "The Cultures of Area Studies in the United States." *Social Text* 41, no. 41 (1994): 91–111.

Ramirez, Francisco O., Yasemin Soysal, and Suzanne Shanahan. "The Changing Logic of Political Citizenship: Cross-National Acquisition of Women's Suffrage Rights, 1890 to 1990." *American Sociological Review* 62, no. 5 (1997): 735–45.

Rampley, Matthew. *The Vienna School of Art History: Empire and the Politics of Scholarship, 1847–1918*. University Park: Pennsylvania State University Press, 2013.

Rancier, Megan. "Resurrecting the Nomads: Historical Nostalgia and Modern Nationalism in Contemporary Kazakh Popular Music Videos." *Popular Music and Society* 32, no. 3 (2009): 387–405.

Randrianja, Solofo, and Stephen Ellis. *Madagascar: A Short History*. London: Hurst, 2009.

Ranzato, Gabriele. "Le elezioni nei sistemi liberali italiano e spagnolo." *Rivista di storia contemporanea*, no. 2 (1989): 244–63.

Reagin, Nancy R. *Sweeping the German Nation: Domesticity and National Identity in Germany, 1870–1945*. New York: Cambridge University Press, 2009.

Régent, Frédéric. "Revolution in France, Revolution in the Caribbean." In *The Routledge Companion to the French Revolution in World History*, edited by Alan Forrest and Matthias Middell, 61–77. Abingdon, UK: Routledge, 2016.

Rehling, Andrea. "Universalismen und Partikularismen im Widerstreit: Zur Genese des UNESCO-Welterbes." *Zeithistorische Forschungen* 8, no. 3 (2011): 414–36.

Reid, Donald Malcolm. *Whose Pharaohs? Archaeology, Museums, and Egyptian National Identity from Napoleon to World War I*. Berkeley: University of California Press, 2002.

Reimers, Fernando. "Education and Social Progress." In *The Cambridge Economic History of Latin America*, vol. 2, *The Long Twentieth Century*, edited by Victor Bulmer-Thomas, John Coatsworth, and Robert Cortes-Conde, 427–80. Cambridge: Cambridge University Press, 2006.

Renes, Hans, and Stefano Piastra. "Polders and Politics: New Agricultural Landscapes in Italian and Dutch Wetlands, 1920s to 1950s." *Landscapes* 12, no. 1 (May 1, 2011): 24–41.

Repp, Kevin. *Reformers, Critics, and the Paths of German Modernity: Anti-politics and the Search for Alternatives, 1890–1914*. Cambridge, MA: Harvard University Press, 2000.

Reynolds, Susan. "The Idea of the Kingdom as a Political Community." In *Power and the Nation in European History*, edited by Len Scales and Oliver Zimmer, 54–67. Cambridge: Cambridge University Press, 2005.

Reyntjens, Filip. "Understanding Rwandan Politics through the Longue Durée: From the Precolonial to the Post-genocide Era." *Journal of Eastern African Studies* 12, no. 3 (2018): 514–32.

Ribeiro de Meneses, Filipe. "The Idea of Empire in Portuguese and Spanish Life, 1890 to 1975." In *The Routledge Companion to Iberian Studies*, edited by Javier Múñoz Basols, Laura Lonsdale, and Manuel Delgado, 401–12. London: Routledge, 2017.

Richard, Anne-Isabelle. "A Global Perspective on European Cooperation and Integration since 1918." In *The Cambridge History of the European Union*, edited by Mathieu Segers and Steven Van Hecke, Vol. 2: 459–480. Cambridge: Cambridge University Press, 2023.

Ricklefs, M. C., Bruce Lockhart, Albert Lau, Portia Reyes, and Maitrii Aung-Thwin. *A New History of Southeast Asia*. Basingstoke, UK: Palgrave Macmillan, 2010.

Ridley, Jane. "Edwin Lutyens, New Delhi, and the Architecture of Imperialism." *Journal of Imperial and Commonwealth History* 26, no. 2 (1998): 67–83.

Rigney, Ann. "The Historical Novel." In *Encyclopedia of Romantic Nationalism in Europe*, edited by Joep Leerssen, 114–16. Amsterdam, 2018.

Rinke, Stefan. *Latin America and the First World War*. Cambridge: Cambridge University Press, 2017.

Riordan, James. "Russia/Soviet Union." In *Routledge Companion to Sports History*, edited by Steven W. Pope and John R. Nauright, 541–53. London: Routledge, 2009.

Rivero, Ángel. "Populism and Democracy in Europe." In *Routledge Handbook of Global Populism*, edited by Carlos de la Torre, 281–95. London: Routledge, 2018.

Robb, Graham. *The Discovery of France: A Historical Geography from the Revolution to the First World War*. New York: W. W. Norton, 2007.

Robelin, Cyril. "La plus petite communauté imaginée du monde: Le territoire neutre de Moresnet." *Language, Discourse and Society* 5 (2017): 71–89.

Roberts, Warren. *Jacques-Louis David, Revolutionary Artist: Art, Politics, and the French Revolution*. Chapel Hill: University of North Carolina Press, 2011.

Rocamora Rocamora, José Antonio. "Un nacionalismo fracasado: El iberismo." *Espacio, tiempo y forma*. Series 5, *Historia contemporánea* 2 (1989): 29–56.

Roces, Mina. "Asian Feminisms: Women's Movements from the Asian Perspective." In *Women's Movements in Asia: Feminisms and Transnational Activism*, edited by Louise P. Edwards and Mina Roces, 1–21. Abingdon, UK: Routledge, 2010.

Roces, Mina, and Louise P. Edwards, eds. *The Politics of Dress in Asia and the Americas*. Eastbourne, UK: Sussex Academic Press, 2010.

Rodogno, Davide. *Against Massacre: Humanitarian Interventions in the Ottoman Empire, 1815–1914*. Princeton, NJ: Princeton University Press, 2012.

———. "Wartime Occupation by Italy." In *The Cambridge History of the Second World War*. Vol. 2, *Politics and Ideology*, edited by Joseph Maiolo and Richard Bosworth, 436–60. Cambridge: Cambridge University Press, 2015.

Rodríguez O., Jaime E. *The Independence of Spanish America*. Cambridge: Cambridge University Press, 1998.

Rogan, Eugene. *The Arabs: A History*. London: Penguin, 2018.

Roncaglia, Alessandro. *The Wealth of Ideas: A History of Economic Thought*. Cambridge: Cambridge University Press, 2005.

Rosanvallon, Pierre. *Le sacre du citoyen: Histoire du suffrage universel en France*. Paris: Gallimard, 1992.

Roshwald, Aviel. *The Endurance of Nationalism: Ancient Roots and Modern Dilemmas*. Cambridge: Cambridge University Press, 2006.

———. *Ethnic Nationalism and the Fall of Empires: Central Europe, Russia and the Middle East, 1914–1923*. London: Routledge, 2001.

———. "Nations Are (Occasionally) Forever: Alternatives to the Modernist Perspective." In *Writing the History of Nationalism*, edited by Stefan Berger and Eric Storm, 83–105. London: Bloomsbury, 2019.

Ross, Robert. *Clothing: A Global History: Or, the Imperialists' New Clothes*. Cambridge: Polity, 2008.

———. *A Concise History of South Africa*. Cambridge: Cambridge University Press, 2008.

Rossi, Luca, Eric Boscaro, and Andrea Torsello. "Venice through the Lens of Instagram: A Visual Narrative of Tourism in Venice." In *Companion Proceedings of the Web Conference 2018*, 1190–97. Geneva: IW3C2, 2018.

Rothermund, Dietmar. *The Routledge Companion to Decolonization*. London: Routledge, 2006.

Rouvière, Nicolas. "Astérix, oeuvre gaullienne ?" In *Le tour du monde d'Astérix*, edited by Bertrand Richet, 73–86. Paris: Presses Sorbonne Nouvelle, 2018.

Rowe, Michael. "The French Revolution, Napoleon, and Nationalism in Europe." In *The Oxford Handbook of the History of Nationalism*, edited by John Breuilly, 131–48. Oxford: Oxford University Press, 2013.

Roy, Olivier. "The Failure of Political Islam Revisited." In *Pathways to Contemporary Islam: New Trends in Critical Engagement*, edited by Mohamed Nawab Mohamed Osman, 167–80. Amsterdam: Amsterdam University Press, 2020.

Rutar, Sabine. "Nationalism in Southeastern Europe, 1970–2000." In *The Oxford Handbook of the History of Nationalism*, edited by John Breuilly, 515–37. Oxford: Oxford University Press, 2013.

Rutjes, Mart. *Door gelijkheid gegrepen: Democratie, burgerschap en staat in Nederland 1795–1801*. Nijmegen: Vantilt, 2012.

Rutten, Gijsbert. *Language Planning as Nation Building: Ideology, Policy and Implementation in the Netherlands, 1750–1850*. Amsterdam: John Benjamins, 2019.

Rydell, Robert W. *All the World's a Fair: Visions of Empire at American International Expositions, 1876–1916*. Chicago: University of Chicago Press, 1984.

Rydell, Robert W., and Rob Kroes. *Buffalo Bill in Bologna: The Americanization of the World, 1869–1922*. Chicago: University of Chicago Press, 2005.

Saada, Emmanuelle. "France: The Longue Durée of French Decolonization." In *The Oxford Handbook of the Ends of Empire*, 85–102. Oxford: Oxford University Press, 2018.

Sahlins, Peter. *Boundaries: The Making of France and Spain in the Pyrenees*. Berkeley: University of California Press, 1989.

———. "The Eighteenth-Century Citizenship Revolution in France." In *Migration Control in the North Atlantic World: The Evolution of State Practices in Europe and the United States from the French Revolution to the Inter-war Period*, edited by Andreas Fahrmeir, Olivier Faron, and Patrick Weil, 11–25. New York: Berghahn, 2003.

Sakwa, Richard. *The Putin Paradox*. London: Tauris, 2020.

Samson, Jim. "Music and Nationalism: Five Historical Moments." In *Nationalism and Ethno-symbolism: History, Culture and Ethnicity in the Formation of Nations*, edited by Steven Grosby and Athena S. Leoussi, 55–68. Edinburgh: Edinburgh University Press, 2007.

Sas, Niek C. F. van. *De metamorfose van Nederland: Van oude orde naar moderniteit, 1750–1900*. Amsterdam: Amsterdam University Press, 2004.

Sayyid-Marsot, Afaf Lutfi. *A History of Egypt: From the Arab Conquest to the Present*. 2nd ed. Cambridge: Cambridge University Press, 2007.

Scheiner, Ethan. "Pipelines of Pork: Japanese Politics and a Model of Local Opposition Party Failure." *Comparative Political Studies* 38, no. 7 (2005): 799–823.

Scheipers, Sibylle, ed. *Heroism and the Changing Character of War: Toward Post-heroic Warfare?* Basingstoke, UK: Palgrave Macmillan, 2014.

Schendel, Willem van. *A History of Bangladesh.* Cambridge: Cambridge University Press, 2009.

Schmidt, Brian C. "On the History and Historiography of International Relations." In *Handbook of International Relations,* edited by Walter Carlsnaes, Thomas Risse, and Beth A. Simmons, 3–29. London: Sage, 2013.

Schmidt Burkhardt, Astrit. "Shaping Modernism: Alfred Barr's Genealogy of Art." *Word and Image* 16, no. 4 (2000): 387–400.

Schneider, Britta. "Methodological Nationalism in Linguistics." *Language Sciences* 76 (November 2019).

Schneider-Mayerson, Matthew. "Popular Fiction Studies: The Advantages of a New Field." *Studies in Popular Culture* 33, no. 1 (2010): 21–35.

Schötter, Peter. "After the Deluge: The Impact of the Two World Wars on the Historical Work of Henri Pirenne and Marc Bloch." In *Nationalizing the Past: Historians as Nation-Builders in Modern Europe,* edited by Stefan Berger and Chris Lorenz, 404–26. Basingstoke, UK: Palgrave Macmillan, 2010.

Schulze, Hagen. *Staat und Nation in der europäischen Geschichte.* Munich: Beck, 1995.

Schulz-Forberg, Hagen. "Embedding the Social Question into International Order: Economic Thought and the Origins of Neoliberalism in the 1930s." In *Nationalism and the Economy: Explorations into a Neglected Relationship,* edited by Stefan Berger and Thomas Fetzer, 249–69. Budapest: Central European University Press, 2019.

Schuster, Sven. "Colombia in the Age of Exhibitions: Envisioning the Nation in a Global Context, 1892–1929." In *World Fairs and the Global Moulding of National Identities: International Exhibitions as Cultural Platforms, 1851–1958,* edited by Joep Leerssen and Eric Storm, 237–64. Leiden: Brill, 2022.

———. *Die Inszenierung der Nation: Das Kaiserreich Brasilien im Zeitalter der Weltausstellungen.* Frankfurt: Peter Lang, 2015.

Schwyter, Jürg Rainer. *Dictating to the Mob: The History of the BBC Advisory Committee on Spoken English.* Oxford: Oxford University Press, 2016.

Seekins, Donald M. "'Runaway Chickens' and Myanmar Identity: Relocating Burma's Capital." *City* 13, no. 1 (2009): 63–70.

Shaffer, Marguerite S. *See America First: Tourism and National Identity, 1880–1940.* Washington, DC: Smithsonian Institution Press, 2002.

Shaw, Annapurna. "Town Planning in Postcolonial India, 1947–1965: Chandigarh Re-examined." *Urban Geography* 30, no. 8 (2009): 857–78.

Shedel, James. "Emperor, Church, and People: Religion and Dynastic Loyalty during the Golden Jubilee of Franz Joseph." *Catholic Historical Review* 76, no. 1 (1990): 71–92.

Shen, Jie, and Fulong Wu. "The Development of Master-Planned Communities in Chinese Suburbs: A Case Study of Shanghai's Thames Town." *Urban Geography* 33, no. 2 (2012): 183–203.

Shennan, J. H. "The Rise of Patriotism in 18th-Century Europe." *History of European Ideas* 13, no. 6 (1991): 689–710.

Shevtsova, Lilia. "Forward to the Past in Russia." In *Authoritarianism Goes Global: The Challenge to Democracy*, edited by Larry Diamond, Marc F. Plattner, and Christopher Walker, 40–57. Baltimore: Johns Hopkins University Press, 2016.

Shiner, Larry. *The Invention of Art: A Cultural History*. Chicago: University of Chicago Press, 2001.

Short, Damien. "When Sorry Isn't Good Enough: Official Remembrance and Reconciliation in Australia." *Memory Studies* 3, no. 5 (2012): 293–304.

Siegelbaum, Lewis H. *Soviet State and Society between Revolutions, 1918–1929*. Cambridge: Cambridge University Press, 1992.

Siekmeier, James F. *Latin American Nationalism: Identity in a Globalizing World*. London: Bloomsbury, 2017.

Silver, Kenneth E. *Esprit de Corps: The Art of the Parisian Avant-Garde and the First World War, 1914–1925*. Princeton, NJ: Princeton University Press, 1989.

Simpson, Gerry J. *Great Powers and Outlaw States: Unequal Sovereigns in the International Legal Order*. Cambridge: Cambridge University Press, 2004.

Sivasundaram, Sujit. *Waves across the South: A New History of Revolution and Empire*. London: William Collins, 2020.

Sivilolu, Murat R. *The Emergence of Public Opinion: State and Society in the Late Ottoman Empire*. Cambridge: Cambridge University Press, 2018.

Skey, Michael. "The Mediation of Nationhood: Communicating the World as a World of Nations." *Communication Theory* 24, no. 1 (2014): 1–20.

———. "Nationalism and Media." *Nationalities Papers*, 2022, 1–11.

———. "Sportswashing: Media Headline or Analytic Concept?" *International Review for the Sociology of Sport* 58, no. 5 (2022): 749–64.

Smith, Allan. "Seven Narratives in North American History: Thinking the Nation in Canada, Quebec and the United States." In *Writing the Nation: A Global Perspective*, edited by Stefan Berger, 63–84. Basingstoke, UK: Palgrave Macmillan, 2007.

Smith, Anthony, ed. *Television: An International History*. Oxford: Oxford University Press, 1995.

Smith, Anthony D. *Chosen Peoples: Sacred Sources of National Identity*. Oxford: Oxford University Press, 2004.

———. *The Ethnic Origins of Nations*. Oxford: Blackwell, 1986.

———. "Nationalism and Classic Social Theory." *British Journal of Sociology* 34, no. 1 (1983): 19–38.

Smith, Benjamin. "Life of the Party: The Origins of Regime Breakdown and Persistence under Single-Party Rule." *World Politics* 57, no. 3 (2005): 421–51.

Smith, Joseph. *The Spanish-American War: Conflict in the Caribbean and the Pacific, 1895–1902*. London: Longman, 1994.

Smith, Sean P. "Landscapes for 'Likes': Capitalizing on Travel with Instagram." *Social Semiotics* 31, no. 4 (2021): 604–24.

Smith, Stephanie J. *The Power and Politics of Art in Postrevolutionary Mexico*. Chapel Hill: University of North Carolina Press, 2017.

Smits, Thomas. *The European Illustrated Press and the Emergence of a Transnational Visual Culture of the News, 1842–1870*. London: Routledge, 2020.

Sobrevilla Perea, Natalia. "Nation-Making and Nationalism." In *The Andean World*, edited by Linda J. Seligmann and Kathleen S. Fine-Dare, 297–310. Abingdon, UK: Routledge, 2019.

Sohrabi, Nader. "Reluctant Nationalists, Imperial Nation-State, and Neo-Ottomanism: Turks, Albanians, and the Antinomies of the End of Empire." *Social Science History* 42, no. 4 (2018): 835–70.

———. *Revolution and Constitutionalism in the Ottoman Empire and Iran.* Cambridge: Cambridge University Press, 2011.

Somerville, Keith. *Africa's Long Road since Independence: The Many Histories of a Continent.* London: Penguin, 2017.

Sorkin, David. *Jewish Emancipation: A History across Five Centuries.* Princeton, NJ: Princeton University Press, 2019.

Soshiroda, Akira. "Inbound Tourism Policies in Japan from 1859 to 2003." *Annals of Tourism Research* 32, no. 4 (2005): 1100–1120.

Sotiropoulos, Michalis, and Antonis Hadjikyriacou. "Patris, Ethnos, and Demos: Representation and Political Participation in the Greek World." In *Re-imagining Democracy in the Mediterranean, 1780–1860,* edited by Joanna Innis and Mark Philp, 99–127. Oxford: Oxford University Press, 2018.

Souchal, François. *Le vandalisme de la Révolution.* Paris: Nouvelles Éditions Latines, 1993.

Sowerwine, Charles. *France since 1870: Culture, Politics and Society.* Basingstoke, UK: Palgrave, 2001.

———. "Revising the Sexual Contract: Women's Citizenship and Republicanism in France, 1789–1944." In *Confronting Modernity in Fin-de-Siècle France: Bodies, Minds and Gender,* edited by Christopher E. Forth and Elinor Accampo, 19–43. Basingstoke, UK: Palgrave Macmillan, 2010.

Spence, Mark David. *Dispossessing the Wilderness: Indian Removal and the Making of the National Parks.* New York; Oxford: Oxford University Press, 2000.

Sperber, Jonathan. *The European Revolutions, 1848–1851.* Cambridge: Cambridge University Press, 2005.

Starr, Kevin. *Material Dreams: Southern California through the 1920s.* New York: Oxford University Press, 1990.

Stauter-Halsted, Keely. *The Nation in the Village: The Genesis of Peasant National Identity in Austrian Poland, 1848–1914.* Ithaca, NY: Cornell University Press, 2004.

Stavans, Ilan. *José Vasconcelos: The Prophet of Race.* New Brunswick, NJ: Rutgers University Press, 2011.

Steber, Martina. *Ethnische Gewissheiten: Die Ordnung des Regionalen im bayerischen Schwaben vom Kaiserreich bis zum NS-Regime.* Göttingen: Vandenhoeck & Ruprecht, 2010.

Steen, Jasper van der. "Remembering the Revolt of the Low Countries: Historical Canon Formation in the Dutch Republic and Habsburg Netherlands, 1566–1621." *Sixteenth Century Journal* 49, no. 3 (2018): 713–42.

Steiner, Christian. "From Heritage to Hyper-Reality? Tourism Destination Development in the Middle East between Petra and the Palm." *Journal of Tourism and Cultural Change* 8, no. 4 (2010): 240–53.

Stern, Fritz. *The Politics of Cultural Despair.* Berkeley: University of California Press, 1961.

Sternhell, Zeev. *La Droite révolutionnaire, 1888–1914: Les origines françaises du fascisme.* Paris: Seuil, 1978.

———. *Maurice Barrès et le nationalisme français.* Rev. ed., Paris: Fayard, 2000.

Stierli, Martino. "Building No Place: Oscar Niemeyer and the Utopias of Brasília." *Journal of Architectural Education* 67, no. 1 (2013): 8–16.

Stolte, Carolien. "Orienting India: Interwar Internationalism in an Asian Inflection, 1917–1937." PhD diss., Leiden University, 2013.

Stolte, Carolien, and Harald Fischer-Tiné. "Imagining Asia in India: Nationalism and Internationalism (ca. 1905–1940)." *Comparative Studies in Society and History* 54, no. 1 (2012): 65–92.

Storm, Eric. "Art History." In *European Regions and Boundaries: A Conceptual History*, edited by Diana Mishkova and Balázs Trencsényi, 372–94. New York; Oxford: Berghahn, 2017.

———. "The Birth of Regionalism and the Crisis of Reason: France, Germany and Spain." In *Region and State in Nineteenth-Century Europe: Nation-Building, Regional Identities and Separatism*, edited by Joost Augusteijn and Eric Storm, 36–57. Basingstoke, UK: Palgrave Macmillan, 2012.

———. *The Culture of Regionalism: Art, Architecture and International Exhibitions in France, Germany and Spain, 1890–1939.* Manchester: Manchester University Press, 2011.

———. *The Discovery of El Greco: The Nationalization of Culture versus the Rise of Modern Art (1860–1914).* Brighton: Sussex Academic Press, 2016.

———. "The Nationalisation of the Domestic Sphere." *Nations and Nationalism* 23, no. 1 (2017): 173–93.

———. *La perspectiva del progreso: Pensamiento político en la España del cambio de siglo (1890–1914).* Madrid: Biblioteca Nueva, 2001.

———. "Tourism and the Construction of Regional Identities." In *Regionalism and Modern Europe: Identity Construction and Movements from 1890 to the Present Day*, edited by Xosé M. Núñez Seixas and Eric Storm, 99–119. London: Bloomsbury, 2019.

———. "The Transnational Construction of National Identities: A Classification of National Pavilions at World Fairs." In *World Fairs and the Global Moulding of National Identities: International Exhibitions as Cultural Platforms, 1851–1958*, edited by Joep Leerssen and Eric Storm, 53–84. Leiden: Brill, 2022.

———. "When Did Nationalism Become Banal? The Nationalization of the Domestic Sphere in Spain." *European History Quarterly* 50, no. 2 (2020): 204–25.

Storm, Eric, and Ali al Tuma, eds. *Colonial Soldiers in Europe, 1914–1945: "Aliens in Uniform" in Wartime Societies.* London: Routledge, 2015.

Stremlau, John J. *The International Politics of the Nigerian Civil War, 1967–1970.* Princeton, NJ: Princeton University Press, 1977.

Suny, Ronald Grigor. *"They Can Live in the Desert but Nowhere Else": A History of the Armenian Genocide.* Princeton, NJ: Princeton University Press, 2015.

Surkis, Judith. *Sex, Law, and Sovereignty in French Algeria, 1830–1930.* Ithaca, NY: Cornell University Press, 2019.

Sutcliffe-Braithwaite, Florence. "Neo-liberalism and Morality in the Making of Thatcherite Social Policy." *Historical Journal* 55, no. 2 (2012): 497–520.

Swart, Sandra. "The Other Citizens: Nationalism and Animals." In *The Routledge Companion to Animal-Human History*, edited by Hilda Kean and Philip Howell, 31–53. London: Routledge, 2018.

Swenson, Astrid. *The Rise of Heritage: Preserving the Past in France, Germany and England, 1789–1914.* Cambridge: Cambridge University Press, 2013.

Switzer, Terri. "Hungarian Self-Representation in an International Context: The Magyar Exhibited at International Expositions and World's Fairs." In *Art, Culture and National Identity in Fin-de-Siècle Europe*, edited by Michelle Facos and Sharon L. Hirsh, 160–86. Cambridge: Cambridge University Press, 2003.

Swyngedouw, Erik. *Liquid Power: Contested Hydro-Modernities in Twentieth-Century Spain, 1898–2010*. Cambridge, MA: MIT Press, 2015.

Takeuchi, Keiichi. "Japanese Geopolitics in the 1930s and 1940s." In *Geopolitics: An Introductory Reader*, edited by Jason Dittmer and Joanna Sharp, 67–75. London: Routledge, 2014.

Tang, Xiaobing. *Global Space and the Nationalist Discourse of Modernity: The Historical Thinking of Liang Qichao*. Stanford, CA: Stanford University Press, 1996.

Tarakçioğlu, Sait. "A Failed Project in Turkey's Sports History: The Law on Physical Education of 1938." *International Journal of the History of Sport* 31, no. 14 (2014): 1807–19.

Tavárez, Fidel J. "Building Nation-Empires in the Eighteenth-Century Iberian Atlantic." In *The Cambridge History of Nationhood and Nationalism*, vol. 2, edited by Cathie Carmichael, Matthew D'Auria, and Aviel Roshwald, 3–24. Cambridge: Cambridge University Press, 2023.

Taylor, Karin. "My Own Vikendica: Holiday Cottages as Idyll and Investment." In *Yugoslavia's Sunny Side: A History of Tourism in Socialism (1950s–1980s)*, edited by Hannes Grandits and Karin Taylor, 171–210. Budapest: Central European University Press, 2010.

Tenorio-Trillo, Mauricio. *Mexico at the World's Fairs: Crafting a Modern Nation*. Berkeley: University of California Press, 1996.

Thapar, Romila. "The Theory of Aryan Race and India: History and Politics." *Social Scientist* 24, no. 1/3 (1996): 3–29.

Ther, Philipp. "Ethnic Cleansing." In *The Oxford Handbook of Postwar European History*, edited by Dan Stone, 141–62. Oxford: Oxford University Press, 2012.

Thiesse, Anne-Marie. *La création des identités nationales: Europe XVIIIe–XXe siècle*. Paris: Seuil, 1999.

———. *Écrire la France: le mouvement littéraire régionaliste de langue française entre la Belle Époque et la Libération*. Paris: Presses Universitaires de France, 1991.

———. *The Transnational Creation of National Arts and Crafts in 19th-Century Europe*. Antwerp: Nise, 2013.

Thom, Martin. *Republics, Nations and Tribes*. London: Verso, 1995.

Tietaah, Gilbert K. M., Margaret I. Amoakohene, and Marquita S. Smith. "Continuity in Change: A History of Radio for National Development." *Radio Journal* 17, no. 2 (2019): 217–34.

Tilly, Charles. *Coercion, Capital, and European States, AD 990–1990*. Cambridge: Blackwell, 1990.

Toews, John Edward. *Becoming Historical: Cultural Reformation and Public Memory in Early Nineteenth-Century Berlin*. Cambridge: Cambridge University Press, 2004.

Toffoletti, Kim. "Sexy Women Sports Fans: Femininity, Sexuality, and the Global Sport Spectacle." *Feminist Media Studies* 17, no. 3 (2017): 457–72.

Tombs, Robert. *France, 1814–1914*. London; New York: Longman, 1996.

Tone, John Lawrence. *The Fatal Knot: The Guerrilla War in Navarre and the Defeat of Napoleon in Spain*. Chapel Hill: University of North Carolina Press, 1994.

———. *La guerrilla española y la derrota de Napoleón*. Madrid: Alianza Editorial, 1999.

Torpey, John C. *The Invention of the Passport: Surveillance, Citizenship and the State*. Cambridge: Cambridge University Press, 2000.

Torre, Carlos de la. "Populism in Latin America." In *The Oxford Handbook of Populism*, edited by Cristóbal Rovira Kaltwasser, Paul Taggert, Paulina Ochoa Espejo, and Pierre Ostiguy, 195–213. Oxford: Oxford University Press, 2017.

Tosaka, Yuji. "The Discourse of Anti-Americanism and Hollywood Movies: Film Import Controls in Japan, 1937–1941." *Journal of American–East Asian Relations* 12, no. 1–2 (2003): 59–80.

Trautsch, Jasper M. "The Origins and Nature of American Nationalism." *National Identities* 18, no. 3 (2015): 289–312.

Trenado Díaz, Marta. "The Cases of 'Stolen Children' in Spain and Ireland—Curtailing the Most Suitable Legal Framework on the Fight for 'Real' Identities." *ICL Journal* 9, no. 2 (2015).

Trigt, Paul van. "Farewell to Social Europe? An Entangled Perspective on European Disability Policies in the 1980s and 1990s." In *Marginalized Groups, Inequalities and the Post-war Welfare State*, edited by Monika Baár and Paul van Trigt, 69–80. London: Routledge, 2019.

Trom, Danny. "Natur und nationale Identität: Der Streit um den Schutz der 'Natur' um die Jahrhundertwende in Deutschland und Frankreich." In *Nation und Emotion: Deutschland und Frankreich im Vergleich 19. und 20. Jahrhundert*, edited by Etienne François, Hannes Siegrist, and Jakob Vogel, 147–68. Göttingen: Vandenhoeck & Ruprecht, 1995.

Tuma, Ali al. *Guns, Culture and Moors: Racial Perceptions, Cultural Impact and the Moroccan Participation in the Spanish Civil War (1936–1939)*. Abingdon, UK: Routledge, 2018.

Turda, Marius. "Race, Science, and Eugenics in the Twentieth Century." In *The Oxford Handbook of the History of Eugenics*, 63–75. Oxford: Oxford University Press, 2010.

Turino, Thomas. "Nationalism and Latin American Music: Selected Case Studies and Theoretical Considerations." *Latin American Music Review* 24, no. 2 (2003): 169–209.

Turnaoğlu, Banu. *The Formation of Turkish Republicanism*. Princeton, NJ: Princeton University Press, 2017.

Turner, Joe, and Dan Bailey. "'Ecobordering': Casting Immigration Control as Environmental Protection." *Environmental Politics* 31, no. 1 (2022): 110–31.

Tyler-McGraw, Marie. *An African Republic: Black and White Virginians in the Making of Liberia*. Chapel Hill: University of North Carolina Press, 2007.

Uduku, Ola. "Modernist Architecture and 'the Tropical' in West Africa: The Tropical Architecture Movement in West Africa, 1948–1970." *Habitat International* 30, no. 3 (2006): 396–411.

Ülker, Erol. "Nationalism, Religion, and Minorities from the Ottoman Empire to the Republic of Turkey." In *Sovereignty, Nationalism, and the Quest for Homogeneity in Interwar Europe*, edited by Emmanuel Dalle Mulle, Davide Rodogno, and Mona Bieling, 61–82. London: Bloomsbury, 2023.

Umbach, Maiken. "Made in Germany." In *Deutsche Erinnerungsorte*, edited by Etienne François and Hagen Schulze, 2:405–19. Munich: Beck, 2001.

Unowsky, Daniel L. *The Pomp and Politics of Patriotism: Imperial Celebrations in Habsburg Austria, 1848–1916*. West Lafayette, IN: Purdue University Press, 2005.

Urbain, Marine. "The Critical Reconstruction of Critical Regionalism (1971–1983)." *Oase*, no. 103 (2019): 41–49.

Urbinati, Nadia. "The Legacy of Kant: Giuseppe Mazzini's Cosmopolitanism of Nations." In *Giuseppe Mazzini and the Globalisation of Democratic Nationalism 1830–1920*, edited by C. A. Bayly and Eugenio F. Biagini, 11–37. Oxford: Oxford University Press, 2008.

Urry, John, and Jonas Larsen. *The Tourist Gaze 3.0*. London: Sage, 2011.

Vaillant, Janet G. *Black, French, and African: A Life of Léopold Sédar Senghor.* Cambridge, MA: Harvard University Press, 1990.

Valdivia Rivera, Soledad. "The Indigenous State: Progress and Limitations in the Promotion of the 'Indigenous' in Contemporary Bolivia." In *The Many Voices of Indigenous Latin America: Reconstruction, Describing, and Preserving Cultural and Linguistic Diversity,* edited by M. Françozo, R. van Gijn, and M. Bruil. Leiden: Brill, forthcoming.

Valiotis, Chris. "South Asia." In *Routledge Companion to Sports History,* edited by Steven W. Pope and John R. Nauright, 571–86. London: Routledge, 2009.

Van Beurden, Jos. *Inconvenient Heritage: Colonial Collections and Restitution in the Netherlands and Belgium.* Amsterdam: Amsterdam University Press, 2022.

Van der Beken, Christophe. "External and Internal Secession in Ethiopia's Multinational Federation." *International Journal on Minority and Group Rights* 28, no. 5 (2021): 944–71.

Van der Linden, Bob. "Non-Western National Music and Empire in Global History: Interactions, Uniformities, and Comparisons." *Journal of Global History* 10, no. 3 (2015): 431–56.

Van der Veer, Peter. "Spirituality in Modern Society." *Social Research* 76, no. 4 (2009): 1097–1120.

Vandewalle, Dirk J. *A History of Modern Libya.* Cambridge: Cambridge University Press, 2012.

Vande Winkel, Roel, and Daniel Biltereyst. "Filmed News and Nationalism in Belgium: Flemish Events At the Crossroads of Politics, Culture, and Commerce (1929–1942)." *Historical Journal of Film, Radio, and Television* 32, no. 3 (2012): 379–99.

Van Ginderachter, Maarten, and Jon E. Fox, eds. *National Indifference and the History of Nationalism in Modern Europe.* Abingdon, UK: Routledge, 2019.

Vanhaute, Eric. *Peasants in World History.* New York: Routledge, 2021.

Van Young, Eric. "Revolution and Imagined Community in Mexico, 1810–21." In *Nationalism in the New World,* edited by Don H. Doyle and Marco Antonio Pamplona, 184–208. Athens: University of Georgia Press, 2006.

Varga, Bálint. "The Habsburg Monarchy." In *The Cambridge History of Nationhood and Nationalism,* vol. 2, edited by Cathie Carmichael, Matthew D'Auria and Aviel Roshwald, 64–88. Cambridge: Cambridge University Press, 2023.

Varga, Somogy. "The Politics of Nation Branding: Collective Identity and Public Sphere in the Neoliberal State." *Philosophy and Social Criticism* 39, no. 8 (2013): 825–45.

Vaughan, Chris. "The Politics of Regionalism and Federation in East Africa, 1958–1964." *Historical Journal* 62, no. 2 (June 2019): 519–40.

Vaughan, William. *Romantic Art.* London: Thames and Hudson, 1988.

Velde, Henk te. *Gemeenschapszin en plichtsbesef: Liberalisme en nationalisme in Nederland, 1870–1918.* The Hague: SDU, 1992.

Vick, Brian E. *The Congress of Vienna: Power and Politics after Napoleon.* Cambridge, MA: Harvard University Press, 2014.

Vickers, Adrian. *Bali: A Paradise Created.* Hong Kong: Periplus, 1989.

Vidacs, Bea. "Banal Nationalism, Football, and Discourse Community in Africa." *Studies in Ethnicity and Nationalism* 11, no. 1 (2011): 25–41.

Vlossak, Elizabeth. *Marianne or Germania? Nationalizing Women in Alsace, 1870–1946.* Oxford: Oxford University Press, 2011.

Waddy, Helena. *Oberammergau in the Nazi Era: The Fate of a Catholic Village in Hitler's Germany.* Oxford: Oxford University Press, 2010.

Wade, Peter. *Race and Ethnicity in Latin America.* London: Pluto, 2015.

Wagenaar, Michiel. *Stedebouw en burgerlijke vrijheid: De contrasterende carrières van zes Europese hoofdsteden*. Bussum: Thoth, 1998.

Wagner, Michael Frederik. "The Rise of Autotourism in Danish Leisure, 1910–1970." *Journal of Tourism History* 5, no. 3 (2013): 265–86.

Walker, Brett L. *A Concise History of Japan*. Cambridge: Cambridge University Press, 2015.

Walraven, Klaas van. *Dreams of Power: The Role of the Organization of African Unity in the Politics of Africa 1963–1993*. Aldershot, UK: Ashgate, 1999.

Wang, Q. Edward. "Between Myth and History: The Construction of the National Past in Modern East Asia." In *Writing the Nation: A Global Perspective*, edited by Stefan Berger, 126–55. Basingstoke, UK: Palgrave Macmillan, 2011.

Warf, Barney, and Santa Arias, eds. *The Spatial Turn: Interdisciplinary Perspectives*. London: Routledge, 2008.

Weber, Eugen. *France, Fin de Siècle*. Cambridge, MA: Belknap Press of Harvard University Press, 1986.

———. *Peasants into Frenchmen: The Modernization of Rural France, 1870–1914*. Stanford, CA: Stanford University Press, 1976.

Webster, Charles. *The National Health Service: A Political History*. Oxford: Oxford University Press, 2002.

Weeda, Claire. *Ethnicity in Medieval Europe, 950–1250: Medicine, Power and Religion*. York: York Medieval Press, 2021.

Weeks, Theodore R. "Russification: Word and Practice 1863–1914." *Proceedings of the American Philosophical Society* 148, no. 4 (2004): 471–89.

———. "Separatist Nationalism in the Romanov and Soviet Empires." In *The Oxford Handbook of the History of Nationalism*, edited by John Breuilly, 199–220. Oxford: Oxford University Press, 2013.

Wehler, Hans-Ulrich. "Bismarck's Imperialism 1862–1890." *Past and Present*, no. 48 (1970): 119–55.

Weinberg, Elizabeth A. *Sociology in the Soviet Union and Beyond: Social Enquiry and Social Change*. London: Routledge, 2017.

Weitz, Eric D. "Self-Determination: How a German Enlightenment Idea Became the Slogan of National Liberation and a Human Right." *American Historical Review* 120, no. 2 (2015): 462–96.

———. *A World Divided: The Global Struggle for Human Rights in the Age of Nation-States*. Princeton, NJ: Princeton University Press, 2019.

Wesseling, Henk L. *The European Colonial Empires, 1815–1919*. Harlow, UK: Longman, 2004.

Wezel, Elsa van. "Het Alte Museum te Berlijn: Wijzigingen in het museumconcept omstreeks 1800." In *Verzamelen: Van rariteitenkabinet tot kunstmuseum*, edited by Ellinoor Bergvelt, Debora J. Meijers, and Mieke Rijnders, 317–32. Heerlen, Netherlands: Open Universiteit, 1993.

Whewell, William. *A History of the Inductive Sciences*. Cambridge: Cambridge University Press, 2010.

Whyte, Christine. "Between Empire and Colony: American Imperialism and Pan-African Colonialism in Liberia, 1810–2003." *National Identities* 18, no. 1 (2016): 71–88.

Wicke, Christian. "Constructivism in the History of Nationalism since 1945." In *Writing the History of Nationalism*, edited by Stefan Berger and Eric Storm, 131–55. London: Bloomsbury, 2019.

Wickramasinghe, Nira. *Sri Lanka in the Modern Age: A History*. Oxford: Oxford University Press, 2015.

Widodo, Johannes. "Modernism in Singapore." *Docomomo*, no. 29 (2003): 54–60.

Wijermars, Mariëlle. *Memory Politics in Contemporary Russia: Television, Cinema and the State*. London: Routledge, 2018.

Wilder, Gary. *The French Imperial Nation-State: Negritude and Colonial Humanism between the Two World Wars*. Chicago: University of Chicago Press, 2005.

Willson, Perry. "The Nation in Uniform? Fascist Italy, 1919–43." *Past and Present* 221, no. 1 (2013): 239–72.

Wils, Lode. "Het aandeel van de 'Flamenpolitik' in de Vlaamse natievorming." *Belgisch Tijd-schrift Voor Nieuwste Geschiedenis* 45 (2015): 216–37.

Wilson, Chris. *The Myth of Santa Fe: Creating a Modern Regional Tradition*. Albuquerque: University of New Mexico Press, 1997.

Wimmer, Andreas. *Nation Building: Why Some Countries Come Together while Others Fall Apart*. Princeton, NJ: Princeton University Press, 2018.

———. *Waves of War: Nationalism, State Formation, and Ethnic Exclusion in the Modern World*. Cambridge: Cambridge University Press, 2013.

Wimmer, Andreas, and Nina Glick Schiller. "Methodological Nationalism and Beyond: Nation-State Building, Migration and the Social Sciences." *Global Networks* 2, no. 4 (2002): 301–34.

Winter, Jay. *Sites of Memory, Sites of Mourning: The Great War in European Cultural History*. Cambridge: Cambridge University Press, 1995.

Witte, Els, Alain Meynen, and Dirk Luyten. *Politieke geschiedenis van België: Van 1830 tot heden*. Antwerp: Manteau, 2016.

Wolff, H. Ekkehard. *Language and Development in Africa: Perceptions, Ideologies and Challenges*. Cambridge: Cambridge University Press, 2016.

Wolschke-Bulmahn, Joachim. "Landscape Design and the Natural Sciences in Germany and the United States in the Early Twentieth Century: 'Reactionary Modernism?'" In *Gardens, Knowledge and the Sciences in the Early Modern Period*, edited by Hubertus Fischer, Volker R. Remmert, and Joachim Wolschke-Bulmahn, 345–65. Cham, Switzerland: Birkhäuser, 2016.

Woolf, Stuart. "Statistics and the Modern State." *Comparative Studies in Society and History* 31, no. 3 (1989): 588–604.

Worboys, Michael, Julie-Marie Strange, and Neil Pemberton. *Invention of the Modern Dog: Breed and Blood in Victorian Britain*. Baltimore: Johns Hopkins University Press, 2018.

Wörner, Martin. *Vergnügung und Belehrung: Volkskultur auf den Weltausstellungen 1851–1900*. Münster: Waxmann, 1999.

Wulf, Andrea. *The Invention of Nature: Alexander von Humboldt's New World*. London: Murray, 2015.

———. *Magnificent Rebels: The First Romantics and the Invention of the Self*. London: Murray, 2022.

Wyrtzen, Jonathan. "Colonial War and the Production of Territorialized State Space in North Africa." In *Rethinking the Colonial State*, edited by Søren Rud and Søren Ivarsson, 151–75. Bingley: Emerald, 2017.

Yasar, Kerim. *Electrified Voices: How the Telephone, Phonograph, and Radio Shaped Modern Japan, 1868–1945*. New York: Columbia University Press, 2018.

Yashar, Deborah J. "Democracy, Indigenous Movements, and Postliberal Challenge in Latin America." *World Politics* 52, no. 1 (1999): 76–104.

Yaycioglu, Ali. *Partners of the Empire: The Crisis of the Ottoman Order in the Age of Revolutions.* Stanford, CA: Stanford University Press, 2016.

Yellen, Jeremy A. *The Greater East Asia Co-prosperity Sphere: When Total Empire Met Total War.* Ithaca, NY: Cornell University Press, 2019.

Yellin, Eric Steven. *Racism in the Nation's Service: Government Workers and the Color Line in Woodrow Wilson's America.* Chapel Hill: University of North Carolina Press, 2013.

Young, Patrick. *Enacting Brittany: Tourism and Culture in Provincial France, 1871–1939.* Farnham: Ashgate, 2012.

Zahra, Tara. "'Condemned to Rootlessness and Unable to Budge': Roma, Migration Panics, and Internment in the Habsburg Empire." *American Historical Review* 122, no. 3 (2017): 702–26.

———. "Imagined Noncommunities: National Indifference as a Category of Analysis." *Slavic Review* 69, no. 1 (2010): 93–119.

Zamoyski, Adam. *Rites of Peace: The Fall of Napoleon and the Congress of Vienna.* London: Harper Perennial, 2008.

Zeller, Thomas. "'The Landscape's Crown': Landscape, Perceptions, and Modernizing Effects of the German Autobahn System, 1934 to 1941." In *Technologies of Landscape: From Reaping to Recycling*, edited by David E. Nye, 218–38. Amherst: University of Massachusetts Press, 1999.

Zeuske, Michael. "The French Revolution in Spanish America." In *The Routledge Companion to the French Revolution in World History*, edited by Alan Forrest and Matthias Middell, 77–96. Abingdon, UK: Routledge, 2016.

Zewde, Bahru. *A History of Modern Ethiopia, 1855–1991.* Oxford: James Currey, 2001.

Zhou, Qingsheng. *Ethnic Minority Languages in China: Policy and Practice.* Boston: De Gruyter, 2020.

Zimmer, Oliver. *Nationalism in Europe: 1890–1940.* Basingstoke, UK: Palgrave Macmillan, 2003.

Zolberg, Aristide R. *A Nation by Design: Immigration Policy in the Fashioning of America.* New York: Russell Sage, 2006.

Zoppi, Marco. "Greater Somalia, the Never-Ending Dream? Contested Somali Borders: The Power of Tradition vs. the Tradition of Power." *Journal of African History, Politics and Society* 1, no. 1 (2015): 43–64.

Zuelow, Eric G. E. *A History of Modern Tourism.* London: Palgrave Macmillan, 2016.

———. *Making Ireland Irish: Tourism and National Identity since the Irish Civil War.* Syracuse, NY: Syracuse University Press, 2009.

Zürcher, Erik Jan. *Turkey: A Modern History.* London: Tauris, 1997.

———, ed. *Jihad and Islam in World War I: Studies on the Ottoman Jihad at the Centenary of Snouck Hurgronje's "Holy War Made in Germany."* Leiden: Leiden University Press, 2016.

INDEX

Ossetia, 291; North, 291; South, 291, 356
Ossian, 62
Ottoman Empire, 8, 13, 29, 68–74, 77–78,
    86–87, 99, 101–2, 104, 106, 110, 112, 117–19,
    121–22, 130, 136, 138, 141–45, 157, 172, 175–80,
    182, 188, 193, 204, 221, 232, 289, 326, 344, 347
Ousmane, Sembene, 267
Owens, Jesse, 223
Oxford, 23, 81, 154
Oyo, 13
Ozenfant, Amédée, 206

Paine, Thomas, 26
painting, 27, 54–57, 59, 83–86, 121–24, 158–161,
    169, 206–7, 209, 263–64, 350, 352–53
Pakistan, 233–34, 252, 254–56, 271, 277; East,
    245; West, 245
Palacký, František, 92, 98
Palestine, 155, 177, 179–80, 204, 227, 233, 246,
    252, 254, 297, 299, 313; Partition of, 225,
    233, 246
Palestine Liberation Organization, 297
Palmer, R.R., 261
Palmyra, 330
pan-Africanism, 242, 353
Panama, 137
Pan American Union, 232
pan-Arabism, 241–42
pan-Celtic, 99, 232
pan-European, 232
pan-Germanism, 136, 232
pan-Scandinavian, 99
pan-Slavism, 99, 232
pan-Turanian, 99
pan-Turkism, 232
Papal States, 68, 91, 97
Paraguay, 44
Paris, 15, 19, 23, 41, 54–59, 74, 77, 84, 86–87,
    90–91, 95, 118, 121–24, 130, 159, 164–65,
    169–71, 183, 207, 209, 218, 238–39, 263–64,
    272, 319, 323, 335
Paris Peace Conference, 175, 179, 181–83, 191
Parma, 68, 97
Parnell, Charles Stewart, 138

Parsons, Talcott, 260
Patagonia, 110–11
Patriotic War, 87
patriotism, 14, 17, 19–20, 31, 33, 35, 38, 41, 43,
    48–50, 62, 65, 79, 207, 247, 276
patronage, political, 109, 137, 151, 254–55, 348
Päts, Konstantin, 186
Pavelić, Ante, 226
Peace of Westphalia, 18
Pedro I, 43
Pelli, César, 324
Peloponnese, 73
Peninsular War, 42, 50
People's Republic of China. See China
People's Republic of Korea. See Korea
Pérez Galdós, Benito, 122
Perón, Eva, 301
Perón, Isabel, 247
Perón, Juan, 301
Perry, Matthew C., 105
Persia, 8, 21, 33, 80, 118, 130, 142, 156–57, 170,
    172, 177, 220–21, 344
Peru, 33, 43, 190, 194, 211, 301
Pessoa, Fernando, 208
Pest, 86. See also Budapest
Petrović, Karageorge, 72
Phan Boi Chau, 151
Phibun Songkhram, 220
Philadelphia, 34, 183
Philippines, 1, 45, 137, 147, 218, 221, 226, 231,
    246, 251, 256, 271, 273, 302, 311, 346; Second
    Republic, 188
philology, 82, 117, 153, 353
philosophy, 28, 30, 60, 62, 82, 117, 134–35,
    259–60, 353
Piano, Renzo, 323
Picardy, 14
Picasso, Pablo, 159, 207, 319
Piedmont, 78, 91, 95–97, 100, 132
Piłsudski, Józef, 186
Pinochet, Augusto, 282
Pirenne, Henri, 205
Plato, 261
Poelaert, Joseph, 124